Counseling the Culturally Different

Counseling the Culturally Different

♦

Theory and Practice

THIRD EDITION

DERALD WING SUE
California School of Professional Psychology, Alameda
California State University, Hayward

DAVID SUE
Western Washington University

JOHN WILEY & SONS, INC.
New York · Chichester · Weinheim · Brisbane · Singapore · Toronto

Copyright © 1999 by John Wiley & Sons, Inc. All rights reserved.

Published simultaneously in Canada.

This publication is designed to provide accurate and authoritative information in regard to the subject matter covered. It is sold with the understanding that the publisher is not engaged in rendering professional services. If legal, accounting, medical, psychological or any other expert assistance is required, the services of a competent professional person should be sought.

Library of Congress Cataloging-in-Publication Data
Sue, Derald Wing.
   Counseling the culturally different : theory and practice / Derald Wing Sue,
David Sue. —3rd ed.
     p.   cm.
   Includes bibliographical references and index.
   ISBN 0-471-14887-3 (hardcover : alk. paper)
   1. Cross-cultural counseling. I. Sue, David. II. Title.
BF637.C6S85 1999
158′.3—dc21   98-41477
                                                          CIP

◆ Contents

◆ *Preface*

Since the publication of the previous editions, *Counseling The Culturally Different: Theory and Practice* has maintained its status as a classic in the field of multicultural counseling and therapy, become the most frequently cited text in the ethnic minority psychology field, and is now the standard reference for nearly all courses in minority mental health and treatment. We believe that the third edition continues the legacy of scholarly excellence without sacrificing its provocative, "hard-hitting," intense, and practice-oriented approach to the field. The balance between the need for mental health professionals to understand cultural differences reflected in worldviews, on the one hand, and the sociopolitical nature of clinical applications, on the other hand, has been maintained. The major thesis of this edition is that counseling and psychotherapy are rooted in, and reflect, the dominant values of the larger society. As a result, forms of treatment may represent cultural oppression and may reflect a primarily Eurocentric worldview that may do great harm to culturally different clients. In order to be culturally competent, mental health professionals must be able to free themselves from the cultural conditioning of their personal and professional training, to understand and accept the legitimacy of alternative worldviews, and to begin the process of developing culturally appropriate intervention strategies in working with a diverse clientele.

We continue to use a large number of clinical and real-life examples to illustrate the concepts of multicultural counseling and therapy. Especially noteworthy is our use of an in-depth case study or real-life example at the beginning of each major chapter to illustrate the concepts and principles related to multicultural mental health practice. Although we have chosen to eliminate the separate chapter on critical incidents, we have integrated many of the cases into the rest of the book.

Readers familiar with the earlier editions will note several major additions, including a more inclusive definition of multiculturalism, along with a discussion of the pros and cons of a general versus a narrow perspective; the most recent statistics on the changing complexion of society (demographics) with a discussion of their implications for clinical practice; a discussion of the culture-bound basis of ACA and APA Code of Ethics and Standards of Practice; a more detailed chapter on multicultural family counseling; a separate chapter on nonwestern forms of healing; and a new chapter on multicultural individual, professional, and organizational development. There is also a new chapter, "Counseling Gays/Lesbians, Women, the Elderly, and Persons with Disabilities". The inclusion of these groups in one chapter in no way implies that we view them as "less important," but rather that we have a greater familiarity with issues related to persons of color. Our continued work in the field has made us realize, however, that principles of multicultural psychology derived from work with racial minorities are applicable to other culturally different groups as well. Likewise, the research on gender, sexual orientation, the aging, and the physically challenged has contributed to a better understanding of issues of prejudice and discrimination.

Because the field has evolved with new developments in research, theory, and practice, the third edition has been reorganized to be more consistent with these changes. Instead of three major divisions, there are now five. "Part I: The Political Dimensions of Mental Health Practice" sets the tone for the entire text. Chapter 1, "The Politics of Counseling and Psychotherapy," probably has the most impact for here the mental health profession is taken to task for its ethnocentric monocultural features. We reveal how counseling and therapy have historically portrayed racial/ethnic minorities as pathological, discuss how mental health practices have oppressed minorities, show how the mental health profession reflects the biases, assumptions, practices, and prejudices of the larger society, and point out the cultural biases in the American Psychological Association and the American Counseling Association's Code of Ethics and Standards of Practice. A "Call to Conscience" for drastic changes in mental health practice is a necessity if we are to provide culturally relevant services to a diverse population. While Chapter 1 deals with the politics of counseling and psychotherapy from a societal and historical perspective, Chapter 2, "Sociopolitical Considerations of Trust and Mistrust in Multicultural Counseling and Therapy," emphasizes how discrimination, prejudice, and stereotyping experienced by various racial/ethnic minority groups have affected their perceptions of the counseling/therapy process. We discuss and outline how the issue of trust and mistrust of mental health professionals is played out in the therapeutic process.

"Part II: The Practice Dimensions of Multicultural Counseling and Therapy" deals specifically with the subject of multicultural therapeutic practice. Updated considerably, Chapter 3, "Barriers to Effective Multicultural Counseling and Therapy," analyzes the culture-bound, class-bound, and linguistic biases in conventional counseling and psychotherapeutic practice. It is gratifying to see how this chapter, first published in 1980, has become a cornerstone in its field: In fact, the concepts presented here have become part of the very knowledge base in the multicultural "helping" field. Chapter 4, "Culturally Appropriate Intervention Strategies," challenges the universal models of helping and suggests that mental health professionals must begin the process of developing appropriate and effective intervention strategies in working with culturally different clients. This means that traditional clinical practice must accept the notion of "culture-specific strategies" in the helping process. Traditional taboos of Eurocentric counseling and therapy are questioned. There are new sections stressing prevention as well as remedial approaches, systems intervention as well as traditional one-to-one relationships, and the use of psychoeducational methods. We stress the importance of mental health practitioners becoming knowledgeable about, and making use of, existing indigenous helping/healing approaches in the minority community. The rationale, importance, description, and use of alternative helping roles in multicultural counseling/therapy are major features of this chapter. Chapter 5, "Multicultural Family Counseling and Therapy," has been completely revised. Much work on family ethnicity and mental health practice has accumulated in recent years. Our basic premise is that the family counselor/therapist must be aware of how racial/ethnic minority groups view the family. Not only do groups differ in defining the family (vs. the nuclear family), but roles and processes differ from Euro-American structures and processes. Specific suggestions and guidelines are proposed for the multicultural family therapist.

Three chapters also comprise "Part III: Worldviews in Multicultural Counseling and Therapy." It is becoming increasingly clear that one's worldview dictates how reality and normality are defined, how problems are perceived, and how forms of treatment are delivered and received. One of the greatest barriers to effective relationships between culturally different groups is the inability to understand another's worldview. Chapter 6, "Racial and Cultural Minority Identity Development: Therapeutic Implications," has been expanded considerably. Much research has now clarified the parameters of the competing theories of racial identity development. Although we discuss the various theories and their pros and cons, the major emphasis is an integrative attempt to describe the various "stages" or "ego states" (a controversy in the field) and their implications for assessment and therapeutic intervention. Chapter 7, "White Racial Identity Development: Therapeutic Implications," is a new chapter that formed a subsection of another chapter in the second edition. White identity development, "White privilege," and how the Euro-American worldview affects perception of race-related issues have become an important aspect of the dialogue in mental health practice. The thesis of this chapter is that multiculturally competent White Euro-American mental health professionals must realize that they are victims of their cultural conditioning and that they have inherited the racial biases, prejudices, and stereotypes of their forebears, must take responsibility for the role they play in the oppression of minority groups, and must move toward actively redefining their Whiteness in a nondefensive and nonracist manner. Discussion of the interplay between varying levels of White awareness and working with culturally different clients is a major part of this chapter. Chapter 8, "Dimensions of Worldviews," discusses how race, culture, ethnicity, gender, and sexual orientation influences worldview. It uses the theory of worldviews that was first described in the 1980 edition and is considered one of the cornerstones of cultural competence. In the field of mental health practice, understanding the worldview of your culturally different clients is considered all-important in delivering culturally relevant services to an increasingly diverse population.

"Part IV: Multicultural Counseling and Therapy Competence," advocates the need to incorporate indigenous wisdom into practice and to see helping from a broader professional/organizational framework. Chapter 9, "Non-western and Indigenous Methods of Healing," challenges conventional therapeutic practice. It takes a giant step in recognizing that all helping originates from a particular cultural context. Within the United States, counseling and psychotherapy are the dominant psychological healing methods; in other cultures, however, indigenous healing approaches continue to be widely used. While there are similarities between Euro-American helping systems and the indigenous practices of many cultural groups, there are major differences as well. Western forms of counseling, for example, rely on sensory information defined by the physical plane of reality (Western science), but most indigenous methods rely on the spiritual plane of existence in seeking a cure. In keeping with the cultural encapsulation of our profession, Western healing has failed to acknowledge or learn from these age-old forms of wisdom. In its attempt to become culturally responsive, however, the field of counseling must begin to put aside the biases of Western science, to acknowledge the existence of intrinsic help-giving networks, and to incorporate the legacy of ancient wisdom which may be contained in indigenous models of healing. The chapter begins with a description of the historic and continuing "shamanic" practice of healers—often called witch, witch doctor, wizard, medicine man/woman, sorcerer, or magic man/woman—who are believed to possess the power to enter an altered state of consciousness and in their healing rituals journey to other planes of existence beyond the physical world. We describe the three major therapeutic approaches which Western science might find helpful: (1) the use of communal, group, and family networks to shelter the disturbed individual, to problem-solve in a group context, and to reconnect them with family or significant others; (2) the use of spiritual and religious beliefs and traditions of the community in the healing process; and (3) the use of shamans who are perceived to be the keepers of timeless wisdom. Within these approaches are embedded some valuable lessons for multicultural counseling and therapy that we extract for the readers.

Chapter 10, "Becoming Multiculturally Competent: Organizational and Professional Development," defines the ultimate goal of a mental health practitioner. At the present time there is a great deal of interest in the development of multicultural competencies in mental health practice. Indeed, the senior author has been fortunate to head the 1982 Division 17 Professional Standards Committee, which produced the first set of multicultural counseling competencies, and the 1992 AMCD Committee, which refined and elaborated them. These competencies have been adopted by two divisions of the American Psychological Association and many divisions of the American Counseling Association. Much work is currently directed at translating them into education and training, science, and practice. The four competencies discussed in this chapter that have strong implications for training are (1) having mental health professionals become culturally aware of their own values, biases, and assumptions about human behavior; (2) having mental health professionals acquire knowledge and understanding of the worldview of minority or culturally different groups and clients; (3) having mental health professionals begin the process of developing appropriate and effective intervention strategies in working with culturally different clients; and (4) understanding how organizational and institutional forces may either enhance or negate the development of multicultural competence.

"Part V: Counseling and Therapy with Specific Populations" contains five chapters that integrate the most recent research and clinical findings on specific culturally different groups with practical suggestions and therapeutic implications. Each of the first four of these chapters specializes in one particular racial/ethnic minority group: Chapter 11, "Counseling African Americans"; Chapter 12, "Counseling American Indians and Alaskan Natives"; Chapter 13, "Counseling Asian Americans"; and Chapter 14, "Counseling Hispanic Americans and Latino Americans".

Chapter 15, "Counseling Gay and Lesbians, Women, the Elderly, and Persons with Disabilities," represents our first step to expand the definition and practice of multicultural counseling/therapy to other culturally distinct groups. While the focus has primarily been on racial/ethnic minorities, the principles of prejudice, racism, oppression, and discrimination applies to other culturally different groups as well. We illustrate this by a discussion of gay/lesbians, women, the physically challenged, and the elderly in our society. Similarities and differences between these groups with respect to the sociopolitical dynamics of being different and how counseling/therapy can be most beneficial utilizing the principles of multiculturalism is a major focus. We make a case that all counseling is, in some respects, multicultural in nature.

There is an African-American proverb that states, "We stand on the head and shoulders of many who have gone on before us." Certainly, this book would not have been possible without their wisdom, commitment, and sacrifice. We thank them for their inspiration, courage, and dedication, and we hope they will look at us and be pleased with our work. We would also like to acknowledge the dedicated pioneers in the field who have journeyed with us along the path of multiculturalism before it became fashionable. While there are too many to name, our professional and/or personal lives have been especially enriched by the following individuals: Patricia Arredondo, Donald Atkinson, Carolyn Attneave, Price Cobbs, William Cross, Ursula Delworth, A. J. Franklin, Leo Goldman, Thomas Gunnings, Robert Guthrie, Janet Helms, Asa Hilliard, Allen Ivey, James Jones, Barbara Kirk, Teresa LaFromboise, Amado Padilla, Thomas Parham, Paul Pedersen, Rene A. Ruiz, Stanley Sue, Ronald Samuda, Dalmas Taylor, Charles Thomas, Joseph Trimble, Melba Vasquez, Clement Vontress, Joe White, and Robert Williams.

Working on this third edition has proven to be a labor of love. It would not have been possible, however, without the love and support of our families who provided the patience and nourishment which sustained us throughout our work on the text. Derald Wing Sue wishes to express his love for his wife, Paulina; his son, Derald Paul; and his daughter, Marissa Catherine. David Sue wishes to express his love to his wife, Diane, his son, Joe and his daughters, Jenni and Christi.

We hope that this third edition of *Counseling the Culturally Different: Theory and Practice,* will stand on "the truth" and continue to be the standard bearer of multicultural therapy texts in the field.

Derald Wing Sue
David Sue

Part One

♦

♦

The Political Dimensions of Mental Health Practice

Chapter One

◆

The Politics of Counseling and Psychotherapy

◆

On January 29, 1996, Thien Minh Ly, a 24-year-old Vietnamese graduate of UCLA was murdered while Rollerblading. He was found lying in a pool of blood from numerous stab wounds to various parts of his body, as well as a slashing wound to his throat. Two White men were later arrested and confessed to the murder. In a letter bragging of the killing, one of the men wrote, "Oh I killed a Jap a while ago, I stabbed him to death." The brutal and torturous killing reflected the sadistic delight the two men took in the cries of pain as they stabbed and stomped Ly to death. In the home of the two assailants were found White supremacist paraphernalia. On September 30, 1997, one of the assailants was sentenced to death for the racially motivated murder.

On August 9, 1997, Abner Louima, a Haitian immigrant, was arrested by New York police officers who took him to their Seventieth Precinct station house. Once there, officers are reported to have dragged the handcuffed Louima to the bathroom, where he was brutally sodomized with a toilet plunger. Four officers were arrested and indicted, charges of police brutality and racism in the media reflected the public outcry that these events inspired. Accused of a pattern of tolerating police brutality, the New York City Police Department has come under civil rights investigation by the U.S. Justice Department. Black, Hispanic, and Asian communities say that such a racially motivated brand of justice is not uncommon and has increased against minority citizens.

In the Superior Court of the State of California in and for the County of Santa Clara Juvenile Division, a judge made highly racist and derogatory comments to a Hispanic family. He said a young Hispanic juvenile was lower than an animal, had no moral upbringing, and his pregnant sister (unmarried) was probably doomed to a life of three or four marriages and half a dozen children before she turned 18. The judge, in a highly charged tone, accused the Mexican people of being "mis-

3

erable, lousy, and rotten," of having no right to live among human beings, and stated that perhaps Hitler was right in advocating genocide.

A White female elementary school teacher in Oklahoma had planned an ethnic minority appreciation day for her sixth-grade class. As there was a large number of American Indian students in her class, part of the day was devoted to a unit on Native American heritage. One of the American Indian students had designed a bonnet and dress of her tribe. While her fellow students expressed appreciation and admiration for her costume and tribal dance demonstration, the teacher was reported to have remained silent. Several days later the female student received a low grade for her participation in the activities. According to the student, the teacher had praised her dance technique and beautiful costume, but had stated that (a) the costume was not typical of her tribe, (b) her dance was not traditional, and (c) the assignment was graded on "authenticity, not fantasy." When the girl's parents heard about the remarks, they demanded a meeting with the teacher and principal. During the meeting, the father expressed anger at "White folks always telling Indians who we are." The teacher's only response was to show the parents an anthropology book with what she claimed to be the typical headgear and costume of the family's tribe.

A merican Airlines was caught "red-faced" over major racial gaffes when it became known in 1998 that their pilots' manual contained derogatory and stereotypic references to their Latin American customers. The manual suggested that Latin Americans "like to get drunk and call in false bomb threats when running late for a plane." American Airlines was forced to make a public apology and stated that future revisions of the manual would remove any such racially charged assertions.

I n 1995, Texaco executives were embarrassed when tapes of boardroom conversations confirmed a common perception by minority employees regarding the prevalence of corporate racism and sexism in the company. In referring to diversity and to employees of color, executives were overheard to express personal and corporate animosity toward diversity training and to make racially derogatory comments, saying that "the black jelly beans" [Black employees] are "stuck to the bottom of the jar" and would never be allowed to move up the corporate ladder. The existence of the embarrassing tapes, worker resistance to such indignities, lawsuits, and a strong consumer boycott that devalued Texaco's stock eventually led to the development of a meaningful diversity plan as settlement of a $176.1 million discrimination lawsuit.

These vignettes outline only a few of the countless examples of the racism and sexism that are alive, well, and thriving in the United States. Indeed, in the 1990s we have seen a historic rise in incidents of overt bigotry throughout the country. The incidents have ranged from murder and mayhem to physical attacks, threats, and racial epithets. A recently released study by Klanwatch and the Militia Task Force (Serrano, 1998) documented a record number of hate groups in 1997, a 20% increase over the previous year; reports of the burning of Black churches in the mid-1990s seemed commonplace; and a recently released report by the National Asian Pacific American Legal Consortium (1997) showed a 17% increase in hate crimes directed toward Asian Americans. These reports are even more disturbing in light of the apparent erosion of the nation's oldest civil rights law. For example, beginning in 1989 the U.S. Supreme Court, with a conservative majority, has ruled that (a) cities may not set aside a fixed percentage of public contracts for minorities, (b) civil rights plaintiffs may not use statistics on job segregation to prove illegal discrimination, (c) White males may file reverse discrimination challenges against court-approved affirmative action programs, and (d) minorities or women may not challenge an unfair seniority policy after it has been in force for 300 days.

More recently, California passed the divisive and mean-spirited Proposition 187 which sought to expel from schools children who were in the United States illegally and would have denied them health care and other social services. While a judge in 1998 struck down the proposition as unconstitutional (only the federal government can regulate immigration), challenges to this ruling will most likely result. And, in 1996, California passed Proposition 209, an anti-affirmative action initiative which effectively eliminates any affirmative action program in the state. Like legislation was passed in the state of Washington. Similar attacks on affirmative action are taking place in legislative halls, courtrooms, and boardrooms. In California, too, Proposition 227, an initiative that would sharply reduce bilingual education in public schools, enjoyed popular support and easily passed in the June 1998 election.

University and college campuses, supposed bastions of enlightenment and democracy, have also reported an alarming rise of racism. Ugly racial incidents, such as the burning of a cross in a Black student's dormitory room, the taunting of a Black female as "dark meat" by Dartmouth football players, the spray painting of racial slurs on the walls of a minority cultural center at Smith College, and the victimizing of Hispanic students with racial epithets and attacks by a fraternity group in Berkeley, have been well documented.

It may seem surprising and unusual for us to open a book on *counseling the culturally different* with these examples. Aren't these incidents only tangentially related to the topic of multicultural counseling and therapy? Why should we give them such prominence? After all, as mental health practitioners, we are here to help people, not oppress them. While these last statements may be correct in philosophy, they fail to recognize several important facets of counseling and psychotherapy with minority clients.

First, the worldview of the culturally different is ultimately linked to the historical and current experiences of racism and oppression in the United States. A culturally different client is likely to approach counseling and therapy with a great deal of healthy suspicion as to the therapist's conscious and unconscious motives in a multicultural context. That a therapist is "supposed to help" or that definitions of therapy encompass certain philosophical assumptions such as (a) a concern and respect for the uniqueness of clients; (b) an emphasis on the inherent worth and dignity of all people regardless of race, creed, color, or sex; (c) a high priority placed on helping others attain their own self-determined goals; (d) valuing freedom and the opportunity to explore one's own characteristics and potentials; and (e) a future-oriented promise of a better life is not enough to foster trust in light of the current sociopolitical climate (Atkinson, Morten, & Sue, 1998; Sue, Ivey, & Pedersen, 1996; Katz, 1985). Many of these goals had their roots in the educational guidance movement of the early 1900s and reflected democratic ideals such as "equal access and opportunity," "pursuit of happiness," "liberty and justice for all," and "fulfillment of personal destiny." While these lofty ideals may seem highly commendable and appropriate for the mental health profession, they have often been translated in such a manner as to justify support for the status quo (D'Andrea & Daniels, 1995; Jackson, 1995; Katz, 1985; D.W. Sue et al., 1998).

That mental health practice has failed to fulfill its promises to the culturally different has been a frequent theme voiced by minority group authors since the mid-1960s and continues to this very day (Jackson, 1995). For example, in reviewing the minority group literature on the delivery of mental health services, we find similar themes throughout all facets of the profession.

At the counseling level:

. . . that it is a waste of time; that counselors are deliberately shunting minority students into dead end nonacademic programs regardless of student potential, preferences, or ambitions; that counselors discourage students from applying to college; that counselors are insensitive to the needs of students and the community; that counselors do not give the same amount of energy and time in working with minority as they do with White-middle-class students; that counselors do not accept, respect, and understand cultural differences; that counselors are arrogant and contemptuous; and that counselors don't know how to deal with their own hangups. (Pine, 1972, p. 35)

At the clinical level:

It makes little sense to speak about American Society as pluralistic and culturally diverse, or to urge the development of mental health services that respect and respond to that diversity, unless we focus attention on the special status of the groups which account for the diversity. . . . A frequent and vigorous complaint of minority people who need care is that they often feel abused, intimidated, and harassed by non-minority personnel. (President's Commission on Mental Health, 1978, pp. 4–6)

At the psychotherapy level:

In the psychotherapy relationship, characterized by close interpersonal interaction, aspects of racism may intrude readily. Differential experiences and effects of racism have not changed appreciably historically even though attention has been called to inequities in practice delivery and therapy process. . . . (Jackson, 1983, p. 143)

At the service delivery level:

Discriminatory practices result from ways in which the services are organized—selection procedures, points of comparison for promotion, etc. (In the case of staff) and diagnostic processes, selective criteria for types of treatment, indicators of "dangerousness" etc. (In the case of patients) Racism may have direct advantage for the dominant (white) population in that, for example, the exclusion of black staff from management, and the easing out of black patients from time-consuming types of "sophisticated" treatment modalities or their labeling as (psychiatrically) dangerous, allows white society to continue its dominance. (Fernando, 1988, p. 147)

At the education and training level:

As we stand at the threshold of the 21st century, mental health professionals, and psychologists more specifically, continue to be predominantly Caucasian; to be trained by predominantly Caucasian faculty members; and to be trained in programs in which ethnic issues are ignored, regarded as deficiencies, or included as an afterthought. (Meyers, Echemendia, & Trimble, 1991, p. 5)

Discouragingly, such minority group perceptions of the helping professions continue to have great legitimacy and indicate a gap existing between the ideals of the mental health profession and its actual operation with respect to the culturally different. While mental health practice enshrines the concepts of freedom, rational thought, tolerance of new ideas, and equality and justice for all, it can be used as an oppressive instrument by those in power to maintain the status quo. In this respect, mental health practice becomes a form of oppression in which there is an unjust and cruel exercise of power to subjugate or mistreat large groups of people. When used to restrict rather than enhance the well-being and development of the culturally different, it may entail overt and covert forms of prejudice and discrimination. Thus, the worldview of the culturally different client who comes for therapy boils down to one important question: "What makes you, a counselor/therapist, any different from all the others out there who have oppressed and discriminated against me?"

This question brings us back to a more personal observation. Just as the two assailants of the Vietnamese youngster, the White police officers, the judge, the teacher, and the Texaco executives could be racist in thought, beliefs, and deeds, so also can counselors and therapists inherit and act out the biases of the society. Racism runs deep and dies hard! Scratch the surface and you'll find beliefs that are evidence of the sociopolitical climate in which we are raised—for example, beliefs that Asians are the cause of U.S. economic woes, that Blacks lack the intellectual "essentials" to advance in our society, that immigrants are to be blamed for draining the resources of our society, that there is nothing worse than the intermingling of races, that Hispanic people are inferior, that American Indians must fit White preconceived definitions, and that persons of color are aliens in their own land. To say that we have somehow escaped our racist upbringing, that we are not perpetrators of racism, or that the racial climate is improving is to deny social reality. As mental health professionals, we have a personal and professional responsibility to (a) confront, become aware of, and take actions in dealing with our biases, stereotypes, values, and assumptions about human behavior; (b) become aware of the culturally different client's worldview, values, biases, and assumptions about human behavior; (c) develop appropriate help-giving practices, intervention strategies, and structures that take into account the historical, cultural, and environmental experiences/influences of the culturally different client; and (d) change the policies, practices, programs, and structures of our institutions that oppress the culturally different.

This book is about providing appropriate mental health care to the culturally different. Its main thesis is that counseling and psychotherapy do not take place in a vacuum isolated from the larger social-political influences of our society. Multicultural counseling often mirrors the state of interracial relationships in the wider society as well as the dominant-subordinate relationships of other marginalized groups (gays/lesbians, women, and the physically challenged). It serves as a microcosm reflecting Black-White, Asian-White, Hispanic-White, American Indian-White, interethnic, and minority-majority relations.

This first chapter explores the many ways in which counseling and psychotherapy have failed with respect to the culturally different. Only by honestly confronting these unpleasant social realities and accepting responsibility for changing them will our profession be able to advance and grow. These failures can be seen in three primary areas: (a) the education and training of mental health professionals, (b) biased and inaccurate therapeutic and mental health literature, and (c) the inappropriate process and practice of counseling and psychotherapy. We deal with only the first two areas in this chapter; therapeutic process and practice is discussed in Chapter 3. Prior to our journey, however, it is important to present some important demographic data regarding the diversification of the United States, and its implications for our society and the mental health profession.

THE DIVERSIFICATION OF THE UNITED STATES

Racial/ethnic minorities have reached critical mass in the United States and their numbers are expected to continue increasing. The rapid increase in the racial/ethnic minority population has been referred to as "the Diversification of the United States" or "the Changing Complexion of Society." The U.S. population will jump 50% from 255 million to 383 million in the year 2050 (U.S. Bureau of the Census, 1992). Most of the population increase will be visible racial/ethnic minority groups (VREG). By the time this book is published, over one-third of the population in the United States will be minorities, with approximately 45% in the public schools (D.W. Sue et al., 1998). From 1980 to 1990, the non-White population grew at a phenomenal rate (African American, 13.18%; Native American, 37.96%; Hispanic/Latino American, 53.02%; Asian American/Pacific Islander, 107.71%) compared to the White population (6.01%). Projections indicate that persons of color will constitute a numerical majority sometime between the years 2030 and 2050 (U.S. Census Bureau, 1992; D.W. Sue et al., 1997).

The rapid demographic shift is due to two major trends: (a) immigration rates and (b) differential birthrates. The current immigration rates (documented immigrants, undocumented immigrants, and refugees) are the highest in U.S. history. Unlike the earlier immigrants, who were primarily White Europeans oriented toward assimilation, the current wave consists primarily of Asian (34%), Latin American (34%), and other visible racial/ethnic groups who may not be readily assimilated (Atkinson, Morten, & Sue, 1998). In addition, the birthrates of White Americans have continued to decline (Euro-American, 1.7 per mother) in comparison to those of racial/ethnic minorities (e.g., African American, 2.4; Mexican American, 2.9; Vietnamese, 3.4; Laotians, 4.6; Cambodians, 7.4; and Hmong, 11.9 per mother).

SOCIETAL IMPLICATIONS

Societal implications of the diversification of the United States are many:

1. Approximately 75% of those now entering the labor force are visible racial/ethnic minorities and women. The changing complexion and feminization of the workforce have become a reality.
2. By the time the so-called baby boomers (those born between 1946 and 1961) retire, the majority of people contributing to Social Security and pension plans will be racial/ethnic minorities. In other words, those planning to retire (primarily White workers) must depend upon their coworkers of color. If racial/ethnic minorities continue to be the most undereducated, underemployed, unemployed, and underpaid, and to encounter the glass ceiling, it bodes poorly for the economic security of retiring White workers.
3. Businesses are aware that their workforce must increasingly be drawn from a diverse labor pool and that the current U.S. minority marketplace equals the gross domestic product of Canada; projections are that it will become immense as the shift in demographics continues.

The economic viability of businesses will depend on their ability to effectively manage a diverse workforce, allow for equal access and opportunity, and appeal to consumers of color.

4. By the year 2000, 45% of the students in our public schools will be racial/ethnic minorities. In school systems (e.g., California) more than 50% of the students were people of color as long ago as the late 1980s. Thus, it appears that our educational institutions must wrestle with issues of multicultural education and the development of bilingual programs.

5. The changes in demographics are uneven and have differential effects on different parts of the country. We have mentioned trends in California several times not because it is more important than other states, but because it represents one of the most diverse regions in the country and is often a precursor for trends as our nation becomes increasingly diverse. Some other parts of the country undergoing rapid transformation are:

- Recent statistics identify 10 states with combined American Indian, Hispanic, Asian and Black populations of 1 million or more (California has 8 million).
- Thirty percent of New York City residents are born outside of this country.
- Seventy percent of the population of the District of Columbia is African American.
- Two thirds of Miami's population is Hispanic.
- One third of the population of San Francisco is Asian/Asian American.
- Nearly 2/3 of the Detroit population is African American.
- Over 10,000 Laotian Hmongs have immigrated to Minneapolis/St. Paul, Minnesota.

The top regions/states in minority representation by the year 2020 are projected to be in the following order:

STATE/REGION	% MINORITY
D.C.	72.6
New Mexico	67.8
Hawaii	64.6
California	62.3
Texas	53.9
Maryland	44.9
Arizona	44.0
New York	43.5
Nevada	42.5
New Jersey	42.0

In recognition of the changing composition of the nation, President Clinton in June 1997 formed his Race Advisory Board in order to facilitate a national dialogue on race and reconciliation. He explained:

. . . I believe the greatest challenge we face . . . is also our greatest opportunity. Of all the questions of discrimination and prejudice that still exist in our society, the most perplexing one is the oldest, and in some ways today, the newest: the problem of race.

The formation of the Race Advisory Board by President Clinton, the movement by business and industry toward diversity training, the infusion of multicultural concepts into school curricula, and the many attempts to fight bigotry, bias, and discrimination in our social, economic, and political systems are healthy and positive signs. Yet, the changing demographics have also caused alarm in many of our White citizens and have often resulted in conflict and major clashes. Perhaps this is to be expected as different worldviews, lifestyles, and value systems challenge the myth of the melting pot concept as we move from a monocultural to a multicultural society.

MENTAL HEALTH IMPLICATIONS

As for our society, the implications for the mental health professions are many.

1. The clash of worldviews, values, and lifestyles is inescapable for therapists not only in their personal lives, but their professional ones as well. It will be impossible for any of us not to encounter client groups who differ from us in terms of race, culture, and ethnicity. Increasingly, therapists will come into contact with culturally different clients who may not share their worldview of what constitutes normality-abnormality; who define helping in a manner that contrasts sharply with our codes of ethics and standards of practice; who require culture-specific strategies and approaches in counseling and psychotherapy; and who may perceive the profession as a sociopolitical tool.

2. If counselors and therapists are to provide meaningful help to a culturally diverse population, we must not only reach out and acquire new understandings, but develop new culturally effective helping approaches. To prepare counselors with multicultural expertise means (a) revamping our training programs to include accurate and realistic multicultural content and experiences, (b) developing multicultural competencies as core standards for our profession, and (c) providing continuing education for our current service providers.

3. Because therapeutic and ethical practice may be culture-bound, therapists who work with culturally different clients may be engaging in cultural oppression using unethical and harmful practices for that particular population. Our professional organizations need to adopt ethical guidelines, codes of ethics, standards of practice, and by-laws that are multicultural in scope. Omission of such standards and failed translation into actual practice are inexcusable and represent a powerful statement of the low priority and lack of commitment to cultural diversity. If we are indeed committed to multiculturalism, then each and every one of us must become an advocate in demanding that our professional associations seriously undertake a major revision of standards used to ascertain counseling competence. Furthermore, these multicultural criteria must be infused into licensing and credentialing standards as well.

4. The education and training of psychologists have, at times, created the impression that their theories and practices are apolitical and value free. Yet, we are often impressed by the fact that the actual practice of therapy can result in cultural oppression; that what happens in the therapist's office may represent a microcosm of race relations in the larger society; that the so-called psychological problems of minority groups may reside not within, but outside of our clients; and that no matter how well intentioned the helping professionals, they are not immune from inheriting the racial biases of their forebears.

5. Since none of us is immune from inheriting the images/stereotypes of the larger society, we can assume that most therapists are prisoners of their own cultural conditioning. As a result, they possess stereotypes and preconceived notions that may be unwittingly imposed upon their culturally different clients. It may affect how they define problems, the goals they

develop, and the standards that they use to judge normal and abnormal behavior. Therapists whose biases and prejudices influence their work with culturally different clients have the potential to oppress and harm them. Thus it is imperative that all therapists explore their own stereotypes and images of various minority groups. Since many of our stereotypes are unconscious, we need to work tirelessly in uncovering them with as much nondefensiveness as possible. One of the greatest obstacles to this process is our fear that others will see our racism, sexism, and biases. Thus we try to deny their existence or hide them from public view. This works against our ability to uncover them.

THE EDUCATION AND TRAINING OF MENTAL HEALTH PROFESSIONALS

While national interest in the mental health needs of ethnic minorities has increased in the past decade, the human service professions, especially clinical and counseling psychology, have historically failed to meet the particular mental health needs of this population (Ponterotto & Casas, 1987; President's Commission on Mental Health, 1978; Samuda, 1998; D. W. Sue et al., 1982). Evidence reveals that the minority population is more likely to encounter problems such as immigrant status, poverty, cultural racism, prejudice, and discrimination, in addition to the common stresses experienced by everyone else. Yet studies continue to reveal that American Indians, Asian Americans, African Americans, and Hispanics tend to underutilize traditional outpatient mental health services (Cheung & Snowden, 1990; Leong 1994). Even more puzzling and disturbing were findings that minority clients tended to terminate counseling/therapy at a rate of more than 50% after only one contact with the therapist. This was in marked contrast to the less than 30% termination rate among White clients (S. Sue, Allen, & Conaway, 1975; S. Sue, Fujino, Hu, Takeuchi, & Zane, 1991; S. Sue & McKinney, 1974; S. Sue, McKinney, Allen, & Hall, 1974).

How are we to explain these startling statistics? One explanation may be that minorities are mentally healthier than their White counterparts, have less need for services, and require fewer sessions to effect a cure. We give this reason with "tongue in cheek," because it is not unusual for researchers to use data to support a point of view that may be quite inaccurate. It is ironic that the mental health literature, as we shall shortly see, has historically portrayed minorities as mentally unhealthy and pathological.

It is our contention that the reasons why minority-group individuals underutilize and prematurely terminate counseling/therapy lie in the biased nature of the services themselves. The services offered are frequently antagonistic or inappropriate to the life experiences of the culturally different client; they lack sensitivity and understanding; and they are oppressive and discriminating toward minority clients.

One of the major reasons for therapeutic ineffectiveness lies in the training of mental health professionals (Korman, 1974; Mio & Morris, 1990; Meyers, Echemendia, & Trimble, 1991). While directors of training report that multicultural coursework has increased in both counseling and clinical psychology programs (Bernal & Castro, 1994; Hills & Strozier, 1992), it is interesting to note that students of graduate programs have a different view. They report few courses offered in multicultural psychology and inadequate coverage of work with diverse populations within required core courses (Allison, Crawford, Echemendia, Robinson, & Knepp, 1994; Mintz, Bartels, & Rideout, 1995). For example, courses in family systems intervention, theories of psychotherapy, assessment, and testing, and research seldom include or infuse multicultural content. Further, the training of mental health professionals has often resulted in therapists' inheriting the racial and cultural bias of their forebears (Guthrie, 1997; Katz, 1985; Wrenn, 1985).

It is our contention that although multicultural coverage is increasing, the reports of its increase are inflated. Most graduate programs continue to give inadequate treatment to mental health issues of ethnic minorities. Cultural influences affecting personality formation, career choice, educational development, and the manifestation of behavior disorders are too often omitted from mental health training or treated in a tangential manner (Bernal & Castro, 1994; White & Parham, 1990). When minority-group experiences are discussed, they are generally seen and analyzed from the "White Euro-American, middle-class perspective." In programs where minority experiences have been discussed, the focus tends to be on their pathological lifestyles and/or a maintenance of false stereotypes. The result is twofold: (a) professionals who deal with mental health problems of ethnic minorities lack understanding and knowledge about ethnic values and their consequent interaction with a racist society, and (b) mental health practitioners are graduated from our programs believing minorities are inherently pathological and that therapy involves a simple modification of traditional White models.

This ethnocentric bias has been highly destructive to the natural help-giving networks of minority communities. Often mental health professionals operate under the assumption that racial and ethnic minorities never had such a thing as counseling and psychotherapy until it was invented and institutionalized in Western cultures. For the benefit of "those" people, the mental health movement has delegitimized natural help-giving networks that have operated for thousands of years by labeling them as unscientific, supernatural, mystical, and not consistent with professional standards of practice. Then mental health professionals are surprised to find that there is a high incidence of psychological distress in the minority community, that their treatment techniques do not work, and that the culturally different do not utilize their services.

Contrary to this ethnocentric orientation, we need to expand our perception of what constitutes mental health practices. Equally legitimate methods of treatment are nonformal or natural support systems so powerful in many minority groups (family, friends, community self-help programs, and occupational networks), folk-healing methods, and indigenous formal systems of therapy (Lee, 1997; Pedersen, 1994; D.W. Sue, Ivey, & Pedersen, 1996; D.W. Sue, et al., 1998). Instead of attempting to destroy them, we should be actively trying to find out why they may work better than Western forms of counseling and therapy.

DEFINITIONS OF MENTAL HEALTH

A number of individuals have pointed out how counseling and psychotherapy tend to often assume universal (*etic*) applications of their concepts and goals to the exclusion of culture-specific (*emic*) views (Trimble, 1990; Wrenn, 1985). Likewise, graduate programs have often been accused of fostering *cultural encapsulation*, a term first coined by Wrenn (1962). The term refers specifically to (a) the substitution of model stereotypes for the real world, (b) the disregarding of cultural variations in a dogmatic adherence to some universal notion of truth, and (c) the use of a technique-oriented definition of the counseling process. As a result, counselor roles are rigidly defined, implanting an implicit belief in a universal concept of "healthy" and "normal."

If we look at criteria used by the mental health profession to judge normality and abnormality, the deficiency of this approach becomes glaring. Several fundamental approaches that have particular relevance to our discussion have been identified (D. Sue, D.W. Sue, & S. Sue, 1997): (a) normality as a statistical concept, (b) normality as ideal mental health, and (c) abnormality as the presence of certain behaviors (research criteria).

First, statistical criteria equate normality with those behaviors that occur most frequently in the population. Abnormality is then defined in terms of those behaviors that occur least frequently. For example, data collected on IQs may be accumulated and an average calculated. IQ scores near the average are considered normal, and relatively large deviations from the norm (in either direction) are considered abnormal. In spite of the word *statistical*, however, these criteria need not be quantitative in nature: Individuals who talk to themselves, disrobe in public, or laugh uncontrollably for no apparent reason are considered abnormal according to these criteria simply because most people do not behave in that way. Statistical criteria undergird our notion of a normal probability curve so often used in IQ tests, achievement tests, and personality inventories.

Statistical criteria may seem adequate in specific instances, but they are fraught with hazards and problems. For one thing, they fail to take into account differences in time, community standards, and cultural values. If deviations from the majority are considered abnormal, then many ethnic and racial minorities that exhibit strong cultural differences from the majority have to be so classified. When we resort to a statistical definition, the dominant or most powerful group generally determines what constitutes normality and abnormality. For example, if a group of African Americans were to be administered a personality test and it was found that they were more suspicious than their White counterparts, what would this mean?

Some psychologists and educators have used such findings to label African Americans as paranoid. Statements by Blacks that "The Man" is out to get them may be perceived as supporting a paranoid delusion. This interpretation, however, has been challenged by many Black psychologists as being inaccurate (Grier & Cobbs, 1968; Guthrie, 1997; A.C. Jones, 1985; White & Parham, 1990). In response to their slave heritage and a history of White discrimination against them, African Americans have adopted various behaviors (in particular, behaviors toward Whites) that have proven important for survival in a racist society. "Playing it cool" has been identified as one means by which Blacks, as well as members of other minority groups, may conceal their true thoughts and feelings. A Black person who is experiencing conflict, anger, or even rage may be skillful at appearing serene and composed. This tactic is a survival mechanism aimed at reducing one's vulnerability to harm and exploitation in a hostile environment (White & Parham, 1990).

The personality test that reveals Blacks as being suspicious, mistrustful, and paranoid needs to be understood from a larger social-political perspective. Minority groups who have consistently been victims of discrimination and oppression in a culture that is full of racism have good reason to be suspicious and mistrustful of White society. In their classic book *Black Rage,* Grier and Cobbs (1968) point out how Blacks, in order to survive in a White racist society, have developed a highly functional survival mechanism to protect them against possible physical and psychological harm. The authors perceive this "cultural paranoia" as adaptive and healthy rather than dysfunctional and pathological. Indeed, some psychologists of color have indicated that the absence of a paranorm among minorities may be more indicative of pathology than its presence. The absence of a paranorm may indicate either poor reality testing (denial of oppression-racism in our society) and/or naiveté in understanding the operation of racism.

Second, the concept of ideal mental health has been proposed as one of the criteria of normality by humanistic psychologists. Such criteria stress the importance of attaining some positive goal. For example, consciousness-balance of psychic forces (Freud, 1960; Jung, 1960), self-actualization/creativity (Maslow, 1968; Rogers, 1961), competence, autonomy, and resistance to stress (Allport, 1961; White, 1963), or self-disclosure (Journard, 1964) have all been historically proposed. The discriminatory nature of such approaches is grounded in the belief of a universal application (all populations in all situations) and reveals a failure to recognize the value base from which the criteria are derived. The particular goal or ideal used is intimately linked with the theoretical frame of reference and values held by the practitioner. For example, the psychoanalytic emphasis on insight as a determinant of mental health is a value in itself (London, 1989). It is important for the mental health professional to be aware, however, that certain socioeconomic groups and ethnic minorities do not particularly value insight. Furthermore, the use of self-disclosure as a measure of mental health tends to neglect the earlier discussion presented on the paranorm. One characteristic often linked to the healthy personality is the ability to talk about the deepest and most intimate aspects of one's life; to self-disclose. This orientation is very characteristic of our counseling and therapy process in which clients are expected to talk about themselves in a very personal manner. The fact that many minorities are reluctant to initially self-disclose can place them in a situation where they are judged to be mentally unhealthy and, in this case, paranoid.

Definitions of mental health such as competence, autonomy, and resistance to stress are related to White middle-class notions of individual maturity. The mental health professions originated from the ideological milieu of individualism (Ivey, Ivey, & Simek-Morgan, 1997). According to this philosophy, individuals make their lot in life. Those who succeed in society do so on the basis of their *own* efforts and abilities. Successful people are seen as mature, independent, and possessing great ego strength. Apart from the potential bias in defining what constitutes competence, autonomy, and resistance to stress, the use of such a person-focused definition of maturity places the blame on the individual. When a person fails in life, it is because of his/her own lack of ability, interest, maturity, or some inherent weakness of the ego. If we see minorities as being subjected to higher stress factors in society and placed in a one-down position by racism, then it becomes quite clear that the definition will tend to portray the lifestyle of minorities as inferior, underdeveloped, and deficient. Ryan (1971) was the first to coin the phrase "blaming the victim" to refer to this process. Yet a broader system analysis would show that the economic, social, and psychological conditions of minorities are related to their oppressed status in America.

Thus, the use of ideal mental health as the sole criterion tends to present multiple problems. Which goal or ideal should be used? The answer depends largely on the particular theoretical frame of reference or values embraced by those posing the criteria. Their unbridled imposition without regard to social-cultural influences would lead us to conclude that almost all minorities in the United States are unhealthy.

Third, an alternative to the previous two definitions of abnormality is a research one. For example, in determining rates of mental illness in different ethnic groups, "psychiatric diagnosis," "presence in mental hospitals," and scores on "objective psychological inventories" are frequently used (Samuda, 1998). Diagnosis and hospitalization present a circular problem. The definition of normality-abnormality depends on what mental health practitioners say it is! In this case, the race or ethnicity of mental health professionals is likely to be different from that of minority clients. Bias on the part of the practitioner with respect to diagnosis and treatment is likely to occur (Cheung & Snowden, 1990; Snowden & Cheung, 1990). The inescapable conclusion is that minority clients tend to be diagnosed differently and to receive less preferred modes of treatment.

Furthermore, the political and societal implications of psychiatric diagnosis and hospitalization were forcefully pointed out over 30 years ago by Laing (1967, 1969) and Szasz (1970, 1971). While it appears that minorities underutilize outpatient services, they appear to face greater levels of involuntary hospital commitments (Snowden & Cheung, 1990). Laing believes that individual madness is but a reflection of the madness of society. He describes schizophrenic breakdowns as desperate strategies by people to liberate themselves from a "false self" used to maintain behavioral normality in our society. Attempts to adjust the person back to the original normality (sick society) are unethical.

Szasz states this opinion even more strongly:

In my opinion, mental illness is a myth. People we label "mentally ill" are not sick, and involuntary mental hospitalization is not treatment. It is punishment. . . . The fact that mental illness designates a deviation from an ethnical rule of conduct, and that such rules vary widely, explains why upper-middle-class psychiatrists can so easily find evidence of "mental illness" in lower-class individuals; and why so many prominent persons in the past fifty years or so have been diagnosed by their enemies as suffering from some types of insanity. Barry Goldwater was called a paranoid schizophrenic . . . Woodrow Wilson, a neurotic . . . Jesus Christ, according to two psychiatrists . . . was a born degenerate with a fixed delusion system. (Szasz, 1970, pp. 167–168)

Szasz sees the mental health professional as an inquisitor, an agent of society exerting social control on those individuals who deviate in thought and behavior from the accepted norms of society. Psychiatric hospitalization is believed to be a form of social control for persons who annoy or disturb us. The label "mental illness" may be seen as a political ploy used to control those who are different, and therapy is used to control, brainwash, or reorient the identified victims to fit into society. It is exactly this concept that many minorities find frightening. For example, many Asian Americans, American Indians, African Americans, and Hispanic/Latino Americans, are increasingly challenging the concepts of normality and abnormality. They believe that their values and lifestyles are often seen by society as pathological and thus are unfairly discriminated against by the mental health professions.

In addition, the use of objective psychological inventories as indicators of maladjustment may also place minorities at a disadvantage. One example concerning the paranorm has already been given. Most minorities are aware that the test instruments used on them have been constructed and standardized according to White middle-class norms. The lack of culturally unbiased instruments makes many feel that the results obtained are invalid. Indeed, in a landmark decision in the State of California (*Larry P. v. California*, 1986), Judge Peckham ruled in favor of the Association of Black Psychologists' claim that individual intelligence tests such as the WISC-R, WAIS-R, and Stanford Binet could not be used in the public schools on Black students. The improper use of such instruments can lead to an exclusion of minorities in jobs and promotion, to discriminatory educational decisions, and to biased determination of what constitutes pathology and cure in counseling/therapy (Halleck, 1971; London, 1989; Samuda, 1998).

D. Sue, D.W. Sue, and S. Sue (1997) have noted some primary objections to testing and the consequent classification that often results. When a diagnosis becomes a label, it can have serious consequences. First, a label can cause people to interpret all activities of the affected individual as pathological. No matter what a Black person may do or say that breaks a stereotype, his or her behavior will seem to reflect the fact that he or she is less intelligent than others around him or her. Second, a label may cause others to treat an individual differently even when he or she is perfectly normal. Third, a label may cause those who are labeled to believe that they do indeed possess such characteristics.

An old study by Rosenthal and Jacobson (1968) has shown how a label can cause differential treatment. They randomly assigned school children to either of two groups. Teachers were told that tests of one group indicated they were intellectual "bloomers" (gaining in competence and maturity); the other group was not given this label. After a one-year interval, children from both groups were retested (they had also been tested the year before). The experimenters found that the group identified as "bloomers" showed dramatic gains in IQ.

How did this occur? Many have speculated that the label led teachers to have higher intellectual expectations for the "bloomers" and thus to treat them differently. Even though there was no significant difference in IQ between the two groups to begin with, differences were present by the end of the year. It is not difficult to speculate that stereotypes of various racial and ethnic minorities will result in differential treatment based on preconceived notions. In addition, the Rosenthal and Jacobson study suggests not only that teachers behave differently, but also that labels may affect the children. It is possible that when people are constantly told by others that they are stupid or smart, they may come to believe such labels (self-fulfilling prophecy). If people ascribe certain stereotypical traits to a racial minority or an ethnic group, then it is reasonable to believe that they will behave differently toward the group and cause cognitive and behavioral changes among members of the group. These factors lend support to the belief that therapy is an ethnocentric part of the Establishment, which interprets behavior exclusively from its reference point and attempts to fit minorities into the "White experience."

These universal definitions of healthy and normal that are accepted unquestioningly in most clinical and counseling graduate programs also guide the delivery of mental health services. Thus the culturally encapsulated therapist may become a tool of his/her own dominant political, social, or economic values. Ethnocentric notions of adjustment tend to ignore inherent cultural-class values, allowing the encapsulated person to be blind to his/her own cultural baggage. The net result has been that mental health services have demanded a type of racial and cultural conformity in client behavior that has been demeaning and that has denied different ethnic minorities the right to their cultural heritage.

CURRICULUM AND TRAINING DEFICIENCIES

It appears that much of the universal definitions of mental health that have pervaded the profession has been primarily due to severe deficiencies in training programs. Various specialists (Arredondo et al., 1996; Mio & Morris, 1990; Ponterotto & Casas, 1987) have asserted that the major reason for ineffectiveness in working with culturally different populations is the lack of culturally sensitive material taught in the curricula. It has been ethnocentrically assumed that the material taught in traditional mental health programs is equally applicable to all groups. Even now, when there is high recognition of the need for multicultural curricula, it has become a battle to infuse such concepts into course content. As a result, course offerings continue to lack a non-White perspective, to treat cultural issues as an adjunct or add-on, to continue portraying cultural groups in stereotypic ways and to create an academic environment that does not support minority concerns, needs, and issues.

It is this very issue of cultural encapsulation and its detrimental effects on minorities that has generated training recommendations from the Vail Conference (Korman, 1974), 1975 Austin Conference, and Dulles Conference (1978). These conferences noted the serious lack and inadequacy of psychology training programs in dealing with religions, racial, ethnic, sexual, and economic groups. Selected recommendations included advocating (a) that professional psychology training programs at all levels provide information on the political nature of the practice of psychology, (b) that professionals need to "own" their value positions, (c) that client populations ought to be involved in helping determine what is "done to them," (d) that evaluation of training programs include not only the content, but also an evaluation of the graduates, and (e) that continuing professional development occur beyond the receipt of any advanced degree.

Perhaps the most important recommendation to arise from these conferences was the importance of identifying and assessing competencies of psychologists as they relate to the culturally different (American Psychological Association, 1993; Arredondo et al., 1996; D.W. Sue et al., 1982; D.W. Sue, Arredondo, & McDavis, 1992; D.W. Sue et al., 1998). In addition, the importance of providing educational experiences that generate sensitivity and appreciation of the history, current needs, strengths, and resources of minority communities was stressed. Students and professionals should be helped to understand the development and behavior of the group being studied, thus enabling them to (a) use their knowledge to develop skills in working with minority groups and (b) develop strategies to modify the effects of political, social, and economic forces on minority groups. The curriculum must focus on immediate social problems and needs. It must stimulate an awareness of minority issues caused by economic, social, and educational deprivation. The curriculum must also be designed to stimulate this awareness not solely at a cognitive level. It must enable students to understand feelings of helplessness and powerlessness, low self-esteem, poor self-concept, and how they contribute to low motivation, frustration, hate, ambivalence, and apathy. Each course should contain (a) a *consciousness-raising* component, (b) an *affective/experiential* component, (c) a *knowledge* component, and (d) a *skills* component.

COUNSELING AND MENTAL HEALTH LITERATURE

Many writers have noted how the social science literature, and specifically research, has failed to create a realistic understanding of various ethnic groups in America (Guthrie, 1997; Jones, 1997; Samuda, 1975, 1998; D.W. Sue & D. Sue, 1972; Thomas & Sillen, 1972). In fact, certain practices are felt to have done great harm to minorities by ignoring them, maintaining false stereotypes, and/or distorting their lifestyles. As mentioned previously, mental health practice may be viewed as encompassing the use of social power and functioning as a handmaiden of the status quo (Halleck, 1971; Highlen, 1996; Katz, 1985). It is clear that organized social science is part of the Establishment from which its researchers are usually drawn; moreover, organized social science often is dependent on the Establishment for financial support. Ethnic minorities frequently see the mental health profession in a similar way—as a discipline concerned with maintaining the status and power of the Establishment (Highlen, 1996). As a result, the persons collecting and reporting data are often perceived as possessing the social bias of their society.

Social sciences, for example, have historically ignored the study of Asians in America (Leong, 1986; Root, 1998). This deficit has contributed to the perpetuation of false stereotypes that has angered many of the younger Asians concerned with raising consciousness and group esteem. When studies have been conducted on minorities, research has been appallingly unbalanced. Many social scientists (Billingsley, 1970; Wilson & Stith, 1991) have pointed out how "White social science" has tended to reinforce a negative view of African Americans among the public by concentrating on unstable Black families instead of on the many stable ones. Such unfair treatment has also been the case in studies on Hispanics that have focused on the psychopathological problems encountered by Mexican Americans (Laval, Gomez, & Ruiz, 1983). Other ethnic groups such as Native Americans (Atkinson, Morten, & Sue, 1998; LaFromboise, 1998) and Puerto Ricans (Christensen, 1975) have fared no better. Even more disturbing is the assumption that the problems encountered by minorities are due to intrinsic factors (racial inferiority, incompatible value systems, etc.) rather than to the failure of society (Katz, 1985; Samuda, 1998).

In a classic study of stereotype evolution, S. Sue and Kitano (1973) analyzed the literature portrayal of the Chinese and Japanese in the United States and concluded that there is a strong correlation between stereotypes and the conditions of society. When economic conditions were poor, Asians were portrayed as nonassimilable, sexually aggressive, and treacherous. However, when economic conditions dictated a cheap labor supply, stereotypes became more favorable. While there are many aspects of how minorities are portrayed in social science literature, two of them seem crucial for us to explore: (a) minorities and pathology and (b) the role of scientific racism in research.

MINORITIES AND PATHOLOGY

When we seriously study the "scientific" literature of the past relating to the culturally different, we are immediately impressed with how an implicit equation of minorities and pathology is a common theme. The historical use of science in the investigation of racial differences seems to be linked with White supremacist notions (Guthrie, 1997; Jones, 1997; Samuda, 1998). The classic work of Thomas and Sillen (1972) refers to this as *scientific racism* and cites several historical examples to support the authors' contention: (a) 1840 census figures (fabricated) were used to support the notion that Blacks living under unnatural conditions of freedom were prone to anxiety; (b) mental health for Blacks was contentment with subservience; (c) psychologically normal Blacks were faithful and happy-go-lucky; (d) influential medical journals presented fantasies as facts supporting the belief that the anatomical, neurological, or endocrinological aspects of Blacks were always inferior to those of Whites; (e) the Black person's brain is smaller and less developed; (f) Blacks were less prone to mental illness because their minds were so simple; and (g) the dreams of Blacks are juvenile in character and not as complex as those of Whites. More frightening, perhaps, is a recent survey that found that many of these stereotypes continue to be accepted by White Americans: 20% publicly expressed a belief that African Americans are innately inferior in thinking ability, 19% believe that Blacks have thicker craniums, and 23.5% believe that Blacks have longer arms than Whites. One wonders how many White Americans hold similar beliefs privately, but because of social pressures do not publicly voice them.

Furthermore, the belief that various human groups exist at different stages of biological evolution was expressed by G. Stanley Hall in 1904. He stated explicitly that Africans, Indians, and Chinese were members of adolescent races and in a stage of incomplete development. In most cases, the evidence used to support these conclusions was fabricated, extremely flimsy, or distorted to fit the belief in non-White inferiority (Thomas & Sillen, 1972). For example, Gossett (1963) reports how, when one particular study in 1895 revealed that the sensory perception of Native Americans was superior to that of Blacks and that of Blacks to Whites, the results were used to support a belief in the mental superiority of Whites. "Their reactions were slower because they belonged to a more deliberate and reflective race than did the members of the other two groups" (p. 364). The belief that Blacks were born athletes as opposed to scientists or statesmen derives from this tradition. The 1987 statement by then Dodger executive Al Campanis that Blacks are not mentally capable of being front-office executives or managers indicates that such stereotypes still operate. More recently, professional golfer Jack Nicklaus is reported to have stated that African American golfers are born with the wrong muscles to play at the highest level in golf (Hatfield, 1996). The fact that Hall was a respected psychologist often referred to as "the father of child study" and first president of the American Psychological Association did not prevent him from inheriting the racial biases of the times.

The Genetically Deficient Model

The portrayal of the culturally different in literature has generally taken the form of stereotyping them as deficient in certain desirable attributes. For example, de Gobineau's (1915) *The Inequality of Human Races* and Darwin's (1859) *On the Origin of Species by Natural Selection* were used to support the genetic intellectual superiority of Whites and the genetic inferiority of the lower races. Galton (1869) wrote explicitly that African "Negroes" were "half-witted men who made childish, stupid and simpleton-like mistakes," while Jews were inferior physically and mentally and only designed for a parasitical existence on other nations of people. In 1916 Terman, using the Binet scales in testing Black, Mexican American, and Spanish Indian families, concluded that they were *uneducable.*

The genetic deficient model is present in the writing of educational psychologists and academicians (Hernstein, 1971; Jensen, 1969; Shockley, 1972; Shuey, 1966). In 1989, Professor Rushton of the University of Western Ontario presented a much-criticized study at the American Association for the Advancement of Science convention. He claimed that human intelligence and behavior were largely determined by race, that Whites have bigger brains than Blacks, and that Blacks are more aggressive. These "scientists" have adopted the position that genes play a predominant role in determination of intelligence. Shockley (1972) has expressed fears that the accumulation of weak or low intelligence genes in the Black population will seriously affect overall intelligence. Thus, he advocates that people with low IQs should not be allowed to bear children; they should be sterilized. This train of thought may have been expressed by Andy Rooney, a well-known commentator on *60 Minutes*, when he said, "Blacks have watered down their genes because the less intelligent ones are the ones that have the most children. They drop out of schools early, do drugs, and get pregnant." In all fairness to Rooney, it must be said that he denies making such comments, although CBS took disciplinary action.

Allegations of scientific racism can also be seen in the work of the late Cyril Burt, eminent British psychologist, who fabricated data to support his contention that intelligence is inherited and that Blacks have inherited inferior brains. Such an accusation is immensely important when one considers that Burt is a major influence in American and British psychology, is considered by many to be the father of educational psychology, was the first psychologist to be knighted, was awarded the American Psychological Association's Thorndike Prize, and that his research findings form the foundation for the belief that intelligence is inherited. The charges, leveled by several people (Dorfman, 1978; Gillie, 1977; Kamin, 1974) can be categorized into four assertions: (a) that Burt guessed at the intelligence of parents he interviewed and later treated his guesses as scientific facts, (b) that two of Burt's collaborators never existed and Burt wrote the articles himself while using their names, (c) that Burt produced figures identical to three decimal points from different sets of data (a statistical impossibility), and (d) that Burt fabricated data to fit his theories. In a thorough review of one of Burt's most influential publications, Dorfman (1978) concludes:

Cyril Burt presented data in his classic paper Intelligence and Social Class *that were in perfect agreement with a genetic theory of IQ and social class. A detailed analysis of these data reveals, beyond reasonable doubt, that they were fabricated from a theoretical normal curve, from a genetic regressions equation, and from figures published more than 30 years before Burt completed his surveys. (p. 1177)*

More recently, the publication of *The Bell Curve: Intelligence and Class Structure in American Life* (Hernstein & Murray, 1994) has reignited the controversy in both the public and academic domains. The assertions by the two authors, again, echo a familiar refrain: Intelligence is inherited to a large degree; race is correlated with intellect; and programs such as Head Start and Affirmative Action should be banished because they do no good. Instead, resources and funding should be reallocated to those who can profit from it. Samuda (1998) concludes about the authors: "Simply stated, they essentially recommend that those of lower intelligence should serve those of higher intelligence" (p. 175). He further concludes: ". . . *The Bell Curve* remains astonishingly antiquated and immune to evidence from the physiological and neurobiological sciences, quantitative genetics, and statistical theory, and it overlooks the significance of environmental factors that research has uncovered" (p. 176). What is problematic about *The Bell Curve* is that it presents a good deal of genuine science sprinkled with science fiction and a political ideology aimed at creating an elite class in America (Gould, 1996; Ryan, 1995; Willie, 1995).

The question of whether there are differences in intelligence between races is both a complex and emotional one. The difficulty in clarifying this question is compounded by many factors. Besides the difficulty in defining race, there exist questionable assumptions regarding whether research on the intelligence of Whites can be generalized to other groups, whether middle-class and lower-class ethnic minorities grow up in similar environments to middle- and lower-class Whites, and whether test instruments are valid for both minority and White subjects. More important, we should recognize that the average values of different populations tell us nothing about any one individual. Heritability is a function of the population, *not* a trait. Ethnic groups all have individuals in the full range of intelligence, and to think of any racial group in terms of a single stereotype goes against all we know about the mechanics of heredity. Yet much of social science literature continues to portray ethnic minorities as being genetically deficient in one sense or another. Those interested in both the issues and consequences in the testing of American minorities and the technical and sociopolitical analyses of *The Bell Curve* are directed to the excellent rebuttal by Samuda (1998).

The Culturally Deficient Model

Well-meaning social scientists who challenged the genetic deficit model by placing heavy reliance on environmental factors nevertheless tended to perpetuate a view of minorities as culturally disadvantaged, deficient, or deprived (Katz, 1985; Mays, 1985). Instead of a biological condition that caused differences, the blame now shifted to the lifestyles or values of various ethnic groups (Baratz & Baratz, 1970; Dana, 1993; Samuda, 1998; Smith, 1977a). The term *cultural deprivation* was first popularized by Riessman's widely read book, *The Culturally Deprived Child* (1962). It was used to indicate that many groups perform poorly on tests or exhibit deviant characteristics because they lack many of the advantages of middle-class culture (education, books, toys, formal language, etc.). In essence, these groups were culturally impoverished! Samuda (1975, 1998) summarizes studies that take the position that a host of factors place many minority persons in a position that hinders their success in school and society at large: (a) nutritional factors—malnutrition contributes to physical and mental impairment; (b) environmental factors—crowded and broken homes, dilapidated and unaesthetic areas (lack of books, toys, pictures, etc.); (c) psychological factors—lower self-concepts, poor motivation, absence of successful male models, lack of parental encouragement and interest in education, and fear of competing with Whites; (d) sociocultural factors— exposure to a culture with slum and ghetto values; and (e) linguistic factors.

While Riessman meant such a concept to add balance to working with minorities and ultimately to improve their condition in America, some educators of the time (Clark, 1963; Clark & Plotkin, 1972; Mackler & Giddings, 1965) strenuously objected to the term. First, the term *culturally deprived* means lacking a cultural background (slaves arrived in America culturally naked), which is impossible because everyone inherits a culture. Second, such terms cause conceptual and theoretical confusions that may adversely affect social planning, educational policy, and research. For example, the oft-quoted Moynihan Report (Moynihan, 1965) asserts that "at the heart of deterioration of the Negro society is the deterioration of the Black family. It is the fundamental source of the weakness in the Negro community" (p. 5). Action thus was directed toward infusing White concepts of the family into the Black ones. Third, Baratz and Baratz (1970) point out that cultural deprivation is used synonymously with the deviation from and superiority of White middle-class values. Fourth, these deviations in values become equated with pathology in which a group's cultural values, families, or lifestyles transmit the pathology. Thus it provides a convenient rationalization and alibi for the perpetuation of racism and the inequities of the socioeconomic system.

The Culturally Diverse or Different Model

There are many who now maintain that the culturally deficient model serves only to perpetuate the myth of minority inferiority. The focus tends to be a person-blame one, an emphasis on minority pathology, and a use of White middle-class definitions of desirable and undesirable behavior. Social science use of a common standard assumption implies that to be different is to be deviant, pathological, or sick. Mercer (1971) claims that intelligence and personality scores for minority group children really measure how Anglicized a person has become. Minorities should no longer be viewed as deficient, but rather as culturally different. The goal of society should be to recognize the legitimacy of alternative lifestyles, the advantages of being bicultural (capable of functioning in two different cultural environments), and the value of differences.

Since publication of the first two editions of this text, there has been increasing use of the term *culturally diverse*. It seems to imply that all racial/ethnic groups operate on a level playing field and that comparisons/descriptions are not made against just one standard (White ethnics).

RELEVANCE OF RESEARCH

So far, our discussion of minority portrayal in the professional literature has been a general one. We have made minimal reference to research as it relates to minorities in particular. Research findings are supposed to form the basis of any profession that purports to be a science. The data generated from research should be objective and free of bias. As we have seen in the last section, what researchers propose to study and how they interpret such findings are intimately linked to personal, professional, and societal value systems. Cheek (1987) goes so far as to assert that "social science is a vehicle of White supremacy."

It is an inescapable conclusion that personal and societal values often affect the interpretation of data as it relates to minorities. A very similar analogy can be drawn with respect to the mental health profession. For example, the profession's preoccupation with pathology tends to encourage the study of personality deficits and weaknesses rather than strengths or assets. Racist attitudes may intensify this narrow view, as minorities may be portrayed in professional journals as neurotics, psychotics, psychopaths, parolees, and so on, instead of as well-rounded persons.

It is not surprising that minority groups are often suspicious of the motives of the researcher. The researchers of ethnic matters may find their attitudes and values toward minority groups being challenged. No longer can the researcher claim that research is solely in the interest of science and morally neutral. The late Carl Rogers, a well-known humanistic psychologist, has stated, "If behavioral scientists are concerned solely with advancing their science, it seems most probable that they will serve the purpose of whatever group has the power" (as quoted in Brecher & Brecher, 1961, p. 20). C. W. Thomas (1970) has voiced this thought in even stronger form:

White psychologists have raped Black communities all over the country. Yes raped. They have used Black people as the human equivalent of rats run through Ph.D. experiments and as helpless clients for programs that serve middle-class White administrators better than they do the poor. They have used research on Black people as green stamps to trade for research grants. They have been vultures. (p. 52)

Williams (1974) discusses two scientific research projects that illustrate this statement: the Tuskegee experiment and the Colville Indian Reservation Study.

The Tuskegee experiment was carried out from 1932 to 1972 by the U.S. Public Health Service. Over 600 Alabama Black men were used as guinea pigs in the study of what damage would occur to the body if syphilis were left untreated. Approximately 399 were allowed to go untreated even when medication was available. Records indicated that seven died as a result of syphilis, and an additional 154 died of heart disease that may have been caused by the untreated syphilis. In a moving ceremony in 1997, President Clinton officially expressed regret for the experiment to the few survivors and apologized to Black America. Experiments of this type are ghastly and give rise to suspicions that minorities are being used as guinea pigs in other experiments of this sort. In view of such experiments, one can understand why so many African Americans continue to believe that HIV infection among Blacks may be caused by the U.S. government.

That exploitation occurs in other ethnic communities is exemplified in the Colville Indian reservation disposition (Williams, 1974). An anthropologist, after gaining the trust and confidence of the Colville Indians in Washington, conducted a study of factionalism among the tribe. A subsequent study by another group of White researchers recommended that the best course of action for the Colville reservation was to liquidate its assets, including land, rather than consider economic development. Part of the justification for liquidation was based on the factionalism results obtained from the first study, and termination of the reservation was recommended. There were several primary issues about the actions that merit attention. First, the reservation was composed of 1.4 million acres of land that was rich in timber and minerals. There was strong pressure on the part of Whites to obtain the land. Second, the problems of factionalism were actually created by a society that attempted to *civilize* the Indians via Christianity and by White businesses that offered promises of riches. Third, many of the Indians confided in the White researcher and were led to believe that the information obtained would not be released.

It is this type of study, as well as the continual portrayal of ethnic communities and groups as deviants, that makes minorities extremely distrustful about the motives of the White researcher. Whereas social scientists in the past have been able to enter ethnic communities and conduct their studies with only minimal justification to those studied, researchers are now being received with suspicion and overt hostility. Minorities are actively raising questions and issues regarding the values systems of researchers and the outcomes of their research.

Concern with the ethics of research has led most educational institutions and government agencies to establish review boards whose purpose is to survey all research being conducted or proposed by investigators. The American Psychological Association adopted a set of guidelines, *Ethical Principles in the Conduct of Research with Human Participants,* part of which is intended to endorse and promote ethical principles in psychological research. The APA has also established a committee on scientific and professional ethics and conduct, which has the power to levy sanctions on members for violations of varying seriousness. The document put out by the APA raises questions such as the following: Under what conditions is it ethically acceptable to study residents of a ghetto, minority group members, the poor, prisoners, intellectually handicapped individuals, or college students? What are the motives of the researcher? Is research conducted for some definable good, or is it opportunistic, exploitative, and potentially damaging to the target populations?

Furthermore, many members of ethnic minorities find it difficult to see the relevance or applicability of much research conducted on them. This is especially true when they view the researcher as a laboratory specialist dealing with abstract, theoretical ideas rather than with the real human condition. Much hostility is directed toward the researcher who is perceived in this way. There is a growing feeling among ethnic minorities that research should go beyond the mere explaining of human behavior. Research should contribute to the concerns and betterment of the groups being studied. This concern is voiced not only by minorities, but also by many students, scholars, and the public. Ethnic minorities often view the researcher as a laboratory specialist interested in abstract theoretical ideas rather than as a person interested in the applicability of his/her findings. Psychological researchers are often guilty of perpetuating this belief by failing to make clear and explicit the goals behind their pursuits. Indeed, many find this task distasteful. Much hostility, therefore, is directed at researchers of ethnic matters whom many minorities feel conduct narrow irrelevant studies that will not improve the human condition. There seems to be much justification for these charges.

First, graduate programs in the social sciences have traditionally been much more concerned with the training of academicians rather than practitioners. Several psychologists (Highlen, 1996; Katz, 1985; Mio & Iwamasa, 1993), in their analysis of graduate education, point out that most programs use as the *root model* the experimental research scientist as the psychological paradigm. This model has frequently hindered research dealing with social and psychological problems facing humankind. Since much exploratory work is needed in investigating complex social problems, the strong emphasis on rigorous methodology discourages much meaningful research dealing with problems of complex social issues (Hoshmand, 1989; Ponterotto & Casas, 1991). This discouragement is often seen in the status hierarchy of graduate programs. Experimental research is at the top of the ladder, with exploratory work at the bottom. Furthermore, manuscripts that may have meaningful implications in social contexts but that may not lend themselves to rigorous experimentation, are difficult to publish in the professional journals. Ethnic minorities who may desire to seek solutions to pressing social problems become alienated from such programs, which they feel are irrelevant and encapsulated from real social settings.

Second, many social researchers feel their responsibility is discharged with the publication of their results. Research data reported in the professional journals may be understandable to fellow professionals, but certainly not to many students and laypeople. All too often the publication of articles is written to impress colleagues and insure promotion and tenure (Goldman, 1977). The individuals and communities in such studies are often forgotten. Feedback in a form that is intelligible and usable by the particular communities is seriously lacking, and this contributes to feelings of exploitation. Researchers are increasingly being asked, "How will this study help us? Tell us in concrete terms, without your professional rationalizations and jargon, and we will decide whether you can have access to us or not."

A CALL TO THE PROFESSION

If the mental health profession is to receive acceptance from racial/ethnic minority groups, it must demonstrate, in no uncertain terms, its good faith and ability to contribute to the betterment of a group's quality of life. This demonstration can take several directions.

First, the mental health profession must take initiative in confronting the potential political nature of counseling (Katz, 1985). For too long we have deceived ourselves into believing that the practice of counseling/therapy and the database that underlie the profession are morally, ethically, and politically neutral. The results have been (a) subjugation of the culturally different, (b) perpetuation of the view that minorities are inherently pathological, (c) perpetuation of racist practices in treatment, and (d) provision of an excuse to the profession for not taking social action to rectify inequities in the system.

Second, psychology must move quickly to challenge certain assumptions that permeate our training programs. We must critically reexamine our concepts of what constitutes normality and abnormality, begin mandatory training programs that deal with these issues, critically examine and reinterpret past and continuing literature dealing with the culturally different, and use research in such a manner as to improve the life conditions of the researched populations.

Many multicultural specialists (Arredondo et al., 1996; D.W. Sue, Arredondo, & McDavis, 1992; D.W. Sue et al., 1982) have made a forceful call for the inclusion of implementing multicultural competence in training programs. Their suggestions involve asking that the American Psychological Association (APA) and the American Counseling Association (ACA) develop an explicit definition of multicultural competence that would be infused in all accreditation standards and into training programs. Requests that all divisions of ACA and APA endorse multicultural competency standards are paying off. As of this writing, two divisions of the APA and six divisions of the ACA have recognized the importance of such standards and formally adopted those created by D.W. Sue, Arredondo, and McDavis (1992).

What this boils down to is that educational programs can no longer present a predominantly White Anglo-Saxon Protestant (WASP) orientation. The study of minority group cultures must receive equal treatment and fair portrayal on all levels of education. Courses dealing with minority group experiences and internship practices must become a required part of the training programs. Training programs also need to reorganize the professional reward structure so that the practitioner receives equal status with the academician, and action or applied research should be encouraged even though it may not involve the epitome of rigorous experimental controls.

Third, research can be a powerful means of combating stereotypes and of correcting biased studies. The fact that previous studies have been used to perpetuate stereotypes does not preclude the usefulness of research. If social scientists believe that research has been poorly conducted or misinterpreted to the detriment of minority groups, they should feel some moral commitment to investigate their beliefs. Unfortunately, this self-correcting process of ethnic research has been underdeveloped, since there is a shortage of minority social scientists contributing a minority-group point of view. The researcher cannot escape the moral and ethical implications of his/her research and must take responsibility for the outcome of his/her study. He/she should guard against misinterpretations and take into account cultural factors and the limitations of his/her instruments.

Fourth, there is a strong need for counseling to attract more ethnic minorities to the profession, complex as this issue is. Although many White professionals have great understanding and empathy for minorities, they can never fully appreciate the dilemmas faced by a minority member. Ethnic minorities can offer a dimension and a viewpoint that act as a counterbalance to the forces of misinterpretation. Furthermore, the cry for more minority professionals demonstrates the presence of a credibility gap between counseling/therapy and minority members (Helms, 1993; Mio & Iwamasa, 1993; Parham, 1993; Ponterotto & Casas, 1990). With this addition of more minority psychologists, trust among ethnic minorities may be enhanced.

Fifth, therapists must realize that many so-called pathological socioemotional characteristics of ethnic minorities can be directly attributed to unfair practices in society. There must be a shift in research, from focusing on the poor and culturally diverse to focusing on the groups and institutions that have perpetuated racism and obstructed needed changes. Another shift in focus can be to study the positive attributes and characteristics of ethnic minorities. Social scientists have had a tendency to look for pathology and problems among minorities. Too much research has concentrated on mental health problems and culture conflict of minorities, while little has been done to determine the advantages of being bicultural. Hopefully, such an orientation will do much to present a more balanced picture of different minority groups. It must be noted, however, that the researcher cannot selectively publish findings that perpetuate *good* characteristics of minority groups and that censure *bad* ones. This selectivity is not only unethical, but also serves to maintain misunderstandings in the long run.

Last, making research with minorities a community endeavor can do much to lower hostility and develop trust between researcher and subject. For example, a social scientist investigating minority groups in the community is often more effective if he/she discusses his/her ideas with community leaders and obtains their cooperation (Mio & Iwamasa, 1993; Ponterotto & Casas, 1990). The inclusion of community members in different phases of research (interviewers, coordinators, etc.) can facilitate trust. This would require that social scientists clearly articulate their goals and methods to the community. Sanford (1970), in his discussion of student activism, notes that many students seldom know the implications or outcomes of the research conducted on them. He points out that research with student involvement can benefit its subjects by (a) helping them answer their questions and concerns, (b) helping them acquire understanding of themselves, and (c) helping them learn research skills. In this way, research will be educational for those being studied as well.

Chapter Two

◆

Sociopolitical Considerations of Trust and Mistrust in Multicultural Counseling and Therapy

◆

"**I** have worked with very few African American clients during my internship at the clinic, but one particular incident left me with very negative feelings. A Black client named Malachi was given an appointment with me. Even though I'm White, I tried not to let his being Black get in the way of our sessions. I treated him like everyone else, a human being who needed help.

"At the onset, Malachi was obviously guarded, mistrustful, and frustrated when talking about his reasons for coming. While his intake form listed depression as the problem, he seemed more concerned about non clinical matters. He spoke about his inability to find a job, about the need to obtain help with job hunting skills, and about advice in how best to write his resume. He was quite demanding in asking for advice and information. It was almost as if Malachi wanted everything handed to him on a silver platter without putting any work into our sessions. Not only did he appear reluctant to take responsibility to change his own life, but I felt he needed to go elsewhere for help. After all, this was a mental health clinic and not an employment agency. Confronting him about his avoidance of responsibility would probably prove counterproductive, so I chose to focus on his feelings. Using a humanistic-existential approach, I reflected his feelings, paraphrased his thoughts, and summarized his dilemmas. This did not seem to immediately help as I sensed an increase in the tension level, and he seemed antagonistic toward me.

"After several attempts by Malachi to obtain direct advice from me, I stated, 'You're getting frustrated at me because I'm not giving you the answers you want.' It was clear that this angered Malachi. Getting up in a very menacing manner, he stood over me and angrily shouted, 'Forget it, man! I don't have time to play your silly games.' For one brief moment, I felt in danger of being physically assaulted before he stormed out of the office.

"This incident occurred several years ago, and I must admit that I was left with a very unfavorable impression of Blacks. I see myself as basically a good person who truly wants to help others less fortunate than myself. I know it sounds racist, but Malichi's behavior only reinforces my belief that they have trouble controlling their anger, like to take the easy way out, and find it difficult to be open and trusting of others. If I am wrong in this belief, I hope this workshop (multicultural counseling and therapy) will help me better understand the Black personality."

A variation of the preceding incident was supplied at an inservice training workshop by a White male therapist and is used here to illustrate some of the major issues addressed in this chapter. In Chapter 1, we asserted that mental health practice is strongly influenced by historical and current sociopolitical forces which impinge upon issues of race, culture, and ethnicity. Specifically, we made a point that (a) the therapeutic session is often a microcosm of race relations in our larger society, (b) the therapist often inherits the biases of his/her forebears, and (c) therapy represents a primarily Euro-American activity that may clash with the worldview of the culturally different client. In this case, we do not question the sincerity of the White therapist nor his desire to help the African American client. However, it is obvious to us that the therapist is part of the problem and not the solution. The male therapist's preconceived notions and stereotypes about African Americans appear to have affected his definition of the problem, assessment of the situation, and therapeutic intervention. Let us analyze this case in greater detail to illustrate our contention.

First, statements that Malachi wants things handed to him on a silver platter, his avoidance of responsibility, and his wanting to take the easy way out are symbolic of social stereotypes that Blacks are lazy and unmotivated. The therapist's statements that African Americans have difficulty controlling their anger, that Malachi was menacing, and that the therapist was in fear of being assaulted seems to paint the picture of the hostile, angry, and violent Black male—again, a societal image of African Americans consciously and unconsciously subscribed to by many in this society. While it is always possible that the client was unmotivated and prone to violence, studies suggest that White Americans continue to cling to the image of the dangerous, violence prone and antisocial image of Black men (Jones, 1997). Is it possible, however, that Malachi has a legitimate reason for being angry? Is it possible that the therapist and the therapeutic process are contributing to Malachi's frustration and anger? Is it possible that the therapist was never in physical danger, but that his own affectively based stereotype of the dangerous Black male caused his unreasonable fear? Is this perhaps a misinterpretation resulting from a clash of different communications styles that triggers unrealistic racial fears and apprehensions?

Second, mental health practice has been characterized as being primarily a White middle-class activity that values rugged individualism, individual responsibility, and autonomy (Atkinson, Morten, & Sue, 1997; Highlen, 1994, 1996; Katz, 1985). Because people are seen as being responsible for their own actions and predicament, clients are expected to make decisions on their own and to be primarily responsible for their fate in life. The role of the traditional therapist should be to encourage self-exploration so that the client can act on his or her own behalf. The individual-centered approach tends to view the problem as residing within the person. If something goes wrong, it is the fault of the client. In the last chapter, we pointed out how many problems encountered by minority clients reside externally to them (bias, discrimination, prejudice, etc.) and that they should not be faulted for the obstacles they encounter. To do so is to engage in *victim blaming* (Lewis, Lewis, Daniels, & D'Andrea, 1998; Ridley, 1995; Ryan, 1971).

Third, therapists are expected to avoid giving advice or suggestions and disclosing their thoughts and feelings not only because they may unduly influence their clients and arrest their individual development, but because they may become emotionally involved, lose their objectivity, and blur the boundaries of the helping relationship (Herlihy & Corey, 1997). Parham (1997) states, however, that a fundamental African principle is that human beings realize themselves only in moral relations to others (collectivity not individuality). "Consequently, application of an African-centered worldview will cause one to question the need for objectivity absent emotions, the need for distance rather than connectedness, and the need for dichotomous relationships rather than multiple roles" (p.110).

In other words, from an African American perspective, the helper and helpee are not separated from one another but are bound together both emotionally and spiritually. The Euro-American style of objectivity encourages separation that Malachi may interpret as uninvolved, uncaring, insincere, and dishonest ("playing silly games"; [Paniagua, 1994]).

Fourth, the more active and involved role demanded by Malachi goes against what the helping profession considers therapy. Studies seem to indicate that clients of color prefer a therapeutic relationship in which the helper is more active, self-disclosing and not averse to giving advice and suggestions when appropriate (D.W. Sue, Ivey, & Pedersen, 1996). The therapist in this scenario fails to entertain the possibility that requests for advice, information, and suggestions may be legitimate and not indicative of pathological responding. The therapist has been trained to believe that his role as a therapist is to be primarily non-directive; therapists do "therapy," not provide job-hunting information. This has always been the conventional counseling and psychotherapy role: one that emphasizes a one-to-one, in-the-office, and remedial relationship aimed at self-exploration and the achievement of insight (Atkinson, Thompson, & Grant, 1993). We will have more to say about how these generic characteristics of counseling and psychotherapy may act as barriers to effective multicultural counseling and therapy in the next chapter.

Many of the above conflicts lead us to our fifth point. If the male therapist is truly operating from unconscious biases, stereotypes, and preconceived notions with his culturally different client, then much of the problem seems to reside within him and not with Malachi. In almost every introductory text on counseling and psychotherapy, lip service is paid to the axiom "therapist, know thyself." In other words, therapeutic wisdom endorses the notion that we become better therapists the more we understand our own motives, biases, values, and assumptions about human behavior (Wehrly, 1995). Unfortunately, most training programs are weak in having their students explore their values, biases, and preconceived notions in the area of racist/sexist/homophobic attitudes, beliefs, and behaviors. We are taught to look at our clients, to analyze them, and to note their weaknesses, limitations, and pathological trends; less often do we look for positive healthy characteristics in our clients or question our conclusions. Questioning our own values and assumptions, the standards we use to judge normality and abnormality, and our therapeutic approach is infrequently done. As mental health professionals, we may find it difficult and unpleasant to explore our racism, sexism, and homophobia, and our training often allows us the means of avoiding it.

When the therapist ends his story by stating that he hopes the workshop will help him better understand the Black personality, his worldview is clearly evident. There is an assumption that multicultural counseling/therapy simply requires the acquisition of knowledge, and that good intentions are all that is needed. This statement represents one of the major obstacles to self-awareness and dealing with one's own biases and prejudices. While we tend to view prejudice, discrimination, racism, and sexism as overt and intentional acts of unfairness and violence, it is the unintentional and covert forms of bias that may be the greater enemy because they are unseen and more pervasive. As a well-intentioned individual, this therapist obviously experiences himself as moral, just, fair-minded, and decent. Thus, it is difficult for him and many other mental health professionals to realize that what they do or say may cause harm to their minority clients.

Unintentional behavior is perhaps the most insidious form of racism. Unintentional racists are unaware of the harmful consequences of their behavior. They may be well-intentioned, and on the surface, their behavior may appear to be responsible. Because individuals, groups, or institutions that engage in unintentional racism do not wish to do harm, it is difficult to get them to see themselves as racists. They are more likely to deny their racism. . . . The major challenge facing counselors is to overcome unintentional racism and provide more equitable service delivery. (Ridley, 1995, p. 38)

Sixth, the therapist states he tried to not let Malachi's "being Black get in the way of the session," and that he treated him like any other "human being." This is a very typical statement made by Whites who unconsciously subscribe to the belief that being Black, Asian American, Latino American, or a person of color is the problem. In reality, color is not the problem. It is society's perception of color that is the problem! In other words, that locus of the problem (racism, sexism, and homophobia) resides not in the culturally different group, but in the society at large. Often, this view of race is manifested in the myth of color blindness: "If color is the problem, let's pretend not to see it." Our contention, however, is that it is nearly impossible to overlook the fact that a client is Black, Asian American, Hispanic, and so forth. When operating in this manner, the color-blind therapist may actually be obscuring his/her understanding of who Malachi really is. To overlook one's racial group membership is to deny an intimate and important aspect of one's identity. Those who advocate a color-blind approach seem to operate under the assumption that "Black is bad" and that to be different is to be deviant.

Last, and central to the thesis of this chapter, is the statement by the counselor that Malachi appears "guarded and mistrustful" and has difficulty being "open" (self-disclosing). We have mentioned several times that the inability of a counselor to establish rapport and a relationship of trust with culturally diverse clients is a major therapeutic barrier. When the emotional climate is negative, and when little trust or understanding exists between the therapist and the client, therapy can be both ineffective and destructive. Yet, if the emotional climate is realistically positive and if trust and understanding exist between the parties, the two-way communication of thoughts and feelings can proceed with optimism. This latter condition is often referred to as *rapport* and sets the stage in which other essential conditions can become effective. One of these, self-disclosure, is particularly crucial to the process and goals of counseling, because it is the most direct means by which an individual makes himself/herself known to another (Carter, 1995; Greene, 1985; Mays, 1985; White & Parham, 1990).

This chapter attempts to discuss the issue of trust as it relates to minority clients. Our discussion does not deal with cultural variables among certain groups (Asian Americans, American Indians, etc.) that dictate against self-disclosure to strangers. This will be presented in Chapter 3. We will first present a brief discussion of the sociopolitical situation as it affects the trust-mistrust dimension of certain culturally different populations. Second, we will look at factors that enhance or negate the therapist's cultural effectiveness as it relates to the theory of social influence. Third, we will systematically examine how therapist credibility and similarity affect a client's willingness to work with a therapist from another race/culture.

EFFECTS OF HISTORICAL AND CURRENT OPPRESSION

Mental health practitioners must realize that racial/ethnic minorities and other marginalized groups (women, gays/lesbians, and the disabled) in our society live under an umbrella of individual, institutional, and cultural forces that oftentimes demeans them, disadvantages them, and denies them equal access and opportunity (Atkinson & Hackett, 1998; Jones, 1972, 1997; Laird & Green, 1996). Experiences of prejudice and discrimination are a social reality for the culturally different and affect their view of the helping professional who attempts to work in the multicultural arena. Thus, mental health practitioners must become aware of the sociopolitical dynamics which not only form the worldview of their clients, but theirs as well. As in the clinical case above, racial/cultural dynamics may intrude into the helping process, causing misdiagnosis, confusion, pain, and a reinforcement of the biases and stereotypes both groups have of one another. It is important for the therapist to realize that the history of race relations in the United States has influenced us to the point of being extremely cautious in revealing our feelings and attitudes about race to strangers. In an interracial encounter with a stranger (i.e., therapy), each party will attempt to discern gross or subtle racial attitudes of the other while minimizing vulnerability. For minorities in the United States, this lesson has been learned well. While White Americans may also exhibit cautiousness similar to their minority counterparts, the structure of society places more power to injure and damage in the hands of the majority culture. In most self-disclosing situations, White Americans are less vulnerable than their minority counterparts.

As the individual chapters on American Indians, Asian Americans, Blacks, Hispanics, and other culturally different groups (gays/lesbians, women, disabled, and elderly) will reveal, the history and experiences of the culturally different have been those of oppression, discrimination, and racism. Institutional racism has created psychological barriers between minorities and White Americans that are likely to interfere with the therapy process. Understanding how the invisibility of ethnocentric monoculturalism has affected race, gender, and sexual orientation relationships is vital to successful multicultural competence.

ETHNOCENTRIC MONOCULTURALISM

It is becoming increasingly clear that the values, assumptions, beliefs, and practices of our society are structured in such a manner as to serve only one narrow segment of the population (D.W. Sue, Ivey, & Pedersen, 1996). Most mental health professionals, for example, have not been trained to work with other than mainstream individuals or groups. This is understandable in light of the historical origins of education, counseling/guidance, and our mental health systems, which have their roots in Euro-American or Western cultures (Highlen, 1994; Wehrly, 1995). As a result, American (U.S.) psychology has been severely criticized as being ethnocentric, monocultural, and inherently biased against racial/ethnic minorities, women, gays/lesbians and other culturally different groups (Carter, 1995; Laird & Green, 1996; Ridley, 1995; D.W. Sue, Arredondo, & McDavis, 1992). As voiced by many multicultural specialists, our educational system and counseling/psychotherapy have often done great harm to our minority citizens. Rather than educate or heal, rather than offer enlightenment and freedom, and rather than allow equal access and opportunities, historical and current practices have restricted, stereotyped, damaged, and oppressed the culturally different in our society.

In light of the increasing diversity of our society, mental health professionals will inevitably be encountering client populations that differ from them in terms of race, culture, and ethnicity. Such changes, however, are believed to pose no problems as long as psychologists adhere to the notion of an unyielding universal psychology that is applicable across all populations. While few mental health professionals would voice such a belief, in reality, the very policies and practices of mental health delivery systems do reflect such an ethnocentric orientation. The theories of counseling and psychotherapy, the standards used to judge normality-abnormality, and the actual process of mental health practice are culture-bound and reflect a monocultural perspective of the helping professions (Highlen, 1994; Katz, 1985; D.W. Sue, 1990). Consequently, they are often culturally inappropriate and antagonistic to the lifestyles and values of minority groups in our society. Indeed, some mental health professionals assert that counseling and psychotherapy may be "handmaidens of the status quo," "instruments of oppression," and "transmitters of society's values" (Halleck, 1971; D.W. Sue & D. Sue, 1990; Thomas & Sillen, 1972).

We believe that *ethnocentric monoculturalism* is dysfunctional in a pluralistic society like the United States. It is a powerful force, however, in forming, influencing, and determining the goals and processes of mental health delivery systems. Consequently, it is very important for mental health professionals to unmask or deconstruct the values, biases, and assumptions that reside in it. Ethnocentric monoculturalism combines what Wrenn (1962, 1985) calls "cultural encapsulation" and Jones' (1972, 1997) description of "cultural racism." In a recent publication by a combined multicultural task group from the American Psychological Association's Division of Counseling Psychology and the Society for the Psychological Study of Ethnic Minority Issues (D.W. Sue et al., 1998), five components of ethnocentric monoculturalism were identified.

Belief in Superiority

First, there is a strong belief in the superiority of one group's cultural heritage (history, values, language, traditions, arts/crafts, etc.). The group norms and values are seen positively and descriptors may include such terms as "more advanced" and "more civilized." Members of the society may possess conscious and unconscious feelings of superiority and that their way of doing things is the best way. In our society, White Euro-American cultures are seen as not only desirable, but normative as well. Physical characteristics such as light complexion, blond hair, and blue eyes; cultural characteristics such as belief in Christianity (single-god concept), individualism, Protestant work ethic, and capitalism; and linguistic characteristics such as standard English, control of emotions, and the written tradition are highly valued components of Euro-American culture (Katz, 1985). People possessing these traits are perceived more favorably and often are allowed easier access to the privileges and rewards of the larger society. McIntosh (1989), a White woman, refers to this condition as "White privilege": an invisible knapsack of unearned assets that can be used to cash in each day for advantages not given to those who do not fit this mold. Among some of these advantages that she enumerates are:

- I can if I wish arrange to be in the company of people of my race most of the time.
- I can turn on the television or open to the front page of the paper and see people of my race widely represented.
- When I am told about our national heritage or about "civilization," I am shown that people of my color made it what it is.
- I can be sure that my children will be given curricular materials that testify to the existence of their race.

Belief in Inferiority of Others

Second, there is a belief in the inferiority of all other groups' cultural heritage that extends to their customs, values, traditions, and language. Other societies or groups may be perceived as "less developed," "uncivilized," "primitive," or even "pathological." The other groups' life-styles or ways of doing things are considered inferior. Physical characteristics such as dark complexion, black hair, and brown eyes; cultural characteristics such as belief in non-Christian religions (Islam, Confucianism, polytheism—many gods, etc.), collectivism, present time orientation, and the importance of shared wealth; and linguistic characteristics such as bilingualism, nonstandard English, speaking with an accent, use of nonverbal and contextual communciation and reliance on the "oral tradition" are usually seen as less desirable by the society. Studies consistently reveal that individuals who are physically different, who speak with an accent, and who adhere to different cultural beliefs and practices are more likely to be evaluated more negatively in our schools and workplaces. Culturally different individuals may be seen as "less intelligent," "less qualified," "more unpopular," and of possessing "more undesirable traits."

Power to Impose Standards

Third, the dominant group possesses the power to impose their standards and beliefs upon the less powerful group. This third component of ethnocentric monoculturalism is very important. All groups are to some extent ethnocentric; that is, they feel positively about their cultural heritage and way of life. Minorities can be biased, can hold stereotypes, and can strongly believe that their way is the best way. Yet, if they do not possess the power to impose their values on others, they theoretically cannot oppress. It is power or the unequal status relationship between groups that defines ethnocentric monoculturalism. The goal here is not to blame, but to speak realistically about how our society operates. Ethnocentric monoculturalism is the individual, institutional, and cultural expression of the superiority of one group's cultural heritage over another, and the possession of power to impose those standards broadly upon less powerful groups. Since minorities, in general, do not possess a share of economic, social, and political power equal to that of Whites in our society, they are generally unable to truly discriminate on a large-scale basis. The damage and harm of oppression is likely to be one-sided: from majority to minority group.

Manifestation in Institutions

Fourth, the ethnocentric values and beliefs are manifested in the programs, policies, practices, structures, and institutions of the society. For example, chain-of-command systems, training and educational systems, communication systems, management systems, and performance appraisal systems often dictate and control our lives. They attain untouchable and Godfather-like status in an organization. Because most systems are monocultural in nature and demand compliance, racial/ethnic minorities and women may be oppressed. Jones (1972, 1997) defines institutional racism as a set of policies, priorities, and accepted normative patterns designed to subjugate, oppress, and force dependence on a larger society onto individuals and groups. It does this by sanctioning unequal goals, unequal status, and unequal access to goods and services. Institutional racism has fostered the enactment of discriminatory statutes, the selective enforcement of laws, the blocking of economic opportunities and outcomes, and the imposition of forced assimilation/acculturation on the culturally different. The sociopolitical system thus attempts to define the prescribed role occupied by minorities. Feelings of powerlessness, inferiority, subordination, deprivation, anger and rage, and overt/covert resistance to factors in interracial relationships are likely to result.

The Invisible Veil

Fifth, since people are all products of cultural conditioning, their values and beliefs (worldview) represent an invisible veil that operates outside the level of conscious awareness. As a result, people assume universality: that the nature of reality and truth are shared by everyone regardless of race, culture, ethnicity, or gender. This assumption is erroneous, but seldom questioned because it is firmly ingrained in our worldview. Racism, sexism, and homophobia may be conscious (intentional) or unconcious (unintentional). The neo-Nazis, Skinheads, and Ku Klux Klan would definitely fall into the first category. While conscious and intentional racism as exemplified by these groups, for example, may cause great harm to culturally different groups, it is the latter form that may ultimately be the most insidious and dangerous. As mentioned previously, it is well-intentioned individuals who experience themselves as moral, decent, and fair-minded that may have the greatest difficulty in understanding how their belief systems and actions may be biased and prejudiced. It is clear that no one was born wanting to be racist, sexist, or homophobic. Misinformation related to culturally different groups is not acquired by our free choice, but rather imposed through a painful process of social conditioning; all of us were taught to hate and fear others who are different in some way (D.W. Sue et al., 1998). Likewise, because all of us live, play, and work within organizations, those policies, practices, and structures that may be less than fair to minority groups are invisible in controlling our lives. Perhaps the greatest obstacle to a meaningful movement toward a multicultural society is our failure to understand our unconscious and unintentional complicity in perpetuating bias and discrimination via our personal values/beliefs and our institutions. The power of racism, sexism, and homophobia is related to the invisibility of powerful forces that control and dictate our lives. In a strange sort of way, we are all victims. Minority groups are victims of oppression. Majority group members are victims unwittingly socialized into the oppressor roles.

HISTORICAL MANIFESTATIONS OF ETHNOCENTRIC MONOCULTURALISM

The Euro-American worldview can be described as possessing the following values and beliefs: rugged individualism, competition, mastery and control over nature, a unitary and static conception of time, religion based on Christianity, and separation of science and religion (Katz,

1985). It is important to note that worldviews are neither right nor wrong, good nor bad. They become problematic, however, when they are expressed through the process of ethnocentric monoculturalism. In the United States, the historical manifestations of this process are quite clear. First, the European colonization efforts toward the Americas operated from the assumption that the enculturation of indigenous peoples was justified because European culture was superior. Forcing the colonized to adopt European beliefs and customs was seen as civilizing them. In the United States, this practice was clearly seen in the treatment of Native Americans where their lifestyles, customs, and practices were seen as backward and uncivilized and attempts were made to make over the "heathens." Such a belief is also reflected in Euro-American culture and has been manifested in attitudes toward other racial/ethnic minority groups in the United States as well: "Racial/ethnic minorities would not encounter problems if they assimilate and acculturate."

Monocultural ethnocentric bias has a long history in the United States and is even reflected as early as the uneven application of the Bill of Rights in favor of White immigrants/descendants as opposed to minority populations (Barongan et al., 1997). Some 222 years ago, Britain's King George III accepted a "Declaration of Independence" from former subjects residing in this country. This proclamation was destined to shape and reshape the geopolitical and sociocultural landscape of the world over many times. The lofty language penned by its principal architect, Thomas Jefferson, and signed by those present was indeed inspiring: "We hold these truths to be self-evident, that all men are created equal. . . ."

Yet, as we now view the historic actions of that time, we cannot but be struck by the paradox inherent in those events. First, all 56 of the signatories were White males of European descent, hardly a representation of the current racial and gender composition of the population. Second, the language of the declaration suggests that only men were created equal, but what about women? Third, many of the founding fathers were slave owners who seemed not to recognize the hypocritical personal standards they used because they considered Blacks to be subhuman. Fourth, the history of this land did not start with the Declaration of Independence or the formation of the United States of America. Yet, our textbooks continue to teach us an ethnocentric perspective "Western Civilization" which ignores over 2/3 of the world's population. Last, it is important to note that those early Europeans who came to this country were immigrants attempting to escape persecution (oppression), but in the process did not recognize their own role in the oppression of indigenous peoples (American Indians) who already resided in this country for centuries.

. . . the natural and inalienable rights of individuals valued by European and European American societies generally appear to have been intended for European Americans only. How else can European colonization and exploitation of Third World countries be explained? How else can the forced removal of Native Americans from their lands, centuries of enslavement and segregation of African Americans, immigration restrictions on persons of color through history, incarceration of Japanese Americans during World War II, and current English-only language requirements in the United States be explained? These acts have not been perpetrated by a few racist individuals, but by no less than the governments of the North Atlantic cultures. . . . If EuroAmerican ideals include a philosophical or moral opposition to racism, this has often not been reflected in policies and behaviors. (Barongan et al., 1997, p. 654)

We do not take issue with the good intentions of the early founders. Nor do we infer in them evil and conscious motivations to oppress and dominate others. Yet, the history of the United

States has been the history of oppression and discrimination against racial/ethnic minorities and women. The Western European cultures that formed the fabric of the United States of America are relatively homogeneous when compared not only to the rest of the world, but to the increasing diversity in this country. This Euro-American worldview continues to form the foundations of our educational, social, economic, cultural, and political systems.

As more and more White immigrants came to the North American continent, the guiding principle of blending the many cultures became codified into such terms as *the melting pot* and *assimilation/acculturation*. The most desirable outcome of this process was a uniform and homogeneous consolidation of cultures: in essence, becoming monocultural. Many psychologists of color, however, have referred to this process as *cultural genocide* an outcome of colonial thought (Guthrie, 1976, 1997; Samuda, 1998; Thomas & Sillen, 1972; White & Parham, 1990). Wehrly states: "Cultural assimilation, as practiced in the United States, is the expectation by the people in power that all immigrants and people outside the dominant group will give up their ethnic and cultural values and will adopt the values and norms of the dominant society— the White, male Euro-Americans." (1995, p. 24)

While ethnocentric monoculturalism is much broader than the concept of "race," it is race and color that have been used to determine the social order (Carter, 1995). The "White race" has been seen as superior and White culture as normative. Thus, a study of U.S. history must include a study of racism and racist practices directed at people of color. The oppression of the indigenous people of this country (Native Americans), enslavement of African Americans, widespread segregation of Hispanic Americans, passage of exclusionary laws against the Chinese, and the forced internment of Japanese Americans are social realities. Thus it should be no surprise that our racial/ethnic minority citizens may view Euro-Americans and our very institutions with considerable mistrust and suspicion. In health care delivery systems and especially in counseling/psychotherapy, which demands a certain degree of trust among therapist and client groups, an interracial encounter may be fraught with historical and current psychological baggage related to issues of discrimination, prejudice, and oppression. Carter (1995) draws the following conclusion related to mental health delivery systems: "Because any institution in a society is shaped by social and cultural forces, it is reasonable to assume that racist notions have been incorporated into the mental health systems" (p. 27).

THERAPEUTIC IMPACT OF ETHNOCENTRIC MONOCULTURALISM

Many multicultural specialists (Herring, 1996; Kochman, 1981; Locke, 1997; Ponterotto & Casas, 1991; Stanback & Pearce, 1985; White & Parham, 1990) have pointed out how African Americans, in responding to their forced enslavement, history of discrimination, and America's reaction to their skin color, have adopted behavior patterns toward Whites important for survival in a racist society. These behavior patterns may include indirect expressions of hostility, aggression, and fear. During slavery, in order to rear children who would fit into a segregated system and who could physically survive, African American mothers were forced to teach them (a) to express aggression indirectly, (b) to discern the thoughts of others while hiding their own, and (c) to engage in ritualized accommodating/subordinating behaviors designed to create as few waves as possible (Willie et al., 1973). This process involves a mild dissociation, where African Americans may separate their true selves from their role as "Negroes" (Pinderhughes, 1973). A dual identity is often used, where the true self is revealed to fellow Blacks, while the dissociated self is revealed to meet the expectations of prejudiced Whites.

From the analysis of African American history, the dissociative process may be manifested in two major ways.

First, "playing it cool" has been identified as one means by which African Americans or other minorities may conceal their true feelings (Greene, 1985; Grier & Cobbs, 1971; A.C. Jones, 1985). The intent of this manner of behavior is to prevent Whites from knowing what the minority person is thinking/feeling and to express feelings/behaviors in such a way as to prevent offending or threatening Whites (Ridley, 1995; White & Parham, 1990). Thus, a culturally different individual who may be experiencing conflict, explosive anger, and suppressed feelings will appear serene and composed on the surface. It is a defense mechanism aimed at protecting minorities from harm and exploitation.

Second, the "Uncle Tom syndrome" may be used by minorities to appear docile, nonassertive, and happy-go-lucky. Especially during slavery, Blacks learned that passivity is a necessary survival technique. To retain the most menial jobs, to minimize retaliation, and to maximize survival of the self and loved ones, many minorities have learned to deny their aggressive feelings toward their oppressors.

We are reminded of the skit performed by Richard Pryor, the Black comedian, in which the issue of Black awareness of personal vulnerability was sarcastically portrayed. In a monologue, Pryor mimicked how he recently purchased a brand-new Cadillac and was proudly driving about when he was pulled over by a White police officer. Aware that many White officers have preconceived notions about dangerous Black males and not wanting to be blown away, Pryor humorously enacted how he immediately raised his arms loudly claiming, "Look, no hidden weapons!" When asked for his driver's license, Pryor stated, "I will now take my right hand and use only two fingers to get my wallet located in the left breast pocket of the jacket." Pryor tipped his body slightly to the left so his jacket flopped open and pronounced "No hidden weapons there, either." Ever so slowly, he advanced his right hand toward the wallet to retrieve it. The skit continued in this very sarcastic but realistic statement about the nature of Black-White relations in our society.

The overall result of the minority experience in the United States has been to increase vigilance and sensitivity to the thoughts and behaviors of Whites in society. We mentioned earlier that African Americans have been forced to discern the thoughts of others accurately in order to survive. This has resulted in some studies (Kochman, 1981; Smith, 1981; D.W. Sue, 1990) revealing that certain minority groups such as African Americans are better readers of nonverbal communication. This will be discussed in greater detail in Chapter 4. Many African Americans have often stated that Whites "say one thing, but mean another." This better understanding and sensitivity to nonverbal communication has allowed Blacks to enhance their survival in a highly dangerous society. As we will later see, it is important for the minority individual to accurately read nonverbal messages, not only for physical survival, but for psychological reasons as well.

In summary, it becomes all too clear that past and continuing discrimination against certain culturally diverse groups is a tangible basis for minority distrust of the majority society (Ridley, 1984, 1995). White people are perceived as potential enemies unless proven otherwise. Under such a sociopolitical atmosphere, minorities may use several adaptive devices to prevent Whites from knowing their true feelings. Because multicultural counseling may mirror the sentiments of the larger society, these modes of behavior and their detrimental effects may be reenacted in the sessions.

The fact that many minority clients are suspicious, mistrustful, and guarded in their interactions with White therapists is certainly understandable in light of the foregoing analysis. In spite of their conscious desire to help, White therapists are not immune from inheriting racist attitudes, beliefs, myths, and stereotypes about Asian American, African American, Latino/Hispanic American, and American Indian clients. For example, White counselors often believe that Blacks are nonverbal, paranoid, and angry and most likely to have character disorders (Carter, 1995; A.C. Jones, 1985) or to be schizophrenic (Pavkov, Lewis, & Lyons, 1989). As a result, they view African Americans as unsuitable for counseling and psychotherapy. Mental health practitioners and social scientists who hold to this belief fail to understand the following facts.

1. As a group, African Americans tend to communicate nonverbally more than their White counterparts, and assume that nonverbal communication is a more accurate barometer of one's true feelings and beliefs (Hall, 1976; Kochman, 1981; Stanback & Pearce, 1985; Weber, 1985). African Americans have learned that verbal intellectual interactions are less trustworthy than the nonverbal messages sent by participants. Hall (1976) observes that African Americans are better able to read nonverbal messages (high context) than their White counterparts and rely less on intellectual verbalizations than on nonverbal communication to make a point. Whites, on the other hand, tune in more to verbal than to nonverbal messages (low context). Because they rely less on nonverbal cues, Whites need greater verbal elaborations to get a point across (D.W. Sue, Ivey, & Pedersen, 1996). Being unaware of and insensitive to these differences, White therapists are prone to feel African Americans are unable to communicate in "complex" ways. This judgment is based on the high value that therapy places on intellectual/verbal activity.

2. Rightly or not, White therapists are often perceived as symbols of the Establishment, who have inherited the racial biases of their forebears. Thus, the culturally different client is likely to impute all the negative experiences of oppression to the them (Katz, 1985; Vontress, 1971). This may prevent the minority client from responding to the helping professional as an individual. While the therapist may be possessed of the most admirable motives, the client may reject the helping professional simply because he/she is White. Thus, communication may be directly or indirectly shut off.

3. Some culturally different clients may lack confidence in the counseling/therapy process because the White counselor often proposes White solutions to their concerns (Atkinson et al., 1989, 1998). Many pressures are placed on culturally different clients to accept an alien value system and reject their own. We have already indicated how counseling and psychotherapy may be perceived as instruments of oppression whose function is to force assimilation and acculturation. As some racial/ethnic minority clients have asked, "Why do I have to become White in order to be considered healthy?"

4. The "playing it cool" and "Uncle Tom" responses of many minorities are also present in the therapy sessions. As pointed out earlier, these mechanisms are attempts to conceal true feelings, to effectively hinder self-disclosure, and to prevent the therapist from getting to know the client. These adaptive survival mechanisms have been acquired through generations of experience with a hostile and invalidating society. The therapeutic dilemma encountered by the helping professional in working with a culturally different client is how to gain trust and break through this maze. What the therapist ultimately does in the sessions will determine his or her trustworthiness.

To summarize, the culturally different client entering counseling or therapy is likely to experience considerable anxiety about ethnic/racial/cultural differences. Suspicion, apprehension, verbal constriction, unnatural reactions, open resentment and hostility, and passive or cool behavior may all be expressed. Self-disclosure and the possible establishment of a working relationship can be seriously delayed and/or prevented from occurring. In all cases, the therapist may be put to severe tests about his/her trustworthiness. A culturally effective therapist is one who is (a) able to view these behaviors in a nonjudgmental manner (they are not necessarily indicative of pathology but a manifestation of adaptive survival mechanisms), (b) able to not personalize any potential hostility expressed toward him/her, and (c) can adequately resolve challenges to his/her credibility. Thus, it becomes important for us to understand those dimensions that may enhance or diminish the culturally different client's receptivity to self-disclosure.

CREDIBILITY AND ATTRACTIVENESS IN MULTICULTURAL COUNSELING

In the last section, we presented a case study to explain how the political atmosphere of the larger society affects the minority client's perception of a multicultural therapy situation. Racial/ethnic minorities in the United States have solid reasons for not trusting White Americans. Lack of trust often leads to guardedness, inability to establish rapport, and lack of self-disclosure on the part of culturally different clients. What a therapist says and does in the sessions can either enhance or diminish his/her credibility and attractiveness. A therapist who is perceived by clients as highly credible and attractive is more likely to elicit trust, motivation to work/change, and self-disclosure. These appear to be important conditions for effective therapy to occur (S. Sue & Zane, 1987).

Theories of counseling and psychotherapy attempt to outline an approach designed to make them effective. It is our contention that multicultural helping cannot be approached through any one theory of counseling (Rogler, Malgady, Constantino, & Blumenthal, 1987; D.W. Sue, Ivey, & Pedersen, 1996). There are several reasons for such a statement. First, theories of counseling are composed of philosophical assumptions regarding the nature of man and a theory of personality. These characteristics, as pointed out earlier, are highly culture-bound (Katz, 1985; D.W. Sue 1995). What is the true nature of people is a philosophical question. What constitutes the healthy and unhealthy personality is also debatable and varies from culture to culture and class to class.

Second, theories of counseling and psychotherapy are also composed of a body of therapeutical techniques and strategies. These techniques are applied to clients with the hope of effecting change in behaviors, perceptions, or attitudes. A theory dictates what techniques are to be used and, implicitly, in what proportions. For example, it is clear that humanistic-existential therapists behave differently from rational-emotive ones. The fact that one school of counseling/therapy can be distinguished from another has implications: It suggests a certain degree of rigidity in working with culturally different clients who might find such techniques offensive or inappropriate. The implicit assumption is that these techniques are imposed according to the theory and not based on client needs and values.

It is very important for the therapist to be aware of the implications in regard to minority reading of nonverbal behavior. "Playing it cool" and the "Uncle Tom" syndrome, as well as other challenges to the counselor, are frequently given in order to assess the counselor's nonverbal message rather than the verbal one. When topics related to racism are brought up in the session, what the therapist says may oftentimes be negated by his/her nonverbal communication. If this is the case, the minority client will quickly perceive the inconsistency and conclude that the therapist is incapable of dealing with cultural/racial diversity.

Third, theories of counseling and psychotherapy have oftentimes failed to agree among themselves about what constitute desirable outcomes. This makes it extremely difficult to determine the effectiveness of counseling and therapy (Herring, 1997; Kleinke, 1994). For example, the psychoanalytically oriented therapist uses insight, the behaviorist uses behavior change, the client-centered person uses self-actualization, and the rational-emotive person uses rational cognitive content/processes. The potential for disagreement over appropriate outcome variables is increased even further when the therapist and client come from different cultures. While the counseling outcome is extremely important, we attempt to concentrate our discussion on process elements. We are more concerned here with *how* change occurs (the process) during therapy rather than with *what* change (the outcomes) results from therapy.

COUNSELING AS INTERPERSONAL INFLUENCE

When people engage in interactions with one another, they inevitably attempt to exert influence. These social-influence attempts may be overt or covert, conscious or unconscious. Whether the intent is to create a favorable impression when meeting people, to toilet train a young child, to convince people that cigarette smoking is harmful, to gain acceptance from a desired group, or to sell goods, these social-influence attempts are all aimed at changing attitudes, perceptions, and/or behaviors.

Likewise, therapy may be conceptualized as an interpersonal-influence process in which the counselor uses his/her social power to influence the client's attitudes and behaviors. Strong (1969) is probably the person most credited with providing a conceptual framework for understanding parallels between the role of the therapist, the process of therapy, and the outcome of therapy with those of the persuasive communicator, the influencing process, and opinion/behavior change, respectively. Specifically, communication attributes that had been established as important determinants of attitude change in the field of social psychology seemed similar to those that make an effective therapist (Heesacker & Carroll, 1997). Counselors who are perceived by their clients as credible (expert and trustworthy) and attractive are able to exert greater influence than those perceived as lacking in credibility and attractiveness. A number of counseling reviews and studies support this contention (Corrigan, Dell, Lewis, & Schmidt, 1980; Heesacker, Conner, & Pritchard, 1995; Heppner & Claiborn, 1989; Heppner & Frazier, 1992; Lent & Maddux, 1997; Schmidt & Strong, 1971; Stoltenberg, McNeill, & Elliot, 1995; Strong & Schmidt, 1970). Using social-influence theory as a means to analyze counseling not only has empirical validity and concentrates on process variables, but also seems to have equal applicability to all approaches. Regardless of the counseling orientation (person-centered, psychoanalytic, behavioral, transactional analysis, etc.), the therapist's effectiveness tends to depend on his/her perceived expertness, trustworthiness, and attractiveness.

Most of the studies mentioned have dealt exclusively with a White population (Heesacher, Conner, & Pritchard, 1995). Thus, findings that certain attributes contribute to a counselor's credibility and attractiveness may not be so perceived by culturally different clients. It is entirely possible that credibility, as defined by credentials indicating specialized training (MFCC, MSW, Psy.D., Ph.D., or M.D.), may mean to a Hispanic client only that the White therapist has no knowledge or expertise in working with Hispanics. This assumption is based on the fact that most training programs are geared for White middle-class clients and are culturally exclusive.

Our focus in this section is twofold: (a) We outline the various ways clients perceive their therapist's attempts to influence them, and (b) we discuss the dimensions of therapist expertness, trustworthiness, and similarity as they relate to culturally different clients. We are then able to lay the foundation for a theory of multicultural counseling, which is presented and discussed later.

PSYCHOLOGICAL SETS OF CLIENTS

Credibility and attractiveness of the therapist are very much dependent on the psychological set or frame of reference for the culturally different client. We all know individuals who tend to value rational approaches to solving problems and others who value a more affective (attractiveness) approach. It would seem reasonable that a client who values rationality might be more receptive to a counseling approach that emphasizes the counselor's credibility. Thus, understanding a client's psychological set may facilitate the therapist's ability to exert social influence in counseling. Collins (1970) has proposed a set of conceptual categories that we can use to understand people's receptivity to pressures for conformity (change). We apply those categories here with respect to the therapy situation. These five hypothetical sets or frames of mind are elicited in clients for several different reasons. Race, ethnicity, and the experience of discrimination often affect the type of set that will be operative in a minority client.

1. *The problem-solving set: information orientation.* In the problem-solving set, the client is cerned about obtaining correct information (solutions, outlooks, and skills) that has adaptive value in the real world. The client accepts or rejects information from the therapist on the basis of its perceived truth or falsity; is it an accurate representation of reality? The processes used in analyzing and attacking the problem tend to be rational and logical. First, the client may apply a consistency test and compare the new facts with information he/she already possesses. For example, a White therapist might try to reassure an African American client that he is not against interracial marriage, but hesitate in speech and tense up whenever the topic is broached. In this case, the verbal or content message is inconsistent with nonverbal cues, and the credibility and social influence of the therapist is likely to decline. Second, the Black client may apply a corroboration test by actively seeking information from others for comparison purposes. If he or she hears from a friend that the therapist has racial hang-ups, the therapist's effectiveness is likely to be severely diminished. The former test makes use of information the individual already has (understanding of nonverbal meanings), while the latter requires him/her to seek out new information (asking a trusted African American friend).

    Through socialization and personal experiences, we have learned that some people are more likely to provide accurate/helpful information (be credible) than others. Sources that have been dependable in the past, that have high status, possess good reputations, occupy certain roles, and are motivated to make accurate representations are more likely to influence us. Minorities, on the other hand, may have learned that many Whites have little expertise when it comes to their lifestyles and that the information/suggestions they give are White solutions/labels. It is highly possible that racial/ethnic groups may vary in their information orientation. For example, D.W. Sue (1981) has indicated that many Puerto Ricans who come for counseling and therapy expect information, advice, and direct sugges-tions. Likewise, it has been found that many Asian Americans tend not only to prefer a structured, direct, and practical orientation, but oftentimes seek advice, consolation, and suggestions from therapists. Therapists who do not value the problem-solving set and who may be affectively oriented may actually have great difficulties in relating to the client.

2. *The consistency set.* People are operating under the consistency set whenever they change an opinion, belief, or behavior in such a way as to make it consistent with other opinions, be-liefs, or behaviors. This principle is best illustrated in Festinger's classic book *A Theory of Cognitive Dissonance* (1957). Stated simply, the theory says that when a person's attitudes, opinions, or beliefs are met with disagreement (inconsistencies), cognitive imbalance or dis-sonance will be created. The existence of dissonance is psychologically uncomfortable and produces tension with drive characteristics. The result is an attempt to reduce the disso-nance. In reality, the consistency set may really be a by-product of the problem-solving set. This is so because we assume that the real world is consistent. For example, since therapists are supposed to help, we naturally believe that they would not do something to hurt us. If they do, then it creates dissonance. To reduce this inconsistency, we may discredit or dero-gate the therapist (he/she is not a good person after all) or in some way excuse the act (he/she did it unintentionally). The rules of the consistency set specify that good people do good things and bad people do bad things. It is important to note that the consistency set states that people are not necessarily *rational* beings but *rationalizing* ones. A therapist who is not in touch with his/her prejudices/biases may send out conflicting messages to a minority client. The counselor may verbally state, "I am here to help you," but at the same time, non-verbally indicate racist attitudes/feelings. This can destroy the credibility of the counselor very quickly in the case of a minority client who accurately applies a consistency set: "White people say one thing, but do another. You can't believe what they tell you."

   Generally, minority clients who enter therapy with a White therapist will tend to apply a consistency test to what the therapist says or does. That is because the client is trying to test the therapist as to whether he or she has the knowledge, understanding, and expertise to work with a minority individual. A culturally different client will actively seek out disclo-sures on the part of the therapist to compare them with the information he/she has about the world. Should the therapist pass the test, then new information may be more readily ac-cepted and assimilated. As we mentioned, culturally different individuals apparently are better readers of nonverbal cues. As a result, the therapist who sends out conflicting verbal and nonverbal messages may easily be dismissed as being unable to help the client.

3. *The identity set.* In the identity set, the individual generally desires to be like or similar to a person or group he/she holds in high esteem. Much of our identity is formed from those ref-erence groups to which we aspire. We attempt to take on the reference group's characteris-tics, beliefs, values, and behaviors because they are viewed as favorable. An individual who strongly identifies with a particular group is likely to accept the group's beliefs and conform to behaviors dictated by the group. If race or ethnicity constitutes a strong reference group for a client, then a counselor of the same race/ethnicity is likely to be more influential than one who is not.

   There are a number of studies (see reviews by Atkinson, 1983, 1985; Atkinson & Schein, 1986) indicating that certain similarities between the counselor and client may actually enhance therapeutic longevity and therapist preference. For example, racial similarity between therapist and client may actually affect willingness to return for therapy and hopefully facilitate effectiveness. The studies on this are quite mixed as there is considerable evidence that membership group similarity may not be as effective as belief or attitude similarity. Furthermore, a number of studies (Parham, 1989; Parham & Helms, 1981, 1985) suggest that the stage of cultural or racial identity affects which dimensions of similarities will be preferred by the racial/ethnic minority client. We will have much more to say about cultural identity development in a following chapter.

4. *The economic set.* In the economic set, the person is influenced because of perceived rewards and punishments the source is able to deliver. In this set, a person performs a behavior or states a belief in order to gain rewards and avoid punishments. In the case of the therapist, he/she controls important resources that may affect the client. For example, a therapist may decide to recommend the expulsion of a student from the school or deny a positive parole recommendation to a prisoner-client. In less subtle ways, the therapist may ridicule or praise a client during a group-counseling session. In these cases, the client may decide to change his/her behavior because the therapist holds greater power. The major problem with the use of rewards and punishments to induce change is that while it may assure behavioral compliance, it does not guarantee private acceptance. As noted, racial/ethnic minorities are well aware of recognizing power differentials and behaving accordingly ("playing it cool" or using the "Uncle Tom" approach). Furthermore, for rewards and coercive power to be effective, the therapist must maintain constant surveillance. Once the surveillance is removed, the client is likely to revert back to previous modes of behavior. For culturally different clients, therapy that operates primarily on the economic set is more likely to prevent the development of trust, rapport, and self-disclosure.

The economic set is probably the strongest indicator of cultural oppression in therapy (D.W. Sue, 1981). We in the mental health professions like to believe that counseling/psychotherapy is aimed at helping people, freeing them, and allowing them greater autonomy and choice in life situations. Unfortunately, in working with culturally diverse clients whose lifestyles and values may differ from our own, we oftentimes engage in cultural oppression. That is, we attempt to make them conform to our standards and ways of behavior. In doing this, we can exercise the economic set strongly by making our clients feel inadequate for being different. As mental health professionals, we need to realize that counseling and therapy can be very oppressive at an unintentional manner.

5. *The authority set.* Under this set, some individuals are thought to have a particular position that gives them a legitimate right to prescribe attitudes and/or behaviors. In our society, we have been conditioned to believe that certain authorities (police officers, chairpersons, designated leaders, etc.) have the right to demand compliance. This occurs via training in role behavior and group norms. Mental health professionals, such as counselors, are thought to have a legitimate right to recommend and provide psychological treatment to disturbed or troubled clients. It is this psychological set that legitimizes the counselor's role as a helping professional. Yet, for many minorities, it is exactly these roles in society that are perceived to be instruments of institutional oppression and racism. The 1996 O.J. Simpson trial and verdict brought out major differences in how African Americans and White Americans perceived the police. African Americans were more likely, as a group, to entertain the notion that police officers deliberately tampered with evidence because Simpson was a Black man; White Americans, however, were much less inclined to believe the police could act in such a

manner. Even when audiotapes of Detective Mark Fuhrman revealed an admission of evidence tampering and racist beliefs, White Americans continued to cling to the belief that it was an isolated incident or that Fuhrman was an exception to the rule.

None of the five sets or frames are mutually exclusive. These sets frequently interact and any number of them can operate at the same time. For example, it is possible that you are influenced by a therapist you find highly credible. It is also possible that you like the therapist or find him/her very attractive. Are you accepting his/her influence because the therapist is credible (problem-solving set), attractive (identification set), or both?

It should be clear at this point that characteristics of the influencing source (therapist) are all-important in eliciting types of changes. In addition, the type of mental or psychological set placed in operation oftentimes dictates the permanency and degree of attitude/belief change. For example, the primary component in getting compliance in the economic and authority set is the power that the person holds over you—the ability to reward or punish; in identification (the identity set), it is the attractiveness or liking of the therapist; and in internalization (the problem-solving and consistency set), credibility or truthfulness is important.

While these sets operate similarly for both majority and minority clients, their manifestations may be quite different. Obviously, a minority client may have great difficulty identifying (identification set) with a counselor from another race or culture. Also, what constitutes credibility to minority clients may be far different from what constitutes credibility to a majority client. We now focus on how counselor characteristics affect these sets as they apply to the culturally different.

Therapist Credibility

Credibility (which elicits the problem-solving, consistency, and identification sets) may be defined as the constellation of characteristics that makes certain individuals appear worthy of belief, capable, entitled to confidence, reliable, and trustworthy. Expertness is an "ability" variable, while trustworthiness is a "motivation" one. Expertness depends on how well-informed, capable, or intelligent others perceive the communicator (counselor) to be. Trustworthiness is dependent on the degree to which people perceive the communicator (therapist) as motivated to make valid assertions. In counseling and therapy, these two components have been the subject of much research and speculation (Barak & Dell, 1977; Barak & La Crosse, 1975; Dell, 1973; Heesacker, Conner, & Pritchard, 1995; La Crosse & Barak, 1976; LaFromboise & Dixon, 1981; Lent & Maddux, 1997; Spiegel, 1976; Sprafkin, 1970; Strong, 1969; Strong & Schmidt, 1970). The weight of evidence supports our commonsense beliefs that the helping professional who is perceived as more expert and trustworthy can have a greater influence on clients more than one who is perceived to have lower levels of these traits.

Expertness. Clients often go to a therapist not only because they are in distress and in need of relief, but also because they believe the counselor is an expert; he/she has the necessary knowledge, skills, experience, training, and tools to help (problem-solving set). Perceived expertness is typically a function of (a) reputation, (b) evidence of specialized training, and (c) behavioral evidence of proficiency/competency. For culturally different clients, the issue of therapist expertness seems to be raised more often than in going to a therapist of one's own culture and race. As mentioned previously, the fact that therapists have degrees and certificates from prestigious institutions (authority set) may not enhance perceived expertness. This is especially true for clients who are culturally different and aware that institutional bias exists in training programs. Indeed, it may have the opposite effect by reducing credibility. Neither is reputation-expertness (authority set) likely to impress a minority client unless the favorable testimony comes from someone of his/her own group.

Thus behavior-expertness, or demonstrating your ability to help a client, becomes the critical form of expertness in effective multicultural counseling (problem-solving set). It appears that using counseling skills and strategies appropriate to the life values of the culturally different client is crucial. We have already mentioned that there is evidence to suggest that certain minority groups prefer a much more active approach to counseling. A counselor playing a relatively inactive role may be perceived as being incompetent and unhelpful. The example presented next shows how the therapist's approach lowers perceived expertness.

ASIAN AMERICAN MALE CLIENT: It's hard for me to talk about these issues. My parents and friends . . . they wouldn't understand . . . if they ever found out I was coming here for help. . . .

WHITE MALE THERAPIST: I sense it's difficult to talk about personal things. How are you feeling right now?

ASIAN AMERICAN CLIENT: Oh, all right.

WHITE THERAPIST: That's not a feeling. Sit back and get in touch with your feelings. [*Pause*] Now tell me, how are you feeling right now?

ASIAN AMERICAN CLIENT: Somewhat nervous.

WHITE THERAPIST: When you talked about your parents' and friends' not understanding and the way you said it made me think you felt ashamed and disgraced at having to come. Was that what you felt?

While this exchange appears to indicate that the therapist (a) was able to see the client's discomfort and (b) interpret his feelings correctly, it also points out the therapist's lack of understanding and knowledge of Asian cultural values. While we do not want to be guilty of stereotyping Asian Americans, many do have difficulty, at times, openly expressing feelings publicly to a stranger. The therapist's persistent attempts to focus on feelings and his direct and blunt interpretation of them may indicate to the Asian American client that the therapist lacks the more subtle skills of dealing with a sensitive topic and/or is shaming the client (see chapter on Asian Americans).

Furthermore, it is possible that the Asian American client in this case is much more used to discussing feelings in an indirect or subtle manner. A direct response from the therapist addressed to a feeling may not be as effective as one that deals with it indirectly. In many traditional Asian groups, subtlety is a highly prized art, and the traditional Asian client may feel much more comfortable when dealing with feelings in an indirect manner.

In many ways, behavioral manifestations of therapist expertness override other considerations. For example, many educators claim that specific therapy skills are not as important as the attitude one brings into the therapeutic situation. Behind this statement is the belief that universal attributes of genuineness, love, unconditional acceptance, and positive regard are the only things needed. Yet the question remains, how does a therapist communicate these things to culturally different clients? While a therapist might have the best of intentions, it is possible that his/her intentions might be misunderstood. Let us use another example with the same Asian American client.

ASIAN AMERICAN CLIENT: I'm even nervous about others seeing me come in here. It's so difficult for me to talk about this.
WHITE THERAPIST: We all find some things difficult to talk about. It's important that you do.
ASIAN AMERICAN CLIENT: It's easy to say that. But, do you really understand how awful I feel,
talking about my parents?
WHITE THERAPIST: I've worked with many Asian Americans and many have similar problems.

In this sample dialogue, we find a distinction between the therapist's intentions and the effects
of his comments. The therapist's intentions were to reassure the client that he understood his
feelings, to imply that he had worked with similar cases, and to make the client not feel isolated
(others have the same problems). The effects, however, were to dilute and dismiss the client's
feelings and concerns, to take the uniqueness out of the situation.

Likewise, a therapist who adheres rigidly to a particular school of counseling, or who relies
primarily on a few therapy responses, is seriously limited in his/her ability to help a wide range
of clients. Advocates of a single school of thought do not realize that when they make statements about their therapeutic orientation (such as "I am Rogerian," "I am behavioral," "I am
rational-emotive in orientation," etc.), they conceptualize people in the same way and respond
toward them in a therapeutic mode that is similar regardless of race, color, creed, religion, and
gender. Counselors and therapists who respond in such a manner fail to take into account that
people differ in a number of ways along these dimensions. While counseling and psychotherapy theories are important, psychology training programs have an equally strong responsibility to teach helping skills that cut across schools of therapy. Only in this way will future
therapists be better able to engage in a wide variety of therapy behaviors when working with
culturally diverse groups.

Trustworthiness.   Perceived trustworthiness encompasses such factors as sincerity, openness,
honesty, or perceived lack of motivation for personal gain. A therapist who is perceived as
trustworthy is likely to exert more influence over a client than one who is not. In our society,
certain roles, such as ministers, doctors, psychiatrists, and counselors, are presumed to exist to
help people. With respect to minorities, self-disclosure is very much dependent on this attribute of perceived trustworthiness. Because mental health professionals are often perceived by
minorities to be "agents of the Establishment," trust is something that does not come with the
role (authority set). Indeed, it may be the perception of many minorities that therapists cannot
be trusted unless otherwise demonstrated. Again, the role and reputation you have as being
trustworthy must be demonstrated in behavioral terms. More than anything, challenges to the
therapist's trustworthiness will be a frequent theme blocking further exploration/movement
until the issue is resolved to the satisfaction of the client. These verbatim transcripts illustrate
the trust issue.

WHITE MALE THERAPIST: I sense some major hesitations . . . it's difficult for you to discuss
your concerns with me.
BLACK MALE CLIENT: You're damn right! If I really told you how I felt about my coach
[White], what's to prevent you from telling him? You Whities are all of the same mind.
WHITE THERAPIST [*angry voice*]:   Look, it would be a lie for me to say I don't know your coach.
He's an acquaintance, but not a personal friend. Don't put me in the same bag with all

Whites! Anyway, even if he was, I hold our discussion in strictest confidence. Let me ask you this question, what would I need to do that would make it easier for you to trust me?
BLACK CLIENT: You're on your way, man!

This verbal exchange illustrates several issues related to trustworthiness. First, the minority client is likely to constantly test the therapist regarding issues of confidentiality. Second, the onus of responsibility for proving trustworthiness falls on the therapist. Third, to prove that one is trustworthy requires, at times, self-disclosure on the part of the mental health professional. That the therapist did not hide the fact that he knew the coach (openness), became angry about being lumped with all Whites (sincerity), assured the client he would not tell the coach or anyone about their sessions (confidentiality), and asked the client how he would work to prove he was trustworthy (genuineness) were all elements that enhanced his trustworthiness.

The "prove to me that you can be trusted" ploy is a most difficult one for therapists to handle. It is difficult because it demands self-disclosure on the part of the helping professional, something graduate training programs have taught us to avoid. It places the focus on the therapist rather than on the client and makes many uncomfortable. It is likely to evoke defensiveness on the part of many mental health practitioners. Here is another verbatim exchange in which defensiveness is evoked, destroying the helping profesional's trustworthiness.

BLACK FEMALE CLIENT: Students in my drama class expect me to laugh when they do "steppin fetchin" routines and tell Black jokes. . . . I'm wondering whether you've ever laughed at any of those jokes.
WHITE MALE THERAPIST [*Long pause*]:   Yes, I'm sure I have. Have you ever laughed at any White jokes?
BLACK CLIENT: What's a White joke?
WHITE THERAPIST: I don't know [*nervous laughter*]; I suppose one making fun of Whites. Look, I'm Irish. Have you ever laughed at Irish jokes?
BLACK CLIENT: People tell me many jokes, but I don't laugh at racial jokes. I feel we're all minorities and should respect each other.

Again, the client tested the therapist indirectly by asking him if he ever laughed at racial jokes. Since most of us probably have, to say no would be a blatant lie. The client's motivation for asking this question was (a) to find out how sincere and open the therapist was and (b) whether the therapist could recognize his racist attitudes without letting it interfere with therapy. While the therapist admitted to having laughed at such jokes, he proceeded to destroy his trustworthiness by becoming defensive. Rather than simply stopping with his statement of "Yes, I'm sure I have," or making some other similar one, he defends himself by trying to get the client to admit to similar actions. Thus the therapist's trustworthiness is seriously impaired. He is perceived as motivated to defend himself rather than help the client.

The therapist's obvious defensiveness in this case has prevented him from understanding the intent and motive of the question. Is the African Amerian female client really asking the therapist whether he has actually laughed at Black jokes before? Or, is the client asking the therapist if he is a racist? Both of these speculations have a certain amount of validity, but it is our belief that the Black female client is actually asking the following important question of the therapist: "How open and honest are you about your own racism, and will it interfere with our session here?" Again, the test is one of trustworthiness, a motivational variable that the White male therapist has obviously failed.

To summarize, expertness and trustworthiness are important components of any therapeutic relationship. In multicultural counseling and therapy, however, the counselor or therapist may not be presumed to possess either. The therapist working with a minority client is likely to experience severe tests of his/her expertness and trustworthiness before serious therapy can proceed. The responsibility for proving to the client that you are a credible therapist is likely to be greater when working with a minority client. How you meet the challenge is important in determining your effectiveness as a multicultural helping professional!

We have come quite a long way in terms of examining how credibility and trustworthiness on the part of the therapist are affected by racial/cultural factors. We have also briefly discussed similarity and the evocation of the identification set. Do minority clients actually prefer a member of their own race in therapy? This is a very important question where the findings seem to be mixed or varying.

It is quite obvious that we know minority individuals who prefer seeing people of their own race and cultural background and some who apparently do not care. We may also know some minority individuals who would prefer to see therapists not of their own race. What are the determining factors that affect this selection process? How important are membership group similarity and attitude similarity in a culturally different client's preference for members of his or her own race? It appears that certain types of similarities and dissimilarities may affect the credibility of the helping professional differentially. Relevant similarities seem more powerful than irrelevant ones. Also, the minority individual's stage of cultural identity may cause him or her to interact quite differently with this question. In a future chapter, we will discuss cultural identity development and how it may affect a minority client's preference for a therapist of his or her own race.

CONCLUSIONS

Since counseling and therapy are White middle-class activities, the factors that may enhance the social influence of the majority therapist might, indeed, lower his/her power base when working with certain culturally different clients. As we have seen, credibility is usually defined in terms of two general dimensions: expertness and trustworthiness. Perceived expertness is typically a function of reputation, behavioral proficiency, or evidence of specialized training (degrees, certificates, and so on). Trustworthiness encompasses such factors as sincerity, openness, honesty, or perceived lack of motivation for personal gain. While majority clients may also be concerned with the therapist's credibility, cultural differences and/or experiences of oppression in U.S. society make the minority client more sensitive to these characteristics of the mental health professional. Tests of credibility may occur frequently in the therapy session, and the onus of responsibility for proving expertness and trustworthiness lies with the therapist.

In multicultural counseling and therapy, the mental health professional may also be unable to use the client's identification set (membership group similarity) to induce change. At times, racial dissimilarity may prove to be so much of a hindrance as to render therapy ineffective. Some have agreed that attitudinal similarity may be more important than racial similarity in counseling. Research in this area is inconclusive. It seems to depend on several factors: (a) the type of presenting problems, (b) the degree and stage of racial/ethnic identity, and (c) certain characteristics of the therapist that may override race differences. Indeed, the difficulties in multicultural counseling may not stem from race factors per se, but from the implications of being a minority in the United States that assigns secondary status to them. In any case, a broad general statement on this matter is oversimplistic. Multicultural therapy by virtue of its definition implies major differences between the client and helper. How these differences can be bridged and under what conditions a therapist is able to work effectively with culturally different clients are key questions.

Part Two

◆

—— ◆ ——

The Practice Dimensions of Multicultural Counseling and Therapy

Chapter Three

◆

Barriers to Effective Multicultural Counseling and Therapy

◆

"One of the most difficult cases I have ever treated was that of a Mexican-American family in southern California. Fernando M. was a 56-year-old recent immigrant to the United States. He had been married some 35 years to Refugio, his wife, and had fathered ten children. Only four of his children, three sons and one daughter, resided with him.

"Fernando was born in a small village in Mexico and resided there until three years ago when he moved to California. He was not unfamiliar with California, having worked as a "bracero" for most of his adult life. He would make frequent visits to the United States during annual harvest seasons.

"The M. family resided in a small, old, unpainted, rented house on the back of a dirt lot that was sparsely furnished with their belongings. The family did not own a car nor was public transportation available in their neighborhood. While their standard of living was far below poverty levels, the family appeared quite pleased at their relative affluence when compared with their life in Mexico.

"The presenting complaints concerned Fernando. He heard threatening voices, was often disoriented, stated the belief that someone was planning to kill him, and that something evil was about to happen. He became afraid to leave his home, was in poor physical health, and possessed a decrepit appearance, which made him essentially unemployable.

"When the M. family entered the clinic, I was asked to see them because the bilingual therapist scheduled that day had called in sick. I was hoping that either Fernando or Refugio would speak enough English to understand the situation. As luck would have it, neither could understand me, nor I them. It became apparent, however, that the two older children could understand English. Since the younger one seemed more fluent, I called upon him to act as a translator during our first session. I noticed that the parents seemed reluctant to participate with the younger son and for some time the discussion among the family members was quite animated. Sensing something wrong and desiring to get the session under way, I interrupted the family and asked the son who spoke the best English, what was wrong. He hesitated for a second, but assured me everything was fine.

"During the course of our first session, it became obvious to me that Fernando was seriously disturbed. He appeared frightened, tense, and, if the interpretations from his son were correct, hallucinating. I suggested to Refugio that she consider hospitalizing her husband, but she was adamant against this course of action. I could sense her nervousness and fear that I would initiate action in having her husband committed. I reassured her that no action would be taken without a follow-up evaluation and suggested that she return later in the week with Fernando. Refugio said that it would be difficult since Fernando was phobic about leaving his home. She had to coerce him into coming this time and did not feel she could do it again. I looked at Fernando directly and stated, "Fernando, I know how hard it is for you to come here, but we really want to help you. Do you think you could possibly come one more time? Dr. Escobedo [the bilingual therapist] will be here with me, and he can communicate with you directly." The youngest son interpreted.

"The M. family never returned for another session and their failure to show up has greatly bothered me. Since that time I have talked with several Latino psychologists who have pointed out multicultural issues that I was not aware of then. Now I realize how uninformed and naive I was in working with Latinos and only hope the M. family has found the needed help elsewhere."

While Chapter 2 dealt with the sociopolitical dynamics affecting multicultural counseling and therapy, this chapter discusses the cultural barriers that may render the helping professional ineffective, thereby denying help to culturally different clients. The preceding vignette illustrates important multicultural issues which are presented in these series of questions.

1. Was it a serious blunder for the therapist to see the M. family or to continue to see them in the session when he could not speak Spanish? Should he have waited until Dr. Escobedo returned?

2. While it may seem like a good idea to have one of the children interpret for the therapist and the family, what possible cultural implications might this have in the Mexican-American family? Do you think one can obtain an accurate translation through family interpreters? What are some of the pitfalls?

3. The therapist tried to be informal with the family in order to put them at ease. Yet, some of his colleagues have stated that how he address clients (last names or first names) may be important. When the therapist used the first names of both husband and wife, what possible cultural interpretation from the family may have resulted?

4. The therapist saw Mr. M.'s symptoms as indications of serious pathology. What other explanations might he entertain? Should he have so blatantly suggested hospitalization? How do Latinos perceive mental health issues?

5. Knowing that Mr. M. had difficulty leaving home, should the therapist have considered some other treatment avenues? If so, what may they have been?

The clash of cultural and therapeutic barriers exemplified in the questions above is both complex and difficult to resolve. They challenge mental health professionals to (a) reach out and understand the worldviews, cultural values, and life circumstances of their culturally different clients; (b) free themselves from the cultural conditioning of what they believe to be correct therapeutic practice; (c) develop new but culturally sensitive methods of working with clients; and (d) play new roles other than the conventional psychotherapy one in the helping process (Atkinson, Thompson, & Grant, 1995; D.W. Sue et al., 1998). Three major potential barriers to effective multicultural therapy (MCT) are illustrated in this vignette: class-bound values, language bias/misunderstanding, and culture-bound values.

First, Fernando's paranoid reactions and suspicions and his hallucinations may have many causes. An enlightened mental health professional must consider whether there are sociopolitical, cultural, or biological reasons for his symptoms? Can his fears, for example, symbolize realistic concerns (fear of deportation, creditors, police, etc.)? How do Latino cultures view hallucinations? Some studies indicate that cultural factors make it more acceptable for some Spanish-speaking populations to admit to hearing voices or seeing visions. Another consideration is the life circumstance of Fernando's work. Could his agricultural work and years of exposure to pesticides and other dangerous agricultural chemicals be contributing to his mental state? Counseling and psychotherapy often focus so much on internal dynamics of clients that there is a failure to consider external sources as causes. These explanations are important for the therapist to consider.

Second, mental health practice has been described as a White middle-class activity that often fails to recognize the economic implications in the delivery of mental health services. Class-bound factors related to socioecomonic status may place those suffering from poverty at a disadvantage and obstruct their efforts to obtain help. For example, Fernando's family is obviously poor; they do not own an automobile; and public transportation is not available in the area where they reside. Poor clients have difficulties traveling to mental health facilities for treatment. Not only is attending sessions a great inconvenience, but it can be costly to arrange private transportation for the family. It might seem that meeting the needs of the M. family could entail home visits or some other form of outreach. If the M. family is unable to travel to the therapist's office for treatment, what blocked the therapist from considering a home visit or a meeting point between the destinations? Many therapists feel disinclined, fearful, or uncomfortable in doing the former. Their training dictates that they practice in their offices and clients come to them. When mental health services are located away from the communities they purport to serve, when outreach programs are not available, and when economic considerations are not addressed by mental health services, institutional bias is clearly evident.

Third, linguistic or language barriers often operate to place culturally different clients at a disadvantage as well. The primary medium by which mental health professionals do their work is through verbalizations (talk therapies). Ever since Freud developed the *talking cure,* psychotherapy has meant that clients must be able to verbalize their thoughts and feelings to a practitioner in order to receive the help required. In addition, because of linguistic bias and monolingualism, the form of talk is via standard English. Clients who do not speak standard English, possess a pronounced accent, or have limited command of English like the M. family may be victimized.

The need to understand the meaning of linguistic differences and language barriers in counseling and psychotherapy has never been greater. As we mentioned previously, changing demographics have resulted in many of our clients being born outside the United States with English as their second language. While the use of interpreters might seem like a solution, such a practice may suffer from certain limitations. For example, can interpreters really give an accurate translation? Cultural differences in mental health concepts are not equivalent in various cultures. In addition, many concepts in English and Spanish do not have equivalent meanings in the other language. Likewise, the well-intentioned efforts of the therapist to communicate with the M. family via the son, who seemed to speak English fluently, might result in a cultural family violation. It may undermine the authority of the father by disturbing the patriarchical role relationships considered sacred in traditional Latino families. There is no doubt that the need for bilingual therapists is great. Yet, the lack of bilingual mental health professionals does not bode well for linguistic minorities.

Fourth, a number of culture-bound issues seemed to be played out in the delivery of services to the M. family. The therapist's attempt to be informal and to put the family at ease resulted in greeting Mr. M. by using his first name, Fernando, as opposed to a more formal one (Mr. M.). In traditional Latino and Asian cultures, such informality or familiarity may be considered a lack of respect for the man as the head of the household. Another cultural barrier might be operative in asking the son whether something was wrong. It is highly probable that the animated family discussion was based upon objections to the son's interpreting by placing the father and mother in a dependency position. Yet, as you recall, the son denied anything wrong. Many traditional Latinos do not feel comfortable airing family issues in public and might consider it impolite to turn down the suggestion of the therapist (having the younger son interpret).

Let us use another case to help illustrate other barriers to effective multicultural counseling and therapy.

◆ *Case Study*

"Several years ago I was asked by a student services committee at a large public university to help identify factors that would make their services more relevant to the needs of minority students. Apparently, the office of student services, especially the Counseling Center, was under considerable pressures from minority groups to make changes amid charges of racism. The Counseling Center director and several staff members reported they had tried to encourage minority students to come for counseling, but their efforts had met with no success. A recent study by the university had revealed that while the student population was comprised of 16% Asian Americans, 17% African Americans, 3% Latino/Hispanic Americans, and less than 1% American Indians, very few minorities used the center's services. The Counseling Center had a nationally known reputation as a fertile training program for interns doing work in socioemotional problems.

"My own investigation revealed that not only were the services heavily clinical (personal/emotional counseling) in nature, but they subscribed to the traditional one-to-one model. When counselors were asked the types of cases they preferred to work with, 85% of the counseling staff listed clinical while only 15% chose educational/vocational ones. Indeed, I quickly sensed a status hierarchy among the staff. At the top of the pecking order were those who primarily did clinical work and at the bottom were the educational/vocational counselors. In addition, the staff of 28 in the center had only three minority members."

The preceding case study identifies another set of possible barriers or impediments that may work against culturally different clients. For example, is the institution discouraging certain culturally different clients from making use of its services? If so, what are these characteristics and why? Is the traditional counselor-client model effective in counseling minorities (nontraditional clients)?

The underrepresentation of minority clients in mental health services is not unusual. As we summarized in Chapter 1, American Indians, Asian Americans, African Americans, and Latinos/Hispanics underutilized traditional mental health services and terminated therapy after only one contact at a rate of over 50% in comparison to a 30% rate for Anglo clients. In this case example, several primary reasons can be identified as to why the Counseling Center has such low utilization rates.

First, it became obvious by a casual inspection of the Counseling Center staff that it was predominantly White. Of the minority group members present, one was an African American counselor, but the others were an African American clerical staff member and an Asian American vocational librarian. The lack of minority professionals in the Counseling Center was a loud and clear message to certain culturally different students concerning the commitment of the institution and Center. The perception of many of the minority students was that the Counseling Center did not care about culturally different students, that it lacked understanding about their lifestyles and experiences, and that its efforts toward encouraging participation were not genuine and sincere. Rightly or wrongly, it was assumed by many of the students that the staff would not be able to relate to the minority-group experience of the students and, indeed, that the low minority representation resulted from racist policies and practices that discriminated against hiring minority staff. Thus, based on these perceptions, many of the students were discouraged from utilizing the services.

Second, how the services were offered to the university community was also crucial in its ability to relate to a culturally diverse student body. The above case study makes it clear that the traditional services were one-to-one in nature, in which the counselor received clients in his or her office. This type of approach, as Atkinson et al. (1998) point out, may actually be less appropriate than meeting the client in a different contextual environment. Like the case of the M. family, rather than demanding that the client adapt to the counselor's culture, it may be better for the counselor to adjust to and work within the client's culture. In other words, alternative roles involve the counselor more actively in the client's life experiences than what we have traditionally been trained to do. Outreach roles, consultant roles, change-agent roles, or the use of the client's indigenous support systems may be more appropriate. Many minority group individuals find the one-to-one/in-office type of counseling very formal, removed, and alien. When counselors move out of their offices into the environments of their clients, it again indicates commitment and interest in the individual. According to this nontraditional view, counseling is not simply sitting down and talking with a client: It may involve shooting basketball with the client in his or her home environment, playing billiards with the client, and working in situations where the minority individual is found (dormitories, the student union, etc.). Unfortunately, most training in counseling and clinical psychology does not give adequate experiences with these types of change-agent outreach programs. Indeed, counselors are often discouraged from meeting clients on their home turf because it is unprofessional and not a part of the counselor's role.

Third, the Counseling Center in this situation is defined as one that is very well known in terms of social-emotional counseling and emphasis. This again is not unusual in most counselor education training programs. Often counselor trainees are more intrigued with personal-emotional (psychiatric) issues than educational or vocational ones. Yet, it appears that many minority individuals are much more concerned with their vocational, educational, and career goals. For example, as we will see in Chapter 12, Asian Americans tend to be much more concerned with educational-vocational counseling and will come for these services at a high rate when offered. Much of this is due to cultural factors operating in the life of Asian Americans. When counseling staff tend to perceive educational-vocational counseling as less prestigious, it is entirely possible that this is communicated to the student population. Additionally, many minority individuals may not trust talking about personal issues with White counselors and may be more amenable to dealing directly with vocational-educational career issues. This subject is discussed further in later chapters.

In Chapter 1 we mentioned how the mental health profession had failed to contribute to the betterment of culturally different groups in America. Psychology training programs and the portrayal of minorities in both the popular and scientific literature have oftentimes instilled within counselor trainees (a) monocultural assumptions of mental health, (b) negative stereotypes of pathology for minority lifestyles, and (c) ineffective, inappropriate, and antagonistic counseling approaches to the values held by minorities. As in the Counseling Center case study, this damage is clearly seen in the actual practice of counseling and therapy.

COUNSELING AND THERAPY CHARACTERISTICS

Counseling/psychotherapy may be viewed legitimately as a process of interpersonal interaction, communication, and social influence. For effective therapy to occur, the therapist and client must be able to *send* and *receive* both *verbal* and *nonverbal* messages *accurately* and *appropriately*. While breakdowns in communication often happen between members who share the same culture, the problem becomes exacerbated between people of different racial or ethnic backgrounds. Many mental health professionals have noted that racial or ethnic factors may act as impediments to therapy by lowering social influence (Trimble, 1981; Vontress, 1981, 1971; D.W. Sue et al., 1982; D.W. Sue, 1995). Misunderstandings that arise from cultural variations in communication may lead to alienation and/or an inability to develop trust and rapport. Culture clashes can often occur between the values of counseling/psychotherapy and the life values of culturally different groups.

At this point, we turn our attention to a much more formal analysis of how these values may distort communication and/or affect the therapeutic relationship. Implications for therapy are discussed. A conceptual scheme is presented that can be used to compare and contrast how language, culture, and class variables can be used to determine appropriate interventions. Such a comparative analysis is helpful in providing a means for examining the appropriateness of counseling approaches, not only for culturally different clients but also for other special populations as well (women, gays/lesbians, the physically handicapped, and the elderly).

GENERIC CHARACTERISTICS OF COUNSELING/THERAPY

We have repeatedly emphasized that counseling/psychotherapy is influenced by the social-cultural framework from which it arises. In the United States, White Euro-American culture holds certain values that are reflected in this therapeutic process. All theories of counseling and psychotherapy are influenced by assumptions that theorists make regarding the goals for therapy, the methodology used to invoke change, and the definition of mental health and mental illness. Counseling and psychotherapy have traditionally been conceptualized in Western individualistic terms (Atkinson et al., 1998; Ivey, 1981, 1986). Whether the particular theory is psychodynamic, existential-humanistic, or cognitive-behavioral in orientation, a number of multicultural specialists (Ivey, Ivey, & Simek-Downing, 1997; Katz, 1985; Sue, 1995;) indicate that they share certain common components of White culture in their values and beliefs. Katz (1985) has described these components of White culture (see Table 8.2, Chapter 8). These values and beliefs have influenced the actual practice of counseling and psychotherapy as can be seen clearly in Tables 3.1 and 3.2.

In the United States and in many countries, psychotherapy and counseling are used mainly with middle- and upper-class segments of the population. As a result, many of the values and characteristics seen in both the goals and process of therapy are not shared by culturally different clients. Schofield (1964) has noted that therapists tend to prefer clients who exhibit the YAVIS syndrome: young, attractive, verbal, intelligent, and successful. This preference tends to discriminate against people from different minority groups or those from lower socioeconomic classes. This has led Sundberg (1981) to sarcastically point out that therapy is not for QUOID people (quiet, ugly, old, indigent, and dissimilar culturally). Three major characteristics of counseling and psychotherapy that may act as a source of conflict for culturally different groups were identified in the early 1970s (D.W. Sue & S. Sue, 1972a).

First, therapists often expect their clients to exhibit some degree of openness, psychological-mindedness, or sophistication. Most theories of helping place a high premium on verbal, emotional, and behavioral expressiveness and the obtaining of insight. These are either the end goals of therapy or are the medium by which cures are effected. Second, therapy is traditionally a one-to-one activity that encourages clients to talk about or discuss the most intimate aspects of their lives. Individuals who fail in or resist self-disclosure may be seen as resistant, defensive, or superficial. Third, the counseling or therapy situation is often an ambiguous one. The client is encouraged to discuss problems while the counselor listens and responds. Relatively speaking, the therapy situation is unstructured and forces the client to be the primary active participant. Patterns of communication are generally from client to therapist.

Table 3.1 GENERIC CHARACTERISTICS OF COUNSELING

Culture	Middle Class	Language
Standard English	Standard English	Standard English
Verbal communication	Verbal communication	Verbal communication
Individual centered	Adherence to time schedules (50-minute sessions)	
Verbal/emotional/behavioral expressiveness	Long-range goals	
Client-counselor communication	Ambiguity	
Openness and intimacy		
Cause-effect orientation		
Clear distinction between physical and mental well-being		
Nuclear family		

Table 3.2   RACIAL/ETHNIC MINORITY GROUP VARIABLES

Culture	Lower Class	Language
Asian Americans		
Asian language	Nonstandard English	Bilingual background
Family centered	Action oriented	
Restraint of feelings	Different time perspective	
One-way communication from authority figure to person	Immediate, short-range goals	
Silence is respect		
Advice seeking		
Well-defined patterns of inter-action (concrete structured)		
Private versus public display (shame/disgrace/pride)		
Physical and mental well-being defined differently		
Extended family		
African American		
Black language	Nonstandard English	Black language
Sense of "people-hood"	Action oriented	
Action oriented	Different time perspective	
Paranorm due to oppression	Immediate, short-range goals	
Importance place on nonverbal behavior	Concrete, tangible, structured approach	
Extended family		
Latino/Hispanic American		
Spanish-speaking	Nonstandard English	Bilingual background
Group centered	Action oriented	
Temporal difference	Different time perspective	
Family orientation	Immediate short-range goals	
Different pattern of communi-cation	Concrete, tangible, structured approach	
A religious distinction between mind and body		
Extended family		

Table 3.2   Continued

Culture	Lower Class	Language
	American Indians	
Tribal dialects	Nonstandard English	Bilingual background
Cooperative, not competitive individualism	Action oriented	
	Different time perspective	
Present-time orientation	Immediate, short-range goals	
Creative/experimental/intuitive/ nonverbal	Concrete, tangible, structured approach	
Satisfy present needs		
Use of folk or supernatural explanations		
Extended family		

Four other factors identified as generally characteristic of therapy are (a) monolingual orientation, (b) emphasis on long-range goals, (c) distinction between physical and mental well-being, and (d) emphasis on cause-effect relationships. Furthermore, since therapy is generally isolated from the client's environment and contacts are brief (50 minutes, once a week), it is by nature aimed at seeking long-range goals and solutions.

Another important and often overlooked factor in therapy is the implicit assumption that a clear distinction can be made between mental and physical illness or health. Contrary to this Western view, many cultures may not make a clear distinction between the two. Such a separation may be confusing to some culturally different clients and cause problems in therapy.

Ornstein's early work (1972) in which he identifies the dual hemispheric functioning of the brain also has intriguing implications for therapy. While the left hemisphere of the brain is involved with linear, rational, and cognitive processes, the right half tends to be intuitive, feeling, and experientially oriented. When both hemispheres are operating in a mutually interdependent fashion, they facilitate our functioning as human beings. Ornstein points out that the linear/logical/analytic/verbal mode of the left brain dominates Western thinking. The functioning of the right brain that is intuitive/holistic/creative/nonverbal has been neglected in Western culture and seen as a less legitimate mode of expression.

An analysis of the various American schools of therapy leads to the inevitable conclusion that Western mental health practice is left-brain oriented (Highlen, 1994; 1996). Such an approach or worldview may clash with Eastern and American Indian philosophy. Thus, a left-brain orientation means a linear emphasis on cause-effect approaches and a linear concept of time. We deal with these concepts in greater detail in a later chapter.

In summary, the generic characteristics of counseling/therapy can be seen to fall into three major categories:

1. Culture-bound values—individual centered, verbal/emotional/behavioral expressiveness, communication patterns from client to counselor, openness and intimacy, analytic/linear/verbal (cause-effect) approach, and clear distinctions between mental and physical well-being;

2. Class-bound values—strict adherence to time schedules (50-minute, once- or twice-a-week meeting), ambiguous or unstructured approach to problems, and seeking long-range goals or solutions; and

3. Language variables—use of standard English and emphasis on verbal communication.

Tables 3.1 and 3.2 summarize these generic characteristics and compare their compatibility to those of four racial/ethnic minority groups. As mentioned previously, such a comparison can also be done for other groups that vary in gender, age, sexual orientation, ability/disability, etc.

SOURCES OF CONFLICT AND MISINTERPRETATION IN THERAPY

While an attempt has been made to clearly delineate three major variables that influence effective therapy, these variables are often inseparable from one another. For example, use of standard English in counseling and therapy definitely places those individuals who are unable to use it fluently at a disadvantage. However, cultural and class values that govern conversation conventions can also operate via language to cause serious misunderstandings. Furthermore, the fact that many African Americans, Latino/Hispanic Americans, and American Indians come from a predominantly lower-class background often compounds class and culture variables. Thus, it is often difficult to tell which characteristics are the impediments in therapy. Nevertheless, this distinction is valuable in conceptualizing barriers to effective MCT.

CULTURE-BOUND VALUES

In simple terms, *culture* consists of all those things that people have learned to do, believe, value, and enjoy in their history. It is the totality of ideals, beliefs, skills, tools, customs, and institutions into which each member of society is born. While D.W. Sue and S. Sue (1972b) have stressed the need for social scientists to focus on the positive aspects of being bicultural, such dual membership may cause problems for many minorities. The term *marginal* person was first coined by Stonequist (1937) and refers to a person's inability to form dual ethnic identification because of bicultural membership. Racial/ethnic minorities are placed under strong pressures to adopt the ways of the dominant culture. The cultural deficit models tend to view culturally different individuals as possessing dysfunctional values/belief systems, and they are often seen as a handicap to be overcome, something to be ashamed of, and to be avoided. In essence, racial/ethnic minorities may be taught that to be different is to be deviant, pathological, or sick.

Many social scientists (Carter, 1995; Guthrie, 1997; Halleck, 1971; Katz, 1985; D.W. Sue et al., 1982; White & Parham, 1990) believe that psychology and therapy may be viewed as encompassing the use of social power and that therapy is a "handmaiden of the status quo." The therapist may be seen as an agent of society transmitting and functioning under Western values. An early outspoken critic, Szasz (1970) believes that psychiatrists are like slave masters using therapy as a powerful political ploy against people whose ideas, beliefs, and behaviors differ from the dominant society. Several culture-bound characteristics of therapy may be responsible for these negative beliefs.

Focus on the Individual

Most forms of counseling and psychotherapy tend to be individual centered—that is, they emphasize the "I-thou" relationship. Pedersen (1987, 1988) notes that U.S. culture and society is based on the concept of individualism and that competition between individuals for status, recognition, achievement, and so forth, forms the basis for Western tradition. Individualism, autonomy, and the ability to become your own person are perceived as healthy and desirable goals. If we look at most Euro-American theories of human development (Piaget, Erickson, etc.), we are struck by how they emphasize "individuation" as normal and healthy development. Pedersen notes that not all cultures view individualism as a positive orientation; rather, it may be perceived in some cultures as a handicap to attaining enlightenment, one that may divert us from important spiritual goals. In many non-Western cultures, identity is not seen apart from the group orientation (collectivism). The personal pronoun *I* in the Japanese language does not seem to exist. The notion of *atman* in India defines itself as participating in unity with all things and not limited by the temporal world.

Many societies do not define the psychosocial unit of operation as the individual. In many cultures and subgroups, the psychosocial unit of operation tends to be the family, group, or collective society. In traditional Asian American culture, one's identity is defined within the family constellation. The greatest punitive measure to be taken out on an individual by the family is to be disowned. What this means in essence is that the person no longer has an identity. While being disowned by a family in Western European culture is equally negative and punitive, it does not have the same connotations as in traditional Asian society. Westerners, while they may be disowned by a family, are always informed and told that they have an individual identity as well. Likewise, many Hispanic individuals tend to see the unit of operation as residing within the family. African American psychologists (Mays, 1985; Parham, 1997; White & Parham, 1990) also point to how the African view of the world encompasses the concept of groupness.

It is our contention that racial/ethnic minorities often use a different psychosocial unit of operation in that collectivism is valued over individualism. This worldview is reflected in all aspects of behavior. For example, many traditional Asian American and Hispanic elders tend to greet one another with the question "How is your family today?" Contrast this with how most U.S. Americans tend to greet each other by asking, "How are you today?" One emphasizes the family (group) perspective, while the other emphasizes the individual perspective.

Affective expressions in therapy can also be strongly influenced by the particular orientation one takes. In the United States, when individuals engage in wrongful behaviors, they are most likely to experience feelings of *guilt.* However, in traditional societies that emphasize collectivism, the most dominant affective element to follow a wrongful behavior is *shame,* not guilt. Guilt is an individual affect, while shame appears to be a group one (it reflects upon the family or group).

Counselors and therapists who fail to recognize the importance of defining this difference between individualism and collectivism will create difficulties in therapy. Often, we are impressed by the number of our colleagues who describe traditional Asian clients as "being dependent," "unable to make decisions on their own," and "lacking in maturity." Many of these judgments are based on the fact that many Asian clients do not see a decision-making process as an individual one. When an Asian client states to a counselor or therapist, "I can't make that decision on my own; I need to consult with my parents or family," he or she is seen as being quite immature. After all, therapy is aimed at helping individuals to make decisions on their own in a mature and responsible manner.

Verbal/Emotional/Behavioral Expressiveness

Many counselors and therapists tend to emphasize the fact that verbal/emotional/behavioral expressiveness is important in individuals. For example, we like our clients to be verbal, articulate, and to be able to express their thoughts and feelings clearly. Indeed, therapy is often referred to as *talk therapies,* indicating the importance placed upon standard English as the medium of expression. Emotional expressiveness is also valued, as we like individuals to be in touch with their feelings and to be able to verbalize their emotional reactions. In some forms of counseling and psychotherapy, it is often stated that if a feeling is not verbalized and expressed by the client, it may not exist. We tend to value and believe that behavioral expressiveness is important as well. We like individuals to be assertive, to stand up for their own rights, and to engage in activities that indicate they are not passive beings.

All these characteristics of therapy can place culturally different clients at a disadvantage. For example, many cultural minorities tend not to value verbalizations in the same way that U.S. Americans do. In traditional Japanese culture, children have been taught not to speak until spoken to. Patterns of communication tend to be vertical, flowing from those of higher prestige and status to those of lower prestige and status. In a therapy situation, many Japanese clients, to show respect for a therapist who is older, wiser, and who occupies a position of higher status, may respond with silence. Unfortunately, an unenlightened counselor or therapist may perceive this client as being inarticulate and less intelligent.

Emotional expressiveness in counseling and psychotherapy is frequently a goal and is highly desired. Yet, there are many cultural groups in which restraint of strong feelings is highly valued. For example, traditional Hispanic and Asian cultures emphasize that maturity and wisdom are associated with one's ability to control emotions and feelings. This applies not only to public expressions of anger and frustration, but also to public expressions of love and affection as well. Unfortunately, therapists unfamiliar with these cultural ramifications may perceive their clients in a very negative psychiatric light. Indeed, these clients are often described as inhibited, lacking in spontaneity, and/or repressed.

The senior author once did a research study at a well-known university in Southern California. The study involved identifying symptomology among Japanese American students using the counseling and psychiatric services. He was quite shocked and surprised when many of the psychiatric staff indicated they were very pleased to see research being done on Japanese American clients because, "Did you know they are one of the most repressed groups we have ever encountered?" We submit that this statement tends to overlook the fact that cultural forces may be operative in the Japanese American clients' overall behavior in the psychiatric session. While the clients may be repressed, the failure to consider cultural factors that dictate against public disclosures and feelings may prove a serious consequence.

In therapy it has become increasingly popular to emphasize expressiveness in a behavioral sense. For example, one need only note the proliferation of cognitive-behavioral assertiveness training programs throughout the United States and the number of self-help books that are being published in the popular mental health literature. Many of these, such as *Stand Up for Your Own Rights* and *When I Say No, I Feel Guilty,* attest to the importance placed on assertiveness and standing up for one's own rights. This orientation fails to realize that there are cultural groups in which subtlety is a highly prized art. Yet, doing things indirectly can be perceived by the mental health professional as evidence of passivity and the need for this individual to learn assertiveness skills.

Therapists who value verbal, emotional, and behavioral expressiveness as goals in therapy may be unaware that they are transmitting their own cultural values. This generic characteristic of counseling is not only antagonistic to lower-class values, but also to different cultural ones. Wood and Mallinckrodt (1990) in their excellent review of assertiveness training, warn that therapists need to make certain that gaining such skills is a value shared by the minority client, and not imposed by therapists. For example, statements by some mental health professionals that Asian Americans are the most repressed of all clients indicate they expect their clients to exhibit openness, psychological-mindedness, and assertiveness. Such a statement may indicate a failure on the part of the therapist to understand the background and cultural upbringing of many Asian American clients. Traditional Chinese and Japanese cultures may value restraint of strong feelings and subtleness in approaching problems.

Insight

Another generic characteristic of counseling is the use of insight in both counseling and psychotherapy. This characteristic assumes that it is mentally beneficial for individuals to obtain insight or understanding into their deep underlying dynamics and causes. Born from the tradition of psychoanalytic theory, many theorists tend to believe that clients who obtain insight into themselves will be better adjusted. While many of the behavioral schools of thought may not subscribe to this, most therapists in their individual practice use insight either as a process of therapy or as an end product or goal.

We need to realize that insight is not highly valued by many culturally different clients. There are also major class differences as well. People from lower socioeconomic classes frequently do not perceive insight as appropriate to their life situations and circumstances. Their concern may revolve around questions such as "Where do I find a job?" "How do I feed my family?" "How can I afford to take my sick daughter to a doctor?" When survival on a day-to-day basis is important, it seems inappropriate for the therapist to use insightful processes. After all, insight assumes that one has time to sit back, to reflect, and to contemplate about motivations and behavior. For the individual who is concerned about making it through each day, this orientation proves counterproductive.

Likewise, many cultural groups do not value insight. In traditional Chinese society, psychology is not well understood. It must be noted, however, that a client who does not seem to work well in an insight approach may not be lacking in insight or lacking in psychological-mindedness. A person who does not value insight is not necessarily one who is incapable of insight. Thus, there tend to be several major factors that affect insight.

First, many cultural groups themselves do not value this method of self-exploration. It is interesting to note that many Asian elders believe that thinking too much about something can cause problems. Lum (1982), in a study of the Chinese in San Francisco's Chinatown, found that many believe the road to mental health was to avoid morbid thoughts. Advice from Asian elders to their children when they encountered feelings of frustration, anger, depression, or anxiety was simply don't think about it. Indeed, it is often believed that the reason why one experiences anger or depression is precisely that one is thinking about it *too much!* The traditional Asian way of handling these affective elements is to keep busy and don't think about it. Granted, it is more complex than this, because in traditional Asian families the reason why self-exploration is discouraged is precisely because it is an individual approach. "Think about the family and not about yourself" is advice given to many Asians as a way of dealing with negative affective elements. This is totally contradictory to Western notions of mental health—that it is best to get things out in the open in order to deal with them.

Second, many racial/ethnic minority psychologists have felt that insight is a value in itself. For example, it was generally thought that insight led to behavior change. This was the old psychoanalytic assumption that when people understood their conflicts and underlying dynamics, the symptoms or behaviors would change or disappear. The behavioral schools of thought have since disproved this one-to-one connection. While insight does lead to behavior change in some situations, it does not always seem to do so. Indeed, behavioral therapies have shown that changing the behavior first may lead to insight (cognitive restructuring and understanding) instead of vice versa. As an example, one of the authors once had considerable difficulties and apprehensions about asking members of the opposite sex out on social occasions. He would find it highly anxiety provoking to call a female friend on the phone and ask her out for a date. This bothered him so greatly that he sought counseling and was able to understand the basis of his anxieties. Briefly, it boiled down to the fact that he feared rejection and that the rejection, if it came, was always in some sense correlated with his own concept of masculinity. This insight made the author feel much better, but did not ever help him pick up the phone to ask a female friend out on a date! Of course, one can claim that the author did not achieve true insight. We would then ask the question, "When does a person have insight?" We submit that the only answer, which is a highly value-based one, is that a client has insight when the therapist says that person has insight. This varies from therapist to therapist and from theory to theory.

Self-Disclosure (*Openness and Intimacy*)

Most forms of counseling and psychotherapy tend to value one's ability to self-disclose and to talk about the most intimate aspects of one's life. Indeed, self-disclosure has often been discussed as a primary characteristic of the healthy personality. The converse of this is that people who do not self-disclose readily in counseling and psychotherapy are seen as possessing negative traits such as being guarded, mistrustful, and/or paranoid. There are two difficulties in this orientation toward self-disclosure. One of these is cultural and the other is sociopolitical.

First, intimate revelations of personal or social problems may not be acceptable, since such difficulties reflect not only on the individual, but also on the whole family. Thus, the family may exert strong pressures on the Asian American client not to reveal personal matters to strangers or outsiders. Similar conflicts have been reported for Hispanics (Laval et al., 1983; Leong et al., 1995) and for American-Indian clients (Everett, Proctor, & Cortmell, 1989; LaFromboise, 1998). A therapist who works with a client from a minority background may erroneously conclude that the person is repressed, inhibited, shy, or passive. Note that all these terms are seen as undesirable by Western standards.

Related to this example is the belief in the desirability of self-disclosure by many mental health practitioners. Self-disclosure refers to the client's willingness to tell the therapist what he/she feels, believes, or thinks. Journard (1964) suggests that mental health is related to one's openness in disclosing. While this may be true, the parameters need clarification. Chapter 1 used as an example the paranorm of Grier and Cobbs (1968). People of African descent are especially reluctant to disclose to Caucasian counselors because of hardships they have experienced via racism (Ridley, 1995; White & Parham, 1990). Few African Americans initially perceive a White therapist as a person of goodwill, but rather as an agent of society who may use the information against them. From the African American perspective, uncritical self-disclosure to others is not healthy.

The actual structure of the therapy situation may also work against intimate revelations. Among many American Indians and Hispanics, intimate aspects of life are shared only with close friends. Relative to White middle-class standards, deep friendships are developed only after prolonged contact. Once friendships are formed, they tend to be lifelong in nature. In contrast, White Americans form relationships quickly, but the relationships do not necessarily persist over long periods of time. Counseling and therapy seem to also reflect these values. Clients talk about the most intimate aspects of their lives with a relative stranger once a week for a 50-minute session. To many culturally different groups who stress friendship as a precondition to self-disclosure, the counseling process seems utterly inappropriate and absurd. After all, how is it possible to develop a friendship with brief contacts once a week?

Scientific Empiricism

Counseling/psychotherapy in Western culture and society has been described as being highly linear, analytic, and verbal in its attempt to mimic the physical sciences. As indicated by Table 3.1, Western society tends to emphasize the so-called scientific method, which involves objective rational linear thinking. Likewise, we oftentimes see descriptions of the therapist as being objective and neutral, rational and logical in thinking (Highlen, 1994; Katz, 1985; Pedersen, 1988). The therapist relies heavily on the use of linear problem solving as well as on quantitative evaluation that includes psychodiagnostic tests, intelligence tests, personality inventories, and so forth. This cause-effect orientation emphasizes left-brain functioning. That is, theories of counseling and therapy are distinctly analytical, rational, and verbal, and strongly stress discovering cause-effect relationships.

The emphasis on symbolic logic is in marked contrast to the philosophy of many cultures that value a more nonlinear, wholistic, and harmonious approach to the world (D.W. Sue, 1995). For example, American Indian worldviews emphasize the harmonious aspects of the world, intuitive functioning, and a holistic approach—a worldview characterized by right-brain activities (Ornstein, 1972), minimizing analytical, reductionistic inquiries. Thus, when American Indians undergo therapy, the analytic approach may violate their basic philosophy of life.

It appears that in U.S. society, the most dominant way of asking and answering questions about the human condition tends to be the scientific method. The epitome of this approach is the so-called experiment. In graduate schools we are often told that only in the experiment can we impute a cause-effect relationship. By identifying the independent and dependent variables and controlling for extraneous factors, we are able to test a cause-effect hypothesis. While correlational studies, historical research, and so forth, may be of benefit, we are told that the experiment represents the epitome of our science. As indicated, other cultures may value different ways of asking and answering questions about the human condition.

Distinctions between Mental and Physical Functioning

Many American Indians, Asian Americans, Blacks, and Hispanics hold a different concept of what constitutes mental health, mental illness, and adjustment. Among the Chinese, the concept of mental health or psychological well-being is not understood in the same way as it is in the Western context. Latino/Hispanic Americans do not make the same Western distinction between mental and physical health as their White counterparts (Rivera, 1984). Thus, nonphysical health problems are most likely to be referred to a physician, priest, or minister. Culturally different clients operating under this orientation may enter therapy expecting therapists to treat them in the same manner that doctors or priests do. Immediate solutions and concrete tangible forms of treatment (advice, confession, consolation, and medication) are expected. For example, both authors, who are psychologists, remember the period in their lives when they entered the field of psychology. Their parents asked one question that drove home the differences in worldview that various cultural groups have concerning this concept of psychology, psychological well-being, psychological adjustment, and mental health and mental illness: "How can you be called a doctor when you're not really a doctor?" This question indicates that for our parents, expectations were that doctors are medical doctors and not doctors of philosophy (Ph.D.). When our work with clients was explained as sitting down and talking with individuals and helping them explore their thoughts and feelings, our father's response was, "Humph, they pay you for that?" Again, it was obvious that to them that this was not a legitimate form of work. After all, avoidance of morbid thoughts is the way to deal with psychological problems, not sitting down and talking about them.

Ambiguity

The ambiguous and unstructured aspect of the therapy situation may create discomfort in clients of color. The culturally different may not be familiar with therapy and may perceive it as an unknown and mystifying process. Some groups, like Hispanics, may have been reared in an environment that actively structures social relationships and patterns of interaction. Anxiety and confusion may be the outcome in an unstructured counseling setting. The following example of a Hispanic undergoing vocational counseling illustrates this confusion:

> Maria W. was quite uncomfortable and anxious during the first interview dealing with vocational counseling. This anxiety seemed more related to ambiguity of the situation than anything else. She appeared confused about the direction of the counselor's comments and questions. At this point, the counselor felt an explanation of vocational counseling might facilitate the process.
>
> COUNSELOR: Let me take some time to explain what we do in vocational counseling. Vocational counseling is an attempt to understand the whole person. Therefore, we are interested in your likes and dislikes, what you do well, your skills, and what they mean with respect to jobs and vocations. The first interview is usually an attempt to get to know you—especially your past experiences and reactions to different courses you've taken, jobs you've worked at, and so forth. Especially important are your goals and plans. If testing seems indicated, as in your case, you'll be asked to complete some tests. After testing we'll sit down and talk about what they mean. When we arrive at possible vocations, we'll use the vocational library and find out what these jobs require in terms of background, training, and so forth.
>
> CLIENT: Oh! I see . . .
>
> COUNSELOR: That's why we've been talking about your high school experiences. Sometimes the hopes and dreams can tell us much about your interests.

After this explanation, Maria participated much more in the interviews.

Patterns of Communication

The cultural upbringing of many minorities dictates different patterns of communication that may place them at a disadvantage in therapy. Counseling, for example, initially demands that communication move from client to counselor. The client is expected to take the major responsibility for initiating conversation in the session, while the counselor plays a less active role.

American Indians, Asian Americans, and Hispanics, however, function under different cultural imperatives that may make this difficult. These three groups may have been reared to respect elders and authority figures and not to speak until spoken to. Clearly defined roles of dominance and deference are established in the traditional family. In the case of Asians, there is evidence to indicate that mental health is associated with exercising willpower, avoiding unpleasant thoughts, and occupying one's mind with positive thoughts. Therapy is seen as an authoritative process in which a good therapist is more direct and active while portraying a father figure (Henkin, 1985; Mau & Jepson, 1988). A racial/ethnic minority client who has been asked to initiate conversation may become uncomfortable and respond with only short phrases or statements. The therapist may be prone to interpret the behavior negatively, when in actuality it may be a sign of respect. We have much more to say about these communication style differences in the next chapter.

CLASS-BOUND VALUES

As mentioned previously, class values are important to consider in therapy because many racial/ethnic minority groups are disproportionately represented in the lower socioeconomic classes. Mental health practices that emphasize assisting the client in self-direction through the presentation of the results of assessment instruments and self-exploration via verbal interactions between client and therapist are seen as meaningful and productive. However, the values underlying these activities are permeated by middle-class ones that do not suffice for those living in poverty. We have already seen how this operates with respect to language. As early as the 1960s, Bernstein (1964) investigated the suitability of English for the lower-class poor in psychotherapy and concluded that it works to the detriment of those individuals.

For the therapist who generally comes from a middle- to upper-class background, it is often difficult to relate to the circumstances and hardships affecting the client who lives in poverty. The phenomenon of poverty and its effects on individuals and institutions can be devastating. For the individual, his/her life is characterized by low wages, unemployment, underemployment, little property ownership, no savings, and lack of food reserves. Meeting even the most basic needs of hunger and shelter is in constant day-to-day jeopardy. Pawning personal possessions and borrowing money at exorbitant interest rates only leads to greater debt. Feelings of helplessness, dependence, and inferiority are easily fostered under these circumstances. Therapists may unwittingly attribute attitudes that result from physical and environmental adversity to the cultural or individual traits of the person.

For example, note the clinical description of a 12-year-old child written by a school counselor.

Jimmy Jones is a 12-year-old Black male student who was referred by Mrs. Peterson because of apathy, indifference, and inattentiveness to classroom activities. Other teachers have also reported that Jimmy does not pay attention, daydreams often, and frequently falls asleep during class. There is a strong possibility that Jimmy is harboring repressed rage that needs to be ventilated and dealt with. His inability to directly express his anger had led him to adopt passive aggressive means of expressing hostility, i.e., inattentiveness, daydreaming, falling asleep. It is recommended that Jimmy be seen for intensive counseling to discover the basis of the anger.

After six months of counseling, the counselor finally realized the basis of Jimmy's problems. He came from a home life of extreme poverty, where hunger, lack of sleep, and overcrowding served to severely diminish his energy level and motivation. The fatigue, passivity, and fatalism evidenced by Jimmy were more a result of poverty than some innate trait.

Likewise, poverty may bring many parents to encourage children to seek employment at an early age. Delivering groceries, shining shoes, and hustling other sources of income may sap the energy of the schoolchild, leading to truancy and poor performance. Teachers and counselors may view such students as unmotivated and potential juvenile delinquents.

Research documentation concerning the inferior and biased quality of treatment to lower-class clients is historically legend (Lerner, 1972; Lorion, 1973, 1974; Pavkov, Lewis, & Lyons, 1989; Powell & Powell, 1983; Rouse, Carter, & Rodriguez-Andrew, 1995; Yamamoto, James, & Palley, 1968). In the area of diagnosis, it has been found that the attribution of mental illness was more likely to occur when the person's history suggested a lower-class rather than higher socioeconomic class origin. Many studies seem to demonstrate that clinicians given identical test protocols tend to make more negative prognostic statements and judgments of greater maladjustment when the individual was said to come from a lower- rather than a middle-class background.

In the area of treatment, Garfield, Weiss, and Pollock (1973) gave counselors identical descriptions (except for social class) of a 9-year-old boy who engaged in maladaptive classroom behavior. When the boy was assigned upper-class status, more counselors expressed a willingness to become ego-involved with the student than when lower-class status was assigned. Likewise, Habemann & Thiry (1970) found that doctoral-degree candidates in counseling and guidance more frequently programmed students from low socioeconomic backgrounds into a noncollege-bound track than a college-preparation one.

In an extensive historic research of services delivered to minorities and low socioeconomic clients, Lorion (1973) found that psychiatrists refer to therapy those persons who are most like themselves: White rather than non-White and those from upper socioeconomic status (SES). Lorion (1974) also points out that the expectations of lower-class clients are often different from those of psychotherapists. For example, lower-class clients who are concerned with survival or making it through on a day-to-day basis expect advice and suggestions from the counselor. Appointments made weeks in advance with short, weekly 50-minute contacts are not consistent with the need to seek immediate solutions. Additionally, many lower-class people, through multiple experiences with public agencies, operate under what is called *minority standard time* (Schindler-Rainman, 1967). This is the tendency of poor people to have a low regard for punctuality. Poor people have learned that endless waits are associated with medical clinics, police stations, and governmental agencies. One usually waits hours for a 10- to 15-minute appointment. Arriving promptly does little good and can be a waste of valuable time. Therapists, however, rarely understand this aspect of life and are prone to see this as a sign of indifference or hostility.

People from a lower SES may also view insight and attempts to discover underlying intraphysic problems as inappropriate. Many lower-class clients expect to receive advice or some form of concrete tangible treatment. When the therapist attempts to explore personality dynamics or to take a historical approach to the problem, the client often becomes confused, alienated, and frustrated. Abad, Ramos, and Boyce (1974) use the case of Puerto Ricans to illustrate this point. They feel the passive psychiatric approach that requires the client to talk about problems introspectively and to take initiative and responsibility for decision making is not what is expected by the Puerto Rican client. Several writers (Menacker, 1971; Schindler-Raimman, 1967) have taken the position that poor people are best motivated by rewards that are immediate and concrete. A harsh environment, where the future is uncertain and immediate needs must be met, makes long-range planning of little value. Many lower SES clients are unable to relate to the future orientation of therapy. To be able to sit and talk about things is perceived to be a luxury of the middle and upper classes.

Because of the lower-class client's environment and past inexperience with therapy, the expectations of the minority individual may be quite different, or even negative. The client's unfamiliarity with the therapy process may hinder its success and cause the therapist to blame the failure on the client. Thus, the minority client may be perceived as hostile and resistant. The results of this interaction may be a premature termination of therapy. Considerable evidence exists that clients from upper socioeconomic backgrounds have significantly more exploratory interviews with their therapists, and that middle-class patients tend to remain in treatment longer than lower-class patients (Gottesfeld, 1995; Leong et al., 1995; Neighbors, Caldwell, Thompson, & Jackson, 1994). Furthermore, the now-classic study of Hollingstead and Redlich (1968) found that lower-class patients tend to have fewer ego-involving relationships and less intensive therapeutic relationships than members of higher socioeconomic classes.

Not only does poverty contribute to the mental health problems among racial/ethnic minority groups and not only does social class determine the type of treatment a minority client is likely to receive, but Atkinson, Morten, & Sue (1998) conclude:

. . . ethnic minorities are less likely to earn incomes sufficient to pay for mental health treatment, less likely to have insurance, and more likely to qualify for public assistance than European Americans. Thus, ethnic minorities often have to rely on public (government-sponsored) or nonprofit mental health services to obtain help with their psychological problems. (p. 64)

LANGUAGE BARRIERS

United States society is definitely a monolingual one. Use of standard English to communicate may unfairly discriminate against those from a bilingual or lower-class background. Not only is this seen in our educational system, but also in the therapy relationship as well. The bilingual background of many Asian Americans, Latino/Hispanic Americans, and American Indians may lead to much misunderstanding. This is true even if a minority group member cannot speak his/her own native tongue. Early language studies (Smith, 1957; Smith & Kasdon, 1961) indicate that simply coming from a background where one or both of the parents have spoken their native tongue can impair proper acquisition of English.

Even African Americans who come from a different cultural environment may use words and phrases (Black English/Ebonics) not entirely understandable to the therapist. While considerable criticism was directed toward the Oakland Unified School District with their short-lived attempt to recognize Ebonics in 1996, the reality is that such a form of communication does exist in many African American communities. In therapy, however, African American clients are expected to communicate their feelings and thoughts to therapists in standard English. For some African Americans, this is a difficult task, since the use of nonstandard English is the norm. Black language code involves a great deal of implicitness in communication, such as shorter sentences and less grammatical elaboration (but greater reliance on nonverbal cues). On the other hand, the language code of the middle and upper classes is much more elaborate, with less reliance on nonverbal cues, and entails greater knowledge of grammar and syntax.

Romero (1985) indicates that counseling psychologists are finding that they must interact with consumers who may have English as a second language, or who may not speak English at all. The lack of bilingual therapists and the requirement that the culturally different client communicate in English may limit the person's ability to progress in counseling/therapy. If bilingual individuals do not use their native tongue in therapy, many aspects of their emotional experience may not be available for treatment. For example, because English may not be their primary language, they may have difficulties using the wide complexity of language to describe their particular thoughts, feelings, and unique situation. Clients who are limited in English tend to feel they are speaking as a child and choose simple words to explain complex thoughts and feelings. If they were able to use their native tongue, they would easily explain themselves without the huge loss of emotional complexity and experience.

White (1984) believes that understanding Black communication styles and patterns is indispensable for therapists working in the African American community. Failure to understand imagery, analogies, and nuances of cultural sayings may render the therapist ineffective in establishing relationships and building credibility.

In therapy, heavy reliance is placed on verbal interaction to build rapport. The presupposition is that participants in a therapeutic dialogue are capable of understanding each other. Therapists oftentimes fail to understand an African American client's language and its nuances for rapport building. Furthermore, those who have not been given the same educational or economic opportunities may lack the verbal skills to benefit from *talk therapy.*

A minority client's brief, different, or poor verbal responses may lead many therapists to impute inaccurate characteristics or motives to him/her. A minority client may be seen as uncooperative, sullen, negative, nonverbal, or repressed on the basis of language expression alone.

Since Euro-American society places such a high premium on one's use of English, it is a short step to conclude that minorities are inferior, lack awareness, or lack conceptual thinking powers. Such misinterpretation can also be seen in the use and interpretation of psychological tests. So-called IQ and achievement tests are especially notorious for their language bias.

GENERALIZATIONS AND STEREOTYPES: SOME CAUTIONS

As can be seen in Table 8.1 (see Chapter 8), White cultural values are reflected in the generic characteristics of counseling (Table 3.1). These characteristics are summarized and can be compared with the values of four racial/ethnic minority groups: American Indians, Asian Americans, Blacks, and Hispanics (see Table 3.2). Although it is critical for therapists to have a basic understanding of the generic characteristics of counseling and psychotherapy and the culture-specific life values of different groups, there is the ever-present danger of overgeneralizing and stereotyping. For example, the listing of racial/ethnic minority group variables does not indicate that all persons coming from the same minority group will share all or even some of these traits. Furthermore, emerging trends such as short-term and crisis intervention approaches and other less verbally oriented techniques differ from the generic traits listed. Yet it is highly improbable that any of us can enter a situation or encounter people without forming impressions consistent with our own experiences and values. Whether a client is dressed neatly in a suit or wears blue jeans, is a man or a woman, or is of a different race will likely affect our assumptions about him/her.

First impressions will be formed that fit our own interpretations and generalizations of human behavior. Generalizations are necessary for us to use; without them, we would become inefficient creatures. However, they are guidelines for our behaviors, to be tentatively applied in new situations, and they should be open to change and challenge. It is exactly at this stage that generalizations remain generalizations or become stereotypes. *Stereotypes* may be defined as rigid preconceptions we hold about *all* people who are members of a particular group, whether it be defined along racial, religious, sexual, or other lines. The belief in a perceived characteristic of the group is applied to all members without regard for individual variations. The danger of stereotypes is that they are impervious to logic or experience. All incoming information is distorted to fit our preconceived notions. For example, people who are strongly anti-Semitic will accuse Jews of being stingy and miserly and then, in the same breath, accuse them of flaunting their wealth by conspicuous spending.

In using Tables 8.1, 3.1, and 3.2, the information should act as guidelines rather than absolutes. These generalizations should serve as the background from which the figure emerges. For example, belonging to a particular group may mean sharing common values and experiences. Individuals within a group, however, also differ. The background offers a contrast for us to see individual differences more clearly. It should not submerge but rather increase the visibility of the figure. This is the figure-ground relationship that should aid us in recognizing the uniqueness of people more readily.

Chapter Four

◆

Culturally Appropriate
Intervention Strategies

◆

The following example of a Black/White interaction, witnessed by one of the authors, illustrates some very powerful and important features about cultural communication styles. While we are concerned about the possibility of overgeneralization, this verbal/nonverbal exchange between an African American faculty member and several White colleagues has occurred with sufficient frequency to suggest that many Blacks and Whites have different styles of communication. Let us briefly analyze the following case study.

◆ Case Study

Dr. Paul S., a Black professor in the doctoral program, was addressing the entire graduate faculty about the need for a multicultural perspective in the department and the need to hire a Latina. Several of his White colleagues raised objections to the inclusion of more minority curriculum in the program because it would either (a) raise the number of units students would have to take to graduate or (b) require the dropping of a course to keep units manageable. At one point, Dr. S. rose from his seat, leaned forward, made eye contact with the most vocal objector and, raising his voice, asked, "What would be wrong in doing that?" The question brought about the following exchange:

WHITE MALE PROFESSOR: The question is not whether it's right or wrong. We need to look at your request from a broader perspective. For example, how will it affect our curriculum? Is your request educationally sound? What external constraints do we have in our ability to hire new faculty? Even if university funds are available, would it be fair to limit it to a Hispanic female? Shouldn't we be hiring the most qualified applicant rather than limiting it to a particular race or sex?

DR. S. [*Raising his voice and pounding the table to punctuate his comments*]:   I've heard those excuses for years and that's just what they are . . . a crock of you-know-what! This faculty doesn't sound very committed to cultural diversity at all!

WHITE MALE PROFESSOR II: Paul, calm down! Don't let your emotions carry you away. Let's address these issues in a rational manner.

DR. S.:   What do you mean? I'm not rational? That pisses me off! All I ever hear is we can't do this, or we can't do that! I want to know where you *all* are coming from. Are we going to do anything about cultural diversity? [Several faculty members on either side of Dr. S. have shifted away from him. At this point, Dr. S. turns to one of them and states:] Don't worry, I'm not going to hit you!

WHITE MALE PROFESSOR: I don't believe we should discuss this matter further, until we can control our feelings. I'm not going to sit here and be the object of anger and insults.

DR. S.:   Anger? What are you talking about? Just because I feel strongly about my convictions, you think I'm angry? All I'm asking for is how *you* stand on the issues.

WHITE MALE PROFESSOR: I already have.

DR. S.:   No you haven't! You've just given me a bunch of intellectual bullshit. Where do you stand?

WHITE PROFESSOR: Mr. Chairman, I move we table this discussion.

First, it is quite obvious from this exchange that the White professor perceived Dr. S. to be angry, out of control, and irrational. How did he arrive at that conclusion? No doubt part of it may have been the language used, but equally important were the nonverbals (raising of the voice, pounding on the table, prolonged eye contact, etc.). In a faculty meeting where White males predominate, the mode of acceptable communication is considered to be low-key, dispassionate, impersonal, and issue oriented. However, many African Americans not only define the issues differently, but also process them in a manner that is misunderstood by many Whites. African American styles tend to be high-key, animated, confrontational, and interpersonal. The differences in style of communication are not limited solely to an academic environment.

For example, in the political arena, noticeable differences can be observed between how Black and White politicians debate and communicate. When the Reverend Jesse Jackson gave the keynote address many years ago at a Democratic convention, many supporters characterized his speech as moving, coming from the heart, and indicative of his sincerity and honesty. Yet, many television commentators (mainly White newsmen) made observations that Jackson's address was like a "Baptist revival meeting" or "pep rally" or was "more style than substance." They seemed to discredit his message because it was too emotional.

These characterizations reveal a value judgment and possible misinterpretations occurring as a result of communication styles. Often, the presence of affect in a debate is equated with emotion (anger and hostility) and seen as counter to reason. Statements that Dr. S. should calm down, not be irrational, and address the issues in an objective fashion are reflective of such an interpretation. Likewise, many African Americans may perceive White communication styles in a negative manner. Dr. S., in his attempt to find out where the White male professor was coming from, is disinclined to believe that his colleague does not have an opinion on the matter. Dealing with the issues on an intellectual level (even if the issues raised are legitimate) may be perceived as "fronting," a Black concept used to denote a person who is purposely concealing how he or she honestly feels or believes.

Second, it is very possible that differences in communication style may trigger off certain preconceived notions, stereotypes, or beliefs we may have about various minority groups. As we have seen, one of the most dominant White stereotypes is that of the angry, hostile Black male who is prone to violence. African Americans are very aware of these stereotypes, as in the case of Dr. S.'s statement to one White colleague, "Don't worry, I'm not going to hit you!"

This example of a Black/White interaction and the misinterpretations is played out in countless everyday situations. They occur with sufficient frequency and consistency to raise the question, "Do African Americans and Euro-Americans differ not only in the content of a debate, but also in the style by which the disagreement is to be resolved?" Likewise, do different racial/ethnic groups differ in their communication styles? If they do, might they not create misunderstandings and misinterpretations of one another's behavior? What implications do communication styles have for helping or therapeutic styles? Do some therapy styles seem more appropriate and effective in working with certain racial/ethnic group members?

COMMUNICATION STYLES

In Chapter 3, we defined therapy as a process of interpersonal interaction, communication, and social influence. For effective therapy to occur, both the therapist and client must be able to *send* and *receive* both *verbal* and *nonverbal* messages *accurately* and *appropriately*. In other words, therapy is a form of communication. It requires that the therapist not only *send* messages (make himself or herself understood), but also *receive* messages (attend to what is going on with the client). The definition for effective therapy also includes *verbal* (content of what is said) and *nonverbal* (how something is said) elements. Furthermore, most therapists seem more concerned with the *accuracy* of communication (let's get to the heart of the matter) rather than whether the communication is *appropriate*. As indicated in the last chapter, traditional Asian culture considers a person's subtlety and indirectness in communication a highly prized art. The direct and confrontive techniques in therapy may be perceived by traditional Asian or Native American clients as lacking in respect for the client, a crude and rude form of communication, and a reflection of insensitivity. In most cases, therapists have been trained to tune in to the content of what is said, rather than how something is said.

When we refer to communication style, we are addressing those factors that go beyond the content of what is said. Some communication specialists believe that only 30–40% of what is communicated conversationally is verbal (Condon & Yousef, 1975; Ramsey & Birk, 1983; Singelis, 1994). What people say and do is usually qualified by other things they say and do. A gesture, tone, inflection, posture, or eye contact may enhance or negate the content of a message. Communication styles have a tremendous impact upon our face-to-face encounters with others. Whether our conversation proceeds in fits and starts, whether we interrupt one another continually or proceed smoothly, the topics we prefer to discuss or avoid, the depth of our involvement, the forms of interaction (ritual, repartee, argumentative, persuasive, etc.), and the channel we use to communicate (verbal-nonverbal vs. nonverbal-verbal) are all aspects of communication style (Douglis, 1987; Wolfgang, 1985). Some refer to it as the "social rhythms" that underlie all our speech and actions. Communication styles are strongly correlated with race, culture, and ethnicity. Gender has also been found to be a powerful determinant of communication style (J.C. Pearson, 1985).

Reared in a Euro-American middle-class society, mental health professionals may assume that certain behaviors or rules of speaking are universal and possess the same meaning. This may create major problems for therapists and culturally different clients. Since differences in communication style are most strongly manifested in nonverbal communication, this chapter concentrates on those aspects of communication that transcend the written or spoken word. First, we explore how race/culture may influence several areas of nonverbal behavior: (a) proxemics, (b) kinesics, (c) paralanguage, and (d) high-low context communication. Second, we spend a brief time discussing the function and importance of nonverbal behavior as it relates to stereotypes and preconceived notions we may have of culturally different groups. Last, we propose a basic thesis that various racial minorities such as Asian Americans, American Indians, African Americans, and Latino/Hispanic Americans possess a unique communication style that may have major implications for mental health practice. These implications suggest that certain therapeutic approaches (person centered, existential, analytic, cognitive, behavioral, etc.) may be more appropriate helping strategies for certain ethnic groups.

NONVERBAL COMMUNICATION

Although language, class, and cultural factors all interact to create problems in communication between the minority client and therapist, an oft-neglected area is nonverbal behavior (Singelis, 1994; Wolfgang, 1985). What a person says can be enhanced or negated by his/her nonverbals. When a man raises his voice, tightens his facial muscles, pounds the table violently, and proclaims, "Goddamn it, I'm not angry!" he is clearly contradicting the content of the communication. If we all share the same cultural and social upbringing, we may all arrive at the same conclusion. Interpreting nonverbals, however, is made difficult for several reasons. First, the same nonverbal behavior on the part of an American Indian client may mean something quite different than if it was made by a White person. Second, nonverbals often occur outside our level of awareness. As a result, it is important that therapists begin the process of recognizing nonverbal communications and their possible cultural meanings. It is important to note that our discussion of nonverbal codes will not include all the possible nonverbal cues. Some of the areas excluded are time considerations, olfaction (taste and smell), tactile cues, and artifactual communication (clothing, hairstyle, display of material things, etc. [DePaulo, 1992; Douglis, 1987; R.E. Pearson, 1985; Ramsey & Birk, 1983]).

Proxemics

The study of *proxemics* refers to perception and use of personal and interpersonal space. Clear norms exist concerning the use of physical distance in social interactions. Hall (1969) has identified four interpersonal distance zones characteristic of U.S. culture: intimate, from contact to 18 inches; personal, from 1.5 feet to 4 feet; social, from 4 to 12 feet; and public (lectures and speeches), greater than 12 feet.

In this society, individuals seem to become more uncomfortable when others stand too close rather than too far away (Goldman, 1980). These feelings and reactions associated with a violation of personal space may include flight, withdrawal, anger, and conflict (J.C. Pearson, 1985). On the other hand, we tend to allow closer proximity or move closer to people whom we like or feel interpersonal attraction toward. Some evidence exists that personal space can be reframed in terms of dominance and status. Those with greater status, prestige, and power may occupy more space (larger homes, cars, or offices). However, different cultures dictate different distances in personal space. For Latin Americans, Africans, Black Americans, Indonesians,

Arabs, South Americans, and French, conversing with a person dictates a much closer stance than normally comfortable for Anglos (Jensen, 1985). A Latin American client may cause the therapist to back away because of the closeness taken. The client may interpret the therapist's behavior as indicative of aloofness, coldness, or a desire not to communicate. In some cross-cultural encounters, it may even be perceived as a sign of haughtiness and superiority. On the other hand, the therapist may misinterpret the client's behavior as an attempt to become inappropriately intimate, a sign of pushiness or aggressiveness. Both the therapist and the culturally different client may benefit from understanding that their reactions and behaviors are attempts to create the spatial dimension to which they are culturally conditioned.

Research on proxemics leads to the inevitable conclusion that conversational distances are a function of the racial and cultural background of the conversants (Susman & Rosenfeld, 1982; Wolfgang, 1985). The factor of personal space has major implications for how furniture is arranged, where the seats are located, where you seat the client, and how far you sit from him or her (LaBarre, 1985). Latin Americans, for example, may not feel comfortable with a desk between them and the person they are speaking to. Euro-Americans, however, like to keep a desk between them and the other person. Some Eskimos may actually prefer to sit side by side rather than across from one another when talking about intimate aspects of their lives.

Kinesics

While proxemics refers to personal space, *kinesics* is the term used to refer to bodily movements. It includes such things as facial expression, posture, characteristics of movement, gestures, and eye contact. Again, kinesics appears to be culturally conditioned, with the meaning of body movements strongly linked to the culture.

Much of our counseling assessment is based upon expressions on people's faces (J.C. Pearson, 1985). We assume that facial cues express emotions and demonstrate the degree of responsiveness and/or involvement of the individual.

For example, smiling is a type of expression in our society which is believed to indicate liking or positive affect. People attribute greater positive characteristics to others who smile, feeling that they are intelligent, have a good personality, and are pleasant (Singelis, 1994). However, when Japanese smile and laugh, it does not necessarily mean happiness but may convey other meanings (embarrassment, discomfort, shyness, etc.). Such nonverbal misinterpretations also fueled much of the conflict in Los Angeles directly after the Rodney King verdict when many African Americans and Korean grocery store owners became at odds with one another. African Americans confronted their Korean American counterparts about exploitation of Black neighborhoods. During one particularly heated exchange, African Americans became incensed when many Korean American store owners would have a constant smile on their faces. They interpreted the facial expression as arrogance, taunting, and lack of compassion for the concerns of Blacks. Little did they realize that a smile in this situation in fact indicated extreme embarassment and apprehension.

On the other hand, some Asians believe that smiling may suggest weakness. Among some Japanese and Chinese, restraint of strong feelings (anger, irritation, sadness, and love or happiness) is considered to be a sign of maturity and wisdom. Children are taught that outward emotional expressions (facial expressions, body movements, and verbal content) are discouraged except for extreme situations (Yamamoto & Kubota, 1983). Therapists who are unaware of this aspect of Asian culture may assume that their Asian American client is lacking in feelings or out of touch with them. More likely, the lack of facial expression may be the basis of stereotypes such as the statement that Asians are inscrutable, sneaky, deceptive, and backstabbers.

A number of gestures and bodily movements have been found to have different meanings when the cultural context is considered (LaBarre, 1985). In the Sung Dynasty in China, sticking out the tongue is a gesture of mock terror and meant as ridicule; to the Ovimbundu of Africa, it means (when coupled with bending the head forward) "you're a fool"; a protruding tongue in the Mayan statues of the gods signifies wisdom; and in our own culture, the sticking out of the tongue is generally considered to be a juvenile quasi-obscene gesture of defiance, mockery, or contempt.

Head movements also have different meanings (Eakins & Eakins, 1985; Jensen, 1985). An educated Englishman may consider the lifting of the chin when conversing as a poised and polite gesture, but to Euro-Americans it may connote snobbery and arrogance (turning up his nose). While we shake our head from side to side to indicate "no," Mayan tribe members say "no" by jerking the head to the right. In Sri Lanka, one signals agreement by moving the head from side to side like a metronome (Singelis, 1994).

Most Euro-Americans perceive squatting (often done by children) as improper and childish. In other parts of the world, people have learned to rest by taking a squatting position. On the other hand, when we put our feet up on a desk, it is believed to signify a relaxed and informal attitude. Yet, Latin Americans and Asians may perceive it as rudeness and arrogance, especially if the bottom of the feet are shown to them.

Shaking hands is another gesture that varies from culture to culture and may have strong cultural/historical significance. Latin Americans tend to shake hands more vigorously, frequently, and for a longer period of time. Interestingly, most cultures use the right hand when shaking. Since most of the population of the world is right-handed, this may not be surprising. However, some researchers believe that shaking with the right hand may be a symbolic act of peace, as in older times it was the right hand that generally held the weapons. In some Moslem and Asian countries, touching anyone with the left hand may be considered an obscenity (the left hand is an aid to the process of elimination or *unclean,* while the right one is used for the intake of food or *clean*). Offering something with the left hand to a Moslem may be an insult of the most serious type.

Eye contact is, perhaps, the nonverbal behavior most likely to be addressed by mental health providers. It is not unusual for us to hear someone say, "notice that the husband avoided eye contact with the wife," or "notice how the client averted his/her eyes when. . . ." Behind these observations is the belief that eye contact or lack of eye contact has diagnostic significance. We would agree with that premise, but in most cases, therapists attribute negative traits to the avoidance of eye contact: shy, unassertive, sneaky, or depressed.

This lack of understanding has been played out in many different situations when Black/White interactions have occurred. In many cases, it is not necessary for Blacks to look at one another in the eye at all times to communicate (Smith, 1981). An African American may be actively involved in doing other things when engaged in a conversation. Many White therapists may be prone to view the African American client as being sullen, resistant, or uncooperative. Smith (1981) provides an excellent example of such a clash in communication styles:

For instance, one Black female student was sent to the office by her gymnasium teacher because the student was said to display insolent behavior. When the student was asked to give her version of the incident, she replied, "Mrs. X asked all of us to come over to the side of the pool so that she could show us how to do the backstroke. I went over with the rest of the girls. Then Mrs. X started yelling at me and said I wasn't paying attention to her because I wasn't looking directly at her. I told her I was paying attention to her (throughout the conversation, the student kept her head down, avoiding the principal's eyes), and then she said that she wanted me to face her and look her squarely in the eye like the rest of the girls [who were all White]. So I did. The next thing I knew she was telling me to get out of the pool, that she didn't like the way I was looking at her. So that's why I'm here." (p. 155)

As this example illustrates, Black styles of communication may not only be different from their White counterparts, but may also lead to misinterpretations. Many Blacks do not nod their heads or say "uh huh" to indicate they are listening (Hall, 1976; Kochman, 1981; Smith, 1981). Going through the motions of looking at the person and nodding the head is not necessary for many Blacks to indicate that one is listening (Hall, 1974, 1976).

Statistics indicate that when White U.S. Americans listen to a speaker, they make eye contact with the speaker about 80% of the time. When speaking to others, however, they tend to look away (avoid eye contact) about 50% of the time. This is in marked contrast to many Black Americans who, when speaking, make greater eye contact and, when listening, make infrequent eye contact.

Paralanguage

The term *paralanguage* is used to refer to other vocal cues that individuals use to communicate. For example, loudness of voice, pauses, silences, hesitations, rate, inflections, and the like, all fall into this category. Paralanguage is very likely to be manifested forcefully in conversation conventions such as how we greet, address, and take turns in speaking. It can communicate a variety of different features about a person, such as age, gender, and emotional responses as well as the race and sex of the speaker (Banks & Banks, 1993; Lass, Mertz, & Kimmel, 1978).

There are complex rules regarding when to speak or yield to another person. For example, U.S. Americans frequently feel uncomfortable with a pause or silent stretch in the conversation, feeling obligated to fill it in with more talk. Silence is not always a sign for you, the listener, to take up the conversation. While it may be viewed negatively by many, other cultures interpret the use of silence differently. The English and Arabs use silence for privacy, while the Russians, French, and Spanish read it as agreement among the parties (Hall, 1969, 1976). In Asian culture, silence is traditionally a sign of respect for elders. Furthermore, silence by many Chinese and Japanese is not a floor-yielding signal inviting others to pick up the conversation. Rather, it may indicate a desire to continue speaking after making a particular point. Often silence is a sign of politeness and respect rather than a lack of desire to continue speaking.

The amount of verbal expressiveness in the United States, relative to other cultures, is quite high. Most Euro-Americans encourage their children to enter freely into conversations, and teachers encourage students to ask many questions and state their thoughts and opinions. This has led many foreigners to observe that Euro-American youngsters are brash, immodest, rude, and disrespectful (Irvine & York, 1995; Jensen, 1985). Likewise, teachers of minority children may see reticence in speaking out as a sign of ignorance, lack of motivation, or ineffective teaching (Banks & Banks, 1993) when, in reality, the students may be showing proper respect (to ask questions is disrespectful because it implies that the teacher was unclear). American Indians, for example, have been taught that to speak out, ask questions, or even raise one's hand in class is an act of immodesty.

A mental health professional who is uncomfortable with silence or who misinterprets it may fill in the conversation and prevent the client from elaborating further. Even greater danger is to impute incorrect motives to the minority client's silence. One can readily see how therapy, which emphasizes talking, may place many minorities at a disadvantage.

Volume and intensity of speech in conversation are also influenced by cultural values. The overall loudness of speech displayed by many Euro-American visitors to foreign countries has earned them the reputation of being boisterous and shameless. In Asian countries, people tend to speak more softly and would interpret the loud volume of a U.S. visitor as aggressiveness, loss of self-control, or anger. When compared to Arabs, however, people in the United States are soft-spoken. Many Arabs like to be bathed in sound, and the volume of their radios, phonographs, and televisions is quite loud. In some countries, where such entertainment units are not plentiful, it is considered a polite and thoughtful act to allow neighbors to hear by keeping the volume high. We in the United States would view such behavior as being thoughtless and an invasion of privacy.

A therapist or counselor working with culturally different clients would be well advised to be aware of possible misinterpretations as a function of speech volume. Speaking loudly may not indicate anger and hostility; speaking in a soft voice may not be a sign of weakness, shyness, or depression.

Directness of a conversation or the degree of frankness also varies considerably among various cultural groups. Observing the English in their parliamentary debates will drive this point home. The long heritage of open, direct, and frank confrontation leads to heckling of public speakers and quite blunt and sharp exchanges. Britons believe and feel that these are acceptable styles and may take no offense at being the object of such exchanges. However, U.S. citizens feel that such exchanges are impolite, abrasive, and not rational. Relative to Asians, Euro-Americans are seen as being too blunt and frank. Great care is taken by many Asians not to hurt the feelings of or embarrass the other person. As a result, use of euphemisms and ambiguity is the norm.

Since many minority groups may value indirectness, the U.S. emphasis on getting to the point and not beating around the bush may alienate others. Asian Americans, American Indians, and some Latino/Hispanic Americans may see this behavior as immature, rude, and lacking in finesse. On the other hand, clients from different cultures may be negatively labeled as evasive and afraid to confront the problem.

High-Low Context Communication

Edward T. Hall, author of such classics as *The Silent Language* (1959) and *The Hidden Dimension* (1969), is a well-known anthropologist who has proposed the concept of high-low context cultures (Hall, 1976). A high-context (HC) communication or message is one that is anchored in the physical context (situation) or internalized in the person. Less reliance is placed on the explicit code or message content. An HC communication relies heavily on nonverbals and the group identification/understanding shared by those communicating. For example, a normal-stressed "no" by a U.S. American may be interpreted by an Arab as "yes." A real negation in Arab culture would be stressed much more emphatically. A prime example of the contextual dimension in understanding communication is exemplified in the following case study.

♦ *Case Study*

"I was asked to consult with a hospital who was having a great deal of difficulty with their Filipino nurses. The hospital had a number of them on their staff and the medical director was concerned about their competence in understanding and following directions from doctors. As luck would have it, when I came to the hospital, I was immediately confronted with a situation which threatened to 'blow up.' Dr. K., a Euro-American physician, had brought charges against a Filipino American nurse for incompetence. He had observed her incorrectly using and monitoring life support systems on a critically ill patient. He relates how he entered the patient's room and told the nurse that she was incorrectly using the equipment and that the patient could die if she didn't do it right. Dr. K. states that he spent some 10 minutes explaining how the equipment should be attached and used. Upon finishing his explanation, he asked the nurse if she understood. The Filipino nurse nodded her head slightly and hesitantly said 'yes, yes, Doctor.' Later that evening, Dr. K. observed the same nurse continuing to use the equipment incorrectly; he reported her to the head nurse and asked for her immediate dismissal. While it is possible that the nurse was not competent, further investigation revealed strong cultural forces affecting the hospital work situation. What the medical administration failed to understand was the cultural context of the situation. In the Philippines, it is considered impolite to say no in a number of situations. In this case, for the nurse to say 'no' to the doctor (a respected figure of high status) when asked whether she understood, would have implied that Dr. K. was a poor teacher. This would be considered insulting and impolite. Thus, the only option the Filipino nurse felt open to her was to tell the doctor 'yes.'"

In Filipino culture, a mild, hesitant "yes" is interpreted by those who understand as a "no" or a polite refusal. In traditional Asian society, many interactions are understandable only in light of high-context cues and situations. For example, to extend an invitation only once for dinner would be considered an affront, because it implies you are not sincere. One must extend an invitation several times, encouraging the invitee to accept. Arabs may also refuse an offer of food several times before giving in. However, most Euro-Americans believe that a host's offer can be politely refused with just a "no, thank you."

If we pay attention to just the explicit coded part of the message, we are likely to misunderstand the communication. According to Hall (1976), low-context (LC) cultures place a greater reliance on the verbal part of the message. In addition, LC cultures have been associated with being more opportunistic, more individual rather than group oriented, and emphasizing rules of law and procedure (Smith, 1981).

It appears that the United States is an LC culture (although it is still higher than the Swiss, Germans, and Scandinavians in the amount of contexting required). China, perhaps, represents the other end of the continuum, where its complex culture relies heavily on context. Asian Americans, African Americans, Hispanics, American Indians, and other minority groups in the United States also emphasize HC cues.

HC communication, in contrast to LC, is faster, as well as more economical, efficient, and satisfying. Because it is so bound to the culture, it is slow to change and tends to be cohesive and unifying. LC communication does not unify but changes rapidly and easily.

Twins who have grown up together can and do communicate more economically (HC) than two lawyers during a trial (LC). Bernstein's (1964) work in language analysis refers to restricted codes (HC) and elaborated codes (LC). Restricted codes are observed in families where words and sentences collapse and are shortened without loss of meaning. However, elaborated codes, where many words are used to communicate the same content, are seen in classrooms, diplomacy, and law.

African American culture has been described as HC. For example, it is clear that many Blacks require fewer words than their White counterparts to communicate the same content (Irvine & York, 1995; Jenkins, 1982; Stanback & Pearce, 1985; Weber, 1985). An African American male who enters a room and spots an attractive lady may stoop slightly in her direction, smile, and may tap the table twice while vocalizing a long drawn out "uh huh." What he has communicated would require many words from his White brother to convey the same message! The fact that African Americans may communicate more by HC cues has led many to characterize them as nonverbal, inarticulate, unintelligent, and so forth.

Another example of how HC and LC orientations may lead to misunderstandings is a situation that occurred during a cross-cultural communications conference. Social scientists from Asia, the Pacific, and the mainland United States were invited to attend a conference in Hawaii. Sessions were run like most at such conferences. All invitees were to present an original piece of research (45 minutes) on cross-cultural communications, and then a respondent would react to it (10 minutes). Contrasting communication styles became immediately apparent. If the presenters were Asian, they would go through an elaborate ritual of expressing gratitude for being invited, derogating the self, praising those in the audience, and so forth. With slight variations, this behavior occurred consistently whether the Asian person was a presenter or respondent. If the latter, the person would apologize for his/her naiveté, praise the paper, and spend only a short time critiquing it. When the presenter or respondent was someone from the U.S. mainland, the White researcher would usually attend directly to the task. Critiques were direct and to the point.

During mealtimes, many of the participants from the mainland would indicate that their Asian counterparts did not seem to realize the weaknesses in some of their colleagues' research papers. On the other hand, many of the Asian participants expressed reluctance to continue because the Americans were too blunt in their remarks. As a result, they could be shamed in public and lose face. They did not want to continue with the conference if the respondent to their paper was from the U.S. mainland. Such reactions were due in large part to the HC-LC differences among participants. The LC participant relied heavily on the explicit code (written and spoken word) as the main means to convey thoughts, ideas, and feelings. The HC participant relied on implicit aspects of the communication. For example, many of the White conferees saw the Asian critiques as "wishy-washy" and lacking in critical analysis. They did not understand that the praises heaped on the person were more form than substance.

The key to understanding the basis of the Asian critiques was not in the words used, but in other factors such as (a) the amount of time used to praise the paper, (b) the amount of time spent to derogate the self, (c) the descriptors used, and (d) the questions that were asked at the end. An Asian might offer a response such as: "I would only ask Dr. Yamamoto two questions. First, how did he decide to use the particular research methodology, and second, how did he select the population to be researched?" Those in the audience who understood the context (HC) knew that the questions indicated that (a) the wrong methodology was used and (b) the population was an unrepresentative one. These examples indicate how important it is for the therapist to understand racial/cultural communication styles.

SOCIOPOLITICAL FACETS OF NONVERBAL COMMUNICATION

There is a common saying among African Americans: "If you really want to know what White folks are thinking and feeling, don't listen to what they say, but how they say it." In most cases, such a statement refers to the biases, stereotypes, and racist attitudes that Whites are believed to possess, but that they consciously or unconsciously conceal.

Rightly or wrongly, many minority individuals through years of personal experience operate from three assumptions. The first assumption is that all Whites in this society are racist. Through their own cultural conditioning, they have been socialized into a culture that espouses the superiority of White culture over all others (Jones, 1997; Parham, 1993; Ridley, 1995). The second assumption is that most Whites find such a concept disturbing and will go to great lengths to deny that they are racist or biased. Some of this is done deliberately and with awareness, but in most cases one's racism is largely unconscious. The last of these assumptions is that nonverbal behaviors are more accurate reflections of what a White person is thinking or feeling than what they say.

There is considerable evidence to suggest that these three assumptions held by various racial/ethnic minorities are, indeed, accurate (McIntosh, 1989; Ridley, 1995; D.W. Sue et al., 1998). Counselors and mental health practitioners need to be very cognizant of nonverbal cues from a number of different perspectives.

In the last section, we discussed how nonverbal behavior is culture-bound, and that the counselor or therapist cannot make universal interpretations about it. Likewise, nonverbal cues are important because they often (a) unconsciously reflect our biases and (b) trigger off stereotypes we have of other people.

NONVERBALS AS REFLECTIONS OF BIAS

Some time back, a TV program called *Candid Camera* was very popular among U.S. audiences. It operated from a unique premise, which involved creating very unusual situations for naive subjects who were then filmed as they reacted to them. One of these experiments involved interviewing housewives about their attitudes toward African American, Latino/Hispanic, and White teenagers. The intent was to select a group of women who, by all standards, appeared sincere in their beliefs that Blacks and Latinos were no more prone to violence than their White counterparts. Unknown to them, they were filmed by a hidden camera as they left their homes to go shopping at the local supermarket.

The creator of the program had secretly arranged for an African American, a Latino, and a White youngster to pass these women on the street. All three youths were dressed casually but nearly identically. The experiment was counterbalanced: That is, the race of the youngster was randomly assigned as to which would approach the shopper first. What occurred was a powerful statement on unconscious racist attitudes and beliefs.

All the youngsters had been instructed to pass the shopper on the purse side of the street. If the woman was holding the purse in her right hand, the youngster would approach and pass on her right. If the purse was held with the left hand, the youngster would pass on her left. Studies of the film revealed consistent outcomes. Many women when approached by the Black or Latino youngster (approximately 15 feet away) would casually switch the purse from one arm to the other! This was an infrequent occurrence with the White youngster. Why?

The answer appears quite obvious to us. The women subjects who switched their purses were operating from biases, stereotypes, and preconceived notions about what minority youngsters are like: They are prone to crime, more apt to snatch a purse or rob, more apt to be juvenile delinquents, and more likely to engage in violence. The disturbing part of this experiment was that the selected subjects were, by all measures, sincere individuals who on a conscious level denied harboring racist attitudes or beliefs. They were not liars, nor were they deliberately deceiving the interviewer. They were normal, everyday people. They honestly believed that they did not possess these biases, yet when tested, their nonverbal behavior (purse switching) gave them away.

The power of nonverbal communication is that it tends to be least under conscious control. Studies support the conclusion that nonverbal cues operate primarily on an unawareness level (DePaulo, 1992; Singelis, 1994), that they tend to be more spontaneous and difficult to censor or falsify (Mehrabian, 1972), and that they are more trusted than words. In our society, we have learned to use words (spoken or written) to mask or conceal our true thoughts and feelings. Note how our politicians and lawyers are able to address an issue without revealing much of what they think or believe. This is very evident in controversial issues such as gun control, abortion, and issues of affirmative action and immigration.

Nonverbal behavior provides clues to conscious deceptions and/or unconscious bias. There is evidence that the accuracy of nonverbal communication varies with the part of the body used: facial expression is more controllable than the hands, followed by the legs and the rest of the body (Hansen, Stevic, & Warner, 1982). The implications for multicultural counseling are obvious. A therapist who has not adequately dealt with his or her own biases and racist attitudes may unwittingly communicate them to his or her culturally different client.

Culturally different clients will often test the therapist through a series of challenges. Many of these challenges are aimed at getting the helping professional to self-disclose. The intent is to ascertain not only the therapist's level of expertness, but of trustworthiness as well. "How open and honest are you about your own racism, and will you allow it to interfere with our relationship?" The minority client, in an attempt to seek an answer to this question, will create situations aimed at getting the counselor to reveal himself or herself. Some very common verbal tests are posed in questions like "How can you possibly understand the minority experience? Have you ever laughed at racist jokes? How do you feel about interracial relationships? Are you a racist? Do you really care what happens to Blacks (Latinos, etc.)?" How you answer the challenge (verbal and nonverbal) will either enhance or diminish your credibility.

If counselors are unaware of their own biases, the nonverbals are most likely to reveal their true feelings. Studies suggest that women and minorities are better readers of nonverbal cues than White males (Hall, 1976; Jenkins, 1982; J.C. Pearson, 1985; Weber, 1985). Much of this may be due to their HC orientation, but another reason may be *survival*. For an African American person to survive in a predominantly White society, he or she has to rely on nonverbal cues more often than on verbal ones.

One of our male African American colleagues gives the example of how he must constantly be vigilant when traveling in an unknown part of the country. Just to stop at a roadside restau rant may be dangerous to his physical well-being. As a result, when entering a diner, he is quick to observe not only the reactions of the staff (waiter/waitress, cashier, cooks, etc.) to his entrance, but the reactions of the patrons as well. Do they stare at him? What type of facial expressions do they have? Do they fall silent? Does he get served immediately or is there an inordinate delay? These nonverbal cues reveal much about the environment around him. He may choose to be himself or play the role of a "humble" Black person who leaves quickly if the situation poses danger.

Interestingly, this very same colleague talks about tuning in to nonverbal cues as a means of *psychological survival.* He believes it is important for minorities to accurately read where people are coming from in order to prevent invalidation of the self. For example, a minority person driving through an unfamiliar part of the country may find himself or herself forced to stay at a motel overnight. Seeing a vacancy light flashing, the person may stop and knock on the manager's door. Upon opening the door and seeing the Black person, the White manager may show hesitation, stumble around in his/her verbalizations, and then apologize for having forgotten to turn off the vacancy light. The Black person is faced with the dilemma of deciding whether the White manager was telling the truth or is simply not willing to rent to a Black person.

Some of you might ask, "Why is it important for you to know? Why don't you simply find someplace else? After all, would you stay at a place where you were unwelcome?" Finding another place to stay might not be as important as the psychological well-being of the minority person. Racial/ethnic minorities have encountered too many situations in which double messages are given to them. For the African American to accept the simple statement, "I forgot to turn off the vacancy light" may be to deny one's own true feelings at being the victim of discrimination. This is especially true when the nonverbals (facial expression, anxiety in voice, and stammering) may reveal other reasons.

Too often culturally different individuals are placed in situations where they are asked to deny their true feelings in order to perpetuate *White deception.* Statements that minorities are oversensitive (paranoid?) may represent a form of denial. When a minority colleague makes a statement such as "I get a strange feeling from John; I feel some bias against minorities coming out," White colleagues, friends, and others are sometimes too quick to dismiss it with statements like "You're being oversensitive." Perhaps a better approach would be to say, "What makes you feel that way?" rather than to negate or invalidate what might be an accurate appraisal of nonverbal communication.

Thus, it is clear that racial/ethnic minorities are very tuned in to nonverbals. For the therapist who has not adequately dealt with his or her own racism, the minority client will be quick to assess such biases. In many cases, the minority client may believe that the biases are too great to be overcome and will simply not continue in therapy. This is despite the good intentions of the White counselor/therapist who is not in touch with his/her own biases and assumptions about human behavior.

NONVERBALS AS TRIGGERS TO OUR BIASES/FEARS

Often people assume that being an effective multicultural therapist is a straightforward process that involves the acquisition of knowledge about the various racial/ethnic groups. If we know that Asian Americans and African Americans have different patterns of eye contact than their Euro-American counterparts and if we know that these patterns signify different things, then we should be able to eliminate biases and stereotypes that we possess. Were it so easy, we might have eradicated racism years ago. While increasing our knowledge base about the lifestyles and experiences of minority groups is important, it is not a sufficient condition in itself. Our racist attitudes, beliefs, and feelings are deeply ingrained in our total being. Through years of conditioning they have acquired a strong irrational base, replete with emotional symbolisms about each particular minority. Simply opening a text and reading about African Americans and Latinos/Hispanics will not deal with our deep-seated fears and biases.

Let us return to the vignette of Black/White interactions given at the beginning of the chapter to illustrate our point. Recall that many of the White faculty members believed that their African American colleague was out of control, too emotional, irrational, angry, and that the meeting should be terminated until the topic could be addressed in an objective manner. On the other hand, the Black faculty member denied being angry and believed that the White faculty members were "fronting," deliberately concealing their true thoughts and feelings. Much of the confusion seemed linked to a difference in communication styles, and how these differences trigger off fears and biases we may possess.

One of the major barriers to effective understanding is the common assumption that different cultural groups operate according to identical speech and communication conventions. In the United States, it is often assumed that distinctive racial, cultural, and linguistic features are deviant, inferior, or embarrassing (Kochman, 1981; Singelis, 1994; Stanback & Pearce, 1985). These value judgments then become tinged with beliefs we hold about Black people (Smith, 1981): racial inferiority, being prone to violence and crime, quick to anger, and a threat to White folks (Irvine & York, 1995; Weber, 1985). The communication style of Black people (manifested in nonverbals) can often trigger off these fears. We submit that the situation presented at the beginning of the chapter represents just such an example.

Black styles of communication are often high-keyed, animated, heated, interpersonal, and confrontational. Much emotion, affect, and feelings are generated (Hall, 1976; Shade & New, 1993; Weber, 1985). In a debate, Blacks tend to act as advocates of a position, and ideas are to be tested in the crucible of argument (Banks & Banks, 1993; Kochman, 1981). White middle-class styles, however, are characterized by being detached and objective, impersonal and non-challenging. The person acts not as an *advocate* of the idea, but as a *spokesperson* (truth resides in the idea). A discussion of issues should be devoid of affect, because emotion and reason work against one another. One should talk things out in a logical fashion without getting personally involved. African Americans perceive their own style of communication as indicating that the person is sincere and honest, while Euro-Americans perceive their own style as reasoned and objective (Irvine & York, 1995).

Many African Americans readily admit that they operate from a point of view and, as mentioned previously, are disinclined to believe that White folks do not. Smith (1981) aptly describes the Black orientation in the following passage:

When one Black person talks privately with another, he or she might say: "Look, we don't have to jive each other or be like White folks; let's be honest with one another." These statements reflect the familiar Black saying that "talk is cheap," that actions speak louder than words, and that Whites beguile each other with words. . . . In contrast, the White mind symbolizes to many Black people deceit, verbal chicanery, and sterile intellectivity. For example, after long discourse with a White person, a Black individual might say: "I've heard what you've said, but what do you really mean?" (p. 154)

Such was the case with the African American professor, who believed his White colleagues were "fronting" and being insincere.

While Black Americans may misinterpret White communication styles, it is more likely that Whites will misinterpret Black styles. The direction of the misunderstanding is generally linked to the activating of unconscious *triggers* or *buttons* about racist stereotypes and fears they harbor. As we have repeatedly emphasized, one of the dominant stereotypes of African Americans in our society is that of the hostile, angry, prone-to-violence Black male. The more animated and affective communication style, closer conversing distance, prolonged eye contact when speaking, greater bodily movements, and the tendency to test ideas in a confrontational/argumentative format, lead many Whites to believe their lives are in danger. It is not unusual for White mental health practitioners to describe their African Americans clients as being hostile and angry. We have also observed that White trainees who work with Black clients may nonverbally respond in such a manner as to indicate anxiety, discomfort, or fear (leaning away from their African American clients, tipping their chairs back, crossing their legs or arms, etc.). These are nonverbal distancing moves that may reflect the unconscious stereotypes they hold of Black Americans. While we would entertain the possibility that a Black client is angry, most occasions we have observed do not justify such a descriptor.

It appears that many Euro-Americans operate from the assumption that when an argument ensues, it may lead to a ventilation of anger with the outbreak of a subsequent fight. When the Black professor was told to calm down, such may have been the fear of the White colleague. When the African American professor stated, "Don't worry, I'm not going to hit you!" it was obvious he knew what was going on in the head of his White colleague. What many Whites fail to realize is that African Americans distinguish between an argument used to debate a difference of opinion and one that ventilates anger and hostility (DePaulo, 1992; Irvine & York, 1995; Kochman, 1981; Shade & New, 1993). In the former, the affect indicates sincerity and seriousness, there is a positive attitude toward the material, and the validity of ideas is challenged. In the latter, the affect is more passionate than sincere, there is a negative attitude toward the opponent, and the opponent is abused.

To understand African American styles of communication and to relate adequately to Black communication would require much study in the origins, functions, and manifestations of Black language (Jenkins, 1982). Weber (1985) believes that the historical and philosophical foundations of Black language have led to several verbal styles among Blacks. "Rappin," not the White usage (rap session), was originally a dialogue between a man and a woman where the intent was to win over the admiration of the woman. Imaginary statements, rhythmic speech, and creativity are aimed at generating interest in the woman for hearing more of the rap. It has been likened to a mating call, an introduction of the male to the female, and a ritual expected by some African American women.

Another style of verbal banter is called "woofing," which is an exchange of threats and challenges to fight. It may be derived from what African Americans refer to as "playing the dozens," which is the highest form of verbal warfare and impromptu speaking considered by many Blacks (Jenkins, 1982; Kochman, 1981; Weber, 1985). To the outsider, it may appear cruel, harsh, and provocative. Yet, to many in the Black community, it has historical and functional meanings. The term "dozens" was used during slavery by slavers to refer to Black persons with disabilities. Because he/she was damaged goods, a disabled Black person would often be sold at a discount rate with eleven other damaged slaves (one dozen; Weber, 1985). It was primarily a selling ploy where "dozens" referred to the negative physical features. Often played in jest, the game requires an audience to act as judge and jury over the originality, creativity, and humor of the combatants.

Say man, your girlfriend so ugly, she had to sneak up on a glass to get a drink of water.

Man, you so ugly, yo mamma had to put a sheet over your head so sleep could sneak up on you. (Weber, 1985, p. 248)

A: *Eat shit.*
B: *What should I do with your bones?*
A: *Build a cage for your mother.*
B: *At least I got one.*
A: *She is the least. (Labov, 1972, p. 321)*

A: *Got a match?*
B: *Yeah, my ass and your face or my farts and your breath. (Kochman, 1981, p. 54)*

Woofing or playing the dozens seems to have very real functional value. First, it allows training in self-control about managing one's anger and hostility in the constant face of racism. In many situations, it would be considered dangerous by an African American to respond to taunts, threats, and insults. Second, woofing also allows a Black person to establish a hierarchy or pecking order without resorting to violence. Last, it can create an image of being fearless where one will gain respect.

This verbal and nonverbal style of communication can be a major aspect of Black interactions. Likewise, other minority groups have characteristic styles that may cause considerable difficulties for White counselors. One way of contrasting communication style differences may be in the overt activity dimension (the pacing/intensity) of nonverbal communication. Table 4.1

Table 4.1 COMMUNICATION STYLE DIFFERENCES
(OVERT ACTIVITY DIMENSION—NONVERBAL/VERBAL)

American Indians	Asian Americans–Hispanics	Whites	Blacks
1. Speak softly/slower	1. Speak softly	1. Speak loud/fast to control listener	1. Speak with affect
2. Indirect gaze when listening or speaking	2. Avoidance of eye contact when listening or speaking to high-status persons	2. Greater eye contact when listening	2. Direct eye contact (prolonged) when speaking, but less when listening
3. Interject less/seldom offer encouraging communication	3. Similar rules	3. Head nods, nonverbal markers	3. Interrupt (turn taking) when can
4. Delayed auditory (silence)	4. Mild delay	4. Quick responding	4. Quicker responding
5. Manner of expression low-key, indirect	5. Low-key, indirect	5. Objective, task oriented	5. Affective, emotional, interpersonal

contrasts five different groups along this continuum. How these styles affect the therapist's perception and ability to work with culturally different clients is important for each and every one of us to consider.

COUNSELING AND THERAPY AS COMMUNICATION STYLE

Throughout this text, we have repeatedly emphasized that counseling and therapy may be perceived as a process of interpersonal interaction, communication, and social influence. As a result, it is not difficult to assume that *different* theories of counseling and psychotherapy represent *different* communication styles. There is considerable early research support for this statement. The *Three Approaches to Psychotherapy* (Shostrom, 1966) and the *Three Approaches to Psychotherapy: II* (Shostrom, 1977) film series, featuring Carl Rogers, Fritz Perls, and Albert Ellis in the former and Rogers, Everett Shostrom, and Arnold Lazarus in the latter, has been the subject of much analysis. In most cases, the studies have focused on the first film and tried to identify differences in verbal response categories among the counselors (Hill, Thames, & Rardin, 1979; Lee & Uhlemann, 1984; Weinrach, 1986), examined consistency and stability of the theorist (Dolliver, Williams, & Gold, 1980; Edwards, Boulet, Mahrer, Chagnon, & Mook, 1982; Weinrach, 1986), and compared perceived expertness, trustworthiness, and attractiveness of the sample counselors (Lee, Uhlemann, & Hasse, 1985; Uhlemann, Lee, & Hett, 1984). Some analyses have also been applied to the comparison of Rogers, Shostrom, and Lazarus (Meara, Pepinsky, Shannon, & Murray, 1981; Meara, Shannon, & Pepinsky, 1979; O'dell & Bhamer, 1981).

While internal consistency of the therapists has been questioned in several cases (Dolliver, Williams, & Gold, 1980; Weinrach, 1986), some general conclusions may be tentatively drawn from all of these studies. Each theoretical orientation (Rogers, Person-Centered Therapy; Perls, Existential Therapy; Ellis, Rational-Emotive Therapy; Shostrom, Actualizing Therapy; Lazarus, Multimodal Therapy) can be distinguished from one another, and the therapy styles/skills exhibited seem to be highly correlated with their theoretical orientation. For example, Rogers's style seemed to emphasize attending skills (encouragement to talk—minimal encouragers, nonverbal markers, paraphrasing, and reflecting feelings), Shostrom relied on direct guidance, providing information, and so forth, while Lazarus took an active, reeducative style. One study, for example, found that Rogers used minimal encouragers 53% of the time; restatements 11% of the time; interpretation, reflection, and information each 7% of the time (Hill, Thames, & Rardin, 1979). These results are highly consistent with person-centered counseling.

Rogers (1980) believes that clients have the innate capacity to advance and grow on their own. The reason they encounter problems in life is that significant others impose conditions of worth upon them. The result is that individuals try to live up to others' expectations, standards, and values while denying their innate actualizing tendency. Rogers's writings suggest his strong belief that people have the capacity to self-correct or grow in a positive direction if left on their own. It is almost as if each and every one of us possesses a genetic blueprint. Counselors must avoid imposing conditions of worth upon their clients; avoid telling them what to do or how to solve problems; and avoid imposing their definition of the problem on them. Rather, counselors need to provide a nurturing and nutritious environment for their clients, accept them for what they are, and provide them with a way to view themselves (a mirror) as they are, and as they were meant to be. In this manner, clients will actively begin to change on their own.

The person-centered philosophy would be expected to be evident in the types of skills exhibited by the helping professional. For example, using Ivey's microcounseling language (Ivey, Ivey, & Simek-Downing, 1987), one would clearly see that Rogers would use primarily attending skills (minimal encouragers, paraphrasing, reflection of feelings, summarization, etc.) over influencing skills (giving advice and direction, expressing content/teaching, expressing feelings on the part of the counselor, and interpreting). Attending skills are person centered and provide a way for the client to see himself or herself. It is highly consistent with Rogerian philosophy. Influencing skills are active attempts to direct the client, and are considered counterproductive in counseling, because their use may be imposing conditions of worth—the precise dynamics which have led the client to suffer difficulties. Likewise, we see that if a theory assumes that the basis of problems resides in cognitions (irrational thoughts and processes), as does the rational-emotive approach, then the therapist would take a more active approach to directly attack the basis of the belief system and to teach the client new ways of thinking. Influencing skills would be highly used and, indeed, analysis of Ellis's style confirms this impression.

As indicated in the last chapter, counselors who are perceived by their clients as expert, trustworthy, and attractive are more influential than those who are perceived to possess lower levels of these attributes. One question we have entertained is: To what extent are these categories a function of the different counseling/therapy styles used by counselors? Limited studies have been conducted to address this question. Those that exist provide some support for the statement that differential verbal and nonverbal behavior affects perceptions of expertness, trustworthiness, and attractiveness (Merluzzi, Banikiotes, & Missbach, 1978; Murphy & Strong, 1972; Uhlemann, Lee, & Hett, 1984). For example, it was found that expertness was consistently the lowest for Rogers and the highest for Ellis and Lazarus in the previously mentioned film series.

DIFFERENTIAL SKILLS IN MULTICULTURAL COUNSELING AND THERAPY

Just as race, culture, ethnicity, and gender may affect communication styles, considerable support exists that theoretical orientations in counseling will likewise influence helping styles as well. There is strong support for the belief that different cultural groups may be more receptive to certain counseling/communication styles because of cultural and sociopolitical factors (R.D. Herring, 1997; D.W. Sue, 1990; Wehrly, 1995). And, indeed, the literature on multicultural counseling/therapy strongly suggests that American Indians, Asian Americans, Black Americans, and Hispanic Americans tend to prefer more active-directive forms of helping than nondirective ones (Cheatham et al., 1997; Ivey, Ivey, & Simek-Morgan, 1997; D.W. Sue et al., 1998). We briefly describe two of these group differences here to give the reader some idea of their implications.

Asian American clients who may value restraint of strong feelings and believe that intimate revelations are to be shared only with close friends may cause problems for the counselor who is oriented toward insight or feelings. It is entirely possible that such techniques as reflection of feelings, asking questions of a deeply personal nature, and making depth interpretations may be perceived as lacking in respect for the client's integrity. The process of insight into underlying processes may not be valued by an Asian American client. For example, some clients who come for vocational information may be perceived by counselors as needing help in finding out what motivates their actions and decisions. Requests for advice or information from the client are seen as indicative of deeper, more personal conflicts. Although this might be true in some cases, the blind application of techniques that clash with cultural values seriously places many Asian Americans in an uncomfortable and oppressed position. Atkinson, Maruyama, and Matsui (1978) tested this hypothesis with a number of Asian American students. Two tape recordings of a contrived counseling session were prepared in which the client's responses were identical, but the counselor's responses differed, being directive in one and nondirective in the other. Their findings indicated that counselors who use the directive approach were rated more credible and approachable than those using the nondirective counseling approach. Asian Americans seem to prefer a logical, rational, structured counseling approach over an affective, reflective, and ambiguous one. Similar conclusions have been drawn by other researchers as well (see the excellent reviews by Leong, 1986; Atkinson & Lowe, 1995).

In a groundbreaking study carried out some 20 years ago, Berman (1979) found similar results with a Black population. The weakness of the previous study was that there was failure to compare equal responses with a White population. Berman's study compared the use of counseling skills between Black and White male and female counselors. A videotape of culturally varied client vignettes was viewed by Black and White counselor trainees. They responded to the question, "What would you say to this person?" The responses were scored and coded according to a microcounseling taxonomy that divided counseling skills into attending and influencing ones. The investigator's hypothesis was that Black and White counselors would give significantly different patterns of responses to their clients. Data supported the hypothesis. Black males and females tended to use the more active expressive skills (directions, expression of content, and interpretation) with greater frequency than their White counterparts. White males and females tended to use a higher percentage of attending skills. Berman concluded that the person's race/culture appears to be a major factor in the counselor's choice of skills, that Black and White counselors appear to adhere to distinctive styles of counseling. The more active styles of the Black counselor tend to include practical advice and allow for the introjection of a counselor's values and opinions.

The implications for therapy become glaringly apparent. Mental health training programs tend to emphasize the more passive attending skills. Therapists so trained may be ill equipped to work with culturally different clients who might find the active approach more relevant to their own needs and values.

IMPLICATIONS FOR MULTICULTURAL COUNSELING AND THERAPY

Ivey's work (Ivey, 1981, 1986; Ivey, Ivey, & Simek-Morgan, 1997) in the field of microcounseling, multicultural counseling, and developmental counseling seems central to our understanding of counseling/communication styles. He believes that different theories are concerned with generating different sentences and constructs, and that different cultures may also be expected to generate different sentences and constructs. Counseling and psychotherapy may be viewed as special types of temporary cultures. When the counseling style of the counselor does not match the communication style of the culturally different client, many difficulties may arise: premature termination of the session, inability to establish rapport, and/or cultural oppression of the client. Thus, it becomes clear that effective multicultural counseling occurs when the counselor and client are able to appropriately and accurately send and receive both verbal and nonverbal messages. When the counselor is able to engage in such activities, his or her credibility and attractiveness will be increased (see previous chapter). Communication styles manifested in the clinical context may either enhance or negate the effectiveness of MCT. It appears that several major implications for counseling can be discerned.

Therapeutic Practice

As practicing clinicians who work with a culturally diverse population, we need to move decisively in educating ourselves as to the differential meanings of nonverbal behavior, and the broader implications for communication styles. We need to realize that proxemics, kinesics, paralanguage, and high-low context factors are important elements of communication; that they may be highly culture bound; and that we should guard against possible misinterpretation in our assessment of culturally different clients. Likewise, it is important that we begin to become aware of and understand our own communication/helping style: What is my clinical/communication style? What does it say about my values, biases, and assumptions about human behavior? How do my nonverbals reflect stereotypes, fears, or preconceived notions about various racial groups? What nonverbal messages might I not be aware of but might be communicating to my client? In what way does my helping style hinder my ability to work effectively with a culturally different client? What culturally- or racially-influenced communication styles cause me greatest difficulty or discomfort? Why?

We believe that therapists need to be able to shift their therapeutic styles to meet the developmental needs of clients. We contend further that effective mental health professionals are those who can also shift their helping styles to meet the cultural dimensions of their clients. Therapists of differing theoretical orientations will tend to use different skill patterns. These skill patterns may be antagonistic or inappropriate to the communication/helping styles of culturally different clients. In previously cited research, it was clear that White counselors (by virtue of their cultural conditioning and training) tend to use the more passive attending and listening skills in counseling/therapy, while racial/ethnic minority populations appear more oriented toward an active influencing approach. There are several reasons why this may be the case.

First, it is our contention that the use of more directive, active, and influencing skills is more likely to provide personal information about where the therapist is coming from (self-disclosure). Giving advice or suggestions, interpreting, and telling the client how you, the counselor or therapist, feel are really acts of counselor self-disclosure. While the use of attending or more nondirective skills may also self-disclose, it tends to be minimal relative to using influencing skills. In multicultural counseling, the culturally different client is likely to approach the counselor with trepidation: "What makes you any different from all the Whites out there who have oppressed me?" "What makes you immune from inheriting the racial biases of your forebears?" "Before I open up to you (self-disclose), I want to know where you are coming from." "How open and honest are you about your own racism and will it interfere with our relationship?" "Can you really understand what it's like to be Asian, Black, Hispanic, American Indian, or the like?" In other words, a culturally different client may not open up (self-disclose) until you, the helping professional, self-disclose first. Thus, to many minority clients, a therapist who expresses his/her thoughts and feelings may be better received in a counseling situation.

Second, the more positive response by minorities to the use of influencing skills appears related to diagnostic focus. In Chapter 8, we propose the concept of locus of responsibility. Studies support the thesis that White therapists are more likely to focus their problem diagnosis in individual, rather than societal, terms (Berman, 1979; Nwachuku & Ivey, 1991; D.W. Sue et al., 1998).

In a society where individualism prevails, it is not surprising to find that Euro-American counselors tend to view their client's problems as residing within the individual rather than society. Thus, the role of the therapist will be person focused because the problem resides within the individual. Skills utilized will be individual centered (attending), aimed at changing the person. Many minorities accept the importance of individual contributions to the problem, but they also give great weight to system or societal factors that may adversely impact their lives. Minorities who have been the victims of discrimination and oppression perceive that the problem resides externally to the person (societal forces). Active systems intervention is called for, and the most appropriate way to attack the environment (stressors) would be an active approach (Lewis et al., 1998). If the counselor shares their perception, he or she may take a more active role in the sessions, giving advice and suggestions, as well as teaching strategies (becoming a partner to the client).

Unfortunately, our mental health training programs are very deficient in teaching therapists the appropriate influencing skills needed for effective multicultural therapy. Much of this resides in a philosophical belief that clients should solve problems on their own, that they are ultimately responsible for the outcomes in their lives, and that therapists who dispense advice/suggestions and disclose their thoughts or feelings are adversely influencing their clients or fostering dependency. As one minority client said to us, "I'm not that weak, stupid, or fragile that what advice you give to me will be unquestioningly accepted."

Finally, while it would be ideal if we could effectively engage in the full range of therapeutic responses, such a wish may prove unrealistic. We cannot be all things to everyone. That is, there are personal limits to how much we can change our communication styles to match those of our culturally different clients. The difficulty in shifting styles may be a function of inadequate practice, inability to understand the other person's worldview, and/or personal biases or racist attitudes that have not been adequately resolved. In these cases, the counselor might consider several alternatives: (a) seek additional training/education, (b) seek consultation with a more experienced counselor, (c) consider the possibility of referring the client to another therapist, and (d) become aware of personal communication style limitations and try to anticipate their possible impact upon the culturally different client. Often, a therapist who is able to recognize the limitations of his/her helping style, and knows how it will impact the culturally different client, can take steps to minimize possible conflicts. Interestingly, one study (Yao, Sue, & Hayden, 1991) found that once rapport and a working relationship are established with a minority client, the counselor may have greater freedom in using a helping style quite different from that of the client. The crucial element appears to be the counselor's ability to acknowledge limitations in his/her helping style, and to anticipate the negative impact it may have on the culturally different client. In this way, the helping professional may be saying to the client, "I understand your worldview, and I know that what I do or say will appear very Western to you, but I'm limited in my communication style. I may or may not understand where you're coming from, but let's give it a try." For some minority clients, this form of communication may be enough to begin the process of bridging the communication-style gap.

Implications for Training and Research

With respect to training, graduate programs need to do several things. First and most important is the recognition that no one style of counseling or therapy will be appropriate for all populations and situations. A program that is primarily psychoanalytically oriented, cognitively oriented, existentially oriented, person-centered oriented, or behaviorally oriented may be doing a great disservice to their trainees. The goals and processes espoused by the theories may not be those held by culturally different groups. The theories tend to be not only culture-bound, but also narrow in how they conceptualize the human condition. In an analysis of the previously mentioned film series (*Three Approaches to Psychotherapy,* Shostrom, 1966), Meara, Shannon, and Pepinsky (1979) concluded that Rogers taught his client to be her "feeling self"; Perls taught her to be her "fighting self"; and Ellis taught her to be her "thinking self."

Each school of counseling and therapy has strengths, but they may be one-dimensional: They concentrate only on feelings, or only on cognitions, or only on behaviors. We need to realize that we are *feeling, thinking, behaving, social, cultural, spiritual* and *political* beings. What we are advocating in training programs is an approach that calls for openness and flexibility both in conceptualizing the issues and in actual skill building. In many respects, it represents a metatheoretical and eclectic approach (D.W. Sue, Ivey, & Pedersen, 1996). Rather than being random, haphazard, and inconsistent, the metatheoretical approach is an attempt to use helping strategies, techniques, and styles that consider not only individual characteristics, but cultural and racial factors as well.

Along with the above training, a number of people have advocated that training programs need a strong antiracism component (Carney & Kahn, 1984; Carter, 1995; Corvin & Wiggins, 1989; Lewis et al., 1998). Simply acquiring information/knowledge of a racial minority and expanding the repertoire of response is not enough. According to Corvin and Wiggins (1989), "White racism is not a result of cultural differences, but the consequences of White ethnocentrism." Attempts to teach multicultural therapy will be doomed to failure unless trainees address their own White racism. Unfortunately, programs seem very reluctant to implement antiracism training because it threatens the very foundations of the program. Racism is a very painful topic for many trainees, and they are likely to react negatively to it. More importantly, many faculty members seem equally threatened and may be a part of the problem, rather than the solution.

With respect to research implications, we would only mention a few. A most fruitful area to research would be to investigate therapy and communication styles with respect to such factors as race, culture, ethnicity, and gender. Most of the studies we have reviewed lend support to the notion that various racial groups do exhibit differences in communication style. What is missing is explicit research exploring the interaction of these styles with various theoretical approaches. Do race and culture affect a culturally different client's receptivity to counseling style? In what ways? How does the style affect a client's perception of therapist expertness, attractiveness, and trustworthiness?

If we are to make progress in understanding these questions, evaluation of therapy approaches can begin only if relevant scoring systems are developed and a common framework is established. While multicultural research in this area has increased, there have been problems associated with the definition of skills that fall under the directive and nondirective divisions (Folensbee, Draguns, & Danish, 1986). In some cases, the skills identified in each category were found to be the same, resulting in contradictory findings.

Last, to develop truly relevant and effective culture-specific approaches may mean a completely different perspective: Before the advent of Western counseling/therapy approaches, how did members of a particular culture solve their problems? What were the intrinsic, natural, help-giving networks? Can we identify specific helping skills in the culture and use that as a frame of reference rather than Western concepts of mental health? We attempt to address some of these questions in Chapter 9. Such a research approach would allow us to eventually develop theories that are different from those we have learned.

Encouragingly, some researchers (C.C. Lee, 1996; Nwachuku & Ivey, 1991) have attempted to answer some of these questions by studying indigenous helping within cultures. For example, Nwachuku & Ivey (1991) studied the African-Igbo culture in order to (a) identify culture-specific means of helping and (b) test whether such helping approaches could be taught to counselor trainees. They systematically identified key behaviors, attitudes, and values of the culture, translated them into identifiable helping skills, and attempted to teach these strategies to counselor trainees. Their preliminary findings suggest that it is possible to identify culture-specific strategies in a given culture, and that these are teachable. Statements that we do not have the research base or technology can no longer be used as excuses for the mental health profession not to move in a direction that addresses cultural diversity in practice, training, and research.

Chapter Five

◆

Multicultural Family Counseling and Therapy

◆

Esteban and Carmen O., a Puerto Rican couple, sought help at a community mental health clinic in the Miami area. Mr. O. had recently come to the United States with only a high school education, but had already acquired several successful printing shops. Carmen, his wife, was a third-generation Latina raised in Florida. The two had had a whirlwind courtship that resulted in marriage after only a three-month acquaintance. She described her husband as handsome, outspoken, confident, and a strong person who could be affectionate and sensitive. Carmen used the term "machismo" several times in describing Esteban.

The couple had sought marital counseling after a series of rather heated arguments over his long work hours and his tendency to go drinking with the boys after work. She missed his companionship, which had been constantly present during their courtship, but now seemed strangely absent. Carmen, who had graduated from the University of Florida with a BA in business, had been working as an administrative assistant when she met Esteban. While she enjoyed her work, Carmen reluctantly resigned the position prior to her marriage, at the urging of Esteban, who stated that "it was beneath her" and that he was capable of supporting them both. Carmen had convinced Esteban to seek outside help with their marital difficulties, and they had been assigned to Dr. Carla B., a White female psychologist. The initial session with the couple was characterized by Esteban doing most of the talking. Indeed, Dr. B. was quite annoyed by Esteban's arrogant attitude. He frequently spoke for his wife and interrupted Dr. B. often, not allowing her to finish questions or make comments. Esteban stated that he understood his wife's desire to spend more time with him, but that he needed to seek financial security for "my children." While the couple did not have any children at the present time, Esteban clearly implied that he expected to have many with his wife. He jokingly stated, "After three or four sons, she won't have time to miss me."

His remark had a strong impact on Carmen, and she appeared quite surprised. Dr. B., who during this session had been trying to give Carmen an opportunity to

97

express her thoughts and feelings, seized the opportunity. She asked Carmen how she felt about having children. As Carmen began to answer, Esteban blurted out quickly, "Of course, she wants children. All women want children."

At this point Dr. B. (obviously angry) confronted Esteban about his tendency to answer or speak for his wife and the inconsiderate manner in which he kept interrupting everyone. "Being a "macho man" is not what is needed here," stated Dr. B. Esteban became noticeably angry and stated, "No woman lectures Esteban. Why aren't you at home caring for your husband? What you need is a *real* man." Dr. B. did not fall for Esteban's baiting tactic and refused to argue with him. She was, nevertheless, quite angry at Esteban and disappointed in Carmen's passivity. The session was terminated shortly thereafter.

During the next few weeks, Carmen came alone to the sessions without her husband, who refused to return. The sessions consisted of dealing with Esteban's sexist attitude and the ways she could be her "own person." Dr. B. stressed that Carmen had an equal right in the decisions made at home, that she should not allow anyone to oppress her, that she did not need her husband's approval to return to her former job, and that having children was an equal and joint responsibility.

During Carmen's six months of therapy, the couple separated. It was a difficult period for Carmen, who came for therapy regularly to talk about her need "to be my own person," a phrase used often by Dr. B.

Carmen and Esteban finally divorced after only a year of marriage.

Like individual therapy, family systems therapy may be culture-bound, and when inappropriately applied, it can have disastrous consequences. Dr. B. failed to understand the gender role relationship between traditional Puerto Rican men and women, unwittingly applied a culture-bound definition of a healthy male-female relationship to Esteban and Carmen, and allowed her own feminist values to influence her therapeutic decisions. While we cannot blame her for the divorce of this couple, one wonders whether this would have been the result if the therapist had clarified the cultural issues/conflicts occurring between the couple, and realized how the values of couple counseling and those manifested in Puerto Rican culture might be at odds with one another.

For example, the egalitarian attitude held by the therapist may be in conflict with Puerto Rican values concerning male-female relationships and the division of responsibilities in the household. Traditional Puerto Rican families are patriarchical, a structure that gives men authority over women, and the ability to make decisions without consulting them (Garcia-Preto, 1996; Ramos-McKay, Comas-Diaz, & Rivera, 1984). Encouraging Carmen to "be her own person" and asserting that she has a right to make independent decisions and to share the decision-making process with Esteban might violate traditional gender role relationships. These men-women relationships are reinforced by the constructs of *machismo* and *marianismo*. *Machismo* is a term used in many Latino cultures to indicate maleness, virility, and that the role of the man is provider and protector of the family. The term connotes male sexual prowess; it indicates men's greater sexual freedom and their responsibility for protecting the honor of women in the family. In the United States, *machismo* has acquired negative connotations; it has been pathologized, and often equated with sexist behavior (De La Cancela, 1991).

The construct *marianismo* is the female counterpart, which is derived from the cult of the Virgin Mary: While men may be sexually superior, women are seen as morally and spiritually superior and capable of enduring greater suffering (Garcia-Preto, 1996). Women are expected to keep themselves sexually pure, and to be self-sacrificing in favor of their children and especially the husband; the woman is the caretaker of the family, and the homemaker. These gender role relationships have existed for centuries within Puerto Rican culture, although intergenerational differences have made these traditional roles an increasing source of conflict.

Dr. B. is obviously unaware that her attempts to interrupt Esteban's dialogue and to encourage Carmen to freely speak her mind, and her implicit derogation of the term *machismo,* may be a violation of Puerto Rican cultural values; it may also be perceived as an insult to Esteban's maleness. The therapist is also unaware that her gender (being a woman) might also be a source of conflict for Esteban. Not only may he perceive Dr. B. as playing an inappropriate role (she should be at home taking care of her husband and children), but it must be a great blow to his male pride to have a female therapist in charge of the sessions.

We are not making a judgment about whether the patriarchical nature of a cultural group is good or bad. We are also not taking the position that egalitarian relationships are better than other culturally sanctioned role relationships. What is important, however, is the realization that personal values (equality in relationships), definitions of desirable male-female role relationships, and the goals of marital or family therapy (independence—"becoming one's own person") may be culture-bound and thus may negatively impact multicultural family counseling/therapy. Effective multicultural family therapy is very difficult not only because of these cultural clashes, but because of the way they interact with class issues. Let us use another family counseling case to illustrate the complexity of this interaction.

Several years ago, a female school counselor sought the senior author's advice about a Mexican American family she had recently seen. She was quite concerned about the identified client, Elena Martinez, a 13-year-old student who was referred for counseling because of alleged peddling of drugs on the school premises. The counselor had formed an impression that the parents did not care for their daughter, were uncooperative, and were attempting to avoid responsibility for dealing with Elena's delinquency. When pressed for how she arrived at these impressions, the counselor provided the following information.

♦ *Case Study*

Elena Martinez was the second-oldest child, with four siblings, ages 15, 12, 10, and 7. The father was an immigrant from Mexico and the mother a natural citizen. The family resided in a blue-collar Latino neighborhood in San Jose, California.

Elena had been reported as having minor problems in school prior to the drug-selling incident. For example, she had "talked back to teachers," refused to do homework assignments, and had "fought" with other students. Her involvement with a group of other Latino students (suspected of being responsible for disruptive school-yard pranks) had gotten her into trouble. Elena was well known to the counseling staff at the school. Because of the seriousness of the drug accusations, the counselor felt that something had to be done, and that the parents needed to be informed immediately.

The counselor reported calling the parents in order to set up an interview with them. When Mrs. Martinez answered the telephone, the counselor had explained how Elena had been caught on school grounds selling marijuana by a police officer. Rather than arrest her, the officer had turned the student over to the vice principal, who luckily was present at the time of the incident. After this explanation, the counselor had asked that the parents make arrangements for an appointment as soon as possible. The meeting would be aimed at informing the parents about Elena's difficulties in school and coming to some decision about what could be done.

During the phone conversation, Mrs. Martinez seemed hesitant about choosing a time to come in and, when pressed by the counselor, excused herself from the telephone. The counselor reported overhearing some whispering on the other end, and then the voice of Mr. Martinez. He immediately asked the counselor how his daughter was and expressed his consternation over the entire situation. At that point, the counselor stated that she understood his feelings, but it would be best to set up an appointment for the following day and to talk about it then. Several times the counselor asked Mr. Martinez about a convenient time for the meeting, but each time he seemed to avoid the answer and to give excuses. He had to work the rest of the day and could not make the appointment. The counselor stressed strongly how important the meeting was for the daughter's welfare, and that the several hours of missed work was not important in light of the situation. The father stated that he would be able to make an evening session, but the counselor informed him that school policy prohibited evening meetings. When the counselor suggested that the mother could initially come alone, further hesitations seemed present. Finally, the father agreed to attend.

The very next day, Mr. and Mrs. Martinez and a brother-in-law (Elena's godfather) showed up together in her office. The counselor reported being upset at the presence of the brother-in-law when it became obvious he planned to sit in on the session. At that point, she explained that a third party present would only make the session more complex and the outcome counterproductive. She wanted to see only the family.

The counselor reported that the session went poorly with minimal cooperation from the parents. She reported, "It was like pulling teeth," trying to get the Martinezes to say anything at all.

The case study of Elena Martinez exemplifies other major misunderstandings that often occur in working with minority families. Like Dr. B. in the earlier vignette, the counselor shows a lack of understanding concerning Hispanic cultural values and how they traditionally affect communication patterns. This lack of knowledge and the degree of insensitivity to the Latino family's experience in the United States can lead to negative impressions such as: "They are uncooperative, avoid responsibility, and do not care for their children." As in the case of Esteban and Carmen, failure to understand cultural differences and the experience of minority status in the United States compounds the problems.

A number of important points need to be made about this case. First, it is entirely possible that the incidents reported by the counselor mean something different from the perspective of traditional Mexican American culture. Like many Euro-Americans, the counselor possesses a value system that emphasizes egalitarianism in the husband-wife relationship. The helping professional must guard against making negative judgments of Mexican American roles that are patriarchal. In reality, division of roles (husband is protector/provider while wife cares for the home/family) allows both to exercise influence and make decisions. Breaking the role divisions (especially by the woman) is done only out of necessity. A wife would be remiss in publicly making a family decision (setting up an appointment time) without consulting or obtaining agreement from the husband. Mrs. Martinez's hesitation on the phone to commit to a meeting time with the counselor may be a reflection of the husband-wife role relationship rather than a lack of concern for the daughter. The counselor's persistence in forcing Mrs. Martinez to decide may actually be asking her to violate cultural dictates about appropriate role behaviors.

Second, the counselor may have seriously undermined the Hispanic concept of the extended family by expressing negativism toward the godfather's attendance at the counseling session. Middle-class White Americans consider the family unit to be nuclear (husband/wife and children related by blood), while most minorities define the family unit as an extended one. A Hispanic child can acquire a godmother (*madrina*) and a godfather (*padrino*) through a baptismal ceremony. Unlike many White Americans, godparents in the Hispanic culture have a more than symbolic role, as they can become co-parents (*compadre*) taking an active part in the raising of the child. Indeed, the role of the godparents is usually linked to the moral, religious, and spiritual upbringing of the child. Who would be more appropriate to attend the counseling session than the godfather? Not only is he a member of the family, but the charges against Elena deal with legal, moral/ethical implications as well.

Third, the counselor obviously did not consider the economic impact that missing a couple of hours' work might have on the family. Again, she tended to consider Mr. Martinez's reluctance to take off work for the "welfare of his daughter" as evidence of the parents' disinterest in their child. Trivializing the missing of work reveals major class/work differences that often exist between mental health professionals and their minority clients. Most professionals (mental health practitioners, educators, white-collar workers) are often able to take time off for a dental appointment, teacher conference, or personal needs without loss of income. Most of us can usually arrange for others to cover for us, or to make up the lost hours on some other day. If we are docked for time off, only a few hours are lost and not an entire afternoon or day's work. This, indeed, is a middle- or upper-class luxury not shared by those who face economic hardships or who work in settings that do not allow for schedule flexibility.

For the Martinez family, loss of even a few hours' wages has serious financial impact. Most blue-collar workers may not have the luxury or option to make up their work. How, for example, would an assembly-line worker make up the lost time when the plant closes at the end of the day? In addition, the worker often does not miss just a few hours, but must take a half or full day off. In many work situations, getting a worker to substitute for just a few hours is not practical. To entice replacement workers, the company must offer more than a few hours (in many cases a full day). Thus, Mr. Martinez may actually be losing an entire day's wages! His reluctance to miss work may actually represent *high concern* for the family rather than *lack of care.*

Fourth, the case of Elena and the Martinez family raises another important question. What obligation do educational and mental health services have toward offering flexible and culturally appropriate services to minority constituents? Mr. Martinez's desire for an evening or weekend meeting brings this issue into clear perspective. Does the minority individual or family always have to conform to system rules and regulations? We are not arguing with the school policy itself—in some schools there are legitimate reasons for not staying after school ends (high crime rate, etc.). What we are arguing for is the need to provide alternative service deliveries to minority families. For example, why not home visits or sessions off the school premises? Social workers have historically used this method with very positive results. It has aided the building of rapport (the family perceives your genuine interest), increased comfort in the family for sharing with a counselor, and allowed a more realistic appraisal of family dynamics. Counselors frequently forget how intimidating it may be for a minority family to come in for counseling. The Martinezes' lack of verbal participation may be a function not only of the conflict over the absence of the godfather, but of the relatively impersonal and formal nature of counseling in the context of the personal orientation of the Hispanic family (*personalismo*).

FAMILY SYSTEMS COUNSELING AND THERAPY

Family systems counseling/therapy encompasses many aspects of the family, which may include marital counseling/therapy, parent-child counseling, or work with more than one member of the family (Nicols & Schwartz, 1995). Its main goal is to modify relationships within a family so as to achieve harmony (Becvar & Becvar, 1996; Foley, 1984). Family systems therapy is based on several assumptions: (a) It is logical and economical to treat together all those who exist and operate within a system of relationships (in most cases, it implies the nuclear family); (b) the problems of the identified patient are only symptoms, and the family itself is the client; (c) all symptoms or problematic behaviors exhibited by a member of the family serve a purpose; (d) the behaviors of family members are tied to one another in powerful reciprocal ways (circular causality emphasized over linear causality); and (e) the task of the therapist is to modify relationships and/or improve communications within the family system (Corey, 1996; Goldenberg & Goldenberg, 1996; McGoldrick, Pearce, & Giordano, 1996).

There are many family systems approaches, but two characteristics seem to be especially important. One of these, the *communications approach,* is based on the assumption that family problems reflect communication difficulties. Many family communication problems are both subtle and complex. Family therapists concentrate on improving not only faulty communications but also interactions and relationships among family members (Satir, 1967, 1983). The way in which rules, agreements, and perceptions are communicated among members may also be important (Haley, 1967). The therapist's role in repairing faulty communications is active, but not dominating. He or she attempts to show family members how they are now communicating with one another; to prod them into revealing what they feel and think about themselves and other family members, and what they want from the family relationship; and to convince them to practice new ways of responding.

The *structural approach* also considers communication to be important, but it especially emphasizes the interlocking roles of family members (Minuchin, 1974). Most families are constantly in a state of change; they are in the process of structuring and restructuring themselves into systems and subsystems. The health of a family is often linked to the members' abilities to recognize boundaries of the various systems—alliances, communication patterns, and so forth. Oftentimes unhealthy family functioning and the symptoms exhibited by members are caused by boundary disputes.

From a philosophical and theoretical perspective, both approaches appear appropriate in working with various minority groups. For example, they appear to:

- highlight the importance of the family (versus the individual) as the unit of identity,
- focus on resolution of concrete issues,
- be concerned with family structure and dynamics,
- assume that these family structures and dynamics are historically passed on from one generation to another,
- attempt to understand the communication and/or alliances via reframing, and
- place the therapist in an expert position.

Many of these qualities, as we have seen, would be consistent with the worldview of racial/ethnic minorities. Such emphasis on the family as the unit of identity and study, understanding of the cultural norms and background of the family system, and the need to balance the system fit well with the worldview of many culturally different families.

Problems arise, however, in translating these goals and strategies into concepts of "the family" or what constitutes the healthy family. Some of the characteristics associated with the White middle-class notion of healthy families may pose problems in therapy with various culturally different groups. These concepts tend to be heavily loaded with value orientations incongruent with the value systems of many culturally different clients (Corey, 1996). They tend to:

- allow and encourage expressing emotions freely and openly,
- view each member as having a right to be his/her own unique self (individuate from the emotional field of the family),
- strive for an equal division of labor among members of the family,
- consider egalitarian role relationships between spouses desirable, and
- hold the "nuclear family" as the standard.

As in the case of Esteban and Carmen and the case of Elena Martinez, these translations in family systems therapy can cause great problems in working with minority clients. It is clear that the culturally effective family systems counselor/therapist must escape from his/her cultural encapsulation, understand the sociopolitical forces that affect minority families, become aware of major differences in the value system he/she possesses when contrasted with racial/cultural family values, and understand structural family relationships that are different from his/her own concepts of family.

ISSUES IN WORKING WITH ETHNIC MINORITY FAMILIES

Effective multicultural family counseling and therapy needs to incorporate the many racial, cultural, economic, and class issues inherent in the two clinical family examples given earlier. While not unique to racial/ethnic minority families, there are distinguishing quantitative and qualitative life events that differentiate the "minority experience" from that of middle-class White families. Several factors have been identified as important for culturally sensitive family therapists to take into consideration (Ho, 1987, 1997; McGoldrick & Giordano, 1996).

1. *Ethnic minority reality* refers to the racism and poverty that dominate the lives of minorities. Lower family income, greater unemployment, increasing numbers falling below the poverty line, etc., have had major negative effects not only on the individuals, but on family structures as well. The relocation of 110,000 Japanese Americans into concentration camps during World War II, for example, drastically altered the traditional Japanese family structures and relationships (D.W. Sue & Kirk, 1973). By physically uprooting these U.S. citizens, symbols of ethnic identity were destroyed, creating identity conflicts and problems. Furthermore, the camp experience disrupted the traditional lines of authority. The elderly male no longer had a functional value as head of household, family discipline and control became loosened, and women gained a degree of independence unheard of in traditional Japanese families.

Likewise, African American families have also been victims of poverty and racism that have done much harm to them. Nowhere is this more evident than in statistics revealing a higher incidence of Black children living in homes without the biological father present—82%, compared with 43% for Whites (Wilkinson, 1993). More Black families are classified as impoverished (46%) compared to Whites (10%), and many more Black males are single, widowed, or divorced (47%) than are Whites (28%). The high mortality rate among Black males has led some to call them an endangered species, and as a result, societal forces have even strained and affected the Black male-female relationship (Gibbs, 1987; White & Parham, 1990). Under slavery, class distinctions were obliterated; the slave husband was disempowered as the head of the household, and the inability of the man to protect and provide for kin had a negative effect on African American family relationships (Wilkinson, 1993).

2. *Conflicting value systems* imposed by White Euro-American society upon minority groups have also caused great harm to them. The case of Elena Martinez reveals how the White counselor's conception of the nuclear family may clash with traditional Latino/Hispanic emphasis on extended families. It appears that almost all minority groups place greater value on families, historical lineage (reverence of ancestors), interdependence among family members, and submergence of self for the good of the family (Kim, 1985; Uba, 1994). African Americans are often described as having a kinship system in which individuals with variety of blood and emotional ties (aunts, uncles, preachers, brothers, sisters, boyfriends, etc.) may act as the extended family (Black, 1996; Hines & Boyd-Franklin, 1996). Likewise, the extended family in the Hispanic culture as evidenced in the case of Elena Martinez includes numerous relatives and friends (Falicov, 1996; Garcia-Preto, 1996). Perhaps most difficult to grasp for many mental health professionals is the American Indian family network, which is structurally open and assumes villagelike characteristics (Red Horse, 1983; Sutton & Broken Nose, 1996). This "family" extension may include from several to many households. Unless therapists are aware of these value differences, they may mislabel behaviors as pathological and/or make decisions detrimental to the family. We will have more to say about this important point shortly.

3. *Biculturalism* refers to the fact that minorities in the United States inherit two different cultural traditions. In the next chapter, we discuss issues of culture conflict, cultural racism, and the melting-pot concept as it affects identity development. The therapist needs to understand how biculturalism influences family structures, communications, and dynamics. The reluctance of a 22-year-old Latino male to go against the wishes of his parents by marrying a woman he loves may not be a sign of immaturity. Rather, it may reflect a conflict resulting from membership in two groups or the positive choice of one cultural dictate over another. A culturally effective therapist is one who understands the possible conflicts that may arise as a result of biculturalism.

Related to biculturalism is the therapist's need to understand the process of acculturation and the stresses encountered by culturally different families. While the term was originally used to indicate the mutual influence of two different cultures on one another, it is best understood in the United States as the interaction between a dominant and nondominant culture. Some questions that family systems therapists need to address when working with culturally different families are: What are the psychological consequences for nondominant families as they encounter the dominant culture? What effects does it have on minority family dynamics and structure? What types of issues or problems are likely to arise as a result of the acculturation process? For example, the parents in a recently migrated family often are aligned with the culture of the country of origin, while their offspring are likely to adapt to the dominant culture more rapidly. In many cases, children may be more oriented to the culture of the larger society, resulting in intergenerational conflicts (Gushue & Sciarra, 1995). However, it is important for the counselor/therapist to understand the sociopolitical dimensions of this process. The problem may not be so much a function of intergenerational conflict, as it is the dominant-subordinate clash of cultures (Gushue & Sciarra, 1995; Szapocznik & Kurtines, 1993). The multiculturally skilled family therapist would focus on the problems created by cultural oppression and reframe the goal as one of stressing the benefits of intergenerational collaboration and alliance against the potentially divisive influence of the dominant culture (Gushue & Sciarra, 1995).

4. *Ethnic differences in minority status* refers to the life experiences and adjustments that occur as a result of a group's minority status in the United States. Different racial/ethnic minority groups have been subjected to a variety of dehumanizing forces:

- The history of slavery for Black Americans has not only negatively impacted their self-esteem, but has contributed to disruption of the Black male-female relationship and the structure of the Black family. Slavery imposed a pathological system of social organization on the African American family, resulting in disorganization and a constant fight for survival and stability. Despite the system of slavery, however, many African Americans overcame these negative forces by sheer force of will, by reasserting their affectional ties, by using extended kinship ties, by their strength of spirit and spirituality, and by their multigenerational networks (Wilkinson, 1993). It would help much if the family systems therapist recognized these strengths in the African American family, rather than stressing its instability and problems.

- Racism and colonialism have made American Indians immigrants in their own land, and the federal government has even imposed a definition of race upon them (they must be able to prove they are at least 1/4 Indian blood). Such a legal definition of race has created problems among Native Americans by confusing issues of identity. Like African Americans, Native Americans have experienced conquest, dislocation, cultural genocide, segregation, and coerced assimilation (Sutton & Broken Nose, 1996). American Indian family life has been strongly affected by government policies that used missionaries, boarding schools, and the Bureau of Indian Affairs in an attempt to "civilize the heathens." The results have been devastating to Native Americans: learned helplessness, gambling, alcohol and drug abuse, suicide, and family relationship problems (Tafoya & Del Vecchio, 1996). A family systems therapist must be aware of the multigenerational disruption the Native American family has experienced through 500 years of historical trauma.

- Immigration status among Latino/Hispanics and Asian refugees/immigrants (legal resident to illegal alien) and the abuses, resentments, and discrimination that they experience are constant sources of stress in their lives. Anti-immigrant feelings have never been more pervasive and intense. As mentioned previously, this negativism was symbolized in California by the passage of Proposition 187 in 1994. Mean-spirited and obviously unfair, the initiative sought to expel from school children who were in the United States illegally, leaving them to fend for themselves; denied nonemergency health care and other social services; and increased fears of deportation and other reprisals. In addition to the hostile climate experienced by recent immigrants, the migration experience can be a source of

stress and/or disappointment. The multicultural family systems therapist must differentiate among reasons for migration, because their impact on the family may be quite different. A family deciding to migrate in order to seek adventure or wealth (voluntary decision)
will experience the change differently from refugees/immigrants who must leave because
of war or religious or political persecution. Attitudes toward assimilation and acculturation might be quite different between two such families.
· Skin color and obvious physical differences are also important factors that determine the
treatment of minority individuals and their families. These physical differences continue
to warp the perception of White America in that persons of color are seen as aliens in their
own land. Recently, MSNBC posted a Web page covering the participation of Tara Lipinski and Michelle Kwan, two American athletes, in the 1998 Nagano Olympics ice-
skating event. The headline of the article, "American Beats Out Kwan," implied that Tara
Lipinski (White) is an American and Michelle Kwan (Asian American) is not. In the end,
MSNBC was forced to issue an apology.

The equation of physical differences and particularly skin color with being alien, negative, pathological, or less than human has a long history. Travel logs of early European sea-
farers describe their encounters with Blacks and the images and judgments associated with
Africans:

*And entering in [a river], we see A number of blacke soules, Whose likelinesse seem'd men to be,
But all as blacke as coles. (Quoted in Jordan, 1969, pp. 4–5)*

Jones (1997) points out that the Oxford English Dictionary definition of the color - black,
prior to the sixteenth century was the following:

*Deeply stained with dirt; soiled, dirty, foul. . . . Having dark or deadly purposes, malignant;
pertaining to or involving death, deadly; baneful, disastrous, sinister. . . . Foul, iniquitous,
atrocious, horrible, wicked. . . . Indicating disgrace, censure, liability to punishment, etc.
(p. 475)*

It is clear, then, that the concept of "blackness" was associated with badness, ugliness, evil-
ness, and the nonhuman. Jones (1997) also observes the relationship between color name
and a classic clinical report of multiple personality disorder. In a classic study of multiple
personalities (Thigpen & Cleckley, 1954), two of the personalities, Eve White and Eve
Black, reflect the positive associations with whiteness and the negative ones with blackness.

*Eve Black is lacking in culture but curiously likable. She is playful, childlike, entertaining. Her
superego is nonfunctional, which makes her a delight, the one who has all the fun. Black is where
the "fun" things go to be. Yet, just as there is a kind of nostalgia and envy directed at Eve Black,
there is judgement and castigation, as well. A certain voyeurism makes Eve Black someone one
would like to be around, but wouldn't want in one's family. Eve White, by contrast, has "all the
right stuff." She is socialized to traditional values, properly "feminine," devoted, even heroic.
Her saintliness is admired, but somehow she is repressed, and one's admiration for her is tinged
with sadness. The personality traits associated differentially with Eve White and Eve Black are
not pulled from thin air; instead, they suggest the content of cultural beliefs about the races as
well as the genders. These cultural beliefs did not, in 1954, depart substantially from the first
conclusions about racial differences by Englishmen in 1550! (Jones 1997, p. 476)*

While skin color is probably the most powerful physical characteristic linked to racism,
other physical features and differences may also determine negative treatment by the wider

society. External societal definitions of race have often resulted in ideological racism that links physical characteristics of groups (usually skin color) to major psychological traits (Feagin, 1989). For example, the expressed beliefs of golfer Jack Nicklaus in 1996 that Blacks are born with the wrong muscles to play golf at the higher levels (apparently he has never seen Tiger Woods play), and those of Al Campanis (former Dodgers executive) and former sportscaster Jimmy "The Greek" Snyder that Blacks are "great athletes" but "poor scholars" represent cultural beliefs that have shaped U.S. treatment of African Americans. Likewise, other physical traits, such as head form, facial features, and color and texture of body hair, contrast with the Euro-American ideal image of "blond haired, fair skinned, slender." Not only is there an external negative evaluation of those who differ from such desired features, but many persons of color may form negative self and body images of themselves and attempt to become westernized in their physical features. One wonders, for example, about the psychological dynamics that have motivated some Asian American women to seek cosmetic surgery to reshape their eyes to appear more western.

5. *Ethnicity and language* refers to the common sense of bonding among members of a group that contributes to a sense of belonging. The symbols of the group (ethnicity) are most manifested in language. Language structures meaning, determines how we see things, is the carrier of our culture, and affects our worldview. Many minority clients do not possess vocabulary equivalents to standard English and when forced to communicate in English may appear "flat," "nonverbal," "uncommunicative," and "lacking in insight" (Romero, 1985). The problem is linguistic, not psychological. In psychotherapy, where words are the major vehicle for effective change, language has been likened to what a baton is to the conductor and what a scalpel is to the surgeon.

Studies in the field of linguistics and sociolinguistics confirm that language conveys a wealth of information other than the primary content of the message: Background, place of origin, group membership, status in the group, and relationship to the speaker can all be determined from cues in language. Thus, use of language reflects the gender, race, and social class of the speaker. More importantly, however, these studies also suggest that the listener utilizes this sociolinguistic information to formulate opinions of the speaker as well as to interpret the message. Because our society values standard English, the use of nonstandard English, dialects, or accented speech is often associated with undesirable characteristics: being less intelligent, uncouth, lower class, unsophisticated, or not insightful. Thus, while racial/ethnic minority groups may use their linguistic characteristics to bond with one another and to permit more accurate communication, the larger society may invalidate, penalize, or directly punish individuals or groups who exhibit bilingualism or the group-idiosyncratic use of language. In Arizona, for example, a law requiring that official state and local business be conducted in English only was passed in 1996 by voters. The law was subsequently ruled unconstitutional by the Arizona Supreme Court in 1998. Unfortunately, Proposition 227, the anti-bilingual education bill, which effectively destroys bilingual education, will come before the California voters shortly. If approved, it would require the state's 1.4 million limited English proficiency students in public schools, who are now in special classes, to be taught in nearly all English. It would also shorten to one year the time that students could remain in special classes. Proponents of such bills play upon the fears of the public that the United States will be overrun by "aliens" and thereby contribute to the climate of antagonism toward racial/ethnic minorities.

6. *Ethnicity and social class* refers to aspects of wealth, name, occupation, and status. Class differences between mental health professionals and their minority clients can often lead to barriers in understanding and communication. This was clearly evident in the case of Elena Martinez, where the counselor had difficulty relating to a missed day of work. Because minorities are disproportionately represented in the lower socioeconomic classes, class differences become even more important for therapists to understand when working with minority families. There are many who argue that class may be a more powerful determinant of values and behavior than race or ethnicity. For example, we know that the wealthiest one million people of the United States earn more than the next 100 million; the top 1% own 40% of the nation's wealth; and the gap between rich and poor is increasing (Thurow, 1995). From a political perspective, some believe that racial conflicts are promulgated by those at the very top, to detract from the real cause of inequities: a social structure that allows the dominant class to maintain power (Bell, 1993). While there is considerable truth to this view, not all differences can be ascribed to class alone. Further, while one cannot change their race or ethnicity, changes in social class can occur. It is our contention that all three traits are important and that the therapist must understand their interaction with one another.

MULTICULTURAL FAMILY COUNSELING AND THERAPY: A CONCEPTUAL MODEL

Effective multicultural family counseling/therapy operates under principles similar to those outlined in earlier chapters. First, counselors need to become culturally aware of their own values, biases, and assumptions about human behavior (especially as it pertains to the definition of family). Second, it is important to become aware of the worldview of the culturally different client and how that client views the definition, role, and function of the family. Last, appropriate intervention strategies need to be devised to maximize success and minimize cultural oppression. While in earlier chapters the focus was on individual clients and their ethnic/racial groups, our concern in this chapter is with the family unit as defined from the group's perspective. In attempting to understand the first two goals, we are using a model first outlined by Kluckhohn and Strodtbeck (1961). This model allows us to understand the worldviews of culturally different families by contrasting the value orientations of the four main groups we are studying (as illustrated in Table 5.1): Asian Americans, Native Americans, African Americans, and Latino/Hispanic Americans.

PEOPLE-NATURE RELATIONSHIP

Traditional Western thinking believes in mastery of and control over nature. As a result, most therapists operate from a framework in which problems are solvable and both therapist and client must take an active part in solving problems via manipulation and control. Active intervention is stressed in controlling and/or changing the environment. As seen in Table 5.1, the four other ethnic groups view "people" as harmonious with nature.

Asian Confucian philosophy, for example, stresses a set of rules aimed at promoting loyalty, respect, and harmony among family members (S. Sue & Morishima, 1982; Uba, 1994). Harmony within the family and the environment leads to harmony within the self. In their analy-

Table 5.1 CULTURAL VALUE PREFERENCES OF MIDDLE-CLASS WHITE EURO-AMERICANS AND RACIAL/ETHNIC MINORITIES: A COMPARATIVE STUDY

Area of Relationships	Middle-Class White Americans	Asian Americans	American Indians	Black Americans	Hispanic Americans
People to Nature/ Environment	Mastery over Future	Harmony with Past-present	Harmony with Present	Harmony with Present	Harmony with Present
Time Orientation	Future	Past-present	Present	Present	Past-present
People Relationships	Individual	Collateral	Collateral	Collateral	Collateral
Preferred Mode of Activity	Doing	Doing	Being-in-Becoming	Doing	Being-in-Becoming
Nature of Man	Good & Bad	Good	Good	Good & Bad	Good

Note. From *Family Therapy with Ethnic Minorities* (P. 232), by M.K. Ho, 1987, Newbury Park, CA: Sage. Copyright 1987 by Sage Publications. Reprinted with permission.

sis of the Japanese family, Kitano and Kimura (1976) go to great lengths to point out how dependence upon the family unit and acceptance of the environment dictate differences in solving problems. Western culture advocates defining and attacking the problem directly. Asian cultures tend to accommodate and/or deal with problems through indirection. In child rearing, it is believed better to avoid direct confrontation and to use deflection. A White family may deal with a child who has watched too many hours of TV by saying, "Why don't you turn the TV off and study?" Or, more threateningly, the parent might say, "You'll be grounded unless the TV goes off!" An Asian parent might say, "That looks like a boring program; I think your friend John must be doing his homework now." Or: "I think Father wants to watch his favorite program." Such an approach stems from the need to avoid conflict and to achieve balance and harmony among members of the family and the wider environment.

In an excellent analysis of family therapy for Asian Americans, Kim (1985) points out how current therapeutic techniques of confrontation and of having clients express thoughts and feelings directly may be inappropriate and difficult to handle. For example, one of the basic tenets of family therapy is that the identified patient (IP) typically behaves in such a way as to reflect family influences and/or pathology. Often, an acting-out child is symbolic of deeper family problems. Yet, most Asian American families come to counseling or therapy *for the benefit of the IP* and *not the family!* Attempts to directly focus on the family dynamics as contributing to the IP will be met with negativism and possible termination. Kim (1985) states:

A recommended approach to engage the family would be to pace the family's cultural expectations and limitations by (1) asserting that the IP's problem (therefore not the IP by implication) is indeed the problem; (2) recognizing and reinforcing the family's concerns to help the IP to change the behavior; and (3) emphasizing that each family member's contribution in resolving the problem is vitally needed, and that without it, the problem will either remain or get worse, bringing on further difficulty in the family. (p. 346)

Thus, it is apparent that Euro-American values that call for us to dominate nature (e.g., conquer space, tame the wilderness, or harness nuclear energy) through control and manipulation of the universe are reflected in family counseling. Family systems counseling theories attempt to describe, explain, predict, and control family dynamics. The counselor/therapist actively attempts to understand what is going on in the family system (structural alliances and communication patterns), identify the problems (dysfunctional aspects of the dynamics), and attack them directly or indirectly through manipulation and control (therapeutic interventions). Ethnic minorities or subgroups that view people as harmonious with nature or believe that nature may overwhelm people ("acts of God") may find the therapist's mastery-over-nature approach inconsistent or antagonistic to their worldview. Indeed, attempts to actively intervene in changing family patterns and relationships may be perceived as the problem because such efforts have the potential to unbalance the *harmony* that existed.

TIME DIMENSION

How different societies, cultures, and people view time exerts a pervasive influence on their lives. U.S. society may be characterized as preoccupied with the future (Katz, 1985; Kluckhohn & Strodtbeck, 1961; Spiegel & Papajohn, 1983). Furthermore, our society seems very compulsive about time in that we divide it into seconds, minutes, hours, days, weeks, months, and years. Time may be viewed as a commodity ("time is money" and "stop wasting time") and/or in fixed and static categories rather than as a dynamic and flowing process. It has been pointed out that the United States' future orientation may be linked to other values as well: (a) stress on youth and achievement in which the children are expected to "better their parents," (b) controlling one's own destiny by future planning and saving for a rainy day, and (c) optimism and hope for a better future (Condon & Yousef, 1975). The spirit of the nation may be embodied in the General Electric slogan, "Progress is our most important product." This is not to deny that people are concerned about the past and the present as well, but rather to suggest that culture, groups, and people may place greater emphasis on one over the other. Nor do we deny that age, gender, occupation, social class, and other important demographic factors may be linked to time perspectives (Gonzalez & Zimbardo, 1985). However, our work with various racial/ethnic minority groups and much published research (Ho, 1987; Inclan, 1985; Kluckhohn & Strodtbeck, 1961) indicate that race, culture, and ethnicity are powerful determinants of whether the group emphasizes the past, present, or future.

Table 5.1 reveals that both American Indians and African Americans tend to value a present time orientation, while Asian Americans and Hispanic Americans have a combination past-present focus. Historically, Asian societies have valued the past as reflected in ancestor worship and the equating of age with wisdom and respectability. Contrast this with U.S. culture, in which youth is valued over the age and the belief that once one hits the retirement years, one's usefulness in life is over. As the U.S. population ages, however, it will be interesting to see whether a shift in the status of the elderly will occur. Compared to Anglo middle-class norms, Latinos also exhibit a past-present time orientation. Strong hierarchical structures in the family, respect for elders and ancestors, and the value of *personalismo* all combine in this direction. American Indians, however, are very grounded in the here and now rather than the future. American Indian philosophy relies heavily on the belief that time is flowing, circular, and harmonious. Artificial division of time, as in making schedules, is disruptive to the natural pattern (Ho, 1987). African Americans also value the present because of the spiritual quality of their existence and their history of oppression by racism. Several difficulties may occur when the counselor or therapist is unaware of differences in time perspective (Hines & Boyd-Franklin, 1996).

First, if time perspective differences exist between the minority family and the White Euro-American therapist, they will most likely be manifested in a difference in the pace of time: Either may feel that things are going too slowly or too fast. An American Indian family who values being in the present and the immediate experiential reality of being may feel that the therapist lacks respect for them and is rushing them (Sutton & Broken Nose, 1996; Herring, 1997) while ignoring the quality of the personal relationship. On the other hand, the therapist may be dismayed by the "delays," "inefficiency," and lack of "commitment to change" among the family members. After all, time is precious, and the therapist has only limited time for interaction with the family. The result is frequently dissatisfaction among the parties, lack of establishing rapport, misinterpretation of the behaviors or situations, and discontinuance of further sessions.

Second, Inclan (1985) points out how confusions and misinterpretations can arise as a result of Hispanics', particularly Puerto Ricans', marking time differently from their U.S. White counterparts. The language of clock time in counseling (50-minute hour, rigid time schedule, once-a-week sessions) can conflict with minority perceptions of time (Garcia-Preto, 1996). The following dialogue illustrates this point clearly:

"Mrs. Rivera, your next appointment is at 9:30 A.M. next Wednesday."
"Good, it's convenient for me to come after I drop off the children at school."

Or:

"Mrs. Rivera, your next appointment is for the whole family at 3:00 P.M. on Tuesday."
"Very good. After the kids return from school we can come right in." (Inclan, 1985, p. 328)

Since school starts at 8:00 A.M., the client is bound to show up very early, while in the second example the client will most likely be late (school ends at 3:00 P.M.). In both cases, the counselor is likely to be inconvenienced, but worse yet is the negative interpretation that may be made of the client's motives (anxious, demanding, or pushy in the first case, or resistant, passive-aggressive, or irresponsible in the second). The counselor needs to be aware that Hispanics may mark time by *events* rather than by the clock.

Third, Ho (1987) suggests that many minorities who overall are present time oriented would be more likely to seek immediate, concrete solutions rather than future-oriented "abstract goals." We have already noted in earlier chapters that goals or processes that are insight oriented assume that the client has time to sit back and self-explore. Career/vocational counseling in which clients explore their interests, values, work temperaments, skills, abilities, and the world of work may be seen as highly future oriented. These approaches, while potentially beneficial to the client, may pose dilemmas for both the minority family and counselor.

RELATIONAL DIMENSION

In general, the United States can be characterized as an achievement-oriented society, a trait most strongly manifested in the Protestant work ethic. Basic to the ethic is the concept of *individualism:* (a) The individual is the psychosocial unit of operation; (b) the individual has primary responsibility for his/her own actions; (c) independence and autonomy are highly valued and rewarded; and (d) one should be internally directed and controlled. In many societies and groups within the United States, however, this value is not necessarily shared. Relationships in Japan and China are often described as being lineal: Identification with others is both wide and linked to the past (ancestor worship). Obeying the wishes of ancestors or deceased parents, and perceiving your existence and identity as linked to the historical past, are inseparable. Almost all racial/ethnic minority groups in the United States tend to be more collateral in their relationships with people. In an individualistic orientation, the definition of the family tends to be linked to a biological necessity (nuclear family), while a collateral and/or lineal view encompasses various concepts of the extended family. Not understanding this distinction and the values inherent in these orientations may lead the family counselor/therapist to erroneous conclusions and decisions. Following is a case study of an American Indian youngster.

◆ *Case Study*

A younger probationer was under court supervision and had strict orders to remain with responsible adults. His counselor became concerned because the youth appeared to ignore this order. The client moved around frequently and, according to the counselor, stayed overnight with several different young women. The counselor presented this case at a formal staff meeting, and fellow professionals stated their suspicion that the client was either a pusher or a pimp. The frustrating element to the counselor was that the young women knew each other and appeared to enjoy each others' company. Moreover, they were not ashamed to be seen together in public with the client. This behavior prompted the counselor to initiate violation proceedings. (Red Horse, Lewis, Feit, & Decker, 1981, p. 56)

Were it not for the fact that a Minneapolis American Indian professional accidentally came upon the case, initiation of a revocation order against the youngster would surely have caused irreparable alienation between the family and the social service agency. The counselor had failed to realize that the American Indian family network is structurally open and may include several households of relatives and friends along both vertical and horizontal lines. The young women were all first cousins to the client, and each was considered a "sister," with all the households representing different units of "the family."

Likewise, African Americans have strong kinship bonds that may encompass both blood relatives and friends. Traditional African culture valued the collective orientation over individualism (Franklin, 1988; Hines & Boyd-Franklin, 1996; Sudarkasa, 1988). This group identity has also been reinforced by what many African Americans describe as the sense of "peoplehood" developed as a result of the common experience of racism and discrimination. In a society that has historically attempted to destroy the Black family, near and distant relatives, neighbors, friends, and acquaintances have arisen in an extended family support network (Black, 1996). Thus, the Black family may appear quite different from the ideal nuclear family. The danger is that certain assumptions made by a White therapist may be totally without merit or may be translated in such a way as to alienate or damage the self-esteem of African Americans.

For example, the absence of a father in the Black family does not necessarily mean that the children do not have a father figure. This function may be taken over by an uncle or male family friend. Thomas and Dansby (1985) provide an example of a group counseling technique that was detrimental to several Black youngsters. Clients in the group were asked to draw a picture of the family dinner table and place circles representing the mother, father, and children in their seating arrangement. They report that even before the directions for the exercise were finished, a young Black girl ran from the room in tears. She had been raised by an aunt. Several other Black clients stated they did not eat dinners together as a family except on special occasions or Sundays—a typical routine in some affluent Black families according to Willie (1982).

The importance of family membership and the extended family system has already been illustrated in the case of Elena Martinez. We give one example here to illustrate that the moral evaluation of a behavior may depend on the value orientation of the subject. Puerto Ricans, because of their collective orientation, view obligations to the family as primary over all other relationships (Garcia-Preto, 1996). When a family member attains a position of power and influence, it is expected that he or she will favor the relatives over "objective criteria." Businesses that are heavily weighted by family members, and appointments of family members in government positions, are not unusual in many countries. Failure to hire a family member may result in moral condemnation and family sanctions (Inclan, 1985). This is in marked contrast to ideals often held in the United States, where appointment of family members over objective criteria of individual achievement is condemned.

It would appear that differences in the relationship dimension between the mental health provider and the minority family receiving services can cause great conflicts. While family therapy may be the treatment of choice for many minorities (over individual therapy), its values may be antagonistic and detrimental to minorities. Family approaches that place heavy emphasis on individualism and freedom from the emotional field of the family may cause great harm. Our approach should be to identify how we might capitalize on collaterality to the benefit of minority families.

ACTIVITY DIMENSION

One of the primary characteristics of White U.S. cultural values and beliefs is an action (doing) orientation: (a) We must master and control nature, (b) we must always do things about a situation, and (c) we should take a pragmatic and utilitarian view of life. In counseling, we expect clients to master and control their own life and environment, to take action to resolve their own problems, and to fight against bias and inaction (Katz, 1985). The doing mode is evident everywhere and is reflected in how White Americans identify themselves by what they *do* (occupations), children are asked what they want to do when they grow up, and higher value is given to inventors over poets and to doctors of medicine over doctors of philosophy. Children returning to school are often assigned to write "what I did on my summer vacation."

It appears that both American Indians and Latinos/Hispanics prefer a being or being-in-becoming mode of activity. The American Indian concepts of self-determination and noninterference are examples. Value is placed on the spiritual quality of being, as manifested in self-containment, poise, and harmony with the universe, on the attainment of inner fulfillment and an essential serenity of one's place in the universe. Because each person is fulfilling a purpose, no one should have the power to interfere or to impose values. Oftentimes those unfamiliar with American Indian values perceive the person as stoic, aloof, passive, noncompetitive, or inactive. In working with families, the counselor role of active manipulator may clash with American Indian concepts of being-in-becoming (noninterference).

Likewise, Latino/Hispanic culture may be said to have a more here-and-now or being-in-becoming orientation. Like American Indians, Hispanics believe that people are born with *dignadad* (dignity) and must be given *respecto* (respect). They are born with innate worth and importance; the inner soul and spirit are more important than the body. People cannot be held accountable for their lot in life (status, roles, etc.), for they are born into this life state (Inclan, 1985). A certain degree of *fatalismo* (fatalism) is present, and life events may be viewed as inevitable ("*Lo que Dios manda*"—What God wills). Philosophically, it does not matter what people have in life or what position they occupy (farm laborer, public official, or attorney). Status is possessed by existing and everyone is entitled to *respecto*.

Since this belief system deemphasizes material accomplishments as a measure of success, it is clearly at odds with Anglo middle-class society. While a doing-oriented family may define a family member's worth by his/her achievement, a being orientation assigns worth to simply belonging. Thus, when a client complains that someone is not an effective family member, what do they mean? This needs to be clarified by the therapist. Is it a complaint that the family member is not performing and achieving (doing), or does it mean that the person is not respectful and accommodating to family structures and values (being)?

Ho (1987) describes both Asian Americans and African Americans as operating from the doing orientation. However, it appears that "doing" in these two groups is manifested differently than in the White American lifestyle. The active dimension in Asians is related not to individual achievement, but to achievement via conformity to family values and demands. Controlling one's own feelings, impulses, desires, and needs to fulfill responsibility to the family is strongly ingrained in Asian children. The doing orientation tends to be more ritualized in the roles and responsibilities toward members of the family. African Americans also exercise considerable control (endure the pain and suffering of racism) in the face of adversity to minimize discrimination and to maximize success.

NATURE OF PEOPLE DIMENSION

Middle-class Euro-Americans generally perceive the nature of people as neutral. Environmental influences such as conditioning, family upbringing, and socialization are believed to be dominant forces in determining the nature of the person. People are neither good nor bad but a product of their environment. While several minority groups may share features of this belief, qualitative and quantitative differences may affect family structure and dynamics. For example, Asian Americans and American Indians tend to emphasize the inherent goodness of people. We have already discussed the Native American concept of noninterference, which is based on the belief that people have an innate capacity to advance and grow (self-fulfillment) and that problematic behaviors are the result of environmental influences that thwart the opportunity to develop. Goodness will always triumph over evil if the person is left alone. Likewise, Asian philosophy (Buddhism and Confucianism) believes in people's innate goodness and prescribes role relationships that manifest the "good way of life." Central to Asian belief is the concept that the best healing source lies within the family (Ho, 1987). Seeking help from the outside (like counseling/therapy) is thus considered nonproductive and against the dictates of Asian philosophy.

Latinos may be described as holding the view that human nature is both good and bad (mixed). Concepts of *dignidad* and *respecto* undergird the belief that people are born with positive qualities. Yet some Hispanics, like Puerto Ricans, spend a great deal of time appealing to supernatural forces so that children may be blessed with a good human nature (Inclan, 1985). Thus, there may be more acceptance of a "bad" child as being destined and less seeking of help from educators or mental health professionals for such problems. The preferred mode of help may be religious consultations and ventilation to neighbors and friends who sympathize and understand the dilemmas (change means reaching the supernatural forces).

African Americans may also be characterized as having a mixed concept of people, but in general, like Whites, they believe that people are basically neutral. Environmental factors have a great influence on how people develop. This orientation is consistent with African American beliefs that racism, discrimination, oppression, and other external factors create problems in living for the individual. Emotional disorders and/or antisocial acts are caused by external forces (system variables) rather than internal intrapsychic psychological ones. For example, high crime rates, poverty, and the current structure of the African American family are the result of historical and current oppression of Black people. White Western concepts of genetic inferiority and pathology (African American people are born that way) hold little validity for the Black person.

MULTICULTURAL FAMILY THERAPY: PRACTICAL IMPLICATIONS

It is extremely difficult to speak specifically about the application of multicultural strategies and techniques in minority families because of the great variations not only among Asian Americans, African Americans, Latino/Hispanic Americans, Native Americans, and Euro-Americans, but because large variations exist within the groups themselves. For example, the term "Asian and Pacific American" covers some 32 distinct subgroups in the United States. To suggest principles of multicultural family systems therapy that would have equal validity to all groups would make our discussion too general and abstract. Worse yet, we might foster overgeneralizations that would border on being stereotypes. Likewise, to attempt an extremely specific discussion would mean dealing with literally thousands of racial, ethnic, and cultural combinations, a task that is not humanly possible. What seems to be required for the helping professional is a balance of these two extremes: a framework that would help us understand differences in communication styles/structural alliances in the family and at the same time help us more specifically pinpoint cultural differences that exist within a particular family. Once that is accomplished, the therapist can turn his or her attention to creatively developing approaches and strategies of family therapy appropriate to the lifestyle of the minority family. To aid therapists in developing competencies in multicultural family therapy, we would like to outline some general principles that may be helpful.

• First, multicultural family therapy requires that the helping professionals free themselves from the cultural conditioning of their past so they can view minority families in a less prejudiced manner. One model we have found useful in working with minority families has been the value-orientation framework described in this chapter. Values are generalized and interrelated conceptions (worldviews) that guide behavior along what are considered desirable and undesirable dimensions. Kluckhohn and Strodtbeck (1961) proposed five general human questions (to be discussed in Chapter 8) to which they propose three potential value-orientation preferences. Whether groups value a lineal, collateral, or individualistic orientation has major implications for their definition of the family and what are considered appropriate goals and strategies (intervention) in family therapy. Other value preferences, such as the time dimension, relationships to nature, and so forth, are equally important and influential. Thus, we believe that a counselor needs a conceptual framework of how to view differences among the various racial minority groups. Other models are racial/cultural identity development (Chapters 6 and 7) and the theory of worldviews (Chapter 8).

- Second, the effective multicultural family therapist needs to be especially attentive to traditional cultural family structure and extended family ties. We have already seen in the case of Elena Martinez how the godfather is an intimate part of the extended family system and should have been included in the therapy session. Understanding husband-wife relationships, parent-child relationships, and sibling relationships from different cultural perspectives is crucial to effective work with minority families. A therapist who is unaware that Asian Americans and Hispanics have a more patriarchal spousal relationship, while Euro-Americans and Blacks have a more egalitarian one, may inappropriately intervene. For example, the concept of equal division of labor in the home between husband and wife or working toward a more equal relationship may be a violation of Hispanic cultural norms, as in the opening vignette with Esteban and Carmen. Another example, given by Ho (1987), and which contrasts sharply with Euro-American norms, is that most minority families view the *wifely* role as *less important* than the *motherly* role. For instance, the existence of children validates and cements the marriage; therefore, motherhood is often perceived as a more important role. Therapists should not judge the health of a family on the basis of the romantic egalitarian model characteristic of White culture.

- Third, family therapists would be well advised to utilize the natural help-giving networks and structures that already exist in the minority culture and community. It is ironic that the mental health field behaves as if minority communities never had anything like mental health "treatment" until the mental health profession came along and invented it. As mentioned in Chapter 1, Western European culture operates from a very ethnocentric framework by defining mental health concepts and by making it unethical and illegal to practice counseling or therapy without proper credentials. It destroys the natural help-giving networks that already exist in a particular culture (declaring them illegal or not recognizing them as legitimate), sets up inappropriate services, waits for minority populations to come to them, and then wonders why minorities do not come for treatment. The mental health profession acts as if only Western European countries have "therapy" and other countries and cultures do not. If that were the case, we wonder how ancient cultures such as those of China and Japan survived through all those years.

It is important for us to we recognize that helping can take many forms. These forms often appear quite different from our own, but they are no less effective or legitimate. In multicultural counseling, modifying our goals and techniques to fit the needs of minority populations is called for. Granted, mental health professionals are sometimes hard-pressed in challenging their own assumptions of what constitutes counseling and therapy and may feel uncomfortable in roles that they are not accustomed to. Yet, the need is great to move in this most positive direction. Atkinson and colleagues (Atkinson, Morten, & Sue, 1998; Atkinson, Thompson, & Grant, 1993) discuss some of these roles in detail (consultant role, ombudsman and change-agent roles, facilitator of indigenous support systems, outreach role, etc.). We will have more to say about this in Chapter 9.

- Fourth, special guidelines related to family ethnicity have been suggested to ensure culturally sensitive family practice (Giordano & Giordano, 1995; McGoldrick & Giordano, 1996). These include assessing the importance of ethnicity to clients and families, validating and strengthening ethnic identity, awareness and use of client's support systems (extended family, friends, and religious groups), serving as a culture broker, awareness of advantages and disadvantages in being of the same or different ethnic group as your client, not feeling you need to know everything about other ethnic groups, and avoiding polarization of cultural issues.
- Last, but not least, the family therapist will need to be creative in the development of appropriate intervention techniques when working with minority populations. With traditional Asian Americans, subtlety and indirectness may be called for rather than direct confrontation and interpretation. Formality in addressing members of the family, especially the father (Mr. Lee rather than Tom), may be more appropriate. For African Americans, a much more interactional approach (as opposed to an instrumental one) in the initial encounter (rather than getting to the goal or task immediately) may be dictated. What we are saying is that approaches are often determined by cultural/racial/system factors, and the more the therapist understands about these areas, the more effective he or she will become.

Part Three

Worldviews in Multicultural Counseling and Therapy

Chapter Six

◆

Racial and Cultural Identity Development: Therapeutic Implications

◆

For nearly all my life I have never seriously attempted to dissect my feelings and attitudes about being a Japanese-American woman. Aborted attempts were made, but they were never brought to fruition, because it was unbearably painful. Having been born and raised in Arizona, I had no Asian friends. I suspect that given an opportunity to make some, I would have avoided them anyway. That is because, I didn't want to have anything to do with being Japanese American. Most of the Japanese images I saw were negative. Japanese women were ugly; they had "cucumber legs," flat yellow faces, small slanty eyes, flat chested, and were stunted in growth. The men were short and stocky, sneaky and slimy, clumsy, inept, "wimpy looking," and sexually emasculated. I wanted to be tall, slender, large eyes, full lips, and elegant looking; I wasn't going to be typical Oriental!

At Cal [University of California, Berkeley], I've been forced to deal with my Yellow-White identity. There are so many "yellows" here that I can't believe it. I've come to realize that many White prejudices are deeply ingrained in me; so much so that they are unconscious. . . . To accept myself as a total person, I also have to accept my Asian identity as well. But what is it? I just don't know. Are they the images given me through the filter of White America, or are they the values and desires of my parents?

. . . Yesterday, I had a rude awakening. For the first time in my life I went on a date with a Filipino boy. I guess I shouldn't call him a "boy" as my ethnic studies teacher says it is derogatory toward Asians and Blacks. I only agreed to go because he seemed different than the other "Orientals" on campus. (I guess I shouldn't use that word either.) He's president of his Asian fraternity, very athletic and outgoing. . . . When he asked me, I figured "why not?" It'll be a good experience to see what it's like to date an Asian boy. Will he be like White guys who will try to seduce me, or will he be too afraid to make any move when it comes to sex? . . . We went to San Francisco's Fisherman's Wharf for lunch. We were seated and our orders were taken before two other White women. They were, however, served first. This was painfully apparent to us, but I wanted to pretend that it was just a mix-up. My friend, however, was less forgiving and made a public fuss with the waiter. Still, it took an inordinate amount of time for us to get our lunches, and the filets were overcooked (purposely?). My date made a very public scene by placing a tip on the table, and then returning to retrieve it. I was both embarrassed, but proud of his actions.

This incident and others made me realize several things. For all my life I have attempted to fit into White society. I have tried to convince myself that I was not different, that I was like all my other White classmates, and that prejudice and discrimination didn't exist for me. I wonder how I could have been so oblivious to prejudice and racism. I now realize that I cannot escape from my ethnic heritage and from the way people see me. Yet, I don't know how to go about resolving many of my feelings and conflicts. While I like my newly found Filipino "male" friend (he is sexy), I continue to have difficulty seeing myself married to anyone other than a White man.

(1989 excerpts from a Nisei student journal)

From reading the journal entry above, it is not difficult for us to conclude that this Nisei (second generation) Japanese American female is experiencing a racial awakening that has strong implications for her racial/cultural identity development. Her previous belief systems concerning Euro-Americans and Asian Americans are being challenged by social reality and the experiences of being a visible racial/ethnic minority. As our focus on this chapter is on racial/cultural identity development, let us briefly analyze this vignette for themes important for our understanding of this process.

First and foremost, a major theme involving societal portrayals of Asian Americans is clearly expressed in the student's beliefs about racial/cultural characteristics: She describes the Asian American male and female in a highly insulting fashion. More importantly, she seems to have internalized these beliefs and to be using White standards to judge Asian Americans as being either desirable or undesirable. For the student, the process of incorporating these standards has not only attitudinal but behavioral consequences. In Arizona, she would not have considered making Asian American friends even if the opportunity presented itself. In her mind, she was not a "typical Oriental"; she disowned or felt ashamed of her ethnic heritage; and finally, she finds it difficult to consider marrying anyone but a White male.

Second, her denial that she is an Asian American is beginning to crumble. Being on a campus where many other Asian Americans attend forces her to explore ethnic identity issues, a process she was able to avoid while living in a predominantly White area. In the past when she encountered prejudice or discrimination, she was able to deny it or to rationalize it away. The differential treatment she received at a restaurant and her male friend's labeling it as "discrimination" make such a conclusion inescapable. The shattering of illusions is manifest in a realization that (a) despite her efforts to fit in, she will not be able to gain social acceptance among many White Americans, (b) she cannot escape her racial/cultural heritage, and (c) she has been brainwashed into believing that one group is superior to another.

Third, the student's internal struggle to cast off the cultural conditioning of her past and the attempts to define her ethnic identity are both painful and conflicting ones. We have clear evidence of her internal turmoil when she refers to her "Yellow-White" identity; writes about her negative images of Asian American males, but winds up dating one; uses the terms "Oriental" and "boy" (in reference to her Asian male friend) but acknowledges their derogatory racist nature; describes Asian men as "sexually emasculated" but sees her Filipino date as "athletic," "outgoing," and "sexy"; expresses embarrassment at confronting the waiter about discrimination, but feels proud of her Asian male friend for doing so; and finally states that she finds her Filipino friend attractive, but finds it difficult to see herself marrying anyone but a White man. Understanding the process by which racial/cultural identity develops in persons of color is crucial for effective multicultural counseling and therapy.

Fourth, it is clear that the Japanese American female is a victim of ethnocentric monoculturalism. As we mentioned previously, the problem that she experiences does not reside in her, but in our society. It resides in a society that portrays racial/ethnic minority characteristics as inferior, primitive, deviant, pathological, or undesirable. The resulting damage strikes at the self-esteem and self/group identity of many culturally different in our society; many, like the student, may come to believe that their racial/cultural heritage or characteristics are burdens to be changed or overcome. This chapter focuses on understanding racial/cultural identity development and its relationship to therapeutic practice.

RACIAL AND CULTURAL IDENTITY DEVELOPMENT MODELS

One of the most promising approaches to the field of multicultural counseling/therapy has been the work on racial/cultural identity development among minority groups (Atkinson, Morten, & Sue, 1998; Carter, 1995; Casas & Pytluk, 1995; Choney, Berryhill-Paapke, & Robbins, 1995; Cross, 1995; Helms, 1984, 1985, 1993; Parham, 1989; Parham & Helms, 1981). Most would agree that Asian Americans, African Americans, Latino/Hispanic Americans, and American Indians each have a distinct cultural heritage that makes them different from each other. Yet, such cultural distinctions can lead to a monolithic view of minority group attitudes and behaviors (Atkinson, Morten, & Sue, 1998). The erroneous belief that all Asians are the same, all Blacks are the same, all Hispanics are the same, or all American Indians are the same has led to numerous therapeutic problems.

First, therapists may often respond to the culturally different client in a very stereotypic manner and fail to recognize within-group or individual differences. For example, research indicates that Asian American clients seem to prefer and benefit most from a highly structured and directive approach rather than an insight/feeling-oriented one (Atkinson, Maruyama, & Matsui, 1978; Kim, 1985; Mau & Jepson, 1988; Root, 1998). While such approaches may generally be effective, they are often blindly applied without regard for possible differences in client attitudes, beliefs, and behaviors. Likewise, conflicting findings in the literature regarding whether a minority client prefers a therapist of his/her own race seem to be a function of our failure to make such distinctions. Preference for a racially or ethnically similar therapist may really be a function of the cultural/racial identity of the minority person (within-group differences) rather than of race or ethnicity per se.

Second, the strength of racial/cultural identity models lies in their potential diagnostic value (Helms, 1984). In a previous chapter, we cited statistics indicating that premature termination rates among minority clients may be attributed to the inappropriateness of transactions that occur between the helping professional and the culturally different client. Research now suggests that a minority individual's reaction to *counseling,* the *counseling process,* and to the *coun selor* is influenced by his/her cultural/racial identity and not simply linked to minority group membership. The high failure-to-return rate of many culturally different clients seems intimately linked to the mental health professional's inability to accurately assess the cultural identity of the client.

A third important contribution derived from racial identity models is their acknowledgment of sociopolitical influences in shaping minority identity (as in the vignette of the Nisei student). As mentioned previously, most therapeutic approaches often do not take into consideration their potential sociopolitical nature. The early models of racial identity development all incorporated the effects of racism and prejudice (oppression) upon the identity transformation of their victims. Vontress (1971), for instance, theorized that African Americans moved through decreasing levels of dependence on White society to emerging identification with Black culture and society (Colored, Negro, and Black). Other similar models for Blacks have been proposed (Cross, 1971; Hall, Cross, & Freedle, 1972; Jackson, 1975; Thomas, 1970, 1971). Various researchers have proposed similar processes for other minority groups, including Asian Americans (Maykovich, 1973; D.W. Sue & S. Sue, 1972; S. Sue & D.W. Sue, 1972), Hispanics (Ruiz, 1990; Szapocznik, Santisteban, Kurtines, Hervis, & Spencer, 1982), and women (Downey & Roush, 1985; McNamara & Rickard, 1989). Their findings may indicate experiential validity for such models as they relate to various oppressed groups.

BLACK IDENTITY DEVELOPMENT MODELS

Early attempts to define a process of minority identity transformation came primarily through the work of Black social scientists and educators (Cross, 1971; Jackson, 1975; Thomas, 1971). Black identity models proposed by Cross (1971) and Jackson (1975) are discussed here because they represent the most highly developed of those proposed.

The Cross model (1971, 1972; Hall, Cross, & Freedle, 1972; Cross, 1995) delineates a four-stage process (originally five-stage) in which Blacks in the United States move from a White frame of reference to a positive Black frame of reference: *preencounter, encounter, immersion-emersion,* and *internalization.* The *preencounter* stage is characterized by individuals (African Americans) who consciously or unconsciously devalue their own Blackness and concurrently value White values and ways. There is a strong desire to assimilate and acculturate into White society. In the *encounter* stage, a two-step process begins to occur. First, the individual encounters a profound crisis or event that challenges his/her previous mode of thinking and behaving; second, the Black person begins to reinterpret the world and a shift in worldview results. Cross points out how the slaying of Martin Luther King Jr. was such a significant experience for many African Americans. The person experiences both guilt and anger over *being* brainwashed by White society. In the third stage, *immersion-emersion,* the person withdraws from the dominant culture and immerses himself or herself in African American culture. Black pride begins to develop, but internalization of positive attitudes toward one's own Blackness is minimal. In the emersion phase, feelings of guilt and anger begin to dissipate with an increasing sense of pride. The final stage, *internalization,* is characterized by inner security as conflicts between the old and new identities are resolved. Global anti-White feelings subside as the person becomes more flexible, more tolerant, and more bicultural/multicultural.

A similar four-stage model has been proposed by Jackson (1975). Like Cross and others, Jackson believed that a Black person's identity is strongly influenced by that person's experiences of racism and oppression. In the *passive-acceptance* stage, the person accepts and conforms to White social, cultural, and institutional standards. Feelings of self-worth come from a White perspective. In the *active-resistance* stage, the person is dedicated toward rejection of White social, cultural, and institutional standards. A great deal of anger (global anti-White feeling) is directed toward White society. The *redirection stage* sees the individual as attempting to develop uniquely African American values, goals, structures, and traditions. This is a period of isolationism in which anger dissipates and is channeled into pride in identity and culture. Once a sense of inner security develops, the person enters the *internalization* stage. The person can own and accept those aspects of U.S. culture that are seen as healthy and can stand against those things that are toxic (racism, sexism, and oppression). White and Black cultures are seen as not necessarily in conflict.

ASIAN AMERICAN IDENTITY DEVELOPMENT MODELS

Asian American identity development models have not advanced as far as those relating to Black identity. One of the earliest heuristic-type models was developed by S. Sue & D.W. Sue (1971a) to explain what they saw as clinical differences among Chinese American students treated at the University of California Counseling Center: (a) Traditionalist—a person who internalizes traditional Chinese customs and values, resists acculturation forces, and believes in the "old ways"; (b) Marginal Person—a person who attempts to assimilate and acculturate into White society, rejects traditional Chinese ways, internalizes society's negativism toward minority groups, and may develop racial self-hatred (like the Nisei student); and (c) Asian American—a person who is in the process of forming a positive identity, who is ethnically and politically aware, and who becomes increasingly bicultural.

Kitano (1982) also proposed a type model to account for Japanese American role behaviors with respect to Japanese and American cultures: (a) positive-positive, in which the person identifies with both Japanese and White cultures without role conflicts; (b) negative-positive, in which there is a rejection of White culture and acceptance of Japanese American culture with accompanying role conflicts; (c) positive-negative, in which the person accepts White culture and rejects Japanese culture with concomitant role conflicts; and (d) negative-negative, in which the person rejects both.

These early type models suffer from several shortcomings (Lee, 1991). First, they fail to provide a clear rationale for how an individual develops one ethnic identity type over another. Although they were useful in describing characteristics of the type, they represented static entities rather than a dynamic process of identity development. Second, the early proposals seem too simplistic to account for the complexity of racial identity development. Third, these models were too population-specific in that they described only one Asian American ethnic group (Chinese American or Japanese American), so that one wonders whether they are equally applicable to Korean Americans, Filipino Americans, Vietnamese Americans, etc. Last, other than a few empirical studies (Lee, 1991; D.W. Sue & Frank, 1973) testing of these typologies is seriously lacking.

In response to these criticisms, theorists have begun to move toward the development of stage/process models of Asian American identity development (Kim, 1981; Lee, 1991; Sodowski, Kwan, & Pannu, 1995). Such models view identity formation as occurring in stages, advancing from less healthy to more healthy. With each stage there exists a constellation of traits and characteristics associated with racial/ethnic identity. They also attempt to explain the conditions or situations that might retard, enhance, or impel the individual's advancement.

After a thorough review of the literature, Kim (1981) used a qualitative narrative approach with third-generation Japanese American women to posit a progressive and sequential five-stage model of Asian American identity development consisting of: ethnic awareness, white identification, awakening to social political consciousness, redirection to Asian American consciousness, and incorporation. Her model incorporates the influence of acculturation, exposure to cultural differences, environmental negativism to racial differences, personal methods of handling race-related conflicts, and the effects of group or social movements on the Asian American individual.

1. The *ethnic awareness* stage begins around the ages of 3–4 where the child's family members serve as the significant ethnic group model. Positive or neutral attitudes toward one's own ethnic origin are formed depending upon the amount of ethnic exposure conveyed by the caretakers.

2. The *white identification* stage begins when children enter school where peers and the surroundings become powerful forces in conveying racial prejudice that negatively impacts their self-esteem and identity. Such interactions result in a recognition of "differentness" that leads to self-blame and a desire to escape their own racial heritage by identifying with White society.

3. The *awakening to social political consciousness* stage means the adoption of a new perspective, often correlated with increased political awareness. Kim believes that significant political events such as the Civil Rights and Women's Movements often precipitate this new awakening. The primary result is an abandoning of identification with White society and a consequent understanding of oppression and oppressed groups.

4. The *redirection to Asian American consciousness* stage means a reconnection or renewed connection with one's Asian American heritage and culture. This is often followed by a recognition of White oppression as the culprit in the negative experiences of youth. Anger against White racism may become a defining theme with an increase in Asian American self and group pride.

5. The *incorporation* stage represents the highest form of identity evolution. It encompasses the development of a positive and comfortable identity as Asian American and consequent respect for other cultural/racial heritages. Identification for or against White culture is no longer an important issue.

LATINO/HISPANIC AMERICAN IDENTITY DEVELOPMENT MODELS

While a number of ethnic identity development models have been formulated to account for Hispanic identity (Bernal & Knight, 1993; Casas & Pytluk, 1995; Szapocznik et al., 1982), the one most similar to those of African Americans and Asian Americans is proposed by Ruiz (1990). His model was formulated from a clinical perspective via case studies of Chicano/Latino subjects. Several underlying assumptions are made by Ruiz. First, he believed in a culture-specific explanation of identity for Chicano, Mexican American, and Latino clients. More general models and those dealing with development of other ethnic groups were helpful, but they lacked characteristics specific to Hispanic cultures. Second, the marginal status of Latinos is highly correlated with maladjustment. Third, negative experiences of forced assimilation are considered destructive to an individual. Fourth, having pride in one's cultural heritage and ethnic identity is positively correlated with mental health. Last, pride in one's ethnicity affords the Hispanic greater freedom to choose freely. These beliefs underlie the five-stage model.

1. *Causal stage.* During this period messages and/or injunctions from the environment or significant others either ignore, negate, or denigrate the ethnic heritage of the person. Affirmation of one's ethnic identity is lacking, and the person may experience traumatic or humiliating experiences related to ethnicity. There is a failure to identify with Latino culture.

2. *Cognitive stage.* As a result of negative/distorted messages, three erroneous belief systems about Chicano/Latino heritage become incorporated into mental sets: (a) association of ethnic group membership with poverty and prejudice, (b) assimilation to White society as the only means of escape, and (c) assimilation as the only possible road to success.

3. *Consequence stage.* Fragmentation of ethnic identity becomes very noticeable and evident. The person feels ashamed of or embarrassed by ethnic markers such as name, accent, skin color, or cultural customs. The unwanted self-image leads to estrangement from and rejection of Chicano/Latino heritage.

4. *Working through stage.* Two major dynamics distinguish this stage. First, the person becomes increasingly unable to cope with the psychological distress of ethnic identity conflict. Second, the person can no longer be a "pretender" by identifying with an alien ethnic identity. The person is propelled to reclaim and reintegrate disowned ethnic identity fragments. Ethnic consciousness increases.

5. *Successful resolution stage.* This last stage is exemplified by greater acceptance of the person's own culture and ethnicity. There is an improvement in self-esteem and a sense that ethnic identity represents a positive and success-promoting resource.

The Ruiz model has a subjective reality that many of the empirically based ones lack. This is expected since it was formulated through a clinical population. It has the added advantage of suggesting intervention focus and direction for each of the stages. For example, the focus of counseling in the causal stage is disaffirming and restructuring of the injunctions; for the cognitive stage it is the use of cognitive strategies attacking faulty beliefs; for the consequence stage it is reintegration of ethnic identity fragments in a positive manner; for the working through stage ethnocultural identification issues are important; and for the successful resolution stage the promotion of a positive identity becomes important.

OTHER IDENTITY DEVELOPMENT MODELS

Although these identity development models pertain specifically to the Black experience, we have already pointed out how various other groups have proposed similar processes. Earlier writers (Berry, 1965; Stonequist, 1937) have observed that minority groups share similar patterns of adjustment to cultural oppression. In the past several decades, Asian Americans, Hispanics, and American Indians have experienced sociopolitical identity transformations so that a "Third World consciousness" has emerged with cultural oppression as the common unifying force. As a result of studying these models and integrating them with their own clinical observations, Atkinson, Morten, and Sue (1989) proposed a five-stage Minority Identity Development Model (MID) in an attempt to identify common features that cut across the popu-

Table 6.1   RACIAL/CULTURAL IDENTITY DEVELOPMENT

Stages of Minority Development Model	*Attitude toward Self*	*Attitude toward Others of the Same Minority*	*Attitude toward Others of Different Minority*	*Attitude toward Dominant Group*
Stage 1— Conformity	Self-depreciating	Group-depreciating	Discriminatory	Group-appreciating
Stage 2— Dissonance	Conflict between self-depreciating and appreciating	Conflict between group-depreciating and group-appreciating	Conflict between dominant-held views of minority hierarchy and feelings of shared experiences	Conflict between group-appreciating and group-depreciating
Stage 3— Resistance and immersion	Self-appreciating	Group-appreciating	Conflict between feelings of empathy for other minority experiences and feelings of culturocentrism	Group-depreciating
Stage 4— Introspection	Concern with basis of self-appreciation	Concern with nature of unequivocal appreciation	Concern with ethnocentric basis for judging others	Concern with the basis of group-depreciation
Stage 5— Integrative Awareness	Self-appreciating	Group-appreciating	Group-appreciating	Selective appreciation

Note. From *Counseling American Minorities: A Cross Cultural Perspective,* 5th ed., by Donald R. Atkinson, George Morten, and Derald Wing Sue, 1998, Dubuque, IA: Wm. C. Brown. All rights reserved. Reprinted with permission.

lation-specific proposals. D.W. Sue & D. Sue (1990) later elaborated on the MID, but renamed it the Racial/Cultural Identity Development Model (R/CID). As we shall see shortly, this model may also be applied to White identity development.

The R/CID model proposed here is not a comprehensive theory of personality, but rather a conceptual framework to aid therapists in understanding their culturally different clients' attitudes and behaviors. The model defines five stages of development that oppressed people experience as they struggle to understand themselves in terms of their *own culture,* the *dominant culture,* and the *oppressive relationship* between the two cultures: *conformity, dissonance, resistance and immersion, introspection,* and *integrative awareness.* At each level of identity, four corresponding beliefs and attitudes that may help therapists understand their minority clients better are discussed. These attitudes/beliefs are an integral part of the minority person's identity and are manifest in how he/she views (a) the self, (b) others of the same minority, (c) others of another minority, and (d) majority individuals. Table 6.1 outlines the R/CID model and the interaction of stages with the attitudes and beliefs.

Conformity Stage

Like individuals in the passive-acceptance stage (Jackson, 1975) and the preencounter stage (Cross, 1971), minority individuals are distinguished by their unequivocal preference for dominant cultural values over their own. White Americans in the United States represent their reference group and the identification set is quite strong. Lifestyles, value systems, and cultural/physical characteristics most like those of White society are highly valued while those most like their own minority group's are viewed with disdain or are repressed. Because the conformity stage represents perhaps the most damning indictment of White racism, and because it has such a profound negative impact upon minority groups, we spend more time discussing it than the other stages. Let us use a case approach to illustrate the social-psychological dynamics of the conformity process.

♦ Case Study

WHO AM I? WHITE OR BLACK

A 17-year-old White high school student, Mary, comes to counseling for help in sorting out her thoughts and feelings concerning an interracial relationship with an African American student. Although she is proud of the relationship and feels that her liberal friends are accepting and envious, Mary's parents are against it. Indeed, the parents have threatened to cut off financial support for her future college education unless she terminates the affair immediately.

During counseling, Mary tells of how she has rid herself of much bigotry and prejudice from the early training of parents. She joined a circle of friends who were quite liberal in thought and behavior. She recalls how she was both shocked by and attracted to her new friends' liberal political beliefs, philosophy, and sexual attitudes. When she first met John, a Black student, she was immediately attracted to his apparent confidence and outspokenness. It did not take her long to become sexually involved with him and to enter into an intense relationship. Mary became the talk of her former friends, but she did not seem to care. Indeed, she seemed to enjoy the attention and openly flaunted her relationship in everyone's face.

Because Mary requested couple counseling, the counselor saw her and John together. John informs the counselor that he came solely to please Mary. He sees few problems in their relationship that cannot be easily resolved. John seems to feel that he has overcome many handicaps in his life, and that this represents just another obstacle to be conquered. When asked about his use of the term "handicap," he responds, "It's not easy to be Black, you know. I've proven to my parents and friends in high school, including myself, that I'm worth something. Let them disapprove—I'm going to make it into a good university." Further probing reveals John's resentment over his own parents' disapproval of the relationship. Even when his relations with them worsened to the point of near-physical assaults, John continued to bring Mary home. He seemed to take great pride in being seen with a "beautiful blond-haired, blue-eyed White girl."

In a joint session, Mary's desire to continue therapy and John's apparent reluctance become obvious. Several times when John mentions the prospect of a "permanent relationship" and both attending the same university, Mary does not seem to respond positively. She does not seem to want to look too far into the future. Mary's constant coolness to the idea and the counselor's attempts to focus on this reluctance anger John greatly. He becomes antagonistic toward the counselor and puts pressure on Mary to terminate this useless talk "crap." However, he continues to come for the weekly sessions. One day his anger boils over, and he accuses the counselor of being biased. Standing up and shouting, John demands to know how the counselor feels about interracial relationships.

There are many approaches to analyzing the preceding case study, but we have chosen to concentrate on the psychological dynamics evidenced by John, the African American student. However, it is clear from a brief reading of this case study that both John and Mary are involved in an interracial relationship as a means of rebellion and as attempts to work out personal and group identity issues. In Mary's case, it may be rebellion against conservative parents and parental upbringing, and the secondary "shock value" it has for her former friends and parents (appearing liberal). John's motivation for the relationship is also a form of rebellion. There are many clues to indicate that John identifies with White culture and feels disdain for Black culture. First, he seems to equate his Blackness with a "handicap" to be overcome. Is it possible that John feels ashamed of who and what he is (Black)? While feeling proud of one's woman friend is extremely desirable, does Mary's being *White, blond-haired,* and *blue-eyed* have special significance? Would John feel equally proud if the woman were beautiful and Black? Being seen in the company of a White woman may represent affirmation to John that he has made it in White society. Perhaps he is operating under the belief that White ways are better and has been sold a false bill of goods.

While John's anger in counseling is multidimensional, much of it seems misdirected toward the counselor. John may actually be angry toward Mary, who seems less than committed to a long-term or permanent relationship. Yet to acknowledge that Mary may not want a permanent relationship will threaten the very basis of John's self-deception (that he is not like the other Blacks and is accepted in White society). It is very easy to blame John for his dilemma and to call him an "Oreo" (Black outside and White inside). However, lest we fall prey to blaming the victim, let's use a wider perspective in analyzing this case.

John is really a victim of larger social psychological forces operating in our society (and, in fact, so is Mary). The key issue here is the dominant-subordinate relationship between two different cultures (Atkinson, Morten, & Sue, 1998; Carter, 1995; Freire, 1970; Jackson, 1975). It is reasonable to believe that members of one cultural group tend to adjust themselves to the group possessing the greater prestige and power in order to avoid inferiority feelings. Yet, it is exactly this act that creates ambivalence in the minority individual. The pressures for assimilation and acculturation (melting-pot theory) are strong, creating possible culture conflicts. John is the victim of ethnocentric monoculturalism (D.W. Sue et al., 1998): (a) belief that one group (White) has a cultural heritage—language, traditions, arts-crafts, and ways of behaving—superior to those of all others; (b) belief in the inferiority of all other lifestyles (non-White); and (c) power of the dominant group to impose such standards onto the less powerful group.

John exemplifies the immense psychological costs of racism on minorities. Constantly bombarded on all sides by reminders that Whites and their way of life are superior and all other lifestyles are inferior, many minority group members begin to wonder whether they themselves are not somehow inadequate, whether members of their own group are not to blame, and whether subordination and segregation are not justified. Clark and Clark (1947) first brought this to the attention of social scientists, stating that racism may contribute to a sense of confused self-identity among Black children. In a study of racial awareness and preference among Black and White children, they found that (a) Black children preferred playing with a White doll over a Black one, (b) the Black doll was perceived as being "bad," and (c) approximately 1/3 when asked to pick the doll that looked like them, picked the White one.

It is unfortunate that the inferior status of minorities is constantly reinforced and perpetuated through television, movies, newspapers, radio, books, and magazines. This contributes to widespread stereotypes that tend to trap minority individuals: Blacks are superstitious, childlike, ignorant, fun loving, or dangerous and criminals; Hispanics are dirty, sneaky, and criminals; Asian Americans are sneaky, sly, cunning, and passive; American Indians are primitive savages. Such portrayals cause widespread harm to the self-esteem of minorities who may incorporate them. That preconceived expectations can set up self-fulfilling prophesies has been demonstrated by Rosenthal and Jacobson (1968). The incorporation of the larger society's standards may lead minority group members to react negatively toward their own racial and cultural heritage. They may become ashamed of who they are, reject their own group identification, and attempt to identify with the desirable "good" White majority. In *The Autobiography of Malcolm X* (Haley, 1966), Malcolm X relates how he tried desperately to appear as White as possible. He went to painful lengths to straighten and dye his hair so he would appear more like White males. It is evident that many minorities do come to accept White standards as a means of measuring physical attractiveness, attractiveness of personality, and social relationships. Such an orientation may lead to the phenomenon of racial self-hatred, in which people dislike themselves for being Asian, Black, Hispanic, or Native American. Like John, individuals operating from the conformity stage experience racial self-hatred and attempt to assimilate and acculturate into White society. People at the conformity stage seem to possess the following characteristics.

1. *Attitude and beliefs toward self.* Self-depreciating attitudes and beliefs. Physical and cultural characteristics identified with one's own racial/cultural group are perceived negatively, as something to be avoided, denied, or changed. Physical characteristics (black skin color, "slant-shaped eyes" of Asians), traditional modes of dress and appearance, and behavioral characteristics associated with the minority group are a source of shame. There may be attempts to mimic what are perceived as White mannerisms, speech patterns, dress, and goals. Low internal self-esteem is characteristic of the person. The fact that John views his own blackness as a "handicap," something bad, and something to deny is an example of this insidious but highly damaging process.

2. *Attitudes and beliefs toward members of the same minority.* Group-depreciating attitudes and beliefs. Majority cultural beliefs and attitudes about the minority group are also held by the person in this stage. These individuals may have internalized the majority of White stereotypes about their group. In the case of Hispanics, for example, the person may believe that members of his or her own group have high rates of unemployment because they are lazy,

uneducated, and unintelligent. Little thought or validity is given to other viewpoints, such as unemployment being a function of job discrimination, prejudice, racism, unequal opportunities, and inferior education. Because persons in the conformity stage find it psychologically painful to identify with these negative traits, they divorce themselves from their own group. The denial mechanism most commonly used is: "I'm not like them; I've made it on my own; I'm the exception."

3. *Attitudes and beliefs toward members of different minorities.* Discriminatory. Because the conformity-stage person most likely strives for identification with White society, he/she not only shares similar dominant attitudes and beliefs toward his/her own minority group, but toward other minorities as well. Minority groups most similar to White cultural groups are viewed more favorably, while those most different are viewed less favorably. For example, Asian Americans may be viewed more favorably than African Americans or Latino/Hispanic Americans in some situations. While a stratification probably exists, we caution readers that such a ranking is fraught with hazards and potential political consequences. Such distinctions often manifest themselves in debates as to which group is more oppressed and which group has done better than the others. Such debates are counterproductive when used to (a) negate another group's experience of oppression, (b) foster an erroneous belief that hard work alone will result in success in a democratic society, (c) shortchange a minority group (e.g., Asian Americans) from receiving the necessary resources in our society, or (d) pit one minority against another (divide and conquer) by holding one group up as an example to others.

4. *Attitudes and beliefs toward members of the dominant group.* Group-appreciating attitudes and beliefs. This stage is characterized by a belief that White cultural, social, and institutional standards are superior. Members of the dominant group are admired, respected, and emulated. White people are believed to possess superior intelligence. Some individuals may go to great lengths to appear White. In *The Autobiography of Malcolm X,* the main character would straighten his hair and primarily date White women (like John in the case study). Reports that Asian women have undergone surgery to reshape their eyes to conform to White female standards of beauty may in some cases typify this dynamic.

Dissonance Stage

No matter how much an individual attempts to deny his/her own racial/cultural heritage, he or she will encounter information or experiences inconsistent with beliefs, attitudes, and values held by the dominant culture. An Asian American who believes that Asians are inhibited, passive, inarticulate, and poor in people relationships may encounter an Asian leader who seems to break all these stereotypes (like the Nisei student). A Latino who may feel ashamed of his cultural upbringing may encounter another Latino who seems proud of his/her cultural heritage. An African American who may have deceived himself or herself into believing that race problems are due to laziness, untrustworthiness, or personal inadequacies of his/her own group may suddenly encounter racism on a personal level. Denial begins to break down, which leads to a questioning and challenging of the attitudes/beliefs of the conformity stage. This was clearly what happened when the Nisei student encountered discrimination at the restaurant.

In all probability, movement into the dissonance stage is a gradual process. Its very name indicates that the individual is in conflict because of disparate pieces of information or experiences that challenge his or her current self-concept. People generally move into this stage slowly, but a traumatic event may propel some individuals to move into dissonance at a much more rapid pace. Cross (1971, 1995) states that a monumental event such as the assassination of a major leader like Martin Luther King Jr. can oftentimes push people quickly from the conformity stage into the ensuing dissonance stage.

1. *Attitudes and beliefs toward self.* Conflict between self-depreciating and self-appreciating attitudes and beliefs. There is now a growing sense of personal awareness that racism does exist, that not all aspects of the minority or majority culture are good or bad, and that one cannot escape one's cultural heritage. For the first time the person begins to entertain the possibility of positive attributes in the minority culture and, with it, a sense of pride in self. Feelings of shame and pride are mixed in the individual, and a sense of conflict develops. This conflict is most likely to be brought to the forefront quickly when other members of the minority group may express positive feelings toward the person: "We like you because you are Asian, Black, American Indian, or Latino." At this stage, an important personal question is being asked: "Why should I feel ashamed of who and what I am?"

2. *Attitudes and beliefs toward members of the same minority.* Conflict between group-depreciating and group-appreciating attitudes and beliefs. Dominant-held views of minority strengths and weaknesses begin to be questioned, as new, contradictory information is received. Certain aspects of the minority culture begin to have appeal. For example, a Latino/Hispanic male who values individualism may marry, have children, and then suddenly realize how Latino cultural values that hold the family as the psychosocial unit possess positive features. Or the minority person may find certain members of his group to be very attractive as friends, colleagues, lovers, and so forth.

3. *Attitudes and beliefs toward members of a different minority.* Conflict between dominant-held views of minority hierarchy and feelings of shared experience. Stereotypes associated with other minority groups become questioned and a growing sense of comradeship with other oppressed groups is shared. It is important to keep in mind, however, that little psychic energy is associated with resolving conflicts with other minority groups. Almost all energies are expended toward resolving conflicts toward the self, the same minority, and the dominant group.

4. *Attitudes and beliefs toward members of dominant group.* Conflict between group-appreciating and group-depreciating attitudes. The person experiences a growing awareness that not all cultural values of the dominant group are beneficial to him/her. This is especially true when the minority person experiences personal discrimination. Growing suspiciousness and some distrust of certain members of the dominant group develops.

Resistance and Immersion Stage

The culturally different individual tends to completely endorse minority-held views and to reject the dominant values of society and culture. The person seems dedicated to reacting against White society and rejects White social, cultural, and institutional standards as having no validity for him or her. Desire to eliminate oppression of the individual's minority group becomes an important motivation of the individual's behavior. During the resistance and immersion stage, the three most active types of affective feelings are *guilt, shame,* and *anger.* There are considerable feelings of guilt and shame that in the past the minority individual has sold out his/her own racial and cultural group. The feelings of guilt and shame extend to the perception that during this past sellout, the minority person has been a contributor and participant in the oppression of his/her own group and other minority groups. This is coupled with a strong sense of anger at the oppression and feelings of having been brainwashed by the forces in White society. Anger toward oppression and racism is directed outward in a very strong way. Movement into this stage seems to occur for two reasons. First, a resolution of the conflicts and confusions of the previous stage allows greater understanding of social forces (racism, oppression, and discrimination) and the person's role as a victim. Second, there is a personal questioning of why people should feel ashamed of themselves. The answer to this question evokes feelings of guilt, shame, and anger.

1. *Attitudes and beliefs toward self.* Self-appreciating attitudes and beliefs. The minority individual at this stage is oriented toward self-discovery of his/her own group's history and culture. There is an active seeking out of information and artifacts that enhance that person's sense of identity and worth. Cultural and racial characteristics that once elicited feelings of shame and disgust become symbols of pride and honor. The individual moves into this stage primarily because he/she asks the question, "Why should I be ashamed of who and what I am?" The original low self-esteem engendered by widespread prejudice and racism most characteristic of the conformity stage is now actively challenged in order to raise self-esteem. Phrases such as "Black is beautiful" represent a symbolic relabeling of identity. Racial self-hatred is actively rejected in favor of the other extreme, which is unbridled racial pride.

2. *Attitudes and beliefs toward members of the same minority.* Group-appreciating attitudes and beliefs. The individual experiences a strong sense of identification with and commitment to his/her minority group as enhancing information about the group is acquired. There is a feeling of connectedness with other members of the racial and cultural group, and a strengthening of new identity begins to occur. Members of one's group are admired, respected, and often viewed now as the new reference group or ideal. Cultural values of the minority group are accepted without question. As indicated, the pendulum swings drastically from original identification with White ways to unquestioning identification with the minority group's ways. Persons in this stage are likely to restrict their interactions as much as possible to members of their own group.

3. *Attitudes and beliefs toward members of a different minority.* Conflict between feelings of empathy for other minority group experiences and feelings of culturocentrism. While members at this stage experience a growing sense of comradeship with persons from other minority groups, a strong culturocentrism develops as well. Alliances with other groups tend to be transitory and based upon short-term goals or some global shared view of oppression. There is not so much an attempt to reach out and understand other racial/cultural minority groups and their values and ways, but more a superficial feeling of political need. Alliances generally are based upon convenience factors and/or are formed for political reasons such as combining together as a group to confront what is perceived as a larger enemy.

4. *Attitudes and beliefs toward members of the dominant group.* Group-depreciating attitudes and beliefs. The minority individual is likely to perceive the dominant society and culture as an oppressor and the group most responsible for the current plight of minorities in the United States. Characterized by both withdrawal from the dominant culture and immersion in one's cultural heritage, there is also considerable anger and hostility directed toward White society. There is a feeling of distrust and dislike for all members of the dominant group in an almost global demonstration of anti-White feeling. White people, for example, are not to be

trusted, because they are the oppressors or enemies. In extreme form, members may advocate complete destruction of the institutions and structures characteristic of White society.

Introspection Stage

Several factors seem to work in unison to move the individual from the resistance and immersion stage into the introspection stage. First, the individual begins to discover that this level of intensity of feelings (anger directed toward White society) is psychologically draining and does not permit one to really devote more crucial energies to understanding themselves or to their own racial/cultural group. The resistance and immersion stage tends to be a reaction against the dominant culture and is not proactive in allowing the individual to use all energies to discover who or what he or she is. Self-definition in the previous stage tends to be reactive (against White racism), so that a need for positive self-definition in a proactive sense emerges.

Second, the minority individual experiences feelings of discontent and discomfort with group views that may be quite rigid in the resistance and immersion stage. Often, in order to please the group, the culturally different individual is asked to submerge individual autonomy and individual thought in favor of the group good. Many group views may now be seen as conflicting with individual ones. A Latino individual who forms a deep relationship with a White person may experience considerable pressure from his or her culturally similar peers to break off the relationship because that person is the "enemy." However, the personal experiences of the individual may in fact not support this group view.

It is important to note that some clinicians often erroneously confuse certain characteristics of the introspective stage with those of the conformity stage. A minority person from the former stage who speaks against the decisions of his/her group may often appear similar to the conformity person. The dynamics are quite different, however. While the conformity person is motivated by global racial self-hatred, the introspective person has no such global negativism directed at his/her own group.

1. *Attitudes and beliefs toward self.* Concern with basis of self-appreciating attitudes and beliefs. While the person originally in the conformity stage held predominantly to majority group views and notions to the detriment of his or her own minority group, the person now feels that he/she has too rigidly held onto minority group views and notions in order to submerge personal autonomy. The conflict now becomes quite great in terms of responsibility and allegiance to one's own minority group versus notions of personal independence and autonomy. The person begins to spend more and more time and energy trying to sort out these aspects of self-identity and begins to demand increased individual autonomy.

2. *Attitudes and beliefs toward members of the same minority.* Concern with unequivocal nature of group appreciation. While attitudes of identification are continued from the preceding resistance and immersion stage, concern begins to build up regarding the issue of group-usurped individuality. Increasingly, the individual may perceive his/her own group's positions as extreme. In addition, there is now increasing resentment over how one's group may attempt to pressure or influence the individual into making decisions that may be inconsistent with the person's own values, beliefs, and outlook. Indeed, it is not unusual for members of a minority group to make it clear that any individual member who does not agree with the group is against it. A common ploy used to hold members in line is exemplified in the questions: "How Asian are you?" "How Black are you?"

3. *Attitudes and beliefs toward members of a different minority.* Concern with ethnocentric basis for judging others. There is now greater uneasiness with culturocentrism and an attempt is made to reach out to other groups in finding out what types of oppression they experience, and how this has been handled. While similarities are important, there is now a movement into understanding potential differences in oppression that other groups might have experienced.

4. *Attitudes and beliefs toward members of the dominant group.* Concern with the basis of group depreciation. The individual experiences conflict between attitudes of complete trust for the dominant society and culture, and attitudes of selective trust and distrust according to a dominant group member's demonstrated behaviors and attitudes. Conflict is most likely to occur here because the person begins to recognize that many elements in U.S. culture are highly functional and desirable, yet there is confusion as to how to incorporate these elements into the minority culture. Would the person's acceptance of certain White cultural values make the person a sellout to his or her own race? There is a lowering of intense feelings of anger and distrust toward the dominant group but a continued attempt to discern elements that are acceptable.

Integrative Awareness Stage

Minority persons in this stage have developed an inner sense of security and now can own and appreciate unique aspects of their culture as well as those of U.S. culture. Minority culture is not necessarily in conflict with White dominant cultural ways. Conflicts and discomforts experienced in the previous stage become resolved, allowing greater individual control and flexibility. There is now the belief there are acceptable and unacceptable aspects in all cultures, and that it is very important for the person to be able to examine and accept or reject those aspects of a culture on their own merits. At the integrative awareness stage, the minority person has a strong commitment and desire to eliminate all forms of oppression.

1. *Attitudes and beliefs toward self.* Self-appreciating attitudes and beliefs. The culturally different individual develops a positive self-image and experiences a strong sense of self-worth and confidence. Not only is there an integrated self-concept that involves racial pride in identity and culture, but the person develops a high sense of autonomy. Indeed, the person becomes bicultural or multicultural without a sense of having sold out his/her integrity. In other words, such persons begin to perceive themselves as autonomous individuals who are unique (individual level of identity); as members of their own racial/cultural group (group level of identity); as members of a larger society; and as members of the human race (universal level of identity).

2. *Attitudes and beliefs toward members of same minority.* Group-appreciating attitudes and beliefs. The individual experiences a strong sense of pride in the group without having to accept group values unequivocally. There is no longer the conflict over disagreeing with group goals and values. Strong feelings of empathy with the group experience are coupled with an awareness that each member of the group is also an individual. In addition, tolerant and empathetic attitudes are likely to be expressed toward members of one's own group who may be functioning in a less adaptive manner toward racism and oppression.

3. *Attitudes and beliefs toward members of a different minority.* Group-appreciating attitudes. There is now literally a reaching out toward different minority groups in order to under-

stand their cultural values and ways of life. There is a strong belief that the more one understands other cultural values and beliefs, the greater is the likelihood of understanding among the various ethnic groups. Support for all oppressed people, regardless of similarity to the individual's minority group, tends to be emphasized.

4. *Attitudes and beliefs toward members of the dominant group.* Attitudes and beliefs of selective appreciation. The individual experiences selective trust and liking for members of the dominant group who seek to eliminate oppressive activities of the group. The individual also experiences an openness to the constructive elements of the dominant culture. The emphasis here tends to be on the fact that White racism is a sickness in society and that White people are also victims who are in need of help.

THERAPEUTIC IMPLICATIONS OF THE R/CID MODEL

Let us first point out some broad general clinical implications of the R/CID model before discussing specific meanings within each of the stages. First, an understanding of cultural identity development should sensitize therapists and counselors to the role that oppression plays in a minority individual's development. In many respects, it should make us aware that our role as helping professionals should extend beyond the office and should deal with the many manifestations of racism. While individual therapy is needed, combating the forces of racism means a proactive approach for both the therapist and client. For the therapist, systems intervention is often the answer. For the culturally different client, it means the need to understand, control, and direct those forces in society that negate the process of positive identity. Thus, a wider sociocultural approach to therapy is mandatory.

Second, the model will aid therapists in recognizing differences between members of the same minority group with respect to their cultural identity. It serves as a useful assessment and diagnostic tool for therapists to gain a greater understanding of their culturally different clients (Atkinson, Morten & Sue, 1998; Helms, 1985; D.W. Sue et al., 1998). In many cases, an accurate delineation of the dynamics and characteristics of the stages may result in better prescriptive treatment. Those therapists familiar with the sequence of stages are better able to plan intervention strategies most effective for a culturally different client. For example, a client experiencing feelings of isolation and alienation in the conformity stage may require a different approach from one experiencing those feelings in the introspection stage.

Third, the model allows helping professionals to realize the potentially changing and developmental nature of cultural identity among clients. If the goal of multicultural therapy is to move a client toward the integrative awareness stage, then the therapist is able to anticipate the sequence of feelings, beliefs, attitudes, and behaviors likely to arise. Acting as a guide and providing an understandable end point will allow the client to more quickly understand and work through issues related to his/her own identity. We now turn our attention to the R/CID model and its implications for the therapeutic process.

CONFORMITY STAGE: THERAPEUTIC IMPLICATIONS

Characteristics of conformity stage individuals (belief in the superiority of White ways and inferiority of minority ways) suggest several therapeutic implications. First, the culturally differ ent client is most likely to prefer a White therapist over a minority therapist. This flows logically from the belief that Whites are more competent and capable than members of one's own race. Such a racial preference can be manifested in the client's reaction to a minority therapist via negativism, resistance, or open hostility. In some instances, the client may even request a change in therapist (preferably someone White). On the other hand, the conformity individual who is seen by a White therapist may be quite pleased about it. In many cases, the culturally different client may be overly dependent upon the White therapist because of his/her identification with White culture. Attempts to please, appease, and seek approval from the helping professional may be quite strong.

Second, most conformity individuals will find attempts to explore cultural identity or to focus in upon feelings very threatening. Clients in this stage generally prefer a task-oriented, problem-solving approach. That is because an exploration of identity may eventually touch upon feelings of low self-esteem, dissatisfaction with personal appearance, vague anxieties, and racial self-hatred, and thus challenge the client's self-deception that he/she is not like the other members of his/her own race. In our earlier case study, for example, when John felt threatened by the idea that Mary might not want a permanent relationship, he used the counselor as a scapegoat for his feelings of anger toward Mary. To recognize that he is really angry at Mary means a breakdown in his denial system and the need to confront his feelings of racial self-hatred, along with the realization that *he is a Black person!*

Whether you are a White or minority counselor working with a conformity individual, the general goal may be the same. There is an obligation to help the client *sort out* conflicts related to racial/cultural identity through some process of reeducation. Somewhere in the process of counseling/therapy, issues of cultural racism, majority-minority group relations, racial self-hatred, and racial cultural identity need to be dealt with in an integrated fashion. We are not suggesting a lecture or a solely cognitive approach to which clients at this stage may be quite intellectually receptive, but exercising good clinical skills that take into account the client's socioemotional state and readiness to deal with feelings. Only in this manner will the client be able to distinguish the difference between positive attempts to adopt certain values of the dominant society and a negative rejection of one's own cultural values (a characteristic of the integrative awareness stage).

While the goals for the White and minority therapist are the same, the way a therapist works toward them may be different. In the case of the minority therapist, he/she is likely to have to deal with hostility from the culturally similar client. The therapist may symbolize all that the client is trying to reject. Because therapy stresses the building of a coalition, establishment of rapport, and to some degree a mutual identification, the process may be especially threatening. The opposite may be true of work with a White therapist. The culturally different client may be overeager to identify with the White professional in order to seek approval. However, rather than being detrimental to multicultural therapy, these two processes may be used quite effectively and productively. If the minority therapist can aid the client in working through his/her feelings of antagonism, and if the majority therapist can aid the client in working through his/her need to overidentify, then the client will be moved closer to awareness rather than self-deception. In the former case, the therapist can take a nonjudgmental stance toward the client and provide a positive minority role model. In the latter, the White therapist needs to model positive attitudes toward cultural diversity. Both need to guard against unknowingly reinforcing the client's self-denial and rejection.

DISSONANCE STAGE: THERAPEUTIC IMPLICATIONS

As individuals begin to become more aware of inconsistencies between dominant-held views and those of their group, a sense of dissonance develops. Preoccupation with and questions concerning self, identity, and self-esteem are most likely to be brought in for therapy. More culturally aware than their conformity counterparts, dissonance clients may prefer a counselor or therapist who possesses good knowledge of the client's cultural group, although there may still be a preference for a White helper. However, the fact that minority helping professionals are generally more knowledgeable of the client's cultural group may serve to heighten the conflicting beliefs and feelings of this stage. Since the client is so receptive toward self-exploration, the therapist can capitalize upon this orientation in helping the client come to grips with his/her identity conflicts.

RESISTANCE AND IMMERSION STAGE: COUNSELING IMPLICATIONS

Minority clients at this stage are likely to view their psychological problems as products of oppression and racism. They may believe that only issues of racism are legitimate areas to explore in therapy. Furthermore, openness or self-disclosure to therapists outside one's own group is considered dangerous because White therapists are "enemies" and members of the oppressing group.

Resistance-and-immersion-stage clients believe society is to blame for their present dilemma and actively challenge the Establishment. They are openly suspicious of institutions, such as mental health services, because they view them as agents of the Establishment. Because they identify mental health services with the status quo, very few of the more ethnically conscious and militant minorities will use them. When they do, they are usually suspicious and hostile toward the helping professional. Before therapy can proceed effectively, the therapist will have to deal with certain challenges from these clients, such as the following:

LATINO/HISPANIC CLIENT: First of all, I don't believe in therapy. I think it's a lot of bullshit. You [therapists] are always trying to adjust people to a sick society, and what is needed is to overthrow these damned oppressive institutions. I feel the same way about those stupid tests you want me to take. Cultural bias—they aren't applicable to minorities. The only reason I came in here was—well, I heard your lecture in Psychology 160, and I think I can work with you.

The male client in this case happened to be hostile and depressed over the recent death of his father. Although he realized he had some need for help, he still did not trust the counseling process.

CLIENT: Psychologists see the problem inside of people when the problem is in society. Don't you think White society has made all minorities feel inferior and degraded?
COUNSELOR: Yes, your observations appear correct. White society has done great harm to minorities.

The client was obviously posing a direct challenge to the counselor. Any defense of White society or explanations of the value of counseling might have aroused greater hostility and mistrust. It would have been extremely difficult to establish rapport without some honest agreement on the racist nature of American society. Later, the counselee revealed that his father had just died. He was beginning to realize that there was no contradiction in viewing society as being racist and in having personal problems. Often, growing pride in self-identity in the extreme makes it difficult for clients who are having emotional problems to accept their personal difficulties.

A therapist working with a client at this stage of development needs to realize several important things. First, he or she will be viewed by the culturally different client as a *symbol* of the oppressive society. If you become defensive and *personalize* the attacks, you will lose your effectiveness in working with the client. It is important to not be intimidated or afraid of the anger that is likely to be expressed; oftentimes, it is not personal and is quite legitimate. White guilt and defensiveness can only serve to hinder effective multicultural therapy. We will have more to say about this in the next chapter. It is not unusual for clients at this stage to make sweeping negative generalizations about White Americans. The White therapist who takes a nondefensive posture will be better able to help the client explore the basis of his/her racial tirades. In general, clients at this stage prefer a therapist of their own race. However, the fact that you share the same race or culture as your client will not insulate you from the attacks. For example, an African American client may perceive the Black counselor as a sellout of his/her own race or as an Uncle Tom. Indeed, the anger and hostility directed at the minority therapist may be even more intense than that directed at a White one.

Second, realize that clients in this stage will constantly test you. In earlier chapters, we described how minority clients will pose challenges to therapists in order to test their sincerity, openness, nondefensiveness, and competence. Because of the active nature of client challenges, therapy sessions may become quite dynamic. Many therapists find this stage the most difficult to deal with because counselor self-disclosure is often a necessary requirement to establish credibility.

Third, individuals at this stage are especially receptive to approaches that are more action oriented and aimed at external change (challenging racism). Also, group approaches with persons experiencing similar racial/cultural issues are well received. It is important that the therapist be willing to help the culturally different client explore new ways of relating to both minority and White persons.

INTROSPECTION STAGE: THERAPEUTIC IMPLICATIONS

Clients at the introspection stage may continue to prefer a therapist of their own race, but they are also receptive to help from therapists of other cultures as long as they understand their worldview. Ironically, clients at this stage may, on the surface, appear similar to conformity persons. Introspection clients are in conflict between their need to identify with the minority group and their need to exercise greater personal freedom. Exercising personal autonomy may occasionally mean going against the wishes or desires of the minority group. This is often perceived by minority persons and their group as a rejection of their own cultural heritage. This is not unlike conformity persons, who also reject their racial/cultural heritage. The dynamics of the two groups, however, are quite different. It is very important for therapists to distinguish the differences. The conformity person moves away from his/her own group because of perceived negative qualities associated with it. The introspection person desires to move away on certain issues, but perceives his/her group positively. Again, self-exploration approaches aimed at helping the client integrate and incorporate a new sense of identity are important. Believing in the functional values of U.S. society does not mean selling out or that you are against your own group.

INTEGRATIVE AWARENESS STAGE: THERAPEUTIC IMPLICATIONS

Clients at this stage have acquired an inner sense of security as to self-identity. They have pride in their racial/cultural heritage yet can exercise a desired level of personal freedom and autonomy. Other cultures and races are appreciated, and there is a development toward becoming more multicultural in perspective. While discrimination and oppression remain a powerful part of their existence, integrative awareness persons possess greater psychological resources to deal with these problems. Being action or systems oriented, clients respond positively to the designing and implementation of strategies aimed at community and society change. Preferences for therapists are not based on race, but on being able to share, understand, and accept their worldviews. In other words, attitudinal similarity between therapist and client is a more important dimension than membership group similarity.

CAUTIONS AND LIMITATIONS IN THE FORMULATION OF RACIAL AND CULTURAL IDENTITY MODELS

In proposing the R/CID model, we have been very aware of some major cautions and possible limitations that readers need to take into account. First, the R/CID model should not be viewed as a global personality theory with specific identifiable stages that serve as fixed categories. While the original Black identity models seemed to imply such a reality by using the term *stages,* Helms (1994a, 1995) has reconceptualized them as *ego-statuses.* Cultural identity development is a dynamic process, not a static one. One of the major dangers that therapists can fall into is to use these stages as fixed entities. In actuality, this should serve as a conceptual framework to help us understand development (Constantine, Richardson, Benjamin & Wilson, 1998). Most culturally different clients may evidence a dominant characteristic, but there are mixtures of the various stages as well. Furthermore, situations and the types of presenting problems may make some characteristics more manifest than others. It is possible that culturally different clients may evidence conformity characteristics in some situations, but resistance and immersion characteristics in others. A question often raised in the formulation of cultural identity development models is whether identity is a linear process. Is it possible for individuals not to begin at one of these stages, or to skip a stage altogether? In general, our clinical experience has been that minority and majority individuals in this society do tend to move at some gross level through each of the identifiable stages. Some tend to move faster than others; some tend to stay predominantly at only one stage; some may regress. This, however, is a question that needs to be tested empirically through research (Constantine et al., 1998; Fisher, Tokar, & Serna, 1998). Parham (1989), for example, has proposed a nigrescence identity model characterized by complex loops to the various stages.

Second, it has become increasingly clear that almost all cultural identity development models begin at a point that involves interaction with an oppressive society. Most of these are weak in formulating a stage prior to conformity characteristics. Recent Asian immigrants to the United States are a prime example of the inadequacy of cultural identity development models.

Many Asian immigrants to the United States tend to hold very positive and favorable views of their own culture and possess an intact racial/cultural identity already. What happens when they encounter a society that views cultural differences as being deviant? Will they or their offspring move through the conformity stage as presented in this model? Again, this is an empirical question.

Third, there is an implied value judgment given in almost all development models. It is clear that all cultural identity development models assume that some cultural resolutions are healthier than others. For example, the R/CID model does believe that the integrative awareness stage represents a higher form of healthy functioning.

Fourth, we need to take into consideration sociocultural forces that affect identity development. Many of the early Black identity development models arose as a result of perceived and real experiences of oppression in our society. The Third World movement (Black power movement, Yellow power movement, Red power movement, and Brown power movement) occurred in a period of our society that heightened racial/cultural pride and awareness. In other words, identity transformations are seen as being triggered by social movements that have powerful effects on the culturally different individual's identity. Does this mean that if social situations change, many of the cultural identity development models would also change? There is a need for exploration and investigation of how interpersonal, institutional, societal, and cultural factors may either facilitate or impede cultural identity development.

Fifth, there is a strong need to understand and refine these models. The roles that class, age, gender, and so forth may play have not been addressed adequately in these models (Constantine et al., 1998). Furthermore, we have talked about identity in a very global manner. A great deal of evidence is mounting that while identity may sequentially move through identifiable stages, affective, attitudinal, cognitive, and behavioral components of identity may not move in a uniform manner. For example, it is entirely possible that the emotions and affective elements associated with certain stages do not have a corresponding one-to-one behavioral impact.

Last, we need to begin looking more closely at the possible therapist and client stage combinations. As mentioned earlier, therapeutic processes and outcomes are often the function of the identity stage of both therapist and client. White identity development (WID) of the therapist can either enhance or retard effective therapy. As yet, the complexity of WID in therapy is in its infancy. We address White Racial Identity Development in the next chapter.

Chapter Seven

⸻ ◆ ⸻

White Racial Identity Development:
Therapeutic Implications

⸻ ◆ ⸻

Miriam Cohen, a young, single, attractive White therapist, had recently graduated from a prestigious Eastern university with a degree in Counseling Psychology. Because of her expressed desire to work with the "disadvantaged," she accepted a position as a psychologist in a community mental health center, whose catchment area included a heavy concentration of African American clients. Some of her White friends had suggested that she accept one of numerous other positions she had been offered. Dr. Cohen decided against going elsewhere, because "these people need help." Her professors commended her public service interest and "social justice" commitment.

Within a period of several weeks, Dr. Cohen had two rather disturbing experiences in working with African American clients. The first involved a Black couple who had come in because of marital difficulties. She found it extremely difficult to establish rapport with them and to get them to open up about their problems. They seemed to view her with suspicion and implied that she could not possibly understand them since she was White. During one session, the husband mentioned that he played in a local jazz band, which took him away from home frequently. His wife did not like his being away at night, and she was fearful that he was fooling around with a female member of the band.

Since Dr. Cohen's undergraduate major had been dramatic arts (she had even had a course on contributions of Black entertainers), she saw this as a good opportunity to establish a sense of commonality between herself and her Black clients. She directed the conversation toward African American movie stars, singers, and athletes. At this juncture, the wife became noticeably agitated and stated, "Stop that shit, honey! You're not Black and you never will be."

Dr. Cohen was surprised at the wife's reaction and apologized to the couple for offending them. She tried to explain that she was just trying to establish a working relationship with them and that she was not unfamiliar with minority experiences. "After all, I'm a Jew, and I know what oppression is. I'm also a woman, like you, and have experienced sex discrimination as well." At this point, the couple rose from their seats, stated that they were wasting time, and left the room.

The second incident occurred with a young African American male client who had been ordered by the court to undergo therapy for "wife beating." He was a handsome, muscular individual who obviously prided himself on his physical appearance. He had been divorced from his wife for nearly a year and had consistently denied that he physically abused her. He stated that he had pleaded guilty and accepted probation and counseling because "those Whites will give me a bum rap if it goes to trial." He had been married to a White woman who he claimed had "used him," and who he had discovered was a racist.

"All of you Whites are racist. What do you care about me?" At these statements Dr. Cohen tried to assure the client that she did care about Black people and that she wouldn't be here unless she cared. The anger and agitation seemed to drain from the client when this was said, and he seemed to open up more fully.

He talked about his boyhood experiences of discrimination, how he had been hurt by his ex-wife, how he couldn't find a good job because of racism, and how he felt so lonely and isolated. "Sometimes I feel like I'm worthless, that no one cares about me. What woman would want an unemployed Black man?" Again, Dr. Cohen reassured the client that everyone was worthwhile, and that he was no different.

Looking up at Dr. Cohen, the Black client asked, "Do you really mean that?" Dr. Cohen responded in the affirmative. This was followed by a series of other questions, "Do you think women would find me attractive? Do you find me attractive?"

While Dr. Cohen answered all of these questions honestly, she felt very uncomfortable at this point. She was totally unprepared for what happened next. The client moved his chair next to her, placed his right hand on her knee and asked, "Do you really like me?" Dr. Cohen recalls that she felt frozen and trapped. She did not answer the question, but firmly removed the hand from her knee and shifted her chair away. At these actions, the following exchange took place.

CLIENT: You Whites are all the same, say one thing, mean another! You're just another racist bitch!

DR. COHEN: I'm not racist. This is a therapy relationship. . . .

CLIENT: You think I'm hitting on you. Well, maybe I am, what's wrong with a man liking a woman? I'm not against interracial relationships, but you seem to be!

DR. COHEN: There's nothing wrong with it, but our relationship is strictly professional. . . . [stammering] I, I, mean . . . I mean, it would not be therapeutic.

CLIENT [Lowering voice]: You mean if we didn't have a doctor-patient relationship you would consider going out with a Black man?

DR. COHEN: Yes, well . . . ah [stammering] . . . ah . . . maybe.

CLIENT: Well, then, I'd like to request seeing another therapist. That way our therapy relationship won't get in the way!

Many important therapeutic issues can be distilled from the preceding vignette and would prove profitable for us to explore. For example, some questions which may be asked are the following:

1. Why did Dr. Cohen's attempt to relate to the African American couple fail? Why did her mention of Black entertainers anger the couple?

2. Doesn't Dr. Cohen have a valid point that Jews and women are also oppressed groups? Shouldn't this allow us to understand and relate to one another in a more meaningful fashion? Why did it seem to have the opposite effect? Dr. Cohen's emphasis on her being a "woman" and "Jew" did not seem to validate the couple's Black experience. Rather, it seemed to negate it. Why and how?

3. Dr. Cohen seemed easily manipulated by the African American male client. While the client was obviously attempting to seduce the therapist and probably treated most women in a sexually objectified manner, a strong case can be made that Dr. Cohen contributed to the problem. For example, the "prove to me that you're not a racist" game instigated by the Black client seemed to tap into an especially vulnerable aspect of the therapist. Can you discern what that might have been?

4. African American clients are often suspicious of the motives of White helping professionals. What motives were behind Dr. Cohen's desire to work with minority clients? In what way did it interfere with the therapist's ability to work effectively with the client? How would you have worked through the suspicions in both cases?

While the first two questions are very important areas to explore (we encourage you to do so), it is the last two concerning Dr. Cohen's image of her White identity that are central to this chapter. Our analysis of the case and similar ones leads us to the inevitable conclusion that part of the problem for the lack of therapeutic effectiveness lies not only with the client, but with the therapist as well. This problem is invisible to many of our White colleagues and can be exemplified in the question "What does it mean to be White?" Let us use this question as a guide to understanding the above vignette.

First, it is clear that Dr. Cohen's image of herself is that of an unbiased individual who does not harbor racist thoughts and feelings; she perceives herself as working toward social justice and possesses a conscious desire to better the life circumstances of those less fortunate than herself. As evidence of her commitment, she chose employment linked to a heavy concentration of racial/ethnic minority clients. These are certainly admirable qualities and, on the surface, are quite commendable. Yet, Dr. Cohen seems to evidence a naiveté that we have observed in many White Euro-American helping professionals. White liberalism is often motivated by "White guilt" and compounded by a lack of self-understanding (Ponterotto & Pedersen, 1993; Ridley, 1995). Dr. Cohen seems wrapped up in her White liberalism, so much so that she fails to understand the almost paternalistic manner in which she wanted to "help these people." We question whether she really is free of personal biases and prejudices and how much she really understands her own motives and values.

Second, being a White person in this society means chronic exposure to ethnocentric monoculturalism as manifested in "White supremacy" (D.W. Sue et al., 1998). It is difficult, if not impossible, for anyone not to inherit the racial biases, prejudices, misinformation, deficit portrayals, and stereotypes of their forebears. To believe that we are somehow immune from inheriting such aspects of White supremacy is to be arrogant, naive, or self-deceived. Such a statement is not intended to assail Dr. Cohen's integrity, but to suggest that she too has been victimized. It is clear to us that no one was born wanting to be racist, sexist, or homophobic. Misinformation is not acquired by our free choice, but is imposed on us through a process of cultural conditioning. While Dr. Cohen is not consciously aware of her own biases and pre-conceived notions regarding African Americans, they are definitely impacting her ability to be therapeutically effective with African American clients. Her decision in working with minority clients, her misguided attempts to form rapport via reference to Black entertainers, and her inability to deal with the "prove to me you're not a racist" game all seem to support a "reaction formation"; an attempt to unconsciously deny aspects of her potential biases. She is so involved in living out her unbiased image of herself that she allows her hang-ups to affect the sessions. The fear that Dr. Cohen suffers from is to be called or be seen as a racist. At a deeper level, however, may be her fear of realizing that she is, indeed, a racist!

". . . the development of White identity in the United States is closely intertwined with the development and progress of racism in this country. The greater the extent that racism exists and is denied, the less possible it is to develop a positive White identity." (Carter, 1995, p. 39)

Third, if Dr. Cohen or White helping professionals are ever able to become effective MCT therapists, they must free themselves from the cultural conditioning of their past and move toward the development of a nonracist White identity. Unfortunately, many White Euro-Americans seldom consider what it means to be "White" in our society. Such a question is vexing to them because they seldom think of race as belonging to them, or of the privileges that come their way by virtue of their white skin. Katz (1985) points out a major barrier blocking the process of White Euro-Americans investigating their own cultural identity and worldview:

Because White culture is the dominant cultural norm in the United States, it acts as an invisible veil that limits many people from seeing it as a cultural system. . . . Often, it is easier for many Whites to identify and acknowledge the different cultures of minorities than accept their own racial identity. . . . The difficulty of accepting such a view is that White culture is omnipresent. It is so interwoven in the fabric of everyday living that Whites cannot step outside and see their beliefs, values, and behaviors as creating a distinct cultural group. (pp. 616–617)

Ridley (1995) asserts that this invisible veil can be manifested in therapy unintentionally with harmful consequences to minority clients:

Unintentional behavior is perhaps the most insidious form of racism. Unintentional racists are unaware of the harmful consequences of their behavior. They may be well-intentioned, and on the surface, their behavior may appear to be responsible. Because individuals, groups, or institutions that engage in unintentional racism do not wish to do harm, it is difficult to get them to see themselves as racists. They are more likely to deny their racism. (p. 38)

We do not want to appear harsh or accusatory, but Dr. Cohen may be an unintentional racist: (a) She is unaware of her biases, prejudices, and discriminatory behaviors; (b) she perceives herself as a moral, good, and decent human being and finds it difficult to ever see herself as racist; (c) she does not have a sense of what her Whiteness means to her; and (d) her therapeutic behavior with culturally different clients is likely to be more harmful (unintentionally) than helpful. These conclusions are often difficult for White helping professionals to accept, because of the defensiveness and feelings of blame that they are likely to engender. Yet, we ask that White therapists and students not be "turned off" to the message and lessons of this chapter.

We ask you to continue your multicultural journey as we explore the question: "What does it mean to be White?"

MODELS OF WHITE RACIAL IDENTITY DEVELOPMENT

Recently, a number of multicultural experts in the field have begun to emphasize the need for White therapists to deal with their concepts of Whiteness and to examine their own racism (Carter, 1995; Corvin & Wiggins, 1989; Helms, 1984, 1990; Ponterotto, 1988; D.W. Sue et al., 1998). These specialists point out that while racial/cultural identity development for minority groups proves beneficial in our work as therapists, more attention has to be devoted to the White therapist's racial identity. Since the majority of therapists and trainees are White middle-class individuals, it would appear that White identity development and its implication for multicultural therapy would be important aspects to consider, both in the actual practice of clinical work and in professional training.

For example, it has been found that the level of White racial identity awareness was predictive of racism: (a) The less aware subjects were of their White identity, the more likely they were to exhibit increased levels of racism, and (b) women were less likely to be racist (Carter, 1990; Pope-Davis & Ottavi, 1994). It was suggested that this last finding was correlated with women's greater experiences with discrimination and prejudice. Evidence also exists that multicultural counseling/therapy competence is correlated with White racial identity attitudes (Ottavi, Pope-Davis, & Dings, 1994). Other research suggests that a relationship exists between a White Euro-American therapist's racial identity and his/her readiness for training in multicultural awareness, knowledge, and skills (Carney & Kahn, 1984; Helms, 1990; Ponterotto, 1988; Sabnani, Ponterotto, & Borodovsky, 1991; D.W. Sue & D. Sue, 1990). Since developing multicultural sensitivity is a long-term developmental task, the work of many researchers has gradually converged toward a conceptualization of the stages/levels/statuses of consciousness of racial/ethnic identity development for White Euro-Americans (Bennett, 1986; Smith, 1991). A number of these models describe the salience of identity for establishing relationships between the White therapist and culturally different client, and some have now linked stages of identity with stages for appropriate training (Bennett, 1986; Carney & Kahn, 1984; Sabnani, Ponterotto, & Borodovsky, 1991).

THE HARDIMAN WHITE RACIAL IDENTITY DEVELOPMENT MODEL

One of the earliest integrative attempts at formulating a White racial identity development model is that of Rita Hardiman (1982). Intrigued with why certain White individuals exhibit a much more nonracist identity than others, Hardiman studied the autobiographies of individuals who had attained a high level of racial consciousness. This led her to identify five White developmental stages: naiveté—lack of social consciousness, acceptance, resistance, redefinition, and internalization.

1. The *naiveté* stage (lack of social consciousness) is characteristic of early childhood when we are born into this world innocent, open, unaware of racism and the importance of race. Curiosity and spontaneity in relating to race and racial differences tend to be the norm. A young

White child who has almost no personal contact with African Americans, for example, may see a Black man in a supermarket and loudly comment on the darkness of his skin. Other than the embarrassment and apprehensions of adults around the child, there is little discomfort associated with this behavior for the youngster. In general, awareness of the meaning of race, racial differences, bias, and prejudice are either absent or minimal. Such an orientation becomes less characteristic of the child as the socialization process progresses. The negative reactions of parents, relatives, friends, and peers toward issues of race begin to convey mixed signals to the child. This is reinforced by the educational system and mass media that instill racial biases in the child and propel him or her into the acceptance stage.

2. The *acceptance* stage is marked by a conscious belief in the democratic ideal; that everyone has an equal opportunity to succeed in a free society and those who fail must bear the responsibility for their failure. White Euro-Americans become the social reference group, and the socialization process consistently instills messages of White superiority and minority inferiority into the child. The underemployment, unemployment, and undereducation of marginalized groups in our society are seen as support that non-White groups are inferior to Whites. Because everyone has an equal opportunity to succeed, the lack of success of minority groups is seen as evidence of some negative personal or group characteristic (low intelligence, inadequate motivation, or biological/cultural deficits). Victim blaming is strong as the existence of oppression and discrimination, and racism is denied. Hardiman believes that while the naiveté stage is brief in duration, the acceptance stage can last a lifetime.

3. Over time, assumptions of White superiority and the denial of racism and discrimination begin to be challenged. Moving from the acceptance to the *resistance* stage can prove to be a painful, conflicting, and uncomfortable transition. The denial system of the White person begins to crumble because of a monumental event or a series of events that not only challenge but shatter the denial system of the individual. A White person may, for example, make friends with a minority coworker and discover that the images he or she has of "these people" are untrue. They may have witnessed clear incidents of unfair discrimination toward persons of color and begin to question assumptions regarding racial inferiority. In any case, the racial realities of life in the United States can no longer be denied. The change from one stage to another might take considerable time, but once completed, the person becomes conscious of being White, is aware that he/she harbors racist attitudes, and begins to see the pervasiveness of oppression in our society. Feelings of anger, pain, hurt, rage, and frustration are present. In many cases, the White person may develop a negative reaction toward his/her own group or culture. While they may romanticize people of color, they cannot interact confidently with them because they fear making racist mistakes. This discomfort is best exemplified in a passage by Sara Winter (1977):

We avoid Black people because their presence brings painful questions to mind. Is it OK to talk about watermelons or mention black coffee? Should we use Black slang and tell racial jokes? How about talking about our experiences in Harlem, or mentioning our Black lovers? Should we conceal the fact that our mother still employs a Black cleaning lady? . . . We're embarrassedly aware of trying to do our best but to "act natural" at the same time. No wonder we're more comfortable in all-White situations where these dilemmas don't arise. (p. 1)

According to Hardiman (1982), the discomfort in realizing that one is White and that one's group has engaged in oppression of racial/ethnic minorities may propel the person into the next stage.

4. Asking the painful question of who one is in relation to one's racial heritage; honestly confronting one's biases and prejudices; and accepting responsibility for one's Whiteness is the culminating mark of the *redefinition* stage. New ways of defining one's social group and membership in that group become important. The intense soul searching is most evident in Sara Winter's personal journey as she writes:

In this sense we Whites are the victims of racism. Our victimization is different from that of Blacks, but it is real. We have been programmed into the oppressor roles we play, without our informed consent in the process. Our unawareness is part of the programming: None of us could tolerate the oppressor position, if we lived with a day-to-day emotional awareness of the pain inflicted on other humans through the instrument of our behavior. . . . We Whites benefit in concrete ways, year in and year out, from the present racial arrangements. All my life in White neighborhoods, White schools, White jobs and dealing with White police (to name only a few), I have experienced advantages that are systematically not available to Black people. It does not make sense for me to blame myself for the advantages that have come my way by virtue of my Whiteness. But absolving myself from guilt does not imply forgetting about racial injustice or taking it lightly (as my guilt pushes me to do). (1977, p. 2)

There is realization that Whiteness has been defined in opposition to people of color by standards of White supremacy. By being able to step out of this racist paradigm and redefining what her Whiteness means to her, Sara Winter is able to add meaning to developing a nonracist identity. The extremes of good/bad or positive/negative attachments to "White" and "people of color" begin to become more realistic. The person no longer denies being White, honestly confronts his/her racism, understands the concept of White privilege, and feels increased comfort in relating to persons of color.

5. The *internalization* stage is the result of forming a new social and personal identity. With the greater comfort in understanding oneself and the development of a nonracist White identity come a commitment to social action as well. The individual accepts responsibility for effecting personal and social change without always relying on persons of color to lead the way.

To end racism, Whites have to pay attention to it and continue to pay attention. Since avoidance is such a basic dynamic of racism, paying attention will not happen naturally. We Whites must learn how to hold racism realities in our attention. We must learn to take responsibility for this process ourselves, without waiting for Blacks' actions to remind us that the problem exists, and without depending on Black people to reassure us and forgive us for our racist sins. In my experience, the process is painful but it is a relief to shed the fears, stereotypes, immobilizing guilt we didn't want in the first place. (Winter, 1977, p. 2)

The racist-free identity, however, must be nurtured, validated and supported in order to be sustained in a hostile environment. Such an individual is constantly bombarded by attempts to be resocialized into the oppressive society.

There are several potential limitations to the Hardiman model: (a) The select and limited sample which she uses to derive the stages and enumerate the characteristics makes potential generalization suspect; (b) the autobiographies of White Americans are not truly representative, and their experiences with racism may be bound by the historical era; (c) the stages are tied to existing social identity development theories and the model proposes a naiveté stage which for all practical purposes exists only in children ages 3–4 (it appears tangential in her model and might better be conceptualized as part of the acceptance stage of socialization); and (d) to date, no exploration of the model using direct empirical or other postmodern methods has occurred. Despite these cautions and potential limitations, Hardiman (1982) has contributed greatly to our understanding of White identity development by focusing attention on racism as a central force in the socialization of White Americans.

THE HELMS WHITE RACIAL IDENTITY MODEL

Janet Helms's White racial identity model (WRID) (Helms, 1984, 1990, 1994b, 1995), developed independently of Hardiman's, is perhaps the most elaborate and sophisticated of those proposed. Helms is arguably the most influential White identity development theorist. Her work has not only led to the development of an assessment instrument to measure White racial identity; it has also been scrutinized empirically (Helms & Carter, 1990) and has generated much research and debate in the psychological literature. Like Hardiman (1982), Helms assumes that racism is an intimate and central part of being a White American. To her, developing a healthy White identity requires movement through two phases: Phase I—Abandonment of Racism, and Phase II—Defining a Nonracist White Identity. There are six specific racial identity statuses equally distributed between the two: *contact, disintegration, reintegration;* and *pseudo-independence, immersion/emersion,* and *autonomy.* Originally, Helms used the term "stages" to refer to the six, but due to certain conceptual ambiguities and the controversy that ensued, she has abandoned that usage.

1. *Contact status.* People in this status are oblivious to and unaware of racism, believe that everyone has an equal chance for success, lack an understanding of prejudice and discrimination, have minimal experiences with persons of color, and may profess to be color-blind. Such statements as "people are people," "I don't notice a person's race at all," and "you don't act Black" exemplify this status. While there is an attempt to minimize the importance or influence of race, there is a definite dichotomy of Blacks and Whites on both a conscious and unconscious level regarding stereotypes and the superior/inferior dimensions of the races. Because of obliviousness and compartmentalization, it is possible for two diametrically opposed belief systems to coexist: (a) uncritical acceptance of White supremist notions that relegate minorities to the inferior category with all the racial stereotypes, and (b) the belief that racial and cultural differences are unimportant. This allows Whites to avoid perceiving themselves as "dominant" group members, or as having biases and prejudices. Such an orientation is aptly described by Peggy McIntosh (1989) in her own White racial awakening:

   My schooling gave me no training in seeing myself as an oppressor, as an unfairly advantaged person, or as a participant in a damaged culture. I was taught to see myself as an individual whose moral state depended on her individual moral will. . . . Whites are taught to think of their lives as morally neutral, normative, and average, and also ideal, so that when we work to benefit others, this is seen as work which will allow "them" to be more like "us." (p. 8)

2. *Disintegration status.* While in the previous status the individual does not recognize the polarities of democratic principles of equality and the unequal treatment of minority groups, such obliviousness may eventually break down. The White person becomes conflicted over unresolvable racial moral dilemmas that are frequently perceived as polar opposites: believing one is nonracist, yet not wanting one's son or daughter to marry a minority group member; believing that "all men are created equal" while perceiving that society treats

Blacks as second-class citizens; and not acknowledging that oppression exists while witnessing it (as in the beating of Rodney King). Conflicts between loyalty to one's group and those of "humanistic ideals" may manifest itself in various ways. The person becomes increasingly conscious of his/her Whiteness and may experience dissonance and conflict resulting in feelings of guilt, depression, helplessness, or anxiety. Statements such as "My grandfather is really prejudiced, but I try not to be" and "I'm personally not against interracial marriages, but I worry about the children" are representative of personal struggles occurring in the White person. This type of conflict is best exemplified in the following passage from Sara Winter (1977):

When someone pushes racism into my awareness, I feel guilty (that I could be doing so much more); angry (I don't like to feel like I'm wrong); defensive (I already have two Black friends . . . I worry more about racism than most whites do—isn't that enough): turned off (I have other priorities in my life with guilt about that thought): helpless (the problem is so big—what can I do?). I HATE TO FEEL THIS WAY. That is why I minimize race issues and let them fade from my awareness whenever possible." (p. 24)

While a healthy resolution might be to realistically confront the "myth of meritocracy," the breakdown of the denial system is painful and anxiety provoking. Attempts at resolution, according to Helms, may involve (a) avoiding contact with persons of color, (b) not thinking about race, and (c) seeking reassurance from others that racism is not the fault of Whites.

3. *Reintegration status.* This status can best be characterized as a regression where the pendulum swings back to the most basic beliefs of White superiority and minority inferiority. In their attempts to resolve the dissonance created from the previous process, there is a retreat to the dominant ideology associated with race and one's own socioracial group identity. This ego status results in idealizing the White Euro-American group and the positives of White culture and society; there is a consequent negation and intolerance of other minority groups. In general, a firmer and more conscious belief in White racial superiority is present. Racial/ethnic minorities are blamed for their own problems.

"I'm an Italian grandmother. No one gave us welfare or a helping hand when we came over [immigrated]. My father worked day and night to provide us with a decent living and to put all of us through school. These negros are always complaining about prejudice and hardships. Big deal! Why don't they stop whining and find a job? They're not the only ones who were discriminated against, you know. You don't think our family wasn't? We never let that stop us. In America everyone can make it if they are willing to work hard. I see these Black welfare mothers waiting in line for food stamps and free handouts. You can't convince me they're starving. Look at how overweight most of them are . . . laziness . . . that's what I see."

4. *Pseudo-independence status.* This status represents the second phase of Helms's White racial identity process, which involves defining a nonracist White identity. As in the Hardiman model, a person is likely to be propelled into this phase by a painful or insightful encounter or event that jars the person from the reintegration status. The awareness of other visible racial/ethnic minorities, the unfairness of their treatment, and a discomfort with the racist White identity may lead a person to identify with the plight of persons of color. There is an attempt to understand racial, cultural, and sexual orientation differences and a purposeful and conscious decision to interact with minority group members. However, the well-intentioned White person at this status may suffer from several problematic dynamics.

While intending to be socially conscious and helpful to minority groups, the White individual may unknowingly perpetuate racism by helping minorities adjust to the prevailing White standards. Also, the person's choice of minority individuals is based on how similar they are to him or her, and the primary mechanism used to understand racial issues is intellectual and conceptual. As a result, understanding does not reach the experiential and affective domains. In other words, understanding Euro-American White privilege, sociopolitical aspects of race, and issues of bias, prejudice, and discrimination tends to be mostly an intellectual exercise.

5. *Immersion/emersion status.* If the person is reinforced to continue a personal exploration of himself/herself as a racial being, questions become focused upon what it means to be White. Helms states that the person searches for an understanding of the personal meaning of racism and the ways by which one benefits from White privilege. There is an increasing willingness to truly confront one's own biases, to redefine Whiteness, and to become more activistic in directly combating racism and oppression. This status is different from the previous one in two major ways: (a) It is marked by a shift in focus from trying to change Blacks to changing the self and other Whites, and (b) it is marked by increasing experiential and affective understanding that were lacking in the previous status. This later process is extremely important. Indeed, Helms believes that a successful resolution of this status requires an emotional catharsis or release that forces the person to relive or reexperience previous emotions that were denied or distorted. The ability to achieve this affective/experiential upheaval leads to a euphoria or even a feeling of rebirth and is a necessary condition to developing a new nonracist White identity. Again, Sara Winter (1977) states:

> *Let me explain this healing process in more detail. We must unearth all the words and memories we generally try not to think about, but which are inside us all the time: "nigger," "Uncle Tom," "jungle bunny," "Oreo"; lynching, cattle prods, castrations, rapists, "black pussy," and black men with their huge penises, and hundreds more. (I shudder as I write.) We need to review three different kinds of material: (1) All our personal memories connected with blackness and black people including everything we can recall hearing or reading; (2) all the racist images and stereotypes we've ever heard, particularly the grossest and most hurtful ones; (3) any race related things we ourselves said, did or omitted doing which we feel bad about today. . . . Most whites begin with a good deal of amnesia. Eventually the memories crowd in, especially when several people pool recollections. Emotional release is a vital part of the process. Experiencing feelings seems to allow further recollections to come. I need persistent encouragement from my companions to continue. (p. 3)*

6. *Autonomy status.* Increasing awareness of one's own Whiteness, reduced feelings of guilt, acceptance of one's role in perpetuating racism, and renewed determination to abandon White entitlement leads to an autonomy status. The person is knowledgeable about racial, ethnic, and cultural differences, values the diversity, and is no longer fearful, intimidated, or uncomfortable with the experiential reality of race. Development of a nonracist White identity becomes increasingly strong. Indeed, the person feels comfortable with their nonracist White identity, does not personalize attacks on White supremacy, and can explore the issues of racism and personal responsibility without defensiveness. A person in this status "walks the talk" and actively values and seeks out interracial experiences. Characteristics of the autonomy status can be found in the personal journey of Kiselica (1998):

> *. . . I was deeply troubled as I witnessed on a daily basis the detrimental effects of institutional racism and oppression on ethnic-minority groups in this country. The latter encounters forced me to recognize my privileged position in our society because of my status as a so-called Anglo. It was upsetting to know that I, a member of White society, benefited from the hardships of others that were caused by a racist system. I was also disturbed by the painful realization that I was, in some ways, a racist. I had to come to grips with the fact that I had told and laughed at racist jokes and, through such behavior, had supported White racist attitudes. If I really wanted to become an effective, multicultural psychologist, extended and profound self-reckoning was in order. At times, I wanted to flee from this unpleasant process by merely participating superficially with the remaining tasks . . . while avoiding any substantive self-examination."* (pp. 10–11)

Helms's model is by far the most widely cited, researched, and applied of all the White racial identity formulations. Part of its attractiveness and value is the derivation of "defenses," "protective strategies" or what Helms (1995) formally labels "Information-Processing Strategies" (IPS) that White people use to avoid or assuage anxiety and discomfort around the issue of race. Each status has a dominant IPS associated with it: contact = obliviousness or denial; disintegration = suppression and ambivalence; reintegration = selective perception and negative out-group distortion; pseudo-independence = reshaping reality and selective perception; immersion/emersion = hypervigilance and reshaping; and autonomy = flexibility and complexity. Table 7.1 lists examples of IPS statements likely to be made by White people in each of the six ego statuses. Understanding these strategic reactions is important for White American identity development, both for understanding the barriers that must be overcome in order to move to another status, and for potentially developing effective training or clinical strategies.

The Helms model, however, is not without its detractors. In an article critical of Helms's model and of most *stage* models of White racial identity development, Rowe, Bennett, and Atkinson (1994) raised some serious objections. First, they claim Helms's model to be erroneously based on racial/ethnic minority identity development models (to be discussed in the next chapter). Because minority identity development occurs in the face of stereotyping and oppression, such models may be inapplicable to White identity, which does not occur under similar conditions. Second, they believe too much emphasis is placed upon the development of White attitudes toward minorities and not much upon the development of White attitudes toward themselves and their own identity. Third, they claim that there is a conceptual inaccuracy in putting forth the model as developmental via stages (linear) and that the progression from less to more healthy seems based upon the creator's ethics.

It is important to note that the critique of Helms' (1984) model has not been left unanswered. Thompson (1995) believes that these criticisms are based on a misrepresentation of Helms's writings and research; that she does emphasize White identity and minority identity development in different contexts; that the task of developing a positive White identity is central to the model; and that the model does meet criteria for a developmental theory that is not necessarily linear. In subsequent writings (1994, 1995), Helms has disclaimed the Rowe, Bennett, and Atkinson (1994) characterization of her model and has attempted to clarify her position.

The continuing debate has proven beneficial for two reasons. First, the Helms model has evolved and changed (whether because of these criticisms or not) so that it has become even more intricate and clear. For example, Helms disclaims ever being a *stage* theorist, but to pre-

Table 7.1 WHITE RACIAL IDENTITY EGO STATUSES AND
INFORMATION-PROCESSING STRATEGIES (IPS)

1. Contact Status: satisfaction with racial status quo, obliviousness to racism and one's participation in it. If racial factors influence life decisions, they do so in a simplistic fashion. IPS: Obliviousness.

Example: "I'm a White woman. When my grandfather came to this country, he was discriminated against, too. But he didn't blame Black people for his misfortunes. He educated himself and got a job: That's what Blacks ought to do. If White callers (to a radio station) spent as much time complaining about racial discrimination as your Black callers do, we'd never have accomplished what we have. You all should just ignore it."

2. Disintegration Status: disorientation and anxiety provoked by unresolvable racial moral dilemmas that force one to choose between own-group loyalty and humanism. May be stymied by life situations that arouse racial dilemmas. IPS: Suppression and ambivalence.

Example: "I myself tried to set a nonracist example (for other Whites) by speaking up when someone said something blatantly prejudiced—how to do this without alienating people so that they would no longer take me seriously was always tricky—and by my friendships with Mexicans and Blacks who were actually the people with whom I felt most comfortable" (Blauner, 1993, p. 8).

3. Reintegration Status: idealization of one's socioracial group, denigration and intolerance for other groups. Racial factors may strongly influence life decisions. IPS: Selective perception and negative out-group distortion.

Example: "So, what if my great-grandfather owned slaves. He didn't mistreat them and besides, I wasn't even here then. I never owned slaves. So, I don't know why Blacks expect me to feel guilty for something that happened before I was born. Nowadays, reverse racism hurts Whites more than slavery hurt Blacks. At least they got three square [meals] a day. But my brother can't even get a job with the police department because they have to hire less-qualified Blacks. That [expletive] happens to Whites all the time."

4. Pseudo-Independence Status: intellectualized commitment to one's own socioracial group and deceptive tolerance of other groups. May make life decisions to "help other racial groups." IPS: Reshaping reality and selective perception.

Example: "Was I the only person left in America who believed that the sexual mingling of the races was a good thing, that it would erase cultural barriers and leave us all a lovely shade of tan? . . . Racial blending is inevitable. At the very least, it may be the only solution to our dilemmas of race" (Allen, 1994, p. C4).

5. Immersion/Emersion Status: search for an understanding of the personal meaning of racism and the ways by which one benefits and a redefinition of whiteness. Life choices may incorporate racial activism. IPS: Hypervigilance and reshaping.

Example: "It's true that I personally did not participate in the horror of slavery, and I don't even know whether my ancestors owned slaves. But I know that because I am White, I continue to benefit from a racist system that stems from the slavery era. I believe that if White people are ever going to understand our role in perpetuating racism, then we must begin to ask ourselves some hard questions and be willing to consider our role in maintaining a hurtful system. Then, we must try to do something to change it."

6. Autonomy Status: informed positive socioracial group commitment, use of internal standards for self-definition, capacity to relinquish the privileges of racism. May avoid life options that require participation in racial oppression. IPS: Flexibility and complexity.

Example: "I live in an integrated (Black-White) neighborhood and I read Black literature and popular magazines. So, I understand that the media presents a very stereotypic view of Black culture. I believe that if more of us White people made more than a superficial effort to obtain accurate information about racial groups other than our own, then we could help make this country a better place for all peoples."

Taken from Helms (1995, p. 185).

Table 7.2 ROWE, BENNETT, AND ATKINSON MODEL OF WHITE
RACIAL CONSCIOUSNESS TYPES AND THEIR CHARACTERISTICS

I. UNACHIEVED
  A. Avoidant types ignore, avoid, deny, or minimize racial issues. They do not consider their own racial identity nor are they seemingly aware of minority issues.
  B. Dependent types have minimal racial attitudes developed through person experience or consideration. They most often follow the lead of significant others in their life, such as would a child with his/her parent.
  C. Dissonant types often feel conflict between their belief system and contradictory experiences. This type may break away from these attitudes depending upon the degree of support or the intensity of the conflict. As such, it is a transitory status for the person.

II. ACHIEVED
  A. Dominative types are very ethnocentric, believe in White superiority and minority inferiority. They may passively act out their biases or actively do so.
  B. Conflictive types oppose direct and obvious discrimination, but would be unwilling to change the status quo. Most feel that discrimination has been eliminated and further efforts constitute reverse racism.
  C. Reactive types have good awareness that racism exists but seem unaware of their personal responsibility in perpetuating it. They may overidentify with or be paternalistic toward minorities.
  D. Integrative types "have integrated their sense of Whiteness with a regard for racial/ethnic minorities . . . [and] integrate rational analysis, on the one hand, and moral principles, on the other, as they relate to a variety of racial/ethnic issues." (p. 141)

vent future confusion, she now prefers the term *status* and describes her thinking on this issue in detail (1995). Second, in responding to the Helms model, Rowe, Bennett, and Atkinson offer an alternative means of conceptualizing White identity that has contributed to the increasing understanding of WRID.

Briefly, Rowe, Bennett, and Atkinson (1994) prefer to conceptualize White racial identity as one of *types* or *statuses* rather than *stages.* They take care in explaining that these types are not fixed entities but are subject to experiential modification. They propose two major groupings with seven types of racial consciousness: unachieved (avoidant, dependent, and dissonant) and achieved (dominative, conflictive, reactive, and integrative). Movement from type to type is dependent on the creation of dissonance, personal attributes, and the subsequent environmental conditions encountered by the person. As a result, the primary gateway for change involves the dissonant type. Persons can move between all types except the two unachieved ones, avoidant and dependent. These latter two are characterized by lack of internalized attitudes. Space does not permit an extended discussion of the model. We have chosen to summarize these types and their characteristics in Table 7.2. A more detailed discussion of the model can be found in Rowe, Bennett, and Atkinson (1994).

THE PROCESS OF WHITE RACIAL IDENTITY DEVELOPMENT: A DESCRIPTIVE MODEL

Analysis of the models proposed by Hardiman and Helms and by Rowe, Bennett, and Atkinson reveals some important differences. First, the identity development models seem to focus on a more definite and sequential movement through stages or statuses. They differ, however, in where they place the particular stages or statuses in the developmental process. Given that almost all models now entertain the possibility that development can vary (looping and re-cycling), the Rowe, Bennett, and Atkinson (1994) consciousness development model allows greater latitude conceptually for movement to various types. It seems to offer a more fluid process of racial experience by White people. Because of this factor, it is also less bound by the context or historical era (identity formed during the Civil Rights movement vs. current times). The addition of nonachieved statuses is something missing in the development theories and may capture more closely the "passive" feeling that White people experience in their racial identity development.

Yet the essential concept of developing a positive White identity is conspicuously absent from the consciousness model. It lacks the richness in explaining or allowing White people to view their developmental history more analytically, to gain a sense of their past, present, and future. Struggling with racial identity and issues of race requires a historical perspective such as development theories offer. It is with this in mind that we have attempted to use aspects of White racial identity/consciousness development in formulating a descriptive model with prac-tice implications.

In our work with White trainees and clinicians, we have observed some very important changes that they seem to move through as they work toward multicultural competence. Like Hardiman (1982), Helms (1990), and Ponterotto (1988), we have been impressed with how Whites also seem to go through parallel racial/cultural identity transformations. This is espe-cially true if we accept that Whites are as much victims of societal forces (socialized into racist attitudes and beliefs) as their minority counterparts. No child is born wanting to be a racist! Yet White people do benefit from the dominant-subordinant relationship evident in our soci-ety. It is this factor that Whites need to confront in an open and honest manner.

Using the formulation of D.W. Sue and D. Sue (1990) and D.W. Sue et al. (1998), we propose a five-stage process whereby many of the characteristics from the other formulations are integrated. We furthermore make some basic assumptions with respect to those models: (a) Racism is an integral part of U.S. life and permeates all aspects of our culture and institu-tions (ethnocentric monoculturalism); (b) Whites are socialized into the society and therefore inherit all the biases, stereotypes, and racist attitudes, beliefs, and behaviors of the larger soci-ety; (c) how Whites perceive themselves as racial beings follows an identifiable sequence that can occur in a linear or nonlinear fashion; (d) the status of White racial identity development in any multicultural encounter affects the process and outcome of interracial relationships; and (e) the most desirable outcome is one in which the White person not only accepts his/her White-ness, but also defines it in a nondefensive and nonracist manner.

1. *Conformity phase.* The White person's attitudes and beliefs in this stage are very ethnocen-tric. There is minimal awareness of the self as a racial being and a strong belief in the uni-versality of values and norms governing behavior. The White person possesses limited accurate knowledge of other ethnic groups, but he/she is likely to rely on social stereotypes as the main source of information. As we saw, Hardiman (1982) describes this stage as an acceptance of White superiority and minority inferiority. Consciously or unconsciously, the White person believes that White culture is the most highly developed, and all others are primitive or inferior. The conformity stage is marked by contradictory and often compart-mentalized attitudes, beliefs, and behaviors. On the one hand a person may believe that he

or she is not racist, yet believe that minority inferiority justifies discriminatory and inferior treatment; that minority persons are different and deviant, yet believe that "people are people" and that differences are unimportant (Helms, 1984). As with their minority counterparts at this stage, the primary mechanism operating here is one of denial and compartmentalization. For example, many Whites deny that they belong to a race that allows them to avoid personal responsibility for perpetuating a racist system. Like a fish in water, White people have difficulty in seeing or are unable to see the invisible veil of cultural assumptions, biases, and prejudices that guide their perceptions and actions. They tend to believe that White Euro-American culture is superior and that other cultures are primitive, inferior, less developed, or lower on the scale of evolution. It is important to note that many Whites in this phase of development are unaware of these beliefs and operate as if they are universally shared. They believe that differences are unimportant and that "people are people," "we are all the same under the skin," "we should treat everyone the same," "problems wouldn't exist if minorities would only assimilate," and that discrimination and prejudice are something that others do. The helping professional with this perspective professes "color blindness" and views counseling/therapy theories as universally applicable and does not question their relevance to other culturally different groups.

Wrenn's (1962, 1985) reference to and description of the culturally encapsulated counselor exemplifies the characteristics of conformity. The primary mechanism used in encapsulation is denial; denial that people are different, denial that discrimination exists, and denial of one's own prejudices. Instead, the locus of the problem is seen to reside in the minority individual or group. Minorities wouldn't encounter problems if they would assimilate and acculturate (melting pot), if they would value education, or if they would only work harder.

2. *Dissonance phase.* Movement into the dissonance phase occurs when the White person is forced to deal with the inconsistencies that have been compartmentalized or encounters information/experiences at odds with his/her denial. In most cases, a person is forced to acknowledge their Whiteness at some level, to examine their own cultural values, and to see the conflict between upholding humanistic nonracist values and their contradictory behavior. For example, a person who may consciously believe that "all men are created equal" and that he/she "treats everyone the same" suddenly experiences reservations about having African Americans move next door or having their son or daughter involved in an interracial relationship. These more personal experiences bring the individual face to face with his/her own prejudices and biases. In this situation, thoughts such as "I am not prejudiced"; "I treat everyone the same regardless or race, creed, or color"; or "I do not discriminate" collide with the denial system. Or some major event (assassination of Martin Luther King Jr., viewing the Rodney King beating, etc.) may force the person to realize that racism is alive and well in the United States. The increasing realization that one is biased and that Euro-American society does play a part in oppressing minority groups is an unpleasant one. Dissonance may result in feelings of guilt, shame, anger, and depression. Rationalizations may become the manner used to exonerate one's own inactivity in combating perceived injustice or personal feelings of prejudice: "I'm only one person, what can I do?" or "Everyone is prejudiced, even minorities." As these conflicts ensue, the White person may retreat into the protective confines of White culture (encapsulation of the previous stage) or move progressively toward insight and revelation (resistance and immersion stage).

Whether a person regresses is related to the strength of positive forces pushing an individual forward (support for challenging racism) and negative forces (fear of some loss) pushing the person backward. For example, challenging the prevailing beliefs of the times may mean risking ostracism from other White relatives, friends, neighbors, and colleagues. Regardless of the choice, there are many uncomfortable feelings of guilt, shame, anger, and depression related to the realization of inconsistencies in one's belief systems. Guilt and shame are most likely related to the recognition of the White person's role in perpetuating racism in the past. Or guilt may result from the person's being afraid to speak out on the issues or to take responsibility for his/her part in a current situation. For example, the person may witness an act of racism, hear a racist comment, or be given preferential treatment over a minority person but decide not to say anything for fear of violating racist White norms. Often, the person may delude himself or herself with rationalizations: "I'm just one person. What can I do about it?" This approach is one frequently taken by many White people in which they rationalize their behaviors by the belief that they are powerless to make changes. There is a tendency to retreat into White culture. If, however, others (which may include some family and friends) are more accepting, forward movement is more likely.

3. *Resistance and immersion.* Should the White person progress to this stage, he/she will begin to question and challenge his/her own racism. For the first time, the person begins to realize what racism is all about, and his/her eyes are suddenly open. Racism is seen everywhere (advertising, television, educational materials, interpersonal interactions, etc.). This phase of development is marked by a major questioning of one's own racism and that of others in society. In addition, increasing awareness of how racism operates and its pervasiveness in U.S. culture and institutions is the major hallmark of this level. It is as if the person has awakened to the realities of oppression; sees how educational materials, the mass media, advertising, etc., portray and perpetuate stereotypes; and recognizes how being White has allowed him/her certain advantages denied to various minority groups.

There is likely to be considerable anger at family and friends, institutions, and larger societal values, which are seen as having sold him/her a false bill of goods (democratic ideals) that were never practiced. Guilt is also felt for having been a part of the oppressive system. Strangely enough, the person is likely to undergo a form of racial self-hatred at this stage. Negative feelings about being White are present, and accompanying feelings of guilt, shame, and anger toward oneself and other Whites may develop. The "White liberal" syndrome may develop and be manifested in two complementary styles: the paternalistic protector role or overidentification with another minority group (Helms, 1984; Ponterotto, 1988). In the former, the White person may devote his/her energies in an almost paternalistic attempt to protect minorities from abuse. In the latter, the person may actually want to identify with a particular minority group (Asian, Black, etc.) in order to escape his/her own Whiteness. The White person will soon discover, however, that these roles are not appreciated by minority groups and will experience rejection. Again, the person may resolve this dilemma by moving back into the protective confines of White culture (conformity stage), again experience conflict (dissonance), or move directly to the introspective stage.

4. *Introspective phase.* This phase is most likely a compromise resulting from having swung from an extreme of unconditional acceptance of White identity to a rejection of Whiteness. It is a state of relative quiescence, introspection, and reformulation of what it means to be White. The person realizes and no longer denies that they have participated in oppression,

that they benefit from White privilege, and that racism is an integral part of U.S. society. However, they become less motivated by guilt and defensiveness, accept their Whiteness, and seek to define their own identity and that of their social group. This acceptance, however, does not mean a less active role in combating oppression. The process may involve addressing such questions as: "What does it mean to be White?" "Who am I in relation to my Whiteness?" "Who am I as a racial/cultural being?"

The feelings or affective elements may be existential in nature and involve feelings of lack of connectedness, isolation, confusion, and loss. In other words, the person knows that they will never fully understand the minority experience but feels disconnected from their Euro-American group as well. In some ways, the introspective phase is similar in dynamics to the dissonance one in that both represent a transition from one perspective to another. The process used to answer the above questions and to deal with the ensuing feelings may involve a searching, observing, and questioning attitude. Answers to these questions involve dialoging and observing one's own social group and actively creating and experiencing interactions with various minority group members as well.

5. *Integrative awareness phase.* Reaching this level of development is characterized by (a) understanding self as a racial/cultural being, (b) awareness of sociopolitical influences with respect to racism, (c) appreciation of racial/cultural diversity, and (d) increased commitment toward eradicating oppression. The formation of a nonracist White Euro-American identity emerges and becomes internalized. The person values multiculturalism, is comfortable around members of culturally different groups, and feels a strong connectedness with members of many groups. Perhaps most important is the inner sense of security and strength that is found in this phase, for it is needed to function in a society that is only marginally accepting of integratively aware White persons.

IMPLICATIONS FOR COUNSELING AND MULTICULTURAL THERAPY

If we acknowledge, as suggested by WRID theorists, that becoming aware of one's own White identity is an important attribute of multicultural competence, then it means several important things in the helping professions. Graduate training programs, for example, would be advised to assess the phase of development for White trainees with respect to WRID. The characteristics associated with one level may dictate the types of objectives and techniques most successful in use with trainees. Linking specific stages of development with ideas for training, Carney and Kahn (1984) described a five-stage development model for trainees who, while not explicitly described as such, are taken to be White. They identified appropriate learning environment features related to each (unnamed) stage of development and discussed points at which it might be important to use same-culture, mixed-culture, and other-culture trainers.

Especially important is the work of Ponterotto and his colleagues (Ponterotto, 1988; Sabnani, Ponterotto, & Borodovsky, 1991), who have focused on integrating general models of White racial identity into a developmental training model specifically designed for White counselors and therapists. Sabnani, Ponterotto, and Borodovsky (1991) have integrated and collapsed the models of Hardiman (1982), Helms (1984), and Ponterotto (1988) into a five-stage developmental model. Stage 1, preexposure/precontact, is characterized by a general lack of awareness of self as a racial being. In stage 2, conflict, there is an expansion of knowledge regarding racial matters incurred through interactions with non-White persons or through

Table 7.3 STAGES OF WHITE IDENTITY DEVELOPMENT AND TRAINING IMPLICATIONS

	Beliefs/attitudes		Knowledge		Skills	
	Goals	*Tasks*	*Goals*	*Tasks*	*Goals*	*Tasks*
Stage 1 Preexposure/ Precontact	Awareness of ones's own cultural heritage Awareness of the cultural heritage of minority groups	Awareness group experience[a][b] "Ethnic dinners"[b] Tours/exhibits of other cultures' crafts/areas Intercultural sharing[c] Multicultural action planning (low level of active involvement)[c] Free drawing test[h] Public and private self-awareness exercise[g] Value statements exercise[h] Decision awareness exercise[g]	Knowledge of the cultural heritage of other minority groups	Research into the history of other cultures Intercultural sharing[c] Multicultural action planning (low level of active involvement)[c] Ethnic literature reviews Field trips Case studies[c] Culture assimilator[i][j][k]	Beginning development of counseling skills	Regular counselor training tasks (microskills training)[d][e][f]
Stage 2 Conflict	Awareness of one's stereotypes and prejudicial attitudes and the impact of these on minorities Awareness of the conflict between wanting to conform to White norms while upholding humanitarian values Dealing with feelings of guilt and depression or anger	Critical incidents exercise[h] Implicit assumptions checklist exercise[h] We and you exercises[h] Exercise for experiencing stereotypes[c] Stereotypes awareness exercise[c] Less structured cross-cultural encounter groups	More extensive knowledge of other cultures Knowledge of the concepts of prejudice and racism Knowledge of the impact of racism on minorities and the privileges of being White	MAP-investigative[e] Tours to other communities Research on racism in the past and present Classes in multicultural issues presenting survey data on minorities Films	Develop more client-specific methods of intervention	Critical incidents method[l] Role-playing exercise[h] Role-playing a problem in a group[h]

	Beliefs/attitudes		Knowledge		Skills	
	Goals	Tasks	Goals	Tasks	Goals	Tasks
Stage 3 Pro-minority Antiracism	Awareness of over-identification and of paternalistic attitudes, and the impact of these on minorities	Interracial encounters[m] Cross-cultural encounter groups Responsible feedback exercise[h] Anonymous feedback from the group exercise[h]	Further immersion into other cultures	Guided self-study Exposure to audio-visual presentations[g] Interviews with consultants and experts[g] Lectures Minority student panels[b] Research into the impact of race on counseling	Continue developing culturally emic and etic approaches to counseling	Role-playing exercises Communication skills training Facilitating interracial groups (FIG)[b] Counseling ethnic minorities (CEM)[b]
Stage 4 Retreat into White culture	Awareness of and dealing with one's own fear and anger	Cross-cultural encounter groups Lump sum[b]	Knowledge of the development of minority identity and White identity	Research into minority identity development models Research into White identity development models	Building culturally etic (transcendent) approaches	Microskills Ponterotto and Benesch (1988)
Stage 5 Redefinition and Integration	Develop an identity that claims Whiteness as a part of it	Feedback-related exercises (see Stage 3)	Expand knowledge on racism in the real world Expand knowledge on counseling methods more appropriate to minorities	Visits to communities with large minority populations Research on ways to transform White-based counseling methods to one more credible to minorities	Deepen more culturally emic approaches Face more challenging cross-cultural counseling interactions	Facilitating interracial groups (FIG)[b] Counseling ethnic minorities individually (CEMI)[b] Triad model[g] Cross-cultural practica

Note: References for exercises suggested in Table 16.2 are indicated by letters, as follows: a. Parker & McDavis, 1979; b. McDavis & Parker, 1977; c. Parker, 1988; d. Ivey & Authier, 1978; e. Egan, 1982; f. Clarkhuff & Anthony, 1979; g. Pedersen, 1988; h. Weeks et al., 1977; i. Albert, 1983; k. Merta, Stringham, & Ponterotto, 1988; l. Sue, 1981; m. Katz & Ivey, 1977. From White racial identity development and cross-cultural counselor training. *The Counseling Psychologist*, 1991, *19*, 76–102. Copyright 1991 by Sage Publications, Inc. Reprinted by permission of Sage Publications.

exposure during training (e.g., a required multicultural course). This stage is characterized by conflict between the desire to conform to majority group norms, while at the same time wishing to represent humanistic, non-racist values. The emotions of guilt, depression, and anger are common in this stage and result from the aforementioned conflict, and/or from an increasing awareness that racism continues in American society.

In stage 3, pro-minority/antiracism, the White individual develops a strong pro-minority stance concomitant with the rejection of internalized racist beliefs and anger directed at the White status quo. This affective reaction serves to alleviate the guilt common to stage 2. Stage 4, retreat into White culture, occurs when a White person perceives rejection from non-White persons or from the minority community. This retreat into the familiarity of same-race relations may also occur in response to a White person's lack of self-assuredness in interracial situations. Feelings of defensiveness, anger, and fear are associated with this stage. Finally, stage 5, redefinition and integration, is characterized by a movement toward the clear development of White racial identity and a culturally transcendent worldview.

Emphasizing the developmental nature of their identity model and acknowledging that different majority group therapists are at varied stages of readiness for incorporating multicultural training, Sabnani, Ponterotto, and Borodovsky (1991) outlined detailed and specific training exercises designed to facilitate movement through the stages. The authors organized their training regimens for each racial identity stage within the context of both training goals and tasks for each of the competency areas (beliefs, attitudes, knowledge, and skills) endorsed by the Division of Counseling Psychology (D.W. Sue et al., 1982). Table 7.3 summarizes the stage-specific training exercises.

Whatever the White racial identity of the therapist, it makes sense that his/her awareness is likely to have major implications for the client and the process of counseling/therapy (Carter, 1995; Helms, 1984; Ponterotto, 1988). A White therapist at the conformity level, for example, may cause great harm to culturally different clients at their levels of identity development. The therapist may intentionally and unintentionally (a) reinforce a conformity client's feelings of racial self-hatred, (b) prevent or block a dissonance client from looking at inconsistent feelings/attitudes/beliefs, (c) dismiss and negate the resistance and immersion client's anger about racism (he/she is a radical), or (d) perceive the integrative awareness individual as having a confused sense of self-identity.

Other combinations of cross-status relationships can lead to confusion in clinical work. What would therapy be like, for example, if the culturally different client were at the conformity level while the White therapist was at the resistance and immersion level? Would the White therapist feel negatively toward the minority client because he or she views the client as having sold out? We are obviously dealing with a highly complex and speculative area, which requires greater research and investigation. (See Helms' [1984] excellent analysis of dyad combinations.) Earlier admonitions for helping professionals to "know thyself" and grow culturally aware of their own biases, values, and assumptions about human behavior become more important.

In closing, it is important to stress again the common assumptions of WRID models. We ask readers to seriously consider the validity of these assumptions and engage one another in a dialogue about them. First, they emphasize how racism is a basic and integral part of U.S. life and permeates all aspects of our culture and institutions. Second, White Euro-Americans are socialized into U.S. society and therefore inherit the biases, stereotypes, and racist attitudes, beliefs, and behaviors of the society. In other words, all White Euro-Americans are racist whether knowingly or unknowingly. Third, the level of White racial identity development in a cross-cultural encounter (working with minorities, responding to multicultural training, etc.) affects the process and outcome of an interracial relationship. Fourth, the most desirable status is the one where the White person not only accepts his/her Whiteness, but defines it in a nondefensive and nonracist manner. Last, how White Americans perceive themselves as racial beings seems to be strongly correlated with how they perceive and respond to racial stimuli. Consequently, their race-related reality represents major differences in worldview, a topic we turn to in the next chapter.

Chapter Eight

◆

Dimensions of Worldviews

◆

Felix Sanchez is a second-generation, 19-year-old Hispanic freshman attending a major university in northern California. He is the oldest of five siblings, all currently residing in Colorado. Felix's father works as a delivery driver for a brewery, and his mother is employed part-time as a housekeeper. Both parents have worked long and hard to make ends meet and have been instrumental in sending their eldest son to college.

Felix is the first in his entire family (including his extended family) to have ever attended an institution of higher education. It is generally understood that the parents do not have the financial resources to send Felix's brothers and sisters to college. His siblings can attend college only by financing it themselves or obtaining help elsewhere. Out of a sense of obligation, Felix obtained a part-time job without the knowledge of his parents in order to secretly save money for his siblings' future education.

During the last two quarters, however, Felix has been experiencing academic difficulties in many of his classes. Felix's inability to obtain grades better than C's or D's greatly discouraged him. Last quarter, he was placed on academic probation and the thought of failing evoked a great sense of guilt and shame in him. While he had originally intended to become a social worker and had looked forward to his course work, he now felt depressed, lonely, alienated, and guilt-ridden. It was not so much his inability to do the work, but the meaninglessness of his courses, the materials in the texts, and the manner in which his courses were taught. Worse yet, he just could not relate to the students in his dormitory and all the rules and regulations.

At the beginning of his last quarter, Felix was referred by his Educational Opportunity Program adviser to the University Counseling Center. Felix's counselor, Dr. Blackburne, seemed sincere enough, but the counseling sessions only made him feel worse. Besides spending time explaining his situation to the counselor, Felix was asked to take a series of vocational interest tests. According to Dr. Blackburne, the tests were "nondefinitive" in that no clear-cut interest pattern seemed to emerge. The counselor had strongly implied several possible reasons for Felix's inability to do well in school. First, it was possible that he was not college material and had to face that fact. After all, Felix was admitted to the University only because the Affirmative Action program allowed less qualified minority students in. Second, the vocational tests supported Dr. Blackburne's belief that Felix lacked the motivation to pursue work in higher education and that this was evident in his lack of desire to pursue social work. Third, his constant "sacrificing" of his time (part-time work) to help his siblings contributed to his poor grades. Fourth, Felix's depression and alienation were symptomatic of serious acculturation problems; he needed to "fit in" and "adjust better to the academic environment," to learn better English skills, and to "think about himself more, rather than doing what he thought would please his parents and family."

In the last chapter, we indicated how White racial identity could influence how a White person perceives the world. While there is a strong relationship between racial/cultural identity development and worldviews, the latter are more global and encompassing. Each and every one of us possesses a worldview that affects how we perceive and evaluate situations and how we determine appropriate actions based upon our appraisal; the nature of clinical reality is very much linked to worldviews (Ivey, Ivey, & Simek-Morgan, 1997; Trevino, 1996). In the preceding vignette, the worldview of Dr. Blackburne affects his assessment and definition of the problem and his proposed solutions. Let us analyze this vignette to illustrate some of the points to be made in this chapter.

First, we would like to acknowledge that Dr. Blackburne is a well-intentioned helping professional. His worldview, however, contains certain philosophical assumptions that may prove detrimental to his culturally different clients. The reasons for Felix's academic problems that the counselor entertains (not being college material, lacking motivation, sacrificing study time, and needing to assimilate more), all imply several things: (a) Success or failure in life is due to individual effort or lack of it; (b) we are all personally responsible for the outcomes in our life; and (c) changing ourselves and our life circumstance is totally within our control. The counselor tends to attribute Felix's academic difficulties to personal deficiencies. Interestingly enough, the reasons are also significantly correlated with stereotypes about many racial/ethnic minorities: not being college material = not very bright; unmotivated = laziness; need to think about himself more = need to be independent; and need to fit in = problems in acculturation.

Such a worldview as evidenced by Dr. Blackburne includes perceiving the individual as the psychosocial unit of operation and an implicit valuing of individualism. Causes of behavior are sought within the individual. As a result, there is a proclivity toward *person blame.* Such a worldview tends to give lesser weight to external explanations as the causes of behavior. The danger here is that we may overlook legitimate systemic (as opposed to individual) factors affecting Felix's feelings of loneliness, isolation, depression, and meaninglessness.

Is it possible, for example, that the academic cultural climate is to blame for Felix's difficulties rather than some personal deficiency? Is it possible that the feelings of alienation and meaninglessness are related to the content of the courses taught and texts used? It is not unusual for many students of color to complain that course content is taught from only one perspective (Euro-American) and that they do not see themselves portrayed in texts, nor in a realistic fashion. Also, how might White middle-class learning/teaching styles clash with those appropriate to a Latino/Hispanic perspective? Likewise, how may institutional rules and regulations clash with Hispanic values of *personalismo?* In many Hispanic groups, human relationships take precedence over institutional policies. That is to say, according to the traditional Latino concept of *personalismo,* people are more important than formal rules and regulations, and people interactions take precedence over such impersonal aspects of existence. Remember that Felix seems bothered by all the rules and regulations in his dormitory residence. Also, is the counselor failing to understand the traditional Hispanic family structure and responsibility, which places great importance upon the eldest son and the ensuing responsibilities and obligations? When the counselor uses the term "sacrifice," has he not turned a cultural value into a deficiency? The counselor may be unintentionally communicating to Felix that his values are outdated and pathological.

If we answer in the affirmative to many of these questions, then we must begin to entertain the notion that contributors to Felix's dilemma lie in the educational system and not in him. We have radically shifted our worldview! At times systemic forces may be so overpowering and stacked against culturally different clients, that they are truly not responsible for their fate and cannot exercise enough systemic control to change or alter the outcome. High unemployment among African American workers, for example, may not be due to some inherent deficits (laziness or stupidity), but to system forces (bias, prejudice, and discrimination). The system is to blame and not the person. From this perspective, the therapeutic solution is to change the system rather than the person (acculturate). We submit that the worldview exemplified by Dr. Blackburne is representative of traditional theories of counseling and psychotherapy.

It has become increasingly clear that many minority persons hold worldviews different from members of the dominant culture. In Chapters 6 and 7, we examined one specific aspect of worldviews—racial/cultural identity. In a broader sense, we can define a worldview (D.W. Sue, 1977b, 1978) as how a person perceives his/her relationship to the world (nature, institutions, other people, etc.). Worldviews are highly correlated with a person's cultural upbringing and life experiences (Ibrahim, 1985; Katz, 1985; Trevino, 1996). Ivey, Ivey, and Simek-Downing (1997) refer to worldviews as "the way you frame the world and what it means to you," "one's conceptual framework," or "how you think the world works." Ibrahim (1985) refers to it as "our philosophy of life," or our "experience within social, cultural, environmental, philosophical, and psychological dimensions." Put in a much more practical way, worldviews are not only composed of our attitudes, values, opinions, and concepts; they may also affect how we think, define events, make decisions, and behave.

For minorities in America, a strong determinant of worldviews is very much related to racism and the subordinate position assigned to them in society. While the intent of this chapter is to discuss racial and ethnic minorities, it must be kept in mind that economic and social class, religion, sexual orientation, and gender are also interactional components of a worldview. Thus, upper- and lower-socioeconomic class Asian Americans, African Americans, Hispanic/Latino Americans, or Native Americans do not necessarily have identical views of the world.

Helping professionals who hold a worldview different from that of their clients and are unaware of the basis for this difference are most likely to impute negative traits to clients. Constructs used to judge "normality" and "healthy" or "abnormality" and "unhealthy" may be inadvertently applied to clients. In most cases, culturally different clients have a greater possibility of holding worldviews different from those of therapists. Yet many therapists are so culturally unaware that they respond according to their own conditioned values, assumptions, and perspectives of reality without regard for other views. What is needed for therapists is for them to become culturally aware, to act on the basis of a critical analysis and understanding of their own conditioning, the conditioning of their clients, and the sociopolitical system of which they are both a part. Without this awareness, counselors who work with the culturally different may be engaging in cultural oppression. Let us begin our exploration of worldviews by continuing with the value orientation model proposed by Kluckhohn and Strodtbeck (1961).

VALUE-ORIENTATION MODEL OF WORLDVIEWS

One of the most useful frameworks for understanding differences among individuals and groups is the Kluckhohn and Strodtbeck model (1961) presented in Chapter 5. It assumes that there exists a set of core dimensions (human questions) that are pertinent for all peoples of all cultures. Differences in value orientations can be ascertained by how we answer them. These questions and the three possible responses to them are given in Table 8.1.

Table 8.1   VALUE-ORIENTATION MODEL

Dimensions	Value Orientations		
1. *Time Focus*	*Past*	*Present*	*Future*
What is the temporary focus of human life?	The past is important. Learn from history.	The present moment is everything. Don't worry about tomorrow.	Plan for the future: Sacrifice today for a better tomorrow.
2. *Human Activity*	*Being*	*Being & In Becoming*	*Doing*
What is the modality of human activity?	It's enough to just be.	Our purpose in life is to develop our inner self.	Be active. Work hard and your efforts will be rewarded.
3. *Social Relations*	*Lineal*	*Collateral*	*Individualistic*
How are human relationships defined?	Relationships are vertical. There are leaders and followers in this world.	We should consult with friends/families when problems arise.	Individual autonomy is important. We control our own destiny.
4. *People/Nature Relationship*	*Subjugation to Nature*	*Harmony with Nature*	*Mastery over Nature*
What is the relationship of people to nature?	Life is largely determined by external forces (God, fate, genetics, etc.)	People and nature co-exist in harmony.	Our challenge is to conquer and control nature.

Note. Adapted from "Effective Cross-Cultural Counseling and Psychotherapy: A Framework," by F.A. Ibrahim, 1985, *The Counseling Psychologist, 13*, pp. 625–638. Copyright 1985 by *The Counseling Psychologist.* Adapted with permission from *Variations in Value Orientations* by F.R. Kluckhohn and F.L. Strodtbeck, 1961, Evanston, IL: Row, Patterson & Co. Copyright 1961 by Row, Patterson & Co. Adapted with permission. Adapted from *Handbook for Developing Multicultural Awareness* (p. 256), by P. Pedersen, 1988, Alexandria, VA: AACD Press. Copyright 1988 by AACD Press. Adapted with permission.

Kluckhohn and Strodtbeck (1961) clearly recognized that racial/ethnic groups vary in how they perceive *time*. Cultures may emphasize *history and tradition,* the *here and now,* or the *distant future.* For example, Puerto Ricans tend to exhibit present time value orientation behaviors that may be different from Anglo future orientation (Garcia-Preto, 1996; Inclan, 1985). Puerto Ricans frequently comment on how Anglos do not seem to know how to have fun because they will leave a party in order to prepare for a meeting tomorrow. Likewise, Anglos will often comment on how Puerto Ricans are poor and disorganized planners. They may notify their boss at the last minute about their need to travel home for the holidays. Worse yet, they may attempt to make airline reservations December 20 for the Christmas holidays only to be forced to fly standby because of poor planning. As we saw in the family therapy chapter, Puerto Ricans and Anglos mark time differently.

Cultures also differ in their attitudes toward *activity.* In White culture, *doing* is valued over *being* or even *being-in-becoming.* There is a strong belief that one's own worth is measured by task accomplishments. In White culture, statements like "do something" indicate the positive value placed on action. Likewise, when someone is involved in *being,* it may be described as "hanging out" or "killing time." In most cases these represent pejorative statements. In counseling and therapy, the perceived inaction of a client who may adhere to a *being* orientation is usually associated with some form of personal inadequacy.

Another dimension of importance is our *relationship with others.* In some cultures, relationships tend to be more *lineal,* authoritarian, and hierarchical (traditional Asian cultures) in which the father is the absolute ruler of the family. Some cultures may emphasize a horizontal, equal, and *collateral* relationship, while others, like U.S. society, value *individual* autonomy. In earlier chapters, we pointed out how a counseling relationship that tends to be more equal and individualistic (I-Thou) may prove uncomfortable for clients who may adhere to a much more formal hierarchical relationship.

The *nature of people* has often been addressed in psychology and philosophy. In theories of personality, for example, Freud saw humans as basically evil or bad; Rogers saw them as innately good; behaviorists tended to perceive human nature as neutral. There is no doubt that cultures, societies, and groups may socialize people into a trusting or suspicious mode. Third World groups, by virtue of their minority status in the United States, may develop a healthy suspiciousness toward institutions and people. Unfortunately, because many mental health professionals may operate from a different value orientation (man is basically neutral or good), they may see the minority clients as evidencing paranoid traits.

The value-orientation model also states that people make assumptions about how they *relate to nature.* Many American Indians, for example, perceive themselves as harmonious with "Mother Earth" and nature (Garrett & Garrett, 1994). Poor Puerto Ricans are governed more by a value of subjugation to nature (Nieto, 1995). White Anglos, however, value conquering and controlling nature (Pedersen, 1988; Ivey, Ivey, & Simek-Morgan, 1997). Such an orientation by the therapist may often lead to difficulties. This aspect of the value dimension presumes that barriers to personal success or happiness may be overcome through hard work and perseverance. Minority or poor clients, however, may perceive this strategy as ineffective against many problems created by racism or poverty. Clients who fail to act in accordance with their therapist's values may be diagnosed as being the source of their own problems. It is precisely this value dimension that we feel has been severely neglected in the mental health field. The reason may lie in its sociopolitical nature.

The remaining part of this chapter deals with a discussion of worldviews as they relate to this central concept. It discusses how race- and culture-specific factors may interact in such a way as to produce people with different worldviews, and it presents a conceptual model that integrates research findings with the clinical literature.

First, we discuss two factors identified as important in understanding persons with different psychological orientations: (a) locus of control and (b) locus of responsibility. Second, we look at how these variables form four different psychological outlooks in life and their consequent characteristics, dynamics, and implications for the clinician. Last, we set forth some conclusions and precautions.

LOCUS OF CONTROL

Rotter's (1966) historic work in the formulation of the concepts internal-external control and the internal-external (I-E) dimension has contributed greatly to our understanding of human behavior. "Internal control" (IC) refers to people's beliefs that reinforcements are contingent on their own actions and that people can shape their own fate. "External control" (EC) refers to people's beliefs that reinforcing events occur independently of their actions and that the future is determined more by chance and luck. Rotter conceived this dimension as measuring a generalized personality trait that operated across several different situations.

Based on past experience, people learn one of two worldviews: The locus of control rests with the individual, or the locus of control rests with some external force. Early researchers (Lefcourt, 1966; Rotter, 1966, 1975) have summarized research findings that correlated high internality with (a) greater attempts at mastering the environment, (b) superior coping strategies, (c) better cognitive processing of information, (d) lower predisposition to anxiety, (e) higher achievement motivation, (f) greater social action involvement, and (g) placing greater value on skill-determined rewards. As can be seen, these attributes are highly valued by U.S. society and constitute the core features of the Euro-American definition of mental health.

Early research on generalized expectancies of locus of control suggests that ethnic group members (Hsieh, Shybut, & Lotsof, 1969; Levenson, 1974; Strickland, 1973; Tulkin, 1968; Wolfgang, 1973), low socioeconomic class people (Battle & Rotter, 1963; Crandall, Katkovsky, & Crandall, 1965; Garcia & Levenson, 1975; Lefcourt, 1966; Strickland, 1971), and women (Sanger & Alker, 1972) score significantly higher on the external end of the locus-of-control continuum. Using the I-E dimension as a criterion of mental health would mean that minority, poor, and female clients would be viewed as possessing less desirable attributes. Thus, a clinician who encounters a minority client with a high external orientation ("it's no use trying," "there's nothing I can do about it," and "you shouldn't rock the boat") may interpret the client as being inherently apathetic, procrastinating, lazy, depressed, or anxious about trying. As we see in the next section, all these statements tend to blame the individual for his/her present condition.

The problem with an unqualified application of the I-E dimension is that it fails to take into consideration the different cultural and social experiences of the individual. This failure may lead to highly inappropriate and destructive applications in therapy (Lewis et al., 1998). While the social-learning framework from which the I-E dimension is derived may be very legitimate, it seems plausible that different cultural groups, women, and lower-class people have learned that control operates differently in their lives than for society at large. In the case of persons of color, the concept of external control takes on a wider meaning (Carter, 1995; Ridley, 1995).

We believe that the locus-of-control continuum must make clearer distinctions on the external end. For example, externality related to impersonal forces (chance and luck) is different from that ascribed to cultural forces and that ascribed to powerful others. Chance and luck operate equally across situations for everyone. However, the forces that determine locus of control from a cultural perspective may be viewed by the particular ethnic group as acceptable and benevolent. In this case, externality is viewed positively. Two ethnic groups may be used as examples to illustrate this point.

For example, we have always known that Chinese, American-born Chinese, and Anglo Americans vary in the degree of internal control they feel (Hsieh, Shybut, & Lotsof, 1969). The first group scores lowest in internality, followed by the Chinese Americans and then Anglo Americans. It is believed that the individual-centered American culture emphasizes the uniqueness, independence, and self-reliance of each individual. It places a high premium on self-reliance, individualism, and status achieved through one's own efforts. In contrast, the situation-centered Chinese culture places importance on the group (an individual is not defined apart from the family), tradition, social roles/expectations, and harmony with the universe (Root, 1998). Thus, the cultural orientation of the more traditional Chinese tends to elevate the external scores. Note, however, that the external orientation of the Chinese is highly valued and accepted (Leong, 1985; Root, 1998; Uba, 1994).

Likewise, one might expect Native Americans to score higher on the external end of the I-E continuum on the basis of their own cultural values. Several writers (Garrett & Garrett, 1994; LaFromboise, 1998) have pointed to American Indian concepts of noninterference and harmony with nature that may tend to classify them as high externals. Anglos are said to be concerned with attempts to control the physical world and to assert mastery over it. To American Indians, accepting the world (harmony) rather than changing it is a highly valued lifestyle.

Support for the fact that Rotter's I-E distinction is not a unidimensional trait has also come from a number of past studies (Gurin, Gurin, Lao, & Beattie, 1969; Mirels, 1970) that indicate the presence of a political influence (powerful others). For example, a major force in the literature dealing with locus of control is that of powerlessness. *Powerlessness* may be defined as the expectancy that a person's behavior cannot determine the outcomes or reinforcements he/she seeks. Mirels (1970) feels that a strong possibility exists that externality may be a function of a person's opinions about prevailing social institutions. For example, lower-class individuals and Blacks are not given an equal opportunity to obtain the material rewards of Western culture (Carter, 1988, 1995; Lewis et al., 1998). Because of racism, African Americans may be perceiving, in a realistic fashion, a discrepancy between their ability and attainment.

In this case, externality may be seen as a malevolent force to be distinguished from the benevolent cultural ones just discussed. It can be concluded that while high external people are less effectively motivated, perform poorly in achievement situations, and evidence greater psychological problems, this does not necessarily hold for minorities and low-income persons (Gurin et al., 1969; White & Parham, 1990). Focusing on external forces may be motivationally healthy if it results from assessing one's chances for success against systematic and real external obstacles rather than unpredictable fate. Three factors of importance for our discussion can be identified.

The first factor, called *control ideology,* is a measure of general belief about the role of external forces in determining success and failure in the larger society. It represents a cultural belief in the Protestant ethic: Success is the result of hard work, effort, skill, and ability. The second factor, *personal control,* reflects a person's belief about his/her own sense of personal efficacy or competence. While control ideology represents an ideological belief, personal control is more related to actual control. Apparently, African Americans can be equally internal to Whites on the control ideology, but when a personal reference (personal control) is used, they are much more external. This indicates that African Americans may have adopted the general cultural beliefs about internal control, but find these cannot always be applied to their own life situations because of racism and discrimination. It is interesting to note that Whites endorse control ideology statements at the same rate as personal control ones. Thus, the disparity between the two forms of control does not seem to be operative for White Americans. A third interesting finding is that personal control, as opposed to ideological control, is more related to motivational and performance indicators. A student high on personal control (internality) tends to have greater self-confidence, higher test scores, higher grades, and so on. Those subjects who are high on the ideological measure are not noticeably different from their externally oriented counterparts.

The I-E continuum is useful for therapists only if they make clear distinctions about the meaning of the external control dimension. High externality may be due to (a) chance/luck, (b) cultural dictates that are viewed as benevolent, or (c) political forces (racism and discrimination) that represent malevolent but realistic obstacles. In each case, it is a mistake to associate an external orientation with inadequacy for a culturally different client. To do so would be to deny the potential influence of cultural values and the effects of prejudice and discrimination. The problem becomes more complex when we realize that cultural and discriminatory forces may both be operative. That is, American Indian cultural values that dictate an external orientation may be compounded by that group's historical experience of prejudice and discrimination in America. The same may be true for poor Puerto Ricans who often perceive a subjugation to nature due to their poverty and religious beliefs (Inclan, 1985).

LOCUS OF RESPONSIBILITY

Another important dimension in world outlooks was formulated from early work on attribution theory (Jones et al., 1972) and can be legitimately referred to as "locus of responsibility." In essence, this dimension measures the degree of responsibility or blame placed on the individual or system. In the case of African Americans, their lower standard of living may be attributed to their personal inadequacies and shortcomings; or the responsibility for their plight may be attributed to racial discrimination and lack of opportunities (Chen, Froehle, & Morran, 1997). The former orientation blames the individual, while the latter explanation blames the system.

The degree of emphasis placed on the individual as opposed to the system in affecting a person's behavior is important in the formation of life orientations. Such terms as *person-centered* or *person-blame* indicate a focus on the individual. Those who hold a person-centered orientation (a) emphasize the understanding of a person's motivations, values, feelings, and goals; (b) believe that success or failure is attributable to the individual's skills or personal inadequacies; and (c) believe that there is a strong relationship between ability, effort, and success in society. In essence, these people adhere strongly to the Protestant ethic that idealizes "rugged individualism." On the other hand, *situation-centered* or *system-blame* people view the sociocultural environment as more potent than the individual. Social, economic, and political forces are powerful; success or failure is generally dependent on the socioeconomic system and not necessarily on personal attributes (Lewis et al., 1998; D.W. Sue et al., 1998).

The causes of social problems in Western society are seen as residing in individuals, and thus they are responsible for them. Such an approach has the effect of labeling that segment of the population (racial and ethnic minorities) that differs in thought and behavior from the larger society as "deviant." Defining the problem as residing in the person enables society to ignore situationally relevant factors and to protect and preserve social institutions and belief systems. Caplan and Nelson (1973) state this point well:

What is done about a problem depends on how it is defined. The way a social problem is defined determines the attempts at remediation—problem definition determines the change strategy, the selection of a social action delivered system, and the criteria for evaluation. . . . Problem definitions are based on assumptions about the causes of the problem and where they lie. If the causes of delinquency, for example, are defined in person-centered terms (e.g., inability to delay gratification, or incomplete sexual identity), then it would be logical to initiate person-change treatment techniques and intervention strategies to deal with the problem. Such treatment would take the form of counselor or other person-change efforts to reach the delinquent, thereby using his potential for self-control to make his behavior more conventional. . . .

If, on the other hand, explanations are situation centered, for example, if delinquency were interpreted as the substitution of extra legal paths for already preempted, conventionally approved pathways for achieving socially valued goals, then efforts toward corrective treatment would logically have a system-change orientation. Efforts would be launched to create suitable opportunities for success and achievement along conventional lines; thus, existing physical, social, or economic arrangements, not individual psyches, would be the targets for change. (pp. 200–201)

A person-centered problem definition has characterized clinical practice (Chen, Froehle, & Morran, 1997; McNamee, 1996; White, 1993). Definitions of mental health, the assumptions of vocational guidance, and most therapy theories stress the uniqueness and importance of the individual. As a result, the onus of responsibility for change in counseling tends to rest on the individual. It reinforces a social myth about a person's ability to control his/her own fate by rewarding the members of the middle class who "made it on their own" and increases complacency about those who have not "made it on their own." Thus, the individual system-blame continuum may need to be viewed differentially for minority groups. An internal response (acceptance of blame for one's failure) might be considered normal for the White middle class, but for minorities, it may be extreme and intrapunitive.

For example, an African American male client who has been unable to find a job because of prejudice and discrimination may blame himself ("What's wrong with me?" "Why can't I find a job?" "Am I worthless?"). An external response may in fact be more realistic and appropriate ("Institutional racism prevented my getting the job"). Early research indicates that African Americans who scored external (blame system) on this dimension (a) more often aspired to nontraditional occupations, (b) were more in favor of group rather than individual action for dealing with discrimination, (c) engaged in more civil rights activities, and (d) exhibited more innovative coping behavior (Gurin et al., 1969). It is important to note that the personal control dimension discussed in the previous section was correlated with traditional measures of motivation and achievement (grades), while individual system-blame was a better predictor of innovative social action behavior. This latter dimension has been the subject of speculation and studies about its relationship to militancy and racial identity.

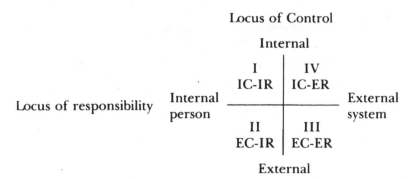

Figure 8.1 Graphic Represenation of Worldviews. *Note:* From "Eliminating Cultural Oppression in Counseling: Toward a General Theory" by D.W. Sue, 1978, *Journal of Counseling Psychology, 25,* p. 422. Copyright 1978 by the *Journal of Counseling Psychology.* Reprinted with persission.

FORMATION OF WORLDVIEWS

The two psychological orientations, locus of control (personal control) and locus of responsibility, are independent of one another. As shown in Figure 8.1, both may be placed on the continuum in such a manner that they intersect, forming four quadrants: internal locus of control–internal locus of responsibility (IC-IR), external locus of control–internal locus of responsibility (EC-IR), internal locus of control–external locus of responsibility (IC-ER), and external locus of control–external locus of responsibility (EC-ER). Each quadrant represents a different worldview or orientation to life. Theoretically, then, if we know the individual's degree of internality or externality on the two loci, we could plot them on the figure. We would speculate that various ethnic and racial groups are not randomly distributed throughout the four quadrants. The previous discussion concerning cultural and societal influences on these two dimensions would seem to support this speculation. Indeed, several studies on African Americans (Helms & Giorgis, 1980; Oler, 1989) and therapists (Latting & Zundel, 1986) offer partial support for this hypothesis. Because our discussion focuses next on the political ramifications of the two dimensions, there is an evaluative "desirable-undesirable" quality to each worldview.

INTERNAL LOCUS OF CONTROL (IC)– INTERNAL LOCUS OF RESPONSIBILITY (IR)

As mentioned previously, high internal personal control (IC) individuals believe that they are masters of their fate and their actions do affect the outcomes. Likewise, people high in internal locus of responsibility (IR) attribute their current status and life conditions to their own unique attributes: Success is due to one's own efforts, and the lack of success is attributed to one's shortcomings or inadequacies. Perhaps the greatest exemplification of the IC-IR philosophy is U.S. society. U.S. culture can be described as the epitome of the individual-centered approach that emphasizes uniqueness, independence, and self-reliance (Herring, 1997; D.W. Sue et al., 1998). A high value for solving all problems is placed on personal resources: self-reliance, pragmatism, individualism, status achievement through one's own effort, and power or control over others, things, animals, and forces of nature. Democratic ideals such as "equal access to opportunity," "liberty and justice for all," "God helps those who help themselves," and "fulfillment of personal destiny" all reflect this worldview. The individual is held accountable for all that transpires. Constant and prolonged failure or the inability to attain goals leads to symptoms of self-blame (depression, guilt, and feelings of inadequacy). Most White middle-class members would fall within this quadrant.

Five American patterns of cultural assumptions and values can be identified (Pedersen, 1988; Stewart, 1971; Wehrly, 1995). These are the building blocks of the IC-IR worldview and typically guide our thinking about mental health services in Western society. As we have seen in the Kluckhohn and Strodtbeck model (1961), these values are manifested in the generic characteristics of counseling. The five systems of assumptions may be described as follows:

1. *Definition of activity.* Western culture stresses an activity modality of "doing," and the desirable pace of life is fast, busy, and driving. A "being" orientation that stresses a more passive, experimental, and contemplative role is in marked contrast to American values (external achievement, activity, goals, and solutions). Existence is in action and not being. Activism is seen most clearly in the mode of problem solving and decision making. Learning is active and not passive. American emphasis is on planning behavior that anticipates consequences.

2. *Definition of social relations.* Americans value equality and informality in relating to others. Friendships tend to be many, of short commitment, nonbinding, and shared. In addition, the person's rights and duties in a group are influenced by his/her own goals. Obligation to groups is limited, and value is placed on one's ability to actively influence the group. In contrast, many cultures stress hierarchical rank, formality, and status in interpersonal relations. Friendships are intense, long-term, and exclusive. Behavior in a group is dictated by acceptance of the constraints on the group and the authority of the leader.

3. *Motivation.* Achievement and competition are seen as motivationally healthy. The worth of an individual is measured by objective, visible, and materialistic possessions. Personal accomplishments are more important than place of birth, family background, heritage, or traditional status. Achieved status is valued over ascribed status.

4. *Perception of the world.* The world is viewed as distinctly separate from "humankind" and is physical, mechanical, and follows rational laws. Thus, the world is viewed as an object to be exploited, controlled, and developed for the material benefit of people. It is assumed that control and exploitation are necessary for the progress of civilized nations.

5. *Perception of the self and individual.* The self is seen as separate from the physical world and others. Decision making and responsibility rest with the individual and not the group. Indeed, the group is not a unit but an aggregate of individuals. The importance of a person's identity is reinforced in socialization and education. Autonomy is encouraged, and emphasis is placed on solving one's own problems, acquiring one's own possessions, and standing up for one's own rights.

Katz (1985) converts many of these characteristics into the components of counseling (and therapy) in Table 8.2.

Therapeutic Implications

It becomes obvious that Western approaches to clinical practice occupy the quadrant represented by IC-IR characteristics. Most therapists are of the opinion that people must take

Table 8.2   THE COMPONENTS OF WHITE CULTURE: VALUES AND BELIEFS

Rugged Individualism:

Individual is primary unit

Individual has primary responsibility

Independence and autonomy highly valued and rewarded

Individual can control environment

Competition:

Winning is everything

Win/lose dichtomy

Action Orientation:

Must master and control nature

Must always do something about a situation

Pragmatic/utilitarian view of life

Communication:

Standard English

Written tradition

Direct eye contact

Limited physical contact

Control emotions

Time:

Adherence to rigid time

Time is viewed as a commodity

Holidays:

Based on Christian religion

Based on White history and male leaders

History:

Based on European immigrants' experience in the United States

Romanticize war

Protestant Work Ethic:

Working hard brings success

Progress & Future Orientation:

Plan for future

Delayed gratification

Value continual improvement and progress

Emphasis on Scientific Method:

Objective, rational, linear thinking

Cause and effect relationships

Quantitative emphasis

Status and Power:

Measured by economic possessions

Credentials, titles, and positions

Believe "own" system is better than other systems

Owning goods, space, property

Family Structure:

Nuclear family is the ideal social unit

Male is breadwinner and the head of the household

Female is homemaker and subordinate to the husband

Patriarchal structure

Aesthetics:

Music and art based on European cultures

Women's beauty based on blond, blue-eyed, thin, young

Men's attractiveness based on athletic ability, power, economic status

Religion:

Belief in Christianity

No tolerance for deviation from single god concept

Note. From *The Counseling Psychologist* (p. 618), by J.H. Katz, 1985, Beverly Hills, CA: Sage. Copyright 1985 by Sage Publications, Inc. Reprinted with permission.

major responsibility for their own actions and can improve their lot in life through their own efforts. The epitome of this line of thought is represented by the numerous self-help approaches currently in vogue in our field.

Clients who occupy this quadrant tend to be White middle-class clients, and for these clients, such approaches might be entirely appropriate. In working with clients from different cultures, however, such an approach might be inappropriate. Diaz-Guerrero (1977), in his attempt to build a Mexican psychology, presents much data on how Mexicans and U.S. Americans differ with respect to their views of life. To be actively self-assertive is more characteristic of Anglo-Saxon sociocultural premises than of the Mexican. Indeed, to be actively self-assertive in Mexican socioculture is to clinically forecast adjustment difficulties. Counselors with a quadrant I orientation are often so culturally encapsulated that they are unable to understand their minority client's worldview. Thus, the possibility of cultural oppression in therapy becomes an ever-present threat.

EXTERNAL LOCUS OF CONTROL (EC) – INTERNAL LOCUS OF RESPONSIBILITY (IR)

Individuals who fall into this quadrant are most likely to accept the dominant culture's definition for self-responsibility but to have very little real control over how they are defined by others. The term *marginal man* (person) was first coined by Stonequist (1937) to describe a person who finds himself/herself living on the margins of two cultures and not fully accommodated to either. Although there is nothing inherently pathological about bicultural membership, Jones (1997) feels that Western society has practiced a form of cultural racism by imposing its standards, beliefs, and ways of behaving onto minority groups. Marginal individuals deny the existence of racism; believe that the plight of their own people is due to laziness, stupidity, and a clinging to outdated traditions; reject their own cultural heritage and believe that their ethnicity represents a handicap in Western society; evidence racial self-hatred; accept White social, cultural, and institutional standards; perceive physical features of White men and women as an exemplification of beauty; and are powerless to control their sense of self-worth because approval must come from an external source. As a result, they are high in person-focus and external control. The same dynamics and characteristics of the conformity stage (see Chapter 6) seem to operate here.

In the past, mental health professionals have assumed that marginality and self-hatred were internal conflicts of the person, almost as if they arise from the individual. In challenging the traditional notion of marginality, Freire (1970) states:

. . . *marginality is not by choice, marginal man has been expelled from and kept outside of the social system and is therefore the object of violence. In fact, however, the social structure as a whole does not "expel," nor is marginal man a "being outside of." . . . [Marginal persons] are "beings for another." Therefore the solution to their problem is not to become "beings inside of," but men freeing themselves; for, in reality, they are not marginal to the structure, but oppressed men within it. (pp. 10–11)*

It is quite clear that marginal persons are oppressed, have little choice, and are powerless in the face of the dominant- subordinate relationship between the middle-class Euro-American culture and their own minority culture. According to Freire (1970), if this dominant-subordinate relationship in society were eliminated, the phenomenon of marginality would also disappear.

For if two cultures exist on the basis of total equality (an ideal for biculturalism), the conflicts of marginality simply do not occur in the person.

Therapeutic Implications

The psychological dynamics for the EC-IR minority client are likely to reflect his/her marginal and self-hate status. For example, White therapists might be perceived as more competent than and preferred to therapists of the client's own race. To EC-IR minority clients, focusing on feelings may be very threatening, since it ultimately may reveal the presence of self-hate and the realization that they cannot escape from their own racial and cultural heritage. A culturally encapsulated White counselor or therapist who does not understand the sociopolitical dynamics of the client's concerns may unwittingly perpetuate the conflict. For example, the client's preference for a White therapist, coupled with the therapist's implicit belief in the values of U.S. culture, becomes a barrier to successive and effective counseling. A culturally sensitive helping professional needs to (a) help the client understand the particular dominant-subordinate political forces that have created this dilemma, and (b) help the client distinguish between positive attempts to acculturate and a negative rejection of one's own cultural values.

EXTERNAL LOCUS OF CONTROL (EC) – EXTERNAL LOCUS OF RESPONSIBILITY (ER)

The inequities and injustices of racism seen in the standard of living tend to be highly damaging to minorities. For example, the standard of living for African Americans, Hispanic Americans, and American Indians is much below that enjoyed by Whites. Discrimination may be seen in the areas of housing, employment, income, and education. In American cities, African Americans are by far the most segregated of the minorities and the inferior housing they are confined to is not the result of free choice or poverty, but discrimination. This inequity in housing is also applicable to other minorities. Contrary to popular belief, Chinatowns in San Francisco and New York City represent ghetto areas with high rates of unemployment, suicide, juvenile delinquency, poverty, and tuberculosis. Inferior jobs, high unemployment rates, and a much lower income than their White counterparts are also the plight suffered by other minorities. Lower income cannot be attributed primarily to less education. African Americans also suffer from segregated and inferior education: class size, qualification of teachers, physical facilities, and extracurricular activities all place them at a disadvantage. Furthermore, extreme acts of racism can wipe out a minority group. American Indians have witnessed widespread massacres that destroyed their leadership and peoples.

A person high in system-blame and external control feels that there is very little one can do in the face of such severe external obstacles as prejudice and discrimination. In essence, the EC response might be a manifestation of (a) having given up, or (b) an attempt to placate those in power. In the former, individuals internalize their impotence even though they are aware of the external basis of their plight. In its extreme form, oppression may result in a form of learned helplessness (Seligman, 1982). Seligman believes that humans exposed to helplessness (underemployment, unemployment, poor quality of education, poor housing) via prejudice and discrimination may exhibit passivity and apathy (poor motivation), may fail to learn that there are events that can be controlled (cognitive disruption), and may show anxiety and depression (emotional disturbance). When minorities learn that their responses have minimal effects on the environment, a phenomenon results that can best be described as an expectation of helplessness. People's susceptibility to helplessness depends on their experience with controlling the environment. In the face of continued racism, many may simply give up in their attempts to achieve personal goals. The basic assumption in the theory of learned helplessness is that organisms exposed to prolonged noncontrol in their lives develop expectations of helplessness in later situations. This expectation, unfortunately, occurs even in situations that are now controllable.

The dynamics of the placater, however, are not related to the giving-up response. Rather, social forces in the form of prejudice and discrimination are seen as too powerful to combat at that particular time. The best one can hope to do is to suffer the inequities in silence for fear of retaliation. "Don't rock the boat," "keep a low profile," and "survival at all costs" are the phrases that describe this mode of adjustment. Life is viewed as relatively fixed, with nothing much the individual can do. Passivity in the face of oppression is the primary reaction of the placater.

Slavery was one of the most important factors shaping the social-psychological functioning of African Americans. Interpersonal relations between Whites and Blacks were highly structured, placing African Americans in a subservient and inferior role. Those Blacks who broke the rules or did not show proper deferential behavior were severely punished. The spirits, however, of most African Americans were not broken. Conformity to White Euro-American rules and regulations was dictated by the need to survive in an oppressive environment. Direct expressions of anger and resentment were dangerous, but indirect expressions were frequently seen.

Therapeutic Implications

EC-ER African Americans are very likely to see the White therapist as symbolic of any other Black/White relations. They are likely to show "proper" deferential behavior and to not take seriously admonitions by the therapist that they are the masters of their own fate. As a result, an IC-IR therapist may perceive the culturally different clients as lacking in courage and ego-strength and as being passive. A culturally effective therapist, however, would recognize the bases of these adaptations. Unlike EC-IR clients, EC-ER individuals do understand the political forces that have subjugated their existence. The most helpful approach on the part of the therapist would be (a) to teach the clients new coping strategies, (b) to have them experience successes, and (c) to validate who and what they represent.

INTERNAL LOCUS OF CONTROL (IC) – EXTERNAL LOCUS OF RESPONSIBILITY (ER)

Individuals who score high in internal control and system-focus believe in their ability to shape events in their own life if given a chance. They do not accept the fact that their present state is due to their own inherent weakness. However, they also realistically perceive that external barriers of discrimination, prejudice, and exploitation block their paths to the successful attainment of goals. There is a considerable body of evidence to support this contention. Recall that the IC dimension was correlated with greater feelings of personal efficacy, higher aspirations, and so forth, and that ER was related to collective action in the social arena area. If so, we would expect that IC-ER people would be more likely to participate in civil rights activities and to stress racial identity and militancy.

Racial Pride and Identity

Pride in one's racial and cultural identity is most likely to be accepted by an IC-ER person. The low self-esteem engendered by widespread prejudice and racism is actively challenged now by these people. There is an attempt to redefine a group's existence by stressing consciousness and pride in their own racial and cultural heritage. Such phrases as "Black is beautiful" represent a symbolic relabeling of identity from Negro and colored to Black or African American. To many African Americans, "Negro" and "colored" are White labels symbolic of a warped and degrading identity given them by a racist society. As a means of throwing off these burdensome shackles, the Black individual and African Americans as a group are redefined in a positive light. Many racial minorities have begun the process in some form and banded together into what is called the "Third World Movement" (Asian Americans, African Americans, Hispanic/Latino Americans, American Indians, and others). Since all minorities share the common experience of oppression, they have formed alliances to expose and alleviate the damage that racism has dealt. Problems like poverty, unemployment, housing, education, and juvenile delinquency, as well as emotional problems, are seen as arising from racism in society. Persons of color have attempted to enhance feelings of group pride by emphasizing the positive aspects of their cultural heritage.

Militancy

Another area seemingly in support of the IC-ER worldview was intimately related to the concept of militancy and collective social action. Between 1964 and 1968 there were 239 violent riots, with racial overtones, resulting in 8,000 injured and 191 dead, mostly Black (National Commission on the Causes and Prevention of Violence, 1969). These events occurred in epidemic proportions that left the American people dazed and puzzled. Rochester in 1964, Chicago in 1965, Los Angeles in 1965, Cleveland in 1966, Detroit in 1967, and Newark in 1967, to name a few, were all struck by a seemingly senseless wave of collective violence in the Black ghettos. Confrontations between the police and Blacks, looting, sniping, assaults, and the burning of homes and property filled television screens across America. In light of these frightening events, many people searched for explanations about what had happened. The basis of the riots did not make sense in terms of rising income, better housing, and better education for Blacks in America. After all, reasoned many, conditions have never been better for Black Americans. Why should they riot?

When the 1960s riots are studied, two dominant explanations seem to arise. The first, called the *riffraff theory* (person-blame), explained the riots as the result of the sick, criminal elements of society: the emotionally disturbed, deviants, communist agitators, criminals, or unassimilated migrants. These agitators were seen as peripheral to organized society and possessing no broad social or political concerns. The agitators' frustrations and militant confrontation were seen as part of their own *personal* failures and inadequacies.

A second explanation, referred to as the *blocked-opportunity theory* (system-blame), views riot participants as those with high aspirations for their own lives and belief in their ability to achieve these goals. However, environmental forces rather than their own personal inadequacies prevent them from advancing in society and bettering their condition. The theory holds that riots are the result of massive discrimination against African Americans that has frozen them out of the social, economic, and political life of America. Caplan and Paige (1968) found that more rioters than nonrioters reported experiencing job obstacles and discrimination that blocked their mobility. Further probing revealed that it was not lack of training or education that accounted for the results. Fogelson (1970) presents data in support of the thesis that the ghetto riots are manifestations of grievances within a racist society. In referring to the riots he states that the rioting

was triggered not only because the rioters issued the protest and faced the danger together but also because the rioting revealed the common fate of Blacks in America. For most Blacks, and particularly northern Blacks, racial discrimination is a highly personal experience. They are denied jobs, refused apartments, stopped-and-searched, and declared ineducable (or so they are told), they are inexperienced, unreliable, suspicious, and culturally deprived, and not because they are Black. (p. 145)

The recognition that ghetto existence is a result of racism and not the result of some inherent weakness, coupled with the rioters' belief in their ability to control events in their own lives, made a situation ripe for the venting of frustration and anger. Several studies support the contention that those who rioted have an increased sense of personal effectiveness and control (Abeles, 1976; Caplan, 1970; Caplan & Paige, 1968; Forward & Williams, 1970; Gore & Rotter, 1963; Marx, 1967). Indeed, a series of studies concerning characteristics of the rioters and nonrioters failed to confirm the riffraff theory (Caplan, 1970; Caplan & Paige, 1968; Forward & Williams, 1970; Turner & Wilson, 1976). In general, the following emerged concerning those who engaged in rioting during the 1960s: (a) Rioters did not differ from nonrioters in income and rate of unemployment, so they appear to be no more poverty stricken, jobless, or lazy; (b) those who rioted were generally better educated, so rioting cannot be attributed to the poorly educated; (c) rioters were better integrated than nonrioters in social and political workings of the community, so the lack of integration into political and social institutions cannot be used as an explanation; (d) long-term residents were more likely to riot, so rioting cannot be blamed on outside agitators or recent immigrants; (e) rioters held more positive attitudes toward Black history and culture (feelings of racial pride) and thus were not alienated from themselves. Caplan (1970) concluded that militants are not more socially or personally deviant than their nonmilitant counterparts. Evidence tends to indicate that they are more healthy according to several traditional criteria measuring mental health. Caplan also believes that attempts to use the riffraff theory to explain riots have an underlying motive. By attributing causes to individual deficiencies, the users of the riffraff theory relieve White institutions of the blame. Such a conceptualization means that psychotherapy, social work, mental hospitalization, or imprisonment should be directed toward the militants. Demands for system-change are declared illegitimate because they are the products of "sick" or "confused" minds. Maintenance of the status quo rather than needed social change (social therapy) is reaffirmed.

Therapeutic Implications

There is much evidence to indicate that minority groups are becoming increasingly conscious of their own racial and cultural identities as they relate to oppression in U.S. society (Atkinson, Morten & Sue, 1998; Carter, 1995; Helms, 1995; D.W. Sue et al., 1998). If the evidence is correct, it is also probable that more and more minorities are likely to hold an IC-ER worldview. Thus, therapists who work with the culturally different will increasingly be exposed to clients with an IC-ER worldview. And, in many respects, these clients pose the most difficult problems for the IC-IR White therapist. Challenges to the therapist's credibility and trustworthiness are likely to be raised by these clients. The helping professional is likely to be seen as a part of the Establishment that has oppressed minorities. Self-disclosure on the part of the client is not likely to come quickly, and more than any other worldview, an IC-ER orientation means that clients are likely to play a much more active part in the therapy process and to demand action from the therapist.

The theory being proposed here predicts several things about the differences between IC-IR and IC-ER worldviews in counseling and therapy. First, these two worldviews may dictate how a clinician and client define problems and how they use and are receptive to different styles of counseling and therapy. For example, IC-IR people will tend to see the problem as residing in the person, while IC-ER people will see the problem as being external to the individual. Furthermore, IC-ER therapists may use and are most receptive to therapy skills, styles, or approaches that are action oriented. This is in contrast to an IC-IR clinician, who may be more nondirective in interactions with clients. Two early studies seem to bear out these predictions.

Berman (1979) cites the example of a study that compared African American and White counselor trainees viewing video vignettes of African American and White clients. The clients presented problems related to vocational choice. To a question of "What would you say next?" White males tended to ask questions, White females tended to reflect feelings and to paraphrase, and African Americans tended to give advice and directions. More importantly, African Americans identified the problem as being in society rather than in the individual, whereas Whites tended to focus more on the individual. The assumption being made is that the Blacks in this study are most likely IC-ER counselor trainees. A similar study conducted by Atkinson, Maruyama, and Matsui (1978) with Asian Americans revealed consistent findings. The more politically conscious Asian Americans (IC-ER) rated counselors using a directive approach (structure, advice, suggestions) rather than nondirective (reflection and paraphrase) more credible and approachable.

CONCLUSIONS

The conceptual model presented in this chapter concerning worldviews and identity development among persons of color is consistent with many of our formulations discussed in the previous two chapters. Racial/cultural identity for minorities in America is intimately related to racism and oppression. Using this model in working with culturally different clients has many practical and research implications.

1. It is obvious that therapy in the United States falls into the IC-IR quadrant. Clients are seen as able to initiate change and are held responsible for their current plight. A therapist operating from this framework will most likely be person-centered. While such a view is not necessarily incorrect or bad, it may be inappropriately applied to clients who do not share this perception. When therapists are culturally-sociopolitically blind and impose their worldviews on clients without regard for the legitimacy of other views, they are engaging in a form of cultural oppression.

   Therefore, what is needed is for therapists to become culturally aware, to understand the basis of their worldviews, and to understand and accept the possible legitimacy of others. Only when graduate training programs begin to incorporate multicultural concepts in their

IC-IR	IC-ER
I. (Assertive/Passive) I'm O.K. and have control over myself. Society is o.k., and I can make it in the system.	*IV. (Assertive/Assertive)* I'm O.K. and have control, but need a chance. Society is not o.k., and I know what's wrong and seek to change it.

EC-IR	EC-ER
II. (Marginal/Passive) I'm O.K., but my control comes best when I define myself according to the definition of the dominant culture. Society is o.k. the way it is; it's up to me.	*III. (Passive-Aggressive)* I'm not O.K. and don't have much control; might as well give up or please everyone. Society is not o.k. and is the reason for my plight; the bad system is all to blame.

Figure 8.2 Transactional Analysis of Sue's Cultural Identity Quadrants. *Note:* From *Counseling and Development in a Multicultural Society* (p. 399), by J.A. Axelson. Copyright © 1993 by Wadsworth, Inc. Reprinted by permission of Brooks/Cole Publishing Company, Pacific Grove, California 93950, a division of Wadsworth, Inc.

training (not from a White perspective, but from the perspective of each culture) will therapy possibly lose its oppressive orientation.

2. Another implication from this conceptual model is its use as an aid to understanding possible psychological dynamics of a culturally different client. Figure 8.2 presents a transactional analysis of the four quadrants.

For example, an EC-IR client who experiences self-hatred and marginality may be a victim of the dominant-subordinate relationship fostered in American society. The problem is not inherent or internal, and counseling may be aimed at a reeducative process to get that client to become aware of the wider social-political forces at the basis of his or her plight.

An EC-IR person, whether he or she has given up or is placating, must be taught new coping skills to deal with people and institutions. Experiences of success are critically important for clients in this quadrant.

IC-ER clients are especially difficult for therapists to handle, because they are most likely to challenge counseling or therapy as acts of oppression. A therapist who is not in touch with these wider social-political issues will quickly lose credibility and effectiveness. In addition, IC-ER clients are externally oriented, and demands for the therapist to take external action on the part of the client will be strong (setting up a job interview, helping the client fill out forms, etc.). While most of us have been taught not to intervene externally on behalf of the client, all of us must look seriously at the value base of this dictate.

3. It is highly possible that problem definitions and specific therapy skills are differentially associated with a particular worldview. Culturally different clients may prematurely terminate therapy (D.W. Sue, 1977a) because therapists not only differ in worldviews, but also use clin-

ical skills inappropriate to their clients' lifestyles. Our next step would be to research the following question: Are there specific counseling/therapy goals, techniques, and skills best suited for a particular worldview? If so, the implications for clinical training are important.

First, this indicates an overwhelming need to teach trainees the importance of being able to understand and share the worldviews of their clients. Second, it is no longer enough to learn a limited number of therapy skills. Ivey, Ivey, and Simek-Downing (1997) make a strong case for this position. The culturally effective therapist is one who is able to generate the widest repertoire of responses (verbal/nonverbal) consistent with the lifestyles and values of the culturally different client. Particularly for minorities, the passive approaches of asking questions, reflecting feelings, and paraphrasing must be balanced with directive responses (giving advice and suggestions, disclosing feelings, etc.) on the part of the therapist.

4. The counselor and therapist need to understand that each worldview has much to offer that is positive. While these four psychological orientations have been described in a highly evaluative manner, positive aspects of each can be found. For example, the individual responsibility and achievement orientation of quadrant I; biculturalism and cultural flexibility of quadrant II; the ability to compromise and adapt to life conditions of quadrant III; and the collective action and social concern of quadrant IV need not be at odds with one another. The role of the counselor or therapist may be to help the client integrate aspects of each worldview that will maximize his/her effectiveness and psychological well-being. Ivey, Ivey, and Simek-Downing (1997) call this person the "culturally effective individual." He/she is a "functional integrator" who is able to combine and integrate aspects of each worldview into a harmonious union. To accomplish this goal, however, the counselor must also be able to share the worldview of his/her clients. In essence, the culturally skilled therapist is also one who is a functional integrator.

SOME CAUTIONS

In closing, there are some precautions that should be observed in using this model. First, the validity of this model has not been directly established through research, although preliminary inquiries are promising (Helms & Giorgis, 1980; Latting & Zundel, 1986; Oler, 1989) and much of the research literature on racial/cultural identity development also supports it. While much empirical and clinical evidence is consistent with the model, many of the assertions in the chapter remain at the speculative level. Second, the behavior manifestations of each quadrant have not been specifically identified. Regardless of a person's psychological orientation, we would suspect that individuals can adapt and use behaviors associated with another worldview. This, indeed, is the basis of training therapists to work with the culturally different. Third, each style represents conceptual categories. In reality, while people might tend to hold one worldview in preference to another, it does not prevent them from holding variations of others. Most persons of color represent mixes of each rather than a pure standard. Fourth, whether this conceptual model can be applied to groups other than minorities in America has yet to be established. Last, we must remember that it is very possible for individuals from different cultural groups to be more similar in worldview than those from the same culture. While race and ethnicity may be correlated with one's outlook in life, the correspondence certainly is not one to one.

Part Four

Multicultural Counseling and Therapy Competence

Chapter Nine

◆

Non-Western and Indigenous Methods of Healing

◆

Renewed interest in indigenous methods of healing has been fueled by both the postmodern movement in psychology and changing demographics in the United States. In the former, the importance of understanding alternative realities, cultural relativism, spirituality, and a holistic perspective has challenged traditional Euro-American science (Highlen, 1994, 1996). In the latter, the increasing numbers of racial/ethnic minority groups in our society, especially recent Asian, Latin American, and African immigrants, have exposed mental health professionals to a host of different belief systems, some radically different from the Euro-American worldview (D.W. Sue, Arredondo, & McDavis, 1992). As counselors and therapists will increasingly come into contact with client groups who differ from them in race, culture, and ethnicity, it seems important to study and understand indigenous healing practices in order to (a) fully understand the worldview of culturally different clients, (b) anticipate potential conflicts in belief systems that might hinder our ability to be therapeutically effective, and (c) develop an appreciation for the richness of these age-old forms of treatment. To prevent our journey from becoming a philosophical and abstract exercise, we will make use of multiple case studies to illustrate alternative belief systems and treatments.

◆ *Case Study*

SPIRIT ATTACKS: THE CASE OF VANG XIONG

Vang Xiong is a Hmong (Laotian) former soldier who, with his wife and child, was resettled in Chicago in 1980. The change from his familiar rural surroundings and farm life to an unfamiliar urban area must have produced severe culture shock. In addition, Vang vividly remembers seeing people killed during his escape from Laos, and he expressed feelings of guilt about having to leave his brothers and sisters behind in that country. Five months after his arrival, the

Xiong family moved into a conveniently located apartment, and that is when Vang's problems began (Tobin & Friedman, 1983).

SYMPTOMS AND CAUSE

Vang could not sleep the first night in the apartment, nor the second, nor the third. After three nights of sleeping very little, Vang came to see his resettlement worker, a young bilingual Hmong man named Moua Lee. Vang told Moua that the first night he woke suddenly, short of breath, from a dream in which a cat was sitting on his chest. The second night, the room suddenly grew darker, and a figure, like a large black dog, came to his bed and sat on his chest. He could not push the dog off and he grew quickly and dangerously short of breath. The third night, a tall, white-skinned female spirit came into his bedroom from the kitchen and lay on top of him. Her weight made it increasingly difficult for him to breathe, and as he grew frantic and tried to call out he could manage but a whisper. He attempted to turn onto his side, but found he was pinned down. After 15 minutes, the spirit left him, and he awoke, screaming. . . . He was afraid to return to the apartment at night, afraid to fall asleep, afraid he would die during the night, or that the spirit would make it so that he and his wife could never have another child. He told Moua that once, when he was 15, he had had a similar attack; that several times, back in Laos, his elder brother had been visited by a similar spirit; and that his brother was subsequently unable to father children due to his wife's miscarriages and infertility. (p. 440)

Moua Lee and mental health workers became very concerned in light of the high incidence of "Sudden Death Syndrome" among Southeast Asian refugees. For some reason, the incidence of unexplained deaths, primarily among Hmong men, would occur within the first two years of residence in the United States. Autopsies produced no identifiable cause for the deaths. All the reports were the same: A person in apparently good health went to sleep and died without awakening. Often, the victim displayed labored breathing, screams, and frantic movements just before death.

Because Vang appeared in danger of suffering such a dire fate, the mental health staff felt they lacked the expertise for so complex and potentially dangerous a case. Conventional Western means of treatment for other Hmong clients had proved minimally effective. As a result, they decided to seek the services of Mrs. Thor, a 50-year-old Hmong woman who was widely respected as a shaman in Chicago's Hmong community. The description of the treatment is given below:

SHAMANIC CURE

That evening, Vang Xiong was visited in his apartment by Mrs. Thor, who began by asking Vang to tell her what was wrong. She listened to his story, asked a few questions, and then told him she thought she could help. She gathered the Xiong family around the dining room table, upon which she placed some candles alongside many plates of food that Vang's wife had prepared. Mrs. Thor lit the candles, and then began a chant that Vang and his wife knew was an attempt to communicate with spirits. Ten minutes or so after Mrs. Thor had begun chanting, she was so intensely involved in her work that Vang and his family felt free to talk to each other, and to walk about the room without fear of distracting her. Approximately one hour after she had begun, Mrs. Thor completed her chanting, announcing that she knew what was wrong. She said that she had learned from her spirit that the figures in Vang's dreams who lay on his chest and who made it so difficult for him to breathe were the souls of the apartment's previous tenants, who had apparently moved out so abruptly they had left their souls behind. Mrs. Thor constructed a cloak out of newspaper for Vang to wear. She then cut the cloak in two, and burned the pieces, sending the spirits on their way with the smoke. She also had Vang crawl through a hoop, and then between two knives, telling him that these maneuvers would make it very hard for spirits to follow. Following these brief ceremonies, the food prepared by Vang's wife was enjoyed by all. The leftover meats were given in payment to Mrs. Thor, and she left, assuring Vang Xiong that his troubles with spirits were over. (p. 441)

Clinical knowledge regarding what is called the Hmong Sudden Death Syndrome indicates that Vang was one of the lucky victims of the syndrome—he survived it. Indeed, since undergoing the healing ceremony in which the unhappy spirits were released, Vang has reported no more problems with nightmares or with his breathing during sleep.

Such a story, to many, might appear unbelievable and akin to mysticism. After all, most of us have been trained in a Western ontology, which does not embrace indigenous or alternative healing approaches. Indeed, if anything, it actively rejects such approaches as unscientific and supernatural; mental health professionals are encouraged to rely on sensory information, which is defined by the physical plane of existence rather than the spiritual one (Highlen, 1996; White & Parham, 1990). Adopting such a rigid stance shows an unfortunate short-sightedness, because there is much that Western healing can learn from these age-old forms of treatment. Let us briefly analyze the case of Vang Xiong to illustrate what these valuable lessons might be and draw parallels between non-Western and Western healing practices.

THE LEGITIMACY OF CULTURE-BOUND SYNDROMES: NIGHTMARE DEATHS AND THE HMONG SUDDEN DEATH PHENOMENON

The symptoms experienced by Vang and the frighteningly high number of Hmong refugees who have died from these "nightmare deaths" have baffled mental health workers for years. Indeed, researchers at the Federal Centers for Disease Control and epidemiologists have tried to study it but remain mystified (Sue, Sue, & Sue, 1997; Tobin & Friedman, 1983). Such tales bring to mind anthropological literature describing "voodoo deaths" and *bangungut,* or Oriental nightmare death. What is clear, however, is that these deaths do not appear to have a primary biological basis and that psychological factors (primarily belief in the imminence of death— either by a curse [as in voodoo suggestion] or some form of punishment and excessive stress) appear to be causative. Belief in spirits and spirit possession is not uncommon among many cultures, especially in Southeast Asia (Fadiman, 1997; Harner, 1990). Such worldview differences pose problems for Western-trained mental health professionals, who may quickly dismiss these belief systems and impose their own explanations and treatments upon culturally different clients. Working outside of the belief system of culturally different clients might not have a desired therapeutic effect, and unintentional harm may occur. In this case there was the risk of death for Vang.

The sudden death phenomenon is a culture-bound reality increasingly being recognized by Western science (Kamarack & Jennings, 1991). Most researchers now acknowledge that attitudes, beliefs, and emotional states are intertwined and can have a powerful effect on physiological responses and physical well-being. Death from bradycardia (slowing of the heartbeat) seems correlated with feelings of helplessness as in the case of Vang (there was nothing he could do to get the cat, dog, or white-skinned spirit off his chest). The following case study shows the impact of this emotion on heart rate.

◆ *Case Study*

The patient was lying very stiffly in bed, staring at the ceiling. He was a 56-year-old man who had suffered an anterior myocardial infarction [heart attack] some 2½ days ago. He lay there with bloodshot eyes, unshaven, and as we walked into the room, he made eye contact first with me and then with the intern who had just left his side. The terror in his eyes was reflected in those of the intern. The patient had a heart rate of 48/min that was clearly a sinus bradycardia. I put my hands on his wrist, which had the effect of both confirming the pulse and making some physical contact with him, and I asked what was wrong. "I am very tired," he said. "I haven't slept in two and one-half days, because I'm sure that if I fall asleep, I won't wake up." I discussed with him the fact that we had been at fault for not making it clear that he was being very carefully monitored, so that we would be aware of any problem that might develop. I informed him further that his prognosis was improving rapidly. As I spoke, his pulse became fuller. (Shine, 1984, p. 27)

It is clear that the patient's physiological response was counteracted by the physician's assurance that his situation was not hopeless—in essence, by removing the source of stress. In other words, the patient believed in the power of the doctor and the monitoring devices attached to him. Likewise, it is apparent that Vang was helped by his belief in the power of Mrs. Thor and the treatment he received. We will return to this important point shortly.

The *Diagnostic and Statistical Manual of Mental Disorders* (DSM-IV, 1994) has made initial strides in recognizing the importance of ethnic and cultural factors related to psychiatric diagnosis. They warn that mental health professionals who work with immigrants and ethnic minorities must take into account (a) the predominant means of manifesting disorders (e.g., possessing spirits, nerves, fatalism, inexplicable misfortune), (b) perceived causes or explanatory models, and (c) preferences for professional and indigenous sources of care. Interestingly, DSM-IV now contains a glossary of culture-bound syndromes in Appendix I (see Table 9.1 for a listing of these disorders). They describe culture-bound syndromes as:

. . . recurrent, locality-specific patterns of aberrant behavior and troubling experience that may or may not be linked to a particular DSM-IV diagnostic category. Many of these patterns are indigenously considered to be "illnesses," or at least afflictions, and most have local names . . .

Table 9.1 DSM-IV CULTURE-BOUND SYNDROMES

Culture-bound syndromes are disorders specific to a cultural group or society, but not easily given a DSM diagnosis. These illnesses or afflictions have local names with distinct culturally sanctioned beliefs surrounding causation and treatment. Some of these are briefly described.

AMOK. A disorder first reported in Malaysia but also found in Laos, the Phillippines, Polynesia, Papua New Guinea, Puerto Rico, and among the Navajo. It is a dissociative episode preceded by introspective brooding and then an outburst of violent, aggressive, or homicidal behavior toward people and objects. Persecutory ideas, amnesia, and exhaustion signal a return to the premorbid state.

ATAQUE DE NERVIOS. A disorder most clearly reported among Latinos from the Caribbean, but recognized in Latin American and Latin Mediterranean groups. It involves uncontrollable shouting, attacks of crying, trembling, verbal or physical aggression, and dissociative or seizure-like and fainting episodes. The onset is associated with a stressful life event relating to family (death of a loved one, divorce, conflicts with children, etc.).

BRAIN FAG. In West Africa, it is a disorder usually experienced by high school or university students in response to academic stress. Students state their brains are "fatigued," and they have difficulties in concentrating, remembering, and thinking.

GHOST SICKNESS. Observed among members of American Indian tribes, this disorder is a preoccupation with death and the deceased. It is sometimes associated with witchcraft and includes bad dreams, weakness, feelings of danger, loss of appetite, fainting, dizziness, anxiety, and a sense of suffocation.

KORO. A Malaysian term describing an episode of sudden and intense anxiety that the penis of the male or the vulva and nipples of the female will recede into the body and cause death. It can occur in epidemic proportions in local areas and has been reported in China, Thailand, and other south and east Asian countries.

MAL DE OJO. Found primarily in Mediterranean cultures, the term refers to a Spanish phrase that means "evil eye." Children are especially at risk, with symptoms that include fitful sleep, crying without apparent cause, diarrhea, vomiting, and fever.

NERVIOS. The disorder includes a range of symptoms associated with distress, somatic disturbance, and inability to function. Common symptoms include headaches, brain aches, sleep difficulties, nervousness, easy tearfulness, dizziness, and tingling sensations. It is a common idiom of distress among Latinos in the United States and Latin America.

ROOTWORK. Cultural interpretations of illness ascribed to hexing, witchcraft, sorcery, or the evil influence of another person. Symptoms include generalized anxiety, gastrointestinal complaints, and fear of being poisoned or killed (voodoo death). Roots, spells, or hexes can be placed on people. It is believed that a cure can be manifested via a "root doctor" who removes the root. Such a belief can be found in the southern United States among both African American and European American populations and in Caribbean societies.

SHEN-K'UEI (TAIWAN); SHENKUI (CHINA). A Chinese-described disorder that involves anxiety and panic symptoms with somatic complaints. There is no identifiable physical cause. Sexual dysfunctions are common (premature ejaculation and impotence). The physical symptoms are attributed to excessive semen loss from frequent intercourse, masturbation, nocturnal emission, or passing of "white turbid urine" believed to contain semen. Excessive semen loss is feared because semen represents one's vital essence; its loss can be life threatening.

SUSTO. The disorder is associated with fright or "soul loss" and is a prevalent folk illness among some Latinos in the United States and found in Mexico, Central America, and South America. *Susto* is attributed to a frightening event that causes the soul to leave the body. Sickness and eventual death may result. Healing is associated with rituals that call the soul back to the body and restoring spiritual balance.

ZAR. This is a term used to describe spirits possessing an individual. Dissociative episodes, shouting, laughing, hitting the head against a wall, weeping, and other demonstrative symptoms are associated with it. It is found in Ethiopia, Somalia, Egypt, Sudan, Iran, and other North African and Middle Eastern societies. People may develop a long-term relationship with the spirit, and their behavior is not considered pathological.

*culture-bound syndromes are generally limited to specific societies or culture areas and are local-
ized, folk, diagnostic categories that frame coherent meanings for certain repetitive, patterned,
and troubling sets of experiences and observations. (p. 844)*

In summary, it is very important for mental health professionals to become familiar not only
with the cultural background of their clients, but to be knowledgeable about specific culture-
bound syndromes. A primary danger from lack of cultural understanding is the tendency to
overpathologize (overestimate the degree of pathology); the mental health professional would
have been wrong in diagnosing Vang as a paranoid schizophrenic suffering from delusions and
hallucinations. Many might have prescribed powerful antipsychotic medication or even insti-
tutionalization. The fact that he was cured so quickly indicates that such a diagnosis would
have been erroneous. Interestingly, it is equally dangerous to underestimate the severity or complexity of a refugee's emotional condition as well.

CAUSATION AND SPIRIT POSSESSION

Vang believed that his problems were related to an attack by undesirable spirits. His story in the
following passage gives us some idea about beliefs associated with the fears:

*The most recent attack in Chicago was not the first encounter my family and I have had with this
type of spirit, a spirit we call Chia. My brother and I endured similar attacks about six years ago
back in Laos. We are susceptible to such attacks because we didn't follow all of the mourning rituals we should have when our parents died. Because we didn't properly honor their memories we have
lost contact with their spirits, and thus we are left with no one to protect us from evil spirits. Without our parents' spirits to aid us, we will always be susceptible to spirit attacks. I had hoped flying
so far in a plane to come to American would protect me, but it turns out spirits can follow even this
far. (Tobin & Friedman, 1983, p. 444)*

Western science remains skeptical of applying supernatural explanations to phenomena and
certainly does not consider the existence of spirits as scientifically sound. Yet, belief in spirits
and its parallel relationship to religious, philosophic, and scientific worldviews have existed in
every known culture, including the United States (as shown in the witchcraft trials of Salem,
Massachusetts). Among many Southeast Asian groups, it is not uncommon to posit the existence of good and evil spirits, to assume that they are intelligent beings, and to believe they are
able to affect the life circumstance of the living (Fadiman, 1997; C.C. Lee, 1996). In the case of
Vang, he believed strongly that his problems were due to spirits who were unhappy and/or pun-
ishing him. Interestingly, among the Hmong, "good spirits" can often help serve a protective
function against susceptibility to the evil ones. Because Vang's parental spirits had deserted
him, he was more susceptible to the workings of evil forces. Many cultures believe that a cure
can come about only through the aid of a shaman or healer with divination skills who can reach
and communicate in the spirit world.

While mental health professionals may not believe in spirits, therapists are similar to the
Hmongs in their need to explain the troubling phenomena experienced by Vang and to con-
strue meaning. Vang's sleep disturbances, nightmares, and fears can be seen as the result of
emotional distress. From a Western perspective, his war experiences, flight, relocation, and
survivor stress (not to mention the adjustment to a new country) may all be contributants
to "combat fatigue" (post-traumatic stress disorder, or PTSD) and survivor guilt (Mollica,
Wyshak, & Lavelle, 1987; Tobin & Friedman, 1983; Uba, 1994). Studies on the hundreds of

thousands of refugees from Southeast Asia, like Vang, suggest that they were severely traumatized during their flight for freedom (Mollica, Wyshak, & Lavelle, 1987). The most frequent diagnoses for this group were generally major affective disorder and post-traumatic stress disorder. In addition to being a combat veteran, Vang is a disaster victim, a survivor of a holocaust in which perhaps 200,000 of the approximately 500,000 Hmongs died. Vang's sleeplessness, breathing difficulties, paranoid belief that something attacked him in bed, and symptoms of anxiety and depression are the result of extreme trauma and stress. Tobin and Friedman (1983) believe that Vang also suffered from survivor's guilt and conclude:

Applying some of the insights of the Holocaust literature to the plight of the Southeast Asian refugees, we can view Vang Xiong's emotional crisis (his breathing and sleeping disorder) as the result not so much of what he suffered as what he did not suffer, of what he was spared. . . . "Why should I live while others died?" so Vang Xiong, through his symptoms, seemed to be saying, "Why should I sleep comfortably here in America while the people I left behind suffer? How can I claim the right to breathe when so many of my relatives and countrymen breathe no more back in Laos?" (*p. 443*)

Although we might be able to recast Vang's problems in more acceptable psychological terminology, the effective multicultural helping professional requires knowledge of cultural relativism and respect for the belief system of culturally different clients. Respecting another's worldview does not mean the helping professional needs to subscribe to it. Yet, the counselor/therapist must be willing and ready to learn from indigenous models of healing and to function as a facilitator of indigenous support or healing systems (Atkinson, Thompson, & Grant, 1993).

THE SHAMAN AS THERAPIST: COMMONALITIES

It is probably safe to conclude that every society and culture has designated individuals or groups considered to be healers: those who comfort the ailing. Their duties involve curing not only physical ailments, but those related to psychological distress or behavioral deviance as well (Harner, 1990). While every culture has multiple healers, the shaman in non-Western cultures is perhaps the most powerful of all, because only he/she possesses the ultimate magico-religious powers that go beyond the senses. Mrs. Thor was a shaman, well known and respected in the Hmong community of the Chicago area. While her approach to treating Vang (use of incense, candle burning, use of newspaper, trance-like chanting, spirit diagnosis, and even her home visit) shows traits that Westerners connect with mysticism, many aspects of her treatment in fact resemble Western psychotherapy.

First, as we saw in Chapter 2, credibility of the healer is crucial to the effectiveness of therapy. In this case, Mrs. Thor had all the cultural credentials signifying her to be a shaman: She was a specialist and professional with long years of training and experience in dealing with similar cases. By reputation and behavior, she acted in a manner familiar to Vang and his family, but more importantly, she shared their worldview as to problem definition. Second, she showed compassion while maintaining a professional detachment, did not pity or make fun of Vang, avoided premature diagnosis or judgement, and listened to his story carefully. Third, like the Western therapist, she offered herself as the chief instrument of cure. She used her expertise and ability to get in touch with the hidden world of the spirits (in Western terms we might call it the unconscious) and aided Vang to understand (become conscious of) the mysterious forces of the spirits (unconscious) to effect a cure.

Because Vang believed in spirits, Mrs. Thor's interpretation that the nightmares and breathing difficulties were spiritual problems was intelligible, desired, and ultimately curative. It is important to note, however, that Vang also continued to receive treatment from the local mental health clinic in coming to grips with the deaths of others (his parents, fellow soldiers, and other family members).

In the case of Vang Xiong, both non-Western and Western forms of healing were combined for maximum effect. The presence of a mental health treatment facility that employed bilingual/bicultural practitioners, its vast experience with Southeast Asian immigrants, and its willingness to use indigenous healers provided Vang with a culturally appropriate form of treatment that probably saved his life. Not all immigrants, however, are so fortunate. Witness the case of the Nguyen family.

♦ *Case Study*

A CASE OF CHILD ABUSE?

Mr. and Mrs. Nguyen and their four children left Vietnam in a boat with 36 other people. Several days later, they were set upon by Thai pirates. The occupants were all robbed of their belongings; some were killed, including two of the Nguyens' children. Nearly all the women were raped repeatedly. The trauma of the event is still very much with the Nguyen family, who now reside in St. Paul, Minnesota. The event was most disturbing to Mr. Nguyen, who had watched two of his children drown and his wife being raped. The pirates had beaten him severely and tied him to the boat railing during the rampage. As a result of his experiences, he continued to suffer feelings of guilt, suppressed rage, and nightmares.

The Nguyen family came to the attention of the school and social service agencies because of suspected child abuse. Their oldest child, Phuoc (age 12), had come to school one day with noticeable bruises on his back and down the spinal column. In addition, obvious scars from past injuries were observed on the child's upper and lower torso. His gym teacher had seen the bruises and scars and reported them to the school counselor immediately. The school nurse was contacted about the possibility of child abuse and a conference was held with Phuoc. He denied he had been hit by his parents and refused to remove his garments when requested to do so. Indeed, he became quite frightened and hysterical about taking off his shirt. Since there was still considerable doubt about whether this was a case of child abuse, the counselor decided to let the matter drop for the moment. Nevertheless, school personnel were alerted to this possibility.

Several weeks later, after four days of absence, Phuoc returned to school. The homeroom teacher noticed bruises on Phuoc's forehead and the bridge of his nose. When the incident was reported to the school office, the counselor immediately called Child Protective Services to report a suspected case of child abuse.

Because of the heavy caseload experienced by the Child Protective Services, a social worker was unable to visit the family until weeks later. The social worker, Mr. P., had called the family and visited the home late on a Thursday afternoon. Mrs. Nguyen greeted Mr. P. upon his arrival. She appeared nervous, tense, and frightened. Her English was poor, and it was difficult to communicate with her. Since Mr. P. had specifically requested to also see Mr. Nguyen as well, he inquired about his whereabouts. Mrs. Nguyen answered that he was not feeling well and was in the room downstairs. She said he was having "a bad day," had not been able to sleep last night, and was having flashbacks. In his present condition, he would not be helpful.

When Mr. P. asked about the bruises on her son Phuoc, Mrs. Nguyen did not seem to understand what he was referring to. The social worker explained in detail the reason for his visit. Mrs. Nguyen explained that the scars were due to the beating given her children by the Thai pirates. She became very emotional about the topic and broke into tears.

While this had some credibility, Mr. P. explained that there were fresh bruises on Phuoc's body as well. Mrs. Nguyen seemed confused, denied there were new injuries, and denied they would hurt Phuoc. The social worker persisted in pressing Mrs. Nguyen about the new injuries when she suddenly looked up and said, "Thúôc Nam." It was obvious that Mrs. Nguyen now understood what Mr. P. was referring to. When asked to clarify what she meant by the phrase, Mrs. Nguyen pointed at several thin bamboo sticks and a bag of coins wrapped tightly in a white cloth. It looked like a blackjack! She then pointed downstairs in the direction of the husband's room. It was obvious from Mrs. Nguyen's gestures that her husband had used these to beat her son.

There are many similarities between the Nguyen family and that of Vang Xiong. One of the most common experiences of refugees forced to flee their country is the extreme stressors they experienced. Constantly staring into the "face of death" was, unfortunately, all too common an experience. Seeing loved ones killed, tortured, and raped; being helpless to change or control such situations; leaving familiar surroundings; living in temporary refugee or resettlement camps; and encountering a strange and alien culture can only be described as multiple severe traumas. There is a high likelihood that Cambodian, Hmong/Laotian, and Vietnamese refugees are likely to suffer from serious post-traumatic stress and other forms of major affective disorders. Mr. and Mrs. Nguyen's behaviors (flashbacks, desire to isolate the self, emotional fluctuations, anxiety and tenseness) might all be symptoms of PTSD. Accurate understanding of their life circumstances will prevent a tendency to overpathologize or underpathologize their symptoms (Mollica, Wyshak, & Lavelle, 1987). These symptoms, along with a reluctance to disclose to strangers and their discomfort with the social worker, should be placed in the context of the stressors they experienced and their cultural background. More importantly, in the case of the Nguyen family, their behaviors should not be interpreted to indicate guilt or a desire not to disclose the truth about child abuse.

There are also potential linguistic and cultural barriers for mental health professionals to consider when working with refugees; a lack of both experience and expertise can exacerbate the difficulty of communicating with such clients. In this case, it is clear that the teacher, school counselor, school nurse, and even the social worker did not have sufficient understanding or experience in working with Southeast Asian refugees. For example, the social worker's failure to understand Vietnamese phrases and the wife's limited English proficiency place serious limitations on their ability to communicate accurately. The social worker might have avoided much of the misunderstanding if an interpreter had been present. In addition, the school personnel may have misinterpreted many culturally sanctioned forms of behavior on the part of the Vietnamese. Phuoc's reluctance to disrobe in front of strangers (the nurse) may have been prompted by cultural taboos rather than by attempts to hide his injuries. Traditional Asian culture dictates strongly that *family matters are handled within the family.* Many Asians believe that family affairs are not discussed publicly and especially not with strangers. Disrobing publicly and telling others about the scars or the trauma of the Thai pirates are not done readily. Yet, such knowledge is required by educators and social service agencies who must make enlightened decisions.

In this case study, both school and social service personnel are obviously uninformed about indigenous healing beliefs and practices. In the case of Vang Xiong, we saw how knowledge and understanding of cultural beliefs led to appropriate and helpful treatment. In the case of the Nguyen family, lack of understanding led to charges of child abuse. But is this really a case of child abuse? When Mrs. Nguyen stated *Thúôc Nam,* what was she referring to? What did the fresh bruises along Phuoc's spinal column, forehead, and bridge of the nose mean? And didn't Mrs. Nguyen admit that her husband used the bamboo sticks and bag of coins to beat Phuoc?

In Southeast Asia, traditional medicine derives from three sources: Western Medicine (*Thúôc Tay*), Chinese or Northern Medicine (*Thúôc Bac*), and Southern Medicine (*Thúôc Nam*). Many forms of these treatments continue to exist among Asian Americans and are even more prevalent among the Vietnamese refugees who brought them to the United States (Nguyen, Nguyen, & Nguyen, 1987). *Thúôc Nam* or traditional medicine involves using natural fruits, herbs, plants, animals, and massage to heal the body. Massage treatments are the most common cause of misdiagnosis of child abuse because they leave bruises on the body. Three common forms of massage treatment are *Băt Gió* ("Catching the Wind"), *Cao Gió* ("Scratching the Wind" or "Coin Treatment"), and *Giác Hoi* ("Pressure Massage" or "Dry Cup Massage"). The latter involves steaming bamboo tubes so the insides are low in pressure, applying them to a portion of the skin which has been cut, and sucking out "bad air" or "hot wind." *Cao Gió* involves rubbing the patient with a mentholated ointment, and coins or spoons are used to lightly strike or scrape along the ribs and both sides of the neck and shoulders. *Băt Gió* involves using both thumbs to rub the temples, then massage toward the bridge of the nose at least 20 times. Fingers are used to pinch the bridge of the nose. All three treatments leave bruises on the parts of the body that they are applied to.

If the social worker had understood Mrs. Nguyen, he would have known that Phuoc's four-day absence from school was due to illness, and that his parents treated him using traditional folk medicine. Massage treatments are widespread customs practiced by not only Vietnamese, but Cambodians, Laotians, and Chinese. These are treatments aimed a curing a host of physical ailments such as colds, headaches, backaches, and fevers. In the mind of the practitioner, such treatments have nothing to do with child abuse. Yet, the question still remains: Is it considered child abuse when traditional healing practices result in bruises to the youngster? This is a very difficult question to answer because it raises a larger question: Can culture justify a practice, especially when it is harmful? While not being able to directly answer this last question (we encourage you to dialogue about it), many medical practitioners in California do not consider it child abuse because (a) medical literature reveals no physical complications as a result of Thúôc Nam; (b) intent is not to hurt the child but to help him/her; and (c) it is frequently used in conjunction with Western medicine (Nguyen, Nguyen, & Nguyen, 1987). However, we would say that health professionals and educators have a responsibility to educate parents concerning the potential pitfalls of many folk remedies and indigenous forms of treatment.

THE PRINCIPLES OF INDIGENOUS HEALING

Ever since the beginning of human existence, all societies and cultural groups have developed not only their own explanations of abnormal behaviors, but culture-specific ways of dealing with human problems and distress (Das, 1987; Harner, 1990; Lee & Armstrong, 1995). Within the United States, counseling and psychotherapy are the predominant psychological healing methods; in other cultures, however, indigenous healing approaches continue to be widely used. While there are similarities between Euro-American helping systems and the indigenous practices of many cultural groups, there are major dissimilarities as well. Western forms of counseling, for example, rely on sensory information defined by the physical plane of reality (Western science), while most indigenous methods rely on the spiritual plane of existence in seeking a cure. In keeping with the cultural encapsulation of our profession, Western healing has been slow to acknowledge and learn from these age-old forms of wisdom (Highlen, 1996). Yet, in its attempt to become culturally responsive, the mental health field must begin to put aside the biases of Western science, to acknowledge the existence of intrinsic help-giving networks, and to incorporate the legacy of ancient wisdom that may be contained in indigenous models of healing.

The work and writings of Lee (Lee, 1996; Lee & Armstrong, 1995; Lee, Oh, & Mountcastle, 1992) are especially helpful in this regard. He has studied what is called the *universal shamanic tradition,* which encompasses the centuries-old recognition of healers within a community. The anthropological term "shaman" includes people referred to by terms such as *witch, witch doctor, wizard, medicine man/woman, sorcerer, or magic man/woman.* These individuals are believed to possess the power to enter an altered state of consciousness and in their healing rituals journey to other planes of existence beyond the physical world. Such was the case of Mrs. Thor, a shaman, who journeyed to the spirit world in order to find a cure for Vang.

In a study of indigenous healing in 16 non-Western countries, it was found that three approaches were often used (Lee, Oh, & Mountcastle, 1992). First, there is heavy reliance on the use of communal, group, and family networks to shelter the disturbed individual (Saudi Arabia), to reconnect them with family or significant others (Korea), and to problem solve in a group context (Nigeria). Second, spiritual and religious beliefs and traditions of the community are used in the healing process. The reading of verses from the Koran and/or use of religious houses/churches are examples. Third, use of shamans (called *piris* and *fakirs* in Pakistan and Sudan), who are perceived to be the keepers of timeless wisdom, is the norm. In many cases, the person conducting a healing ceremony may be a family member or a respected elder of the community.

An excellent example that illustrates the incorporation of these approaches is the Native Hawaiian *ho'oponopono* healing ritual (Nishihara, 1978; Shook, 1985). A literal translation of the word means "a setting to right, to make right, to correct." In cultural context, *ho'oponopono* attempts to restore and maintain good relations among family members and between the family and the supernatural powers. It is a kind of family conference (family therapy) aimed at restoring good and healthy harmony in the family; it is considered by many Native Hawaiians to be one of the soundest methods of restoring and maintaining good relations that any society has ever developed. Such a ceremonial activity usually occurs among members of the immediate family but may involve the extended family and even nonrelatives if they were involved in the *pilikia* (trouble). The process of healing includes the following:

1. The *ho'oponopono* begins with *pule weke* (opening prayer) and ends with *pule ho'opau* (closing prayer). The *pule* creates the atmosphere for the healing and involves asking the family gods for guidance. These gods are not asked to intervene but to grant wisdom, understanding and honesty.

2. The ritual elicits *oia'i'o* or "truth telling" sanctioned by the gods and makes compliance among participants a serious matter. The leader states the problem, prays for spiritual fu-

sion among members, reaches out to resistant family members, and attempts to unify the group.

3. Once this occurs, the actual work begins through *mahiki*, a process of getting to the problems. Transgressions, obligations, righting the wrongs, and forgiveness are all aspects of *ho'oponopono*. The forgiving-releasing-severing of wrongs, hurts, and conflicts produces a deep sense of resolution.

4. Following the closing prayer, the family participates in *pani*, the termination ritual in which food is offered to the gods and to the participants.

In general we can see several principles of indigenous Hawaiian healing illustrated: (a) Problems reside in relationships with people and spirits; (b) harmony and balance in the family and nature are desirable; (c) healing must involve the entire group and not just an individual; (d) spirituality, prayer, and ritual are important aspects of healing; (e) the healing process comes from a respected elder of the family; and (f) the method of healing is indigenous to the culture.

Indigenous healing can be defined as helping beliefs and practices that originate within the culture or society; it is not transported from other regions; and it is designed for treating the inhabitants of the given group. Those who study indigenous psychologies do not make an a priori assumption that one particular perspective is superior to another (Kim & Berry, 1993). The Western ontology of healing (counseling/therapy), however, does consider its methods to be more advanced and scientifically grounded than those found in many cultures. It has traditionally operated from several assumptions. First, reality consists of distinct and separate units or objects (the therapist and client, the observer and observed); second, reality consists of what can be observed and measured via the five senses; third, space and time are fixed and are absolute constructs of reality; and fourth, science operates from universal principles and is culture-free (Highlen, 1994, 1996). While these guiding assumptions of Western science have contributed much to human knowledge and to the improvement of the human condition, most non-Western indigenous psychologies appear to operate from a different perspective. For example, many non-Western cultures do not separate the observer from the observed and believe that all life forms are interrelated with one another, including Mother Nature and the cosmos; that the nature of reality transcends the senses; that space and time are not fixed; and that much of reality is culture-bound (Sue, Carter et al., 1998). Let us briefly explore several of these parallel assumptions and see how they are manifested in indigenous healing practices.

HOLISTIC OUTLOOK, INTERCONNECTEDNESS, AND HARMONY

The concepts of separation, isolation and individualism are hallmarks of the Euro-American worldview. On an individual basis, modern psychology takes a reductionistic approach to describing the human condition (e.g., id, ego, and superego; belief, knowledge, and skills; cognitions, emotions, and behaviors). In Western science, the experimental design is considered the epitome of methods used to ask and answer questions about the human condition or the universe. The search for cause-effect is linear and allows us to identify the independent variables, the dependent variables, and the effects of extraneous variables that we attempt to control. It is analytical and reductionistic in character. The attempt to maintain objectivity, autonomy, and independence in understanding human behavior is also stressed. Such tenets have resulted in separation of the person from the group (valuing of individualism and uniqueness), science from spirituality, and man/woman from the universe.

Most non-Western indigenous forms of healing take a holistic outlook on well-being in that they make minimal distinction between physical and mental functioning and believe strongly in the unity of spirit, mind, and matter. The interrelatedness of life forms, the environment, and the cosmos is a given. As a result, the indigenous peoples of the world tend to conceptualize reality differently. As mentioned in Chapter 3, the psychosocial unit of operation for many culturally different groups, for example, is not the individual but the group (collectivism). In many cultures, acting in an autonomous and independent manner is seen as "the problem" because it creates disharmony within the group. The following case description by a Chinese counselor trainee (international student) reveals just such a difference in worldview perspectives.

♦ *Case Study*

WHO HAS THE PROBLEM?

Carol, 29 years of age, blames herself for her family's tension and dissension. Her father is out of work and depressed most of the time; her mother feels overburdened and ineffective. In the past Carol has assumed responsibility for the problems and has done a lot for her parents. She is convinced, however, that if she were more hardworking and more competent, most of the family problems would diminish greatly. The fact that she is increasingly unable to effect change bothers her, and she has come to a counselor for help. When my professor asked the class to analyze what the woman's problem was, everybody, except me, said that Carol was too submissive, that she should not continue to put family interests above her own. When the teacher played to the class two model tapes of interviews based on the case, much to my dismay, the student counselors, implicitly or explicitly, encouraged the client to think of her own needs first, leave her family and live alone, and make sure not to let her parents override her wishes. Almost the entire class agreed that the client needed assertiveness training, which I felt was quite unacceptable.

I just cannot understand why putting the family's interest before one's own is not correct or "normal" in the dominant American culture. I believe a morally responsible son or daughter has the duty to take care of his or her parents, whether it means sacrifice on his or her own part or not. . . . What is wrong with this interdependence? To me, it would be extremely selfish for Carol to leave her family when the family is in such need of her.

Although I do not think the client has a significant psychological problem, I do believe that the parents have to become more sensitive to their daughter's needs. It is not very nice and considerate for the parents to think only of themselves at the cost of their daughter's well-being. If I were the counselor of this client, I would do everything in my power to try to help change the parents, rather than the client. I feel strongly that it is the selfish person who needs to change, not the selfless person.

I was criticized by some of my American classmates for being judgmental; I think they are probably right. I would argue, however, that as soon as they defined Carol's problem as one of putting her family's interests before her own and suggested assertiveness training as a way of solving her problem, they had made a judgement, too. No? (Zhang, 1994, pp 79–80)

The author concludes: "In contemporary China, where submergence of self for the good of the family, community, and country is still valued, and individualism condemned, our beginning counseling practice could fail should we adopt American counseling theories and skills without considerable alteration" (p. 80).

Illness, distress, or problematic behaviors are seen as an imbalance in people relationships, a disharmony between the individual and his/her group, or of being out of synchrony with internal or external forces. The seeking of harmony or balance is the healer's goal. Among American Indians, for example, harmony with nature is symbolized by the circle, or hoop of life (Heinrich, Corbin, & Thomas, 1990; Sutton & Broken Nose, 1996). Mind, body, spirit, and nature are seen as a single unified entity with little separation between the realities of life, medicine, and religion. All forms of nature, not just the living, are to be revered because they reflect the creator or deity. Illness is seen as a break in the hoop of life, an imbalance or separation between the elements. Many indigenous beliefs come from a metaphysical tradition. They accept the interconnectedness of cosmic forces in the form of energy or subtle matter (less dense than the physical) that surrounds and penetrates the physical body and world. The ancient Chinese use of acupuncture and references to chakras in Indian yogic texts involve the use of subtle matter to rebalance and heal the body and mind (Highlen, 1996). Chinese medical theory is concerned with the balance of yin (cold) and yang (hot) in the body, and it is believed that strong emotional states and an imbalance in the type of foods eaten may create illness (E. Lee, 1996; Mullavey-O'Byrne, 1994). Treatment might involve eating specific types or combinations of foods and/or, as in the case of Phuoc Nguyen, using massage treatment to suck out "bad" or "hot" air. Such ideas of illness and health can also be found in the Greek theory of balancing body fluids (blood, phlegm, black bile, and yellow bile; Bankart, 1997).

Likewise, the Afrocentric perspective also teaches that human beings are part of a wholistic fabric, that they are interconnected and should be oriented toward collective rather than individual survival (Asante, 1987; Hines & Boyd-Franklin, 1996; White & Parham, 1990). The indigenous Japanese assumptions and practices of Naikan and Morita therapy attempt to move clients toward being more in tune with others and society, to move away from individualism, and to move toward interdependence and connectedness (harmony with others; Bankart, 1997; Walsh, 1995). Naikan therapy, which derives from Buddhist practice, requires the client to reflect on three aspects of human relationships: (a) what other people have done for them, (b) what they have done for others, and (c) how they cause difficulties to others (Ishiyama, 1986; Walsh, 1995). The overall goal is to expand awareness as to how much we receive from others, the gratitude due them, and how little we demonstrate such gratitude. This ultimately leads to a realization of the interdependence of the parts to the whole. Working for the good of the group ultimately benefits the individual.

BELIEF IN METAPHYSICAL LEVELS OF EXISTENCE

Several years ago, two highly popular books—*Embraced by the Light* (Eadie, 1992) and *Saved by the Light* (Brinkley, 1994)—and several television specials described fascinating cases of "near death experiences." All had certain commonalities: The individuals who were near death experienced leaving their physical bodies, observed what was happening around them, saw a bright beckoning light, and journeyed to higher levels of existence. Despite the fact that the popularity of such books and programs might indicate the American public's inclination to believe in such phenomena, science has not been able to validate these personal accounts and remains skeptical toward them. Yet many societies and non-Western cultures accept the existence of different levels or planes of consciousness, experience, or existence as a given. Understanding and ameliorating the causes of illness or problems of life may involve looking to a different plane of reality rather than the physical world of existence.

Asian psychologies posit detailed descriptions of states of consciousness, and outline developmental levels of enlightenment extending beyond that of Western psychology. Asian perspectives concentrate less on psychopathology and more on enlightenment and ideal mental health (Tart, 1986; Walsh & Vaughan, 1993). The normal state of consciousness, in many ways, is not considered optimal and may be seen as a "psychopathology of the average" (Maslow, 1968). Moving to higher states of consciousness has the effect of enhancing perceptual sensitivity and clarity, concentration, sense of identity, and emotional, cognitive and perceptual processes. Such movement, according to Asian philosophy, frees one from the negative pathogenic forces of life. Attaining enlightenment and liberation can be achieved through the classic practices of meditation and yoga. Research findings indicate that they are the most widely used of all therapies (Walsh, 1995). They have been shown to reduce anxiety, specific phobias, and substance abuse (Kwee, 1990; Shapiro, 1982; West, 1987), have benefited those with medical problems by reducing blood pressure and aided in the management of chronic pain (Kabat-Zinn, 1990), and have enhanced self-confidence, sense of control, marital satisfaction, etc. (Alexander, Rainforth, & Gelderloos, 1991). They may even extend longevity (Alexander, Langer, Newman, Chandler, & Davies, 1989). Today, meditation and yoga in the United States have become accepted practices among millions, especially for relaxation and stress management. For practitioners of meditation and yoga, altered states of consciousness are unquestioned aspects of reality.

Nonordinary reality states, according to some cultures, allow some healers to access an invisible world surrounding the physical one. Puerto Ricans, for example, believe in *espiritismo* (spiritism), a world where spirits reside and can have major impact on the people in the physical world (Ramos-McKay, Comas-Diaz, & Rivera, 1988). *Espiritistas*, or mediums, are culturally sanctioned indigenous healers who possess special faculties that allow them to intervene positively or negatively on behalf of their clients. Many cultures strongly believe that human destiny is often decided in the domain of the spirit world. Mental illness may be attributed to the activities of hostile spirits, often in reaction to transgressions of the victim or the victim's family (C.C. Lee, 1996; Mullavey-O'Byrne, 1994). As in the case of Mrs. Thor, shamans, mediums, or indigenous healers often enter these realities on behalf of their clients in order to seek answers, to enlist the help of the spirit world, or to aid in realigning the spiritual energy field that surrounds the body and extends throughout the universe. Ancient Chinese methods of healing and Hindu chakra work also acknowledge another world of etheric reality that parallels the physical one (Highlen, 1996). Accessing this world allows the healer to use these special energy centers to balance and heal the body and mind. Occasionally, the shaman may aid the helpee or novice in accessing that plane of reality, so that he or she may find the solutions. The "vision quest" in conjunction with the sweat lodge experience is used by American Indians as religious renewal or a rite of passage (Hammerschlag, 1988; Heinrich, Corbin, & Thomas, 1990). Behind these practices, however, is the human journey to another world of reality. Rituals and sacred symbols, prayers to the Great Spirit, isolation, fasting, and personal reflection: These elements of the vision quest ceremony are intended to induce in the young man the proper frame of mind. Whether in a dream state or in full consciousness, another world of reality is said to reveal itself. Hindu mantras, chants, and meditation, and the taking of certain drugs (peyote) all have as their purpose allowing a journey into another world of existence.

SPIRITUALITY IN LIFE AND THE COSMOS

Native American Indians look on all things as having life, as having spiritual energy and importance. A fundamental belief is that all things are connected. The universe consists of a balance among all of these things and a continuous flow of cycling of this energy. Native American Indians believe that we have a sacred relationship with the universe that is to be honored. All things are connected, all things have life, and all things are worthy of respect and reverence. Spirituality focuses on the harmony that comes from our connection with all parts of the universe in which everything has the purpose and value exemplary of "personhood" including plants (e.g., "tree people"), the land ("Mother Earth"), the winds ("the Four powers"), "Father Sky," "Grandfather Sun," "Grandmother Moon," "The Red Thunder Boys." . . . Spiritual being essentially requires only that we seek our place in the universe; everything else will follow in good time. Because everyone and everything was created with a specific purpose to fulfill, no one should have the power to interfere or to impose on others the best path to follow. (Garrett & Garrett, 1994, p. 187)

The sacred Native American beliefs concerning spirituality embody concepts truly alien to modern Euro-American thinking. The United States has had a long tradition of believing that one's religious beliefs should not enter into scientific or rational decisions. Incorporating religion in the rational decision-making process or in the conduct of therapy has generally been seen as unscientific and unprofessional. The schism between religion and science occurred centuries ago, resulting in a split between science/psychology and religion (Highlen, 1994, 1996). This is reflected in the phrase "separation of Church and State." The separation has become a serious barrier to incorporation of indigenous forms of healing into mainstream mental health practice, especially when religion is confused with spirituality. Independent of any formal religion, indigenous helpers believe that spirituality is an intimate aspect of the human condition. While Western psychology acknowledges the behavioral, cognitive, and affective realms, it makes only passing reference to the spiritual realm of existence. Yet indigenous helpers believe that spirituality transcends time and space, transcends mind and body, and transcends our behaviors, thoughts, and feelings (Lee & Armstrong, 1995).

These contrasting worldviews are perhaps most clearly seen in definitions of "the good life" and how our values are manifested in evaluating the worth of others. In the United States, for example, the "pursuit of happiness" is most likely manifested in material wealth and physical well-being, while other cultures value spiritual or intellectual goals. The worth of a person is anchored in the number of separate properties he/she owns, net worth, and the ability to acquire increasing wealth. Indeed, it is often assumed that such an accumulation of wealth is a sign of divine approval (Condon & Yousef, 1975). In cultures where spiritual goals are strong, the worth of people is unrelated to materialistic possessions; it resides within, emanates from their spirituality, and is a function of whether they live the "right life." People from capitalistic cultures who travel abroad to countries like India, for example, often do not understand self-immolations and other acts of suicide. They are likely to make statements such as "life is not valued here" or even "life is cheap." These statements indicate a lack of understanding about actions that arise from cultural forces rather than personal frustrations; they may be symbolic of a spiritual-valuing rather than a material-valuing orientation.

One does not have to leave the United States, however, to note that many racial/ethnic minority groups in this country are strongly spiritual. As a group, African Americans, Asian Americans, Latino/Hispanic Americans, and Native Americans place strong emphasis on the interplay and interdependence of spiritual life and healthy functioning. Puerto Ricans, for example, may sacrifice material satisfaction in favor of values pertaining to the spirit and soul. The Lakota Sioux often say *"Mitakuye Oyasin"* at the end of a prayer or as a salutation. Translated, it means "To all my relations," which acknowledges the spiritual bond between speaker and all people present, to forebears, the tribe, the family of man, and to Mother Nature. It speaks to the philosophy that all life forces, Mother Earth, and the cosmos are sacred beings and the spiritual is the thread that binds all together.

Likewise, a strong spiritual orientation has always been a major aspect of life in Africa, and especially during the slavery era in the United States (Hines & Boyd-Franklin, 1996):

Highly emotional religious services conducted during slavery were of great importance in dealing with oppression. Often signals as to the time and place of an escape were given then. Spirituals contained hidden messages and a language of resistance (e.g., "Wade in the Water" and "Steal Away"). Spirituals (e.g., "Nobody Knows the Trouble I've Seen") and the ecstatic celebrations of Christ's gift of salvation provided Black slaves with outlets for expressing feelings of pain, humiliation, and anger. (p. 74)

The African American church has a strong influence over the lives of Black people and is often the hub of religious, social, economic, and political life. Religion is not separated from the daily functions of the church, as it acts as a complete support system for the African American family with its minister, deacons, deaconesses, and church members operating as one big family. A strong sense of peoplehood is fostered via social activities, choirs, Sunday School, health-promotion classes, day care centers, tutoring programs, and counseling. To many African Americans the road to mental health and the prevention of mental illness lie in the health potentialities of their spiritual life.

Increasingly, mental health professionals are becoming open to the potential benefits of spirituality as a means for coping with hopelessness, identity issues, and feelings of powerlessness. As an example of this movement, the Association for Counselor Education and Supervision recently adopted a set of competencies related to spirituality. They define spirituality as

the animating force in life, represented by such images as breath, wind, vigor and courage. Spirituality is the infusion and drawing out of spirit in one's life. It is experienced as an active and passive process. Spirituality is also described as a capacity and tendency that is innate and unique to all persons. This spiritual tendency moves the individual towards knowledge, love, meaning, hope, transcendence, connectedness, and compassion. Spirituality includes one's capacity for creativity, growth, and the development of a values system. Spirituality encompasses the religious, spiritual, and transpersonal. (ACES Spectrum, 1997, p. 14)

Interestingly enough, it appears that many in the United States are experiencing a spiritual hunger or a strong need to reintegrate spiritual or religious themes into their lives (Gallup, 1995; Thoreson, 1998). For example, it appears that there is a marked discrepancy between what patients want from their doctors and what doctors supply. Often, patients want to talk about the spiritual aspects of their illness and treatment, while doctors are either unprepared or disinclined to do so (Marwick, 1995). Likewise, most mental health professionals feel equally uncomfortable, disinclined, or unprepared to speak with their clients about religious or spiritual matters. Thoresen (1998) reports that in a meta-analysis of over 200 published studies, the relationship between spirituality and health is highly positive. Those with higher levels of spirituality have lower disease risk, fewer physical health problems, and higher levels of psychosocial functioning. It appears that people require faith as well as reason to be healthy, and that psychology may profit from allowing the spirit to rejoin matters of the mind and body (Strawbridge, Cohen, Shema, & Kaplan, 1997).

INDIGENOUS HEALING: GUIDELINES FOR MULTICULTURAL COUNSELING AND PSYCHOTHERAPY

We have repeatedly stressed that worldviews of culturally different clients may often be worlds apart from the dominant society. When clients attribute disorders to a cause quite alien from the Euro-American one, when their definitions of a healer are different from that of conventional therapists, and when the role behaviors (process of therapy) are not perceived as therapeutic, major difficulties are likely to occur in the provision of therapeutic services to culturally different groups in the United States. As a Western-trained therapist, for example, how would you treat a culturally different client who believed (a) that their mental problems were due to spirit possession, (b) that only a shaman with inherited powers could deal with the problem, and (c) that a cure could only be effected via a formal ritual (chanting, incense burning, symbolic sacrifice, etc.) and a journey into the spirit world? Most of us, who have had very little experience with indigenous methods of treatment, would find great difficulty in working effectively with such clients. There are, however, some useful guidelines that may help bridge the gap between contemporary forms of therapy and traditional non-Western indigenous healing.

DO NOT INVALIDATE THE INDIGENOUS CULTURAL BELIEF SYSTEMS OF YOUR CULTURALLY DIFFERENT CLIENT

On the surface, the assumptions of indigenous healing methods might appear radically different from our own. When we encounter them, we are often shocked find such beliefs to be "unscientific," and are likely to negate, invalidate, or dismiss them. Such an attitude will have the effect of invalidating our clients as well, since these beliefs are central to their worldview and reflect their cultural identity. It is important that therapists be open and able to entertain alternative worldviews and understand that such beliefs reflect the realities of a different culture. Such an orientation does not mean the therapist must subscribe to that belief system; it does mean, however, that the helping professional avoids being judgmental. This will encourage and allow the client to more readily share his/her story; to feel validated; and to encourage the building of mutual respect and trust. Remember, one of the key components of multicultural competence is the ability to understand the worldview of your culturally different client. This must entail a willingness to hear the stories your client has to tell. Cultural storytelling and personal narratives have always been inherent in the process of helping in all cultures.

BECOME KNOWLEDGEABLE ABOUT INDIGENOUS BELIEFS AND HEALING PRACTICES

Therapists have a professional responsibility to become knowledgeable about and conversant with the assumptions and practices of indigenous healing so that a desensitization and normalization process can occur. By becoming knowledgeable and understanding of indigenous helping approaches, the therapist will avoid equating differences with deviance! Furthermore, we have found that the therapist must do two things. First, they must understand that there is often a logical consistency between treatment approaches and philosophical explanations of human behavior. If one believes that mental illness is due to biological factors (chemical imbalance, genetic transmission, or malfunction of internal organs), then medication or some other form of medical intervention is called for. If one believes that mental disorders are due to psychological factors (stress, unconscious conflicts, guilt, or abuse), then counseling/therapy may be dictated. Likewise, if one believes that abnormal behavior is a function of a supernatural force, then shamanic practices seem natural. Second, as we indicated in the example of Mrs. Thor, the shamanic healer, many similarities exist between Western and non-Western healing practices. Rather than perceiving non-Western indigenous forms of healing as abnormal, we can see them as a normal process within a particular cultural context.

LEARNING ABOUT INDIGENOUS HEALING AND BELIEFS ENTAILS EXPERIENTIAL OR LIVED REALITIES

While reading books about non-Western forms of healing and attending seminars and lectures on the topic is valuable and helpful, understanding culturally different perspectives must be supplemented by lived experience. Even when we travel abroad, few of us actively place ourselves in situations that are unfamiliar because it evokes discomfort, anxiety, and a feeling of differentness. Yet this is one of the few means by which to truly understand and relate to others. Because the United States has become so diverse, one need not leave the country to experience the richness of different cultures. Opportunities abound. We suggest that you consider attending cultural events, meetings, and activities of the culturally different groups in your community. Such actions allow you to view culturally different individuals interacting in their community and witness how their values are expressed in relationships. Hearing from church leaders, attending open community forums, and attending the community celebrations allow you to sense the strengths of the minority community and observe leadership in action. Such experiences can enable you to personalize your understanding, and allow you to identify potential guides and advisors to your own self-enlightenment.

AVOID OVERPATHOLOGIZING AND UNDERPATHOLOGIZING A CULTURALLY DIFFERENT CLIENT'S PROBLEMS

A therapist or counselor who is culturally unaware and who believes primarily in a universal psychology may often be culturally insensitive and inclined to see differences as deviance. They may be guilty of overpathologizing a culturally different client's problems by seeing them as more severe and pathological than they truly may be. There is a danger, however, of also underpathologizing a culturally different client's symptoms as well. While being understanding of a client's cultural context, having knowledge of culture-bound syndromes, and being aware of cultural relativism are desirable, being oversensitive to these factors may predispose the therapist to minimize problems, thereby underpathologizing disorders.

BE WILLING TO SEEK THE ADVICE OR UTILIZE THE SERVICES OF TRADITIONAL HEALERS

Mental health professionals must be willing and able to form partnerships with indigenous healers or develop community liaisons. Such an outreach has several advantages. Traditional healers may provide knowledge and insights into client populations that would prove of value to the delivery of mental health services. Such an alliance will also ultimately enhance the cultural credibility of therapists. Additionally, it allows for referral to traditional healers (shamans, religious leaders, etc.) in which treatment is rooted in cultural traditions. To accomplish these goals, therapists must respect the universal shamanic tradition while remaining embedded in a Western psychological tradition as well. Most culturally different clients are open to a blend of both Western and non-Western approaches. For example, in Oakland, California's, Asian Community Mental Health Services, a Buddhist monk serves on the staff. Not only does his presence lend credibility to the service delivery organization, but the monk provides for the spiritual needs of the Asian American/Pacific Islander community.

SPIRITUALITY MUST BE SEEN AS AN INTIMATE ASPECT OF THE HUMAN CONDITION AND A LEGITIMATE ASPECT OF MENTAL HEALTH WORK

Spirituality is a belief in a higher power that allows us to make meaning of life and the universe. It may or may not be linked to a formal religion, but there is little doubt that it is a powerful force in the human condition. As indicated previously, many groups accept the prevalence of spirituality in nearly all aspects of life; thus, separating it from one's existence is not possible. A counselor or therapist who does not feel comfortable in dealing with spiritual needs of the clients, or who believes in an "artificial" separation of the spirit (soul) from the everyday life of the culturally different client, may not be providing the help needed. Just as therapists might inquire about the physical health of their clients, they should feel free and comfortable to inquire about their client's values and beliefs as they relate to spirituality. We do not, however, advocate indoctrination of the client. Nor do we endorse having the therapist prescribe any particular pathway to embracing, validating, or expressing spirituality and spiritual needs. What we suggest is that a mental health professional be open to exploring this aspect of the human condition and actively seek to integrate it into his/her practice.

HAVING THE ABILITY TO EXPAND OUR DEFINITION OF THE HELPING ROLE TO COMMUNITY WORK AND INVOLVEMENT

More than anything else, indigenous healing is community oriented and focused. Culturally competent mental health professionals must begin to expand their definition of the helping role to encompass a greater community involvement. The in-the-office setting is, often, nonfunctional in minority communities. Culturally sensitive helping requires making home visits, going to community centers, and visiting places of worship and areas within the community. The types of help most likely to prevent mental health problems are building and maintaining healthy connections with one's family, one's god(s), and one's universe. It is clear that we live in a monocultural society; a society that invalidates and separates us from one another, from our spirituality and from the cosmos. There is much wisdom in ancient forms of healing that stress that the road to mental health is through becoming united and in harmony with the universe. Activities that promote these attributes involve community work. They include client advocacy and consultation, preventive education, developing outreach programs, becoming involved in systemic change and aiding in the formation of public policy that allows for equal access and opportunities for all.

In general, indigenous healing methods have much to offer to Euro-American forms of mental health practice. The contributions are valuable not only because of the multiple belief systems that now exist in our society, but because counseling and psychotherapy have neglected to deal with the spiritual dimension of human existence. Our heavy reliance on "science" and the reductionistic approach to treating clients have made us view human beings and human behavior as composed of separate noninteracting parts (cognitive, behavioral, and affective). There has been a failure to recognize our spiritual being and to take a holistic outlook on life. Indigenous models of healing remind us of these shortcomings and challenge us to look for answers in other realms of existence besides the physical world.

Chapter Ten

♦

Becoming Multiculturally Competent: Organizational and Professional Development

♦

"**S**everal years after receiving my doctorate in counseling psychology, I accepted a position at a well-known private university on the West Coast. The university was located in an area with a large Latino population, but the student body was over 90% White. Having previously been employed at a northern California university, I had been exposed to the aftermath of the Free Speech Movement, and had been involved with the Third World Strike, a movement begun in the late 1960s aimed at multicultural curriculum reform, and increasing representation of minorities in students, faculty, and staff alike.

"With these goals in mind, several colleagues and I confronted the university administration with the low numbers of Hispanic/Latino American students on the college campus and (a) suggested there was bias in the admission criteria, (b) asked for a change in the standards used to admit students of minority cultural background, (c) demanded the placement of minority faculty members on admissions committees, (d) requested the formation of outreach groups to recruit minority students, and (e) asked for creation of an ethnic studies department.

"Being a very conservative institution, the university strongly resisted all of our demands. I recall countless hours of meetings, debates, and even community demonstrations concerning the underrepresentation of minority student admissions to the university. Academic senate meetings became very emotional, with the majority of faculty and administrators claiming that our group wanted to "lower the standards" of the university. We, in turn, took the position that current admission criteria were biased against minority applicants, and that what we sought was not a lowering but a changing of standards that could be fairly applied to a culturally different student population. Indeed, many of our other requests such as curriculum reform, increased minority faculty and staff, culturally relevant student services, etc., soon were dropped as the battleground was fought on the frontiers of traditional admission criteria (GPA, SAT scores, recommendations, extracurricular activities, etc.).

"After nearly a year of sustained debate on this issue, the university administration relented in the face of community pressures and developed what was called a "special accommodated category," which allowed the admission of large numbers of primarily Latino students onto the campus. While many of us celebrated this development, our victory was short lived. By the end of the first quarter, nearly 50% of the minority students admitted under the new standard were placed on academic probation. By the end of the academic year, many of those on probation had failed, and even those students who had maintained a C average had decided not to return to the university. Encouraged by these results, our opponents used them to buttress their arguments: Minority students were not to be admitted to the university unless they met the same standards as their White counterparts. The next year, the university dropped the special category provision. I also left the following year, and accepted a position at another higher education institution.

"This incident has always haunted me for several reasons. First, there was my own guilt at having started a movement that suddenly backfired and left all those involved (proponents and opponents alike) with negative feelings toward concepts of affirmative action and diversity. Second, for years after my departure, I could not fully understand what had happened to derail our movement. I was left with a bitter taste in my mouth; I was confused about what had gone wrong; and I was at a loss as to what else we might have done to effect a more positive outcome. It was only years later, as I became increasingly involved with multicultural organizational development, that I came to fully understand some of the reasons that led to our downfall."

The preceding vignette demonstrates strongly the need for purveyors of institutional change to understand systemic principles and forces. It is our contention that clinical practice has too long accepted an extremely narrow view of helping, leaving us with tunnel vision and ill-prepared to work with organizations and larger social systems. For example, it does little good to be culturally competent in clinical work when the very organizations that employ us are nonreceptive to multicultural practice and/or directly punish therapists when they choose to exercise those helping skills. System forces can be powerful and oppressive; the following vignette illustrates how a failure to understand systemic dynamics may derail productive change regardless of the good intentions involved and/or the willingness to push a multicultural agenda. As we noted earlier, becoming multiculturally competent requires not only changes at an individual practice level, but changes associated with how we define our helping role. That role is significantly different from the conventional counselor/therapist one and entails roles that impact the system directly rather than affecting the individual alone. Let us briefly discuss why this change in focus is needed.

First, there is a common belief supported by actual practice that therapists work primarily with individuals or small groups (Atkinson, Morten, & Sue, 1998). The practice of counseling and psychotherapy has arisen from the study of individual differences and reflects the value of individualism in U.S. society. Traditional Euro-American schools of counseling and therapy have implicitly or explicitly glamorized and defined the clinician as one who conducts his/her trade, working with individuals, in an office environment. While the development of individual intervention skills has been the main focus in graduate training programs, little emphasis is given to other roles, activities, or settings. Thus, not only are therapists lacking in systems-intervention knowledge and skills, but they are unaccustomed to, and uncomfortable in, leaving their offices (D.W. Sue, Ivey, & Pedersen, 1996). Yet work with racial/ethnic minority groups suggests that out-of-office sites/activities (client homes, churches, volunteer organizations, etc.) and alternative helping roles (ombudsmen, advocates, consultants, organizational change agents, facilitators of indigenous healing systems, etc.) may prove more therapuetic and effective (Atkinson, Thompson, & Grant, 1993).

Second, and related to the above point, is that clinical work should be concerned primarily with internal or intrapsychic dynamics and conflicts. When the focus of therapy is on the individual, however, there is a strong tendency to see the locus of the problem as residing solely in the person (Berman, 1979; Ivey, 1986; Ivey, Ivey, & Simek-Morgan, 1997; Lewis et al., 1998) rather than in the organization or social structures. As a result, well-intentioned counselors may mistakenly blame the victim ("the problem is a deficiency of the person") when the fault may in fact reside in the environment. For example, African Americans who are unemployed are often perceived as being lazy, unmotivated, or lacking in skills to acquire a job when prejudice and discrimination may in fact account for their difficulty in getting jobs. When the problems and practices of an organization (employer) are biased against minority groups, shouldn't attempts at change be directed against the "discriminating" organizational structures?

Third, training programs often imbue trainees with the belief that the role of therapists is relatively free of organizational influences or pressures. In the privacy of their offices, counselors may be under the illusion that they are free to help clients attain their full potential; that their allegiance is to the individual client seeking help. Yet it is becoming clear that what we can or cannot do is often dictated by the rules and regulations of our employing agencies (length of sessions, maximum number of sessions, types of problems treated, definition of counseling role, limits of confidentiality, etc.). The managed health care environment has forced us to confront this reality much more than ever before. The policies of an organization or a superordinate group (insurance carrier, HMO, state or professional organization, etc.) may conflict with the therapuetic help needed by our clients. This is especially true in an organization that lacks sensitivity toward culturally different groups.

In addition, clinicians may find themselves in conflict when the needs of their clients differ from that of the organization or employer. The fact that a therapist's livelihood depends on the employing agency creates additional pressures to conform. Thus, how do therapists handle such conflicts? Who truly are their clients? Organizational knowledge and skills become a necessity if the therapist is to be truly effective.

Fourth, conventional therapy continues to be oriented toward remediation rather than prevention. While no one would deny the importance of biological and internal psychological factors contributing to personal problems, more research now acknowledges the importance of sociocultural factors (inadequate or biased education, poor socialization practices, biased values, and discriminatory institutional policies) in creating many of the difficulties encountered by individuals. As helping professionals, we are frequently placed in a position of treating clients who represent the aftermath of failed and oppressive policies and practices (D.W. Sue, 1991a, 1995). We have been trapped in the role of remediation (attempting to cure clients once they have been damaged by sociocultural biases). While treating troubled clients (remediation) is a necessity, our task would be an endless and losing venture unless the true sources of the problem (stereotypes, prejudice, discrimination, and oppression) are changed. Would it not make more sense to take a proactive and preventive approach by attacking the cultural and institutional bases of the problem?

Finally, many of us behave as if the main focus of therapy should be on individual or small group change; organizational change is the province of industrial/organizational (I/O) psychologists. The arguments presented thus far challenge this point of view; acquisition of organizational knowledge and skills is a therapeutic necessity. Intraprofessional divisions (professional territoriality) should not prevent us from developing and adopting organizational development strategies in our work. We can profit much from I/O principles developed in the business world. Indeed, many counseling and clinical psychologists have recently advocated increasing roles for professionals in business and industry. As psychologists move into the areas of occupational health (Osipow, 1982; Toomer, 1982) and diversity training (Katz & Miller, 1988; D.W. Sue, 1991b, 1995), the artificial distinctions between the roles of I/O psychologists and clinicians may become blurred. Let us briefly return to the opening vignette to analyze how a lack of appreciation of organizational dynamics may lead to failure.

1. *A realistic assessment of the level of multicultural development is needed.* Before advocating a change in admission standards at the university for prospective minority students, proponents should have conducted a thorough assessment of the institutional climate with respect to multiculturalism. All organizations differ in their receptivity to diversity concepts, and premature intervention may result in devasting consequences (D'Andrea, Daniels, & Heck, 1991). The supporters of multiculturalism should have known that not only are institutions conservative (resist change): In this case, the institution was in fact hostile to multicultural concerns. Indeed, most multicultural organizational development (MOD) models would have characterized the university as monocultural: (a) Cultural diversity issues are either ignored or purposefully undermined; (b) most workers (faculty and staff) are either ethnocentric or highly assimilated tokens; (c) hiring and admission practices are highly discriminatory; (d) the curriculum is taught from a Euro-American perspective without regard for other cultural views; and (e) there is a strong organizational belief that there is only one best way to run a university.

Under these conditions, it is little wonder that attempts to implement change met with such swift failure. The proponents' tunnel vision and narrow focus prevented them from seeing the larger picture. They were motivated by naive idealism without a full understanding of systems intervention. Their task was much larger than getting the university to adopt different admissions criteria. It was much greater than trying to convince key members of committees to accept their suggestions. As novices, they failed to realize that the effective introduction of change depends not only on what is introduced and how, but on the readiness and commitment of an organization. The stage of MOD of an organization (to be presented shortly) often dictates the type of interventions deemed most effective.

2. *The interrelationships of subsystems need to be understood.* In family therapy, students are often warned that treating the "identified patient" without intervening in the family system may prove to be futile. The assumption is that the problems or pathology observed in one member of the family are not necessarily due to internal conflicts, but to unhealthy values and pressures of family life (Sue, Sue, & Sue, 1997). Treating a child in individual sessions, for example, may appear to eradicate the symptoms as long as the child remains outside of the family. Once the child reenters the family, however, he/she may again be forced to play the sick role because the subsystems and rules of the family remain unchanged. Treating the child has unbalanced the family homeostasis and family dynamics will again strive for balance.

Like family systems, organizations are also composed of many interacting subsystems (Levinson, 1994). Over time, these subsystems have worked out a homeostatic relationship held together by institutional policies and practices (formal and informal) governing their relationship to one another. These rules and regulations seemingly attain a "functional autonomy" that dictates what we can or cannot do in an organization (D.W. Sue, 1994). Changing only one aspect of a system does not guarantee change in others. For example, at a very simplistic level, the university can be seen as having three major functions: recruitment, retention, and graduation of students. Within each of these three functions are multiple systems that theoretically support the activities. Student support services, grading standards and processes, teaching and learning styles, curriculum content, and campus culture may all be seen as subsystems. One very important subsystem is that of the admissions process and criteria used to select students. Attempts to get the university to change one of these subsystems (standards for admission) was doomed to fail because advocates for diversity did not have the understanding or foresight to recognize that the other systems did not change. Indeed, these other subsystems worked against the changes (attempts to reestablish equilibrium) and eventually succeeded in reinstituting the original monocultural standards. The low enrollment of Latino students at the university may have initially been due to biased admissions criteria (the recruitment system), but failure to consider the influence of other university systems led to the loss of minority students. The subsequent high dropout rates were due largely to characteristics of a monocultural university. The curriculum alienated many minority students; the teaching styles were culturally biased; grading practices emphasized individual competition; the campus climate was hostile to minority students (they were also perceived as less qualified); support services (counseling, study skills, etc.) were not geared for nontraditional students; and lack of role models (minority faculty, staff, and administrators) left minority students feeling isolated and alienated. The large group of Latino students who were admitted were subjected to all these antagonistic systems, which eventually took their toll. What advocates should have done was to somehow make existing systems more sensitive and receptive to multicultural issues (curriculum reform and introducing varying teaching styles that recognize diversity) or create new subsystems that would support the students. Organizational change must occur throughout to be effective.

3. *Commitment must come from the top.* Diversity implementation is most effective when strong leadership is exerted on behalf of multiculturalism. For private businesses, the board of directors, CEO, and management team are the principals; for governmental agencies, it is often the head of the service or unit (Secretary of Labor, Housing, etc.); for education, it is the school board, superintendent, principal, etc.; and for our nation it is the President of the United States, the Congress, judiciary, and local, state, and federal leaders.

In the vignette, the university administrators were either publicly or privately resentful and antagonistic toward the goals of multiculturalism. The deans and department chairs were usually adamant in their vocal opposition to proposed changes, while those in the higher echelons of the university (president, academic vice president, and governing board) kept silent. The old saying, "silence can be deafening," was heard throughout. Even when the changed standards were adopted, many leaders in the university voiced only lukewarm support.

It also is important to note that faculty, staff, and students alike are most likely to watch the actions (not just words) of their leaders. Commitment must be manifested in action. There is more to affirmative action than a written policy or statements that we are an "equal opportunity employer." What specific steps has the leadership taken to implement diversity goals at the university? It was clear that the university was not prepared to make any other adjustments in its operation to accommodate minority students. The message was quite clear: "Minority students are not wanted on this campus." Such a message from the leadership gave permission for those in the lower ranks (faculty, staff, and even White students) to resist and/or sabotage proposed changes.

4. *Premature introduction of change may only support the mistaken/biased beliefs of the opposition.* One of the greatest lessons learned from this incident was that lack of an overarching plan for change can backfire with devasting consequences. Many of the more well-meaning and receptive colleagues harbored grave doubts about changing admission standards. Advocates for change felt that attempts to work on those who were adamantly opposed was a waste of time, so they concentrated their efforts on the more receptive group. With such a high dropout rate among the minority students, the "we told you so" cry was used by the opposition in reaffirming three points: (a) The standards of the university had been lowered; (b) less qualified students were admitted solely because of their race; and (c) these students were incapable of handling university work. All of these beliefs became reinforced, and even the "borderline" allies finally concluded that reinstituting traditional admission criteria was a necessity. Thus, the negative beliefs regarding minority students and implementing diversity became more firmly entrenched as a result of the good intentions of proponents of change. It might have been better if they had not attempted any intervention at all!

5. *White people are also victims and under strong institutional pressures to conform.* Even the most well-intentioned White educators or administrators are not immune from inheriting the racial biases, stereotypes, and prejudices of the larger society. During the brief time the senior author was in the psychology department, he had made a number of friends. When the issue of accepting more minority students came up, he was quite surprised to find that many of his faculty friends expressed biases against various minority groups. Subsequently, proponents saw these individuals as enemies and unfortunately grouped them in a *good* or *bad* dichotomy. This artificial category failed to recognize a simple fact: While minorities are often seen as being the victims of prejudice and discrimination, White people may be victims as well. Their victimization is different, however, because they have been socialized into oppressor roles. It is our belief that no one was ever born wanting to be racist, sexist, or prejudiced. White people are programmed into roles without their informed consent (D.W. Sue, 1992, 1993). While this does not absolve them from taking responsibility for their biases, this understanding may make it easier to avoid seeing them as "evil beings." Many educators who might have been enlightened with some effort on the part of the proponents were pushed away and dismissed as potential allies.

Furthermore, the advocates' failure to understand the power of institutional forces (forced compliance) led to continued loss of potential allies. For example, in many informal discussions with White faculty and staff, things were said that often suggested their sympathies with the cause of diversity. When asked for their support, they would often readily agree (in private). Yet, when more formal meetings were held with committees and university representatives, these very same White faculty members would either say nothing or couch their responses in a very ambiguous or guarded manner. When votes were taken, they would vote against diversity proposals, abstain, or not show for the meetings (always with a very convenient excuse). Advocates were enraged by their actions and saw this as deceit, insincerity, and hypocrisy. Years later, the senior author has gained greater clarity on such behaviors. Again, these were not "bad" people, but individuals exposed to a punitive system. They may personally have believed in our cause, but the institution had great ability to reward or punish them (promotion, tenure, treatment at the university, etc.). Indeed, it is not much different from a person who hears a racist joke told by a group of friends. While finding the joke offensive, the person fails to voice any objections for fear of losing friends or being ridiculed. Inspiring indifference, fear, and lack of action on the part of well-meaning individuals is a major mechanism by which institutional forces preserve the status quo.

DEVELOPING MULTICULTURAL ORGANIZATIONAL COMPETENCE

Just as MCT has become a "fourth force" in individual and group counseling/therapy (Pedersen, 1991b), so too must it increasingly influence organizational development. If our society is to truly value diversity and to become multicultural, then our organizations (mental health care delivery systems, businesses, industries, schools, universities, governmental agencies, and even professional organizations like the American Counseling Association and the American Psychological Association) must move toward becoming multicultural. The lessons learned from the painful vignette at the beginning of this chapter have taught the senior author the importance of developing organizational knowledge and skills. Multicultural organizational development is different from traditional organizational development work in that it (a) takes a social justice perspective (ending of oppression and discrimination in organizations), (b) believes that inequities that arise within organizations may not be primarily due to poor communication, lack of knowledge, poor management, person-organization fit problems, etc., but to monopolies of power, and (c) assumes that conflict is inevitable and not necessarily unhealthy. MOD is increasingly subscribed to by diversity trainers, consultants, and mental health practitioners.

MOD is based on the premise that organizations vary in their awareness of how racial, cultural, ethnic, sexual orientation, and gender issues impact their clients or workers. Institutions that recognize and value diversity in a pluralistic society will be in a better position to avoid many of the misunderstandings and conflicts characteristic of monocultural organizations. They will also be in a better position to offer culturally relevant services to their culturally different clients and allow mental health professionals to engage in organizationally sanctioned roles and activities without the threat of punishment. Moving from a monocultural to a multicultural organization requires the therapist or change agent to understand the characteristics of both. It is crucial to ascertain what the organizational culture is like, what policies or practices either facilitate or impede cultural diversity, and how to implement change.

MODELS OF MULTICULTURAL ORGANIZATIONAL DEVELOPMENT

Some of the more helpful MOD models have arisen from a variety of areas, including the business sector (Adler, 1986; Foster, Jackson, Cross, Jackson, & Hardiman, 1988; Jackson & Holvino, 1988; Sue, 1991b), education (Barr & Strong, 1987; Highlen, 1994; D'Andrea, Daniels, & Heck, 1991), and mental health agencies (Cross, Bazron, Dennis, & Isaacs, 1989). Interestingly, nearly all of these models seem to describe stages or a process similar to the racial/cultural identity models for individual development (Atkinson et al., 1998; Cross, 1971, 1991; Helms, 1984, 1986, 1990; Jackson, 1975; Parham & Helms, 1981) and for White racial identity development (Hardiman, 1982; Helms, 1995; Rowe, Bennett, & Atkinson, 1994; Sabnani, Ponterotto, & Borodovsky, 1991).

Table 10.1 STAGES OF MULTICULTURAL ORGANIZATIONAL DEVELOPMENT

Author	*Stages*				
Adler (1986)	Parochial		Ethnocentric		Synergistic
Foster, Jackson, Cross, Jackson, and Hardiman (1988)	Monocultural		Nondiscriminatory		Multicultural
Barr and Strong (1987)	Traditional		Liberal, Managing Diversity		Radical
Cross, Bazron, Dennis, and Isaacs (1989)	Cultural Destructiveness	Cultural Incapacity	Cultural Blindness	Cultural Precompetence	Cultural Competence	Cultural Proficiency
Characteristics typical of organizations at particular stages	Cultural diversity is either deliberately ignored or destroyed. Organization members are monocultural or highly assimilated "tokens." Hiring practices are discriminatory, and services or products are inadequate or inappropriate for cultural minorities. Organizations believe there is only one right way to do things.		Organizations acknowledge that diversity exists and have "good intentions," but operate from a sense that "our way is the best way." Focus is on meeting affirmative action and EEO goals, with a legalistic approach to nondiscrimination. There may be attempts at cross-cultural sensitivity training for individuals, but no focus on organizational change. Staff may be culturally diverse but are judged by traditional (White, male) standards		Organizations value diversity, view it as an asset rather than a problem. Staff diversity is evident at all levels, and staff are evaluated and promoted for meeting diversity criteria. Training focuses on the personal and organizational dynamics of racism, sexism, and so on. Planning is creative, flexible, to accommodate ongoing cultural change.	

Note. From *Multicultural Counseling Competencies: Individual and Organizational Development* (p. 101), by D.W. Sue et. al., 1998, Thousand Oaks, CA: Sage Publications. Reprinted with permission.

In comparing a number of these MOD models, D.W. Sue & Carter et al. (1998), note some very strong similarities. First, most describe a developmental stage process by which organizations move from a primarily monocultural orientation to a more multicultural one. The labels or terms for the stages differ, but their descriptors are primarily the same (see Table 10.1). The following characteristics of organizations as they move toward diversity implementation have been distilled from Adler (1986), Katz and Miller (1988), Foster et al. (1988), Barr and Strong (1987), Cross et al. (1989), D'Andrea, Daniels, & Heck (1991), D.W. Sue (1991b) and Highlen (1994).

1. *Monocultural organizations.* At the one extreme are organizations that are primarily Eurocentric and ethnocentric. They believe in the following premises and practices:

- There is an implicit or explicit exclusion of racial minorities, women, and other oppressed groups.
- Many organizations are rigged to the advantage of the dominant majority. In this case, Whites are privileged.
- There is only one best way to deliver health care, manage, teach, or administrate.
- Culture does not impact management, mental health, or education.
- Clients, workers, or students should assimilate.
- Culture-specific ways of doing things are neither recognized nor valued. Everyone should be treated the same.
- Strong belief in the melting-pot concept.

2. *Nondiscriminatory organizations.* As organizations become more culturally aware and enlightened, they enter another stage, often referred to as "nondiscriminatory." These organizations are characterized by the following premises and practices:

- The organization has inconsistent policies and practices regarding multicultural issues. Certain departments or mental health practitioners/managers/teachers are becoming sensitive to minority issues, but it is not an organizational priority.
- Leadership may recognize the need for some action but lacks a systematic program or policy addressing the issue of prejudice and bias.
- There is an attempt to make the climate or services of an organization less hostile or different, but these changes are superficial and often without conviction. They are more for public relations or perception.
- EEO, affirmative action, numerical symmetry of minorities and women, etc., are implemented grudgingly.

3. *Multicultural organizations.* As organizations become progressively more multicultural, they begin to value diversity and evidence continuing attempts to accommodate ongoing cultural change. Their basic premises and practices reflect these values:

- In the process of working on a vision that reflects multiculturalism.
- Reflects the contributions of diverse cultural and social groups in its mission, operations, products, or services.
- Values diversity and views it as an asset.
- Actively engages in visioning, planning, and problem-solving activities that allow for equal access and opportunities.
- Realizes that equal access and opportunity is not equal treatment.
- Values diversity (not just tolerates it) and works to diversify environment.

These models are helpful as heuristic devices, but they still beg the question of describing what a culturally competent system of care should look like and how best to move an organization toward multiculturalism.

CULTURALLY COMPETENT MENTAL HEALTH ORGANIZATIONS

The many issues identified in the earlier part of this book are among the motivations for mental health organizations to become multicultural; unmet needs of minority populations are foremost among them. To meet those needs, not only must a mental health organization employ individuals with multicultural therapy skills, but the agency itself needs to have a multicultural culture.

Alvarez et al. (1976) offer a general description of a mental health system that would meet community needs, including those of a multicultural population:

A system that is more effective in reaching people and in allocating resources because of improved organization, redefined relationships, continued evaluation, and improved communications will be the hallmark of a functioning [health care] system. This can be successful only if the system's staff and board will engage in education of and by the community and its own affiliates for understanding the system and its potential. Comprehensive community mental health has value only if, beyond the concept, program implementation is compatible with the community's understanding of mental health and its interpretation of mental illness. There must be a meaningful relationship between the center's practices, consumers' problems, and community concerns. The programs and services must have the potential to provide solutions that the community accepts as valid. In the center's effort to respond to problems in sub-units of a community, it must also explore the consequences of implementing a partial solution to a large community problem. (p. 69)

Cross et al. (1989) have incorporated the insights of many researchers and gone beyond the three-stage business models to describe a detailed six-stage developmental continuum of cultural competence for care-giving organizations such as mental health agencies. They call these stages (1) cultural destructiveness, (2) cultural incapacity, (3) cultural blindness, (4) cultural pre-competence, (5) cultural competence, and (6) cultural proficiency.

1. *Cultural destructiveness.* Cross et al. acknowledge the checkered history of organizations and research ostensibly designed to help certain racial/ethnic groups by identifying the first stage of (in)competence as cultural destructiveness. This is represented by programs that have participated in culture/race-based oppression, forced assimilation, or even genocide. Historically, many federal government programs aimed at American Indians fit this description (Allen, 1994), as do the infamous Tuskegee experiment, in which Black men with syphilis were deliberately left untreated, and Nazi-sponsored medical "experiments" that singled out Jews, Gypsies, gays/lesbians, and the disabled, among other groups, for systematic torture and death under the guise of medical research.

2. *Cultural incapacity.* Cross et al.'s second stage is cultural incapacity. Organizations may not be intentionally culturally destructive, but they lack the capacity to help minority clients or communities because the system remains extremely biased toward the racial/cultural superiority of the dominant group. The characteristics of cultural incapacity include: discriminatory hiring and other staffing practices; subtle messages to people of color that they are not valued or welcome, especially as manifested by environmental cues (building location, decoration, publicity that uses only Whites as models, etc.), and generally lower expectations of minority clients, based on unchallenged stereotypical beliefs.

3. *Cultural blindness.* The third stage in Cross et al.'s continuum, is one in which agencies provide services with the express philosophy that all people are the same, and the belief that helping methods used by the dominant culture are universally applicable. Despite the agency's good intentions, services are so ethnocentric as to make them inapplicable for all but the most assimilated minority group members.
   Such services ignore cultural strengths, encourage assimilation, and blame the victim for their problems. . . . Outcome is usually measured by how closely a client approximates a middle-class, non-minority existence. Institutional racism restricts minority access to professional training, staff positions, and services (Cross et al., p. 15)

Foster et al.'s nondiscriminatory stage fits here, and they note that organizations at this stage may have more of a fixation on "getting the numbers right" and eliminating any apparent signs of hostility toward new groups. While there may be a sincere desire to eliminate a majority group's unfair advantages, the focus may end up on limited and legalistic attempts to comply with equal employment or affirmative action regulations. It is difficult for organizations to move past this stage if Whites or other cultural majority members are not willing to confront the ways they have benefited from institutional racism, and to risk trying new ways of sharing power (Barr & Strong, 1987).

4. *Cultural pre-competence.* Agencies at this stage have, as Schein (1990) might say, at least looked at the "artifacts" and values of their organization, to recognize their weaknesses in serving minorities and developing a multicultural staff. They may experiment with hiring more minority staff beyond the minimal numbers required to comply with EEO goals, may recruit minorities for boards of directors or advisory committees, might work cooperatively to perform needs assessments with minority groups in their service area, and may institute cultural sensitivity training for staff, including management. They may propose new programs specifically for a particular ethnic/cultural group, but if planning is not done carefully, this program may end up marginalized within the agency.

It is at this stage that the level of individuals' racial/ethnic identity awareness comes more clearly to the forefront, where individuals who are less aware of their stage of development may remain unchallenged within a system that overall is pleased with its accomplishments. "One danger at this level is a false sense of accomplishment or of failure that prevents the agency from moving forward along the continuum. . . . Another danger is tokenism" (Cross et al., 1989, p. 16) when minority professionals are expected to raise the agency's level of cross-cultural efficacy by simply being present in slightly greater numbers. However, minority staff may lack training in many of the skills or knowledge areas that would allow them to translate their personal experience into effective counseling, not to mention training of coworkers. If the task of developing cultural awareness has been given to minority staff (or motivated majority staff) who do not have the clout to involve all elements of the agency, "this pattern of program development allows for the phony embracing of multiculturalism because the dominant group can remain on the sidelines judging programs and helping the institution to continue on its merry way" (Barr & Strong, 1987, p. 21). These staff may sacrifice job performance in other areas and then be criticized, or work doubly hard because of taking on the extra burden of cultural awareness activities, and then may not receive any acknowledgment, in patterns that continue the oppression of minorities (Gallegos, 1982).

5. *Cultural competence.* Agencies at this stage show "continuing self-assessment regarding culture, careful attention to the dynamics of difference, continuous expansion of cultural knowledge and resources, and a variety of adaptations to service models in order to better meet the needs of culturally diverse populations (Cross et al., 1989, p. 17).

Organizations at this stage will have a diverse staff at all levels, and most individuals will have reached the higher stages of individual racial/cultural identity awareness: They are aware of and able to articulate their cultural identity, values, and attitudes toward cultural diversity issues. This will be true for both majority and minority culture members. Staff will regularly be offered or seek out opportunities to increase their cross-cultural skills and knowledge. There is recognition that minority group members have to be at least bicultural in U.S. society, and that this creates its own mental health issues concerning identity, assimilation, values conflicts, etc., for staff as well as clients. There will be enough multilingual staff available to offer clients choices in relating to service providers. If the agency has culture-specific programs under its umbrella, these programs are perceived by agency staff and clients as integral to the agency, and not just junior partners.

6. *Cultural proficiency.* This stage encompasses the highest goals of Adler's (1986) synergistic and Foster et al.'s (1988) multicultural stages. As Adler notes, these organizations are very uncommon, given that both the organizational culture and the individuals within it are operating at high levels of multicultural competence, having overcome many layers of racism, prejudice, discrimination, and ignorance.

Organizations at this stage seek to add to the knowledge base of culturally competent practices by "conducting research, developing new therapeutic approaches based on culture, and disseminating the results of demonstration projects" (Cross et al., 1989, p. 17), and follow through on their "broader social responsibility to fight social discrimination and advocate social diversity" in all forums (Foster et al., 1988, p. 3). Staff are hired who are specialists in culturally competent practices, or are trained and supervised systematically to reach competency. Every level of an agency (board members, administrators, counselors, and consumers) regularly participates in evaluations of the agency's cross-cultural practices and environment, and all are able to articulate the agency's values and strategies concerning cultural diversity. If the agency runs culture-specific programs, these programs are utilized as resources for everyone in the agency and community, and not perceived as belonging just to that ethnic community (Muñoz & Sanchez, 1996).

CONCLUSIONS

As can be seen, the task before us is immense. To be successful means getting organizations to review their policies, practices, and organizational structures to remove potential barriers. They may need to create new policies, practices, and internal structures that will support and advance cultural diversity. To truly value diversity, however, means altering the power relations in organizations to minimize structural discrimination. This may mean the following developments: (a) the inclusion of minorities in decision-making positions and the sharing of power with them and (b) constructing diversity programs and practices with the same economic and maintenance priorities as other valued aspects of the organization. More importantly, there is a need to implement programs that directly attack the biases, prejudices, and stereotypes of mental health administrators, staff, and professional workers. Any diversity initiative that does not contain a strong antiracism component, for example, will not be successful. Eliminating prejudice and discrimination is not simply an acquisition of new knowledge and information (cognitive exercise). If that were the case, we would have eradicated racism years ago. Euro-American mental health professionals need to realize that they have directly or indirectly benefited from individual, institutional, and cultural racism. While many Whites may acknowledge that minorities and women are placed at a disadvantage in the current system, few realize or recognize "White privilege" (invisible systems that confer dominance on Whites; McIntosh, 1989). Although no one was ever born wanting to be biased or prejudiced, White Euro-Americans have been socialized in a racist society and need to accept responsibility for their own racism and to deal with it in a nondefensive, guilt-free manner (see Chapter 7). Movement toward valuing and respecting differences, becoming aware of one's own values and biases, and becoming comfortable with differences that exist in terms of race and culture, among other characteristics, are essential.

PROFESSIONAL MULTICULTURAL COMPETENCE

Becoming a multiculturally competent mental health professional, educator, administrator, or member of society requires a constant and ongoing commitment to change in awareness, knowledge, and skills (D.W. Sue, Arredondo, & McDavis, 1992). This change must occur not only at an organizational level, but a professional one as well. Professionally, the culturally competent mental health professional must (a) be aware of the sociopolitical forces that have impacted the minority client; (b) understand that culture, class, and language factors can act as barriers to effective MCT; (c) point out how expertness, trustworthiness, and lack of similarity influence the minority client's receptivity to change/influence; (d) emphasize the importance of worldviews/cultural identity in the helping process; (e) understand culture-bound and communication style differences among various racial groups; and (f) become aware of his/her own racial biases and attitudes (D.W. Sue & Carter et al., 1998). All these variables seem to imply one thing: Clinical work with culturally different clients may require a different combination of skills (process) and goals. Yet the question still remains, How do we determine relevant processes and goals in MCT? While a specific answer would not be possible, D.W. Sue (1977b, 1981) has presented a conceptual model that may be of help in answering this question.

To be more responsive to the culturally different, clinicians must begin the much-needed task of systematically determining the appropriateness or inappropriateness of intervention approaches. Graduate training programs, mental health delivery systems, and therapists themselves must take major responsibility to examine and evaluate the relevance of their particular theoretical framework with respect to the client's needs and values. This statement implies several things. First, there must be knowledge of minority group cultures and experiences. The earlier chapters are intended to provide insights into this area for mental health practitioners. Likewise, the following chapters on American Indians, Asian Americans, African Americans, Hispanic Americans, and other culturally diverse groups are also designed to address this point. Second, we must make clear and explicit the generic characteristics of counseling/therapy and the particular value assumptions inherent in the different schools of thought. Third, when these two aspects of our work are complete, we can compare and contrast them to see which approaches are (a) consistent, (b) conflicting, or (c) new to one another. Implicit in these statements is the assumption that different cultural and subcultural groups require different approaches. From there a decision can be made about how to work with a culturally different individual.

Figure 10.1 reveals four conditions that may arise when counseling a person from a different culture. This schema is proposed as one approach to looking at clinical interventions and the culturally different. The model can also be used for examining the appropriateness of alternative theoretical models of counseling and therapy for different individuals within a single culture.

At the preentry level, culturally different clients inherit a whole constellation of cultural and class values, language factors, and life experiences. Those factors form the person's cultural identity and his/her worldview. Often, the minority client's communication style is a function of these factors. Further, the helping professional is also a product of his or her culture, class,

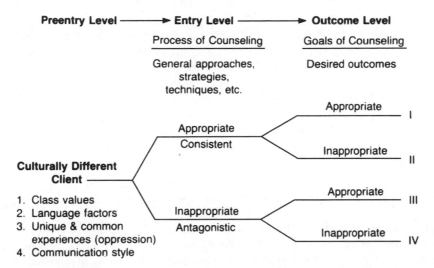

Figure 10.1 Processes and Goals in Counseling. *Note.* From *Counseling the Culturally Different: Theory and Practice,* 3d ed. (p. 99), by D.W. Sue, 1981, New York: John Wiley. Copyright 1981 by John Wiley. Reprinted with permission.

language, and experiences. In the case of a White helping professional, this is what may be referred to as White identity development. This will influence the intervention, as will the particular school of therapy chosen by the therapist. On entering the process of treatment, mental health practitioners choose a general approach, style, or strategy in working with clients. All theories of counseling and therapy rely heavily on some basic techniques in the therapeutic session (existentialists may disagree). Closely linked to the actual process of clinical work are certain implicit or explicit goals such as insight, self-actualization, or behavior change. Or there may be more specific goals, such as how to study better, deal with aggression, or interview for jobs. As can be seen in Figure 10.1, a culturally different client may be exposed to one of four conditions: (I) appropriate process, appropriate goals; (II) appropriate process, inappropriate goals; (III) inappropriate process, appropriate goals; (IV) inappropriate process, inappropriate goals.

CONDITION I—APPROPRIATE PROCESS, APPROPRIATE GOALS

In condition I the client is exposed to a helping process that is consistent with his or her values, life experiences, and culturally conditioned way of responding. An African American male student from the ghetto who is failing in school and getting into fights with other students can be treated by a school counselor in a variety of ways. Sometimes such a student lacks the academic skills necessary to get good grades. The constant fighting is a result of peers' teasing him about his "stupidity." A counselor who is willing to teach the student study and test-taking skills as well as give advice and information may be using an appropriate process consistent with the expectations of the student. The appropriate goals defined between counselor and client, besides acquisition of specific skills, may be an elevation of grades. Notice that this particular activity (teaching, giving advice, etc.) is not traditionally seen as a legitimate part of counseling. Working with the culturally different, counselors must break away from their narrow definition of counseling activities or order to be effective (Sue et al., 1998). The expectations of a poverty-stricken client are often different from those of therapists. Such clients are more concerned with survival and making it on a day-to-day basis. They may expect immediate, concrete suggestions and advice. Getting job interviews for clients, teaching specific educational skills, and helping them to understand and fill out unemployment forms may be the desired and preferred help. In addition, if the problem resides in the environment (racism, oppression, discrimination, etc.), it would appear appropriate that a more action-oriented approach to change the environment would be called for in this case. Thus, a counselor who uses strategies that make sense to the client (consistent with his or her values) and defines suitable goals will be an effective and helpful one.

CONDITION II—APPROPRIATE PROCESS, INAPPROPRIATE GOALS

Often, a helping strategy may be chosen by the therapist that is compatible with the client's life experiences, but the goals are questionable. Again, let us take the aforementioned example of the African American ghetto student. Here the counselor may define the goal as the elimination of "fighting behavior." The chosen technique may be behavior modification. Since the approach stresses observable behaviors and provides a systematic, precise, and structured approach to the problem, much of the nebulousness and mystique of counseling is reduced for the Black student. Rather than introspection and self-analysis, which many people of color may find unappealing, the concrete tangible approach of behavioral counseling is extremely attractive.

While the approach may be a positive experience for many minorities, there is danger here regarding control and behavioral objectives. If the Black student is being teased and forced to fight because he is a minority group member, then the goal of "stopping fighting behavior" may be inappropriate. The counselor in this situation may inadvertently be imposing his or her own standards and values on the client. The end goals place the problem in the hands of the individual rather than society, which produced the problem. Some have termed these approaches "pacification" programs (Bardo, Bryson, and Cody, 1974; Steiner, 1975).

To what extent does the client assume responsibility for deciding the direction of change? To what extent is the counselor forcing the client to adapt or adjust to a "sick" situation that ought to be changed? These are not easy questions to answer. They point out the complexity of certain social issues in counseling and therapy and the concern that many minorities express about cultural oppression.

CONDITION III—INAPPROPRIATE PROCESS, APPROPRIATE GOALS

More often than not, counselors tend to use inappropriate strategies in working with the culturally different. Early termination of therapy is most likely to occur when the process is antagonistic to the values of the client and forces him or her to violate some basic personal values. The mental health practitoner, with the best of intentions and appropriate goals, may fail because the process is incompatible with values of the client. For example, many American Indians view the person as harmonious with nature. The world is accepted in its present form without undue attempts to change it. Unlike American Indian society, Anglos are concerned with controlling and mastering the physical world. The more nature is controlled, the better. American Indians, who may operate under the principle of noninterference, find coercion and the use of suggestion in counseling to be rude, ill-mannered, and hostile. The therapist who leans heavily on some form of intervention, such as behavioral techniques, may be seen as coercive and manipulative. American Indian clients exposed to therapists who stress individual responsibility for changing and mastering the environment are, in effect, being asked to violate a basic value. This may be one reason why American Indians have such a high dropout rate in our educational system.

Another example illustrates this condition with respect to person-centered counseling and therapy. The Rogerian conditions of respect for individuals, empathy, genuineness, and warmth may be very compatible with the values of many persons of color. However, the Rogerian process of paraphrasing, reflecting feelings, and summarizing can be incompatible with cultural patterns. African Americans, for example, may find the patient, waiting, and reflective type of nondirective technique to be antagonistic to their values. Furthermore, empathy is difficult to establish when the therapist does not understand African American idioms or nonverbal modes of expression and the traditions and values of a Black lifestyle. In this case, other techniques to arrive at empathy may be called for. Some (Greene, 1985; Mays, 1985) contend that if a therapist is to be effective with African Americans, techniques that bring a client to a level of awareness and action would be best. Directive, confrontive, and persuasive approaches are more compatible.

There is some question about whether it is possible to use an inappropriate process to arrive at an appropriate goal. If a client, for whatever reason, stays in the counseling relationship, then does not his or her exposure to a process that violates a basic value change the person? Can the client ever attain an appropriate goal? If we look only at the techniques and goals of different counseling/therapy theories, then the answer may appear to be yes. For example, Gestalt approaches emphasize the end goals of the "here and now" (present-time orientation) and getting in touch with bodily feelings. These goals may appear consistent with Native American values. Yet the body of techniques used in Gestalt therapy tend to be confrontive and controlling—actions that may prove embarrassing to American Indian clients.

The problem with looking solely at a particular theory is that doing so is "static." Therapy is a dynamic process, an activity that is ongoing. The relationships between process and goals are highly interrelated and complex. The question of whether condition III can ever exist cannot be easily answered. If the answer, however, is yes, then another issue presents itself: Do the ends justify the means?

CONDITION IV—INAPPROPRIATE PROCESS, INAPPROPRIATE GOALS

Approaches that are clearly inappropriate in terms of techniques and goals generally lead to early termination of therapy. For example, Vietnamese clients who may value restraint of strong feelings and believe that intimate revelations are to be shared only with close friends may cause problems for the insight- or feeling-oriented therapist. Not only are the techniques inappropriate (reflecting feelings, asking questions of a deeply personal nature, making in-depth interpretations, and so on) and seen as lacking in respect for the client's integrity, but the goal of insight into deep underlying processes may not be valued by the person. For example, Vietnamese clients who come for vocational information may be perceived by counselors as needing help in finding out what motivates their actions and decisions. Requests for advice or information from the client are seen as indicative of deeper, more personal conflicts. Although this may be true in some cases, the blind application of techniques that clash with cultural values and the rigid adherence to a goal such as insight seriously places many Vietnamese at a disadvantage. This analysis indicates three important things.

First, it is important for therapists to attend to group differences in working with racial or ethnic minorities. A culturally skilled therapist is one who is able to relate to minority group experiences and has knowledge of cultural and class factors. Second, therapists need to recognize that working with individuals from different cultures does not dictate the same approach, but one that is differentially consistent with lifestyles. In therapy, *equal treatment may be discriminatory*. Third, it is important to systematically look at racial and ethnic differences as they relate to (a) the therapist's own approach and values and (b) the various schools of counseling/therapy. One way we can do this is to more clearly understand what therapists do in therapy (process) and what particular goals therapists hold for their clients. It is hoped that a comparative analysis as proposed in Figure 10.1 will lead to a more realistic appraisal of the appropriateness of counseling/therapy approaches (psychodynamic, Gestalt, cognitive-behavioral, humanistic-existential, etc.) in working with the culturally different.

CHARACTERISTICS OF THE CULTURALLY COMPETENT MENTAL HEALTH PROFESSIONAL

Understanding of minority group experiences and the issues raised throughout this book can be implemented only by enlightened, nondefensive, open, and skilled mental health professionals. Until recently, a systematic attempt to identify characteristics of the culturally skilled therapist was lacking. This served as a major impediment to training programs that were receptive to multicultural training but had difficulty identifying what the program goals should be. It was not until 1980 that the Division of Counseling Psychology of the American Psychological Association directly addressed this issue (D.W. Sue et al., 1982) and outlined 11 characteristics of a culturally skilled counselor. Since this article's publication, however, work on the development of cultural competence has become a dynamic and important area of work, resulting in major publications: "Multicultural Competencies/Standards: A Call to the Profession" (Sue, Arredondo, & McDavis, 1992), "Guidelines for Providers of Psychological Services to Ethnic, Linguistic, and Culturally Diverse Populations" (APA, 1993), "Operationalization of the Multicultural Counseling Competencies" (Arredondo et al., 1996), *Multicultural Counseling Competencies: Assessment, Education and Training, and Supervision* (Pope-Davis & Coleman, 1997), and *Multicultural Counseling Competencies: Individual and Organizational Development* (Sue & Carter et al., 1998). Those interested in a more detailed specification of cultural competencies are encouraged to check out these sources. Table 10.2 also summarizes many of the multicultural counseling competencies endorsed by several divisions of the American Psychological Association and the American Counseling Association. We summarize several considered of major importance in the next few sections.

Consistent with the thesis stressed throughout this book, a culturally competent therapist is seen as working toward these primary goals. First, a culturally competent helping professional is one who is actively in the process of becoming aware of his/her own assumptions about human behavior, values, biases, preconceived notions, personal limitations, and so forth. Second, a culturally competent helping professional is one who actively attempts to understand the worldview of his/her culturally different client. In other words, what are the client's values and

Table 10.2   MULTICULTURAL CONSELING COMPETENCES

I. COUNSELOR AWARENESS OF OWN CULTURAL VALUES AND BIASES

A. *Attitudes and Beliefs*
1. Culturally skilled counselors have moved from being culturally unaware to being aware and sensitive to their own cultural heritage and to valuing and respecting differences.
2. Culturally skilled counselors are aware of how their own cultural backgrounds and experiences and attitudes, values, and biases influence psychological processes.
3. Culturally skilled counselors are able to recognize the limits of their competencies and expertise.
4. Culturally skilled counselors are comfortable with differences that exist between themselves and clients in terms of race, ethnicity, culture, and beliefs.

B. *Knowledge*
1. Culturally skilled counselors have specific knowledge about their own racial and cultural heritage and how it personally and professionally affects their definitions of normality-abnormality and the process of counseling.
2. Culturally skilled counselors possess knowledge and understanding about how oppression, racism, discrimination, and stereotyping affect them personally and in their work. This allows them to acknowledge their own racist attitudes, beliefs, and feelings. Although this standard applies to all groups, for White counselors it may mean that they understand how they may have directly or indirectly benefited from individual, institutional, and cultural racism (White identity development models).
3. Culturally skilled counselors possess knowledge about their social impact on others. They are knowledgeable about communication style differences, how their style may clash or foster the counseling process with minority clients, and how to anticipate the impact it may have on others.

C. *Skills*
1. Culturally skilled counselors seek out educational, consultative, and training experience to improve their understanding and effectiveness in working with culturally different populations. Being able to recognize the limits of their competencies, they (a) seek consultation, (b) seek further training or education, (c) refer out to more qualified individuals or resources, or (d) engage in a combination of these.
2. Culturally skilled counselors are constantly seeking to understand themselves as racial and cultural beings and are actively seeking a nonracist identity.

II. COUNSELOR AWARENESS OF CLIENT'S WORLDVIEW

A. *Attitudes and Beliefs*
1. Culturally skilled counselors are aware of their negative emotional reactions toward other racial and ethnic groups that may prove detrimental to their clients in counseling. They are willing to contrast their own beliefs and attitudes with those of their culturally different clients in a nonjudgmental fashion.
2. Culturally skilled counselors are aware of their stereotypes and preconceived notions that they may hold toward other racial and ethnic minority groups.

B. *Knowledge*
1. Culturally skilled counselors possess specific knowledge and information about the particular group they are working with. They are aware of the life experiences, cultural heritage, and historical background of their culturally different clients. This particular competency is strongly linked to the "minority identity development models" available in the literature.
2. Culturally skilled counselors understand how race, culture, ethnicity, and so forth may affect personality formation, vocational choices, manifestation of psychological disorders, help-seeking behavior, and the appropriateness or inappropriateness of counseling approaches.

Table 10.2   Continued

3. Culturally skilled counselors understand and have knowledge about sociopolitical influences that impinge upon the life of racial and ethnic minorities. Immigration issues, poverty, racism, stereotyping, and powerlessness all leave major scars that may influence the counseling process.

C. *Skills*
1. Culturally skilled counselors should familiarize themselves with relevant research and the latest findings regarding mental health and mental disorders of various ethnic and racial groups. They should actively seek out educational experiences that foster their knowledge, understanding, and cross-cultural skills.
2. Culturally skilled counselors become actively involved with minority individuals outside of the counseling setting (community events, social and political functions, celebrations, friendships, neighborhood groups, and so forth) so that their perspective of minorities is more than an academic or helping exercise.

III. CULTURALLY APPROPRIATE INTERVENTION STRATEGIES

A. *Attitudes and Beliefs*
1. Culturally skilled counselors respect clients' religious and/or spiritual beliefs and values, including attributions and taboos, because they affect worldview, psychosocial functioning, and expressions of distress.
2. Culturally skilled counselors respect indigenous helping practices and respect minority community intrinsic help-giving networks.
3. Culturally skilled counselors value bilingualism and do not view another language as an impediment to counseling (monolingualism may be the culprit).

B. *Knowledge*
1. Culturally skilled counselors have a clear and explicit knowledge and understanding of the generic characteristics of counseling and therapy (culture bound, class bound,

and monolingual) and how they may clash with the cultural values of various minority groups.
2. Culturally skilled counselors are aware of institutional barriers that prevent minorities from using mental health services.
3. Culturally skilled counselors have knowledge of the potential bias in assessment instruments and use procedures and interpret findings keeping in mind the cultural and linguistic characteristics of the clients.
4. Culturally skilled counselors have knowledge of minority family structures, hierarchies, values, and beliefs. They are knowledgeable about the community characteristics and the resources in the community as well as the family.
5. Culturally skilled counselors should be aware of relevant discriminatory practices at the social and community level that may be affecting the psychological welfare of the population being served.

C. *Skills*
1. Culturally skilled counselors are able to engage in a variety of verbal and nonverbal helping responses. They are able to *send* and *receive* both *verbal* and *nonverbal* messages *accurately* and *appropriately*. They are not tied down to only one method or approach to helping but recognize that helping styles and approaches may be culture bound. When they sense that their helping style is limited and potentially inappropriate, they can anticipate and ameliorate its negative impact.
2. Culturally skilled counselors are able to exercise institutional intervention skills on behalf of their clients. They can help clients determine whether a "problem" stems from racism or bias in others (the concept of health paranoia) so that clients do not inappropriately personalize problems.
3. Culturally skilled counselors are not averse to seeking consultation with traditional healers and religious and spiritual leaders and practitioners in the treatment

Table 10.2   *Continued*

of culturally different clients when appropriate. 4. Culturally skilled counselors take responsibility for interfacing in the language requested by the client and, if not feasible, make appropriate referral. A serious problem arises when the linguistic skills of a counselor do not match the language of the client. This being the case, counselors should (a) seek a translator with cultural knowledge and appropriate professional background and (b) refer to a knowledgeable and competent bilingual counselor. 5. Culturally skilled counselors have training and expertise in the use of traditional assessment and testing instruments. They not only understand the technical aspects	of the instruments but are also aware of the cultural limitations. This allows them to use test instruments for the welfare of the diverse clients. 6. Culturally skilled counselors should attend to as well as work to eliminate biases, prejudices, and discriminatory practices. They should be cognizant of sociopolitical contexts in conducting evaluation and providing interventions and should develop sensitivity to issues of oppression, sexism, elitism, and racism. 7. Culturally skilled counselors take responsibility in educating their clients to the processes of psychological intervention, such as goals, expectations, legal rights, and the counselor's orientation.

Note. From "Multicultural Counseling Competencies and Standards: A Call to the Profession," by D.W. Sue, P. Arredondo, and R.J. McDavis, 1992, *Journal of Counseling and Development, 70,* pp. 484–486. Copyright American Counseling Association, 1992. Reprinted with permission.

assumptions about human behavior, biases, and so on? Third, a culturally competent helping professional is one who is in the process of actively developing and practicing appropriate, relevant, and sensitive intervention strategies/skills in working with his/her culturally different client.

These three goals stress the fact that becoming culturally competent is an *active process,* that it is *ongoing,* and that it is a process that *never reaches an end point.* Implicit is recognition of the complexity and diversity of the client and client populations, and acknowledgment of our own personal limitations and the need to always improve.

THERAPIST AWARENESS OF OWN ASSUMPTIONS, VALUES, AND BIASES

In almost all human service programs, counselors, therapists, and social workers are familiar with the phrase, "Counselor, know thyself." Programs stress the importance of not allowing our own biases, values, or hang-ups to interfere with our ability to work with clients. In most cases, the adage stays primarily on an intellectual level with very little training directed at having trainees get in touch with their own values and biases about human behavior. In other words, it appears easier to deal with trainees' cognitive understanding of their own cultural heritage, the values they hold about human behavior, their standards for judging normality and abnormality, and the culture-bound goals they strive toward.

What makes examination of the self difficult is the emotional impact of attitudes, beliefs, and feelings associated with cultural differences and, in particular, racism. For example, as a member of a White Euro-American group, what responsibility do you hold for the racist, oppressive, and discriminatory manner in which you personally and professionally deal with minorities? This is a threatening question for many White people to entertain. Yet to be effective in MCT means one has adequately dealt with this question and worked through the biases, feelings, fears, guilt, and so forth associated with it. It would appear, then, that a culturally competent therapist will have developed beliefs and attitudes consistent with the following characteristics.

1. *The culturally competent mental health professional is one who has moved from being culturally unaware to being aware and sensitive to his/her own cultural heritage and to valuing and respecting differences.* The therapist has begun the process of exploring his/her values, standards, and assumptions about human behavior. Rather than being ethnocentric and believing in the superiority of his/her group's cultural heritage (arts, crafts, traditions, language), there is acceptance and respect for cultural differences. Other cultures are seen to be as valuable and legitimate as his/her own. It is clear that a counselor/therapist who is culturally unaware is most likely to impose his or her values and standards onto a minority client. As a result, an unenlightened therapist may be engaging in an act of cultural oppression.

2. *The culturally competent mental health professional is aware of his/her own values and biases, and how they may affect minority clients.* The therapist actively and constantly attempts to avoid prejudices, unwarranted labeling, and stereotyping. Beliefs that African Americans and Hispanic Americans are intellectually inferior and will not do well in school, or that Asian Americans make good technical workers but poor managers, are examples of widespread stereotyping that may hinder equal access and opportunity. Culturally competent providers try not to hold preconceived limitations/notions about their minority clients. As a check upon this process, they actively challenge the assumptions they are working on, and they monitor their functioning via consultations, supervision, and/or continuing education.

3. *Culturally competent mental health professionals are comfortable with differences that exist between themselves and their clients in terms of race and beliefs.* Differences are not seen as being deviant! The culturally competent counselor/therapist does not profess "color blindness" or negate the existence of differences that exist in attitudes and beliefs. The basic concept underlying color blindness is the humanity of all people. Regardless of color or other physical differences, each individual is equally human. While its original intent was to eliminate bias from treatment, it has served to deny the existence of differences in clients' perceptions of society arising from membership in different racial groups. The message tends to be, "I will like you only if you are the same," instead of, "I like you because of and in spite of your differences."

It is important that therapists begin to recognize the different levels of identity each possesses. Each therapist's *individual* identity makes him or her unique and unlike others. *Group* identity acts as a reference base that may incorporate such things as family, race, ethnicity, gender, religion, and so forth. *Universal* identity emphasizes those common aspects that all share as human beings. Therapists often deny the group identity of the client (race and culture) only to concentrate on the individual or universal level. While these levels do constitute aspects of the client, and while they are important and beneficial to consider, focusing on these to the exclusion of race or culture may be indicative of discomfort in dealing with these issues (i.e., differences are deviant, negative, and create barriers).

4. *The culturally competent mental health practitioner is sensitive to circumstances (personal biases, stage of ethnic identity, sociopolitical influences, etc.) that may dictate referral of the minority client to a member of his/her own race/culture or to another therapist.* A culturally

competent helper is aware of his/her limitations in MCT and is not threatened by the prospect of referring a client to someone else. This principle, however, should not be used as a cop-out for therapists who do not want to work with culturally different clients, or who do not want to work through their own personal hang-ups.

5. *The culturally competent mental health professional acknowledges and is aware of his/her own racist attitudes, beliefs, and feelings.* A culturally competent helper does not deny the fact that he/she has directly or indirectly benefited from individual, institutional, and cultural racism and that he/she has been socialized in a racist society. As a result, the culturally competent provider possesses racist elements that may be detrimental to his/her culturally different client. Culturally competent counselors accept responsibility for their own racism, and attempt to deal with it in a nondefensive, guilt-free manner. They have begun the process of defining a racism-free, nonoppressive, and nonexploitative attitude. Addressing one's Whiteness as in the models of White identity development is crucial for effective MCT.

UNDERSTANDING THE WORLDVIEW OF THE CULTURALLY DIFFERENT CLIENT

It is crucial that counselors and therapists understand and can share the worldview of their culturally different clients. This statement does not mean that providers have to hold these worldviews as their own, but rather that they can see and accept other worldviews in a nonjudgmental manner. In a process that some have referred to as cultural role-taking, the therapist acknowledges that he/she has not lived a lifetime as an Asian American, African American, American Indian, or Hispanic American person. It is almost impossible for the therapist to think, feel, react, and so forth, as a minority individual. Yet cognitive empathy, as distinct from affective empathy, may be possible. It represents cultural role-taking, in which the therapist acquires practical knowledge concerning the scope and nature of the client's cultural background, daily living experience, hopes, fears, and aspirations. Inherent in cognitive empathy is the understanding of how therapy relates to the wider sociopolitical system that minorities contend with every day of their lives.

1. *The culturally competent mental health professional must possess specific knowledge and information about the particular group he/she is working with.* He/she must be aware of the history, experiences, cultural values, and lifestyle of various racial/ethnic groups. The greater the depth of knowledge of a cultural group and the more knowledge he/she has of many groups, the more likely it is that the therapist can be an effective helper. Thus, the culturally competent counselor is one who continues to explore and learn about issues related to various minority groups throughout his/her professional career.

2. *The culturally competent mental health professional will have a good understanding of the sociopolitical system's operation in the United States with respect to its treatment of minorities.* It is important to understand the impact and operation of oppression (racism, sexism, etc.), the politics of counseling, and the racist concepts that have permeated the mental health helping professions. Especially valuable for the therapist is an understanding of the role ethnocentric monoculturalism plays in the development of identity and worldviews among minority groups.

3. *The culturally competent mental health professional must have a clear and explicit knowledge and understanding of the generic characteristics of counseling/therapy.* These encompass lan-

guage factors, culture-bound values, and class-bound values. The therapist should clearly understand the value assumptions (normality and abnormality) inherent in the major schools of therapy and how they may interact with values of the culturally different. In some cases, the theories or models may limit the potential of persons from different cultures. Likewise, being able to determine those that may have usefulness to culturally different clients is important.

4. *The culturally competent mental health professional is aware of institutional barriers that prevent minorities from using mental health services.* Such factors as the location of a mental health agency, the formality or informality of the decor, the language(s) used to advertise the services, the availability of minorities among the different levels, the organizational climate, the hours and days of operation, the offering of services needed by the community, and so forth, are important.

DEVELOPING APPROPRIATE INTERVENTION STRATEGIES AND TECHNIQUES

Effectiveness is most likely to be enhanced when the therapist uses therapeutic modalities and defines goals consistent with the life experiences/cultural values of the client. Throughout this chapter, this basic premise has been emphasized. Studies have consistently revealed that (a) economically and educationally marginalized clients may not be oriented toward "talk therapy"; (b) self-disclosure may be incompatible with cultural values of Asian Americans, Hispanic Americans, and American Indians; (c) the sociopolitical atmosphere may dictate against self-disclosure; (d) the ambiguous nature of counseling may be antagonistic to life values of the culturally different client; and (e) many minority clients prefer an active/directive approach to an inactive/nondirective one in treatment. Therapy has too long assumed that clients share a similar background and cultural heritage and that the same approaches are equally effective with all clients. This is an erroneous assumption that needs to be buried.

Because groups and individuals differ from one another, the blind application of techniques to all situations and all populations seems ludicrous. In the interpersonal transactions between the counselor and client, differential approaches consistent with the life experiences of the person are needed (Sue, Ivey, & Pedersen, 1996). In this particular case and as mentioned earlier, it is ironic that equal treatment in therapy may be discriminatory treatment! Therapists need to understand this. As a means to prove discriminatory mental health practices, racial/ethnic minority groups have in the past pointed to studies revealing that minority clients are given less preferential forms of treatment (medication, electroconvulsive [shock] therapy, etc.). Somewhere confusion has occurred, and it was believed that to be treated differently is akin to discrimination. The confusion centered around the distinction between equal access and opportunities versus equal treatment. Racial/ethnic minority groups may not be asking for equal treatment so much as they are for equal access and opportunities. This dictates a differential approach that is truly nondiscriminatory.

1. *At the skills level, the culturally competent mental health professional must be able to generate a wide variety of verbal and nonverbal responses.* There is mounting evidence to indicate that racial/ethnic minority groups may not only define problems differently from their Anglo counterparts, but respond differently to counseling therapy styles. It appears that the wider the repertoire of responses the therapist possesses, the better the helper he/she is likely to be.

We can no longer rely on a very narrow and limited number of skills in counseling and therapy. We need to practice and be comfortable with a multitude of response modalities.

2. *The culturally competent mental health professional must be able to send and receive both verbal and nonverbal messages accurately and appropriately.* The key words "send," "receive," "verbal," "nonverbal," "accurately," and "appropriately" are important. These words recognize several things about MCT.

First, communication is a two-way process. The culturally skilled counselor/therapist must not only be able to communicate (send) his/her thoughts and feelings to the client, but must also be able to read (receive) messages from the client. Second, MCT effectiveness may be highly correlated with the counselor's ability to recognize and respond not only to verbal, but also to nonverbal messages. Third, sending and receiving a message accurately means the ability to consider cultural cues operative in the setting. Fourth, accuracy of communication must be tempered by its appropriateness. This is a difficult concept for many to grasp. It deals with communication styles. In many cultures, subtlety and indirectness of communication is a highly prized art. Likewise, directness and confrontation are prized by others.

3. *The culturally competent mental health professional is able to exercise institutional intervention skills on behalf of his/her client when appropriate.* This implies that help-giving may involve out-of-office strategies (outreach, consultant, change agent, ombudsman roles, and facilitator of indigenous support systems) that discard the intrapsychic counseling model and view the problems/barriers as residing outside the minority client.

4. *The culturally competent mental health professional is aware of his/her helping style, recognizes the limitations he/she possesses, and can anticipate the impact upon the culturally different client.* All helpers have limitations in their ability to relate to culturally different clients. It is impossible to be all things to everyone; that is, no matter how skilled we are, our personal helping style may be limited. This is nothing to be ashamed of, especially if a therapist has tried and continues to try to develop new skills. When therapy-style adjustments appear too difficult, the next best thing to do may be to (a) acknowledge the limitations, and (b) anticipate your impact upon the client. These things may communicate several things to the culturally different client: (a) that you are open and honest about your style of communication and the limitations or barriers that it may cause, (b) that you, the therapist, understand enough about the client's worldview to anticipate how this may adversely affect your client; and (c) that you will communicate your desire to help despite your limitations. Surprisingly, for many culturally different clients, this may be enough to allow rapport building and greater freedom on the part of counselors to use techniques that are less than optimal for a particular client.

5. *The culturally competent mental health professional is able to play helping roles characterized by an active systemic focus that leads to environmental interventions.* They are not trapped into the conventional counselor/therapist mode of operation. In the *consultant role,* for example, helping professionals attempt to serve as resource persons to other professionals and/or minority populations in developing programs that would improve their life conditions through prevention and remediation. The *outreach role* requires that counselors and therapists move out of their offices and into their clients' communities (Atkinson, Thompson, & Grant, 1993). For example, since many African Americans are deeply involved in their church and respect their Black ministers, outreach and preventive programs could be

delivered through the support of interdenominational Black ministerial alliances or personnel in the churches (Thomas & Dansby, 1985). Home visits are an outreach tactic traditionally used by social workers. Therapists who use this method would be meeting the needs of minority clients (financial difficulties with transportation), allowing the helping professional to see the family in their natural environment, making a positive statement about their own personal commitment and involvement with the family, avoiding the intimidating atmosphere of large formal and unfamiliar institutions, and perhaps allowing the therapist to directly observe the environmental factors that are contributing to the families problems. The *ombudsman role,* which originated in Europe, functions to protect citizens against bureaucratic mazes and procedures. In this situation, the therapist would attempt to identify institutional policies and practices that may discriminate against or oppress a minority constituency. As a *facilitator of indigenous support systems,* the counselor would structure their activities to supplement, not supplant, the already existing system of mental health. Collaborative work with folk healers, medicine persons, or community leaders would be very much a part of the therapist's role.

CONCLUSIONS

Characteristics of cultural competence in this chapter stress dissimilarities between the helping professional and the culturally different client. Some criticisms have been leveled at the advocacy of criteria that emphasize differences between the helper and the client. Most such criticisms seem to be along the following lines: (a) Concentrating on differences fosters a backlash of racism, sexism, or homophobia; (b) by focusing on racial/cultural/gender/sexual orientation characteristics, the counselor may lose sight of the individual client; (c) there are so many differences and the field is so complex that one cannot possibly work with all culturally different groups; (d) counselors and therapists may be limited in their ability to adopt a different therapy style; (e) concentrating on culture-specific techniques may lead to a technique-oriented definition of therapy devoid of a conceptual framework; (f) technique approaches may be distal to the goal of therapy; and (g) playing alternative helping roles may blur the boundaries of therapy (dual role conflicts and loss of objectivity).

There is much truth to many of these warnings, but let us not be guilty of "blaming the victim." Differences are not the problem. Being Asian American is not the problem. Being American Indian is not the problem. Being African American is not the problem. Being Hispanic American is not the problem. The problem lies in the perception of what differences mean and in society's perception of the attributes attached to being a minority group member! MCT implies major differences between the helper and client. Not only are there major differences, but those dissimilaries are associated with minority status in the United States. As a result, therapists who are afraid to face these facts squarely, who deny that they exist, who perceive these as the problem, and who feel uncomfortable working out these differences will meet with failure. Mental health practitioners who are willing to address cultural differences directly are those who do not perceive them as impediments. Instead, therapists who view these differences as positive attributes will most likely meet and resolve the challenges that arise in MCT. Such a helper is what we consider to be culturally competent.

Part V

♦

Counseling and Therapy with Specific Populations

Thus far our journey into multicultural counseling/therapy has been concerned with providing a broad conceptual and theoretical base from which to analyze counseling/therapy and its relationship to the culturally different. While differences among minority groups have been mentioned, we have dealt mainly with concepts and issues that seem applicable to all minority experiences in the United States. This has been necessary to supply us with an analytic framework from which to view multicultural counseling and therapy. Yet it is equally important for us to recognize that while commonalities exist among varying cultural groups, differences are also present. These differences seem intimately correlated with (a) cultural values unique to an ethnic group, (b) historical experiences in the United States, and (c) society's negative treatment and stereotyping of the culturally different. In this book, we have included a chapter on *other groups* that also have been subject to oppression and a devalued status (gay men and lesbian women, elderly adults, individuals with disabilities, and women). With each of the ethnic and other diverse groups described in the forthcoming chapter, we suggest that you apply concepts learned from the earlier sections and ask yourself the following question:

1. What are the cultural values and norms of the groups? What life experiences do they have that may be similar to those of other culturally different groups? What life experiences may be unique or specific to them?

2. How has the experience of this group been shaped by society's reaction to it? What contributed to the negative view by the larger society?

3. How may the norms, values, and historical experiences affect the group's behavior and motivation, and its perception of mental health practice?

4. Are the concepts of racial/cultural identity applicable to each of the groups?

5. Review the generic characteristics of counseling. Which seem to be potential barriers? Why?

6. In what ways do indigenous belief systems or healing practices affect the particular groups being discussed? How may they affect the delivery of Euro-American mental health practices?

7. What types of professional and organizational changes might need to occur in order to deliver relevant services to the specific populations in the following chapters?

We hope that these questions will help you begin to address the issues raised in multicultural counseling.

Chapter 11

◆

Counseling African Americans

◆

In Jasper, Texas, James Byrd Jr. was savagely beaten, chained to a pickup truck, and then dragged to death. Two of the three suspects had racist tattoos. (Fields-Meyer, 1998)

A human rights commission successfully brought a civil lawsuit against two Klan groups for harassing and threatening African Americans who had moved into an all-white housing project. (Baldauf & Johnson, 1998)

At the Advisory Board to President Clinton's Initiative on Race, statistics were presented that indicated that racism exists in law enforcement. For example, in Maryland African American motorists are four times more likely to have to submit to searches than White drivers. (Anonymous, 1998)

The Supreme Court agreed to decide whether a suit involving "environmental racism" can be brought in federal courts. Chester, Pennsylvania, is a town of 42,000 that is 65% African American and has five major waste facilities. The rest of the county, which is 91% white, has 500,000 people but has only two waste facilities. (Watson, 1998)

The African American population is expected to have reached 35.5 million by the year 2000. Of the increase since 1980, 16% was due to immigration. The poverty rate for African Americans remains nearly three times higher than that of White Americans (33.1% versus 12.2%) and the unemployment rate twice as high (11% versus 5%; U. S. Bureau of the Census, 1995). Their disadvantaged status, as well as racism and poverty, contribute to the following statistics. About 1/3 of African American men in their 20s are in jail, on probation, or on parole. This rate has increased by over 1/3 during the past five years (Freeberg, 1995). The lifespan of

African Americans is five to seven years shorter than that of White Americans (Anderson, 1995; Felton, Parson, Misener & Oldaker, 1997).

Other health statistics are equally dismal. Twenty percent of African Americans have no health insurance (Giachello & Belgrave, 1997). About 40% of new cases of AIDS cases in 1995 were African Americans (Talvi, 1995). Rates of hypertension (National Center for Health Statistics, 1996) and obesity (Kumanyika, 1993) are higher than those of the White population. Although hypertension has been thought to be primarily biological in African Americans, psychological factors may also be involved. African Americans exposed to videotaped or imaginal depictions of racism showed increases in heart rate and digital blood flow (Jones et al., 1996). Systolic blood pressure also appears to be influenced by response to discrimination. African Americans who responded by accepting discrimination showed higher blood pressure than those who challenged the situation (Krieger and Sidney, 1996). Medical researchers (Ayanian et al., 1993; Harris, Andrews and Elixhauser, 1997) have found that compared to White patients, African American patients were less likely to undergo corrective surgeries or major therapeutic procedures. Since all had insurance coverage, the reason for the difference in care is unclear, although race-based decisions remain as one possibility.

Although these statistics are grim, Ford (1997) points out that much of our literature is based on individuals of the lower social class who are on welfare or unemployed and not enough on other segments of the African American population. The focus on one segment of African Americans masks the great diversity that exists among African Americans, who may vary greatly from one another on factors such as socioeconomic status, educational level, cultural identity, family structure, and reaction to racism. More than 1/3 of African Americans are now middle-class or higher. They tend to be well educated, homeowners, and married. In 1989, one out of seven African American familes had an income of $50,000 or higher (Hildebrand, Phenice, Gray & Hines, 1997). These are important distinctions. Many middle- and upper-class African Americans are receptive to the values of the dominant society, believe that advances can be made through hard work, feel that race has a relative rather than a pervasive influence in their lives, and embrace their heritage. However, they may feel bicultural stress. As Leanita McClain, the first African American elected to the Board of Directors of the Chicago Tribune, reported

". . . I run a gauntlet between two worlds, and I am cursed and blessed by both. I travel, observe, and take part in both; I can also be used by both. I am a rope in a tug of war . . . whites won't believe that I remain culturally different; Blacks won't believe that I remain culturally the same. . . ." (*Ford, 1997, p. 93*)

However, middle-class African Americans are also exposed to feelings of guilt of having "made it," frustrations by the limitations imposed by the "glass ceiling," and feelings of isolation. Often upward mobility can produce unintentional effects, as shown in the following case study.

◆ *Case Study*

A 14-year-old African American boy, Joseph, came into counseling because of feelings of depression and anger. His parents are professionals and moved to a predominantly white suburb.

Prior to the move, Joseph attended a mainly Black school where he received many awards for academic achievement. Since his enrollment in a primarily white school, Joseph's performance has fallen. His teachers report him to be disruptive, off-task, and argumentative—particularly on issues of justice and minority groups. Joseph complains that they are insensitive and resents being the "expert" on Blacks. He has been asked why Blacks commit so many crimes and why they are so good in sports. He is also teased when he visits friends at his first school for speaking "proper English." Joseph has stolen money from his parents in an attempt to "buy" friendship with his white peers (Ford, 1997).

The move from his predominantly Black school to one that is primarily white has exposed Joseph to issues of racism and the feeling of being different from both White Americans and African Americans. Issues of racial identity are also evident. It is also apparent that Joseph's parents are not aware of the racial issues that have surfaced with the change in schools. These factors need to be addressed with both the parents and Joseph.

Ford believes that middle- and upper-class African Americans may suffer a negative impact on mental health from issues such as: believing a double standard exists (having to work twice as hard to succeed); feelings of isolation (being the only African American in the organization); powerlessness (given responsibility only on tasks pertaining to minorities); being an "expert" or a "representative" on minority issues (African American professor might be asked to teach multicultural classes even if it is not their area of expertise); and "survival guilt" in moving to a higher class and neighborhood. Because of this, middle- and upper-class African Americans may occupy a marginal status where they are not fully accepted by White Americans and are rejected by African Americans.

AFRICAN AMERICANS: CONCERNS FOR COUNSELING AND THERAPY

STAGES OF RACIAL IDENTITY

Some researchers (Atkinson, Morten, & Sue, 1989; Cross, 1971, 1995) believe that minorities go through several stages of racial identity or consciousness. There is some controversy over whether racial identity is a linear process and whether individuals at the earlier stages can be mentally healthy. For African Americans, the stages involve a transformation of a non-Afrocentric identity to one that is Afrocentric (although some African Americans already have a Black identity through early socialization). Cross (1995) has recently modified his stage theory to incorporate more of the research findings in describing five stages of identity for African Americans.

1. *Pre-encounter.* Individuals at this stage have a Eurocentric perspective and accept most of the values of the majority culture. In Cross's (1971) model, individuals at this stage had self-hatred, poor mental health, and anti-Black sentiments. In his revision, Cross (1995) indicates that only a minority of individuals show these characteristics. For many, race may merely be of low salience and of little importance in their daily lives. Individuals may acknowledge prejudice and discrimination but can still achieve high self-esteem. They may

identify more with their religion, profession, or social class than with being Black. Most are not aware that they have been miseducated about African Americans in the United States and believe that African Americans contribute to their own problems. An individual with this set of beliefs can be mentally healthy. They may not feel the need for any change in identity.

2. *Encounter.* Movement to this stage involves two elements: a series of events that are racist and discriminatory in nature and personalizing of these events. Only then will an individual at the pre-encounter stage start to question their set of beliefs. They may become distressed, depressed, confused, and angry at themselves for not recognizing racism.

3. *Immersion-emersion.* During this stage the old identity is shed and a new frame of reference develops. The majority culture is faulted and seen as evil and the individual seeks Black experiences in books, meetings, or art. Immersion in the Black culture is sought and African features are now seen as beautiful. Confrontation with White individuals and their culture is a frequent mode of communication. Resentment is expressed toward other African Americans who do not demonstrate appropriate levels of Black identity. Some may remain fixated at this stage. However, for most, this degree of emotional intensity can not be maintained and the individual recognizes that they are not in control. Others may revert back to their previous identity if the experience is negative. Still others may drop out of involvement with Black issues.

4. *Internalization.* At this stage the new identity is completely internalized. However, there is a range of responses, from being totally committed to Black issues to emphasizing those with a bicultural or multicultural orientation. Other concerns, such as career, religion, and gender, may also be considered. The individual feels more at ease, calmer, and comfortable with their personal standard of Black identity.

5. *Internalization-commitment.* The fifth stage is characterized by a long-term interest in and commitment to African American affairs.

Psychological functioning in African Americans has been associated with the stage of racial identity (Carter, 1991). Additionally, African American preferences for counselor ethnicity are related to the stage of racial identity (Atkinson & Lowe, 1995). Similarly, Parham and Helms (1981) found that African Americans at the pre-encounter stage preferred a White counselor, while those in the other stages preferred a Black counselor. Pomales, Claiborn, and LaFromboise (1986), however, found that the most important counselor characteristic for African American students was cultural sensitivity. A culturally sensitive counselor (one who acknowledges the possibility that race or culture might play a role in the client's problem) is seen as more competent than a "culture-blind" counselor (one who focuses on factors other than culture and race when dealing with the presenting problem). In this study, stage of racial identity played only a minor role in preference for counselor ethnicity. An assessment of racial identity may be useful for a counselor to hypothesize the types of conflict the client may be undergoing and the way the world is viewed.

EDUCATION

The gap in educational attainment between Black and White children is gradually narrowing. The high school dropout rate for African Americans declined from 11% in 1970 to 5% in 1994 and is now not significantly different from that of Whites. In 1994, approximately 73% of

African Americans 25 years and older had completed at least high school and 13% had completed at least a bachelor's degree. The corresponding rates in 1980 were 51% and 8% (U.S. Bureau of the Census, 1995). However, problems are still found in academic performance. Especially at risk are African American boys who show a tendency toward "disidentification" (the disengagement of academic performance from self-esteem), subsequently losing interest in academics during middle and high school. In a longitudinal study Osbourne (1997) studied Hispanic and African American students and found that African American males were the only group to show no relationship between academic performance and global self-esteem. This may lead to lower academic performance.

A study of African American and White middle school students in one school district found that 56.3% of the former had grade point averages below 2.0, versus 20.9% for the latter group. Only 9.67% of African American students had a grade point average above 3.0, versus 43.5% for White students. In addition, African American students are more than twice as likely as White students to be suspended or expelled. At some grade levels, up to 56% of African American students are referred to special education classes (Seattle Public Schools, 1986). Several factors may have contributed to the findings. The school system has a predominantly White teaching staff, and the student population has changed from predominantly White to predominantly minority. Because of this, teaching skills effective in the past may no longer work. Many teachers are also not sensitive to cultural differences and may respond inappropriately to minority group members. Curriculum may also not be meaningful to the experiences of minority group children. Drug abuse may also contribute to the lack of achievement in Black children. The Seattle school district is currently working on a program that addresses these problems.

The gap in educational attainment between Whites and African Americans is also evident in higher education and may increase with the dismantlement of affirmative action policies in admission. At University of California, Berkeley, the number of African American freshmen admitted dropped to 98 in 1998 from 260 in 1997 (Healy, 1998). Only 131 African American students indicated an interest in enrolling at UCLA, the lowest number in 25 years (Brandon, 1998). Unless ways are found to increase minority enrollments, the number of African Americans in higher education will plummet. The percentage of African American enrollment has already declined from a peak in 1978 and has been decreasing through the mid-1980s (U.S. Department of Education, State Task Force on Minority Student Achievement, 1987), although there was some improvement from 1990 to 1995. As of 1995, 13% of African Americans have four or more years of college, compared to 23% for White students (U.S Bureau of the Census, 1995).

Many educators believe that recent cutbacks in financial support and educational programs for minorities, along with an erosion of moral support, have led to this decrease. There is a feeling that society is less interested in the plight of minorities. This has been accompanied by increasing numbers of reported instances of racism on major university campuses. Across five different universities, African Americans report feelings of discomfort and racial hostility on the campuses (Mack et al., 1997). Reasons for this were discussed by a panel of prominent individuals at the University of Michigan (Lockard, 1987). They concluded that racism on campuses has been affected by several factors, including: (1) a decline in interest in civil rights issues in the United States, (2) a backlash to advances that have been made by minorities, (3) declining levels of financial support, (4) a university environment that does not provide emotional support for minority students, and (5) a lack of African American faculty members and mentors. The University of Michigan did commit itself to the recruitment and retention of African American students and faculty members in hopes of increasing enrollment. Unfortunately, their affirmative action program has also come under attack recently.

FAMILY CHARACTERISTICS

Increasingly larger percentages of African American families are headed by females or males with no spouse present. In 1994, 47% of all African American families involved married couples as compared to 68% in 1970 and 56% in 1980 (U.S. Bureau of the Census, 1995). The African American family has been generally described as matriarchal and blamed for many of the problems faced by Black Americans today. Among lower-class African American families, over 70% are headed by women. Black females who are unmarried account for nearly 60% of births and, of these mothers, the majority are teenagers.

What is missed with these statistics, however, is an acknowledgment of the strengths in the African American family structure. For many, there exists an extended family network that provides emotional and economic support. Among families headed by females, the rearing of children is often undertaken by a large number of relatives, older children, and close friends. Within the Black family there exists an adaptability of family roles, strong kinship bonds, a strong work and achievement ethic, and strong religious orientation (Hildebrand, Phenice, Gray, & Hines, 1996; McCollum, 1997). African American men and women value behaviors such as assertiveness, and within a family, males are more accepting of women's work roles and more willing to share in the responsibilities traditionally assigned to women, such as picking up children from school. In spite of the problems with racism and prejudice, many African American families have been able to instill positive self-esteem in their children.

Thomas and Dansby (1985) indicate that much of our reaction to African American families is due to our nuclear family orientation. They relate an incident in which children were asked to draw a picture of their mother and father and the rest of the family eating dinner together. A Black girl left the room in tears. She had been raised by her aunt. Many forms of our assessment and evaluation are still based on the middle-class Euro-American perspective of what constitutes a family. Thomas and Dansby indicate that some families do not eat dinner together because both parents have to work, and in many families the child is raised by someone other than the parent. The different family structures that exist indicate the need to consider various alternative treatment modes and approaches in working with Black Americans. In working with African American families, the counselor often has to assume various roles, such as advocate, case manager, problem solver, and facilitating mentor (Ahai, 1997). In many cases the counselor not only has to intervene in the family but has to deal with community interventions as well. A number of African American families who go into counseling are required to do so by the schools, courts, or police. Issues that may need to be dealt with are feelings about differences in ethnicity between the client and counselor and clarification of the counselor's relationship to the referring agency. Clients should be told what to expect during the initial session. Assessment may have to be made to determine not only how community resources can be better utilized, but also the impact of socioeconomic issues such as food, housing, and areas of strengths of the family members (Grevious, 1985; Paniagua, 1994).

If the family is heavily involved in church activities or has strong religious beliefs, the counselor could enlist resources such as the pastor or minister to deal with problems involving conflicts within the family and health issues such as family planning (Richardson & June, 1997). For many African American families, spiritual beliefs play an important role in their lives and may have developed as part of a coping strategy to deal with stressors. Churches should be considered as much a potential source of information as clinics, schools, hospitals, or other mental health professionals. The church personnel may have an understanding of the family dynamics and living conditions of the parishioners. A pastor or minister can help create sources of social support for family members and help them with social and economic issues. In addition, programs for the enrichment of family life may be developed jointly with the church.

Family Therapy

For family therapy to be successful, counselors must first identify their own set of beliefs and values regarding appropriate roles and communication patterns within a family. One must be careful not to impose these beliefs on a family. For example, African American parents, especially those of the working class, are more likely than White parents to use physical punishment to discipline their children. However, while some types of physical discipline have been related to more acting out behavior in White children, this was not found in African American children (Deater-Deckard, Dodge, Bates & Pettit, 1996). Physical discipline should not be seen as necessarily indicative of a lack of parental warmth or negativity. Parent education approaches based on White, intact, nuclear families are often inappropriate for African American families. In fact, they may perpetuate the view that minorities have deficient child-rearing skills. Attempts are being made to develop culturally sensitive parent education programs for African Americans that focus on responses to racism by the family, culture conflicts, single parenting, drug abuse, and different types of discipline. Differences in family functioning should not be automatically seen as deficits (Gorman & Balter, 1997).

Family therapy can be particularly difficult for many African American families who feel that issues such as out-of-wedlock births, marital status of adult members of a family, and the paternity of children may be reacted to negatively by the counselor. These are in addition to other trust issues that may be involved. Knowledge of the family structure can aid in therapy. In addition, the impact of racism, economic difficulties, and identity issues should also be explored in the family. Boyd (1982) suggests the use of a method of inquiry that allows important information to be gathered about the extended family.

◆ Case Study

A mother, Mrs. J., brought in her 13-year-old son, Johnny, who she said was having behavioral problems at home and in school. During the interview, the therapist found out that Johnny had five brothers and sisters living in the home. In addition, his stepfather, Mr. W., also lived in the house. The mother's sister, Mary, and three children had recently moved in with the family until their apartment was repaired. The question "Who is living in the home?" caught this. The mother was also asked about other children not living at home. She also had a daughter living with an aunt in another state. The aunt was helping the daughter raise her child. When asked, "Who helps you out?" the mother responded that a neighbor watches her children when she has to work and that both groups of children had been raised together. Mrs. J.'s mother also assisted with her children.

Further questioning revealed that Johnny's problem developed soon after his aunt and her children moved in. Before this, Johnny had been the mother's primary helper and took charge of the children until the stepfather returned home from work. The changes in the family structure that occurred when the sister and her children moved in produced additional stress on Johnny. Treatment included Mrs. J. and her children, Mr. W., Mary and her children, and Mrs. J.'s mother. Pressures on Johnny were discussed and alternatives were considered. Mrs. J.'s mother agreed to take in Mary and her children temporarily. To deal with the disruption in the family, follow-up meetings were conducted to help clarify roles in the family system. Within a period of months, behavioral problems in the home and school had stopped for Johnny. He once again assumed a parental role to help out his mother and stepfather.

Montague (1996) points out several important considerations to make in working with Black families. Because of the possibility of an extended or nontraditional family arrangement, questions should be directed to finding out who is living in the home and who helps out. It is also important to work to strengthen the original family structure and to try to make it more functional rather than to try to change it. One of the strengths of the African American family is that men, women, and children are allowed to adopt multiple roles within the family. An older child like Johnny could adopt a parental role while the wife might take on the role of the father. The grandmother may be a very important family member who also helps raise the children. Her influence and help should not be eliminated, but the goal should be to make more efficient the working alliance with the other caregivers. A family therapist should remember that flexibility of roles is a strength but can also produce problems if roles conflict with one another.

AFRICAN AMERICAN YOUTH

For many urban Black adolescents, life is complicated by problems of poverty, illiteracy, and racism. The homicide rate for African American youth between the ages of 15 and 24 was nearly 10 times that of White youth in 1989; their suicide rate increased to over twice that of other teenagers between 1980 and 1992; and they are more likely to contract sexually transmitted diseases than other groups of teenagers (Harvey & Rauch, 1997). Unemployment can range from 37% to nearly 50% among Black teenagers. Most African American youth feel strongly that race is still a factor in how people are judged (Gannet News Service, 1998).

Issues presented in counseling may differ to some extent between males and females. African American adolescent females, like other females, are burdened by living in a male-dominated society, face issues with racial identity and negative stereotypes, and strive to succeed in relationships and careers.

Well, in this time I think it's really hard to be an African American woman . . . we are what you call a double negative; we are Black and we are a woman and it's really hard. . . .

I'd rather say I'm African-American than I'm Black because of the connection with the land, knowing that I come from somewhere. . . .

That [racial identity] is important to me because society sees African-American females as . . . always getting pregnant and all that kind of thing and being on welfare. . . . (Shorter-Gooden and Washington, 1996, p. 469)

In this sample of young African American females, Shorter-Gooden and Washington (1996) found that the struggle over racial identity was a more salient factor than gender identity in establishing self-definition. These adolescents believed that they had to be strong and determined to overcome the obstacles in being Black. About half had been raised by their mother and most indicated the importance of the mother-daughter relationship. Careers were also important to 2/3 of the females; most felt that the motivation to succeed academically was instilled by their parents. In counseling young African American women, issues involving racial identity and conflict should be explored, and their sense of internal strength should be increased since it appears to serve as a buffer to racism and sexism.

The type of socialization that African American children and teenagers receive from their parents has been found to be related to social anxiety. Facing racism, African American parents may: (a) address racism and prejudice directly and help their children identify with their own race; (b) discuss race only when the issue is brought up by their children and consider it to be of minor importance; (c) focus on human values and ignore the role of race. Neal-Barnett found that the third approach was related to higher levels of social anxiety, particularly with African American peers. Ignoring racial issues in socialization left children vulnerable to anxiety when Black peers accused them of "acting White." They had not had the opportunity to develop coping strategies.

African American females often have to deal with the double issue of being both Black and female. They have to fight against negative images to prevent them from being incorporated into their belief system, and simultaneously, develop pride and dignity in Black womanhood (Jordan, 1997).

◆ Case Study

A 16-year-old African American female, Brenda, was referred for counseling by her case manager. Brenda had lived in a foster home for three years due to the arrest of her mother for drug use. In school, Brenda was reported to be aggressive and combative and had had a confrontation with her teacher over the portrayal of African Americans in books.

Brenda had a number of problems and was still fighting for her self-identity. The counselor was supportive and worked to help counteract the negative messages that Brenda was receiving at home and in school. Because of this intervention, these messages were not internalized, and she was able to focus on her strengths. She graduated from high school (Jordan, 1997).

Black youth often do not come to counseling willingly. Often they do so because they have been referred or brought in by their parents. Because of this, cooperation may be difficult to obtain.

♦ *Case Study*

Michael is a 19-year-old African American male who was brought to counseling by his aunt, Gloria, with whom he has lived for the past 2 years. Gloria is concerned about Michael's future as a result of his being present during a recent drug raid at the home of some friends. . . . Although Michael graduated from high school and is employed part-time at a fast food restaurant, he is frustrated with this work and confused about his future. He believes that Black men "don't get a fair shake" in life, and therefore is discouraged about his prospects about getting ahead. . . . Michael's aunt . . . is concerned that Michael's peers are involved in gangs and illegal activities. She thinks the rap music he listens to is beginning to fill his head with hate and anger. . . . Michael's major issues center around developing a positive identity as an African American man and discovering his place in the world (Frame & Williams, 1996, p. 22).

Frame and Williams suggest several strategies in working with Black youth. The first involves the use of metaphors and is based on the African tradition of storytelling. Instead of just responding to "Black men don't get a fair shake," the counselor could get Michael to help identify family phrases or Biblical stories that instill hope. Additional metaphors could be generated from the writings of contemporary African American figures. The second strategy could be support for Michael's struggle with societal barriers. He could envision himself as a crusader for human rights and learn how to direct his anger in appropriate ways. Third, Michael could be asked to bring in his rap music and discuss what is appealing about it. Issues addressed in the lyrics could be explored and the counselor could help with decisions regarding healthy outlets for his feelings of anger or despair. Fourth, family and community support systems could be generated. Members of the extended family, the pastor, teachers, and other important individuals in Michael's life could be asked to meet together in Aunt Gloria's home. All the members could share information about their struggles and search for identity. Use of these techniques, derived from African American experiences, can lead to personal empowerment.

Paster (1985) makes several recommendations in working with Black youth. First, the youth's expectations about the usefulness of counseling should be discussed. Second, a negotiated contract on counseling duration and goals should be obtained. Paster recommends making it a short-term (6- to 8-week) trial period. Third, the counselor should set firm limits, especially when dealing with verbal abuse. A streetwise youth might deliberately attempt to frighten or shock the counselor by describing use of drugs and sexual behaviors in graphic detail. Others might adopt a highly confrontive and aggressive stance or tell tales as a means of testing out the therapist. In addition, Paster feels that it is important for the counselor to act as an advocate for the youth and deal as an intermediary with agencies such as the school and the court. When possible, community resources should be utilized.

Paster indicated how she applied some of these suggestions in working with a 13-year-old boy, "J.," who was referred for counseling by his probation officer.

♦ *Case Study*

J. had had a history of problems with the authorities since the age of 7. He had been involved in a number of gang fights, had committed burglaries, and had been arrested carrying a weapon. In school, he spent most of his time wandering in the schoolyard and halls. The judge had given him the option of counseling or incarceration. The counselor indicated that J. had the right not to attend the sessions, but that she would have to communicate that decision to the judge. Negotiations were made concerning expectations, attendance, and goals. J. indicated that he did not feel that counseling would be of any benefit but did agree to attend. Together, they decided that two absences in attendance would result in a report to the judge of this fact. J. was asked to bring back a list of what he wanted to achieve in treatment. He came back the next session with a list requesting food and candy, becoming a football hero, and winning the lottery. Paster discussed these seriously with the boy but also with a sense of humor and felt that the excitement of discussion helped to engage J. in the counseling process. He remained in treatment for three years and showed substantial gains. In working with J., Paster had been able to achieve gains even with the initial resistance. She had discussed expectations, negotiated goals, and, most important, was able to get J. involved in the counseling process.

VALUES

African American values have been shaped by cultural factors, social class variables, and experience with racism. As a group, African Americans tend to be more group centered and sensitive to interpersonal matters, to have strong kinship bonds, be work and education oriented, and to have a strong commitment to religious values and church participation (McCollum, 1997). Todisco and Salomone (1991) believe that some of these values are due to their African heritage, which stresses groupness, community, cooperation and interdependence, and being one with nature. In contrast, White middle-class values focus on individuality, uniqueness, competition, and control over nature.

African Americans have also been influenced by exposure to racism and prejudice in American society and by their struggle for identity. Because of these difficulties, African Americans often display a differential response according to the race of the individual that they are interacting with. With other Blacks, they are often open, responsive, playful, and expressive. In interacting with White Americans, Blacks are often more guarded and formal, and less verbal. However, these behavioral differences in Black-Black and Black-White interaction patterns are also influenced by social class and the degree to which Black Americans have accepted white middle-class values.

The existence of racism has produced a variety of defense and survival mechanisms among

Black Americans. A.C. Jones (1985) believes that it is important for the counselor or therapist to acknowledge the existence of these factors and to help the client identify maladaptive means of dealing with racism. For example, an individual may have only a limited or reflexive response in dealing with these situations. In counseling a client about dealing with situations in which racism plays a part, the counselor must assist the client in developing a wider range of options and encourage the development of a more conscious, problem-solving mode. The client must consider the way he/she usually deals with racism and consider other options that might be more productive. The following case study by Jones demonstrates this approach.

◆ *Case Study*

A recently divorced, 25-year-old African American medical student sought therapy for migraine headaches that were stress related. He felt that the racist environment of the training school and a particular professor were responsible for his problem. He proposed to deal with the problem by directly confronting his professor and accusing him of racism. It did appear that the professor had engaged in prejudicial behavior. However, it is very possible that directly confronting the professor in this manner would have led to the student's dismissal from the school. Jones also found that the client's choice of this strategy was at least partially related to his unresolved feeling of anger over his recent divorce. This event had made him feel more vulnerable, and the resulting bitter feelings helped in his choice of directly confronting the professor. As the client understood the impact of his divorce, he was able to consider a wider range of options that were open to him. He decided that it would be best to file a complaint with the minority affairs office. Although the tension between the student and the professor remained high, the student felt that he had chosen the best option and remained in school.

A.C. Jones (1985) feels that in working with an African American client, four sets of interactive factors must be considered (see Figure 11.1). The first factor involves the reaction to racial oppression. Most African Americans have faced racism, and the possibility that this factor might play a role in the present problem should be examined. Vontress and Epp (1997) describe this factor as "historical hostility," a reaction in response to current and past suffering endured by the group. Because of this, problems are often perceived through this filter. The second factor is the influence of Afro-American culture on the client's behavior. Clients may vary greatly in their identification with Afro-American traditions. The third factor involves the degree of adoption of majority culture values. The task of the therapist is to help the client understand his or her motivation and make conscious, growth-producing choices. The fourth factor involves the personal experiences of the individual. African Americans differ significantly in their family and individual experiences. For some, this last category may be much more significant than racial identity.

Although all four factors may influence an African American client, the degree of overlap or importance of each of the factors may vary greatly from individual to individual. A middle-class

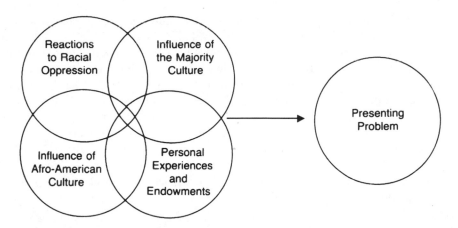

Figure 11.1 The Interaction of Four Sets of Factors in the Jones Model. From "Psychological Functioning in Black Americans: A Conceptual Guide for Use in Psychotherapy" by A.C. Jones, 1985, *Psychotherapy, 22,* p. 367. Copyright 1982 by *Psychotherapy.* Reprinted by permission of the Editor, *Psychotherapy.*

African American living in a predominantly White neighborhood may show a different pattern from a lower-class African American living in a Black neighborhood. The advantage of this model is that it includes the elements involved in the studies on identity and forces the counselor to more completely assess external and internal influences on a Black American's problem.

COUNSELING ATTITUDES AND PROBLEMS

African Americans who seek counseling are often thought to have a negative view of mental health services. Some may have a "historical hostility" response because of their prolonged inferior treatment in American society (Vontress & Epp, 1997). "A non-Black counselor may always trigger mistrust and trepidation in the African American client" (p. 171), and it is recommended that the counselor consider "interpretation of the influence of historical hostility as a necessary part of effective psychotherapy of African Americans" (p. 180). Vontress and Epp believe that acting-out behaviors, substance abuse, and violence are, in part, a response to historical hostility. However, it is also possible that African Americans regard counseling positively but find a problem with the counseling process. Differences in the types of problems presented by African American and White clients do not appear to be responsible for the less favorable response by the former to counseling. Baum and Lamb (1983) found that for 170 African American students seeking help at a university counseling center, the majority of problems revolved around career and vocational choice, academic problems, anxiety, depression, and relationship problems. A comparison with White students found that they expressed very similar concerns. Evans, Acosta, Yamamoto, and Hurwicz (1986) likewise reported few differences between reasons of African American and White patients for coming to a psychiatric outpatient clinic. However, Black clients had a tendency to want the counselor to resolve the problem and felt that counselors had less to offer in this area.

The attitude African Americans have toward mental health clinics does not appear to be highly negative. In a representative sample of African Americans, approximately 50% indicated neutral attitudes toward community mental health centers, 34% had positive attitudes, and less than 20% had negative attitudes (Gary, 1985). Parker and McDavis (1983) also found that most African American respondents were aware of the location of mental health agencies and had realistic views of their function. They believed that help could be obtained at the centers and that "normal" individuals utilize their services. They also felt that counseling could be helpful, that both African American and White counselors could be effective, that one of the goals of therapy is self-understanding, and that therapy involves more than just talking. Slight sex differences were found. African American females were somewhat more comfortable with a White counselor than African American males, and the latter indicated a slightly greater preference than did African American females for seeing an African American counselor. Overall, it appears that African Americans view counseling positively but may encounter difficulties during the counseling process itself.

BARRIERS TO EFFECTIVE CROSS-CULTURAL COUNSELING

COUNSELOR VARIABLES

A variety of factors involving the counselor, the African American client, their interaction, and the expectations of both counselor and client are probably responsible for the less-than-optimal outcome in counseling. In discussing these variables, we first focus on problems that might occur with a non-African American counselor. The counselor must initially deal with issues of racism and feelings of the Black client about working with someone of different ethnicity. It is very important for the counselor to examine the personal values that he/she brings to counseling, particularly values pertaining to work with minority clients.

Cultural perceptions often influence clinical or counseling judgments. In one study (Atkinson et al., 1996), African American and Euro-American psychologists were presented a photograph and case information on an African American female and asked to rate the client. African American psychologists rated the client more attractive, more likely to benefit from counseling, and had more positive feelings about the individual than the Euro-American psychologists. The latter professionals also believed that the client suffered from more severe mental disorders than did the African American counselors. The study clearly indicates that clinical judgment can be influenced by cultural factors. Because of these results, Atkinson and his colleagues believe that in some cases African American clients may be better served by mental health professionals of the same ethnicity. Greene (1985) describes several attitudes and responses that might have a negative impact on counseling. None of these stances is helpful to the African American client, and they necessitate a closer examination of one's motivation and personal feelings when working with African American clients.

1. *Racism or prejudice.* Feelings of superiority over another group may exist at either a conscious or an unconscious level. Underlying this feeling may be the belief that African Americans are an inferior group who create their own problems. Cultural differences involving a different lifestyle may be viewed negatively and interpreted as an indication of pathology. A limited number of options may be discussed with the African American client, and the focus may be on intrapsychic conflicts without any examination of external influences on the

problem. Positive aspects and strengths of the individual may not be acknowledged or recognized. A "blaming the victim" approach is taken. Often the influence is subtle and involves the evaluation of behaviors such as lifestyle, parenting methods, and family practices according to the counselor's own system of values.

2. *Color blindness.* A counselor taking this stance argues that an African American client is the same as any client. Possible influences of culture and racism on the problem are not acknowledged or explored. Solutions that are suggested are based on a White middle-class perspective. Many African Americans have lifestyles very different from those of mainstream Americans. Minority group status and experiences of and with racism must be acknowledged. Unless this occurs, realistic strategies to deal with real-life situations may not develop.

3. *Paternalism.* In this stance, the counselor interprets the client's problems as always stemming from racism or prejudice. Severe disorders are excused as merely a reaction to racism or minority status. Possible personal contributions of the individual to his or her problem are not examined. The therapist may become the protector of the individual, which fosters dependence. In this event, clients are prevented from developing independent problem-solving skills or from understanding their own role in their problems.

4. *Unquestioning acceptance of the Black perspective.* Associated with paternalism is a counselor who has the view that because of racism and prejudice, the client should have the right to achieve a personal goal without considering the rights and feelings of others. The African American client is allowed to freely express hostility or take any action that is felt to be justified. This stance may involve feelings of racial guilt on the part of the counselor, who is attempting to prove that he/she is open and accepting. This approach is also not helpful to the client.

Another barrier in cross-cultural counseling is that the process, goals, and expectations of the majority counselor might also not fit the worldview of the client. Most therapies are directed toward the middle-class White client, who is educated and employed. Because of this, African Americans may feel that the therapist does not understand issues such as economic deprivation. The goals of personal growth and self-exploration may be insufficient, since lower-class African Americans tend to focus more on external conditions than on intrapsychic concerns. Clients may need more help in dealing with socioeconomic issues such as housing, food stamps, and employment and may need concrete assistance rather than insight therapy. Problem-solving and behavioral approaches appear to be recommended treatment modalities for most African Americans (Paniagua, 1994).

Berman (1979) has found that African American counseling students used a different set of microskills than their White counterparts. The former tended to rely more on active expression skills such as giving directions and interpretation, whereas White males and females used more attending skills and reflection of feelings. Berman reached several conclusions: (1) Current counseling training programs place a heavy emphasis on nondirective attending skills; (2) the counseling style preferred by minorities may lie outside the narrow range of skills emphasized in the counseling profession; and (3) counseling programs may have to consider incorporating some of the more active elements if they wish to be sensitive to cultural differences. Counselors who work with African American clients will have to display a wider range of skills than they do in working with white clients.

CLIENT VARIABLES

Because of past experiences with racism and prejudice, African American clients are often distrustful of white counselors. To make headway in therapy, the therapist must establish a trusting relationship. Black clients are especially sensitive to interpersonal processes and will size up the counselor and test the relationship. They may directly challenge the therapist's values and qualifications or act in a very guarded and aloof manner. The counselor cannot merely sit back and expect a commitment to evolve. In particular, African American males may consider participation in counseling to be an admission of weakness and "unmanly," and therefore be reluctant to furnish personal information (Lee, 1990). These behaviors are part of a protective mechanism. The nonresponsiveness is not resistance but an active means of evaluating the counselor. If the counselor is able to respond in a straightforward manner, a relationship may develop. It has to be understood that self-disclosure is very difficult for many African American clients since it leaves them vulnerable to racism.

♦ *Case Study*

A 50-year-old African American male, Curtis, is currently a midlevel manager in an electronics firm. He is married with three children, one of whom is attending a prestigious university. Curtis served in the Marine Corps during the Vietnam War and was wounded in action. His boss recommended that he see the employee assistance counselor because of a deterioration in the quality of his work. Curtis was reluctant to talk to the counselor and attended the session only because of his supervisor's request (Lee & Bailey, 1997).

Curtis's initial behavior was that of being aloof and wary. The counselor dealt with this by engaging in a conversation about events in the community and sharing some of his background such as family origins and military experience. The counselor wanted Curtis to see him as an individual first and then a mental health professional. Developing an egalitarian relationship is important for some African American clients. Later, after trust had developed, introspection over current problems were discussed. The meaning of life was discussed in terms of how Curtis viewed the things that gave him meaning in life and how he saw himself as a man and an African American. Later, issues around racism and the "glass ceiling" at his workplace as well as the increased financial and personal responsibility in taking care of his mother were discussed. With Curtis's help, more healthy ways of dealing with these stressors were identified.

GROUP COUNSELING

For African Americans, groups for children, adolescents, and adults can be of great value because of the cultural orientation to communal work. The members are encouraged to see themselves as part of the larger social community, which can enhance self-esteem and racial identity

(Ford, 1997). Topics involving introspection about the minority experience in their school or community along with healthy ways of dealing with these issues can be raised in a group setting. This is especially useful in groups where all the members are African Americans. Lee (1990) uses a group interaction model to help raise Black male consciousness. In leading such a group the facilitator or co-facilitator must be an African American male. During the sessions, members reflect on the challenges associated with their being Black and male. Masculinity from the African American perspective is discussed, as well as the hazards that Black men face in psychological, social, and health areas. As African American males, the members explore the roles, responsibilities, and relationships they have in their lives. Healthy and beneficial ways of defining their roles are identified. After the group ends, the members should be able to benefit from participating in groups with African American females and also White peers.

Because group goals can be culturally biased (individualistic versus collectivistic and intrapsychic rather than external orientation reflect White middle-class values), changes have to be made when African Americans are involved. McRoy and Oglesby (1984) indicated some modifications in procedures that had to be employed before a group approach that was developed for White couples in evaluating prospective adoptive couples could be used for an African American population. The orientation of the program was primarily a client-centered approach, which was combined with values clarification exercises, transactional analysis, and parent effectiveness training (PET). The African American couples had wanted to adopt children and participated in this program. The group was composed of five African American couples who had an average family income of $30,000 to $45,000. Most had at least some college education. The group was led by a White and a Black social worker. Several problems occurred during the group sessions. First, most of the participants did not agree with the approach of the parent effectiveness training. They had problems with what they interpreted as lengthy parent-child negotiations and also disagreed with the prohibition against the use of physical punishment. Most of the couples had already successfully raised children and felt that PET principles did not reflect "Black values in child rearing." Second, the couples indicated discomfort with role-playing and felt that the activity was "childish."

Because of these problems, modifications were made. The couples who had reared children were asked to present their method of handling problems with children and to discuss alternative ways it could be done. In place of role-playing, the African American social worker gave examples of active listening from his own experiences with his wife and then encouraged feedback and discussion from the participants. The couples were also asked to practice active listening at home and to discuss how it worked.

The African American participants were distrustful of the adoption process and concerned about whether or not they would be evaluated fairly. All of them had experienced racism before and felt that the White social worker would make the decision as to whether a specific couple would make good adoptive parents. The interaction by group members was initially directed only to the Black social worker. The White social worker was accepted after making a humorous self-disclosure and when the roles and expectations were more clearly explained. Cohesiveness in the group was strong. Phone numbers and addresses were exchanged after the first meeting, and all participants indicated the importance of a feeling of belongingness.

This study indicates the importance of discussing with African American participants the purpose of the group and roles of the group leaders. In addition, group goals and processes may have to be modified with Black participants because of differences in cultural values. Because of experiences with racism, African American participants in a group setting may be suspicious, especially when there might be an element of evaluation. Cohesiveness and good inter-personal relationships can quickly develop in the group and serve as a support for the partici-pants.

CONSULTATION

In consultation, as in counseling, we have to be aware of our own values and realize that they provide the lenses through which we view other cultural groups. We may have to alter our par-adigm to make it appropriate for our consultees. In doing so, we need to have an understand-ing of their values and behavior (Brown, 1997; Warner & Morris, 1997). Gibbs (1980) describes some of her experiences in school consultation. She observes that African Americans tend to focus more on interpersonal factors, while White Americans respond more to the instrumen-tal skills demonstrated by the consultant. Her observations are based on a presentation of a proposed school project made to both Black and White teachers at an inner-city school. She found that the same five-stage consultation sequence occurred but that each group focused on separate issues.

1. *Appraisal stage.* During this stage, both African American and White teachers evaluated the consultant. Gibbs observed that African American teachers tended to be aloof and cool. They responded minimally and did not indicate interest through questions about the proj-ect. They wanted to know about the potential harm of the project for the African American children in the school. White teachers were much more attentive and asked questions related to the methods and goals of the project.

2. *Investigation stage.* During this stage, the consultant was checked out. The African Ameri-can consultees focused on the consultant's personal life and her background and values. For example, the African American principal asked Gibbs personal questions and then also re-lated her own experiences with teaching. After this discussion, the African American prin-cipal said she would support Gibbs because she "liked her." Another African American teacher, who was initially critical about the project, became friendlier and supportive after a discussion that revealed areas of commonality with the consultant. White teachers con-tinued to focus on the technical aspects of the project and did not seek personal informa-tion except about the expertise and experiences of the consultant.

3. *Involvement stage.* If a favorable evaluation occurred during stages 1 and 2, the consultees became involved. For African American teachers it revolved around whether or not a per-sonal relationship had been established. Part of their involvement included exchanges of personal information and social interactions during coffee breaks and lunch. White teach-ers maintained a formal professional relationship and were interested in what they would gain from their involvement. One teacher indicated that the approach could be used in work-ing with emotionally disturbed children. Another indicated the belief that the project might help the school achieve goals.

4. *Commitment stage.* During this stage, African American teachers exhibited more interest in the goals of the project and less in the consultant's personality. White consultees also ex-pressed willingness to participate.

5. *Engagement stage.* Final commitment was made by the teachers to support the project. For African American teachers this commitment was based on interpersonal qualities of the consultant; and for White teachers, it was based on the instrumental competence displayed.

Because African American teachers focused on interpersonal relationships, Gibbs feels that it is important for the consultant to be genuine and down to earth, and to establish an equal relationship. The consultant must also be open to interpersonal approaches and questioning by Black consultees. Gibbs's observations are useful in (1) helping understand the ways African American and White individuals differ during the consultation stages, (2) pointing out the differences between instrumental and interpersonal orientations, (3) providing training models for consultants who will work with African Americans, and (4) providing a cross-cultural orientation useful in training both African American and White consultants in working with different cultural groups.

CONCLUSIONS

In working with African American youth and adults in counseling situations, certain suggestions can be made about the elements necessary during the vital first few sessions. Although the order of these elements can be modified or some omitted, these steps may be helpful to the counselor and client:

1. During the first session, it may be beneficial to bring up the reaction of the client to a counselor of a different ethnic background. (Although African Americans show a same-race preference, being culturally competent has been shown to be even more important.) A statement such as "sometimes clients feel uncomfortable working with a counselor of a different race; would this be a problem for you?" or a variant can be used.

2. If the clients are referred, determine their feelings about counseling and how it can be made useful for them. Explain your relationship with the referring agency and the limits of confidentiality.

3. Identify the expectations and worldview of the African American clients, find out what they believe counseling is, and explore their feelings about counseling. Determine how they view the problem and the possible solutions.

4. Establish an egalitarian relationship. In contrast to other ethnic groups, most African Americans tend to establish a personal commonality with the counselor. This may be accomplished by self-disclosure. If the client appears hostile or aloof, discussing some non-counseling topics may be useful.

5. Determine whether and how the client has responded to discrimination and racism both in unhealthy and healthy ways. Also examine issues around racial identity (many clients at the pre-encounter stage will not believe that race is an important factor). For some, the identification with Afrocentricity may be important in establishing a positive self-identity. In these cases, elements of African/African American culture should be incorporated in counseling. This can be achieved through readings, movies, music, and discussions of African American mentors.

6. Assess the positive assets of the counselee, such as family (including relatives and nonrelated friends), community resources, and the church.

7. Determine the external factors that might be related to the presenting problem. This may involve contact with outside agencies for financial and housing assistance. Do not dismiss issues of racism as "just an excuse"; instead, help the client identify alternative means of dealing with the problems.

8. Help the client define goals and appropriate means of attaining them. Assess ways in which the client, family members, and friends handled similar problems successfully.

9. After the therapeutic alliance has been formed, problem-solving approaches and time-limited approaches seem to be the most useful.

The first sessions are crucial in determining whether or not the client will return. The steps above help by explaining what counseling is and by enlisting the assistance of the client. Because of prior experiences, issues of trust may become very important. The counselor can deal with these issues by discussing them directly and by being open, authentic, and empathetic. The African American client will often make a decision by making an interpersonal evaluation of the counselor. The role of the counselor may have to be much broader for the African American client than for the White client. He or she may have to be more directive, serve in an educative function, and/or help the client deal with agencies or with issues involving employment and health. Although these steps may be helpful in working with most African American clients, it must also be remembered that large within-group differences exist in the African American population. As A.C. Jones (1985) points out:

Knowing that a client is black fails to inform adequately about his views of psychotherapy, about his personality and psychological conflict, and about his aspirations and goals in therapy, let alone about educational level, social background, or environmental context. There is enormous within-group variability. The question is not how to treat the black client, but how to treat this black client. (p. 175)

Chapter 12

♦

Counseling Asian Americans

♦

$\mathbf{E}$ric Liu, the son of immigrants from Taiwan, graduated from Yale and has written speeches for President Clinton and doesn't feel like an "Asian American." He believes the identity is contrived and unnecessary. (Chang, 1998)

$\mathbf{D}$avid Mura (1996) was relieved when he had a daughter. He felt that he would be able to help her deal with female Asian stereotypes. A son would be exposed to a culture that would attempt to emasculate him. He later did have two sons and resolved to help them face the issue of Asian American identity and masculinity. (Mura, 1996)

$\mathbf{A}$t a gathering at the White House, Asian Americans with approved clearances were initially prevented from entering even though their names were on a list that showed that they were U.S. citizens. They "looked foreign." (Sun, 1997)

The Asian American population is growing rapidly and has been projected to reach 12.1 million, or 4% of the U.S. population by the year 2000 (U.S. Bureau of the Census, 1995) and 20 million by the year 2020 (Ong & Hee, 1993). The large increase is due to the changes in immigration laws that occurred in 1965 and the entry of over 1.5 million Southeast Asian refugees since 1975 (Chung, Bemak, & Okazaki, 1997). With the relaxation of immigration laws, the population of Asian Americans increased fivefold from 1973 to 1993. The immigration pattern has changed the characteristics of the Asian American population. Because of this, the majority of Asian Americans are foreign born (2/3 of Filipinos and Chinese and 3/4 of Asian Indians, Koreans, and Southeast Asians; U.S. Commerce Department, 1993). In fact, with the exception of Japanese Americans, Asian American populations are now principally composed of foreign-born individuals.

Between-group differences within the Asian American population may be quite great, since the population is composed of at least 40 distinct subgroups that differ in language, religion, and values (Sandhu, 1997). They include the larger Asian groups in the United States (Chinese, Filipinos, Koreans, Asian Indians, and Japanese), refugees and immigrants from Southeast Asia (Vietnamese, Laotians, Cambodians, and Hmongs), and Pacific Islanders (Hawaiians, Guamanians, and Samoans). Compounding the difficulty in making any generalization about the Asian American population are within-group differences. Individuals diverge on variables such as migration or relocation experiences, degree of assimilation or acculturation, identification with the home country, facility in their native language and in English, family composition and intactness, amount of education, and degree of adherence to religious beliefs.

ASIAN AMERICANS: A SUCCESS STORY?

In contrast to many Third World groups, the contemporary image of Asian Americans is that of a highly successful minority who have "made it" in society. For example, the belief that Asian Americans represent a "model" minority has been played up by the popular press in such headlines as "Asian! To America with Skills" (Doerner, 1985) and "The Oriental Express" (McLeod, 1986). Indeed, a close analysis of census figures (U.S. Bureau of the Census, 1995) seems to support this contention. In 1994, of those individuals over 25, 40% of Asians/Pacific Islanders had at least a bachelor's degree, a proportion one and one half times higher than that of their white counterparts. Approximately 10% of all students at Harvard, 22% of those at Berkeley, and 19% of those at MIT are Asian Americans (Sandhu, 1997). Terms such as "intelligent," "hardworking," "enterprising," and "disciplined" are frequently applied to this population (Morrissey, 1997).

Even more striking evidence of success is the apparent reduction of social distance between Asians and Whites. Bogardus (1925) developed a social distance scale that is presumably a measure of prejudice and/or discrimination against minority groups. If members of a minority group are allowed to marry and form intimate relationships with the dominant group, then a reduction in social distance is said to have occurred. The incidence of interracial marriages for Asian Americans in 1989 for Los Angeles County has approached 50%, with the rate about twice as high among Asian females as males (33% males and 66% females; Kitano & Maki, 1996).

Besides these educational and social indicators of success, other mental health statistics reinforce the belief that Asians in America are relatively well adjusted, function effectively in society, and experience few difficulties. Studies consistently reveal that Asian Americans have low official rates of juvenile delinquency (Abbott & Abbott, 1968; Kitano, 1969), low rates of psychiatric contact and hospitalization (Kimmich, 1960; Kitano, 1969a; D.W. Sue & Kirk, 1975; S. Sue & McKinney, 1975; Yamamoto, James, & Palley, 1969), and low rates of divorce (S. Sue & Kitano, 1973). Indeed, there seems to be a prevalent belief that Asian Americans are somehow immune to the forces of prejudice and discrimination. These beliefs seem ironic in light of the massive discrimination that has historically been directed at Asians. Denied the rights of citizenship, denied ownership of land, assaulted, murdered, and placed in concentration camps during World War II, Asians in America have at one time or another been subjected to the most appalling forms of discrimination ever perpetrated against any immigrant group (Ina, 1997; Kitano, 1969b; D.W. Sue , 1994).

A closer analysis of the status of Asian Americans reveals disturbing truths that contrast with popular views of their success story. First, economically, reference to the higher median income of Asian Americans do not take into account (a) the higher percentage of Asian American families having more than one wage earner, (b) a higher prevalence of poverty despite the higher median income (14% versus 8% for the U.S. population), and (c) the discrepancy between education and income. The poverty rate of certain Southeast Asian groups is in fact five times higher than that of the general population (Sandhu, 1997), and education-income disparity exists in that while Asian wage earners may have higher levels of education, their wages are not commensurate with their training (Atkinson, Morten, & Sue, 1989; U.S. Bureau of the Census, 1995). Due to a lack of job skills or English proficiency, Southeast Asians are three times more likely to be on welfare than the general population (Sandhu, 1997).

Second, in the area of education, Asian Americans show a disparate picture of extraordinary high educational attainment and a large undereducated mass. Among the Hmong, only 31% have completed high school, and less than 6% of Tongans, Cambodians, Laotians, and Hmongs 25 years and older have a bachelor's degree (U.S. Bureau of the Census, 1995). This bimodal distribution when averaged out indicates how misleading statistics can be.

Third, there is now widespread recognition that, apart from being tourist attractions, Chinatowns, Manilatowns, and Japantowns in San Francisco and New York represent ghetto areas with prevalent unemployment, poverty, health problems, and juvenile delinquency. People outside these communities seldom see the deplorable social conditions that exist behind the bright neon lights, restaurants, and quaint shops. Over 1/3 of the residents complain of depression and emotional tension (S. Sue, D.W. Sue, L. Sue, & Takeuchi, 1995). Mass murders committed over the years have been traced to Chinese juvenile gangs operating in Chinatowns, and recent news reports show this trend to be on the increase.

Fourth, whether underutilization of mental health facilities is due to low rates of socioemotional adjustment difficulties, discriminatory mental health practices, and/or cultural values inhibiting self-referral is not known. It is possible that much of the mental illness, the adjustment problems, and the juvenile delinquency among Asians is hidden. The discrepancy between official and real rates may be due to such cultural factors as the shame and disgrace associated with admitting to emotional problems, the handling of problems within the family rather than relying on outside resources, and the manner of symptom formation, such as a low prevalence of acting-out disorders. Many Southeast Asian refugees show psychiatric symptoms associated with past traumas and current resettlement problems. Very high levels of PTSD and major depression have been in this population (S. Sue, D.W. Sue, L. Sue, & Takeuchi, 1996).

The myths and stereotypes about Asians in America, such as the popular belief that they represent a model minority and that they experience no difficulties in society, must be dispelled. Asian Americans view these stereotypes as having functional value for those who hold power in society. First, these stereotypes reassert the erroneous belief that any minority can succeed in a democratic society if the minority group members work hard enough. Second, the Asian American success story is seen as a divisive concept used by the Establishment to pit one minority group against another by holding one group up as an example to others. Third, the success myth has shortchanged many Asian American communities from receiving the necessary moral and financial commitment due them as a struggling minority with unique concerns. It is especially important for counselors, pupil personnel workers, and educators who work with Asian Americans to look behind the success myth and to understand the Asian experience in America. The matter is even more pressing for counselors when we realize that Asian Americans are more likely to seek help at a counseling service rather than at a psychiatric service.

The approach of this chapter is twofold. First, it attempts to investigate how certain forces have served to shape and define the lifestyle of recent immigrants/refugees and United States–born Asian Americans. Second, this chapter explores how an understanding of the Asian American experience suggests the need for major modifications in counseling and psychotherapeutic practices to fit the needs of Asians in America.

FORCES SHAPING THE IDENTITY OF ASIAN AMERICANS

It is widely accepted that sociopolitical forces have a strong impact on the behavioral expression of different racial or ethnic groups. Although most social scientists pay lip service to the idea that psychological development is not an isolated phenomenon apart from sociocultural forces, most theories of human behavior tend to be culturally exclusive. Therefore, in order to understand the Asian American experience, it is necessary to discuss the wider social milieu in which behavior and identity originate.

HISTORICAL EXPERIENCE IN AMERICA

Many in the American public are unaware that Asians in America have suffered from some of the most inhumane treatment ever accorded any immigrant group. Beginning in the 1840s, the Chinese were the first Asian group to arrive in large numbers. Because of the high demand for cheap labor (the discovery of gold in the Sacramento Valley and building of the transcontinental railroad) and the political unrest and overpopulation in certain provinces of China, a large steady stream of Chinese male peasants began to immigrate to the United States (Daniels, 1971; DeVos & Abbott, 1966). In the 1860s nearly all the Chinese lived and settled on the West Coast, with the heaviest concentrations in California. Because their presence in the labor force served to fill a void in the labor market, these early Chinese peasants were not particularly mistreated.

However, a series of business recessions, coupled with the completion of the Union-Central Pacific Railroad in 1869, made competition for jobs fierce. Because the Chinese constituted a large fraction of the California population and labor force, white workingmen saw them as an economic threat. The Chinese were especially vulnerable as scapegoats because of their "strange" customs and appearance; that is, they wore their hair in queues (pigtails), spoke in a "strange tongue," and ate "unhealthy" food. As a result, labor began to agitate against the Chinese with rallying cries such as "the Chinese must go." Although it was originally based on economics, Daniels (1971) feels that "the movement soon developed an ideology of white supremacy/Oriental inferiority that was wholly compatible with the mainstream of American racism" (p. 3).

The systematic harassment of the Chinese resulted in legal discrimination that denied them the rights of citizenship; Chinese testimony in court was ruled inadmissible as evidence. Indeed, the Chinese were seen as "heathens" and "subhuman aliens" who were detrimental to the well-being of America. Exclusionist legislation was passed at all levels of government and culminated in the passing of an immigration law, the Chinese Exclusion Act of 1882, which was not repealed until 1943. Kagiwada and Fujimoto (1973) point out that the phrase "not a Chinaman's chance" alludes to these conditions. They point out further that these actions did not seem to satisfy the prejudiced elements of society. Individual and mob violence such as mass murder, physical attacks, and destruction of homes and property were common occurrences. Large-scale massacres of the Chinese in Los Angeles in 1851 and Rock Springs, Wyoming, in 1885 are examples of such abuse (Daniels, 1971; Kitano, 1969b).

The next Asian group to immigrate in large numbers to the United States was the Japanese. By the time the Japanese came in larger numbers to the United States, beginning in the 1890s, the "Chinese problem" had been largely solved. Most of the early Japanese immigrants found employment in railroads, canneries, mining, and so on. Since many of the Japanese had previously come from a farming class, their gravitation toward farming and gardening could be predicted (Kitano, 1969b). The Japanese immigrants' knowledge of agriculture and their perseverance made them highly successful in these fields, where they subsequently became economic competitors. The now-familiar pattern of violence and harassment previously directed at the Chinese was now channeled toward the Japanese. This pervasive anti-Oriental feeling became labeled as "the Yellow Peril."

Because Japan was a rising international power, the anti-Japanese feeling did not manifest itself in direct governmental legislation to restrict immigration, but led to a "gentlemen's agreement" to stop the flow of Asians to the United States. To further harass the Japanese, California passed the Alien Land Law in 1913 that forbade aliens to own land. The discrimination and prejudice toward the Japanese was evident in the incarceration of 110,000 Japanese American citizens in concentration camps during World War II. The effects of this action perpetrated against the Japanese are still very much evident today in the suspiciousness that many Asians have for the American mainstream. Indeed, nothing in the Constitution forbids such an action from being taken again.

Likewise, the historical treatment of Filipinos and Koreans was no better than that given their Chinese and Japanese counterparts. The Chinese Exclusion Act of 1882 and the gentlemen's agreement eventually created another imbalance in the labor situation (Rabaya, 1971; Shin, 1971). The Hawaiian super-plantation owners (mainly White) and the mainland businesses were forced to find another cheap source of labor. The two potential reservoirs of labor were Puerto Rico and the Philippines. The Filipino immigrants who came to the United States also encountered much prejudice and discrimination. Labor unions led by the American Federation of Labor condemned the Filipinos as "cheap labor" that lowered the standard of living for White workers.

More recently, some 1.5 million refugees from Southeast Asia have arrived in the United States since 1975. The majority are Vietnamese, Cambodian or Khmer, and Laotian (Chung, Bemak, & Okazaki, 1997). In general, refugees are under more stress than immigrants. As Bemak, Chung, and Bornemann (1996) point out, immigrants are individuals who have had time to prepare to move to the United States. However, refugees are often not in control of their own fate. For example, the vast majority of Vietnamese, who left just before the fall of Saigon in 1975, had only a few days to decide whether or not to leave their country. Refugees often had to wait in camps for years before immigrating to countries such as the United States, Australia, and France. Many Cambodians have experienced death in their immediate family from starvation or conflict with the Vietcong since they had worked with the Central Intelligence Agency (Cheung, 1987). Over 92% of the Hmong have stress-related illnesses. In fact, 75% are unemployed and 86% indicate they would return to Laos if possible (Smalley, 1984).

Significant immigration increases in the Asian American population have led to a swell in current anti-Asian sentiment. The killing of Vincent Chin in 1982, the murder of Jim Loo in 1989, the Stockton, California, massacre of five Cambodian and Vietnamese children at Cleveland Elementary School (1989) by a White male who "hated and blamed" Asians for the loss of American jobs (see Chapter 1), increases in racial slurs, and the portrayal of Asians as sub-human "gooks" in such award-winning movies as *Platoon* and *Full Metal Jacket* attest to the tenor of current times. In 1995, the number of hate crimes against Asian Americans rose, with assaults increasing by 11% and aggravated assaults by 14% (Matthee, 1997). In addition, Asian Americans continue to be seen as foreigners. During the 1998 Olympics in Nagano, MSNBC reported the gold medal outcome in skating between U.S. competitors Michele Kwan and Tara Lipinski as "American beats Kwan."

Unfortunately, space limitations do not allow us to focus on the diversity of Asian groups in the United States. We will first concentrate on recent immigrants/refugees and then on the large group of Asian Americans (Chinese, Filipinos, Japanese, Koreans, etc.) who have lived here for some time (many were born and raised in the United States) and have experienced long-term effects of cultural racism. While recent immigrants and refugees have had experiences similar to those who came here in the past, and while Asian immigrants share many similar cultural values with those born and raised here, there appears to be a qualitative difference in their experience of cultural racism in the United States. Let us turn our attention to the special problems faced by immigrants/refugees and then to the United States–born Asian Americans.

SPECIAL PROBLEMS OF RECENT IMMIGRANTS AND REFUGEES

Mrs. N. is a 48-year-old Vietnamese woman who sought help at a mental health clinic for depression and frequent nightmares of atrocities and the death of her husband. She and her two daughters fled Vietnam in 1982. During the escape, one of her daughters died. She spent 2½ years in a refugee camp in Thailand before locating in the United States.

Although Mrs. N.'s daughter is now a teenager and appears to have adjusted well, Mrs. N. continues to suffer from suicidal thoughts and disturbed memories involving her husband and dead daughter. She has a few Vietnamese women friends and works as a janitor. Her "only reason for living" appears to be to take care of her remaining daughter. (Chung, Bemak, & Okazaki, 1997)

Cheung (1987) indicates that three waves of Southeast Asian refugees, each with their own set of problems, came to the United States. The first wave came from Vietnam in 1975 with the fall of Saigon. Many of them had worked for the U.S. government and were acquainted with Western culture. Many fled at a moment's notice and left family members and their possessions behind. Depression is very high among Vietnamese refugees because of the method of departure from Vietnam and life in refugee camps (ACMH, 1987; Atkinson, Ponterotto, & Sanchez, 1984). Over 40% of Vietnamese patients seen at the Oregon Health Sciences University Clinic have a major affective disorder.

The second wave occurred from 1979 to 1982 and included not only Vietnamese, but also Cambodians, Laotians, and Hmongs. Hundreds had escaped by cramming themselves into small boats. Many drowned, starved to death, or were killed by Thai pirates. The second wave was different from the first and was more likely to include those who were less educated, possessed fewer job skills, were more rural, had had little contact with Western culture, and were less likely to be proficient in English and more likely to have spent relatively long periods of time in relocation camps.

In a study of 40,000 Southeast Asian refugees in San Diego County, Rumbaut (1985) found that nearly 80% of one group of Khmer were uncertain of the fate of family members left behind in their home country and had been unable to contact them. This compares to 29.5% of the Hmong, 20.7% of the Chinese, and 4.6% of the Vietnamese. During and after the exodus, 40% of the refugees reported one or two deaths, and 9% had from three to six deaths in their immediate family—usually due to violent circumstances. The Khmer and Hmong reported the greatest number of losses among close family members. Rumbaut (1985) found that among the Hmong, 75% had incomes below the poverty level in 1982.

A study by Nguyen and Henkin (1983) of 285 heads of households among refugees found that 80% complained of homesickness, 72% indicated being worried about the future, 55% felt lonely, and 40% indicated feeling sad most of the time. Many of the problems facing the refugees appear to be related to personal losses and culture conflict. In a sample of 118 Southeast Asian refugee clients, major concerns involved: (a) being separated from or deaths of members of the family, (b) marital and family problems, (c) worries about the future, (d) problems with English, and (e) job dissatisfaction. Among this sample, 25% had made suicide attempts, and behavioral problems in the schools among their children had increased. Vietnamese refugees report that their children display less politeness and obedience, that respect for elders is fading, and that the changing role of women is producing problems (Nguyen & Henkin, 1983). The third wave of refugees occurred after the Vietnamese initiated the Orderly Departure Program in 1982. These refugees are composed mainly of the elderly and Amerasian and unaccompanied minors. Most are illiterate.

The greatest increase in the Asian/Pacific Island population was due to the relaxation of immigration laws. During the 20-year period from 1973 to 1993, there was more than a fivefold increase in population. The initial group of immigrants during this period consisted largely of highly educated and skilled professionals. Holders of professional degrees constituted a significant proportion of immigrants from China (46%), India (90%), Korea (75%), and the Philipines (67%). The next group of immigrants, however, were much less educated and were more likely to be unskilled. They entered under the category of "close family members and other relatives" (Sandhu, 1997). Although immigrants confront many of the same problems faced by refugees, most of them have not experienced traumatic wartime events.

♦ Case Study

Mr. G. is a 40-year-old Korean American who came to the United States about 5 years ago. Although he was employed as a high school teacher in Korea, his lack of English proficiency limited his job opportunities. He bought and operates a Laundromat working about 60 hours a week. He has children in the third and fifth grades. Mr. G. is resentful of the changes in his family. His wife has had to get a job and works in a sandwich shop. He feels his children are separating from him. They speak in English, a language that he barely understands. He feels that his wife sides with the children when differences arise in the family. He has started to drink heavily and was recently visited by social service representatives, after his children reluctantly described his disciplinary methods to the school counselor. (Toarmino & Chun, 1997)

In Mr. G.'s case, the following issues should be addressed in the counseling session: (a) the loss of his traditional role as head of the family (his wife works and is no longer totally dependent upon him, and he can no longer communicate well with his children); (b) feelings of shame and betrayal that his children relayed information of a personal nature to someone outside the family; (c) the downward shift in his occupation from teacher to laundry operator; (d) the wife's differences in expectations about the move to the United States; (e) her being caught between her husband's frustration and his manner of dealing with his children; (f) the children's exposure to different values. Although many of the recent immigrants are professional and well educated, adjustment problems produced by differences in cultural values, the inability to utilize their skills, more rapid acculturation of children, and changes in the roles of family members are common difficulties.

VALUE CONFLICTS AND COUNSELING

Although the Asian immigrants and refugees form very diverse groups, there are certain areas of commonality, such as deference to authority, emotional restraint, specified roles, and hierarchical family structure, gender-specific roles, and extended family orientation (Chang, 1997; Kinzie, 1985; Sandhu, 1997; Tsui & Schultz, 1985). The areas in which the traditionally oriented Asian American client and the American-trained counselor may differ are shown in Table 12.1.

Although cultural knowledge is important in helping the counselor identify potential conflict areas, one must be careful not to apply cultural information in a stereotypic manner. Cultural difficulties, such as the degree of assimilation, socioeconomic background, family experiences, and educational level, impact each individual in a unique manner. Knowledge of cultural values can help generate hypotheses about the way an Asian might view a disorder and his or her expectations of treatment, but it must not be applied in a rigid fashion.

Mental health and psychotherapy are foreign concepts to the Asian countries. Because of the unfamiliarity with mental health concepts, many refugees and immigrants have limited faith in talking about problems. In contrast to Caucasian students, Vietnamese students in the United States were less likely to recognize the need for mental health services, more concerned about the stigma attached to counseling, less open about personal problems, and less confident that mental health professionals would be of any help (Atkinson, Ponterotto, & Sanchez, 1984). In many Southeast Asian countries, having a psychological problem is the same as being insane, an overt admission of inferiority (Nguyen, 1985), or a genetic defect (Cheung, 1989). Because of these differences in values and orientation, a therapeutic alliance may not be formed. Nisio and Bilmer (1987) present several cases in which the traditional approach was not successful.

In the first case, a Vietnamese family was referred to a Western therapist after their daughter had displayed bizarre behaviors. As part of the assessment, the counselor began to explore the possibility that the daughter's behavior might be affected by the dynamics between the husband and wife. Questions were asked about their marital relationship. The couple did not return for the next session. They indicated a willingness to continue therapy as long as marital problems were not discussed. The parents felt that their relationship was a private matter and not related to their daughter's problem.

Table 12.1   AREAS OF DIFFERENCE BETWEEN ASIAN AMERICAN CLIENTS AND WESTERN-TRAINED COUNSELORS

Asian American Clients	*Western-Trained Counselors*
• Collectivism—Family and group focus, Interdependence	• Individual Focus, Independence
• Hierarchical Relationships	• Equality of Relationships
• Restraint of Emotions = Maturity	• Emotional Expression = Healthy
• Counselors should provide solutions	• Clients develop solutions through introspection
• Mental illness is shameful and represents family failure	• Mental illness is the same as any other problem

Note. Adapted from Chang & Myers, 1997; Kinzie, 1985; Leong, Wagner, & Kim, 1995; Sandu, 1997.

In another case, the patients were a Laotian couple whose husband was alcoholic and physically abusive to his wife. The Western therapist encouraged the wife to become more independent and to consider leaving her husband. The couple did not return and instead sought the help of an Asian therapist. The therapist understood that an unhealthy situation existed, but was also aware of cultural norms and expectations. Greater independence for the wife in certain areas was reframed as an opportunity for the husband to have more time for himself. The husband's initial objections were eliminated when the changes were presented in this manner. It was also determined that the problems of abuse and alcohol intake were related to the stresses he felt in the new culture and the loss of his status. As these frustrations were addressed and dealt with, the husband stopped abusing his wife and terminated his drinking.

Physical complaints are a common and culturally accepted means of expressing psychological and emotional stress. It is believed that physical problems cause emotional disturbances, and that these will disappear as soon as there is appropriate treatment of the physical illness. Instead of talking about anxiety and depression, the mental health professional will often hear complaints involving headaches, fatigue, restlessness, and disturbances in sleep and appetite (D. Sue, 1997; Toarmino & Chun, 1997). Even psychotic patients typically made somatic complaints and sought treatment for those physical ailments (Nguyen, 1985). In the following case study, Tsui and Schultz (1985) indicate how the differences in perspective can produce problems for both the patient and the mental health worker.

◆ *Case Study*

A female client complained about all kinds of physical problems such as feeling dizzy, having a loss of appetite, an inability to complete household chores, and insomnia. She asked the therapist if her problem could be due to "nerves." The therapist suspected depression since these are some of the physical manifestations of the disorder and asked the client if she felt depressed and sad. At this point, the client paused and looked confused. She finally stated that she feels very ill and that these physical problems are making her sad. Her perspective is that it was natural for her to feel sad when sick. As the therapist followed up by attempting to determine if there was a family history of depression, the client displayed even more discomfort and defensiveness. Although the client never directly contradicted the therapist, she did not return for the following session.

In working with clients who have somatic complaints, it would be helpful to acknowledge them and recommend physical treatments before dealing with possible emotional factors.

TREATMENT STRATEGIES

Treatment strategies for immigrants and refugees have many elements of similarity. It is important to prepare the clients for counseling by engaging in role preparation. Lambert and Lambert (1984) found that Asian immigrants who were told about (a) what happens in therapy, (b) the need for verbal disclosure, (c) problems typically encountered by clients in therapy, (d) the role of the therapist and client, (e) misconceptions about therapy, and (f) the need for attendance adjusted better to counseling than a control group who did not receive role preparation. The clients who were prepared developed more accurate perceptions of therapy, saw their therapist as more interested and respectful, perceived more positive changes on their part, and were more satisfied with their adjustment. The necessity to give immigrants an overview of the counseling process was also stressed by Chung, Bemak, and Okazaki (1997). Although role preparation and a discussion of counseling expectations is important, modifications to adjust for cultural differences should be made. The following suggestions are from Chung, Bemak, and Okazaki (1997); Ishisaka, Nguyen and Okimoto (1985), Lorenzo and Adler (1984), Nidorf (1985), and Tung (1985).

1. Use restraint when gathering information. Because of the stigma against mental illness, the norm against sharing private matters with outsiders, and the lack of client knowledge of the mental health field, the therapist should refrain from asking too many personal questions during the initial session.

2. Do a thorough analysis of current environmental concerns, such as the need for food and shelter. The clients may need information on services that are available to them and help in filling out forms and interacting with agencies. Assess financial and social needs.

3. Assess the worldview of the client, the way they view the problem; determine appropriate solutions and positive assets within the individual, family, and community. Work within the framework of the client.

4. Focus on the specific problem brought in by the client, and help the client develop his or her goals for therapy. This allows the concerns of the client to be presented and reduces the chance that the worldview of the therapist will be imposed on the client.

5. Take an active and directive role. Because of cultural expectations and a lack of experience with mental health therapy, the clients will rely on the counselor to furnish direction.

6. In working with families, consider intergenerational conflicts, particularly with respect to changes in role, culture conflict, and differences in acculturation levels. Be willing to accept

the hierarchical structure of the family and initially focus on cultural conflict as the "identified client."

7. The therapy should be time limited, focus on concrete resolution of problems, and deal with the present or immediate future.

8. In the case of refugees, it is important to do a careful history and gather information on their family life in their home country, their escape or immigration and how this was experienced, reasons for leaving, losses and expectations, their life in camps, the method of sponsorship, and their expectations in the United States. Also important would be difficulties refugees have had in adjusting to the new culture, their methods of coping, and marital and family problems that have developed. Taking a good history is important to help the counselor understand some of the issues involved in working with Southeast Asian refugees.

Many of the refugees suffered great personal losses involving property, business, identity, and family members. A great many have strong feelings of regret, especially in cases in which family members were left behind. Lin, Masuda, and Tazuma (1982) report the case of a 56-year-old Vietnamese woman who was living with her husband, two sons, and daughter. She had been suffering from a large number of physical symptoms and was in a depressed mood for two years. On a wall in her house was a picture of a daughter who had died during the evacuation. The mother was especially upset that her daughter's body had to be thrown into the sea and did not receive a proper burial. It was clear that the family was still in active mourning.

Nidorf (1985) feels that adolescents are at special risk of suffering problems. Young women may have been attacked sexually during the escape process and may present suicidal symptoms or have become sexually promiscuous. Young males may also display a variety of affective responses that may have been related to their helpless observation of the victimization of family members. Careful analysis of the past history of immigrants and refugees may be very helpful in developing a treatment plan for the Asian clients.

FAMILY CHARACTERISTICS

When she does something wrong, I think, something like misbehavior, something not good, I will sit down first, think about how to solve this problem. If I have difficulty, I will consult an expert on how to solve this problem. . . . (Kass, 1998, p. 3)

Hou-Lin Li and his wife, Luying Deng, had completed a parent education course after being accused of using a slap to discipline their 8-year-old daughter for lying and forging their signature on a disciplinary note from a teacher. For this, the state prosecutor, Richard Devine, charged the parents with child abuse and threatened them with deportation back to China (the Cook County public guardian, Patrick Murphy, had asked the prosecutor to drop the case). We don't know if the charge of child abuse was appropriate in this case, but it is important to realize that ethnic variations in child-rearing practices exist. As Gray and Cosgrove (1985) point out:

The protective services system in the United States may be committing a form of institutional abuse of minority families if the professionals who work in that system are not sufficiently well versed in the unique childrearing practices of each culture in the communities the system represents. It is easy for misunderstandings to occur from an ethnocentric perspective, and these misunderstandings are unlikely to be in the minority group's favor. (p. 389)

Traditional Asian American families tend to be hierarchical in structure, with males and older individuals occupying a higher status. The sons are expected to carry on the family name and tradition. Even when they are married, their primary allegiance is to the parents. Although acculturation has weakened this value, second-generation Chinese American high school students place a higher priority on filial piety and obedience to their parents and authorities than their Caucasian counterparts (Feldman & Rosenthal, 1990). Third-generation Japanese Americans still feel the pressure of parental obligations (Ina, 1997). Daughters are expected to be passive and occupy a less important role in the family, since they are expected to adhere to the expectations of their husbands' families. More acculturated Asian American females often have problems with their parents over the issue of the equality of the sexes (Hildebrand et al., 1996).

In many Asian families, there is generally less open display of emotions to older children. Care and concern is shown by supplying the physical needs of family members. The father maintains an authoritative and distant role and is less emotionally demonstrative and involved with his children. His role is to provide for the economic and physical needs of the family. Shame and guilt are used to control and train the children. Mothers are more responsive to the children but use less nurturance and more verbal and physical punishments than Caucasian mothers (Kelly & Tseng, 1992). However, they are expected to meet the emotional needs of the children and often serve as the intermediary between the father and the children. When the children are exposed to different parenting styles, they begin to question their parents. Chang-Rae Lee (1995), in a novel, describes his father as *"unencumbered by the needling questions of existence and self-consciousness. . . . I wasn't sure he had the capacity to love"* (p. 58). Relationships between an Asian husband and wife may be different from those of White couples. In one study, care and concern between an Asian couple was shown more by taking care of the physical needs of the partner than by expressing it verbally. Western marital therapy, which emphasizes verbal expressiveness as the main goal, may not be adequate in dealing with some Asian couples (Juang & Tucker, 1991).

Problems in Asian American families can involve the following issues (Chandras, 1997; Lee, 1988):

1. Conflicts over values as children acculturate more rapidly than their parents. The parents may have lower English proficiency and feel at loss in terms of how to deal with their children. They have lost their status, and now even being an adequate parent is questioned (Salvador, Omizo, & Kim, 1997). Some respond by becoming more rigid. One Asian Indian daughter described her parents as displaying a "museumization of practices." On a trip to India, she discovered that there was a wide difference between the parents' version of "Indian" and what Indians in India actually did. Her parents' version was much more restrictive (Das Gupta, 1997). However, many parents do become more democratic and less dominant with their children with increased exposure to mainstream values (Chandras, 1997).

2. Conflicts over dating and marriage. Traditionally oriented Asian parents still demand to have an active part in the selection of dating and marriage partners. The increase in interracial marriage and dating is especially distressing to them, since it is perceived as a failure on the part of the parent and is often interpreted as an end to the lineage.

3. Academic expectations. There is a great deal of emphasis placed on academic achievement. Although Asian American students had the highest levels of academic achievement, they also had the highest fear of academic failure compared to their Caucasian peers. They spend twice as much time each week on academics as their non-Asian counterparts (Eaton & Dembo, 1997).

FAMILY THERAPY

For many traditionally oriented Asian American families, problems arise because the family is unable to negotiate or deal with cultural differences between family members and/or the larger community. Western-trained counselors working with an Asian family should be willing to alter the therapeutic approach or a therapeutic alliance will not be formed.

♦ *Case Study*

A Chinese American family was referred to a counselor because of their son's acting-out behavior at school. The father spoke English but it was clearly his second language. He appeared stern whenever his son spoke and otherwise appeared to be uncomfortable and noncommunicative. The son was quite verbal and complained about the restrictions on his dating and the expectation that he should study "all the time." He complained that his father was "old-fashioned." The mother stated that there was a great deal of tension at home and appeared to try to mediate between her husband and son. Because of the father's attitude, the counselor began to view the father as rigid and asked him about his view of child rearing. The father just stated that his son was "bad." The mother showed increasing discomfort with the personal questions. The family did not return for further sessions. (D. Sue, 1990)

In this case, the counselor did not consider cultural values and their impact on counseling. Traditional Asian families have a hierarchical structure and negotiate differences through mediation. To expect personal problems to be discussed openly before trust has developed is too confrontive. The counselor needs to function as a negotiator and follow the family structure. The father should be addressed first to gain his perceptions of the problem. Direct statements from family members would go through the counselor. In general, it is not helpful to have family members address one another. A statement from the son, such as "you don't care about me," can be reframed into "Your son is wondering what he can do to make you proud of him" (Ho, 1987, p. 52). To focus on positive aspects, a parent can be asked about the positive aspects of a family member. Complaints about the parent's being "old-fashioned" can be interpreted from a traditional value perspective (Jung, 1984, 1998). The problem becomes cast as one involving the struggle of family members to adapt to competing sets of values. As trust is gained in the "negotiator," the role of parents as educators of their children can be broached. The family may be more willing to accept a broader definition of what constitutes appropriate behaviors from the members.

ACCULTURATION CONFLICTS

As Asians become progressively exposed to the standards, norms, and values of the wider society, increasing assimilation and acculturation are frequently the result. Bombarded on all sides by peers, schools, and the mass media upholding Western standards as better than their own, Asian Americans are frequently placed in situations of extreme culture conflict that may lead to much pain and agony. Because of the existence of racism, David Mura (1996) reported being relieved when his baby was a girl rather than a boy. He believed that girls were less constricted by stereotypes than boys and pointed out the lack of positive Asian role models on mass media. Later, he did have two sons and resolved to have them face the issues around Asian American identity. Chang-Rae Lee (1995), a novelist, described his experiences as *"straddling two worlds and at home in neither."* He felt alienated from both American and Korean cultures.

Kitano and Maki (1996) believe that the culture conflict involving assimilation (process of becoming Americanized) and ethnic identity (retention of customs, attitudes, and beliefs of culture of origin) is generally resolved in one of four ways: Type A—high in assimilation, low in ethnic identity; Type B—high in assimilation, high in ethnic identity; Type C—high in ethnic identity, low in assimilation; and Type D—low in ethnicity, low in assimilation.

Type A individuals are fully Westernized in value orientation, dress, and manner. They tend to have egalitarian relationships with their spouses and children. Eric Liu grew up in a predominately White community, has married a White woman, and believes that the Asian American identity is "contrived" and "unnecessary." He has become fully Americanized. Liu belongs to the group of Asians in which ethnic identity is unimportant or not salient. Others may react against their ethnic identity in a different manner. Individuals who are caught up in a culture conflict may often attempt to become over-Westernized by rejecting traditional Asian values. Their pride and self-worth are defined by the ability to acculturate into White society. In their attempts to assimilate and acculturate into White society, they are often forced to reject the Asian side of themselves and thus feel ashamed of anything that reminds them of being an Asian. They come to view their ethnicity as a handicap that may lead to various forms of racial self-hatred. Lee (1994) describes the "New Wavers," primarily Southeast Asian refugees, who rebelled against Asian values in order to be accepted by the White students and culture. They rejected family obligations and instead were peer oriented. Instead of focusing on academics, they would cut classes in order to be "more American . . . more cool" (p. 423), to party and to have fun, anything that would help them escape from Asian stereotypes.

Counselors working with individuals with high assimilation and low ethnic identity can generally use the same techniques and approaches they employ for mainstream value clients. Some, such as those who have completely rejected their ethnic identity, may show a preference for a White counselor. However, ethnic issues may still be a problem for these individuals. Some values and behaviors such as filial piety, emotional restraint, and self-consciousness disappear more slowly and may still be necessary issues to assess. Even in mixed marriage situations, problems can occur because of remnants of traditional Asian values that remain. Completely rejecting one's ethnic identity (as opposed to having it as a low salience factor) may be unhealthy and may indicate an excessive need to be accepted by members of the majority culture. Clients should be helped to sort out their identity conflict and to consider the impact of cultural racism and its effect on minority group members. The client must be helped to distinguish between attempts to acculturate and a wholesale rejection of his or her own cultural values, and perhaps try to find the healthiest resolution.

Type B individuals are both high on assimilation and high in cultural identity. They are bicultural and feel comfortable with members of either cultural group. These individuals may respond well to traditional counseling. Roughly fitting into this category are what Sue and Sue (1990) describe as "Asian Americans."

I have experiences that are similar to other Asians that live in America: that my culture is not all Asian and it's not all American. It's entirely different. And it's not like some people say, that it's a mixture. It's like a whole different thing. When I say I'm Asian American, I feel like I establish a root for myself here. Many parents think of themselves as Vietnamese because their roots are in Vietnam. Being Asian American is like a way to feel I belong. (Lee, 1994, p. 427)

The "Asian American" is aware of the political, social, and economic forces that have shaped his or her identity. Because of this, he/she is more sensitive to the effects of racism and often reacts to injustice with anger and militancy. The emphasis on the inequities of society and the feeling that change must be instituted in racist institutions make many Asian Americans suspicious of counseling services. Many feel that counseling services are agents of the Establishment and that their primary goal is to adjust clients to society. This can cause difficulties for both the client, whose political beliefs may mask his/her problems, and for the counselor, who must deal appropriately with certain challenges before counseling can proceed effectively. In the former, growing pride in self-identity frequently makes it difficult for many Asian students to accept their difficulties as personal rather than external. The client should be led to realize that although many problems of minorities are rooted in the shortcomings of society, there is no inherent contradiction in viewing society as racist and having personal problems. On the other hand, the counselor must be sensitive enough to know that many problems encountered by his or her clients are caused by society and that he or she must act accordingly. Militancy and emphasis on group pride are not signs of maladjustment, as many individuals would have us believe. It is imperative, however, that counselors be able to distinguish between the two types of confusion.

Type C individuals are low on assimilation and high on ethnic identity. They are more likely to include recent immigrants, those living in ethnic communities, or even many second-, third-, and fourth-generation Asian Americans. Individuals in this group adhere closely to the norms, standards, and values of the traditional Asian family. Among Asian college students, this was shown by placing a high value on doing well in school. They worked hard to achieve good grades and felt obligated to their families because of their sacrifices. They also talked about wanting to get good jobs so that they could support their parents (Lee, 1994).

♦ *Case Study*

John C. is a 20-year-old junior student majoring in electrical engineering. He is the oldest of five children born and raised in San Francisco. The parents have always had high expectations for their eldest son and constantly transmitted these feelings to him. Ever since he can remember, John's parents had decided that he would go to college and become an engineer—a job they held in high esteem. Throughout his early school years, John was an outstanding student and was constantly praised by his teachers. However, his parents seemed to take John's school successes for granted. In fact, they would always make statements such as, "You can do better still."

John first came to the counseling center during the latter part of his junior year because of severe headaches and a vague assortment of bodily complaints. A medical checkup failed to reveal any organic malfunctioning, which led the psychologist to suspect a psychophysiological reaction. John exhibited a great deal of anxiety throughout the interviews. He seemed suspicious of the psychologist and found it difficult to talk about himself in a personal way. As the sessions progressed, it became evident that John felt a great deal of shame about having come to a therapist. John was concerned that his family not be told since they would be disgraced.

Throughout the interviews, John appeared excessively concerned with failing to meet his parents' expectations. The parents frequently made statements such as, "Once you are out of school and making good money, it would be nice if you could help your brothers and sisters through college." John's resentment of these imposed responsibilities was originally denied and repressed. When he was able to clearly see his anger and hostility toward his parents, much of his physical complaints vanished. However, with the recognition of his true feelings, he became extremely depressed and guilty. John could not see why he should be angry at his parents after all they had done for him.

The counselor who works with John C. is most likely working with an individual with a strong Asian orientation. First, the counselor must be aware that when an Asian-oriented client seeks counseling or therapy, this person is most likely to experience intense feelings of shame and guilt. Issues of confidentiality are important to deal with. Second, the client may find it difficult to directly admit to problems and will present them in an indirect manner—for example, psychophysiological reactions, declining grades, vocational indecision, and so on. It may be wise for the counselor to initially respond to these problems, since they are less threatening to the traditionalist, until a degree of rapport and trust can be formed. Third, it is imperative that the counselor recognize that vocational indecision, often presented by Asian Americans, may mask deeper conflicts. In the case of John C., it tends to be a conflict between his own desires for independence and the extremely strong obligations he feels toward his parents. Last, counselors working with a person of traditional background must be willing to alter their usual style of counseling and therapy. The actual practice of counseling and psychotherapy may be inherently discriminating to ethnic minorities. Since the counseling/therapy situation is essentially a White middle-class activity that values verbal expressiveness, openness, and a certain degree of psychological-mindedness, these values may cause problems between the counselor and the minority client For example, the traditionalist may find it difficult to talk about feelings and may find counseling so ambiguous that the counselor must take a much more active approach in structuring the interview sessions. Techniques that may be helpful include: (a) normalizing the problem—indicating that the problem is typical of that faced by Asian students; and (b) focusing on cultural conflicts— talking about different sets of expectations, including family obligations and individual needs.

Type D individuals are low on both assimilation and ethnic identity. They feel alienated from both cultures and tend to be mentally unhealthy. This may be a transitory stage for many who are still searching for an identity. Counselors working with these individuals should address issues of cultural racism and its impact on the ethnic identity of Asian individuals. Ways of coping other than a rejection of both sets of values need to be considered.

CONCLUSIONS

It is hoped that the foregoing discussion has provided an idea of the complexity of human behavior and how futile it is to attempt an understanding of ethnic minorities without an adequate exploration of their historical background, subcultural values, and unique conflicts. The lack of knowledge and the insensitivity of Western society to the plight of minorities have done much harm to Asian Americans. Educators and social scientists have a moral obligation to enlighten themselves and others to the life experiences of disadvantaged groups. Only in an atmosphere of trust and understanding can different groups live together in health and harmony.

Chapter 13

◆

Counseling American Indians and Alaskan Natives

◆

Most American Indian adults experienced attempts by the U.S. government to eliminate their cultural customs, language, and values. They were forbidden to practice their religious ceremonies until the 1974 Indian Freedom of Religion Act. (Johnson et al., 1995)

Of the 175 Indian languages spoken in the United States, only about 20 are passed on from mothers to babies. James Jackson Jr. remembered his experience in a boarding school when a teacher grabbed him when he was speaking his native language and threatened to wash out his mouth with soap. "That's where we lost it [our language]." (Brooke, 1998)

At a U.S. Senate hearing, an elder sang and beat a drum while hundreds of American Indians stood. On the other side of the aisle, a similar number of Euro-Americans rose and sang "The Star-Spangled Banner." Thus began a hearing regarding whether tribal immunity should be terminated from lawsuits from members of the outside community. American Indians believe that conflicts over fishing rights, gambling restrictions on reservations, and the rights of tribal courts to deal with Indian affairs has been an attempt to further break "solemn promises" made in treaties. (Shukovsky, 1998)

In North America, the American Indian population was decimated by wars and diseases that resulted from contact with Europeans. It is estimated that the large population of American Indians had decreased to only 10% of its original number by the end of the eighteenth century (Richardson, 1981; Swinomish Tribal Mental Health Project, 1991). The experience of American Indians in America is not comparable to that of any other ethnic group. In contrast to immigrants who arrived with few resources and struggled to gain equality, American Indians had resources. They had land and status that were gradually eroded by imperial, colonial, and then federal and state policies (Johnson et al., 1995). Extermination and seizure of lands seemed to be the primary policy of the North Americans. Experience with this type of contact prompted this observation from a Delaware warrior: *"I admit that there are good White men, but they bear no proportion to the bad; the bad must be the strongest, for they rule."* Indians suffered massive losses of their land.

During the 1930s, over 125,000 Indians from different tribes were forced from their homes in many different states to a reservation in Oklahoma. The move was traumatic for Indian families and, in many cases, disrupted their cultural traditions. Assaults against the Indian culture occurred in attempts to "civilize" the Indians. Many Indian children were forced to be educated in English-speaking boarding schools. They were not allowed to speak their own language and had to spend eight continuous years away from their family and tribes. Children were also removed from their homes and placed with non-Indian families until the Indian Child Welfare Act of 1978 (Blanchard, 1983; Choney, Berryhill-Paapke, & Robbins, 1995; Johnson et al., 1995). These practices had a great negative impact on family and tribal cohesion and prevented the transmission of cultural values from the parents to their children. The following case study illustrates some of the disruptions caused by a boarding school experience.

♦ *Case Study*

Mary was born on the reservation. She was sent away to school when she was 12 and did not return to the reservation until she was 20. By the time she returned, her mother had died from pneumonia. She didn't remember her father, who was the medicine man of the tribe, very well. Shortly after she returned, she became pregnant by a non-Indian man she met at a bar. . . . Mary's father . . . looked forward to teaching and leaving to his grandson John the ways of the medicine man. . . . John felt his grandfather was out of step with the 20th century. . . . Mary . . . could not validate the grandfather's way of life . . . she remembered having difficulty fitting in when she returned to the reservation. . . . In response to the growing distance between the two men, she became more and more depressed and began to drink heavily. . . . (Sage, 1997, p. 48)

In the past, the tribe, through the extended family, was responsible for the education and training of the children. The sense of identity developed through this tradition has been undermined. In addition, even recent history is full of broken treaties, the seizure or misuse of Indian land, and battles (often led by the U.S. government) to remove or severely limit fishing and hunting rights. These acts have made the American Indians very suspicious of the motives of the majority culture, and most of them do not expected to be treated fairly by non-Indian agencies (Johnson et al., 1995).

THE AMERICAN INDIAN/THE ALASKAN NATIVE

American Indians/Alaskan Natives form a highly heterogeneous group composed of over 450 distinct tribes, some of which are comprised only four or five members. The American Indian, Eskimo, and Aleut population grew rapidly to nearly two million in 1990 and is expected to reach 4.3 million by the year 2050. The population is young, with 39% under 29 years of age as compared to 29% of the total U.S. population. About 6 in 10 were married couple families versus 8 in 10 of the nation's families overall. Female householders with no husband present represented 27% of families versus 17% of the U.S. average. Fewer American Indians are high school graduates than the general U.S. population (66% versus 75%). Their income level is only 62% of the U.S. average, and the poverty rate is nearly three times as high (U.S. Bureau of the Census, 1995).

There are large within-group and between-group differences among the different tribes in customs, language, and type of family structure. Although tribes differ from one another in customs and values, they all share the experience of having lost their ancestral lands, forced education in boarding schools, systematic attempts to eradicate their language and religion, and restrictions on their traditional means of obtaining a livelihood (Norton & Manson, 1996). Over 60% of American Indians are of mixed heritage, having Black, White, and Hispanic backgrounds. In addition, American Indians differ in their degree of acculturation (Trimble, Fleming, Beauvais, & Jumper-Thurman, 1996). The majority of American Indians do not live on reservations, in part because of the lack of economic opportunities (Johnson et al., 1995).

What constitutes an Indian is often an area of controversy. The U.S. Census depends on self-report of racial identity; some tribes specify either tribal enrollment or blood quantum levels (Norton & Manson, 1996). As Trimble and Fleming (1989) point out, unlike other ethnic groups, American Indians have had a legal definition formulated for them by Congress. An individual has to have an Indian blood quantum of at least 25% to be considered an Indian. This definition has caused problems both within and outside the Indian community. Many in both groups feel that only an Indian who is of pure Indian blood is a true Indian. The arbitrary blood requirement established by the U.S. government has sometimes resulted in dissension among Indians due to the limited amount of funds available for social, economic, and educational development. More than 60% of American Indians are of mixed ethnicity as a result of inter-marriages with Black, Hispanic, and Caucasian individuals (Trimble, 1990).

Indians are often thought to have specific physical characteristics such as black hair and eyes, brown skin, and high cheekbones. Trimble (1981) indicates that for many, it is difficult to accept as an Indian an individual who has light hair, blue eyes, and fair skin. However, American Indians display a wide range of phenotypic characteristics in terms of body size, skin and hair color, and facial features. Conflicts in identity are often great for individuals who do not fit the traditional physical stereotypes. They may meet with prejudice and rejection from Indians and non-Indians alike.

TRIBE

For the many Indians living on reservations and for those living in urban areas, the tribe is of fundamental importance. The relationship that Indians have with their tribes is different from that between non-Indians and their society. Indians see themselves as an extension of their tribe. This identity provides them with a sense of belonging and security, with which they form an interdependent system. Status and rewards are obtained by adherence to tribal structure. Indians judge themselves in terms of whether or not their behaviors are of benefit to the tribe. Personal accomplishments are honored and supported if they serve to benefit the tribe. Indians who leave the reservation to seek greater opportunities often lose their sense of personal identity, since they lose their tribal identity (Anderson & Ellis, 1995; Blanchard, 1983).

FAMILY CHARACTERISTICS

It is difficult to describe "the Indian family." It varies from matriarchal structures seen in the Navajo, where women govern the family, to patriarchal in which men are the primary authority figures. Some generalizations can be made, however. American Indians are characterized by a high fertility rate, a large percentage of out-of-wedlock births, and a strong role for women. For most tribes, the extended family is the basic unit. Children are often raised by relatives such as aunts, uncles, and grandparents who live in separate households (Hildebrand et al., 1996). The living conditions for most American Indians are poor, especially for those on reservations. The per capita income in 1989 for American Indians living on all reservations or trust lands was $4,478, versus $8,328 for all American Indians. Between 1979 and 1989, the poverty rate for American Indians increased from 24% to 27%, and the median family income declined by 5%. Of the families maintained by females with no husband present, 50% were poor, compared with 31% of all families maintained by women with no husbands present (U.S. Bureau of the Census, 1995). In one tribe, over 90% of the grandparents lived in separate households but were involved and fulfilled traditional family roles on a daily basis with their children, grandchildren, and great-grandchildren. The existence of high unemployment on reservations has forced many to move into urban areas. However, cultural conflict and the loss of contact with the extended family and tribe may be responsible for the fact that 40% return to the reservation (Miller, 1980).

The concept of the extended family is often misunderstood by those in the majority culture who operate under the concept of the nuclear family. The extended family often extends through the second cousin. For the American Indian, it is not unusual to have youngsters stay in a variety of different households. Misinterpretations can be made if one thinks that only the parents should raise and be responsible for the children. Red Horse (1982) presents a case of a 15-year-old girl who was doing very well in school. However, she chose not to live with her parents, who had problems with alcohol, but lived instead in five different households of relatives during a 3-year period. The White caseworker felt the pattern of moving around was an indication of irresponsibility on the part of the girl and neglect on the part of the parents. If the girl was a member of the majority culture, such an interpretation would not be out of line. At the age of 17, Linda requested a place of her own. This request was resisted by the social worker, who cited her view that Linda was irresponsible and had displayed a pattern of instability. However, Indian professionals pointed out that Linda was doing very well in school and that many members of her extended family lived within an eight-block radius of her apartment. Further, she had the support of the school counselor and Indian professionals. It was also pointed out that a pattern of living in the households of the extended family was not uncommon.

In this example, there are several factors to note. First, the pattern of behavior has to be considered in a cultural context. Second, the decision regarding Linda's request was based not only on cultural knowledge but also on her individual strengths and weaknesses. If she had not done well in school or had not displayed responsible behavior, the decision would most likely have been different. Red Horse cautions that in working with American Indians, the consideration of Indian values as well as specific problem behaviors should be reviewed before a treatment plan is developed.

PROBLEMS OF CHILDREN AND ADOLESCENTS

Indian children and adolescents not only face the developmental problems faced by all young people, they are also in a state of conflict over exposure to two very different cultures. They are caught between expectations of their parents to maintain traditional values and the necessity to adapt to the majority culture. In one study of American Indian adolescents, the most serious problems identified involved family relationships, grades, and concerns about the future. In addition, boys frequently cited their Indianness or being Indian as being a problem. Surprisingly, 1/3 of the girls reported feeling that they did not want to live (Bee-Gates, Howard-Pitney, LaFramboise, & Rowe, 1996). These and other stressors may account for the fact that among Indian youth, truancy, delinquency and arrest rates, school failure, drug use, and suicide are high (Red Horse, 1982; Shore, 1988).

American Indian children appear to do well during the first few years of school. However, by the fourth grade, a pattern of decline and dropouts occurs. A significant drop in achievement motivation occurs around the seventh grade. This reduction is associated with a perception that school is not important to them for their future life plans (Wood & Clay, 1996). This view produces feelings of hopelessness and despair. In the Seattle School District, nearly 59% of American Indian students in middle school had a grade point average below 2.00 (9% had GPAs above 3.00), compared to 21% of White students. American Indian students were also more likely to be suspended (34%) than White students (17%; Seattle Public Schools, 1989). Red Horse (1982) feels that the decline is also due to the exposure to negative stereotypes as the children begin to identify themselves as Indians. For adolescent Indian girls, a particular problem is pregnancies at school age. In one study in Minneapolis, 40% of all school-age pregnancies occurred in Indian girls. This figure did not include girls who had dropped out of school because of pregnancy (Red Horse, 1982). The inability to complete an education perpetuates the cycle of poverty and lack of opportunities and may contribute to the high suicide rate among American Indian adolescents (Keane, Dick, Bechtold, & Manson, 1996).

VALUES

Because of the great diversity and variation among American Indians, it is difficult to describe a set of values that encompasses all groups. However, certain generalizations can be made regarding Indian values (Herring, 1997; Swinomish Tribal Mental Health Project, 1991).

1. *Sharing.* Among Indians, honor and respect is gained by sharing and giving, while in the dominant culture, status is gained by the accumulation of material goods. Once enough money is earned, Indians may stop working and spend time and energy in ceremonial activities. Refusing to accept an invitation to share drinks or substances with a member of the same tribe would be considered an affront to the individual making the offer and considered a violation of the value of sharing and giving.

2. *Cooperation.* Indians believe that the tribe and family take precedence over the individual. Indian children may be seen as unmotivated in schools because of a reluctance to compete with peers in the classroom. To compete could be seen as an expression of individuality and suggest that the student is better than the tribe. Because of this value, American Indian students may also feel it necessary to show their answers to another tribe member. Instead of going to an appointment, they may instead assist a family member needing help. Indians work hard to prevent discord and disharmony. In a counseling setting, they may find it easier to agree with the counselor, but will not follow through with the suggestions. In contrast, in the majority culture, individual achievement and competition are seen as important.

3. *Noninterference.* Indians are taught not to interfere with others and to observe rather than react impulsively. Rights of others are respected. They are often seen as permissive in child rearing. In the majority culture, action and taking charge are valued.

4. *Time orientation.* Indians are very much involved in the present rather than the future. Ideas of punctuality or planning for the future may be unimportant. Life is to be lived in the here and now. Long-term plans such as going to college are seen as acts of egoism rather than future planning. Things get done according to a rational order and not according to deadlines. In the majority culture, delay of gratification and planning for future goals are seen as important qualities.

5. *Extended family orientation.* Interrelationships between a large number of relatives are important, and there is strong respect for elders and their wisdom and knowledge. In the majority culture, the nuclear family is the basic unit of family structure and elders are not held in great esteem.

6. *Harmony with nature.* Rather than seeking to control the environment, Indians accept things as they are. In the majority culture, there are attempts to master and control the environment. The more nature can be controlled, the better.

These value differences can produce certain problems, especially when Indian behaviors are interpreted from a non-Indian perspective. For example, a teacher referred an Indian girl for counseling because of social anxiety and shyness. When asked the reason for the referral, the teacher indicated that the girl would not look her in the eye when she spoke to her. This interpretation was premature, since the teacher was not aware that among many Indian groups, eye contact between a child and an elder indicated a lack of respect. There have been reported cases in which the lack of eye contact has been regarded as a deficit. A behavior modification procedure was employed to shape eye contact in a Navaho girl (Everett, Proctor, & Cortmell, 1989). Indian children tend to display sensitivity to the opinions and attitudes of their peers. They will actively avoid disagreements or contradictions. Most do not like to be singled out and made to perform in school unless the whole group would benefit.

Within-Group Differences

Although some of the value differences between Indians and non-Indians have been presented, many Indians are acculturated and hold the values of the larger society. The degree of Indian identity versus acculturation and assimilation should always be considered, since it influences receptivity in counseling (Trimble et al., 1996). For example, Lowrey (1983) points out the wide differences within the Navaho people. Some have had minimal contact with the majority culture and are strongly oriented to their own culture. Others are acculturated, do not identify with Navaho values, and wish to move the Navaho nation into the modern world. Another group is able to move comfortably between the two cultures. They are also interested in "advancing" their tribe but want to be able to retain their traditional religious and family values. They want the freedom to choose from both cultures.

It is clear that within-group differences have to be considered in working with American Indians. Because of differences in acculturation, approaches that might be appropriate for a given individual might not be appropriate for all Indians (Choney, Berryhill-Paapke, & Robbins, 1995). Zitzow and Estes (1981) have expressed concern that by presenting the cultural values of American Indians, counselors and mental health workers will develop a set of stereotyped notions about the appropriate method of counseling for members of this population. They suggest that it is necessary to assess the degree of assimilation of the specific American Indian client. For example, the types of problems and the process and goals appropriate for an American Indian living on a rural reservation may be very different from those appropriate for an urbanized Indian who retains few of the traditional beliefs. The inappropriate application of cultural knowledge can mislead professionals into developing preconceived notions of how to counsel American Indians.

Zitzow and Estes (1981) emphasize the importance of recognizing individual differences in American Indians but also feel that it might be useful to develop a typology for conceptualizing this group. They offer suggestions to assess assimilation in American Indians and develop a two-point continuum. The first is the Heritage Consistent Native American (HCNA), whose predominant orientation is the American Indian tribal culture. The second is the Heritage Inconsistent Native American (HINA), whose behaviors and lifestyles reflect the dominant American culture. These types are not mutually exclusive, and overlaps occur. Signs indicative of heritage consistency may include: growing up on or near a reservation, extended family orientation, involvement in tribal religious and cultural activities, education on or near a reservation, social activities primarily with other Native Americans, being knowledgeable about or willing to learn about own culture, placing low priority on materialistic goals, and using shyness and silence as signs of respect.

Specific issues that may be involved in counseling the HCNA include: (a) the sense of security for the individual may be limited to the reservation and the extended family; (b) nonverbal communication may be more important, and the individual may have difficulty with the English language; (c) socialization may involve only other American Indians, and the individual may feel uncomfortable communicating with a non-Indian; (d) basic academic learning skills may be underdeveloped; (e) the value of education may not fit into the individual's belief system, and the individual might feel a conflict between motivation to learn and values on the reservation; (f) the individual might be concerned about failure and its impact on the extended family and the tribe; (g) the individual may have difficulty in establishing long-term goals; (h) the holding back of emotions may be perceived as a positive characteristic; (i) paternalism from government agencies may have diminished feelings of personal responsibility in decision making; and (j) the individual may be unfamiliar with the expectations of the dominant culture.

As opposed to HCNA individuals, issues that a HINA may face include: (a) denial and lack of pride in being a Native American; (b) pressure to adopt the majority cultural values; (c) guilty feelings over not knowing or participating in his/her culture; (d) negative views of Native Americans; and (e) a lack of a support and belief system.

Being able to identify the degree of acculturation or self-identity for an individual client is important. Zitzow and Estes (1981) present an example of two American Indian sisters, one of whom is adopted and raised by a White family away from the reservation. She is not knowledgeable about her culture and is not interested in participating in traditional activities. She is not totally comfortable with her White friends but is less comfortable with her native culture. The other sister was raised on the reservation within an extended family. She participates in tribal activities and is proud of her identity. However, she is uncertain and uneasy when interacting with the dominant culture. Each of the sisters would require a different intervention. The first would have to examine value and self-identity conflicts. The second requires skills in coping with the dominant society.

In addition, Zitzow and Estes (1981) feel that there are common counseling issues that should be explored with all American Indians, such possible feelings of distrust toward mental health professionals (especially non–Native American), prejudice and discrimination, possible lack of strong self-identity, fear of failure and ridicule, alcohol and substance abuse, a lack of exposure to successful American Indian role models, feelings of frustration that others are responding to them in a stereotypic fashion rather than as an individual, and possible conflicts over commitment to long-term goals such as education, with feelings of alienation from tribal and extended family values. American Indians should be responded to as individuals first. Cultural knowledge serves only to indicate areas of potential difficulty and allows the mental health professional to be sensitive to cultural issues and values.

PROBLEM AREAS

Robert Jaycob Jensen was first. The lanky 17-year-old Sioux Indian, who'd been drinking heavily and having run-ins with police all summer, slipped into his family's dank basement last Aug. 30. Over toward the corner, past the rusted-out furnace and broken sewer line, he threaded a braided leather belt over a board nailed between floor beams, buckled it around his neck and hanged himself.

On Nov. 16, in the same basement with the same type of belt, Robert's 16-year-old cousin and best friend, Charles Gerry, hanged himself. Three other Indian youths have since taken their lives. . . . In the five months since Robert's death, 43 reservation boys and girls have attempted suicide. . . . ("Rash of Indian," 1998, p. A5)

The suicide epidemic is thought to be the result of alcohol abuse, poverty, boredom, and family breakdown. American Indian youth have twice the rate of attempted and completed suicide as other youth. Adolescence to adulthood is the time of greatest risk for suicide (EchoHawk, 1997; Shore, 1988). A promising culturally tailored suicide intervention program was implemented by LaFromboise and Howard-Pitney (1995) at the request of the Zuni Tribal High School. The participants were involved in either an intervention or no-intervention condition. Scores on a suicide probability measure indicated that 81% of the students were in the moderate to severe ranges. Of the participants, 18% reported having attempted suicide and 40% reported knowing of a relative or friend who had committed suicide. The program involved the development of suicide intervention skills through role-playing. Other components included self-esteem building, identifying emotions and stress, recognizing and eliminating negative thoughts or emotions, receiving information on suicide and intervention strategies, and setting personal and community goals. The program was effective in reducing feelings of hopelessness and suicidal probability ratings. However, scores on depression did not change. The students in the intervention condition were also able to demonstrate behaviorally problem solving and

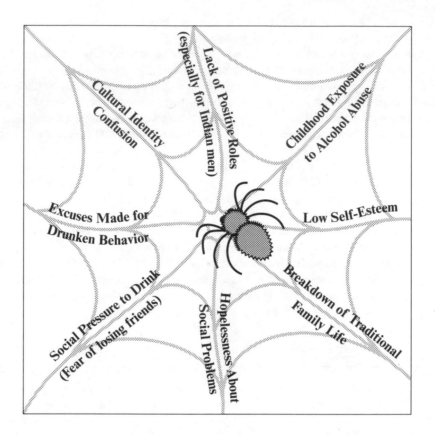

Figure 13.1   Strands in the web of alcohol abuse. From *A gathering of wisdoms,* Swimonish Tribal Mental Health Project, 1991. Reprinted by permission.

suicide intervention strategy. Although the long term-effects of the program are not known, the approach seems promising in the prevention of suicide.

Substance abuse is one of the greatest problems faced by the American Indian. They are considerably more likely to die of alcohol-related causes than the general U.S. population (Penn et al., 1995). In Indian Health Service Hospitals approximately 21% of hospitalizations are for alcohol-related problems (MMWR, 1997). In Alaska, 32% of American Indian/Alaskan Natives of childbearing age reported heavy drinking, which is responsible for the disproportionately high percentage of cases of fetal alcohol syndrome reported in this population (MMWR, 1994). In addition, drug abuse and dependence are very high among young Indian clients. In one survey, up to 70% of Indian adolescents in an urban school setting were involved in drug and alcohol abuse (Red Horse, 1982). Alcohol use is associated with fighting, vandalism, and delinquency (Manson, Tatum, & Dinges, 1982). However, it must be remembered that many American Indian/Alaskan Natives do not drink or only drink moderately. Abstinence is high among certain tribes such as the Navajo (Myers et al., 1995).

A variety of explanations have been put forth to indicate possible reasons for the rise in alcohol abuse (see Figure 13.1).

The drinking of alcoholic beverages may have been initially incorporated into cultural practices in that it was seen as a an activity of sharing, giving, and togetherness (Swinomish Tribal Mental Health Project, 1991). Turning down an offered drink is considered to be an act of individual autonomy and disruptive to group harmony. Other explanations have focused on the release of feelings of frustration and boredom, allowing Indians to express emotions that are normally under control; drinking of alcohol as a social event; and the acceptance of drinking in many tribal groups (Anderson & Ellis, 1995). Manson, Tatum, and Dinges (1982) indicate that among many American Indians, drinking is an accepted practice and is encouraged among family members. Parents are often heavy drinkers and allow their children to drink. Manson and his colleagues feel that a major etiologic component of childhood abuse of alcohol is the Indian respect for autonomy and permissiveness, which then allows a child to determine how much alcohol to consume.

TREATMENT OF SUBSTANCE ABUSE

Substance abuse is often related to low self-esteem, cultural identity conflicts, lack of positive role models, abuse history, social pressure to use substances, hopelessness about life, and a breakdown in the family (Swinomish Tribal Mental Health Project, 1991; Yee et al., 1995). The use of illicit substances is related to the 50% dropout rate from school by American Indian youth (Beauvais et al., 1996).

Successful residential drug treatment programs have incorporated appropriate cultural elements. Gutierres and Todd (1997) found that including the use of a sweat lodge and talking circle with American Indian substance abuse increased successful treatment completion. Schinke et al. (1985) believe that prevention and treatment of substance abuse is best accomplished in groups of Indian youth, preferably led by Indian social workers, teachers, or school counselors. The process would involve six steps. The first would provide the students with accurate information on drugs and alcohol. Respected elders and older youth might be invited to talk about some of the dangers of drug use. Suggestions can be made that natural highs can be gained by spirit dancing, singing, and dancing. Second, problem-solving skills in rejecting alcohol would be developed. Schinke and his colleagues give an example of a teenager who would share a six-pack of beer with friends during the school lunch hour. He did not like the feelings of sleepiness in class after consuming the beer. He is asked to brainstorm solutions. Suggestions he comes up with are that he could drink only a little, pretend to drink, stay in class during the lunch break, pretend that he had a stomachache, or not drink at all. He chooses the last solution but decides to stand beside his cousin who will not pressure him to drink. The development of alternative responses can be very helpful in reducing the chances of abuse. The third step would be to develop a cognitive rehearsal strategy. Coping statements can be thought of, expressed subvocally, and then aloud. The individual thinks of what he or she can say to refuse to participate and then rehearses it aloud. The fourth step involves behavioral rehearsal with coaching and reinforcement. For example, a student might be told to consider a situation such as: "A friend of yours wants you to smoke pot with her. How would you indicate that you do not wish to do so?" In this situation another American Indian student supports and reinforces the student who is practicing refusal skills. The fifth step would involve establishing a positive social network. Family and friends who will support nondrinking are identified and brought into the social network. Involvement in alternative activities such as dance, intertribal sports, and clan activities is encouraged. Pairs and groups of individuals are formed to assist one another in rejecting the use of alcohol and other drugs in the last step.

COUNSELING AMERICAN INDIAN CHILDREN AND YOUTH

In working with American Indian adolescents, ethnic identity issues should be explored. For many, "Indianness" or the emphasis he or she places on being Indian is a very important feature in the development of self-identity (Bigfoot-Sipes, 1992). Considering identity issues serves several purposes. First, it allows the client to be aware of potential problems if the therapist is of different ethnicity. Second, it gets the client to consider his/her own feelings about values, self-identity, and relationship with the majority society. Problems involving identity formation may be great and swing back and forth, with the Indian youths sometimes seeing themselves as primarily Indian, and sometimes moving in the direction of White values. The therapist has to help recognize and clarify the conflicts so that the client can make an individual resolution. Many Indians do not prefer assimilation or individuality, as they see themselves as an extension of the tribe. Harmony, cooperation, and the prevention of discord is important (Anderson & Ellis, 1995).

Indian youths may have a difficult time with assertion or the expression of strong emotions. However, Katz (1981) believes that a major loophole occurs when the individual becomes drunk. In this condition, an individual is not considered to be responsible for his/her behavior and can openly express anger. A case study of a 17-year-old Cree male, Chris, was presented to illustrate this point. Chris was attempting to save money on the job that he had so he could buy a car. However, he found this difficult to do since he was supporting his unemployed brother who was living with him. His brother contributed nothing to the living expenses and did not seek employment. Chris was caught between his personal desire and the cultural expectation of sharing with others. He was unable to express his feelings of anger. However, one day he allowed himself to get drunk and then angrily denounced his brother. Within a few days, the brother moved out. Neither discussed the incident, and they remained close. Although the outcome was a success, a more meaningful solution would have been to make the conflict conscious and decide what would be possible alternatives to the problem.

Because of the importance of the extended family, counseling may be more successful in homes and with family members or friends present. Group counseling seems to be a promising modality, as can be seen in the pilot project described by Yvonne Red Horse (1982). This prevention program involved increasing the interdependence of Indian girls with their extended family. Nine Indian girls between the ages of 15 and 17, who were having adjustment problems in school, participated. All came from dysfunctional families in which there were problems with alcohol and drug abuse, unemployment, and inadequate housing. However, they all had in common an intact extended family network.

The pilot project involved working on the strengths that existed in the families and using a culturally accepted group format to promote social cohesion. Culture was used to strengthen group ties. Group identity was built through the participation of the members in cultural activities such as powwows, feasts, and intertribal dancing. As trust was built up in the groups, exploration of feelings and frustrations could be explored. A problem-solving approach was used to determine solutions that could be implemented. Extended family ties were strengthened by having the girls share their feelings with aunts, uncles, cousins, parents, and grandparents. Members of the extended family were consulted whenever problems arose. Reliance on help from extended family members increased. The Indian adolescents developed confidence and learned to be more independent through becoming more interdependent with family members.

COUNSELING ISSUES

Before working with American Indians, it is important to be aware of our own cultural biases. Much of what we do is based on Western values and influences. We expect clients to establish good eye contact, to discuss inner feeling, and to verbalize concerns. American Indians often will not display these behaviors. In working with adolescents, we often work toward having them develop increasing independence from their parents. We also see the nuclear family as the basic unit. For American Indians, interdependence with the extended family might be the goal. As parents, they are often much more permissive in their child-rearing practices.

One woman pointed out that children are watched but that their parents do not tell them to behave. . . . One respondent gave the example of a child at a pow-wow sticking his finger in the fire as several adults, including the mother, watched but did not warn the child or otherwise prevent him from burning himself. Once burned . . . he stayed away from the fire. According to several Blackfeet respondents, the belief in allowing children to learn from experience rather than "doing as the parent says" has been part of the Indian childrearing philosophy for generations. (Gray and Cosgrove, p. 395)

It is important to be aware of how cultural influences have shaped our perception of what is "right" or "wrong" in parent-child relationships. American Indians are more indulgent and less punitive to their children than parents from other ethnic groups (MacPhee, Fritz, and Miller-Heyl, 1996). A culturally sensitive parent education program has been developed for American Indians that involves: (a) use of the oral tradition by storytelling to teach lessons for children; (b) understanding the spiritual nature of child rearing and the spiritual value of children; and (c) use of the extended family in child rearing. The eight-session program involves a half-hour social time for parents and children before each session. Storytelling and a potluck meal are included. The focus is the application of traditional teaching methods (nurturing, use of nature to teach lessons, and use of harmony as a guiding principle for family life; Gorman & Balter, 1997). For traditionally oriented or even marginally identified American Indian parents, this approach may be more appropriate than our traditional methods of parent education.

It is also important to avoid stereotypes of what an individual Indian is like. Instead, it is critical to respond to the individual and identify and explore his or her values. Many American Indians adhere completely to mainstream values; others, especially those on or near reservations, are more likely to hold to traditional values. In discussing a typology regarding the degree of assimilation by American Indians, Zitzow and Estes (1981) indicate possible problems and issues faced by American Indians with different orientations. We also presented some of the value differences between American Indians and the majority culture. Cultural knowledge should not be used in a stereotypic fashion. The value of cultural knowledge is to help the counselor be more flexible in outlook and be able to generate more alternative definitions about possible problems with a specific individual.

Can current counseling skills that most counselors have learned be appropriate in working with members of the American Indian population?

Is it conceivable that a traditional Indian, one steeped in the culture of the tribe, would respond to conventional techniques regardless of the theoretical underpinnings? If not, is it possible to modify conventional techniques to render them appropriate for use with traditional clients? (Trimble & LaFramboise, 1985, pp. 129–130)

There is controversy surrounding the answer to this question. Trimble & LaFramboise (1985) feel that client-centered approaches are often "disastrous" in working with American Indians. In contrast, Wise and Miller (1983) feel that a nondirective approach would be more effective than directive counseling. These statements indicate the current confusion over attempts to develop culturally relevant approaches in working with American Indians.

Trimble & LaFramboise are pointing out problems with expectations. Many American Indians are not socialized to express inner thoughts and feelings, while Wise and Miller are equating the directive approach with confrontation and forcing the client to reveal sensitive material before trust has developed. Part of the disagreement is over the matter of timing. American Indians cannot be expected to talk about issues in a meaningful manner until trust has developed. Qualities such as respect and acceptance of the individual, unconditional positive regard, understanding the problem from the individual's perspective, allowing the client to explore his or her own values, and arriving at an individual solution are core qualities that may transcend cultures. However, American Indian clients may need more guidance than is usually offered by client-centered approaches. Expectations of rapid discussion of sensitive material will not be fulfilled. It may be more helpful to first talk about other matters until trust has developed. The appropriate combination of client-centered with behavioral approaches might be very effective.

In working with American Indians, issues of ethnic differences between the therapist and client should be explored indirectly, the client's value structure should be identified, and possible issues of culture conflict and identity should be investigated. Do they live on or near a reservation? Is tribal connectiveness important to them? Acculturation occurs in four domains: (a) cognitive—understanding of customs and language; (b) behavioral—participation in tribal or White activities; (c) affective/spiritual—degree of emotional connectiveness with tribe; and (d) social/environmental—socialization patterns (Choney, Berryhill-Paapke, & Robbins, 1995). American Indians may have made different accommodations to these areas and have sets of different problems. Some acculturated families may do well with mainstream therapies, but traditional American Indians may first have to deal with the issue of trust. Many believe that government agencies and their representatives are not trustworthy.

Basic needs may have to be addressed first. Problems resulting from poverty, such as food, shelter, child care and employment, should be discussed as well as possible solutions. Prevalent problems such as use of substances, depression, and suicide should be assessed. The degree of tribal or family responsibility should be determined. More traditional American Indians may miss counseling sessions to help out a family or tribal member. They may work only seasonally and may leave the area. These issues should be discussed and the appropriate ways of dealing with them developed. Many of the traditional American Indians are more present- rather than future-oriented. Determine if this is the case, and if so, develop strategies that work in the here and now.

American Indians may respond best to a cooperative approach that offers a combination of client-centered and behavioral approaches. With its emphasis on external influences, issues such as racism and other environmental stressors can be identified and dealt with. Allow the client to express his or her view of the goals for counseling. For children and adolescents, attempt to have them help determine if some of their problems are due to cultural values (not speaking out in class, sharing answers on tests with friends, using substances). Strategize different ways of dealing with the value conflicts. Family therapy and processes that involve the extended family are often indicated. In working with parents, determine whether child-rearing practices are consonant with traditional Indian methods. Discuss the strengths of the traditional methods, how they can be applied to their children, and how they view recommendations from mainstream parent education programs. Other recommendations include: (a) the client's cultural conceptualization of treatment and outcome should be explored; (b) counseling techniques should be culturally acceptable to the client and goals should be consistent with cultural expectations; (c) acculturation conflicts for the client and family members should be assessed; (d) religious and spiritual beliefs should be considered; (e) for some American Indians, coordination with traditional healers in the treatment may be necessary; (f) some American Indians will have problems with the limits of a 50-minute session; (g) in dealing with a dysfunctional family, attempt to strengthen it by use of the extended family; (h) during the initial session, keep a low profile and do not press the client; (i) allow the client time to finish statements and thoughts—do not interrupt; and (j) confrontation is considered to be rude and should be kept to a minimum (Swinomish Tribal Mental Health Project, 1991). Most importantly, it is crucial that mental health professionals remember to respond to the American Indian client as an individual.

Chapter 14

◆

Counseling Hispanic Americans

◆

Ron Taber, in his 1996 failed campaign for superintendent of public instruction in Washington, referred to Spanish as "The language of doormen, dishwashers and fruit pickers." (Zimmerman, 1998)

State representative Cindy Watkins, in a letter complaining of water pollution in her district, identified the culprits as ". . . hogs, chickens, turkeys, cows, goats and Hispanics. . . ." (Burritt, 1998). She later apologized.

A thick scar below his right elbow reminds him of his first days in the fields, when he slipped and fell on some sharp farming tools. . . . Like many farm-worker children, Gonzales went to work to help his family pay the bills. He was a good student until he dropped out at age 15. He hasn't given up hope—but his family comes first. (Kramer, 1998, p. A6). Only about 10% of children of migrant workers complete high school.

In this chapter, the term "Hispanic" encompasses individuals living in the United States with ancestry from Mexico, Puerto Rico, Cuba, El Salvador, the Dominican Republic, and other Latin American countries. However, the term is not accepted by all groups, with some individuals preferring to be referred to as "Latinos" or "La Raza" (the race). Even within specific subgroups, there are different opinions on the appropriate terms of identification. Some Hispanics from Mexico may refer to themselves as "Mexicano," "Mexican American," "Chicano" or "Spanish American" (Gonzalez, 1997; Padilla & DeSnyder, 1985). The designation "Chicano" often produces a mixed reception. It is used by some Mexican Americans to indicate racial pride and consciousness, but it is rejected by others, primarily older Mexican Americans, who consider it to be an insulting term that refers to uneducated, exploited farmhands (Avila & Avila, 1995). Even the term "Hispanic" is controversial, since it does not indicate the influence of the indigenous cultures. However, the term will be employed in this chapter to indicate the common background of Spanish language and customs. Although Hispanics share common characteristics, there are distinct differences between and within the different groups.

HISPANIC AMERICANS: COMMONALITIES AND DIFFERENCES

In physical characteristics, the appearance of Hispanics varies greatly and may include resemblance to North American Indians, Blacks, Asians, or Latins and Europeans depending on their country of origin (Casas & Vasquez, 1996). Mexican Americans are mostly of Mestizo ancestry (mixed Spanish and native Aztec-Indian blood). In Mexico, it is estimated that 55% are Mestizo, 29% Indian, and 15% of European background (Avila & Avila, 1980). Among Cuban Americans, most are of Spanish descent, with the rest of Black or mixed ancestry. In Latin America, the immigration of African and Asian populations has resulted in a wide range of physical characteristics. Puerto Ricans generally are of Spanish descent, but influences from Indians and Blacks can also be seen.

DEMOGRAPHICS

According to the U.S. Census (U.S. Bureau of the Census, 1995), Hispanic Americans comprise a population of 22.8 million, of whom nearly 2/3 are of Mexican descent, 10.5% are from Puerto Rico (Puerto Rico became a commonwealth on July 25, 1952, and its residents are U.S. citizens who can move between the island and the mainland without any restrictions), 4.8% are Cuban, and about 13.6% are from Latin American countries. Because of the high birthrate and ongoing immigration patterns, it is estimated that Hispanics will be the largest minority group in the United States by the year 2005 and will reach a population of 96 million by the year 2050.

As a group, Hispanic Americans are a very young population, with an average age almost 9 years younger than that of White Americans. However, the median age of the subpopulations differ, ranging from the Cuban population, with an average age of 43.6 years, to the Mexican population, which averages 24.6 years. Because of their religious background as well as strong emphasis on large families and youth, nearly twice as many Hispanic households (54%) are composed of four or more people compared to 28% for the country as a whole (Church, Goodgame, Leavitt, & Lopez, 1985).

The vast majority of Hispanic Americans are situated in metropolitan areas of the United States and populate every state, including Alaska and Hawaii. In certain states and cities, they make up a substantial percentage of the population. The population of Arizona is 16% Hispanic; of New Mexico, 36%; of Denver, Colorado, 19%; of Hartford, Connecticut, 20%; and of Miami, Florida, 64%. Mexican Americans reside primarily in the Southwest and Great Lakes regions and in various metropolitan areas throughout the United States. Cubans populate the Miami Beach area and other large cities in Florida. Puerto Ricans reside primarily in the large northeastern cities. In 1990, the majority of Mexican Americans lived in California; they make up about 1/4 of the population of California and Texas. They number 619,000 in Arizona, 612,000 in Illinois, and 329, 233 in New Mexico (Gonzalez, 1997).

Hispanics are overrepresented among the poor, have high unemployment, and often live in substandard housing. Most are blue-collar workers and hold semiskilled or unskilled occupations. There is a significant discrepancy between the annual incomes of Hispanics and Caucasians. In 1992, the median annual salary for a full-time Hispanic worker was $20,054 for males and $17,124 for females, compared to $31,765 for White males and $21,930 for White females. Nearly 40% of Hispanic children live in poverty, compared to 13.2% of White children (U.S. Bureau of the Census, 1995). Puerto Ricans appear to have the highest rate of poverty, while Cubans have the highest incomes. About half of the native Hispanic families in Southern California are middle-class, and 2/3 of those in the United States live above the poverty line (Robinson, 1998).

Hispanic Americans have disproportionately high rates of tuberculosis, AIDS, and obesity. Certain subgroups also show higher health risks. Among Hispanic farmworkers, infant mortality rates are reported as to be as high as 25%, and they are 50 times more likely than the general population to have parasitic infections (Johnson et al., 1995). Among Puerto Ricans, death rates for heart disease, pneumonia, asthma, liver disease, and homicide exceed those of other Hispanic groups (Flack et al., 1995). Asthma, especially in children, occurs at a higher than expected rate (Christiansen et al., 1997). Among recent immigrants and migrant workers, health information is often inaccurate or inadequate. In one sample of infected Hispanic immigrants enrolled in a county health department program, 50% did not know how they contracted tuberculosis (Ailinger, 1997). In one study, from 1/3 to 1/2 of female migrant workers surveyed believed that individuals could contract AIDS from mosquito bites, by using public restrooms, kissing, and by being tested for AIDS (Organista, Organista, & Soloff, 1998).

EDUCATION

Peer pressure to drop out can be nearly overwhelming in the Hispanic community, as DeAnza Montoya, a pretty Santa Fe teen, can attest. In her neighborhood, it was considered "anglo" and "nerdy" to do well in school. . . . "In school they make you feel like a dumb Mexican," she says, adding that such slights only bring Hispanics closer together. (Headden, 1997, p. 64)

Educationally, Hispanic Americans have not been faring well in the public schools. Hispanic students have a very high dropout rate. Nearly 1/3 drop out before completing high school. This is more than double the rate for Blacks and three times higher than the rate for White students. Only 10% of children of migrant workers complete school. Twenty-five percent of Hispanic eighth graders have repeated one grade, and over 15% have been retained two or more times in their school careers (Gersten & Woodward, 1994). Among Hispanic groups, Puerto Rican students have the highest dropout rate. Although there has been a great deal of emphasis on the importance of nondiscriminatory assessment, in Texas, Mexican Americans are overrepresented by 300% in the special education programs under the learning disabilities classification (Cummins, 1986). Many of these students were placed in these programs because of their lack of English proficiency (tests were conducted in English or they were unable to perform adequately from classroom material in a language they were just beginning to learn; Gersten & Woodward, 1994).

A number of problems contribute to the high dropout rate of Hispanic students. As was mentioned earlier, many of the educational difficulties faced by Hispanics relate to their varied proficiency with English. Spanish is the primary language spoken in the homes of over half of Hispanic Americans, and a much larger percentage regularly listen to or speak Spanish on a more limited basis. Second-generation Hispanics are often bilingual. However, their command of the English language is often limited. Many are exposed first to Spanish in the home and then to English in the school. Immigrant parents may speak in Spanish and be responded to by their child in a combination of Spanish and English. Of the Hispanic eighth-graders who scored poorly on an academic test, almost half had parents who had not completed high school (Gersten & Woodward, 1994).

A 1974 Supreme Court case (*Lau v. Nichols*) mandated that public schools provide a program that would not prevent non-English-speaking students from receiving a meaningful education. Subsequently, a document, popularly called the Lau Remedies, was developed by the U.S. Office of Civil Rights in 1975, dictating bilingual education as an appropriate means of correcting past practices. Bilingual education programs, which have been in effect for more than a decade, have been and continue to be the subject of much controversy and debate.

In 1998, California recently voted to ban bilingual education, eliminating a 30-year-old program. Spanish-speaking students will be given a one-year transition class and then will be exposed to an English immersion program. In contrast with California's former system of providing years of instruction in the child's native language, the programs in Washington state are transitional and designed to keep students current with their studies with the goal of getting them into all-English classes within 3 years.

Cummins (1986) feels that a variety of factors, including intergroup power relationships, have much to do with the lack of educational success of Hispanic Americans. For example, Finnish students have a relatively poor academic performance in Sweden, where they are considered a low-status group, but are successful academically in Australia, where they are a high-status group. Since change of status is not possible in the United States, Cummins feels that it is possible to "empower" students in schools through four components: (a) incorporation of the language and culture of the minority group into the school programs; (b) participation of the ethnic community in the children's education; (c) implementation of methods to increase motivation in students by having them use their own language to achieve greater knowledge; and (d) emphasis on having the professionals involved in assessment become advocates for the students instead of using tests to legitimize localizing the problem "in the student."

The poor performance of Hispanic Americans has often been blamed on their culture or the parents for failing to prepare or to motivate their children academically. However, their parents do have high aspirations for their children. Most want their children to complete college (Retish & Kavanaugh, 1992). Hispanic children also lack role models. Hispanic Americans constitute just 1.5% of all college faculty and 1.1% of all tenured faculty (Kavanaugh & Retish, 1991).

In general, schools have been poorly equipped to deal with large numbers of Spanish-speaking students. Teachers who do not have proficiency in Spanish have a difficult time preparing understandable lessons for students and have no means of effectively evaluating their performance. The inability to communicate with Hispanic parents compounds the problem and hampers information passed through parent-teacher conferences. Many low-income Hispanic parents feel they have no right to question the teacher or school decisions. This may be interpreted as a lack of caring or parental involvement in the child's education. To engage parents, the conferences should be scheduled at flexible hours. Child care should be made available, as well as interpreters if the teacher is not bilingual. Face-to-face communication or other personal contact is more successful than written material (even if written in Spanish). Trust develops slowly, and it is important to identify and support the family's strengths rather than focusing on the shortcomings (Espinosa, 1998). Altering instructional strategy to fit cultural values is important. Instead of saying to a child, "Good work, you should be proud of yourself," the teacher could respond, "Good work, your family will be proud of you" and have the child bring the work home to show the parents. Teachers often don't know how to respond when they observe cultural characteristics in children. Vasquez (1998) has a three-step procedure to modify instructional strategy (See Figure 14.1).

FAMILY AND VALUES

For Hispanic Americans, family tradition is an important aspect of life. Family unity is seen as very important, as is respect for and loyalty to the family. Cooperation rather than competition among family members is stressed. Interpersonal relationships are maintained and nurtured within a large network of family and friends. For the family, a critical element is to develop and maintain interpersonal relationships. There is deep respect and affection among friends and family. Hispanic American students are more likely to endorse the following items than White students: loyalty to the family, strictness of child rearing, religiosity, and respect to adults (Negy, 1993). For many Hispanic Americans, the extended family includes not only relatives but often nonblood "relatives" such as the best man (*padrino*), maid of honor (*madrina*), and godparents (*compadre* and *comadre*). Each member of the family has a role: grandparents (wisdom), mother (abnegation), father (responsibility), children (obedience), and godparents (resourcefulness; Ruiz, 1995). Because of these relationships and resources, outside help is generally not sought until advice is obtained from the extended family and close friends (Carillo, 1982).

However, Padilla and DeSnyder (1985) point out that although there are many positive features of the extended family, emotional involvement and obligations with a large number of family and friends may also function as an additional source of stress. Since family relationships are so important, decisions may be made that impact the individual negatively. Allegiance to the family is of primary importance, taking precedence over any outside concerns, such as school attendance or work (Avila & Avila, 1995). For example, older children may be kept at home in order to help care for ill siblings or parents. They may be absent from school to attend family functions (Hildebrand et al., 1996) or to meet a family financial obligation (Headden, 1997).

The Catholic religion often has a major influence in Hispanic groups and is a source of comfort in times of stress. There is strong belief in the importance of prayer, and most participate in Mass. This religious belief is related to the view that: (a) sacrifice in this world is helpful to salvation, (b) being charitable to others is a virtue, and (c) you should endure wrongs done against you (Yamamoto & Acosta, 1982). The consequences of these beliefs are that many Hispanics have difficulty behaving assertively. They feel that problems or events are meant to be and cannot be changed. The strong reliance on religion can be a resource. Sometimes a priest can help deal with counseling issues. Acosta and Evans (1982) report the case of a 35-year-old, Spanish-speaking Mexican American, José, who came into the clinic complaining of anxiety attacks. The precipitating event appeared to be his impending marriage, which would necessitate reducing the amount of money he could send to his parents in Mexico. He felt that it would be a sin to reduce his assistance. The counselor suggested that José talk to his priest about this issue. With short-term counseling, along with assurance from the priest that he would not be committing a sin, José was able to marry and reconcile sending less to his parents. In addition to an extended family orientation and a fatalistic outlook, Hispanics also hold values that differ from those held by middle-class White Americans. For example, Inclan (1985) compares the latter with the values of traditional Puerto Ricans (see Table 14.1).

THREE-STEP PROCEDURE FOR ADAPTING INSTRUCTION TO CULTURAL TRAITS

Step 1	Step 2	Step 3
Teacher observes/identifies student trait.	Trait is passed through "filter" of three questions to identify which aspect of teaching (content, context, mode) should be affected.	Teacher verbalizes/ writes out the new instruction strategy.

1. Carlos is very concerned about pleasing his family.

Content

a. Does any aspect of the trait suggest the kind of material I should be teaching?

1. I'll tell Carlos that I'll inform his parents when he does really good work. (Carlos should work with great effort and expectation and thus for him the context is changed).

2. Sammy and Joanna seem disinterested when given individual work and more "turned on" when interacting with others.

Context

b. Does any aspect of the trait suggest the physical or psychological setting I should create in the classroom?

2. I'll provide more activities that allow Sammy and Joanna to work on projects with others in small groups. (Mode is changed since the means of instruction has shifted to include more student input.)

3. Ben seems intimidated and shy when I ask him questions to which he may not know the answer.

Mode

c. Does any aspect of the trait suggest the manner in which I should be teaching?

3. I'll ask Ben questions in class that I'm fairly sure he can answer correctly, and work with him individually in areas in which he is less knowledgeable. (This strategy affects both the mode of instruction and the psychological context for Ben.)

4. Charlotte does better when the material I teach involves people interacting with one another; she is not strongly "object" oriented.

4. I'll teach more math concepts in the context of people dealing with one another, as in buying, trading, borrowing. (The mode is basically changed to suit Charlotte's preferred style of learning.)

Figure 14.1 Three-step Procedure for Adapting Instruction to Cultural Traits. By J.A. Vasquez, 1998, *The Prevention Researcher,* 5(1), p. 3. Reprinted by permission of the Editor, *The Prevention Researcher.*

Table 14.1 COMPARISON OF VALUE-ORIENTATION PROFILES FOR FIRST-GENERATION POOR PUERTO RICANS AND MIDDLE-CLASS ANGLO AMERICANS

Dimension	First-Generation Poor Puerto Rican	Middle-Class American
Time	Present > Future > Past	Future > Present > Past
Activity	Being > Doing > Being-in-Becoming	Doing > Being > Being-in-Becoming
Relational	Lineal > Collateral > Individual	Individual > Collateral > Lineal
Person-Nature	Subjugated > Harmony > Dominant Over	Dominant Over > Subjugated > Harmony
Basic Human Nature	Mixed > Evil > Good	Neutral > Evil > Good

From "Variations in Value Orientations in Mental Health Work with Puerto Ricans" by J. Inclan, 1985, *Psychotherapy, 22,* p. 328. Copyright 1985 by *Psychotherapy.* Reprinted by permission of the Editor, *Psychotherapy.*

Middle-class White Americans are usually concerned with time and planning for the future. Puerto Ricans often find it humorous that Anglos will leave a party because they have to be ready for the coming day. Puerto Ricans prefer to enjoy the present activities. Activity is also viewed differently; being is valued more than doing. Middle-class White Americans tend to stress the importance of doing something during a vacation. For the Puerto Rican, being with the family and experiencing this is more important than doing something. Among White middle-class families, individual achievement in the workplace is important, while for Puerto Rican families prestige and status are gained by demonstrating respect and cooperation in the family. Family members are given priority. If a member is in a position to hire someone, it is expected that the relative will be selected. In the person-nature dimension, the view is that humans must accommodate nature and are not able to change events, in contrast to the White middle-class view that nature can and should be changed. Puerto Ricans feel that human nature is mixed and that whether an individual is good or bad is dependent upon supernatural forces. In the White middle class it is felt that basic human nature is neutral and can be changed.

The orientation of Hispanics to the family and values produces certain consequences. First, the family is valued over the individual. Second, divorce is much less acceptable and less often seen as an alternative to marital difficulties. Third, conflicts in values can occur between family members at different levels of acculturation. Fourth, life's misfortunes are seen as inevitable, and Hispanics often feel resigned to their fate.

Inclan (1985) presents the following case study in which knowledge of a family's value orientation was helpful in treating a problem.

◆ *Case Study*

During family therapy, a Puerto Rican mother indicated to her son, "You don't care for me anymore. You used to come by every Sunday and bring the children. You used to respect me and teach your children respect. Now you go out and work, you say, always doing this or that. I don't know what spirit (*que diablo*) has taken over you." (p. 332)

In response the son indicated that he was working hard and sacrificing for the children; that he wanted to be a success in the world and an individual that his children could be proud of. In examining the case, it is clear that the mother is expressing disappointment. She defines love as being with her, having the family gather together, and the subordination of individual desires for the family. The son has adopted a middle-class set of values stressing individual achievement, doing, and the future. The clash in value differences was at the root of the problem.

In working with the family, the therapist provided an alternative way of viewing the conflict instead of using terms such as right or wrong. He explained that our views are shaped by the values that we hold. He asked about the socialization process that the mother had undergone. She emphasized the "good old days" and the socialization and values of her childhood. The son indicated the pain he felt in losing the understanding of the parents, but he felt he had to change in order to succeed in the United States. The therapist pointed out that different adaptive styles may be necessary for different situations and what is right is dependent on the social context. Both of them began to acknowledge that they still loved one another but might have to show it in different ways. As a result of the sessions, the mother and son accepted one another and understood the nature of the original conflict.

FAMILY STRUCTURE

In 1994, about 71% of Hispanics had two married parents. Approximately 25% of Hispanic families have a female head of household (Gonzalez, 1997). Traditional Hispanic families are hierarchical in form with special authority given to the elderly, the parents, and males. Within the family, the father assumes the role of the primary authority figure. Sex roles are clearly delineated (Avila & Avila, 1995; Carillo, 1982; Green, Trankina, & Chavez, 1976; Mejia, 1983; Mizio, 1983). Children are expected to be obedient and are usually not consulted on family decisions. The sexual behaviors of adolescent females are severely restricted. Male children are afforded greater freedom to come and go as they please. Children are expected to contribute financially to the family when possible. Parents reciprocate by providing for them through young adulthood and even during marriage. This type of reciprocal relationship is a lifelong expectation (Mizio, 1983). Older children are expected to take care of and protect their younger siblings when away from home. The older sister may function as a surrogate mother. Adolescent children are expected to take responsibility at an early age. Even though they may be adolescents, many think of themselves and function as young adults. Marriage and parenthood are entered into early in life and are seen as stabilizing influences. Children are welcome and a source of pride. However, youthful marriages are vulnerable to dissolution (Vega, Hough, & Romero, 1985).

SEX-ROLE CONFLICTS

In working with Hispanic Americans, the counselor will often face problems dealing with conflicts over sex roles. In their traditional culture, men are expected to be strong, dominant, and the provider for the family, whereas women are expected to be nurturant, submissive to the male, and self-sacrificing. As head of the family, the male expects the members to be obedient to him. However, the following pattern of migration among Hispanics has produced strain and stress with this role expectation. The male leaves the family in search of work, leaving behind his wife and children. This forced separation often becomes permanent, with the wife becoming the head of the household. This change in family structure and exposure to the majority culture with differing sex-role expectations can produce problems. Areas in which males may have sex-role conflicts include (Avila & Avila, 1995; Carillo, 1982; Hildebrand et al., 1996):

1. *Submissiveness or assertion in the area of authority.* The Hispanic male may have difficulty interacting with agencies and individuals outside of the family and may feel that he is not fulfilling his role. In addition, changes involving greater responsibility of the wife and children may produce problems related to his authority.

2. *Feelings of isolation and depression because of the need to be strong.* Talking about or sharing views of problems with others may be seen as a sign of weakness. With the additional stress of living in a very different culture, the inability to discuss feelings of frustration and anxiety produces isolation.

3. *Conflicts over the need to be consistent in his role.* As ambiguity and stresses increase, the need to adjust and to seek security in a more rigid adherence to the role produces anxiety.

4. *Anxiety over questions of sexual potency.*

The traditional feminine role in the Hispanic family is to be submissive to the male, self-sacrificing, and restrained (Avila & Avila, 1995; Mejia, 1983; Mizio, 1983). For females, conflicts may involve (a) expectations to meet the requirements of her role, (b) anxiety when unable to live up to these standards, (c) depression over not being able to live up to these standards, and (d) the inability to act out her feelings of anger. Espin (1985) feels that Hispanic women are socialized to feel that they are inferior and that suffering and being a martyr are characteristics of a good woman. With greater exposure to the dominant culture, such views may be questioned. Certain roles may change more than others. For example, Espin indicates that some women are very modern in their views of education and employment, but remain traditional in the area of sexual behavior and personal relationships. Others remain very traditional in all areas. Other writers (Gonzalez, 1997; McCurdy & Ruiz, 1980; Ruiz, 1981) caution that Hispanic sex roles are not as inflexible and rigid as has often been described. For example, the concept of masculinity or *machismo* includes being a good provider. Egalitarian decision making appears to be increasing with later generations of Mexican Americans (Gonzalez, 1997). Also, many Hispanic women assert their influence indirectly and "behind the scenes," thus preserving the appearance of male control (Hayes, 1997).

The double standard is decreasing rapidly in the urban class. Part of the reason for the change is that many women are required to act independently in the work setting and to deal with schools and other agencies. In some cases, the woman may become the wage earner, which produces problems since this role traditionally belongs to the male. Conversely, as the wife becomes more independent, the husband may feel anxiety. Both may feel that the man is no longer fulfilling his role. The counselor must be able to help the family deal with the anxiety and suspiciousness associated with role change. For both males and females, role conflict is likely to occur if the male is unemployed, if the female is employed, or both. In addition, it may be easier for the female to obtain a job than for the male to do so. Since both feel that the male should be the provider for the family, an additional source of stress can occur.

In dealing with sex-role conflicts, the counselor faces a dilemma and potential value conflict. If the counselor believes in equal relationships, should he or she move the clients in this direction? Green, Trankina, & Chavez (1976) point out some of the aspects of the situation that have to be taken into consideration. "If clearly differentiated sex roles are accepted as desirable in the culture, too much deviance will obviously cause rejection. Counselors working with cultural mores different from their own must be particularly careful not to impose their views on the clients. Rather, they must try to help the client achieve change to the degree that the client seeks it but not to a degree that will cause alienation from the ethnic group" (p. 232).

Green and his colleagues make a valuable point in that the consequences of too much of a change might be seen as the individual's rejection of the ethnic group. The degree of change should be left to the client. The responsibility of the counselor is to let the client know the consequences of the change. For example, Espin (1985) cautions that in working with women, changes in their role may be perceived as threatening to their family. Any counselor who works to help a female client achieve more independence without apprising her of potential problems within her family and community is not fulfilling his/her obligations.

Espin points out that Hispanic culture allows a certain range of behaviors and that a Hispanic woman may place herself anywhere within this range. A determination should also be made to see if a specific behavior is a result of personal choice or adherence to norms. An error can be made by a counselor in interpreting behaviors as personal choice when they might be merely adherence to cultural norms. Behaviors that are being maintained only at the cost of high anxiety and frustration can be interpreted as a matter of personal choice and not due to cultural factors. If cultural norms are used to explain behavior, it is possible that other factors influencing the individual's life will not be explored. Appropriate reactions to norm violations may be interpreted as neurotic behavior. As Espin puts it, ". . . although there is a danger of being insensitive to cultural differences, there is also a danger of accepting as 'cultural' some behaviors or attitudes that might be self-defeating and damaging" (pp. 169–170). Therefore a careful assessment must be made to determine and distinguish between personal choice within a cultural context.

ACCULTURATION

To live in the Borderlands means you
are neither hispana india negra espanola
ni gabacha, eres mestiza, mulata, half-breed
caught in the crossfire between camps
while carrying all five races on your back
not knowing which side to turn to, run from . . .
To survive the Borderlands
you must live sin fronteras
be a crossroads.
  Gloria Anzaldua (1987)

At a school assembly composed mainly of Hispanic students, teachers asked who among them was Hispanic. Only a few raised their hands, and they looked uncertain and embarrassed. The teachers believed that this was an indication that the Hispanic culture that they loved was in danger of being forgotten and formed Amigas de la Cultura (Friends of Culture) to attempt to educate others about Hispanic customs (Bold, 1996).

♦ *Case Study*

A teenager, Mike, was having difficulty knowing who he was or what group he belonged with. His parents had given him an Anglo name to ensure his success in American society. They only spoke to him in English because they were fearful that he might have an accent. During his childhood, he felt estranged from his relatives. His grandparents, aunts, and uncles could speak only Spanish and so they were able to communicate only through nonverbal means. At school, he did not fit in with his African American peers and he also felt different from the Mexican American students who would ask him why he was unable to speak Spanish. The confusion over his ethnic identity was troublesome for him. He attempted to learn Spanish in college but was unable to do so. (Avila & Avila, 1995)

During middle school Hispanic children begin to have questions about their identity. Should they adhere to mainstream values? Few role models exist for Hispanic Americans. The representation of Hispanic Americans on television has actually decreased over the last 30 years. They account for only 2% of characters in 139 prime-time series. In depictions, they are more likely to behave criminally or be violent (Espinosa, 1997). The mixed heritage of many Hispanic Americans raises additional identity questions. If they are of Mexican/Indian heritage, should they call themselves "Mexican American," "Chicano," "Latino," or "Spanish American"? What about mixtures involving other racial backgrounds? An ethnic identity provides a sense of belonging and group membership. Many Hispanic youngsters undergo this process of searching for an identity. This struggle may be responsible for such problems as: (a) Mexican American adolescents report more depressive symptoms and conduct disorders than White youth; (b) small-town Mexican American youth have more severe and elevated rates of alcohol and drug abuse; and (c) suicidal behaviors are high in Hispanic female adolescents and Puerto Rican males (Roberts & Sobhan, 1992).

Ethnic identity issues should be recognized and incorporated within the school curriculum with modules on ethnicity, focusing on what it means to be Hispanic, Chicano, or Spanish speaking. Case studies of contributions made by different ethnic groups can be presented. Conflicts between mainstream values and ethnic group values can be discussed, and students can engage in brainstorming for methods to bridge the differences. Teaching styles can be altered to accommodate different cultural learning styles. It should be stressed that ethnic identity is part of the normal development process. In many cases, a bicultural perspective may be the most functional, since such a perspective does not involve the wholesale rejection of either culture (Galan, 1998; Gay, 1998).

Ponterotto (1987) found that the level of acculturation is related to variables such as dropout rate, experienced level of stress, and attitude toward counselors. The degree of acculturation can influence the types of problems that may be faced by Hispanic Americans, the way the problems are interpreted, and the appropriate process and goals in counseling. Hispanic Americans with minimal acculturation rarely present mental health issues to counselors and believe that counseling will take only one session (Gonzalez, 1997). Second-generation Hispanic Americans are usually bilingual, but often with only functional use of English. They are often exposed to Spanish at home and exposed to English in the school and on television. Second-generation Hispanic Americans are often marginal in both native and majority cultures. Acculturation also may influence perceptions of counseling and responses to counseling. Mexican Americans with a strong traditional orientation may have more difficulty being open and self-disclosing than those with a strong orientation toward the dominant culture (Gonzalez, 1997).

Women have more positive attitudes toward counseling and are more likely to self-disclose (Zimmerman & Sodowsky, 1993). A study has also found that acculturated Hispanic American wives were more likely to perceive themselves as equal partners in making decisions (O'Guinn, Imperia, & MacAdams, 1987). Because of this, the impact of the level of acculturation on the individual and the entire family (in family therapy) is an important consideration. However, Miranda and Umhoefer (1998) believe that a bicultural orientation may be the "healthiest" resolution. In their study, they found that both high- and low-acculturated Mexican Americans scored high on social dysfunction, alcohol consumption, and acculturative stress. Bicultural individuals appeared to fare much better because of an ability to accept and negotiate aspects of both cultures.

Because knowledge of acculturation level is important, a variety of acculturation measures have been developed. One formal assessment measure is the Acculturation Rating Scale for Mexican Americans (Cuellar, Harris, & Jasso, 1980). Scores on this 20-item questionnaire allow categorizing on a five-point scale: "Very Mexican," "Bicultural, Mexican oriented," "True Bicultural," "Bicultural, Anglo oriented," and "Very Anglicized." Measures of acculturation also exist for Puerto Ricans (Inclan, 1979) and Cubans (Szapocznik, Scopetta, Kurtines, & Aranalde, 1978). If the counselor feels uncomfortable using a formal measure, it is also possible to inquire about the specific Hispanic group that they are from, length of time in the country or generational status, primary language, religious orientation and strength of religious beliefs, whether they live in a barrio, the reason for immigration (if immigrants), if they are in an extended family situation, and other information related to acculturation (Dominguez-Ybarra & Garrison, 1977; Juarez, 1985). However, it must be remembered that acculturation is often not a straightforward process. On values such as family solidarity, ethnic identification, religious orientation, and sex roles, a single individual might score very traditional in some areas and more Anglicized in others. What this means is that even though acculturation information is helpful, it is the responsibility of the counselor to examine individual patterns of acculturation and to develop individual counseling plans. The danger exists that acculturation measures will be given and that the client will be seen in a stereotypic manner. Cultural information is important in alerting the counselor to possible issues and conflicts. As with any client, information can be obtained that assists in the conceptualization of problems. However, an individual treatment plan must be developed on the basis of all information available.

CLIENT PROBLEMS

Mrs. Lopez, age 70, and her 30-year-old daughter, sought counseling because they had a very conflictual relationship . . . the mother was not accustomed to a counseling format. . . . At a pivotal point in one session, she found talking about emotional themes overwhelming and embarrass-

ing. . . . In order to reengage her, the counselor asked what resources she used when she and her daughter quarreled. She . . . prayed to Our Lady of Guadalupe. (Zuniga, 1997, p. 149)

The counselor used a culturally adapted strategy of having Mrs. Lopez use prayer to understand her daughter and to find solutions for the counseling sessions. This format allowed Mrs. Lopez to discuss spiritual guidance and possible solutions to the problem. The use of a cultural perspective allowed the sessions to continue.

It is important to remember that many of the problems of Hispanic Americans are from external sources. Because the majority are poor, they often suffer stresses attributable to inadequate food and shelter or from dealing with bureaucracies and unemployment (De La Cancela, 1985; Vazquez, 1997). LeVine and Padilla (1980) point out that symptoms of stress displayed by Hispanics to external factors are often similar to those caused by personal conflicts. "If extrapsychic conflict is predominant, therapy aimed at social action and the alleviation of discrimination and poverty may be appropriate. If intrapsychic conflict is more basic, introspective or behavioral therapy is the treatment of choice" (p. 256). Careful assessment of the source of emotional disturbance is necessary before appropriate action can be taken, and this should be done very early in the counseling session. For example, Ruiz (1981) presents the case of a married migrant worker in his mid-50s who comes into therapy complaining of hearing threatening voices. He refuses to leave his home because of anxiety. In working with many Hispanics, Ruiz recommends an analysis of external causes first. In this case, it is suggested that the worker undergo a complete physical with special attention to exposure to pesticides and other agricultural chemicals that might result in mental symptoms. It is also possible that the feelings of fear displayed by the individual stem from factors such as suspiciousness of outside authorities, fear of deportation of self or others in the family, or recent encounters with creditors. External factors that are specific to the experience of Hispanic Americans must first be examined.

Recent immigrants often have feelings of estrangement and displacement in the United States due to culture conflict and disruption of the extended family. For example, Cuban elders expected that they would be accorded a high status later in life and be the ultimate authority in the family. This expectation has not been met. Instead, they are often considered to be burdens to the family, resulting in feelings of isolation and depression (Szapocznik, et al., 1982). Intergenerational conflicts due to differences in rates of acculturation are common. *Vergzsenza* (shame) is a common problem among Mexican Americans and is evident during the initial process of acculturation. Dominguez-Ybarra and Garrison (1977) feel that it is important to provide a link with Mexican values in working with these clients and to help them understand the conflict as a function of differences between Mexican and Anglo values. However, Green, Trankina, and Chavez (1976) indicate that in working with an *agringado* (acculturated Mexican American) the counselor should not attempt to reinstate traditional values but rather should indicate potential areas of conflict and the consequences of their stance. LeVine and Padilla (1980) feel that the pressures in acculturation versus the pressures to remain ethnically loyal are common in Hispanics. They recommend that a determination be made with the client in terms of how much acculturation or separation from the dominant culture will produce personal growth.

COUNSELING CONSIDERATIONS, STRATEGIES, AND MODALITIES

ASSESSMENT

Sandra G. is a 24-year-old female college student. . . . She identified herself as "Mexican" although she has lived in this country for about 11 years. . . . She reported a very negative experience in adjusting to life in this country . . . especially in the area of friendships with U.S. born Chicanos or Mexican American (whom she considered to be sexist). . . . Sandra sought treatment . . . for several issues, including chronic depression, anxiety, low self-esteem and a "combative relationship" with her boyfriend. . . . She had no history of mental illness . . . and displayed no symptoms of psychosis. (Valasquez et al., 1997, pp. 115–116)

During the counseling sessions, Sandra would use Spanish when discussing issues that involved emotional content. Because she used English primarily, the MMPI-2, English version, was given to her. Her profile appeared valid and showed peaks on schizophrenia, psychasthenia, and paranoia. Such a profile might result in neuroleptic medication or hospitalization. However, this pattern did not seem indicative of the mental status of the client and so the Spanish version of the MMPI-2 was given. The new profile indicated maladjustments more suggestive of dysthymia (depression) and personality disorder, which had a better fit with the clinical impressions. She was successfully treated with cognitive and interpersonally based therapies. It appears that in choosing between the English and Spanish versions of the MMPI-2 for bilingual clients, the selection should be based upon the language employed for emotional issues. Assessments should always be interpreted within a sociocultural context and be supported by additional data.

SOCIOCULTURAL ISSUES

Because many Hispanics suffer from factors beyond their control such as prejudice, discrimination, and poverty, some professionals have argued for social change. Rivera (1984) argues that the goal in working with Puerto Rican patients should be to help them become more aware of the oppression they face and to attain personal and collective liberation. Espin (1985) feels that oppression also exists against women in the Hispanic culture and that the counselor should help women empower themselves. Ponterotto (1987) and Vazquez (1997) believe that an important part of counseling Hispanics is the consideration of psychosocial, economic, and political needs of the clients.

In working with traditional Hispanics, the most appropriate counselor would be bilingual and bicultural. Unfortunately, there are few therapists who fit this description. It is important that the counselor be knowledgeable and understanding of both minority and majority cultural values and beliefs. Objectivity and the ability to integrate the different value systems as they relate to the problems presented by the client are critical. Because of the lack of bilingual counselors, problems in communication occur with Hispanic clients who are not conversant in English. For example, Marcos (1973) found that Mexican American patients were seen as suffering from greater psychopathology when interviewed in English than when interviewed in Spanish. However, interpreters may present difficulties themselves in the counseling process. They are often responsible for distortions in communication. Personal relationships may also develop between the interpreter and the client. In one case, a client offered to care for the translator's child (Cooper & Costas, 1994). Marcos (1979) found that distortions may result from

(a) the interpreter's language competence and translation skills, (b) the interpreter's lack of psychiatric knowledge, and (c) the attitudes of the counselor. For example, relatives used as interpreters often answer the questions put to the client without waiting for a response. The following example occurred in an actual exchange:

CLINICIAN (To Spanish-speaking Patient):   What about worries, do you have many worries?
INTERPRETER (To PATIENT):   Is there anything that bothers you?
PATIENT: I know, I know that God is with me, I'm not afraid. They cannot get me [pause].
    I'm wearing these new pants and I feel protected. I feel good, I don't get headaches anymore.
INTERPRETER (To CLINICIAN):   He says he is not afraid, he feels good, he doesn't have
    headaches anymore. (Marcos, 1979, p. 173)

To reduce some of these errors, Marcos (1979) and Cooper and Costas (1994) recommend that the mental health professional meet with the interpreter to discuss goals, areas to be assessed, and possible sensitive areas that may need to be explored. The language proficiency of the interpreter should also be assessed. It might also be helpful to have as part of the team an indigenous worker who is knowledgeable about the community and can provide help in contacting social service agencies or assistance when this is needed in working with a client.

In developing treatment strategies it is important to consider the expectation of the clients. Traditional Hispanic Americans are accustomed to being treated by physicians. They are unclear as to the purpose of counseling and may expect medication, a quick solution to their problem, and advice as to what to do (Acosta & Evans, 1982; Gonzalez, 1997). To increase the "fit" between expectations and techniques, the counselor should (a) carefully explain the difference between the physician and the counselor, (b) indicate the role of the counselor and client in counseling, (c) discuss the goals for counseling, and (d) select techniques that are appropriate to the cultural norms of Hispanics.

Most mental health professionals (Casas & Vasquez, 1996; De La Cancela, 1985; Juarez, 1985; Ponterotto, 1987; Ruiz & Casas, 1981; Yamamoto & Acosta, 1982) feel that techniques should be employed that are active, concrete, and problem solving in their orientation. Juarez feels that behavior therapy has these characteristics and fits client expectations of direct intervention and guidance to change behaviors. Specific tasks are assigned and counselors take a very active and directive role. Other advantages are a focus on the impact of the environment on behavior and a here-and-now emphasis. Ponterotto also feels that these procedures and methods of treatment and goal selection work well with Hispanics. Boulette (1976) found that behavioral approaches such as assertiveness training are more effective for Mexican American women than nondirective therapy. Montijo (1985) feels that a cognitive behavioral approach would be effective with Puerto Ricans in raising self-esteem by eliminating self-defeating thoughts and promoting more accurate perceptions of the environment. In terms of length, Yamamoto and Acosta recommend short-term therapy lasting four to five sessions.

Because of the importance of the extended family and the relationships among its members, family therapy is often recommended in working with Hispanics. This is especially important since changes in the client in an individual session may have profound effects on the family (De La Cancela, 1985; Padilla & DeSnyder, 1985). Structural family approaches are useful, since the hierarchical structure is considered along with the impact of socioeconomic and cultural factors. This approach has been used effectively with Puerto Rican families (Canino & Canino, 1982).

COUNSELING CHILDREN AND ADOLESCENTS

In family therapy, it is important to determine the degree of hierarchical structure that exists and to work within that framework. Often the conflicts among family members involve differences in acculturation. In less acculturated families, Paniagua (1994) recommends interviewing the father for a few minutes during the beginning of the first session. This would show a recognition of the father's authority and indicate that the counselor is sensitive to cultural factors in counseling. In a more acculturated family, the father could still be addressed first and then the mother and the children. It also must be remembered that in traditionally oriented Hispanic American families, there is less importance placed on shared interests and joint activities between husband and wife, although a great deal of socialization occurs during social events involving families and friends (Negy & Woods, 1992). Szapocznik and Kurtines (1993) recommend that acculturation play the role of the "identified patient" and solutions be obtained that involve the reframing and negotiation of the conflicting cultural norms and values.

Counselors working with Hispanic students must determine whether a complaint is real or imagined. For example, if a student feels that he/she is encountering prejudice, intervention will depend on the reality of the complaint. If it is real, several steps may be taken. The source of the prejudice can be directly confronted and/or the individual can learn to respond appropriately when treated unfairly. If, however, the student is in fact troubled by feelings of inferiority and the prejudice is only imagined, a cognitive behavior approach to correct perceptions would be appropriate. The same type of determination has to be made for all complaints.

Relationship problems with family members are often presented. In working with the child or adolescent, it must be remembered that attempts to deal with the problem can produce additional problems in the family. In this situation, the use of family therapy would be a possibility. In a case that Ruiz and Casas (1981) present, a student stated, "My father never asks me for help around the home . . . but expects me to be around every weekend in case there's something to be done. He doesn't understand that studying is a full-time job" (pp. 197–198). Assertiveness training was employed but modified in that it was performed to present the student's view in a manner that did not show disrespect. The son stated that he was willing to help but needed advance notice because of school obligations. This was practiced in a manner that would show no disrespect to the father. There was no attempt to state personal desires in all areas. Assertiveness training should emphasize the importance of situational assertiveness to the student, indicating that it might be appropriate to be assertive in a classroom or on job interviews but that it may not be necessary to do so with parents.

Cuento (folklore therapy), an interesting program that involved a culturally sensitive approach, was used in working with at-risk Puerto Rican children (Rogler et al., 1987). The program attempted to reduce the stress and anxiety felt by second-generation Hispanic children who were marginal to both cultures. The *cuento* involved reading folktales to the children. The stories were then discussed in terms of cultural values and the specific ways that the characters encountered and solved problems. It was hoped that pride in culture as well as developing means of dealing with the environment would occur. To develop this second aspect, children were asked to role-play the various characters in the story and to role-play positive solutions to the situations faced. In another group, the same procedures were involved. However, an additional feature was present in that adapted folktales were used. The cultural values remained the same, but contemporary situations were presented. The setting of the stories approximated the actual environment that the children lived in, and the types of problems presented were urban in nature. Again, the values and problems were discussed and the children role-played solutions. Both of these groups produced greater reduction in anxiety in the children than did traditional group therapy or a no-treatment control. The most effective group involved the adapted story. This approach appears promising, since cultural values are maintained and stressed, and children learn to develop adaptable behaviors in stressful situations.

INITIAL INTERVIEWS

Several writers (Padilla & DeSnyder, 1985; Paniagua, 1994; Ruiz, 1995; Velasquez et al., 1997; Yamamoto & Acosta, 1982) have made suggestions as to how to conduct the initial session with Hispanic Americans.

1. It is important to engage in a respectful, warm, and mutual introduction with the client. Be sure to pronounce the client's name correctly. It is difficult to establish rapport when the client winces every time you say his or her name. With less acculturated Hispanic Americans a more formal relationship is expected. The counselor will be seen as an authority figure and should be formally dressed.

2. Give a brief description of what counseling is and the role of each participant. Less acculturated Hispanic Americans often expect medication and to meet for only one or two sessions. Also explain the notion of confidentiality. Even immigrants with legal status have inquired about whether the information shared during counseling would "end up in the hands of the Border Patrol or other immigration authorities" (Velasquez et al., 1997, p. 112). Immigrant families may also be uncertain about the limits of confidentiality, especially as it applies to child abuse or neglect issues. Physical discipline is used more often in Hispanic families (this is also the case for lower-class Whites) than in middle-class White families. They may be fearful about how their child-rearing practices will be perceived. Many of them also live in poverty. Furnishing clothing and sometimes even food may be a problem for these families, and they may be concerned that their difficulties in these areas might be viewed as neglect. In fact, these concerns may be legitimate. Gray and Cosgrove (1985) found that culturally normative practices such as having infants and small children cared for by younger siblings and parents calling their children by names based on physical attributes could be considered to be neglect or emotionally harmful by child protective services.

3. Have the client state in his/her own words the problem or problems as he/she sees it. How is it dysfunctional? Are there cultural or societal aspects to the problem? What is the impact of racism, poverty, and acculturative stress on the problem? Conflicts with acculturation and ethnic identity are common. Determine whether there a need for a formal assessment and select culturally appropriate materials. Determine whether a translator is needed. Be careful not to interpret slow speech or long silences as indicators of depression or cognitive dysfunction. The individual may just have problems with English.

4. Determine the positive assets and resources available to the client and his/her family. Have they, other family members, or friends dealt with similar problems? How was a successful outcome defined? Use paraphrasing to summarize the problem as you understand it and make sure that the client knows you understand it.

5. Help the clients prioritize the problems and determine what they perceive as the important goals. What are their expectations? How will they know when the goals have been achieved?

6. Discuss possible consequences of achieving the goals for the individual, family, and community.

7. Discuss the possible participation of family members and consider family therapy. Within the family, determine the hierarchical structure as well as the degree of acculturation of the different members. Focus on the problems produced by conflicting values.

8. Assess possible problems from external sources, such as need for food, shelter, or employment, or stressful interactions with agencies. Provide necessary assistance in developing and maintaining environmental supports.

9. Explain the treatment to be used, why it was selected, and how it will help achieve the goals.

10. With the client's input, determine a mutually agreeable length of treatment.

11. *Personalismo* is a basic cultural value of Hispanic Americans. Although the first meetings may be quite formal, once trust has developed, the clients may develop a close personal bond with the counselor. He or she may be perceived as a family member or friend and invited to family functions and given gifts. These behaviors are not evidence of dependency or a lack of boundaries.

CONCLUSION

In working with Hispanic populations, it must be remembered that there are large between- and within-group differences in terms of values, acculturation level, and problems faced. These differences must be examined before counseling can proceed. Although this information is vital, it can also be misused if generalizations are made in a stereotypic fashion. Background information provides the counselor only with potential issues and problems faced by the client. An individual treatment plan must be developed. With Hispanics and other minority group members, the assessment of possible environmental factors is critical. Problems presented in response to the stresses of poverty, poor housing, lack of facility with English, and dealing with agencies often produce symptoms that are similar to those produced by intrapsychic conflicts. The more traditional the Hispanic, the more likely the necessity for treatment strategies that are concrete, goal oriented, and structured. Family and group therapy are other useful modalities. In considering goals, it is important to consider and discuss with the client the consequences of changes on the individual, his/her family, and the relationship with his/her cultural group.

Chapter 15

◆

Counseling Gays and Lesbians, Women, the Elderly, and Persons with Disabilities

---
◆

In this chapter, we will consider four other groups who have experienced systematic marginalization and oppression by the dominant culture. The groups include gay men and lesbian women, elderly persons, women, and individuals with disabilities. All of these groups have been impacted by negative stereotypes and have been devalued, often resulting in lower self-esteem and a negative view of the self. An individual may belong to several of these groups and suffer from multiple layers of discrimination (Atkinson & Hackett, 1998). The four groups were selected for discussion in this chapter because they have received the most interest from the American Psychological Association and the American Counseling Association (Hayes, 1996).

We are aware that there is some controversy over the inclusion of factors other than race/ethnicity in discussions of multiculturalism and multicultural counseling and psychotherapy. Some believe that MCT should include only racial/ethnic minority groups. Proponents of this position point out that multiculturalism can become diluted to the point of uselessness if expanded to include more than race and ethnicity. This warning is well taken, for consideration of other factors can be used to divert attention away from matters related to racism. Helms (1994) warns that broad definitions of multiculturalism obscure and ignore race, that this may be done intentionally or unintentionally; such definitions allow White people to avoid dealing with their own biases, and they continue to perpetuate misinformation in the professional literature. Despite the legitimacy of this position, we have chosen to include other oppressed groups for several reasons.

First, the sociopolitical dynamics related to the treatment of marginalized or oppressed groups in our society share many similarities. Prejudice, stereotyping, and discrimination and their negative effects on these groups operate from a common foundation with frightening effects. Second, we accept the definition of multicultural counseling and therapy as proposed by Sue et al. (1998):

Multicultural counseling and therapy (MCT) is a metatheoretical approach that (a) recognizes that all modes and theories of helping arise from a particular cultural context; (b) refers specifi-

cally to a helping relationship in which two or more of the participants are of different cultural backgrounds; (c) includes any counseling combination that fulfills the definition of "culture"; (d) recognizes the use of both Western and non-Western approaches to helping; and (e) is characterized by the helping professional's culturally appropriate awareness, knowledge, and skills. . . . (p. 12–13)

We accept the notion that individuals of certain sexual orientations and some physically challenged individuals (e.g., the deaf) can legitimately claim to be culturally distinct. Third, in order to prevent misunderstanding and invalidation due to an overinclusive definition, we try to clearly distinguish between the types of diversity we refer to (i.e., race, sexual orientation, gender, age). Last, it is our position that truly understanding oppression from the perspective of one group should allow us to relate better to other culturally different groups. It should allow us to build bridges of mutual understanding rather than create divisiveness, jealousy, and separation. If the latter happens, then we have become caught up in a societal divide and conquer dynamic. It is our conviction that all forms of oppression are detrimental and that playing the "who's more oppressed?" game is counterproductive to all.

COUNSELING GAY MEN AND LESBIAN WOMEN

Pat Robertson, a religious broadcaster, warned that hurricanes, tornadoes, or even a meteor might strike Orlando because of the "Gay Days" event that was held there. "I don't think I'd be waving those flags in God's face if I were you." ("Robertson warns," 1998, p. 1)

Mathew Shepard, a gay student attending the University of Wyoming, died five days after being savagely beaten and tied to a split rail fence. At his funeral service, a dozen protesters held up anti-gay signs such as "God Hates Fags." ("Mourners gather," 1998)

Homosexuality involves the affectional and/or sexual orientation to a person of the same sex. In self-definitions, most males prefer the term gay to homosexual and most females prefer the term lesbian. It is estimated that approximately 4% to 10% of the U.S. population are homosexual (Norton, 1995). According to the National Gay and Lesbian Task Force, during the past 20 years there has been increasing support for equal rights in employment, housing, and the military. Disapproval of homosexuality has dropped from 75% in the mid-1980s to about 56% in 1996. In New Jersey, two gay men were awarded custody of a 3-year-old boy after a 2-year effort. They successfully challenged the state law that did not allow adoption by same-sex couples (Smothers, 1998).

Even with progress occurring on these fronts, discrimination and violence against this population remains high. Gay men and lesbians still constitute one of the least liked groups in the country (Goldberg, 1998). In the city of Los Angeles in 1994, there were 332 reported incidents of hate crimes ranging from harassment to murder directed at gay men and lesbians, a 53% increase from the previous year (Boxall, 1995). Gay-bashing is hard to understand and is often described as an extreme homophobic reaction. One victim, Arthur Dong, responded: "I was stunned. I was never attacked as an Asian man, and I'm obviously an Asian man. . . . But I was attacked as a gay man. . . . Why do people do this?" (Graham, 1997, p. D11)

Dong was so disturbed by this that he produced *License to Kill,* an award-winning film that showed interviews with six men explaining why they had murdered gay men. One of the cases involved a man who had murdered two gay men. He was raised in a strict, religious household where his father denounced homosexuality. Jay Johnson, the killer, was himself gay.

Gay and lesbian youths also face discrimination and harassment in schools. In a study of Massachusetts high school students (Massachusetts Youth Risk Behavior Survey Results, 1995), gay, lesbian, and bisexual students were more likely than their peers to be confronted with a weapon at school (66.7% versus 28.8%), or not attend school because of safety concerns (20.1% versus 4.5%). In addition, they were over four times more likely to have attempted suicide during the past year than their heterosexual-identified counterparts (36.5% versus 8.9%).

Although the American Psychiatric Association and the American Psychological Association no longer consider homosexuality to be a mental disorder, some individuals still harbor the belief that it is. Trent Lott, the Senate majority leader, recently described homosexuality as a disorder akin to alcoholism, kleptomania, and sexual addiction—a condition that should be treated (Mitchell, 1998). The American Psychiatric Association first voted in 1973 to remove homosexuality from the *Diagnostic and Statistical Manual* (*DSM*). However, it did create a new category, ego-dystonic homosexuality in *DSM-III* (1980) for individuals with: (a) a lack of heterosexual arousal that interferes with heterosexual relationships and (b) persistent distress from unwanted homosexual arousal. This category was eliminated in the face of the argument that societal pressure and prejudice created the condition.

The American Psychological Association took an even stronger stand and adopted a official policy statement that "Homosexuality per se implies no impairment in judgement, stability, reliability or general social or vocational capabilities" and indicated that mental health professionals should take the lead in removing the stigma of mental illness that has long been associated with homosexual orientations (Conger, 1975). A number of studies (Berube, 1990; Gonsiorek, 1982; Hooker, 1957; Reiss, 1980) have demonstrated few adjustment differences between individuals with a homosexual or heterosexual orientation. As one researcher, Gonsiorek, concluded: "Homosexuality in and of itself is unrelated to psychological disturbance or maladjustment. Homosexuals as a group are not more psychologically disturbed on account of their homosexuality" (p. 74).

The intimate relationships of gay and lesbian couples appear to be similar to those of heterosexual individuals. Among lesbian couples, there is a more egalitarian relationship. Household chores and decision making are equally shared. Their children show healthy cognitive and behavioral functioning. It has been concluded that traditional family structures are not necessary for healthy child development (Strickland, 1995).

Unfortunately, counselors who work with gay men and lesbian women often display societal prejudices or are uninformed about issues associated with this population. Liddle (1996) summarized the reports of 392 lesbian women and gay men who reported their experiences with 923 therapists. Gay and lesbian therapists, bisexual therapists of both genders, and heterosexual female therapists were all rated more helpful than heterosexual male therapists (although 30% of heterosexual males were rated very helpful). Issues that were identified as important to the client included: (a) understanding the effects of societal prejudice on development and health; (b) recognizing and dealing with the issue of internalized homophobia; (c) assisting the client in developing a positive gay or lesbian identity; and (d) being aware of community resources. However, they warn that counselors should not focus on sexual orientation if it is not a present issue.

Garnets, Hancock, Cochran, Goodchilds, and Peplau, (1998) also conducted a survey of instances of biased or beneficial responses that therapists heard of or "knew" of from other therapists or clients in counseling gay or lesbian clients. The following biased or inappropriate practices were reported:

1. Belief that homosexuality is a form of mental illness. Some therapists continue to believe that homosexuality represents a personality or other disorder and is not just a different lifestyle.

2. Attributing a client's problem to sexual orientation without evidence that this is the case.

3. Failure to understand that a client's problem, such as depression or low self-esteem, can be a result of the internalization of society's view of homosexuality.

4. Assuming that the client is heterosexual, thereby making it harder to bring up issues regarding sexual orientation.

5. Focusing on sexual orientation when it is not relevant. Problems may be completely unrelated to sexual orientation, but some therapists continue to focus on it as the major contributor to all presented problems.

6. Attempting to have clients renunciate or change their sexual orientation. For example, a lesbian was asked by the therapist to date men.

7. Trivializing or demeaning homosexuality. A therapist responded to a lesbian who brought up that she was "into women" that he didn't care, since he had a client who was "into dogs."

8. Transferring clients to another therapist without dealing with the emotional aspects of the change.

9. Lacking an understanding of identity development in lesbian women and gay men or viewing homosexuality solely as sexual activity.

10. Not understanding the impact of possible internalized negative societal pressures or homophobia on identity development.

11. Underestimating the consequences of "coming out" for the client. Such suggestion should be provided only after a careful discussion of the pros and cons of this disclosure.

12. Misunderstanding or underestimating the importance of intimate relationships for gay men and lesbians. One therapist reportedly advised a lesbian couple who were having problems in their relationship to not consider it a permanent relationship and consider going to a gay bar to meet others.

13. Using the heterosexual framework inappropriately when working with lesbian and gay male relationships. One couple was given a book to read dealing with heterosexual relationships.

14. Presuming that clients with a different sexual orientation cannot be good parents and automatically assuming that their children's problems are a result of the orientation.

15. Insensitivity to the degree of prejudice and discrimination faced by lesbians and gay males and their children.

16. Displaying inaccurate or insufficient information about gay and lesbian issues.

PROBLEMS FACED BY LESBIAN WOMEN AND GAY MEN

Losses

The discovery that one's sexual orientation is different from that accepted by society can produce a profound feeling of loss. One woman who discovered her sexual orientation after 25 years of marriage writes:

Several years ago my husband and I attended the 50th birthday for one of our oldest friends. Everyone was sharing anecdotes about the guest of honor, Jeff, as he stood arm in arm with his wife, Sherry. She looked at him lovingly: Suddenly my eyes filled with tears and I fled the room . . . during my 25th year of marriage, I fell in love with my best friend. . . . My confession to her destroyed our friendship. . . . My tears were for . . . the isolation my silence condemned me to, my internalized homosexuality. (Strock, 1998, p. 16)

For this individual, the heterosexual ideal of a "picture perfect" relationship was lost forever. Gay men and lesbian women, after realizing their sexual orientation, may feel isolated from their families and friends who adhere to the heterosexual standard. Many no longer feel welcome in churches and are concerned about having their orientation discovered in the workplace (Ritter & O'Neill, 1989). The counselor must help the client discover new sources of support.

Identity Issues

The slow discovery of being different is agonizing. As one individual observed, "Imagine learning about love and sexuality in a heterosexual world when your preference is for people of the same gender" (Parker & Thompson, 1990). Awareness of the sexual orientation of gay males and lesbian females tends to occur in the early teens with the first sexual relationship occurring in middle to late teens. Acknowledgment of their sexual identity generally happens by the early 20s. Disclosure to parents tends to occur by the age of 30, although even at that age, over half had not disclosed (Norton, 1995). The struggle for identity involves one's internal perceptions, in contrast to the external perceptions or assumptions of others about your sexual orientation. The individual must learn to accept their internal identity, often struggling with the society's definition of what is "healthy." To come to an appropriate resolution, the individual ceases struggling to be "straight" and begins to establish a new identity and self-concept and understanding of what constitutes a good life. Often during this period of time, issues of grief over letting go of the old identity must be dealt with (Browning, Reynolds, & Dworkin, 1998; Parker & Thompson, 1990).

Coming Out

The decision to "come out" is extremely difficult and is often influenced by the overwhelming sense of isolation the individual feels. In maintaining the secret, relationships with friends and family may be seriously affected. Coming out is especially difficult for adolescents who are emotionally and financially dependent on their family. They have less access to appropriate role models and to support systems in the gay and lesbian community (Browning, Reynolds, & Dworkin, 1998). Coming out to parents and friends can lead to rejection, anger, and grief. Most recipients of the information will also experience grief at the loss of the individual they thought they knew. Parents may feel a loss for their children in terms of the picture that society has painted of appropriate relationships. They may be concerned about their parenting as the cause of the sexual orientation (Shannon & Woods, 1998).

The decision of when to come out should be carefully considered. To whom does the individual want to reveal the information? What are the possible effects and consequences of the self-disclosure for the individual and the recipient of the information? What new sources of support among family, friends, or community are available for them? If the individual is already in a relationship, how will the disclosure affect his/her partner? Have they also considered the consequences? If the individual has considered the implications of coming out and still desires to do so, the counselor should offer specific help and preparation in determining how this should be accomplished. Role-plays and the discussion of possible reactions should be practiced (Murphy, 1989). If parents are open, counseling sessions would be helpful for them in dealing with their feelings of loss involving past goals for their children, weddings, grandchildren, and feelings of guilt. They will have to deal with the stigma of having a homosexual family member and may benefit from receiving information and education regarding myths and stereotypes of homosexuality (Coleman & Ramafedi, 1989). If the parents are rejecting, the individual must strengthen other sources of social support.

HELPFUL PRACTICES FOR GAY MEN AND LESBIAN WOMEN

Lesbian women and gay men have identified certain practices by counselors as helpful (Garnets et al., 1998).

- Helping the client work through societal biases and toward an understanding that gay men and lesbian women can have long-lasting relationships. Having materials available that portray healthy and satisfying homosexual relationships can be helpful.
- Addressing possible societal issues and their role in the problems faced by lesbians and gay men.
- Assessing all factors in the problems presented by lesbian women and gay men so as not to pay an inordinate amount of attention to sexual orientation.
- Helping the client deal with internalized homophobia and establish a new affirming identity.
- Identifying and utilizing community resources and support groups, including religious organizations.

COUNSELING ELDERLY CLIENTS

We are an ageist society where the young are valued much more than the old; youth is glorified and older people are seen as incompetent, inflexible, wedded to the past, desexed, uncreative, poor, sick, and slow." (Dychtwald, 1989, p. 26)

Loyd Botimer, 103, walked in carrying the medal he had won in the javelin throw in the Senior Olympics three years ago. Essie Brown, 105, who wore a blue dress and heels, let it be known she was looking for a dance partner. And 101-year-old Lenore Schaeffer brought news clippings attesting to her fame as a ballroom-dancing centenarian ("No longer a rarity," 1998, p. A1)

The older population in the United States is growing. The increase in the number of the elderly (those aged 65 and more) has exceeded the growth rate of the population as a whole. In 1994, the elderly population included 29.8 million Euro-Americans, 2.7 million African Americans, 1.5 million Hispanic Americans, 615,000 Asian Americans and Pacific Islanders, and 137,000 American Indians/Alaskan Natives. It increased from 3 million in 1900 to 33 million in 1994. By the year 2030, those over 65 years of age will constitute 20% of the population. Those 85 years and older are the fastest growing part of the elderly population, and this trend will continue into the next century. Because females live longer than males, at age 65, there are only 39 elderly men for every hundred women. This ratio increases with increasing age (U.S. Census Bureau, 1995).

As with other minority groups, elderly individuals are subject to negative stereotypes and discrimination. The media described 54-year-old Mick Jagger of the Rolling Stones as "defying nature" during a recent concert; a 16-year-old commented, "I honestly thought, you know, all those grandads looking disgusting up there, but they bowled me over" (Currie, 1997, p. 7115).

Ageism has been defined as negative attitudes toward the process of aging or elderly people (Doty, 1987). In a review of attitudes towards older individuals, Atkinson and Hackett (1998) found that elderly persons are considered to be rigid and not adaptable in their thought processes; they are thought to be in poor health and not very intelligent or alert; sexual interest or activity is not thought to be appropriate for this population; negative attitudes toward elderly persons were present in college students; many medical staff members feel uncomfortable around elderly patients; and jokes about old age abound and are primarily negative in nature. These negative stereotypes lead to elderly people's being viewed as less valued members of society. Older women are even more likely to be viewed negatively by society as a whole. Elderly individuals may come to accept these views and suffer a loss of self-esteem. In fact, they also believe that they will suffer mental decline. When a group of older individuals were asked if they felt that there was a strong possibility that they would become senile, 90% responded affirmatively (Grant, 1996).

Our visual entertainment, news, and advertising media are dominated by youth, with few exceptions. Information about older people often comes from youthful interviewers who do not have the appropriate perspective for the experiences of the older generation. One exception is Donald M. Murray, 73 years old, a Boston columnist who covers issues of age and some of its positive aspects. In his column, he often corrects the misperceptions of the young about older adults.

I am not elderly, I am old and proud of it. I am aged, like a good cheese. I am a walking history book, an elder of the tribe, tested, tempered, wise. . . . I can leave parties early. . . . I enjoy melancholy, even revel in it. . . . (Frankel, 1998, p. 16)

We are an aging society, yet poorly prepared to handle our currently aged population and certainly not equipped for the coming baby boomer generation (Ponzo, 1992). The elderly population is underserved and little understood. Few resources have been devoted to determine their needs. In a review, Kim and Atkinson (1998) noted that few training programs in counseling deal with older populations. In fact, the topic of sexuality and the aging process appears to be given even less consideration now than it was 10 years ago. Underlying this neglect is the belief that sexuality should not be considered in the aged. One physician notes:

I recently worked in an infectious disease clinic where I met a patient in her late 60s who was infected with the human immunodeficiency virus (HIV). My surprise at seeing an older woman with HIV, an infection associated with unprotected sex or injecting drug use, made me realize I had preconceptions about aging and the elderly . . . my attitudes could be construed as sexist in nature. (McCray, 1998, p. 1035–1036)

Information is lacking on therapies and medications for older individuals. As a group, they are less likely to receive new treatments for heart attacks or other illnesses, and elderly women are less likely to receive radiation and chemotherapy after breast cancer surgery. This is surprising, since a healthy 70-year-old individual can be expected to live at least 10 years more (People's Medical Society, 1998).

PROBLEMS OF THE ELDERLY PERSON

Physical and Economic Health

There is a major difference between the "young-old" and the "old-old." Most older individuals are able to live independent lives and require only minimal assistance. Only 5% of people 65 and over live in nursing homes; this increases to only 22% by age 85 (Heller, 1998). Approximately 9% of those between the ages of 65 and 69 require personal assistance for daily activities; at the age of 85 and over, about 50% require assistance. In all age categories, women are more likely to need assistance than men (U.S. Bureau of the Census, 1995).

The rate of poverty for elderly individuals has been decreasing, from 25% in 1970 to 13% in 1992. However, economic difficulties remain for many older individuals, especially women and minority members. Elderly women are more likely to be poor than elderly men (16% versus 9%). Among elderly minority group members, rates of poverty for African Americans were 27% for men and 38% for women; for Hispanic Americans, 27% for men and 25% for women (U.S. Bureau of the Census, 1995).

Mental Health

There is a perception that rates of mental illness are high among elderly persons. This may be due to observation of the small number of mentally ill adults living in nursing homes. In actuality, elderly individuals have rates of affective disorders lower than that of younger adults, although their rates for anxiety disorders approximate that of the general population (Robins & Regier, 1991). Only about 6% of older adults are in the community mental health system which is far below the proportion predicted according to their percentage in the population (Heller, 1998). Part of the problem may be that physicians are less likely to identify psychological problems in older as opposed to younger adults or may attribute symptoms to age. The consequences are that older adults are not very likely to be referred for treatment by physicians to mental health professionals. Service providers also lack gerontological training and appear to believe that psychotherapy is not very effective with older adults. Both the providers and elderly individuals tend to conceptualize their problems as due to physical health or aging rather than psychological factors (Heller, 1998).

Mental Deterioration or Incompetence

After 49 years of teaching in Whatcom County school, including the last 26 as a substitute, Mitch Evich has come across all kinds of students. "Recently I've worked in classes that were lovely, you can't beat them," Evich said. "Of course other classes, I wish I could," he said with a laugh. Evich, now 81, has no immediate plans on ending his substitute teaching career. (Lane, 1998, p. A1)

A common view of elderly persons is that they are mentally incompetent. Terms such as "senile" reflect this perspective. However, only a minority of elderly persons have dementia. Most are still mentally sharp and benefit from the store of knowledge that they have acquired over a lifetime. Some 5% to 10% of individuals over the age of 65 have mild to moderate dementia;

this increases to 15%–20% for those over 75 years of age and 25%–50% of those over 85 (American Psychiatric Association, 1997; Saunders, 1998). Saunders found that patients with dementia attempt to maintain a sense of competence and dignity despite their memory problems. They would blame their confusion on external events such as being pressured too much. Older persons with dementia can still show varied aspects of themselves. One woman responded to an inability to recall her husband's name humorously, by using a metaphor, stating that her brain was "off key." Another responded to memory problems by joking that "My brain is gone on strike, I think" (p. 67). Despite their memory impairment, older individuals often use humor and demonstrate their competence and verbal sophistication through their use of metaphors.

Dementia

One of the areas requiring treatment in the elderly is dementia. Although dementia has a gradual progression, the effects of this disorder impact both the afflicted individual and family members. Caretaking may be stressful and increase conflict among family members. In working with family members, a counselor should address the following issues (American Psychiatric Association, 1997):

1. The need for patience and understanding in working with individuals with dementia.
2. The potential stresses on family members.
3. Education of family members regarding the neurological problems involved, how they are manifested in behavior, and available treatments. In the early stages, memory problems are primary symptoms. Language and spatial dysfunction tend to occur later. Delusions and hallucinations may also occur in the late stage.
4. Practical solutions for problems such as how to deal with agitation, wandering, and other safety issues. Exercise is helpful but should be supervised. Identification on clothing and medical alert bracelets are helpful if unsupervised departures do occur. In the beginning stages of dementia, the individual should be advised not to drive.
5. The family dynamics as they relate to the caregiving situation and how responsibilities should be allocated.
6. Improving communication of the family members.
7. Community resources such as the Alzheimer's Association and other support groups.
8. Financial and legal matters involving the patient, such as the power of attorney.
9. Decisions that may need to be made, such as under what circumstance the afflicted person would need to be cared for in a nursing home or other outside agency.

Substance Abuse

"I wouldn't get up in the morning," she said. "I realized I was using alcohol to raise my spirits. It raises your spirits for a little while, and then you become depressed. . . . With people dying around you, you feel more lonely and isolated." (Wren, 1998, p. 12)

Alcohol abuse can begin after a loss. Genevieve May, a psychiatrist, started abusing alcohol after the death of her husband. Finding that this was not the solution, Dr. May entered the Betty Ford Center and was successfully treated at age 83. She is now 88 and has been sober for

5 years. It is estimated that 17% of adults aged 60 and older abuse alcohol or prescription drugs. Some of the misuse of prescription drugs may involve confusion over or misunderstanding of the directions. Because older adults take an average of five different prescription drugs a day, the chance of negative drug interactions or reactions with alcohol increases dramatically (Guerra, 1998). Often these reactions resemble psychological or organic conditions.

Elderly problem drinkers are more likely to be unmarried, report more stress, have more financial problems, report persistent interpersonal conflicts with others, and have fewer social resources (Brennan & Moos, 1996). About 30% started drinking after the age of 60 because of depression and negative life changes (Guerra, 1998). Older adults rarely seek treatment for substance abuse problems because of shame and perhaps because they may feel uncomfortable in programs that also deal with drugs such as heroin or crack cocaine. One 74-year-old woman who was in group therapy with younger drug abusers asked "What is crack?" She was successfully treated only after entering a program for older adults (Wren, 1998). As compared to younger substance abusers, older patients responded better to more structured program policies, more flexible rules regarding discharge, more comprehensive assessment, and more outpatient mental health aftercare (Moos, Mertens, & Brennan, 1995). Older adults who receive appropriate treatment respond well and return to their previous lifestyle.

Depression and Suicide

Suicide rates are high in the older population and accounted for about 20% of all suicides in 1992. Factors associated with suicide included: being separated, divorced, or alone; depression; having an anxiety disorder; physical or medical problems; and family conflict or loss of a relationship. Caucasian men were at greater risk for suicide than non-Caucasian men or women (Florio, Hendryx, Jensen, & Rockwood, 1997). Although rates of depression are lower among older individuals than in the population as a whole, depression still plays a role in many suicides. In women, depression is related to financial loss; for men, the loss of health is the greatest stressor (Ponzo, 1992). Healthy, normally functioning older adults do not appear to be at greater risk for depression than younger adults. What seems to be age-related depression is often depression over physical health problems and the related disability. Aging, independent of declining health problems, does not increase the risk of depression (Roberts, Kaplan, Shema, & Strawbridge, 1997). Reynolds, Dew, Frank, and Begley (1998) found that both early onset (first time major depression at 59 or less) and late onset (first time major depression after age 60) responded well to a combination of psychotherapy and antidepressants. However, individuals in the early onset group required 5 to 6 weeks longer to achieve remission.

Sexuality in Old Age

In our youth-oriented society, sexual activity among older persons is thought rare and even considered to be inappropriate. The elderly are not expected to be interested in sex. However, sexual interest and activity continues well into the 80s and 90s for many individuals (Diokno, Brown, & Herzog, 1990; Kun & Schwartz, 1998). In a study of 1,216 elderly people with a mean age of 77.3, nearly 30% had participated in sexual activity during the past month, and 67% were satisfied with their current level of sexual activity. Men were more sexually active than women but less satisfied with their level of sexual activity. Age did not appear to be related to sexual satisfaction (Matthias, Lubben, Atchison, & Schweitzer, 1997). Most had positive reactions such as "Physical satisfaction is not the only aim of sex . . . it is the nearness of someone throughout the lonely nights of people in their 70s and 80s"; and "I believe sex is a wonderful outlet for love and physical health and worth trying to keep alive in advancing age . . . it makes one feel youthful and close to one's mate and pleased to 'still work'" (Johnson, 1995, p. A23). Of the more than 600 older women surveyed, 35% had said that their present level of sexual interest had decreased. However, Johnson found that 2/3 said they were very interested in sexual intercourse and that most believed they had liberal sexual attitudes.

Changes do occur in sexual functioning in both older men and women (Kim & Atkinson, 1998). In men, erections occur more slowly and need more continuous stimulation, but can be maintained for longer periods of time without the need for ejaculation. The refractory period increases, so that it may take a day or two for the man to become sexually responsive again. Antihypertensive drugs, vascular diseases of the penile arteries, and diabetes are common causes of impotence in men. For women, aging is associated with a decline of estrogens, and vaginal lubrication decreases. However, sexual responsiveness by the clitoris is similar to that of younger women. Sexual activities remain important for older men and women. Medical and psychological methods have been successful in treating sexual dysfunctions in older adults.

Multiple Discrimination

Minority status in combination with older age can produce a double burden. For example, older lesbian women may still encounter discrimination on the basis of their sexual orientation. Some remain distressed over their lack of acceptance from the heterosexual community and even family members. They observe that neighbors interact with them but do not invite them over socially. In addition, they may feel isolated from the lesbian community.

I was shocked and hurt when one of them [a young lesbian] who considers herself quite liberated didn't want to dance with me at a local lesbian bar, but she did dance with others. (Jacobson & Samdahl, 1998, p. 242)

The woman attributed this rejection to her being older than the other women. She points out that in lesbian newsletters or activities, there was seldom anything about older women. Unfortunately, even minority members who have experienced discrimination themselves can display ageism.

COUNSELING OLDER ADULTS

Older adults have to deal with issues such as the loss of friends and other significant individuals, the cultural devaluation of their group, health and physical problems, forced isolation, and having more limited financial resources (Butler & Lewis, 1983; Moye & Brown, 1995). However, many develop alternative support systems in the community and in having grandchildren. Social contacts are important, and engaging in either paid or volunteer work enhances the self-esteem and life satisfaction of older individuals (Acquino, Russell, Cutrona, & Altmaier, 1996). Issues that face older adults may include chronic illness and disability, loss of loved ones, caregiving for a loved one, and change of roles (Knight & McCallum, 1998).

Butler and Lewis (1983), Knight and McCallum (1998), and Qualls (1998) offer some suggestions in counseling older adults.

1. Medical conditions and cognitive assessments should be obtained.
2. If necessary, slow the pace of therapy to accommodate cognitive slowing.

3. Help couples negotiate issues regarding time spent alone and together (especially after retirement). When working or raising children, time was structured. Arguments over recreation are common. There is too much "couple time" and no "legitimate" reason for separateness.

4. It is important to have individuals who are alone establish support systems in the community.

5. Help the older adult develop a sense of fulfillment in life by discussing the positive aspects of their experiences. "Success" can be defined as having done one's best or having met and survived challenges. A life review is often helpful.

6. Assist in interpreting the impact of cultural issues such as ethnic group membership, gender, and sexual orientation on their lives.

7. For adults very close to the end of their lives, help them deal with a sense of attachment to familiar objects by having them decide how heirlooms, keepsakes, and photo albums will be distributed and cared for. Counseling can improve the quality of life for older adults or help them resolve late-life issues.

COUNSELING WOMEN

Congresswoman Patricia Schroeder won a seat to the Armed Services Committee along with Ron Dellums, an African American. According to Pat Schroeder, the Chairperson of the committee was not pleased with the new members. "He said that women and blacks were worth only half of one 'regular' member, so he added only one seat to the committee room and made Ron and me share it. . . . Nobody else objected." (Mann, 1998, p. E03)

During a visit to a Denver High School, the basketball coach asked the players to "show Mrs. Schroeder what you think of Title Nine" (Mann, 1998, p. E03). The boys turned around and "mooned" her. Title IX had just passed in Congress, mandating equal funding for educational programs including sports for males and females.

Although progress has been made in promoting gender equality, sexual discrimination continues. The National Coalition for Women and Girls in Education (1998) published a report indicating that: (a) Girls and women continue to be underrepresented in areas such as math and sciences; (b) women continue to predominate in low-wage, traditional female tracks; (c) women comprise 73% of elementary and secondary school teachers but only 35% of principals; (d) pay disparities between male and female educators persist at all levels; (e) female students continue to receive less attention, encouragement, and praise than male students; and (f) sexual harassment continues to be pervasive. Studies indicate that 81% of 8th through 11th graders, 30% of undergraduates, and 40% of graduate students have been sexually harassed, a situation that often negatively impacts interest in academics and school.

PROBLEMS FACED BY WOMEN

Economic Status

About 1/3 of families headed by single women live in poverty. In terms of income, females make less than their male counterparts across all racial groups; this disparity is most pronounced between White women and White men, with women earning less than 3/4 of the salaries earned by men (U.S. Bureau of the Census, 1995). Nontraditional career fields are often not hospitable to women, resulting in the larger percentage of women who remain in "feminine" careers. Females are overrepresented in occupations such as secretary (98.5%), cashier (78.3%), nurse's aide (89.4%), elementary school teacher (83.9%), and receptionist (96.5%) and underrepresented in administrative positions (U.S. Department of Labor, 1998). Even in occupations where women represent the numerical majority, they earn less than men in the same field (Atkinson & Hackett, 1998).

The underrepresentation of women in certain fields is due in part to gender role stereotypes. Some jobs require characteristics not generally associated with females. Femininity includes the qualities of emotionality, sensitivity, nurturance, and interdependence (Cook, 1990). When a woman behaves in a manner that is not considered to be "feminine," negative consequences may result. If a woman displays a task-oriented style of leadership that violates the gender norm of modesty, she is rated as competent but incurs cost in low social attraction and likableness ratings. Men displaying the same leadership style are rated high in competence and are better liked (Rudman, 1998). Similar results were found by Forsyth, Heiney, and Wright (1997) in a comparison of responses to male and female group leaders displaying task-oriented or relationship-oriented leadership styles. Group members favored men over women when selecting leaders and evaluating leaders, even when the leadership behaviors were held constant. However, group members with a liberal attitude toward women's roles responded positively to either leadership style by women. It was also interesting to observe that biases against the task-oriented style for women leaders was not restricted to male group members.

Discrimination and Victimization

From 15% to 45% of females suffer abuse involving physical contact before the age of 18 (Brock, Mintz, & Good, 1997). Survivors often suffer from depression and other emotional difficulties. The majority of women who are in treatment for childhood sexual abuse suffer from post-traumatic stress disorder (Rodriguez, Ryan, Vande Kemp, & Foy, 1997). Sexual harassment is also quite prevalent in the work environment.

One woman who suffered six years of harassment from her male colleagues that included lewd behavior and suggestive comments finally threatened to to report them. They responded by saying, "Fine. We know where your your car is, and we know where you live." (Lewis, 1998, p. D5)

As with many women in the same circumstances, the woman decided not to fight back. Over 70% of women office workers have reported harassment at their place of employment (Piotrkowski, 1998). Women respond to the harassment by attempting to ignore it, taking a leave of absence, or using alcohol to cope. Lower job satisfaction, poorer physical health, and higher levels of depression and anxiety can be the result of harassment (Fitzgerald, Drasgow, Hulin, Gelfand, & Magley, 1997). Even low-frequency sexual harassment has been found to have a significant negative impact on the psychological well-being of the victims (Schneider, Swan, & Fitzgerald, 1997).

Gender issues

The stereotyped standards of beauty expressed through advertisement and the mass media have had an impact on the health and self-esteem of girls and women. Societal pressure for females to achieve a thin body has led to the internalization of an unrealistic body shape as the ideal and has resulted in body dissatisfaction and disordered eating patterns and dieting (Stice, Shaw, & Nemeroff, 1998). It is estimated that 35% of women engage in disordered eating, and many attempt to control their weight through self-induced vomiting and the use of laxatives (Kendler et al., 1991). Bulimia nervosa is ten times more common in females than in males and affects up to 3% of women between the ages of 13 and 20 (McGilley & Pryor, 1998). The need to meet societal standards for thinness or beauty becomes more intense when girls at the ages of 12 and 13 begin to date and to experience the physical changes associated with puberty. They become more concerned about their physical appearance and are more likely to start dieting (Heatherton, Mahamedi, Striepe, Field, & Keel, 1997). Interestingly, African American females appear to have a different standard for attractiveness than White females. Nearly 3/4 of African American females in one study were satisfied with their current weight or body shape. Most had a broad definition of beauty that included being well groomed, demonstrating the right attitude and personality, and style. They also felt that they would become more beautiful with age (Parker, Nichter, Vuckovic, Sims, & Ritenbaugh, 1995).

Several programs have been developed to combat the restricted view of body image. In the YMCA's leadership camp, middle school girls perform community service projects, are exposed to women in leadership roles, and participate in communication and problem-solving exercises. Part of the discussion involves the feelings of inadequacy produced by the body image portrayed by mass media and their deviation from that standard. The camp is useful in helping participants realize that they have similar reactions to societal pressures and learn to develop internal standards that they can feel good about (Steinberg, 1998). In another program, marketing students from different high schools have approached several large department stores requesting that the displays show a more diverse range of body types than just the super-thin image. The students pointed out to store managers that half of the teens and adult women in the United States wear a size 14 or larger and that the mannequins and models were size 8 or less. In support of their position, they cited a survey done at their schools that indicated that 93% of the students wanted to see more diverse body types in advertisements and in magazines. Only one department store, the Union Bay, advertised using a range of body types or "healthy looking" models (Cronin, 1998). Programs directed at changing the unrealistically thin female image promoted by advertisers, magazines, and other mass media may be effective ways of reducing body dissatisfaction in females.

Affective Disorders

The prevalence of affective disorders in White women is about twice as high as found in White men. The same ratio has been found between African American women and men. However, no clear-cut gender differences for affective disorders have been found for Hispanic Americans (Robins & Regier, 1991). Factors contributing to depression in women include poor socioeconomic status, unhealthy societal gender standards, and post-traumatic stress (Culbertson, 1997). Women feel the pressure to fulfill stereotyped feminine social roles in which they are evaluated according to physical beauty, modesty, and marriageability. The punishment for deviating from these standards can lead to self-doubt, poor self-image, and depression (Sands, 1998). Cook (1990) also believes that women devalue their relationship capabilities. Depression may result from their socialization to try to maintain relationships at the cost of their own needs and wishes. Failures in relationships are often seen as personal failures, compounding stress and affecting mood.

Minority women have multiple characteristics that are subject to discrimination and prejudice and see additional obstacles to their achieving their life goals. African American teenagers who were interviewed concerning their multiple minority status were quite aware of the discrimination that they face.

I'm a black female and black females are the lowest. The black female has a hard time, for one, because she's black, two, because she's a female, and I think it would take more for me to strive to get what I want. . . . (Olsen, 1996, p. 113)

These African American teenagers were aware of the negative messages regarding their ethnicity and also the disparagement of the female gender role. Although they acknowledged the disadvantages of their gender, none of them wanted to be a boy.

Aging

With the emphasis on youth and the sexism that exists in our society, older women are viewed more negatively than older men. There are relatively few positive images of older women. In addition, older women are thought to face additional stressors such as the "empty nest" syndrome and menopause (Lippert, 1997). However, these are actually not difficult transitions for most women. Of a group of women ages 40 to 59 asked about how they felt about "this time in life," nearly 3/4 felt "very happy" or "happy" and nearly 2/3 found it "not very confusing" or "not confusing at all." Only 13.7% felt "unhappy" or "very unhappy." Most were enjoying midlife because of increased independence, freedom from worrying about what others think, freedom from parenting, and the ability to define their own identity based on their own interests (McQuaide, 1998). Transitions through midlife for older women seem to be easier than previously assumed. It does not appear to be a time of increased difficulty for most but instead a time of increased freedom.

FEMINIST IDENTITY THEORY

An identity development model comparable to that for ethnic minority members has been developed for women. Feminist therapists believe that the patriarchal aspect of U.S. society is responsible for many of the problems faced by women. They believe women show a variety of reactions to their subordinate status in society. The following stages represent an evolution of consciousness of societal subjugation of women and the development of the feminist identity (McNamara & Rickard, 1998).

1. *Passive-Acceptance.* During this stage, the female accepts traditional gender roles, sees them as advantageous to her, and considers men to be superior to women. She is unaware of or denies prejudice or discrimination. Male contributions to the arts, business, and theater are valued more than those of women.
2. *Revelation.* Events involving sexism occur in a way that cannot be denied or ignored. The individual becomes personally awakened to prejudice, becomes angry, and feels guilty at not being previously aware. There is intense self-examination and dichotomous thinking. All men are seen as oppressive and all women as positive.

3. *Embeddedness-Emanation.* The woman begins to form close emotional relationships with other women. With their help she is able to express her emotions in a supportive environment. Her feminist identity is becoming solidified, and she engages in more relativistic rather than dualistic thinking regarding males.

4. *Synthesis.* During this stage, a positive feminist identity is fully developed. Sexism is no longer considered the cause of all social and personal problems, and other causal factors are considered. The woman can take a stance different from that of other feminists and still maintain her feminist identity.

5. *Active commitment.* The woman is now interested in turning her attention to making societal changes.

Although some women go through these stages, it is not clear how applicable this model is to most women. This theory is based on Cross's 1971 view of the development of African American identity. Since then, Cross has revised his model (Cross, 1995), particularly as it applies to the passive-acceptance stage (pre-encounter). Individuals at this stage may feel that characteristics of race (gender) are of low salience or not more important than other things such as religion, lifestyle, or social status. They may see progress as due to personal effort and motivation. Many individuals at this stage who have this attitude are mentally healthy. Feminist identity theory is of fairly recent origin, and there is need for research to determine whether it is applicable to most women.

THERAPY FOR WOMEN

Feminist therapists have been instrumental in pointing out the sexist nature of our society, even in the counseling process. It is important for counselors to be aware of possible biases in working with female clients. For example, what are the attributes believed to be aspects of a "healthy" female? In past research, qualities such as submissiveness and being more emotional and relationship oriented were seen as positive qualities in women (Atkinson & Hackett, 1998). If counselors adhere to these standards, consciously or unconsciously, these attitudes may be conveyed to clients in the counseling session. In one study of family therapy sessions, it was observed that counselors interrupted women more often than men (Werner-Wilson, Price, Zimmerman, & Murphy, 1997). Even though the therapists were not aware of this behavior, they were subtly conveying gender role expectations to the family. Female counselor trainees have also been shown to demonstrate bias in counseling men and women who seem to be seeking nontraditional roles. For example, a greater number of questions regarding parenting were posed to women than to male clients (Seem & Johnson, 1998). Gender role expectations are difficult to eliminate.

Biases can also exist for certain diagnostic categories. Some of the personality disorders may be based on exaggerated gender characteristics. Self-dramatization, exaggerated emotional expressions; intense fluctuations in mood, self-image, and interpersonal relationships; reliance on others and the inability to assume responsibilities are aspects of Histrionic, Borderline, and Dependent personality disorders, respectively. Not surprisingly, women are more likely to be diagnosed with these disorders. Another problematic category is Premenstrual Dysphoric Disorder, which is included as a diagnosis that requires "further study" in *DSM-IV.* The essential features include marked change in mood, anger, and depression or anxiety, accompanied by complaints of breast tenderness and bodily aches that interfere with work or social activities. The symptoms occur a week before menses and remit a few days afterwards. Critics of this category acknowledge that many women have some of these symptoms, but argue that the symptoms should be accepted as a physical reaction. Labeling premenstrual symptoms as a psychological disorder promotes the view that women are emotional and controlled by "raging" hormones (Sue, Sue, & Sue, 1997).

GUIDELINES FOR COUNSELING WOMEN

Both male and female counselors must be careful not to foster traditional sex roles and must be aware of sexist assumptions. Presenting problems need to be understood within a societal context in which devaluation of women is a common occurrence; gender conceptualizations need to be considered integral aspects of counseling and mental health. Both rigid traditional and nontraditional gender roles can be confining. Each female client must choose what is best for her, despite gender conceptions or political correctness (Good, Gilbert, & Scher, 1990).

As DeVoe (1998) points out, both feminist and nonsexist counseling approaches may be helpful for women clients. Feminist counseling can be especially useful in working with women who are dissatisfied with gender role restrictions and are interested in effecting societal changes. However, the feminist perspective should not be imposed on a client who believes her problem is not related to gender. Nonsexist counseling incorporates less of the feminist philosophy, but attempts to reduce the impact of sexism when counseling women. Fitzgerald and Nutt (1998) have identified some guidelines for counselors who counsel women. Counselors or therapists should:

1. Possess up-to-date information regarding the biological, psychological, and sociological issues that impact women. For example, knowledge about menstruation, pregnancy, birth, infertility and miscarriage, gender roles and health, and discrimination, and their impact on women, is important.

2. Recognize that most counseling theories are male-centered and require modification in work with women.

3. Attend workshops to explore gender-related factors in mental health and be knowledgeable about issues related to women.

4. Maintain awareness of all forms of oppression and understand how they interact with sexism.

5. Utilize skills that may be particularly appropriate for the needs of women, such as assertiveness training, gender role analysis, and consciousness-raising groups. As with any approach in which traditional perspectives are challenged, clients need to understand the consequences in making changes.

6. Refrain from expressing counseling attitudes that constrain life goals or careers for women.

7. Assess when a female counselor may be the most appropriate match for a female client. For example, a male counselor should be aware of when a female client is best served by a female counselor (rape, pregnancy issues, domestic violence).

These guidelines indicate the importance of incorporating features of feminist and nonsexist components in all our counseling programs.

COUNSELING PERSONS WITH DISABILITIES

> *In 1988 I became obviously disabled. I walk with crutches and a stiff leg. Since that time I no longer fulfill our cultural standard of physical attractiveness. But worse, there are times when people who know me don't acknowledge me. When I call their name and say, "Hello," they often reply, "Oh, I didn't see you." I have also been mistaken for people who do not resemble me. For example, I was recently asked, "Are you a leader in the disability movement?" While I hope to be that someday, I asked her, "Who do you believe I am?" She had mistaken me for a taller person with a different hair color, who limps but does not use a walking aid. The only common element was our disability. My disability had become my persona. This person saw it and failed to see me. . . . (Buckman, 1998, p. 19)*

Danielle Buckman is a psychotherapist who teaches university courses on counseling people with disabilities and, due to her own struggle with multiple sclerosis, has firsthand experiences with discriminatory reactions from the general public. Since Ms. Buckman is in midlife, she also expresses concern about the triple whammy involving gender, disability, and aging issues. Attitudes toward individuals with disabilities run the gamut from ignorance to lack of understanding to being overprotective or overly sympathetic. People without handicaps often don't know how to respond to people with disabilities, especially with their accomplishments. Kerry Clifford (Vacc & Clifford, 1995) who has a physical disability, believes that the public's reaction is similar to that of Samuel Johnson to a dog walking on two legs. He is reported to have said, "it is not done well, but you are surprised to see it done at all."

A national survey (National Organization on Disability/Harris Survey, 1998) reported dismal statistics on the well-being of Americans with disabilities. Of adults with disabilities, only 29% have any type of employment, compared to 79% of the general public. This 50-point difference is not due to a lack of interest in working; in fact, 72% of individuals with disabilities want to work. Over 1/3 of adults with disabilities have incomes of $15,000 or less, compared to 12% of those without disabilities. Only about 1/3 of adults with disabilities are very satisfied with life, compared to 61% of the nondisabled public. Worse, 20% of adults with disabilities have not finished high school, compared to 9% of those without disabilities—a ratio of more than two to one. Individuals with disabilities earn only 2/3 the income of coworkers without disabilities; minorities with disabilities have an even lower income than Whites with disabilities (Atkinson & Hackett, 1998). It was in part due to dismal statistics like these that Congress passed the Americans with Disabilities Act.

THE AMERICANS WITH DISABILITIES ACT

The Americans with Disabilities Act (ADA) was signed into law in 1990, extending the federal mandate of nondiscrimination toward individuals with disabilities to state and local governments and the private sector. Congress defined disability as "a physical or mental impairment that substantially limits one or more of the major life activities of such individual." It includes individuals with mental retardation, hearing impairment or deafness, orthopedic impairments, learning disabilities, speech impairment, and other health or physical impairments. Psychiatric disorders covered include major depression, bipolar disorder, panic and obsessive-compulsive disorders, personality disorders, schizophrenia, and rehabilitation from drug use or addiction. Conditions not covered include sexual behavior disorders, compulsive gambling, kleptomania, pyromania, and current substance abuse (Sleek, 1998). Under this definition, there are 49 million Americans with disabilities, of whom 24 million have a severe form. The prevalence of disability ranges from 5.8% for children under 18 to 53.9% for those 65 and over (U.S. Bureau of the Census, 1995). The number recognized by ADA is in fact now higher, since HIV has recently been added as a disability.

The Americans with Disabilities Act has had an impact on businesses with employees with disabilities. Many have made adjustments and accommodations.

Mike Johnson wasn't asking for special treatment at work, but his bosses thought they'd better provide it anyway. Two months after being hospitalized for bipolar disorder, Johnson, an accomplished, 35-year-old sales executive, told his boss that he was feeling "stressed out." The boss also noticed that Johnson overbooked his schedule during his manic phases and would wake up late and miss appointments during depressive periods. . . . (Sleek, 1998, p. 15)

Mike Johnson's employer was able to retain a valuable executive with bipolar disorder by developing a flexible work schedule that allowed him to have time off for therapy.

Congress passed the Americans with Disabilities Act in 1990 to address the following issues:

1. Historically, society has tended to isolate and segregate individuals with disabilities, and, despite some improvements, such forms of discrimination against individuals with disabilities continue to be a serious and pervasive social problem.
2. Unlike individuals who have experienced discrimination on the basis of race, color, sex, national origin, religion, or age, individuals who have experienced discrimination on the basis of disability have often had no legal recourse to redress such discrimination.
3. Individuals with disabilities continually encounter various forms of discrimination, including intentional exclusion, the discriminatory effects of architectural, transportation, and communication barriers, overprotective rules and policies, failure to make modifications to existing facilities and practices, exclusionary qualification standards and criteria, segregation, and relegation to lesser services, programs, activities, benefits, jobs, or other opportunities.
4. Census data, national polls, and other studies have documented that people with disabilities, as a group, occupy an inferior status in our society, and are severely disadvantaged socially, vocationally, economically, and educationally.
5. The nation's goals regarding individuals with disabilities are to assure equality of opportunity, full participation, independent living, and economic self-sufficiency. The act prohibits discrimination in employment, telecommunication, transportation, and public services and accommodations. (Atkinson & Hackett, 1998)

MYTHS ABOUT PEOPLE WITH DISABILITIES

There are many myths associated with people with disabilities (American Friends Service Committee, 1998).

1. *Most are in wheelchairs.* Actually, of the 49 million individuals with disabilities, only about 10% use a wheelchair, crutches, or a walker. The majority have disabilities related to cardiovascular problems, blindness, developmental disabilities, or "invisible" disabilities such as asthma, learning disabilities, or epilepsy.

2. *People with disabilities are a drain on the economy.* It is true that 71% of working-age persons with disabilities are not working. However, 72% of those want to work. Discrimination has kept them out of the workforce.

3. *The greatest barriers to people with disabilities are physical ones.* In actuality, negative attitudes and stereotypes are the greatest impediments and the most difficult to change.

4. *Businesses dislike the Americans with Disabilities Act.* Actually, 82% of executives surveyed believe it worth implementing and that expenses with implementation are minimal.

5. *Government health insurance covers people with disabilities.* Of the 29.5 million individuals with disabilities between the ages of 15 and 64, 18.4 million have private insurance, 4.4 million are covered by Medicaid, and 5.1 million have no health insurance.

PROGRAMS FOR INDIVIDUALS WITH DISABILITIES

In the past, programs for persons with disabilities focused on rehabilitation rather than assisting them to develop independent living skills. There has been gradual recognition that deficient experiences and opportunities limit the development of the individual. The services received by individuals with disabilities are most effective when they enable independence, self-determination, and productive participation in society (Humes, Szymanski, & Hohenshil, 1989). However, the statistics on the outcome of educational programs have not been very positive. One survey found that only 27% of individuals with disabilities go to college, compared to 68% of those without disabilities; 30% drop out of high school. Three to 5 years after graduation from high school, only 57% are employed, compared to 69% of youth without disabilities (Wagner & Blackorby, 1996). Clearly, there are needs for new approaches. Several programs have obtained promising results.

Ted Stabelfeldt is a 19-year-old, paralyzed from the shoulders down, who discovered the DO-IT program at the University of Washington. This program links high school students with disabilities who are interested in science and math with computer technology that is designed to work from their areas of strength. Todd is able to operate his computer with a hollow mouth wand. He types by pointing the wand to letters on the screen and blowing into the wand to make it operate like a computer mouse. One puff represents a single click and two puffs a double-click. Todd has learned to operate the computer efficiently but admits that the most difficult part was not learning the new technology but getting over his own negative attitudes toward disability.

When I attended DO-IT, that all changed. I met 40 other gimps—that's what I call them. I realized, hey, man, they're cool. They're real people too. (H.T. George, 1998, p. B2)

Todd's computer skills helped him obtain a job writing medical software. Of the 136 students who participated in the program, over 50% are going into technical schools or colleges and over 25% have found employment. There has been a shift in the orientation of programs for people with disabilities from remediation or "making them as normal as possible" to identifying and strengthening skills that they possess.

The "Bridges from School to Work" program that involved 2,258 students also was successful. The disabilities included learning disability (52%), mental retardation (22%), emotional disability (14%), and other disabilities (12%); the last category included epilepsy, sensory impairments, head injury, and orthopedic and mobility impairments. Participants had moderate to severe disabilities. The program involved prevocational orientation for both the family and the student. Information on job preparation, job expectations, and skills training was followed by internship placement in local businesses. The 12-week internship involved job skills training and monitoring of performance by the employers. Of the 76% of participants who completed their internships, 71% were offered jobs by the same or a different employer. In a 6-month follow-up, 84% of the participants were employed or had enrolled in college. The program was successful both in helping youths with disability make the transition to employment or further education and in opening doors in the business community (Fabian, Lent, & Willis, 1998).

COUNSELING ISSUES WITH INDIVIDUALS WITH DISABILITIES

Many counselors and other mental health professionals do not know how to deal with clients with disabilities.

A 33-year-old hard of hearing client has problems at work. Her employer claims she does not follow orders and inquires about attention or memory problems. The psychologist administers the Wechsler Adult Intelligence Scale—Revised (WAIS-R), the Wechsler Memory Scale—Revised and the Minnesota Multiphasic Personality Inventory (MMPI) and finds no evidence of memory or attentional deficits. The MMPI results suggest mild paranoid and depressive tendencies. (Leigh, Corbett, Gutman, & Morere, 1996)

In this case the psychologist concluded that the problems at work were a result of the woman's depression and paranoid tendencies. There is no mention in his report of the possible impact of her hearing loss on both the findings of the assessments and her ability to adapt to the work environment. In fact, it is likely that the woman's hearing impairment accounted for the majority of the presenting symptoms. Helping professionals often have the same attitude as the general public toward individuals with disabilities and may feel uncomfortable or experience guilt or pity when working with them. As in working with other oppressed groups, the counselor must examine his or her own view of clients with disabilities and identify and question prejudicial assumptions. A client's disability should not be the sole focus for counseling. Environmental contributions to problems should also be identified. Issues involving frustrations with architectural barriers or with negative stereotypes or prejudices against individuals with disabilities need to be addressed in counseling (Vacc & Clifford, 1995).

Kemp and Mallinckrodt (1996) point out some of the errors that can occur in counseling relationships with individuals with disabilities. First, errors involving omission may be made. The counselor may fail to ask questions about critical aspects of the client's life because the assumption is made that the issue is unimportant due to the presence of the disability. For example, sexuality and relationship issues may be ignored because of the belief that the individual lacks the ability or interest in pursuing these intimacies. Affective issues may also be avoided, since the counselor may be uncomfortable addressing the impact of the disability on the client. The counselor may display a lowered expectation of the client's capabilities. Second, errors of commission may be made. In this case, the counselor assumes without justification that certain issues should be important because of the presence of the disability, when they are not. Personal problems faced by the client are all assumed to be a result of the disability. Career and academic counseling may become a focus even when it is not the interest of the client. Other errors identified by Kemp and Mallinckrodt that may be made in working with clients with disabilities are: not addressing the disability at all; encouraging dependency and the "sick" role; countertransference in wanting to "rescue" the client; and having a lowered expectation of the client's capabilities.

Family Counseling

With family members, emotional issues such as guilt, self-punishment, or anger may need to be dealt with (Hulnick & Hulnick, 1989). Family members may feel responsible for the condition and have a primarily negative focus. For both the individual with the disability and the family members, choices have to be made. They can decide to withdraw from or reach out to others. Hulnick and Hulnick suggest focusing on choices that can be made. For example, the counselor can ask questions such as "What are you doing that perpetuates the situation?" and "Are you aware of other choices that would have a different result?" These questions are empowering, since clients realize that they have the ability to make choices. Instead of viewing disability as a problem, reframing can be used to identify opportunities through questions such as "In what ways could you use this situation to your advancement?" or "What can you learn from this experience?"

Albert Ellis, the founder of rational-emotive therapy, has suffered from the disabilities of diabetes, tired eyes, deficient hearing, and other physical handicaps but has successfully utilized cognitive approaches, such as reframing, to deal with his disabilities. For example, because he cannot keep his eyes open for any length of time, he focuses on the positive aspects of conducting therapy sessions with his eyes closed. He tells himself that with his eyes shut he can: (a) focus "unusually well" on his clients' verbalizations (tone of voice, hesitations, etc.); (b) identify more easily their irrational thoughts; (c) help clients feel more relaxed; and (d) serve as a healthy model of an individual with a disability (Ellis, 1997). In Ellis's case, he has been able to look at the positive aspects of a disability.

Mental health professionals working with individuals with disabilities should know the federal and state legislation applicable to these individuals. They should know the rights of individuals with disabilities in school and work settings. Under the Americans with Disabilities Act, employers cannot discriminate against an individual with a disability during employment or promotion if they are otherwise qualified, cannot inquire about a disability but only about the ability to perform the job, need to make "reasonable" accommodation for people with disabilities, and cannot use tests that will cause individuals to be screened out due to disabilities (Vacc & Clifford, 1995). The counselor should also be aware of problems in using standardized assessment tools with individuals who have disabilities. Finally, it is important for counselors to understand that individuals with the same disability may show a wide range of functional difficulties and accomplishments.

References

Abad, V., Ramos, J., & Boyce, E. (1974). A model for delivery of mental health services to Spanish-speaking minorities. *American Journal of Orthopsychiatry, 44,* 584–595.

Abbott, K., & Abbott, E. (1968). Juvenile delinquency in San Francisco's Chinese-American community. *Journal of Sociology, 4,* 45–56.

Abeles, R.P. (1976). Relative deprivation, rising expectations and black militancy. *Journal of Social Issues, 32,* 119–137.

ACMH. (1987). The California Southeast Asian mental health needs assessment. Oakland, California: Asian Community Mental Health Services.

Acosta, F.X., & Evans, L.A. (1982). Effective psychotherapy for low-income and minority patients. In F.X. Acosta, J. Yamamoto, & L.A. Evans (Eds.), *Effective psychotherapy for low-income and minority patients* (pp. 51–82). New York: Plenum Press.

Acquino, J.A., Russell, D.W., Cutrona, C.E., & Altmaier, E.M. (1996). Employment status, social support, and life satisfaction among the elderly. *Journal of Counseling Psychology, 43,* 480–489.

Adler, N.J. (1986). Cultural synergy: Managing the impact of cultural diversity. *The 1986 annual: Developing human resources.* San Diego, CA: University Associates.

Ahai, C.E. (1997). A cultural framework for counseling African Americans. In C.C. Lee (Ed.), *Multicultural issues in counseling* (2d ed., pp. 73–80). Alexandria, VA: American Counseling Association.

Ailinger, R.L. (1997). Latino immigrants' explanatory models of tuberculosis infection. *Qualitative Health Research, 7,* 521–526.

Alexander, C., Langer, E., Newman, R., Chandler, H., & Davies, J. (1989). Transcendental meditation, mindfulness and longevity: An experimental study with the elderly. *Journal of Personality and Social Psychology, 57,* 950–964.

Alexander, C., Rainforth, M., & Gelderloos, P. (1991). Transcendental meditation, self actualization and psychological health: A conceptual overview and statistical meta-analysis. *Journal of Social Behavior and Personality, 6,* 189–247.

Allen, A. (1994, May 29). Black unlike me: Confessions of a white man confused by racial etiquette. *Washington Post,* p. C1.

Allison, K.W., Crawford, I., Echemendia, R., Robinson, L., & Knepp, D. (1994). Human diversity and professional competence: Training in clinical and counseling psychology revisited. *American Psychologist, 49,* 792–796.

Allport, G.W. (1961). *Pattern and growth in personality.* New York: Holt, Rinehart & Winston.

Alvarez, A., Batson, R.M., Carr, A.K., Parks, P., Peck, H.B., Shervington, W., Tyler, R.B., & Zwerling, I. (1976). *Racism, elitism, professionalism: Barriers to community mental health.* New York: Jason Aronson.

American Friends Service Committee. (1998). *People with disabilities.* Philadelphia, PA: Affirmative Action Office.

American Psychological Association. (1993). Guidelines for providers of psychological services to ethnic, linguistic, and culturally diverse populations. *American Psychologist, 48,* 45–48.

American Psychiatric Association. (1997). Practice guidelines for the treatment of patients with Alzheimer's disease and other dementias of late life. *American Journal of Psychiatry, 154,* 1–39.

Anderson, M.J., & Ellis, R. (1995). On the reservation. In N.A. Vacc, S.B. DeVaney, & J. Wittmer (Eds.), *Experiencing and counseling multicultural and diverse populations* (3d ed., pp. 179–198). Bristol, PA: Accelerated Development.

Anderson, N.B. (1995). Behavioral and sociocultural perspectives on ethnicity and health: Introduction to the special issue. *Health Psychology, 14,* 589–591.

Anonymous. (1998). President Clinton's race panel cites disparity in treatment of Blacks and Whites by nation's law enforcement system. *Jet, 94,* p. 36.

Anzaldúa, G. (1987). *Borderlands.* (pp. 194–95). San Francisco, CA: Spinsters/Aunt Lute.

Arredondo, P., Toporek, R., Brown, S.P., Jones, J., Locke, D.C., Sanchez, J., & Stadler, H. (1996). Operationalization of the multicultural counseling competencies. *Journal of Multicultural Counseling and Development, 24,* 42–78.

Asante, M. (1987). *The Afrocentric idea.* Philadelphia: Temple University Press.

Atkinson, D.R. (1983). Ethnic similarity in counseling psychology: A review of research. *The Counseling Psychologist, 11,* 79–92.

Atkinson, D.R. (1985). Research on cross-cultural counseling and psychotherapy: A review and update of reviews. In P.B. Pederson (Ed.), *Handbook of cross-cultural counseling and therapy* (pp. 191–197). Westport, CT: Greenwood Press.

Atkinson, D.R., Brown, M.T., Parham, T.A.,

Matthews, L.G., Landrum-Brown, J., & Kim, A.U. (1996). African American client skin tone and clinical judgments of African American and European American Psychologists. *Professional Psychology: Research and Practice, 27,* 500–505.

Atkinson, D.R., & Hackett, G. (1998). *Counseling diverse populations* (2d ed.). Boston: McGraw-Hill.

Atkinson, D.R., & Lowe, S.M. (1995). The role of ethnicity, cultural knowledge, and conventional techniques in counseling and psychotherapy. In J.G. Ponterotto, J.M. Casas, L.A. Suzuki, & C.M. Alexander (Eds.), *Handbook of Multicultural Counseling* (pp. 387–414). Thousand Oaks, CA: Sage.

Atkinson, D.R., Maruyama, M., & Matsui, S. (1978). The effects of counselor race and counseling approach on Asian Americans' perceptions of counselor credibility and utility. *Journal of Counseling Psychology, 25,* 76–83.

Atkinson, D.R., Morten, G., & Sue, D.W. (1989). A minority identity development model. In D.R. Atkinson, G. Morten, & D.W. Sue (Eds.), *Counseling American Minorities* (pp. 35–52). Dubuque, IA: W.C. Brown.

Atkinson, D.R., Morten, G., & Sue, D.W. (1998). *Counseling American Minorities.* (5th ed.). Boston: McGraw-Hill.

Atkinson, D.R., Ponterotto, J.G., & Sanchez, A.R. (1984). Attitudes of Vietnamese and Anglo-American students toward counseling. *Journal of College Student Personnel, 25,* 448–452.

Atkinson, D.R., & Schein, S. (1986). Similarity in counseling. *The Counseling Psychologist, 14,* 319–354.

Atkinson, D.R., Thompson, C.E., & Grant, S.K. (1993). A three-dimensional model for counseling racial/ethnic minorities. *The Counseling Psychologist, 21,* 257–277.

Avila, D.L., & Avila, A.L. (1980). The Mexican-American. In N.A. Vacc & J.P. Wittmer (Eds.), *Let me be me* (pp. 225–281). Muncie, IN: Accelerated Development.

Avila, D.L. & Avila, A.L. (1995). Mexican Americans. In N.A. Vacc, S.B. DeVaney, & J. Wittmer (Eds.), *Experiencing and counseling multicultural and diverse populations* (3d ed., pp. 119–146). Bristol, PA: Accelerated Development.

Axelson, J.A. (1993). *Counseling and Development in a Multicultural Society.* Pacific Grove, CA: Brooks/Cole.

Ayanian, J.Z., Udvarhelyi, I.S., Gatsonis, C.A., Pashos, C.L. & Epstein, A.M. (1993). Racial differences in the use of revascularization procedures after coronary angiography. *JAMA, 269,* 2642–2646.

Baldauf, S., & Johnson, K. (1998, June 11). Texas case highlights US problem race hate. *Christian Science Monitor,* p. 1.

Bankart, C.P. (1997). *Talking Cures: A History of Western and Eastern Psychotherapies.* Pacific Grove, CA: Brooks/Cole.

Banks, J.A., & Banks, C.A. (1993). *Multicultural Education.* Boston: Allyn Bacon.

Barak, A., & Dell, D.M. (1977). Differential perceptions of counselor behavior: Replication and extension. *Journal of Counseling Psychology, 24,* 288–292.

Barak, A., & La Crosse, M.B. (1975). Multidimensional perception of counselor behavior. *Journal of Counseling Psychology, 22,* 471–456.

Baratz, S., & Baratz, J. (1970). Early childhood intervention: The social sciences base of institutional racism. *Harvard Educational Review, 40,* 29–50.

Bardo, J., Bryson, S.L., & Cody, J.J. (1974). Black concerns with behavior modification. *Personnel and Guidance Journal, 53,* 334–341.

Barongan, C., Bernal, G., Comas-Diaz, L., Iijima Hall, C.C., Nagayama Hall, G.C., LaDue, R.A., Parham, T.A., Pedersen, P.B., Porche-Burke, L.M., Rollock, D., & Root, M.P.P. (1997). Misunderstandings of multiculturalism: Shouting fire in crowded theaters. *American Psychologist, 52,* 654–655.

Barr, D.J., & Strong, L.J. (1987, May). Embracing multiculturalism: The existing contradictions. *ACU-I Bulletin,* pp. 20–23.

Battle, E., & Rotter, J. (1963). Children's feelings of personal control as related to social class and ethnic group. *Journal of Personality, 31,* 482–490.

Baum, M.C., & Lamb, D.H. (1983). A comparison of the concerns presented by Black and White students to a university counseling center. *Journal of College Student Personnel, 24,* 127–131.

Beauvais, F., Chavez, E.L., Oetting, E.R., Deffenbacher, J.L., & Cornell, G.R. (1996). Drug use, violence, and victimization among white American, Mexican American, and American Indian dropouts, students with academic problems, and students in good academic standing. *Journal of Counseling Psychology, 43,* 292–299.

Becvar, D.S., & Becvar, R.J. (1996). *Family Therapy: A systemic Integration* (3rd ed.). Needham Heights, MA: Allyn & Bacon.

Bee-Gates, D., Howard-Pitney, B., LaFromboise, T., & Rowe, W. (1996). Help-seeking behavior of Native American Indian high school students. *Professional Psychology: Research and Practice, 27,* 495–499.

Bell, D. (1993). *Faces at the bottom of the well: The permanence of racism.* New York: Basic Books.

Bemak, F., Chung, R.C-Y., & Bornemann, T. (1996). Counseling and psychotherapy with refugees. In P. Pedersen, J. Draguns, W. Lonner, & J. Trimble (Eds.), *Counseling across cultures* (4th Edition, pp. 243–265). Thousand Oaks, CA: Sage.

Bennett, M.J. (1986). A developmental approach to training for intercultural sensitivity. *International Journal of Intercultural Relations, 10,* 179–196.

Berman, J. (1979). Counseling skills used by Black and White male and female counselors. *Journal of Counseling Psychology, 26,* 81–84.

Bernal, M.E., & Castro, F.G. (1994). Are clinical psychologists prepared for service and research with ethnic minorities? A report of a decade of progress. *American Psychologist, 49,* 797–805.

Bernal, M.E., & Knight, G.P. (1993). *Ethnic identity: Formation and transmission among Hispanics and other minorities.* Albany, NY: State University of New York Press.

Bernstein, B. (1964). Elaborated and restricted codes: Their social origins and some consequences. In J.J. Gumperz & D. Hymes (Eds.), The ethnography of communication, *American Anthropologist, 66,* 55–69.

Berry, B. (1965). *Ethnic and race relations.* Boston: Houghton Mifflin.

Berube, A. (1990). *Coming out under fire: The history of gay men and women in World War II.* New York: Free Press.

BigFoot-Sipes, D.S., Dauphinais, P., LaFromboise, T.D., Bennett, S.K. & Rowe, W. (1992). American Indian secondary school students preferences for counselor. Journal of Multicultural Counseling and Development, 20, 113–122.

Billingsley, A. (1970). Black families and White social science. *Journal of Social Issues, 26,* 127–142.

Black, L. (1996). Families of African origin: An overview. In M. McGoldrick, J. Giordano, & J.K. Pearce (Eds.), *Ethnicity and Family Therapy* (pp. 57–65). New York: Guilford.

Blanchard, E.L. (1983). The growth and development of American Indians and Alaskan Native children. In G.J. Powell, J. Yamamoto, A. Romero, & A. Morales (Eds.), *The psychosocial development of minority group children.* New York: Brunner/Mazel.

Blauner, B. (1993). But things are much worse for the negro people: Race and radicalism in my life and work. In J.H. Stanfield II (Ed.), *A history of race relations research: First generation recollections* (pp. 1–36). Newbury Park: Sage.

Bogardus, E. (1925). Measuring social distance. *Journal of Applied Sociology, 9,* 229–308.

Bold, K. (1996, October 25). Friends of the culture: To preserve Hispanic traditions and to educate others about what they perceive as an endangered way of life, three Orange County teachers have formed Amigas de la Cultura. *The Los Angeles Times,* p. E1.

Boulette, R.R. (1976). Assertive training with low income Mexican-American women. In M.R. Mirand (Ed.), *Psychotherapy with the Spanish-speaking: Issues in research and service delivery* (pp. 67–71). Los Angeles: Spanish-Speaking Mental Health Center.

Boxall, G. (1995, March 7). Report shows 53% rise in anti-gay hate crimes in L.A. *The Los Angeles Times,* p. 3.

Boyd, N. (1982). Family therapy with Black families. In E.E. Jones & S.J. Korchin (Eds.), *Minor-*

ity mental health (pp. 227–249). New York: Praeger.

Brandon, K. (1998, May 21). Student date stoke re-segregation fear: Fewer California Blacks and Hispanics plan to enroll at the state's leading universities. *Chicago Tribune,* p. 8.

Brecher, R., & Brecher, E. (1961). The happiest creatures on earth? *Harpers, 222,* 85–90.

Brennan, P.L., & Moos, R.H. (1996). Late-life drinking behavior. *Alcohol Health and Research World, 20,* 197–204.

Brinkley, D. (1994). *Saved by the light.* New York: Villard Books.

Brock, K.J., Mintz, L.B., & Good, G. (1997). Differences among sexually abused and nonabused women. *Journal of Counseling Psychology, 44,* 425–432.

Brolin, D.E. & Gysbers, N.C. (1989). Career education for students with disabilities. *Journal of Counseling and Development, 68,* 155–159.

Brooke, J. (1998, April 9). Indians strive to save their languages. *The New York Times,* p. 1.

Brown, D. (1997). Implications of cultural values for cross-cultural consultation with families. *Journal of Counseling and Development, 76,* 29–35.

Browning, C., Reynolds, A.L., & Dworkin, S.H. (1998). Affirmative psychotherapy for lesbian women. In D.R. Atkinson & G. Hackett (Eds.), *Counseling diverse populations* (2d ed., pp. 317–334). Boston: McGraw-Hill.

Burntt, C. (1998, April 19). Special Report: 1998 Southern economic survey: The Latin influence. *The Atlanta Journal/Atlanta Constitution,* p. O5.

Buckman, D.F. (1998). The see-through syndrome. *Inside MS, 16,* p. 19.

Butler, R.N., & Lewis, M.I. (1983). *Aging and mental health.* St. Louis: C.V. Mosby Company.

Canino, I., & Canino, G. (1982). Cultural syntonic family therapy for migrant Puerto Ricans. *Hospital and Community Psychiatry, 33,* 299–303.

Caplan, N. (1970). The new ghetto man: A review of recent empirical studies. *Journal of Social Issues, 26,* 59–73.

Caplan, N., & Nelson, S.D. (1973). On being useful—The nature and consequences of psychological research on social problems. *American Psychologist, 28,* 199–211.

Caplan, N., & Paige, J.M. (1968, August). A study of ghetto rioters. *Scientific American, 219,* 15–21.

Carillo, C. (1982). Changing norms of Hispanic families. In E.E. Jones & S.J. Korchin (Eds.), *Minority mental health* (pp. 250–266). New York: Praeger.

Carney, C.G., & Kahn, K.B. (1984). Building competencies for effective cross-cultural counseling: A developmental view. *The Counseling Psychologist, 12,* 111–119.

Carter, R.T. (1988). The relationship between racial identity attitudes and social class. *Journal of Negro Education, 57,* 22–30.

Carter, R.T. (1990). The relationship between racism and racial identity among White Americans: An exploratory investigation. *Journal of Counseling and Development, 69,* 46–50.

Carter, R.T. (1991). Racial identity attitudes and psychological functioning. *Journal of Multicultural Counseling and Development, 19,* 105–114.

Carter, R.T. (1995). *The influence of race and racial identity in psychotherapy.* New York: John Wiley.

Casas, J.M., & Pytluk, S.D. (1995). Hispanic identity development. In J.G. Ponterotto, J.M. Casas, L.A. Suzuki, & C.M. Alexander (Eds.), *Handbook of multicultural counseling* (pp. 155–180). Thousand Oaks, CA: Sage.

Casas, J.M. & Vasquez, M.J.T. (1996). Counseling the Hispanic. In P.B. Pedersen, J.G. Draguns, W.J. Lonner, & J.E. Trimble (Eds.), *Counseling across cultures* (4th ed., pp. 146–176). Thousand Oaks, CA: Sage Publications.

Chandras, K.V. (1997). Training multiculturally competent counselors to work with Asian Indian Americans. *Counselor Education and Supervision, 37,* 50–59.

Chang, C.Y. & Meyer, J.E. (1997). Understanding and Counseling Korean Americans: Implications for Training. *Counselor Education and Supervision, 37,* 35–49.

Chang, Y. (1998, June 22). Asian identity crisis. *Newsweek,* p. 68.

Cheatham, H., Ivey, A.E., Ivey, M.B., Pedersen, P., Rigazio-DiGilio, S., Simek-Morgan, L., & Sue, D.W. (1997). Multicultural counseling and therapy I: Metatheory—Taking theory into practice. In A.E. Ivey, M.B. Ivey, & L. Simek-Morgan (Eds.), *Counseling and Psychotherapy: A Multicultural Perspective* (pp. 133–169). Boston: Allyn Bacon.

Cheek, D. (1987). *Assertive White... puzzled White.* San Luis Obispo, CA: Impact.

Chen, M., Froehle, T., & Morran, K. (1997). Deconstructing dispositional bias in clinical inference: Two interventions. *Journal of Counseling and Development, 76,* 74–81.

Cheung, F.K., & Snowden, L.R. (1990). Community mental health and ethnic minority populations. *Community Mental Health Journal, 26,* 277–291.

Cheung, L.-R.L. (1987). *Assessing Asian language performance.* Rockville: Aspen Publishers.

Choney, S.K., Berryhill-Paapke, E., & Robbins, R.R. (1995). The acculturation of American Indians: Developing frameworks for research and practice. In J.G. Ponterotto, J.M. Casas, L.A. Suzuki, & C.M. Alexander (Eds.), *Handbook of multicultural counseling* (pp. 73–92). Thousand Oaks, CA: Sage.

Christensen, E.W. (1975). Counseling Puerto Ricans. *Personnel and Guidance Journal, 55,* 412–415.

Christiansen, S.C., Martin, S.B., Schleicher, N.C., Koziol, J.A., Mathews, K.P. & Zuraw, B.L. (1996). Current prevalence of asthma-related symptoms in San Diego's predominantly Hispanic inner-city children. *Journal of Asthma, 33,* 17–26.

Chung, R.C.-Y., Bemak, F., & Okazaki, S. (1997). Counseling Americans of Southeast Asian descent. In C.C. Lee (Ed.), *Multicultural issues in counseling* (2d ed., pp. 207–231). Alexandria, VA: American Counseling Association.

Church, G.J., Goodgame, D., Leavitt, R., & Lopez, J. (1985, July 8). Hispanics: A melding of cultures. *Time, 126,* 36–39.

Clark, K.B. (1963). Educational stimulation of racially disadvantaged children. In A.H. Passow (Ed.), *Education in depressed areas* (pp. 142–162). New York: Teachers College Press.

Clark, K.B., & Clark, M.K. (1947). Racial identification and preference in Negro children. In T.M. Newcomb & E.L. Hartley (Eds.), *Readings in social psychology* (pp. 169–178). New York: Holt, Reinhart & Winston.

Clark, K.B., & Plotkin, L. (1972). A review of the issues and literature of cultural deprivation theory. In K.B. Clark (Ed)., *The educationally deprived* (pp. 47–73). New York: Metropolitan Applied Research Center.

Coleman, E. & Ramafedi, G. (1989). Gay, lesbian, and bisexual adolescents: A critical challenge to counselors. *Journal of Counseling and Development, 68,* 36–40.

Collins, B.E. (1970). *Social Psychology.* Reading, MA: Addison-Wesley.

Condon, J.C., & Yousef, F. (1975). *An introduction to intercultural communication.* New York: Bobbs-Merrill Co.

Conger, J. (1975). Proceedings of the American Psychological Association, Incorporated, for the year 1974: Minutes of the annual meeting of Council of Representatives. *American Psychologist, 30,* 620–651.

Constantine, M.C., Richardson, T.Q., Benjamin, E.M., & Wilson, J.W. (1998). An overview of Black racial identity theories: Limitations and considerations for future theoretical conceptualizations. *Applied and Preventive Psychology, 7,* 95–99.

Cook, E.P. (1990). Gender and psychological distress. *Journal of Counseling and Development, 68,* 371–375.

Cooper, C., & Costas, L. (1994). Ethical challenges when working with Hispanic/Latino families: Personalismo. *The Family Psychologist, 10,* 32–34.

Corey, G. (1996). *Theory and Practice of Counseling and Psychotherapy* (5th ed.). Pacific Grove, CA: Brooks/Cole.

Corrigan, J.D., Dell, D.M., Lewis, K.N., & Schmidt, L.D. (1980). Counseling as a social influence process: A review. *Journal of counseling Psychology, 27,* 391–441.

Corvin, S., & Wiggins, F. (1989). An antiracism training model for White professionals. *Journal of Multicultural Counseling and Development, 17,* 105–114.

Crandall, V., Katkovsky, W., & Crandall, V. (1965). Children's beliefs in their own control of reinforcements in intellectual achievement situations. *Child Development, 36,* 91–109.

Cronin, M.E. (1998, June 11) Body type–body hype—Local high-school students challenge marketing of super-thin image. *Seattle Times,* p. E1.

Cross, T.L., Bazron, B.J., Dennis, K.W., & Isaacs, M.R. (1989). *Towards a culturally competent system of care.* Washington, DC: Child and Adolescent Service System Program Technical Assistance Center.

Cross, W.E. (1971). The Negro-to-Black conversion experience: Towards a psychology of Black liberation. *Black World, 20,* 13–27.

Cross, W.E. (1991). *Shades of Black: Diversity in African American identity.* Philadelphia: Temple University Press.

Cross, W.E. (1995). The psychology of Nigrescence: Revising the Cross model. In J.G. Ponterotto, J.M. Casas, L.A. Suzuki, & C.M. Alexander (Eds.), *Handbook of Multicultural Counseling* (pp. 93–122). Thousand Oaks, CA: Sage.

Cuellar, I., Harris, L.C., & Jasso, R. (1980). An acculturation scale for Mexican American normal and clinical populations. *Hispanic Journal of Behavioral Sciences, 2,* 199–217.

Culbertson, F.M. (1997). Depression and gender. *American Psychologist, 52,* 25–31.

Cummins, J. (1986). Empowering minority students: A framework for intervention. *Harvard Educational Review, 56,* 18–36.

Currie, C. (1997). Old fools, lovers, and sages. *British Medical Journal, 315,* 7115.

Dana, R.H. (1993). *Multicultural assessment perspectives for professional psychology.* Needham Heights, MA: Allyn & Bacon.

D'Andrea, M., & Daniels, J. (1995). Promoting multiculturalism and organizational change in the counseling profession: A case study. In J.G. Ponterotto, J.M. Casas, L.A. Suzuki, & C.M. Alexander (Eds.), Handbook of Multicultural Counseling (pp. 17–33). Thousand Oaks, CA: Sage.

D'Andrea, M., Daniels, J., and Heck, R. (1991). Evaluating the impact of multicultural counseling training. *Journal of Counseling and Development, 70,* 143–150.

Daniels, R. (1971). *Concentration camps USA: Japanese Americans and World War II.* New York: Rinehart & Winston.

Darwin, C. (1859). *On the origin of species by natural selection.* London: Murray.

Das, A.K. (1987). Indigenous models of therapy in traditional Asian societies. *Journal of Multicultural Counseling and Development, 15,* 25–37.

Das Gupta, M. (1997). "What is Indian about you?": A gendered, transnational approach to ethnicity. *Gender and Society, 11,* 572–596.

Deater-Deckard, K., Dodge, K.A., Bates, J.E., & Pettit, G.S. (1996). Physical discipline among African American and European American mothers: Links to children's externalizing behaviors. *Developmental Psychology, 32,* 1065–1072.

de Gobineau, A. (1915). *The inequality of human races.* New York: Putnam.

De La Cancela, V. (1985). Toward a sociocultural psychotherapy for low-income ethnic minorities. *Psychotherapy, 22,* 427–435.

De La Cancela, V. (1991). Working affirmatively with Puerto Rican men: Professional and personal reflections. In M. Bograd (Ed.), *Feminist approaches for men and women in family therapy* (pp. 195–211). New York: Harrington Park Press.

Dell, B.M. (1973). Counselor power base, influence attempt, and behavior change in counseling. *Journal of Counseling Psychology, 20,* 399–405.

DePaulo, B.M. (1992). Nonverbal behavior and self-presentation. *Psychological Bulletin, 111,* 203–243.

DeVoe, D. (1998). Feminist and nonsexist counseling: Implications for the male counselor. In D.R. Atkinson & G. Hackett (Eds.), *Counseling diverse populations* (2d ed., pp. 283–291). Boston: McGraw-Hill.

DeVos, G., & Abbott, K. (1966). The Chinese family in San Francisco. Unpublished master's dissertation, University of California, Berkeley.

Diaz-Guerrero, R. (1977). A Mexican psychology. *American Psychologist, 32,* 934–944.

Diokno, A.C., Brown, M.B., & Herzog, A.R. (1990). Sexual functioning in the elderly. *Archives of Internal Medicine, 150,* 197–200.

Dolliver, R.H., Williams, E.L., & Gold, D.C. (1980). The art of Gestalt therapy or: What are you doing with your feet now? *Psychotherapy: Theory, Research & Practice, 17,* 136–142.

Dominguez-Ybarra, A., & Garrison, J. (1977). Toward adequate psychiatric classification and treatment of Mexican-American patients. *Psychiatric Annals, 7,* 86–89.

Dorfman, D.D. (1978). The Cyril Burt question: New findings. *Science, 201,* 1177–1186.

Doty, L. (1987). *Communication and assertion skills for older persons.* New York: Hemisphere.

Douglis, R. (1987, November). The beat goes on. *Psychology Today.*

Downey, N.E., & Roush, K.L. (1985). From passive acceptance to active commitment: A model of feminist identity development for women. The Counseling Psychologist, 13, 695–709.

Dulles Conference Task Force (1978). *Expanding the roles of culturally diverse peoples in the profession of psychology.* Report submitted to the Board of Directors of American Psychological Association, Washington, DC: American Psychological Association.

Dychtwald, K. (1989). *Age Wave.* Los Angeles: J.P. Tarcher.

Eadie, B.J. (1992). *Embraced by the light.* Carson City, NV: Gold Leaf Press.

Eakins, B.W., & Eakins, R.G. (1985). Sex differences in nonverbal communication. In L.A. Samovar & R.E. Porter (Eds.), *Intercultural communication: A reader* (pp. 290–307). Belmont, CA: Wadsworth.

Eaton, M.J., & Dembo, M.H. (1997). Differences in the motivational beliefs of Asian Americans. *Journal of Educational Psychology, 89,* 433–440.

Ebert, B. (1978). The healthy family. Family therapy, 5, 227–232.

EchoHawk, M. (1997). Suicide: The scourge of Native American people. *Suicide and Life Threatening Behavior, 27,* 60–67.

Edwards, H.P., Boulet, D.B., Mahrer, A.R., Chagnon, G.J. & Mook, B. (1982). Carl Rogers during initial interviews: A moderate and consistent therapist. *Journal of Counseling Psychology, 29,* 14–18.

Ellis, A. (1997). Using rational emotive behavior therapy techniques to cope with disability. *Professional Psychology: Research and Practice, 28,* 17–22.

Ellison, R. (1966). Harlem is nowhere. In Shadow and Act. New York: Random House.

Espin, O.M. (1985). Psychotherapy with Hispanic women. In P.B. Pedersen (Ed.), *Handbook of cross-cultural counseling and therapy* (pp. 165–171). Westport, CT: Greenwood Press.

Espinosa, P. (1997). School involvement and Hispanic parents. *The Prevention Researcher, 5,* 5–6.

Evans, L.A., Acosta, F.X., Yamamoto, J., & Hurwicz, M.L. (1986). Patient requests: Correlates and therapeutic implications for Hispanic, Black, and Caucasian patients. *Journal of Clinical Psychology, 42,* 213–221.

Everett, F., Proctor, N., & Cortmell, B. (1989). Providing psychological services to American Indian children and families. In D.R. Atkinson, G. Morten, & D.W. Sue (Eds.), *Counseling American minorities* (3d ed., pp. 53–71). Dubuque, IA: W.C. Brown.

Fabian, E.S., Lent, R.W. & Willis, S.P. (1998). Predicting work transition outcome for students with disabilities: Implications for counselors. *Journal of Counseling and Development, 76,* 311–316.

Fadiman, A. (1997). *The spirit catches you and you fall down.* New York: Farrar, Straus & Giroux.

Falicov, C.J. (1996). Mexican Families. In M. McGoldrick, J. Giordano, & J.K. Pearce (Eds.), *Ethnicity and Family Therapy* (pp. 169–182). New York: Guilford.

Feagin, J.R. (1989). *Racial and ethnic relations.* Englewood Cliffs, NJ: Prentice-Hall.

Feldman, S.S., & Rosenthal, D.A. (1990). The acculturation of autonomy expectations in Chinese high schoolers residing in two western nations. *International Journal of Psychology, 25,* 259–281.

Felton, G.M., Parson, M.A., Misener, T.R. & Oldaker, S. (1997). Health promoting Behavior of black and white college women. *Western Journal of Nursing Research, 19,* 654–664.

Fernando, S. (1988). *Race and culture in psychiatry.* London: Croom Helm.

Festinger, L. (1957). *A theory of cognitive dissonance.* Evanston, IL: Row & Peterson.

Fields-Meyer, T. (1998, June 29). One deadly night. *People Weekly, 49,* 46–47.

Fisher, A.R., Tokar, D.M., & Serna, G.S. (1998). Validity and construct contamination of the Racial Identity Attitude Scale—Long Form. *Journal of Counseling Psychology, 45,* 212–224.

Fitzgerald, L.F., Drasgow, F., Hulin, C.L., Gelfand, M.J., & Magley, V.J. (1997). Antecedents and consequences of sexual harassment in organizations: A test of an integrated model. *Journal of Applied Psychology, 82,* 578–589.

Fitzgerald, L.F. & Nutt, R. (1998). The Division 17 principles concerning the counseling/psychotherapy of women: Rationale and implementation. In D.R. Atkinson & G. Hackett (Eds.), *Counseling diverse populations* (2d ed., pp. 239–270). Boston: McGraw-Hill.

Flack, J.M., Amaro, H., Jenkins, W., Kunitz, S., Levy, J., Mixon, M., and Yu, E. (1995). Panel I: Epidemiology of mental health. *Health Psychology, 14,* 592–600.

Florio, E.R., Hendryx, M.S., Jensen, J.E. & Rockwood, T.H. (1997). A comparison of suicidal and nonsuicidal elders referred to a community mental health center program. *Suicide and Life, 27,* 182–193.

Fogelson, R.M. (1970). Violence and grievances: Reflections on the 1960's riots. *Journal of Social Issues, 26,* 141–163.

Folensbee, R., Draguns, J.G., & Danish, S. (1986). Counselor interventions in three cultural groups. *Journal of Counseling Psychology, 33,* 446–453.

Foley, V.D. (1984). Family therapy. In R.J. Corsini (Ed.), *Current psychotherapies.* Itasca, IL: F.F. Peacock Publishers.

Ford, D.Y. (1997). Counseling middle-class African Americans. In C.C. Lee (Ed.), *Multicultural issues in counseling* (2d ed., pp. 81–108). Alexandria, VA: American Counseling Association.

Forsyth, D.R., Heiney, M.M. & Wright, S.S. (1997).

Biases in appraisals of women leaders. *Group Dynamics: Theory, Research, and Practice, 1,* 98–103.

Forward, J.R., & Williams, J.R. (1970). International external control and Black militancy. *Journal of Social Issues, 26,* 74–92.

Foster, B.G., Jackson, G., Cross, W.E., Jackson, B., & Hardiman, R. (1988). Workforce diversity and business. Alexandria, VA: American Society for Training and Development. (Reprinted from *Training and Development Journal,* April 1988).

Frame, M.W. & Williams, C.B. (1996). Counseling African Americans: Integrating spirituality in therapy. *Counseling and Values, 41,* 16–28.

Frankel, M. (1998, May 24). The oldest bias. *New York Times Magazine,* p. 16–17.

Franklin, A.J. (1982). Therapeutic interventions with urban Black adolescents. In E.E. Jones & S.J. Korchin (Eds.), *Minority mental health* (pp. 267–295). New York: Praeger.

Franklin, J.H. (1988). A historical note on black families. In H.P. McAdoo (Ed.), *Black families* (pp. 3–14). Newbury Park, CA: Sage.

Freeberg, L. (1995, October 5). 1 of 3 blacks in 20s has had trouble with law. *Seattle Post-Intelligencer,* pp. A1, A8.

Freire, P. (1970). *Cultural action for freedom.* Cambridge: Harvard Educational Review Press.

Freud, S. (1960). *Psychopathology of everyday life.* In J. Strachey (ed. and trans.), The Standard edition of the complete psychological works of Sigmund Freud. *6,* London: Hogarth Press.

Galan, F.J. (1998). An empowerment prevention approach for Hispanic youth. *The Prevention Researcher, 5,* 10–12.

Gallegos, J.S. (1982). Planning and administering services for minority groups. In M.J. Austin & W.E. Hershey (Eds.), *Handbook on mental health administration* (pp. 87–105). San Francisco: Jossey-Bass.

Gallup, G. (1995). *The Gallup poll: Public opinion 1995.* Wilmington, DE: Scholarly Resources.

Galton, F. (1869). *Hereditary genius: An inquiry into its laws and consequences.* London: Macmillan.

Gannett News Service (1998, May 26). Young Americans optimistic, but face deep racial divisions. *The Bellingham Herald,* p. A7.

Garcia, D., & Levenson, H. (1975). Differences between Black's and White's expectations of control by chance and powerful others. *Psychological Reports, 37,* 563–566.

Garcia-Preto, N. (1996). Puerto Rican Families. In M. McGoldrick, J. Giordano, & J.K. Pearce (Eds.), *Ethnicity and Family Therapy* (pp. 183–199). New York: Guilford.

Garfield, J.C., Weiss, S.L., & Pollock, E.A. (1973). Effects of a child's social class on school counselors' decision making. *Journal of Counseling Psychology, 20,* 166–168.

Garnets, L., Hancock, K.A., Cochran, S.D., Goodchilds, J., & Peplau, L.A. (1998). Issues in psychotherapy with lesbians and gay men: A survey of psychologists. In D.R. Atkinson & G. Hackett (Eds.), *Counseling diverse populations* (2d ed., pp. 297–316). Boston: McGraw-Hill.

Garrett, J.T., & Garrett, M.W. (1994). The path of good medicine: Understanding and counseling Native American Indians. *Journal of Multicultural Counseling and Development, 22,* 134–144.

Gary, L.E. (1985). Attitudes toward human service organizations: Perspectives from an urban Black community. *Journal of Applied Behavioral Science, 21,* 445–458.

Gay, G. (1998). Coming of age ethnically: Teaching young adolescents of color. *The Prevention Researcher, 5,* 7–9.

George, H.T. (1998, July 14). Young quadriplegic has a dream. *Seattle Post-Intelligencer,* p. B2.

George, K. (1998, June 18). Parenthood and scholarship out at Taholah. *Seattle Post-Intelligencer,* pp. B1, B3.

Gersten, R. & Woodward, J. (1994). The language-minority student and special education: Issues, trends, and paradoxes. *Exceptional Children, 60,* 310–308.

Giachello, A.L. & Belgrave, F. (1997). Task Group VI: Health Care Systems and Behavior. Journal of Gender, Culture, and Health, 2, 163–173.

Gibbs, J.T. (1980). The interpersonal orientation in mental health consultation: Toward a model of ethnic variations in consultation. *American Journal of Orthopsychiatry, 45,* 430–445.

Gibbs, J.T. (1987). Identity and marginality: Issues in the treatment of biracial adolescents. *American Journal of Orthopsychiatry, 57,* 265–278.

Gillie, D. (1977). The IQ issue. *Phi Delta Kappan, 58,* 469.

Giordano, J., & Giordano, M.A. (1995). Ethnic dimensions in family therapy. In R. Mikesell, D. Lusterman, & S. McDaniel (eds.), *Integrating family therapy.* Washington, DC: American Psychological Association.

Goldberg, C. (1998, May 31). Acceptance of gay men and lesbians is growing, study says. *New York Times,* p. 21.

Goldenberg, I, & Goldenberg, H. (1996). *Family Therapy: An overview* (4th ed.). Pacific Grove: Brooks/Cole.

Goldman, L. (1977). Toward more meaningful research. *Personnel and Guidance Journal, 55,* 363–368.

Goldman, M. (1980). Effect of eye contact and distance on the verbal reinforcement of attitude. *The Journal of Social Psychology, 111,* 73–78.

Gonsiorek, J.C. (1982). Results of psychological testing on homosexual populations. *American Behavioral Scientist, 25,* 385–396.

Gonzalez, A. & Zimbardo, P.G. (1985, March). Time in perspective. *Psychology Today,* pp. 21–26.

Gonzalez, G.M. (1997). The emergence of Chicanos in the twenty-first century: Implications for counseling, research, and policy. *Journal of Multicultural Counseling and Development, 25,* 94–106.

Good, G.E., Gilbert, L.A., & Scher, M. (1990). Gender aware therapy: A synthesis of feminist therapy and knowledge about gender. *Journal of Counseling and Development, 68,* 376–380.

Gore, P.M., & Rotter, J.B. (1963). A personality correlate of social action. *Journal of Personality, 31,* 58–64.

Gorman, J.C. & Balter, L. (1997). Culturally sensitive parent education: A critical review of quantitative research. *Review of Educational Research, 67,* 339–369.

Gossett, T.F. (1963). *Race: The history of an idea in America.* Dallas, TX: Southern Methodist University Press.

Gottesfeld, H. (1995). Community context and the underutilization of mental health services by minority patients. *Psychological Reports, 76,* 207–210.

Gould, S.J. (1996). *The mismeasure of man.* New York: Norton.

Graham, R. (1997, May 4). Speaking with the enemy, Arthur Dong's film about gay bashing. *Boston Globe,* p. D, 11:3.

Grant, L.D. (1996). Effects of ageism on individual and health care providers' responses to healthy aging. *Health and Social Work, 21,* 9–14.

Gray, E. & Cosgrove, J. (1985). Ethnocentric perception of childrearing practices in protective services. *Child Abuse and Neglect, 9,* 389–396.

Green, J.M., Trankina, F.J., & Chavez, N. (1976). Therapeutic intervention with Mexican-American children. *Psychiatric Annals, 6,* 227–234.

Greene, B.A. (1985). Considerations in the treatment of Black patients by White therapists. *Psychotherapy, 22,* 389–393.

Grevious, C. (1985). The role of the family therapist with low-income Black families. *Family Therapy, 12,* 115–122.

Grier, W., & Cobbs, P. (1968). *Black rage.* New York: Basic Books.

Grier, W., & Cobbs, P. (1971). *The Jesus bag.* San Francisco: McGraw-Hill.

Guerra, P. (1998, July). Older adults and substance abuse: Looking at the "invisible epidemic." *Counseling Today,* pp. 38, 43.

Gurin, P., Gurin, G., Lao, R., & Beattie, M. (1969). Internal-external control in the motivational dynamics of negro youth. *Journal of Social Issues, 25,* 29–54.

Gushue, G.V., & Sciarra, D.T. (1995). Culture and families: A multidimensional approach. In J.G. Ponterotto, J.M. Casas, L.A. Suzuki & C.M. Alexander (Eds.), *Handbook of Multicultural Counseling* (pp. 586–606). Thousand Oaks, CA: Sage.

Guthrie, R.V. (1997). *Even the rat was white: A his-*

torical view of psychology (2nd ed.). New York: Harper and Row.

Gutierres, S.F. & Todd, M. (1997). The impact of childhood abuse on treatment outcomes. *Professional Psychology: Research and Practice, 28,* 348–354.

Habemann, L., & Thiry, S. (1970). The effect of socioeconomic status variables on counselor perception and behavior. Unpublished master's thesis. Madison: University of Wisconsin.

Haley, A. (1966). *The autobiography of Malcolm X.* New York: Grove Press.

Haley, J. (1967). Marriage therapy. In H. Greenwald (Ed.), *Active psychotherapy* (pp. 189–223). Chicago: Aldine.

Hall, E.T. (1959). *The silent language.* Greenwich, CT: Premier Books.

Hall, E.T. (1969). *The hidden dimension.* Garden City, New York: Doubleday.

Hall, E.T. (1974). *Handbook for proxemic research.* Washington, DC: Society for the Ontology of Visual Communications.

Hall, E.T. (1976). *Beyond culture.* New York: Anchor Press.

Hall, W.S., Cross, W.E., & Freedle, R. (1972). Stages in the development of Black awareness: An exploratory investigation. In R.L. Jones (Ed.), *Black Psychology* (pp. 156–165). New York: Harper & Row.

Halleck, S.L. (1971, April). Therapy is the handmaiden of the status quo. *Psychology Today, 4,* 30–34, 98–100.

Hammerschlag, C.A. (1988). *The dancing healers.* San Francisco: Harper & Row.

Hansen, J.C., Stevic, R.R., & Warner, R.W. (1982). *Counseling: Theory and process.* Toronto: Allyn-Bacon.

Hardiman, R. (1982). White identity development: A process oriented model for describing the racial consciousness of White Americans. *Dissertation Abstracts International, 43,* 104A. (University Microfilms No. 82-10330).

Harner, M. (1990). *The way of the shaman.* San Francisco: Harper and Row.

Harris, D.R., Andrews, R., & Elixhauser, A. (1997). Racial and gender differences in use of procedures for black and white hospitalized adults. *Ethnicity and Disease, 7,* 91–105.

Harvey, A.R., & Rauch, J.B. (1997). A comprehensive Afrocentric rites of passage program for Black male adolescents. *Health and Social Work, 22,* 32–37.

Hatfield, D. (1996, July/August). The Jack Nicklaus syndrome. *The Humanist,* p. 38.

Hayes, L.L. (1997, August). The unique counseling needs of Latino clients. *Counseling Today,* pp. 1, 10.

Hays, P.A. (1996). Addressing the complexities of culture and gender in counseling. *Journal of Counseling and Development, 74,* 332–338.

Headden, S. (1997). The Hispanic dropout mystery. *U.S. News & World Report, 123,* 64–65.

Healy, P. (1998). Berkeley struggles to stay diverse in post-affirmative action era. *The Chronicle of Higher Education, 44,* A31–A33.

Heatherton, T.F., Mahamedi, F., Striepe, M., Field, A.E., & Keel, P. (1997). A 10-year longitudinal study of body weight, dieting, and eating disorders. *Journal of Abnormal Psychology, 106,* 117–125.

Heesacker, M., & Carroll, T.A. (1997). Identifying and solving impediments to the social and counseling psychology interface. *The Counseling Psychologist, 25,* 171–179.

Heesacker, M., Conner, K., & Pritchard, S. (1995). Individual counseling and psychotherapy: Allocations from the social psychology of attitude change. *The Counseling Psychologist, 23,* 611–632.

Heinrich, R.K., Corbin, J.L., & Thomas, K.R. (1990). Counseling Native Americans. *Journal of Counseling & Development, 69,* 128–133.

Heller, K. (1998). Prevention activities for older adults: Social structures and personal competencies that maintain useful social roles. In D.R. Atkinson & G. Hackett (Eds.), *Counseling diverse populations* (2d ed., pp. 183–198). Boston: McGraw-Hill.

Helms, J.E. (1984). Toward a theoretical explanation of the effects of race on counseling: A Black and White model. *The Counseling Psychologist, 12,* 153–165.

Helms, J.E. (1985). Cultural identity in the treatment process. In P.B. Pedersen (Ed.), *Handbook of cross-cultural counseling and therapy* (pp. 239–245). Westport, CT: Greenwood Press.

Helms, J.E. (1986). Expanding racial identity theory to cover counseling process. *Journal of Counseling Psychology, 33,* 62–64.

Helms, J.E. (1990). *Black and White racial identity: Theory, research, and practice.* New York: Greenwood Press.

Helms, J.E. (1993). I also said, "White racial identity influences White researchers" [Reaction]. *The Counseling Psychologist, 21,* 240–243.

Helms, J.E. (1994a). How multiculturalism obscures racial factors in the therapy process: Comment on Ridley et al. (1994), Sodowsky et al. (1994), Ottavi et al. (1994), and Thompson et al. (1994). *Journal of Counseling Psychology, 41,* 162–165.

Helms, J.E. (1995). An update of Helms's White and people of color racial identity models. In J.G. Ponterotto, J.M. Casas, L.A. Suzuki, & C.M. Alexander (Eds.), *Handbook of Multicultural Counseling* (pp. 181–191). Thousand Oaks, CA: Sage.

Helms, J.E., & Carter, R.T. (1990). Development, of the White racial identity attitude inventory. In J.E. Helms (Ed.), *Black and White racial identity: Theory, research and practice* (pp. 67–80). Westport, CT: Greenwood.

Helms, J.E., & Giorgis, T.W. (1980, November). A comparison of the locus of control and anxiety level of African, Black American, and White American college students. *Journal of College Student Personnel,* pp. 503–509.

Henkin, W.A. (1985). Toward counseling the Japanese in America: A cross-cultural primer. *Journal of Counseling & Development, 63,* 500–503.

Heppner, P.P., & Claiborn, C.D.(1989). Social influence research in counseling: A review and critique. *Journal of Counseling Psychology, 36,* 365–387.

Heppner, P.P., & Frazier, P.A. (1992). Social psychological processes in psychotherapy: Extrapolating basic research to counseling psychology. In S.D. Brown & R.W. Lent (Eds.), *Handbook of counseling psychology* (2nd ed., pp. 141–175). New York: John Wiley.

Herlihy, B., & Corey, G. (1997). *Boundary issues in counseling.* Alexandria, VA: American Counseling Association.

Herring, R.D. (1997). *Counseling Diverse Ethnic Youth.* Fort Worth, TX: Harcourt Brace.

Hernstein, R. (1971). IQ. *Atlantic Monthly,* pp. 43–64.

Hernstein, R., & Murray, C. (1994). *The bell curve: Intelligence and class structure in American life.* New York: Free Press.

Highlen, P.S. (1994). Racial/ethnic diversity in doctoral programs of psychology: Challenges for the twenty-first century. *Applied and Preventive Psychology, 3,* 91–108.

Highlen, P.S. (1996). MCT theory and implications for organizations/systems. In D.W. Sue, A.E. Ivey, & P.B. Pedersen (Eds.), *A theory of multicultural counseling and therapy* (pp. 65–85). Pacific Grove, CA: Brooks/Cole.

Hildebrand, V., Phenice, L.A., Gray, M.M., & Hines, R.P. (1996). *Knowing and serving diverse families.* Englewood Cliffs, NJ: Prentice-Hall.

Hill, C.E., Thames, T.B., & Rardin, D.K. (1979). Comparison of Rogers, Perls, and Ellis on the Hill Counselor Verbal Response Category System. *Journal of Counseling Psychology, 26,* 198–203.

Hills, H.I., & Strozier, A.A. (1992). Multicultural training in APA approved counseling psychology programs: A survey. *Professional Psychology: Research and Practice, 23,* 43–51.

Hines, P.M., & Boyd-Franklin, N. (1996). African American families. In M. McGoldrick, J. Giordano, & J.K. Pearce (Eds.), *Ethnicity and family therapy* (pp. 66–84). New York: Guilford Press.

Ho, M.K. (1987). *Family therapy with ethnic minorities.* Newbury Park, CA: Sage.

Ho, M.K. (1997). *Family therapy with ethnic minorities.* (2nd ed). Thousand Oaks, CA: Sage.

Hollingshead, A.R., & Redlich, F.C. (1968). Social class and mental health. New York: John Wiley.

Hooker, E. (1957). The adjustment of the male overt homosexual. *Journal of Projective Techniques, 21,* 18–31.

Hoshmand, L.S.T. (1989). Alternate research paradigms: A review and teaching proposal. *The Counseling Psychologist, 17,* 3–79.

Hsieh, T., Shybut, J., & Lotsof, E. (1969). Internal versus external control and ethnic group membership: A cross-cultural comparison. *Journal of Consulting and Clinical Psychology, 33,* 122–124.

Hulnick, M.R., & Hulnick, H.R. (1989). Life's challenges: Curse or opportunity? Counseling families of persons with disabilities. *Journal of Counseling and Development, 68,* 166–170.

Humes, C.W., Szymanski, E.M., & Hohenshil, T.H. (1989). Roles of counseling in enabling persons with disabilities. *Journal of Counseling and Development, 68,* 145–150.

Ibrahim, F.A. (1985). Effective cross-cultural counseling and psychotherapy: A framework. *The Counseling Psychologist, 13,* 625–638.

Ina, S. (1997). Counseling Japanese Americans. In C.C. Lee (Ed.), *Multicultural issues in counseling* (2d ed., pp. 189–206). Alexandria, VA: American Counseling Association.

Inlan, J. (1979). Adjustment to migration: Family organization, acculturation, and psychological symptomatology in Puerto Rican women of three socioeconomic class groups. Unpublished doctoral dissertation. New York: New York University.

Inclan, J. (1985). Variations in value orientations in mental health work with Puerto Ricans. *Psychotherapy, 22,* 324–334.

Irvine, J.J., & York, D.E. (1995). Learning styles and culturally diverse students: A literature review. In J.A. Banks & C.A. McGee Banks (Eds.), *Handbook of Research on Multicultural Education* (pp. 484–497). New York: McMillan.

Ishisaka, H.A., Nguyen, Q.T., & Okimoto, J.T. (1985). The role in the mental health treatment of Indochinese refugees. In T.C. Owan (Ed.), *Southeast Asian mental health treatment, prevention services, training, and research.* Washington, DC: National Institute of Mental Health.

Ishiyama, F. (1986). Morita therapy. *Psychotherapy, 23,* 375–380.

Ivey, A.E. (1981). Counseling and psychotherapy:

Toward a new perspective. In A.J. Marsella and P.B. Pedersen (Eds.), *Cross-cultural counseling and psychotherapy.* New York: Pergamon.

Ivey, A.E. (1986). *Developmental therapy.* San Francisco: Jossey-Bass.

Ivey, A.E., Ivey, M.B., & Simek-Downing, L. (1987). *Counseling and psychotherapy: Skills, theories, and practice.* Englewood Cliffs, NJ: Prentice-Hall.

Ivey, A.E., Ivey, M.B., & Simek-Morgan, L. (1997). *Counseling and psychotherapy: A multicultural perspective.* Boston: Allyn Bacon.

Jackson, A.M. (1983). A theoretical model for the practice of psychotherapy with Black populations. *Journal of Black Psychology, 10,* 19–27.

Jackson, B. (1975). Black identity development. *Journal of Educational Diversity, 2,* 19–25.

Jackson, B.W., & Holvino, E. (1988). Developing multicultural organizations. *Journal of Religion and the Applied Behavioral Sciences, 9,* 14–19.

Jackson, M.L. (1995). Multicultural Counseling: Historical Perspectives. In J.G. Ponterotto, J.M. Casas, L.A. Suzuki, & C.M. Alexander (Eds.), *Handbook of Multicultural Counseling* (pp. 3–16). Thousand Oaks, CA: Sage.

Jacobson, S., & Samdahl, D.M. (1998). Leisure in the lives of old lesbians: Experiences with and responses to discrimination. *Journal of Leisure Research, 30,* 233–255.

Jenkins, A.H. (1982). *The psychology of the Afro-American.* New York: Pergamon.

Jensen, A. (1969). How much can we boost IQ and school achievement? *Harvard Educational Review, 39,* 1–123.

Jensen, J.V. (1985). Perspective on nonverbal intercultural communication. In L.A. Samovar & R.E. Porter (Eds.), *Intercultural communication: A reader* (pp. 256–272). Belmont, CA: Wadsworth.

Johnson, B. (1995, January 19). Elderly women need not abandon sexuality. *Seattle Post-Intelligencer.*

Johnson, K.W., Anderson, N.B., Bastida, E., Kramer, B.J., Williams, D., & Wong, M. (1995). Macrosocial and environmental influences on minority health. *Health Psychology, 14,* 601–612.

Jones, A.C. (1985). Psychological functioning in Black Americans: A conceptual guide for use in psychotherapy. *Psychotherapy, 22,* 363–369.

Jones, D.R., Harrell, J.P., Morris-Prather, C.E., Thomas, J. & Omowale, N. (1996). Affective and physiological responses to racism: The roles of afrocentrism and mode of presentation. *Ethnicity and Disease, 6,* 109–122.

Jones, E.E., Kanouse, D., Kelley, H.H., Nisbett, R.E., Valins, S., & Weiner, B. (Eds.). (1972). *Attribution: Perceiving the causes of behavior.* Morristown, NJ: General Learning Press.

Jones, J.M. (1972). *Prejudice and racism.* Reading, MA: Addison Wesley.

Jones, J.M. (1997). *Prejudice and racism* (2nd ed.). New York: McGraw-Hill.

Jordon, J.M. (1997). Counseling African American Women from a cultural sensitivity perspective. In C.C. Lee (Ed.) Multicultural issues in counseling (2d ed.), pp. 109–122. Alexandria, VA: American Counseling Assoc.

Jordan, W.D. (1969). *White over Black: American attitudes toward the Negro, 1550–1812.* Baltimore: Penguin Books.

Journard, S.M. (1964). *The transparent self.* Princeton, NJ: D. Van Nostrand.

Juang, S.-H., & Tucker, C.M. (1991). Factors in marital adjustment and their interrelationships: A comparison of Taiwanese couples in America and Caucasian American couples. *Journal of Multicultural Counseling and Development, 19,* 22–31.

Juarez, R. (1985). Core issues in psychotherapy with the Hispanic child. *Psychotherapy, 22,* 441–448.

Jung, C.G. (1960). The structure and dynamics of the psyche. In Collected Works, 8. Princeton, NJ: Princeton University Press.

Kabat-Zinn, J. (1990). *Full catastrophe living.* New York: Delacorte.

Kagiwada, G., & Fujimoto, I. (1973). Asian-American studies: Implications for education. *Personnel and Guidance Journal, 51,* 400–405.

Kamarck, T., & Jennings, J.R. (1991). Biobehavioral factors in sudden cardiac death. *Psychological Bulletin, 109,* 42–75.

Kamin, L. (1974). *The science and politics of I.Q.* Potomac, MD: Erlbaum.

Kass, J. (1998, May 11). State's attorney needs some sense knocked into him. *Chicago Tribune,* p. 3.

Katz, J. (1985). The sociopolitical nature of counseling. *The Counseling Psychologist, 13,* 615–624.

Katz, J.H., & Miller, F.A. (1988). Between monoculturalism and multiculturalism: Traps awaiting the organization. *O.D. Practitioner, 20,* 1–5.

Katz, P. (1981). Psychotherapy with Native adolescents. *Canadian Journal of Psychiatry, 26,* 455–459.

Kavanaugh, P.C., & Retish, P.M. (1991). The Mexican American ready for college. *Journal of Multicultural Counseling and Development, 19,* 136–144.

Keane, E.M., Dick, R.W., Bechtold, D.W. & Manson, S.M. (1996). Predictive and concurrent validity of the Suicide Ideation Questionnaire among American Indian Adolescents. *Journal of Abnormal Child Psychology, 24,* 735–747.

Kelly, M., & Tseng, H. (1992). Cultural differences in childrearing: A comparison of immigrant Chinese and Caucasian American mothers. *Journal of Cross-Cultural Psychology, 23,* 444–455.

Kemp, N.T., & Mallinckrodt, B. (1996). Impact of professional training on case conceptualization of clients with a disability. *Professional Psychology: Research and Practice, 27,* 378–385.

Kendler, K.S., MacLean, C., Neal, M., Kessler, R., Heath, A., & Eaves, L. (1991). The genetic epidemiology of bulimia nervosa. *American Journal of Psychiatry, 148,* 1627–1637.

Kim, A.U., & Atkinson, D.R. (1998). What counselors need to know about aging and sexuality. In D.R. Atkinson & G. Hackett (Eds.), *Counseling diverse populations* (2d ed., pp. 217–233). Boston: McGraw-Hill.

Kim, J. (1981). The process of Asian American identity development: A study of Japanese-American women's perceptions of their struggle to achieve personal identities as Americans of Asian ancestry. *Dissertation Abstracts International, 42,* 1551A. (University Microfilms No. 81-18080)

Kim, S.C. (1985). Family therapy for Asian Americans: A strategic structural framework. *Psychotherapy, 22,* 342–356.

Kim, U., & Berry, J.W. (1993). *Indigenous psychologies.* Newbury Park: Sage.

Kimmich, R.A. (1960). Ethnic aspects of schizophrenia in Hawaii. *Psychiatry, 23,* 97–102.

Kinzie, J.D. (1985). Overview of clinical issues in the treatment of Southeast Asian refugees. In T.C. Owan (Ed.), *Southeast Asian mental health: Treatment, prevention services, training, and research* (pp. 113–136). Washington, DC: National Institute of Mental Health.

Kiselica, M.S. (1998). Preparing anglos for the challenges and joys of multiculturalism. *The Counseling Psychologist, 26,* 5–21.

Kitano, H.H.L. (1969b). *Japanese-Americans: The evolution of a subculture.* Englewood Cliffs, NJ: Prentice-Hall.

Kitano, H.H.L. (1982). Mental health in the Japanese American community. In E.E. Jones & S.J. Korchin (Eds.), *Minority mental health* (pp. 149–164). New York: Praeger.

Kitano, H.H.L., & Kimura, A. (1976). The Japanese American family. In C.H. Mindle & R.W. Haberstein (Eds.), *Ethnic families in America.* New York: Elsevier.

Kitano, H.H.L., & Maki, M.T. (1996). Continuity, change, and diversity: Counseling Asian Americans. In P.B. Pedersen, J.G. Draguns, W.J. Lonner, & J.E. Trimble (Eds.), *Counseling across cultures* (4th ed., p. 124–145). Thousand Oaks, CA: Sage.

Kleinke, C.L. (1994). *Common principles of psychotherapy.* Pacific Grove, CA: Brooks/Cole.

Kluckhohn, F.R., & Strodtbeck, F.L. (1961). *Variations in value orientations.* Evanston, IL: Row, Patterson, & Co.

Knight, B.G., & McCallum, T.J. (1998). Adapting psychotherapeutic practice for older clients: Implications of the contextual, cohort-based, maturity, specific challenge model. *Professional Psychology: Research and Practice, 29,* 15–22.

Kochman, T. (1981). *Black and White Styles in Conflict.* Chicago: University of Chicago Press.

Korman, M. (1974). National conference on levels and patterns of professional training in psychology. *American Psychologist, 29,* 441–449.

Kramer, F. (1998, May 24). On nation's farms, some workers give up childhood—"I just want to go back to school," a youngster tells child-labor forum. *Seattle Times,* p. A6.

Krieger, N., & Sidney, S. (1996). Racial discrimination and blood pressure: the CARDIA study of young black and white adults. *American Journal of Public Health, 86,* 1370–1308.

Kumanyika, S.K. (1993). Special issues regarding obesity in minority populations. *Annuals of Internal Medicine, 119,* 650–654.

Kun, K.E., & Schwartz, R.W. (1998). Older Americans with HIV/AIDS. *SIECUS Report, 26,* 12–14.

Kwee, M. (1990). *Psychotherapy, meditation and health.* London: East-West.

LaBarre, W. (1985). Paralinguistics, kinesics and cultural anthropology. In L.A. Samovar & R.E. Porter (Eds.), *Intercultural communication: A reader* (pp. 272–279). Belmont, CA: Wadsworth.

Labov, W. (1972). *Language in the inner city: Studies in the Black English vernacular.* Philadelphia: University of Pennsylvania Press.

La Crosse, M.B., & Barak, A. (1976). Differential perception of counselor behavior. *Journal of Counseling Psychology, 23,* 170–172.

LaFromboise, T. (1998). American Indian mental health policy. In D.A. Atkinson, G. Morten, & D.W. Sue (Eds.), *Counseling American minorities: A cross-cultural perspective* (pp. 137–158). Boston: McGraw-Hill.

LaFromboise, T., & Howard-Pitney, B. (1995). The Zuni Life Skills Development Curriculum. *Journal of Counseling Psychology, 42,* 479–486.

LaFromboise, T.D., & Dixon, D.N. (1981). American Indian perception of trustworthiness in a counseling interview. *Journal of Counseling Psychology, 28,* 135–139.

Laing, R.D. (1967). *The divided self.* New York: Pantheon.

Laing, R.D. (1969). *The politics of experience.* New York: Pantheon.

Laird, J., & Green, R. (1996). *Lesbians and gays in couples and families.* San Francisco: Jossey-Bass.

Lambert, R.G., & Lambert, M.J. (1984). The effects of role preparation for psychotherapy on immigrant clients seeking mental health services in Hawaii. *Journal of Community Psychology, 12,* 263–275.

Lane, M. (1988, June 22). At age 81, teacher's lessons are timeless. *Bellingham Herald,* p. A1.

Lass, N.J., Mertz, P.J., & Kimmel, K. (1978). The effect of temporal speech alterations on speaker race and sex identification. *Language and Speech, 21,* 279–290.

Latting, J.E. & Zundel, C. (1986). Worldview differences between clients and counselors. *Social Casework, 12,* 66–71.

Laval, R.A., Gomez, E.A., & Ruiz, P. (1983). A language minority: Hispanics and mental health care. *The American Journal of Social Psychiatry, 3,* 42–49.

Lee, C-R. (1995). *Native speaker.* New York: Berkley Publishing Group.

Lee, C.C. (1996). MCT Theory and implications for indigenous healing. In D.W. Sue, A.E. Ivey, & P.B. Pedersen (Eds.), *A theory of multicultural counseling and therapy* (pp. 86–98). Pacific Grove, CA: Brooks/Cole.

Lee, C.C., & Armstrong, K.L. (1995). Indigenous models of mental health intervention: Lessons from traditional healers. In J.G. Ponterotto, J.M. Casas, L.A. Suzuki, & C.M. Alexander (Eds.), *Handbook of Multicultural Counseling* (pp. 441–456). Thousand Oaks, CA: Sage.

Lee, C.C., & Bailey (1997). Counseling African American male youth and men. In C.C. Lee (Ed.), *Multicultural issues in counseling* (2d ed., pp. 123–154). Alexandria, VA: American Counseling Association.

Lee, C.C., Oh, M.Y., & Mountcastle, A.R. (1992). Indigenous models of helping in nonwestern countries: Implications for multicultural counseling. *Journal of Multicultural Counseling and Development, 20,* 1–10.

Lee, D.Y., & Uhlemann, M.R. (1984). Comparison of verbal responses of Rogers, Shostrom, and Lazarus. *Journal of Counseling Psychology, 31,* 91–94.

Lee, D.Y., Uhlemann, M.R., & Hasse, R.F. (1985). Counselor verbal and nonverbal responses and perceived expertness, trustworthiness, and attractiveness. *Journal of Counseling Psychology, 32,* 181–187.

Lee, E. (1988). Cultural factors in working with Southeast Asian refugee adolescents. *Journal of Adolescents, 11,* 167–179.

Lee, E. (1996). Chinese Families. In M. McGoldrick, J. Geordano, & J.K. Pearce (Eds.), *Ethnicity and Family Therapy* (pp. 249–267). New York: Guilford.

Lee, F.Y. (1991). *The relationship of ethnic identity to social support, self-esteem, psychological distress, and help-seeking behavior among Asian American college students.* Unpublished doctoral dissertation, University of Illinois, Urbana-Champaign.

Lee, S.J. (1994). Behind the model-minority stereotype: Voices of high- and low-achieving Asian American students. *Anthropology and Education Quarterly, 25,* 413–429.

Lefcourt, H. (1966). Internal versus control of reinforcement: A review. *Psychological Bulletin, 65,* 206–220.

Leigh, I.W., Corbett, C.A., Gutman, V., & Morere, D.A. (1996). Providing psychological services to deaf individuals: A response to new perceptions of diversity. *Professional Psychology: Research and Practice, 27,* 364–371.

Lent, R.W., & Maddux, J.E. (1997). Self efficacy: Building a sociocognitive bridge between social and counseling psychology. *The Counseling Psychologist, 25,* 240–255.

Leong, F. (1985). Career development of Asian Americans. *Journal of College Student Personnel, 26,* 539–546.

Leong, F.T. (1986). Counseling and psychotherapy with Asian-Americans: Review of literature. *Journal of Counseling Psychology, 33,* 196–206.

Leong, F.T.L. (1994). Asian Americans' differential patterns of utilization of inpatient and outpatient public mental health services in Hawaii. *Journal of Community Psychology, 22,* 82–96.

Leong, F.T.L., Wagner, N.S., & Kim, H.H. (1995).

Group counseling expectations among Asian American students: The role of culture-specific factors. *Journal of Counseling Psychology, 42,* 217–222.

Leong, F.T.L., Wagner, N.S., & Tata, S.P. (1995). Racial and ethnic variations in help-seeking attitudes. In J.G. Ponterotto, J.M. Casas, L.A. Suzuki, & C.M. Alexander (Eds.), *Handbook of multicultural counseling* (pp. 415–438). Thousand Oaks, CA: Sage.

Lerner, B. (1972). *Therapy in the ghetto.* Baltimore: Johns Hopkins University Press.

Leung, P. (1990). Asian Americans and psychology: Unresolved issues. *The Journal of Training and Practice in Professional Psychology, 4,* 3–13.

Levenson, H. (1974). Activism and powerful others. *Journal of Personality Assessment, 38,* 377–383.

LeVine, E.S., & Padilla, A.M. (1980). *Crossing cultures in therapy: Pluralistic counseling for the Hispanic.* Monterey, CA: Brooks/Cole.

Levinson, H. (1994). Why the behemoths fell: Psychological roots of corporate failure. *American Psychologist, 49,* 428–436.

Lewis, J.A., Lewis, M.D., Daniels, J.A., & D'Andrea, M.J. (1998). *Community Counseling.* Pacific Grove: Brooks/Cole.

Liddle, B.J. (1996). Therapist sexual orientation, gender, and counseling practices as they relate to ratings of helpfulness by gay and lesbian clients. *Journal of Counseling Psychology, 43,* 394–401.

Lin, K.-M., Masuda, M.I., & Tazuma, L. (1982). Adaptational problems of Vietnamese refugees, Part III. Case studies in clinic and field: Adaptive and maladaptive. *The Psychiatric Journal of the University of Ottawa, 7,* 173–183.

Lippert, L. (1997). Women at midlife: Implications for theories of women's adult development. *Journal of Counseling and Development, 76,* 16–22.

Lockard, J.O. (1987). Racism on campus: Exploring the issues. *Michigan Alumnus, 93,* 22–33.

Locke, D.C. (1997). *Increasing multicultural understanding.* Thousand Oaks, CA: Sage.

London, P. (1989). *Modes and morals of psychotherapy.* New York: Holt, Rinehart & Winston.

Lorenzo, M.K., & Adler, D.A. (1984). Mental health services for Chinese in a community health center. *Social Casework, 65,* 600–610.

Lorion, R.P. (1973). Socioeconomic status and treatment approaches reconsidered. *Psychological Bulletin, 79,* 263–280.

Lorion, R.P. (1974). Patient and therapist variables in the treatment of low-income patients. *Psychological Bulletin, 81,* 344–354.

Lowrey, L. (1983). Bridging a culture in counseling. *Journal of Applied Rehabilitation Counseling, 14,* 69–73.

Lum, R.G. (1982). Mental health attitudes and opinions of Chinese. In E.E. Jones & S.J. Korchin (Eds.), *Minority mental health.* New York: Praeger.

Mack, E.E., Tucker, T.W., Achuleta, R., DeGroot, G., Hernandez, A.A., and Cha, S.O. (1997). Interethnic relations on campus: Can't we all get along? *Journal of Multicultural Counseling and Development, 25,* 256–268.

Mackler, B., & Giddings, M.G. (1965). Cultural deprivation: A study in mythology. *Teachers College Record, 66,* 608–613.

MacPhee, D., Fritz, J., & Miller-Heyl, J. (1996). Ethnic variations in personal social networks and parenting. *Child Development, 67,* 3278–3295.

Mann, J. (1998, July 10). A proud pioneer looks back. *The Washington Post,* p. E03.

Manson, S.M., Tatum, E., & Dinges, N.G. (1982). Prevention research among American Indian and Alaska Native communities: Charting further courses for theory and practice in mental health: In S.M. Manson (Ed.), *New directions in prevention among American Indian and Alaska Native Communities* (pp. 1–61). Portland, OR: Oregon Health Sciences University.

Marcos, L.R. (1973). The language barrier in evaluating Spanish-American patients. *Archives of General Psychiatry, 29,* 655–659.

Marcos, L.R. (1979). Effects of interpreters on the evaluation of psychopathology in non-English-speaking patients. *American Journal of Psychiatry, 136,* 171–174.

Marwick, C. (1995). Should physicians prescribe prayer for health? Spiritual aspects of well-being considered. *Journal of the American Medical Association, 273,* 1561–1562.

Marx, G.T. (1967). *Protest and prejudice: A study of belief in the Black community.* New York: Harper & Row.

Maslow, A.H. (1968). *Toward a psychology of being.* Princeton: Van Nostrand.

Matthee, I. (1997, Sept 9). Anti-Asian hate crimes on rise in U.S. but state sees decline in such offenses. *Seattle Post-Intelligencer,* p. A3.

Matthias, R.E., Lubben, J.E., Atchison, K.A., & Schweitzer, S.O. (1997). Sexual satisfaction among very old adults: Results from a community-dwelling Medicare population survey. *The Gerontologist, 37,* 6–14.

Mau, W.C., & Jepson, D.A. (1988). Attitudes toward counselors and counseling processes: A comparison of Chinese and American graduate students. *Journal of Counseling and Development, 67,* 189–192.

Maykovich, M.H. (1973). Political activation of Japanese American youth. *Journal of Social Issues, 29,* 167–185.

Mays, V.M. (1985). The Black American and psychotherapy: The dilemma. *Psychotherapy, 22,* 379–388.

McCollum, V.J.C. (1997). Evolution of the African American family personality: Considerations for family therapy. *Journal of Multicultural Counseling and Development, 25,* 219–229.

McCray, C.C. (1998). Ageism in the preclinical years. *Journal of the American Medical Association, 279,* 1035. Copyright 1998. American Medical Association.

McCurdy, P.C., & Ruiz, R.A. (1980). Sex role and marital agreement. In R.A. Ruiz & R.E. Cromwell (Eds.), *Anglo, Black, and Chicano families in the urban community.*

McGilley, B.M., & Pryor, T.L. (1998). Assessment and treatment of bulimia nervosa. *American Family Physician, 57,* 2743–2750.

McGoldrick, M., & Giordano, J. (1996). Overview: Ethnicity and Family Therapy. In M. McGoldrick, J. Giordano, & J.K. Pearce (Eds.), *Ethnicity and Family Therapy* (2d ed., pp. 1–27). New York: Guilford Press.

McIntosh, Peggy (1989, July/August). White privilege: Unpacking the invisible knapsack. *Peace and Freedom,* pp. 8–10.

McNamara, K., & Rickard, K.M. (1989). Feminist identity development: Implications for feminist therapy with women. *Journal of Counseling and Development, 68,* 184–193.

McNamara, K., & Rickard, K.M. (1998). Feminist identity development: Implications for feminist therapy with women. In D.R. Atkinson & G. Hackett (Eds.), *Counseling diverse populations* (2d ed., pp. 271–282). Boston: McGraw-Hill.

McNamee, S. (1996). Psychotherapy as a social construction. In H. Rosen & K.T. Kuehlwein (Eds.), *Constructing realities: meaning-making perspective for psychotherapists* (pp. 115–137). San Francisco: Jossey-Bass.

McQuaide, S. (1998). Women at midlife. *Social Work, 43,* 21–31.

McRoy, R.G., & Oglesby, Z. (1984). Group work with Black adoptive applicants. *Social Work with Groups, 7,* 125–134.

Meara, N.M., Pepinsky, H.B., Shannon, J.W., & Murray, W.A. (1981). Semantic communication and expectations for counseling across three theoretical orientations. *Journal of Counseling Psychology, 28,* 110–118.

Meara, N.M., Shannon, J.W., & Pepinsky, H.B. (1979). Comparison of the stylistic complexity of the language of the counselor and client across three theoretical orientations. *Journal of Counseling Psychology, 26,* 181–189.

Mehrabian, A. (1972). *Nonverbal communication.* Chicago: Aldene-Atherton.

Mejia, D. (1983). The development of Mexican-American children. In G.J. Powell, J. Yamamoto, A. Romero, & A. Morales (Eds.), *The psychosocial development of minority group children* (pp. 77–114). New York: Brunner/Mazel.

Menacker, J. (1971). *Urban poor students and guidance.* Boston: Houghton Mifflin.

Mercer, J.R. (1971). Institutionalized anglocentrism. In P. Orleans & W. Russel (Eds.), *Race, change, and urban society.* Los Angeles: Sage.

Merluzzi, T.V., Banikiotes, P.G., & Missbach, J.W. (1978). Perceptions of counselor characteristics:

Contributions of counselor sex, experience, and disclosure level. *Journal of Counseling Psychology, 25,* 479–482.

Meyers, H., Echemedia, F., & Trimble, J.E. (1991). American Indians and the counseling process. In P.B. Pedersen (Ed.), *Handbook of cross-cultural counseling* (pp. 3–9). Westport, CT: Greenwood.

Miller, D. (1980). The Native American family: The urban way. In E. Corfman (Ed.), *Families today* (pp. 441–484). Washington, DC: U.S. Government Printing Office.

Mintz, L.B., Bartels, K.M., & Rideout, C.A. (1995). Training in counseling ethnic minorities and race-based availability of graduate school resources. *Professional Psychology: Research and Practice, 26,* 316–321.

Minuchin, S. (1974). *Families and family therapy.* Cambridge, MA: Harvard University Press.

Mio, J.S., & Iwamasa, G. (1993). To do, or not to do: That is the question for White cross-cultural researchers. *The Counseling Psychologist, 21,* 197–212.

Mio, J.S., & Morris, D.R. (1990). Cross-cultural issues in psychology training programs: An invitation for discussion. *Professional Psychology: Theory and Practice, 21,* 434–441.

Miranda, A.O. & Umhoefer, D.L. (1998). Depression and social interest differences between Latinos in dissimilar acculturation stages. *Journal of Mental Health Counseling, 20,* 159–171.

Mirels, H. (1970). Dimensions of internal versus external control. *Journal of Consulting and Clinical Psychology, 34,* 226–228.

Mitchell, A. (1998, June 17). Controversy over Lott's view of homosexuality. *New York Times,* p. 24.

Mizio, E. (1983). The impact of macro systems on Puerto Rican families. In G.J. Powell, J. Yamamoto, A. Romero, & A. Morales (Eds.), *The psychosocial development of minority group children* (pp. 216–236). New York: Brunner/Mazel.

MMRW-Morbidity and Mortality Weekly Report (1992). Alcohol-related hospitalizations—Indian Health Service and Tribal Hospitals, United States, May 1992, *41,* 757–760.

MMRW-Morbidity and Mortality Weekly Report (1994). Prevalence and characteristic of alcohol consumption and fetal alcohol awareness—Alaska, 1991 and 1993, *43,* 3–6.

Mollica, R.F., Wyshak, G., & Lavelle, J. (1987). The psychosocial impact of war trauma and torture on Southeast Asian refugees. *American Journal of Psychiatry, 144,* 1567–1572.

Montague, J. (1996). Counseling families from diverse cultures. A nondeficit approach. *Journal of Multicultural Counseling and Development, 24,* 37–41.

Montijo, J.A. (1985). Therapeutic relationships with the poor: A Puerto Rican perspective. *Psychotherapy, 22,* 436–440.

Moos, R.H., Mertens, J.R., & Brennan, P.L. (1995). Program characteristics and readmission among older substance abuse patients: Comparisons with middle-aged and younger patients. *Journal of Mental Health Administration, 22,* 332–346.

Morrissey, M. (1997, October). The invisible minority: Counseling Asian Americans. *Counseling Today,* pp. 1, 21–22.

Mourners gather to honor gay murdered in Wyoming (1998, October 17). *Bellingham Herald,* p. A8.

Moye, J., & Brown, E. (1995). Postdoctoral training in geropsychology: Guidelines for formal programs and continuing education. *Professional Psychology: Research and Practice, 26,* 591–597.

Moynihan, D.P. (1965). Employment, income and the ordeal of the Negro family. *Daedalus,* pp. 745–770.

Mullavey-O'Byrne, C. (1994). Intercultural Communication for Health Care Professionals. In R.W. Brislin & T. Yoshida (Eds.), *Improving Intercultural Interactions* (pp. 171–196). Thousand Oaks, CA: Sage.

Muñoz, R.H., & Sanchez, A.M. (1996). *Developing culturally competent systems of care for state mental health services.* Boulder, CO: Western Interstate Commission for Higher Education.

Mura, D. (1996, June 28–30). Of racism, sexism and fatherhood. *USA Weekend,* pp. 8–9.

Murphy, B.C. (1989). Lesbian couples and their parents: The effects of perceived parental attitudes on the couple. *Journal of Counseling and Development, 68,* 46–51.

Murphy, K.C., & Strong, S.R. (1972). Some effects of similarity self-disclosures. *Journal of Counseling Psychology, 19,* 121–124.

Myers, H.F., Kagawa-Singer, M., Kumanyika, S.K., Lex, B.W., & Markides, K.S. (1995). Panel III: Behavioral risk factors related to chronic diseases in ethnic minorities. *Health Psychology, 14,* 613–621.

National Asian Pacific American Legal Consortium (1997). *Audit of violence against Asian Pacific Americans.* Washington, DC: NAPA.

National Coalition for Women and Girls in Education (1998). *Title IX at 25: Report card on gender equity.* Washington, DC: National Coalition for Women and Girls in Education.

National Center for Health Statistics (1996). *Health, United States, 1995.* Hyattsville, MD: Public Health Service.

National Commission on the Causes and Prevention of Violence. (1969). *To establish justice, to insure domestic tranquility.* New York: Award Books.

National Organization on Disability/Louis Harris Survey (1998). Americans with disabilities still face sharp gaps in securing jobs, education, transportation, and in many areas of daily life. National Organization on Disability.

Negy, C. (1993). Anglo- and Hispanic-Americans' performance on the Family Attitude Scale and its implications for improving measurements of acculturation. *Psychological Reports, 73,* 1211–1217.

Negy, C., & Woods, D.J. (1992). The importance of acculturation in understanding research with Hispanic-Americans. *Hispanic Journal of Behavioral Sciences, 14,* 224–247.

Neighbors, H.W., Caldwell, C.H., Thompson, E., & Jackson, J.S. (1994). Help-seeking behavior and unmet need. In Sriedman (Ed.), *Disorders in African Americans* (pp. 26–39). New York: Springer Publishing Co.

Nguyen, L.T., & Henkin, L.B. (1983). Change among Indochinese refugees. In R.J. Samada & S.C. Woods (Eds.), *Perspectives in immigrant and minority education.* New York: University Press of America.

Nguyen, S.D. (1985). Mental health services for refugees and immigrants in Canada. In T.C. Owen (Ed.), *Southeast Asian mental health: Treatment, prevention, services, training, and research* (pp. 261–282). Washington, DC: National Institute of Mental Health.

Nicols, M.P., & Schwartz, R.C. (1995). *Family therapy: Concepts and methods* (3rd ed.), Boston: Allyn & Bacon.

Nidorf, J.F. (1985). Mental health and refugee youths: A model for diagnostic training. In T.C. Owan (Ed.), *Southeast Asian mental health: Treatment, prevention, services, training, and research* (pp. 391–430). Washington, DC: National Institute of Mental Health.

Nieto, S. (1995). A history of the education of Puerto Rican students in U.S. mainland schools: "Losers," "Outsiders," or "Leaders"? In J.A. Banks & C.A. McGee Banks (Eds.), *Handbook of research on multicultural education* (pp. 388–411). New York: McMillan.

Nishihara, D.P. (1978). Culture, counseling, and ho'oponopono: An ancient model in a modern context. *Personnel and Guidance Journal, 56,* 562–566.

Nisio, K., & Bilmer, M. (1987). Psychotherapy with Southeast Asian American clients. *Professional Psychology: Research and Practice, 18,* 342–346.

No longer a rarity, centenarians change face of aging. (1998, June 22). *Bellingham Herald,* p. A1.

Norton, I.M., & Manson, S.M. (1996). Research in American Indian and Alaskan Native communities: Navigating the cultural universe of values and process. *Journal of Consulting and Clinical Psychology, 64,* 856–860.

Norton, J.L. (1995). The gay, lesbian, bisexual populations. In N.A. Vacc, S.B. DeVaney, & J. Wittmer (Eds.), *Experiencing and counseling multicultural and diverse populations* (3d ed., pp. 147–177). Bristol, PA: Accelerated Development.

Nwachuku, U., & Ivey, A. (1991). Culture specific counseling: An alternative approach. *Journal of Counseling and Development, 70,* 106–111.

O'dell, J.W., & Bahmer, A.J. (1981). Rogers,

Lazarus, and Shostrom in content analysis. *Journal of Clinical Psychology, 37,* 507–510.

O'Guinn, T.C., Imperia, G., & MacAdams, E.A. (1987). Acculturation and perceived family decision-making input among Mexican-American wives. *Journal of Cross-Cultural Psychology, 18,* 78–92.

Oler, C.H. (1989). Psychotherapy with Black clients' racial identity and locus of control. *Psychotherapy, 26,* 233–241.

Olsen, C.S. (1996). African-American adolescent women: Perceptions of gender, race, and class. *Marriage and Family Review, 24,* 105–121.

Ong, P. & Hee, S.J. (1993). Twenty million in 2020. In *The State of Asian Pacific America. (pp.* 11–24). Los Angeles: Leadership Education for Asian Pacifics and UCLA Asian American Studies Center.

Organista, P.B., Organista, K.C., & Soloff, P.R. (1998). Exploring AIDS-related knowledge, attitudes, and behaviors of female Mexican migrant workers. *Health and Social Work, 23,* 96–103.

Ornstein, R.E. (1972). *The psychology of consciousness.* San Francisco: Freeman.

Osbourne, J.W. (1997). Race and academic disidentification. *Journal of Educational Psychology, 89,* 728–735.

Osipow, S.H. (1982). Counseling psychology: Applications in the world of work. *The Counseling Psychologist, 10,* 19–25.

Ottavi, T.M., Pope-Davis, D.B., & Dings, J.G. (1994). Relationship between White racial identity attitudes and self-reported multicultural counseling competencies. *Journal of Counseling Psychology, 41,* 149–154.

Padilla, A.M., & DeSnyder, N.S. (1985). Counseling Hispanics: Strategies for effective intervention. In P.B. Pedersen (Ed.), *Handbook of cross-cultural counseling and therapy* (pp. 157–164). Westport, CT: Greenwood Press.

Paniagua, F.A. (1994). *Assessing and treating culturally diverse clients.* Thousand Oaks, CA: Sage.

Parham, T.A. (1989). Cycles of psychological nigrescence. *The Counseling Psychologist, 17,* 187–226.

Parham, T.A. (1993). White researchers conducting multi-cultural counseling research: Can their efforts be "Mo Betta"? [Reaction]. *The Counseling Psychologist, 21,* 250–256.

Parham, T.A. (1997). An African-centered view of dual relationships. In B. Herlihy & G. Corey (Eds.), *Boundary issues in counseling* (pp. 109–112). Alexandria, VA: American Counseling Association.

Parham, T.A., & Helms, J.E. (1981). The influence of black students' racial attitudes on preferences for counselor's race. *Journal of Counseling Psychology, 28,* 250–257.

Parham, T.A., & Helms, J.E. (1985). Relation of racial identity attitudes to self-actualization and affective status of Black students. *Journal of Counseling Psychology, 32,* 431–440.

Parham, T.A., & McDavis, R.J. (1987). Black men and endangered species: Who's really pulling the trigger? *Journal of Counseling and Development, 66,* 24–27.

Parker, S., Nichter, M., Vuckovic, N., Sims, C., & Ritenbaugh, C. (1995). Body image and weight concerns among African American and White adolescent females: Differences that make a difference. *Human Organization, 54,* 103–114.

Parker, S., & Thompson, T. (1990). Gay and bisexual men: Developing a healthy identity. In D. Moore & F. Leafgren (Eds.), *Men in conflict* (pp. 113–121). Alexandria, VA: American Counseling Association.

Parker, W.M., & McDavis, R.J. (1983). Attitudes of Blacks toward mental health agencies and counselors. *Journal of Non-White Concerns, 11,* 89–98.

Parnetti, L., Brooks, J.O., Pippi, M., Caputo, N. (1997). Diagnosing Alzheimer's disease in very elderly patients. Gerontology, 43, 335–338.

Paster, V.S. (1985). Adapting psychotherapy for the depressed, unacculturated, acting-out, Black male adolescent. *Psychotherapy, 22,* 408–417.

Pavkov, T.W., Lewis, D.A., & Lyons, J.S. (1989). Psychiatric diagnosis and racial bias: An empirical investigation. *Professional Psychology: Research & Practice, 20,* 364–368.

Pearson, J.C. (1985). Gender and communication. Dubuque, IA: W.C. Brown.

Pearson, R.E. (1985). The recognition and use of natural support systems in cross-cultural counseling. In P.B. Pedersen (Ed.), *Handbook of cross-cultural counseling and therapy* (pp. 299–306). Westport, CT: Greenwood Press.

Pedersen, P.B. (1988). *Handbook for developing multicultural awareness.* Alexandria, VA: American Association for Counseling and Development Press.

Pedersen, P. (1991a). Multiculturalism as a generic approach to counseling. *Journal of Counseling and Development, 70*(1), 6–12.

Pedersen, P. (1991b). Multiculturalism as a fourth force in counseling [Special issue]. *Journal of Counseling and Development, 70.*

Pedersen, P. (1994). *A handbook for developing multicultural awareness* (2nd ed.). Alexandria, VA: American Counseling Association.

Pedersen, P.B. (1987). Ten frequent assumptions of cultural bias in counseling. *Journal of Multicultural Counseling and Development, 15,* 16–24.

Penn, N.E., Kar, S., Kramer, J., Skinner, J. & Zambrana, R.E. (1995). Panel VI: Ethnic minorities, health care systems, and behavior. *Health Psychology, 14,* 641–646.

People's Medical Society Newsletter (1998). Are seniors being shortchanged? *People's Medical Society Newsletter, 17,* p. 1, 6.

Pinderhughes, C.A. (1973). Racism in psychotherapy. In C. Willie, B. Kramer, & B. Brown (Eds.), *Racism and mental health* (pp. 61–121). Pittsburgh, PA: University of Pittsburgh Press.

Pine, G.J. (1972). Counseling minority groups: A review of the literature. *Counseling and Values, 17,* 35–44.

Piotrkowski, C.S. (1998). Gender harassment, job satisfaction, and distress among employed White and minority women. *Journal of Occupational Health Psychology, 3,* 33–43.

Pomales, J., Claiborn, C.D., & LaFromboise, T.D. (1986). Effects of Black students' racial identity on perceptions of White counselors varying in cultural sensitivity. *Journal of Counseling Psychology, 34,* 123–131.

Ponterotto, J.G. (1987). Counseling Mexican-Americans: A multimodal approach. *Journal of Counseling and Development, 65,* 308–312.

Ponterotto, J.G. (1988). Racial consciousness development among white counselors' trainees: A stage model. *Journal of Multicultural Counseling and Development, 16,* 146–156.

Ponterotto, J.G., & Casas, J.M. (1987). In search of multicultural competence within counselor education programs. *Journal of Counseling and Development, 65,* 430–434.

Ponterotto, J.G., & Casas, J.M. (1991). *Handbook of racial/ethnic minority counseling research.* Springfield, IL: Charles C. Thomas.

Ponterotto, J.G., & Pedersen, P.B. (1993). *Preventing prejudice.* Newbury Park, CA: Sage.

Ponzo, Z. (1992). Promoting successful aging: Problems, opportunities, and counseling guidelines. *Journal of Counseling and Development, 71,* 210–213.

Pope-Davis, D.B., & Coleman, H.L.K. (1997). *Multicultural counseling competencies: Assessment, education and training, and supervision.* Thousand Oaks, CA: Sage.

Pope-Davis, D.B., & Ottavi, T.M. (1994). Examining the association between self-reported multicultural counseling competencies and demographic and educational variables among counselors. *Journal of Counseling and Development, 72,* 651–654.

Powell, G., & Powell, R. (1983). Poverty: The greatest and severest handicapping condition in childhood. In G. Powell (Ed.), *The psychosocial development of minority group children* (pp. 573–580). New York: Brunner/Mazel.

President's Commission on Mental Health. (1978). *Report from the President's Commission on Mental Health.* Washington, DC: U.S. Government Printing Office.

Qualls, S.H. (1998). Marital therapy with later life couples. In D.R. Atkinson & G. Hackett (Eds.), *Counseling diverse populations* (2d ed., pp. 199–216). Boston, MA: McGraw-Hill.

Rabaya, V. (1971). Filipino immigration: The creation of a new social order. In A. Tachiki, E. Wong, F. Odo, & B. Wong (Eds.), *Roots: An Asian American reader.* Los Angeles: UCLA.

Ramos-McKay, J.M., Comas-Diaz, L., & Rivera, L.A. (1988). Puerto Ricans. In L. Comas-Diaz & E.E.H. Griffith (Eds.), *Clinical Guidelines in Cross-Cultural Mental Health* (pp. 204–232). New York: Wiley.

Ramsey, S., & Birk, J. (1983). Preparation of North Americans for interaction with Japanese: Considerations of language and communication style. In D. Landis & R.W. Brislin (Eds.), *Handbook of intercultural training: Volume III* (pp. 227–259). New York: Pergamon.

Rash of Indian teen suicides (1998, Feb. 8) *The Bellingham Herald*, p. A5.

Red Horse, J. (1983). Indian family values and experiences. In G.J. Powell, J. Yamamoto, A. Romero, & A. Morales (Eds.), *The psychosocial development of minority group children* (pp. 258–272). New York: Brunner/Mazel.

Red Horse, J.G., Lewis, R., Feit, M. & Decker, J. (1981). In R.H. Dana (ed.), *Human services for cultural minorities.* Baltimore: University Park Press.

Red Horse, Y. (1982). A cultural network model: Perspectives for adolescent services and paraprofessional training In S.M. Manson (Ed.), *New directions in prevention among American Indian and Alaska Native Communities* (pp. 173–184). Portland, OR: Oregon Health Sciences University.

Reiss, B.F. (1980). Psychological tests in homosexuality. In J. Marmor (Ed.), *Homosexual behavior: A modern reappraisal* (pp. 296–311). New York: Basic Books.

Retish, P. & Kavanaugh, P. (1992). Myth: America's public schools are educating Mexican American students. *Journal of Multicultural Counseling and Development, 20,* 89–96.

Reynolds, C.F., III, Dew, M.A., Frank, E., & Begley, A.E. (1998). Effects of age at onset of first lifetime episode of recurrent major depression on treatment response and illness course in elderly patients. *American Journal of Psychiatry, 155,* 795–799.

Richardson, B.L. & June, L.N. (1997). Utilizing and maximizing the resources of the African American church: Strategies and tools for counseling professionals. In C.C. Lee (Ed.), *Multicultural issues in counseling* (2d ed., pp. 155–169). Alexandria, VA: American Counseling Association.

Richardson, E.H. (1981). Cultural and historical perspectives in counseling American Indians. In D.W. Sue (Ed.), *Counseling the culturally different: Theory & practice* (pp. 216–255). New York: John Wiley.

Ridley, C.R. (1984). Clinical treatment of the nondisclosing Black client. *American Psychologist, 39,* 1234–1244.

Ridley, C.R. (1995). *Overcoming unintentional racism in counseling and therapy: A practitioner's guide to intentional intervention.* Thousand Oaks, CA: Sage.

Riessman, F. (1962). *The culturally deprived child.* New York: Harper & Row.

Ritter, K.Y. & O'Neill, C.W. (1989). Moving through loss: The spiritual journey of gay men and lesbian women. *Journal of Counseling and Development, 68,* 9–15.

Rivera, A.N. (1984). *Toward a psychotherapy for Puerto Ricans.* Rio Piederis, PR: CEDEPP.

Roberts, R.E., Kaplan, G.A., Shema, S.J., & Strawbridge, W.J. (1997). Does growing old increase the risk for depression? *American Journal of Psychiatry, 154,* 1384–1390.

Roberts, R.E., & Sobhan, M. (1992). Symptoms of depression in adolescence: A comparison of Anglo, African, and Hispanic Americans. *Journal of Youth and Adolescents, 21,* 639 650.

Robertson warns of disaster from "Gay Days." (1998, June 10) *Columbian,* p. 1.

Robins, L.N., & Regier, D.A. (1991). *Psychiatric disorders in America.* New York: The Free Press.

Robinson, L. (1998, May 11). "Hispanics" don't exist. *U.S. News & World Report, 124,* 26–32.

Rodriguez, N., Ryan, S.W., Vande Kemp, H. & Foy, D.W. (1997). Posttraumatic stress disorder in adult female survivors of child sexual abuse: A comparison study. *Journal of Consulting and Clinical Psychology, 65,* 53–59.

Rogers, C. (1980). *A way of being.* Boston: Houghton Mifflin.

Rogers, C.R. (1961). *On becoming a person.* Boston: Houghton Mifflin.

Rogler, L.H., Malgady, R.G., Constantino, G., & Blumenthal, R. (1987). What do culturally sensitive mental health services mean? The case of Hispanics. *American Psychologist, 42,* 565–570.

Romero, D. (1985). Cross-cultural counseling: Brief reactions for the practitioner. *The Counseling Psychologist, 13,* 665–671.

Root, M.P.P. (1998). Facilitating psychotherapy with Asian American clients. In D.R. Atkinson, G. Morten, & D.W. Sue (Eds.), *Counseling American Minorities: A Cross-Cultural Perspective* (pp. 214–234). Boston: McGraw-Hill.

Rosenthal, R., & Jacobson, L. (1968). *Pygmalion in the classroom.* New York: Holt, Rinehart, & Winston.

Rotter, J. (1966). Generalized expectancies for internal versus external control of reinforcement. *Psychological Monographs, 80,* 1–28.

Rotter, J. (1975). Some problems and misconceptions related to the construct of internal versus external control of reinforcement. *Journal of Consulting and Clinical Psychology, 43,* 56–67.

Rouse, B.A., Carter, J.H., & Rodriguez-Andrew, S. (1995). Race/ethnicity and other sociocultural influences on alcoholism treatment for women. *Recent developments in alcoholism, 12,* 343–367.

Rowe, W., Bennett, S., & Atkinson, D.R. (1994). White racial identity models: A critique and alternative proposal. *The Counseling Psychologist, 22,* 120–146.

Rudman, L.A. (1998). Self-promotion as a risk factor for women: The costs and benefits of counter-stereotypical impression management. *Journal of Personality and Social Psychology, 74,* 629–645.

Ruiz, A. (1981). Cultural and historical perspectives in counseling Hispanics. In D.W. Sue (Ed.), *Counseling the culturally different: Theory & practice* (pp. 186–215). New York: John Wiley.

Ruiz, A.S. (1990). Ethnic identity: Crisis and resolution. *Journal of Multicultural Counseling and Development, 18,* 29–40.

Ruiz, P. (1995). Assessing, diagnosing and treating culturally diverse individuals: A Hispanic perspective. *Psychiatric Quarterly, 66,* 329–341.

Ruiz, R.A., & Casas, J.M. (1981). Culturally relevant and behavioristic counseling for Chicano college students. In P.B. Pedersen, J.G. Draguns, W.J. Lonner, & J.E. Timble (Eds.), *Counseling across cultures.* Honolulu, HI: University of Hawaii Press.

Rumbaut, R.B. (1985). Research concerns associated with the study of Southeast Asian refugees. In T.C. Owan (Ed.), *Southeast Asian mental health: Treatment, prevention, services, training, and research.* Washington, DC: National Institute of Mental Health.

Ryan, A. (1995). Apocalypse now? In R. Jacoby & N. Glauberman (Eds.), *The bell curve debate* (pp. 14–29). New York: Times Book.

Ryan, W. (1971). *Blaming the victim.* New York: Pantheon.

Sabnani, H.B., Ponterotto, J.G., & Borodovsky, L.G. (1991). White racial identity development and cross-cultural counselor training. *The Counselor Psychologist, 19,* 76–102.

Sage, G.P. (1997). Counseling American Indian adults. In C.C. Lee (Ed.), *Multicultural issues in counseling* (2d ed., pp. 35–52). Alexandria, VA: American Counseling Association.

Salvador, D.S., Omizo, M.M., & Kim, B.S.K. (1997). Bayanihan: Providing effective counseling strategies with children of Filipino ancestry. *Journal of Multicultural Counseling and Development, 25,* 201–209.

Samuda, R.J. (1975). From ethnocentrism to a multicultural perspective in educational testing. *Journal of Afro-American Issues, 3,* 4–18.

Samuda, R.J. (1998). *Psychological testing of American minorities.* Thousand Oaks, CA: Sage.

Sandhu, D.S. (1997). Psychocultural profiles of Asian and Pacific Islander Americans: Implications for counseling and psychotherapy. *Journal of Multicultural Counseling and Development, 25,* 7–22.

Sands, T. (1998). Feminist counseling and female adolescents: Treatment strategies for depression. *Journal of Mental Health Counseling, 20,* 42–54.

Sanger, S.P., & Alker, H.A. (1972). Dimensions of internal-external locus of control and the women's liberation movement. *Journal of Social Issues, 28,* 15–129.

Satir, V. (1967). *Conjoint family therapy.* Palo Alto: Science & Behavior Books.

Satir, V. (1983). *Conjoint family therapy* (3rd ed.). Palo Alto: Science and Behavior Books.

Saunders, P.A. (1998). "My brain's on strike." The construction of identity through memory accounts by dementia patients. *Research on Aging, 20,* 65–90.

Schein, E.H. (1990). Organizational Culture. *American Psychologist, 45*(2), 109–119.

Schindler-Rainman, E. (1967). The poor and the PTA. *PTA Magazine, 61*(8), 4–5.

Schinke, S.P., Schilling, R.F., II, Gilchrist, L.D., Barth, R.P., Bobo, J.K., Trimble, J.E., & Cvetkovich, G.T. (1985). Preventing substance abuse with American Indian youth. *Social Casework, 66,* 213–217.

Schmidt, L.D., & Strong, S.R. (1971). Attractiveness and influence in counseling. *Journal of Counseling Psychology, 18,* 348–351.

Schneider, K.T., Swan, S., & Fitzgerald, L.F. (1997). Job-related and psychological effects of sexual harassment in the workplace: Empirical evidence from two organizations. *Journal of Applied Psychology, 82,* 401–415.

Schofield, W. (1964). *Psychotherapy: The purchase of friendship.* Englewood Cliffs, NJ: Prentice Hall.

Seattle Public Schools (1986). *Disproportionality task force preliminary report.* Seattle: Seattle Public Schools.

Seem, S.R. & Johnson, E. (1998). Gender bias among counseling trainees: A study of case conceptualization. *Counselor Education and Supervision, 37,* 257–268.

Seligman, M.E.P. (1982). *Helplessness: On depression, development and death.* San Francisco: Freeman.

Serrano, R.A. (1998, March 4). Study counts record number of hate groups, 20% jump in year. *San Francisco Chronicle,* p. A5.

Shade, B.J., & New, C.A. (1993). Cultural influences on learning: Teaching implications. In J.A. Banks & C.A. McGee Banks (Eds.), *Multicultural Education* (pp. 317–331). Boston: Allyn Bacon.

Shannon, J.W., & Woods, W.J. (1998). Affirmative psychotherapy for gay men. In D.R. Atkinson &

G. Hackett (Eds.), *Counseling diverse populations* (2d ed., pp. 335–351). Boston: McGraw-Hill.

Shapiro, D.H. (1982). Overview: Clinical and physiological comparison of meditation with other self control strategies. *American Journal of Psychiatry, 139,* 267–274.

Shin, L. (1971). Koreans in America: 1903–1945. In A. Tachiki, E. Wong, F. Odo, & B. Wong (Eds.), *Roots: An Asian American reader.* Los Angeles: UCLA.

Shine, K.I. (1984). Anxiety in patients with heart disease. *Psychosomatics, 25,* 27–31.

Shockley, W. (1972). Determination of human intelligence. *Journal of Criminal Law and Criminology, 7,* 530–543.

Shook, V.E. (1985). *Ho'oponopono.* Honolulu, HI: University of Hawaii Press.

Shore, J.H. (1988). Introduction. *American Indian and Alaskan Native Mental Health Research, 1,* 3–4.

Shorter-Gooden, K., & Washington, N.C. (1996). Young, Black, and female: The challenge of weaving an identity. *Journal of Adolescence, 19,* 465–475.

Shostrom, E.L. (Producer). (1966). *Three approaches to psychotherapy: II* [Film]. Santa Ana, CA: Psychological Films.

Shuey, A. (1966). *The testing of Negro intelligence.* New York: Social Science Press.

Shukovsky, P. (1998, April 8). Indians, neighbors square off: Drums, singing enliven hearing on Gorton bill. *Seattle Post-Intelligencer,* p. B1.

Singelis, T. (1994). Nonverbal communication in intercultural interactions. In R.W. Brislin & T. Yoshida (Eds.), *Improving intercultural interactions* (pp. 268–294). Thousand Oaks, CA: Sage.

Sleek, S. (1998, July). Mental disabilities no barrier to smooth and efficient work. *Monitor,* p. 15.

Smalley, W.A. (1984). Adoptive language strategies of the Hmong: From Asian mountains to American ghettos. *Language Science, 1,* 241–269.

Smith, E.J. (1977a). Counseling Black individuals: Some stereotypes. *Personnel and Guidance Journal, 55,* 390–396.

Smith, E.J. (1977b). Counseling Black women. In

P.B. Pedersen (Ed.), *Handbook of cross-cultural counseling and therapy* (pp. 213–237). Westport, CT: Greenwood Press.

Smith, E.J. (1981). Cultural and historical perspectives in counseling Blacks. In D.W. Sue (Ed.), *Counseling the culturally different: Theory and practice* (pp. 141–185). New York: John Wiley.

Smith, E.J. (1991). Ethnic identity development: Toward the development of a theory within the context of majority/minority status. *Journal of Counseling and Development, 70,* 181–188.

Smith, M.E. (1957). Progress in the use of English after twenty-two years by children of Chinese ancestry in Honolulu. *Journal of Genetic Psychology, 90,* 255–258.

Smith, M.E., & Kasdon, L.M. (1961). Progress in the use of English after twenty years by children of Filipino and Japanese ancestry in Hawaii. *Journal of Genetic Psychology, 99,* 129–138.

Smothers, R. (1998, June 22). Church blesses union of 2 men in adoption case. *New York Times,* p. 5.

Snowden, L.R., & Cheung, F.H. (1990). Use of inpatient mental health services by members of ethnic minority groups. *American Psychologist, 45,* 347–355.

Sodowsky, G.R., Kwan, K.K., & Pannu, R. (1995). Ethnic identity of Asians in the United States. In J.G. Ponterotto, J.M. Casas, L.A. Suzuki, & C.M. Alexander (Eds.), *Handbook of Multicultural Counseling* (pp. 123–154). Thousand Oaks, CA: Sage.

Spiegel, J., & Papajohn, J. (1983). *Final report: Training program on ethnicity and mental health.* Waltham, MA: The Florence Heller School, Branders University.

Spiegel, S.B. (1976). Expertness, similarity, and perceived counselor competence. *Journal of Counseling Psychology, 23,* 436–441.

Sprafkin, R.P. (1970). Communicator expertness and changes in word meaning in psychological treatment. *Journal of Counseling Psychology, 17,* 191–196.

Stanback, M.H., & Pearce, W.B. (1985). Talking to "the man": Some communication strategies used by members of "subordinate" social groups. In

L.A. Samovar & R.E. Porter (Eds.), *Intercultural communication: A reader* (pp. 236–253). Belmont, CA: Wadsworth.

Steinberg, L. (1998, July 18). A summer of promise: YMCA camp helps adolescent girls gain confidence in themselves and their abilities. *Seattle Post-Intelligencer,* p. C1.

Steiner, C. (Ed.). (1975). *Readings in radical psychiatry.* New York: Grove Press.

Stewart, E.C. (1971). *American cultural patterns: A cross-cultural perspective.* Pittsburgh, PA: Regional Council for International Understanding.

Stice, E., Shaw, H., & Nemeroff, C. (1998). Dual pathway model of bulimia nervosa: Longitudinal support for dietary restraint and affect-regulation mechanisms. *Journal of Social and Clinical Psychology, 17,* 129–149.

Stoltenberg, C.C., McNeill, B.W., & Elliot, T.R. (1995). Selected translations of social psychology to counseling psychology. *The Counseling Psychologist, 23,* 603–610.

Stonequist, E.V. (1937). *The marginal man.* New York: Charles Scribner's Sons.

Strawbridge, W.J., Cohen, R.D., Shema, S.J., & Kaplan, G.A. (1997). Frequent attendance at religious services and mortality over 28 years. *American Journal of Public Health, 87,* 957–961.

Strickland, B. (1971). Aspiration responses among Negro and White adolescents. *Journal of Personality and Social Psychology, 19,* 315–320.

Strickland, B. (1973). Delay of gratification and internal locus of control in children. *Journal of Counseling and Clinical Psychology, 40,* 338.

Strickland, B.R. (1995). Research on sexual orientation and human development: A commentary. *Developmental Psychology, 31,* 137–140.

Strock, C. (1998, May 18). A painful discovery. *Newsweek,* p. 16.

Strong, S.R. (1969). Counseling: An interpersonal influence process. *Journal of Counseling Psychology, 15,* 215–224.

Strong, S.R., & Schmidt, L.D. (1970). Expertness and influence in counseling. *Journal of Counseling Psychology, 15,* 31–35.

Sudarkasa, N. (1988). Interpreting the African heritage in Afro-American family organization. In

H.P. McAdoo (Ed.), *Black families* (pp. 27–43). Newbury Park, CA: Sage.

Sue, D. (1990). Culture in transition: Counseling Asian-American men. In D. Moore and F. Leafgren (Eds.), *Men in Conflict* (pp. 53–165). Alexandria, VA: American Association for Counseling and Development.

Sue, D. (1994). Incorporating cultural diversity in family therapy. The Family Psychologist, 10, 19–21.

Sue, D. (1997). Counseling strategies for Chinese Americans. In C.C. Lee (Ed.), Multicultural issues in counseling (2d ed., pp. 173–187). Alexandria, VA: American Counseling Association.

Sue, D. (1997). Multicultural training. *International Journal of Intercultural Relations, 21,* 175–193.

Sue, D., Bernier, J., Durran, A., Feinberg, L., Pedersen, P., Smith, E., & Vasquez-Nuttal, E. (1982). Position paper: Cross-cultural counseling competencies. *The Counseling Psychologist, 10,* 45–52.

Sue, D.W. (1977a). Barriers to effective cross-cultural counseling. *Journal of Counseling Psychology, 24,* 420–429.

Sue, D.W. (1977b). Counseling the culturally different: A conceptual analysis. *Personnel and Guidance Journal, 55,* 422–424.

Sue, D.W. (1978). Eliminating cultural oppression in counseling: Toward a general theory. *Journal of Counseling Psychology, 25,* 419–428.

Sue, D.W. (1981). Evaluating process variables in cross-cultural counseling and psychotherapy. In A.J. Marsell & P.B. Pedersen (Eds.), *Cross-cultural counseling and psychotherapy.* New York: Pergamon.

Sue, D.W. (1990). Culture specific techniques in counseling: A conceptual framework. *Professional Psychology, 21,* 424–433.

Sue, D.W. (1991a). A conceptual model for cultural diversity training. *Journal of Counseling and Development, 70,* 99–105.

Sue, D.W. (1991b). A diversity perspective on contextualism. *Journal of Counseling and Development, 70,* 300–301.

Sue, D.W. (1992). The challenge of multiculturalism: The road less traveled. *American Counselor, 1,* 7–14.

Sue, D.W. (1993). Confronting ourselves: The White and racial/ethnic minority researcher. *The Counseling Psychologist, 21,* 244–249.

Sue, D.W. (1994). Asian-American mental health and help-seeking behavior: Comment on Solberg et al. (1994), Tata and Leong (1994), and Lin (1994). *Journal of Counseling Psychology, 41,* 292–295.

Sue, D.W. (1994). U.S. business and the challenge of cultural diversity. *The Diversity Factor,* pp. 24–28.

Sue, D.W. (1995). Multicultural organizational development: Implications for the counseling profession. In J.G. Ponterotto, J.M. Casas, L.A. Suzuki, & C.M. Alexander (Eds.), (pp. 474–492). Thousand Oaks, CA: Sage.

Sue, D.W. (1995). Toward a theory of multicultural counseling and therapy. In J.A. Banks & C.A.M. Banks (Eds.), *Handbook of research on multicultural education* (pp. 647–659). New York: Macmillan.

Sue, D.W. (1997). Multiculturalism and discomfort, *Spectrum, 57*(3), 7–9.

Sue, D.W., Arredondo, P., & McDavis, R.J. (1992). Multicultural competencies/standards: A Call to the Profession. *Journal of Counseling and Development, 70*(4), 477–486.

Sue, D.W., Bernier, J.B., Durran, M., Feinberg, L., Pedersen, P., Smith, E., & Vasquez-Nuttall, E. (1982). Position paper: Cross-cultural counseling competencies. *The Counseling Psychologist, 10,* 45–52.

Sue, D.W., Carter, R.T., Casas, J.M., Fouad, N.A., Ivey, A.E., Jensen, M., LaFromboise, T., Manese, J.E., Ponterotto, J.G., & Vasquez-Nuttall, E. (1998). *Multicultural Counseling Competencies: Individual and Organizational Development.* Thousand Oaks, CA: Sage.

Sue, D.W., & Frank, A.C. (1973). A topological approach to the study of Chinese- and Japanese-American college males. *Journal of Social Issues, 29,* 129–148.

Sue, D.W., Ivey, A.E., & Pedersen, P.B. (1996). *A Theory of Multicultural Counseling and Therapy.* Pacific Grove, CA: Brooks Cole.

Sue, D.W., & Kirk, B.A. (1973). Differential characteristics of Japanese-American and Chinese-

American college students. *Journal of Counseling Psychology, 20,* 142–148.

Sue, D.W., & Kirk, B.A. (1975). Asian Americans: Use of counseling and psychiatric services on a college campus. *Journal of Counseling Psychology, 22,* 84–86.

Sue, D.W., & Sue, D. (1972). Ethnic minorities: Resistance to being researched. *Professional Psychology, 2,* 11–17.

Sue, D.W., & Sue, D. (1973). Understanding Asian Americans: The neglected minority. *Personnel and Guidance Journal, 51,* 386–389.

Sue, D.W., & Sue, D. (1977). Barriers to effective cross-cultural counseling. *Journal of Counseling Psychology, 24,* 420–429.

Sue, D.W., & Sue, D. (1977b). Ethnic minorities: Failures and responsibilities of the social sciences. *Journal of Non-White Concerns in Personnel and Guidance, 5,* 99–106.

Sue, D.W., & Sue, D. (1990). *Counseling the culturally different: Theory and practice.* New York: John Wiley & Sons.

Sue, D., Sue, D.W., & Sue, S. (1994). *Understanding abnormal behavior.* (4th ed.). Boston: Houghton-Mifflin.

Sue, D., Sue, D.W., & Sue, S. (1997). *Understanding abnormal behavior.* (5th ed.). Boston: Houghton-Mifflin.

Sue, D.W., & Sue, S. (1972a). Counseling Chinese-Americans. *Personnel & Guidance Journal, 50,* 637–644.

Sue, S. (1977). Community mental health services to minority groups: Some optimism, some pessimism. *American Psychologist, 32,* 616–624.

Sue, S., Allen, D., & Conaway, L. (1975). The responsiveness and equality of mental health care to Chicanos and Native Americans. *American Journal of Community Psychology, 45,* 111–118.

Sue, S., Fujino, D.C., Hu, L., Takeuchi, D.T., & Zane, N.W.S. (1991). Community mental health services for ethnic minority groups: A test of the cultural responsiveness hypothesis. *Journal of Consulting and Clinical Psychology, 59,* 533–540.

Sue, S., Ito, J., & Bradshaw, C. (1984). Ethnic minority research: Trends and directions. In E.E. Jones & S.J. Korchin (Eds.), *Minority mental health.* New York: Praeger.

Sue, S., & Kitano, H.H.L. (1973). Stereotypes as a measure of success. *Journal of Social Issues, 29,* 83–98.

Sue, S., & McKinney, H. (1974). Delivery of community health services to black and white clients. *Journal of Consulting and Clinical Psychology, 42,* 794–801.

Sue, S., & McKinney, H. (1975). Asian Americans in the community mental health care system. *American Journal of Orthopsychiatry, 45,* 111–118.

Sue, S., McKinney, H., Allen, D., & Hall, J. (1974). Delivery of community health services to Black & White clients. *Journal of Consulting Psychology, 42,* 794–801.

Sue, S., & Morishima, J.K. (1982). *The mental health of Asian Americans.* San Francisco: Jossey-Bass.

Sue, S., & Sue, D.W. (1971a). Chinese-American personality and mental health. *Amerasian Journal, 1,* 36–49.

Sue, S., & Sue, D.W. (1971b). *The reflection of culture conflicts in the psychological problems of Chinese and Japanese students.* Paper presented at the American Psychological Association Convention, Honolulu, HI.

Sue, S. & Sue, D.W. (1972). Chinese American personality and mental health: A reply to Tong's criticisms. *Amerasian Journal, 1,* 60–65.

Sue, S., Sue, D.W., & Sue, D. (1975). Asian Americans as a minority group. *American Psychologist, 31,* 906–910.

Sue, S., Sue, D.W., Sue, L. & Takeuchi, D.T. (1995). Psychopathology among Asian Americans: A model minority? *Cultural diversity and mental health, 1,* 39–51.

Sue, S., & Zane, N. (1987). The role of culture and cultural techniques in psychotherapy: A reformation. *American Psychologist, 42,* 37–45.

Sun, L.H. (1997, September 11). Asian names scrutinized at White House; Guards stopped citizens who looked "foreign." *The Washington Post,* p. A1.

Sundberg, N.D. (1981). Cross-cultural counseling and psychotherapy: A research overview. In A.J. Mansella & P.B. Pedersen (Eds.), *Cross-cultural counseling and psychotherapy* (pp. 29–38). New York: Pergamon.

Susman, N.M., & Rosenfeld, H.M. (1982). Influence of culture, language and sex on conversation distance. *Journal of Personality and Social Psychology, 42,* 66–74.

Sutton, C.T., & Broken Nose, M. (1996). American Indian families: An overview In M. McGoldrick, J. Giordano, & J.K. Pearce (Eds.), *Ethnicity and Family Therapy* (pp. 31–54). New York: Guilford Press.

Swinomish Tribal Mental Health Project (1991). *A gathering of wisdoms.* LaConner, WA: Sinomish Tribal Community.

Szapocznik, J., & Kurtines, W.M. (1993). Family psychology and cultural diversity: Opportunities for theory, research, and application. *American Psychologist, 48,* 400–407.

Szapocznik, J., Santisteban, D., Kurtines, W.M., Hervis, O.E., & Spencer, F. (1982). Life enhancements counseling: A psychosocial model of services for Cuban elders. In E.E. Jones & S.J. Korchin (Eds.), *Minority mental health* (pp. 296–329). New York: Praeger.

Szapocznik, J., Scopetta, M.A., Kurtines, W., & Aranalde, M.A. (1978). Theory and measurement of acculturation. *International Journal of Psychology, 12,* 113–130.

Szasz, T.S. (1970). The crime of commitment. In *Readings in Clinical Psychology Today* (pp. 167–169). Del Mar, CA: CRM Books.

Szasz, T.S. (1971). *The myth of mental illness.* New York: Hoeber.

Tafoya, N. & Del Vecchio, A. (1996). Back to the future: An examination of the Native American Holocaust. In M. McGoldrick, J. Giordano, & J.K. Pearce (eds). 45–54. *Ethnicity and Family Therapy.* New York: Guilford.

Talvi, S.J.A. (1997). The silent epidemic: The challenge of HIV prevention within communities of color. *The Humanist, 57,* 6–10.

Tart, C. (1986). *Waking up: Overcoming the obsta-cles to human potential.* Boston: New Science Library.

Thigpen, C.H., & Cleckley, H.M. (1954). A case of multiple personality. *Journal of Abnormal Social Psychology, 49,* 135–151.

Thomas, A., & Sillen, S. (1972). *Racism and psychiatry.* New York: Brunner/Mazel.

Thomas, C.W. (1970). Different strokes for different folks. *Psychology Today, 4,* 49–53, 80.

Thomas, C.W. (1971). *Boys no more.* Beverly Hills, CA: Glencoe Press.

Thomas, M.B., & Dansby, P.G. (1985). Black clients: Family structures, therapeutic issues, and strengths. *Psychotherapy, 22,* 398–407.

Thompson, C.E. (1995). Helms' White racial identity development (WRID) theory: Another look. *The Counseling Psychologist, 22,* 645–649.

Thoresen, C.E. (1998). Spirituality, health and science: The coming revival? In S.R. Roemer, S.R. Kurpius & C. Carmin (eds.), *The Emerging Role of Counseling Psychology in Health Care.* New York: Norton.

Thurow, L. (1995, November 19). Why their world might crumble. *New York Times Magazine.*

Toarmino, D., & Chun, C.-A. (1997). Issues and strategies in counseling Korean Americans. In C.C. Lee (Ed.), *Multicultural issues in counseling* (2d ed., pp. 233–254).

Tobin, J.J., & Friedman, J. (1983). Spirits, shamans, and nightmare death: Survivor stress in a Hmong refugee. *American Journal of Orthopsychiatry, 53,* 439–448.

Todisco, M., & Salomone, P.R. (1991). Facilitating effective cross-cultural relationships: The White counselor and Black client. *Journal of Multicultural Counseling and Development, 19,* 146–157.

Toomer, J.E. (1982). Counseling psychologists in business and industry. *The Counseling Psychologist, 10,* 9–18.

Trevino, J.G. (1996). Worldview and change in cross-cultural counseling. *The Counseling Psychologist, 24,* 198–215.

Trimble, J.E. (1981). Value differentials and their importance in counseling American Indians. In P.B. Pedersen, J.G. Draguns, W.J. Lonner, & J.E.

Trimble (Eds.), *Counseling across cultures* (pp. 203–243). Honolulu, HI: University of Hawaii Press.

Trimble, J.E. (1990). Application of psychological knowledge for American Indians and Alaska Natives. *The Journal of Training and Practice in Professional Psychology, 4,* 45–63.

Trimble, J.E., & Fleming, C.M. (1989). Providing counseling services for Native American Indians: Client, counselor, and community characteristics. In P.B. Pedersen, J.G. Draguns, W.J. Lonner, & J.E. Trimble (Eds.), *Counseling across cultures,* (3d ed., pp. 177–204). Honolulu, HI: University of Hawaii Press.

Trimble, J.E., Fleming, C.M., Beauvais, F., & Jumper-Thurman, P. (1996). Essential cultural and social strategies for counseling Native American Indians. In P.B. Pedersen, J.G. Draguns, W.J. Lonner, & J.E. Trimble (Eds.), *Counseling across cultures* (4th ed., pp. 177–209). Thousand Oaks, CA: Sage Publications.

Trimble, J.E., & LaFromboise, T. (1985). American Indians and the counseling process: Culture, adaptation, and style. In P.B. Pedersen (Ed.), *Handbook of cross-cultural counseling and therapy* (pp. 127–134). Westport, CT: Greenwood Press.

Tsui, P., & Schultz, G.L. (1985). Failure of rapport: When psychotherapeutic engagement fails in the treatment of Asian clients. *American Journal of Orthopsychiatry, 55,* 561–569.

Tulkin, S. (1968). Race, class, family and school achievement. *Journal of Personality and Social Psychology, 9,* 31–37.

Tung, T.M. (1985). Psychiatric care for southeast Asians: How different is different? In T.C. Owan (Ed.), *Southeast Asian mental health, treatment, prevention services, training, and research* (pp. 5–40). Washington, DC: National Institute of Mental Health.

Turner, C.B., & Wilson, W.J. (1976). Dimensions of racial ideology: A study of urban Black attitudes. *Journal of Social Issues 32,* 193–252.

Uba, L. (1994). *Asian Americans.* New York: Guilford Press.

Uhlemann, M., Lee, D.Y., & Hett, G.G. (1984). Perception of theoretically derived counseling approaches as a function of preference for counseling orientation. *Journal of Clinical Psychology, 40,* 1111–1116.

U.S. Bureau of the Census. (1995). *Population profile of the United States.* Washington, DC: U.S. Government Printing Office.

U.S. Census Bureau. (1992). *Statistical abstract of the United States: The national data book* (112th ed.). Washington, DC: Bureau of the Census.

U.S. Commerce Department. (1997). Census Bureau Current Population Reports, Series P-60. Washington, DC: U.S. Government Printing Office.

U.S. Commerce Department. (1998). Census Bureau Current Population Reports, Series P-60, Selected Issues. Washington, DC: U.S. Government Printing Office.

U.S. Department of Education. (1987). Percent of minority enrollment in U.S. colleges and universities, Fall 1968–1984. State Task Force on Minority Student Achievement. Washington, DC: U.S. Government Printing Office.

U.S. Department of Labor. (1998). *Bureau of Labor Statistics.* Washington, DC: U.S. Government Printing Office.

Vacc, N.A., & Clifford, K. (1995). Individuals with a physical disability. In N.A. Vacc, S.B. DeVaney, & J. Wittmer (Eds.), *Experiencing and counseling multicultural and diverse populations* (3d ed., pp. 251–272). Bristol, PA: Accelerated Development.

Vasquez, J.A. (1998). Distinctive traits of Hispanic students. *The Prevention Researcher, 5,* 1–4.

Vazquez, J.M. (1997). Puerto Ricans in the counseling process: The dynamics of ethnicity & its societal context. In C.C. Lee (Ed.) *Multicultural issue in counseling* (2d Ed.) (pp. 315–330). Alexandria, VA: American Counseling Association.

Vega, W.A., Hough, R.L., & Romero, A. (1985). Family life patterns of Mexican-Americans. In G.J. Powell, J. Yamamoto, A. Romero, & A. Morales (Eds.), *The psychosocial development of minority group children* (pp. 194–215). New York: Brunner/Mazel.

Velasquez, R.J., Gonzales, M., Butcher, J.N., Castillo-Canez, I., Apodaca, J.X., & Chavira, D. (1997). Use of the MMPI-2 with Chicanos: Strategies for counselors. *Journal of Multicultural Counseling and Development, 25,* 107–120.

Vontress, C. (1981). Racial and ethnic barriers in counseling. In P. Pedersen, J.G. Draguns, W.J. Lonner, & J.E. Trimble (Eds.), *Counseling across cultures.* Honolulu, HI: University of Hawaii Press.

Vontress, C.E. (1971). Racial differences: Impediments to rapport. *Journal of Counseling Psychology, 18,* 7–13.

Vontress, C.E., & Epp, L.R. (1997). Historical hostility in the African American client: Implications for counseling. *Journal of Multicultural Counseling and Development, 25,* 170–184.

Wagner, M.M. & Blackorby, J. (1996). Transition from high school to work or college: How special education students fare. *The Future of Students, 6,* 103–120.

Walsh, R. (1995). Asian psychotherapies. In R.J. Corsini & D. Wedding (Eds.), *Current Psychotherapies.* Itasca, IL: F.E. Peacock.

Walsh, R., & Vaughan, F. (Eds.), (1993). *Paths beyond ego. The transpersonal vision* (pp. 387–398). Los Angeles: J.P. Tarcher.

Warner, C.M. & Morris, J.R. (1997). African-Americans and consultation. *Journal of Multicultural Counseling and Development, 25,* 244–255.

Watson, T. (1998, June 9). Justices to hear "environmental racism" case. *USA Today,* 3A.

Weber, S.N. (1985). The need to be: The socio-cultural significance of Black language. In L.A. Samovar & R.E. Porter (Eds.), *Intercultural communication: A reader* (pp. 244–253). Belmont, CA: Wadsworth.

Wehrly, B. (1995). *Pathways to multicultural counseling competence.* Pacific Grove, CA: Brooks Cole.

Weinrach, S.G. (1986). Ellis and Gloria: Positive or negative model? *Psychotherapy, 23,* 642–647.

Werner-Wilson, R.J., Price, S.J., Zimmerman, T.S., & Murphy, M.J. (1997). Client gender as a process variable in marriage and family therapy: Are women clients interrupted more than men clients? *Journal of Family Psychology, 11,* 373–377.

West, M. (1987). *The psychology of meditation.* Oxford: Clarendon Press.

White, J.L., & Parham, T.A. (1990). *The psychology of Blacks.* Englewood Cliffs, NJ: Prentice Hall.

White, M. (1993). Deconstruction and therapy. In S. Gilligan, & R. Price (Eds.), *Therapeutic Conversations* (pp. 22–61). New York: Norton.

White, R.W. (1963). Ego and reality in psychoanalytic theory: A proposal regarding independent ego energies. *Psychological Issues, 3,* 1–210.

Wilkinson, D. (1993). Family ethnicity in American. In H.P. McAdoo (Ed.), *Family Ethnicity: Strength in Diversity.* Newbury Park, CA: Sage.

Williams, R.L. (1974). The death of White research in the Black community. *Journal of Non-White Concerns in Personnel and Guidance, 2,* 116–132.

Willie, C.V. (1995). The relativity of genotypes and phenotypes. *Journal of Negro Education, 64,* 267–276.

Willie, C.V., Kramer, B.M., & Brown, B.S. (1973). Racism and mental health. Pittsburgh, PA: University of Pittsburgh Press.

Wilson, L.L., & Stith, S.M. (1991). Culturally sensitive therapy with Black clients. *Journal of Multicultural Counseling and Development, 19,* 32–43.

Winter, S. (1977). Rooting out racism. *Issues in Radical Therapy, 17,* 24–30.

Wise, F., & Miller, N.B. (1983). The mental health of American Indian children. In G.J. Powell, J. Yamamoto, A. Romero, & A. Morales (Eds.), *The psychosocial development of minority group children* (pp. 344–361). New York: Brunner/Mazel.

Wolfgang, A. (1973). Cross-cultural comparison of locus of control, optimism towards the future, and time horizon among Italian, Italo-Canadian, and new Canadian youth. *Proceedings of the 81st Annual Convention of the American Psychological Association, 8,* 229–330.

Wolfgang, A. (1985). The function and importance of nonverbal behavior in intercultural counseling. In P.B. Pedersen (Ed.), *Handbook of cross-*

cultural counseling and therapy (pp. 99–105). Westport, CT: Greenwood Press.

Wong, H.Z. (1985). Training for mental health service providers to Southeast Asian refugees: Models, strategies, and curricula. In T.C. Owan (Ed.), *Southeast Asian mental health: Treatment, prevention, services, training, and research* (pp. 345–390). Washington, DC: National Institute of Mental Health.

Wood, P.B., & Clay, W.C. (1996). Perceived structural barriers and academic performance among American Indian high school students. *Youth and Society, 28,* 40–61.

Wood, P.S., & Mallinckrodt, B. (1990). Culturally sensitive assertiveness training for ethnic minority clients. *Professional Psychology: Research & Practice, 21,* 5–11.

Wren, C.S. (1998, June 5). Many women 60 and older abuse alcohol and prescribed drugs, study says. *New York Times,* p. 12.

Wrenn, C.G. (1962). The culturally-encapsulated counselor. *Harvard Educational Review, 32,* 444–449.

Wrenn, C.G. (1985). Afterward: The culturally-encapsulated counselor revisited. In P.B. Pedersen (Ed.), *Handbook of cross-cultural counseling and therapy* (pp. 323–329). Westport, CT: Greenwood Press.

Yamamoto, J., & Acosta, F.X. (1982). Treatment of Asian-Americans and Hispanic-Americans: Similarities and differences. *Journal of the Academy of Psychoanalysis, 10,* 585–607.

Yamamoto, J., James, Q.C., & Palley, N. (1968). Cultural problems in psychiatric therapy. *Archives of General Psychiatry, 19,* 45–59.

Yamamoto, J., & Kubota, M. (1983). The Japanese American family. In J. Yamamoto, A. Romero, & A. Morales (Eds.), *The psychosocial development of minority group children.* (pp. 237–247). New York: Brunner/Mazel.

Yao, T., Sue, D. & Hayden D. (in progress). Untitled research.

Yee, B.W.K., Castro, F.G., Hammond, W.R., John, R., Wyatt, G.E. & Yung, B.R. (1995). Risk-taking and abusive behavior among ethnic minorities. *Health Psychology, 14,* 622–631.

Zhang, W. (1994). American counseling in the mind of a Chinese counselor. *Journal of Multicultural Counseling and Development, 22,* 79–85.

Zimmerman, J.E. & Sodowsky, G.R. (1993). Influences of acculturation on Mexican-American drinking practices: Implications for counseling. *Journal of Multicultural Counseling and Development, 21,* 22–35.

Zimmerman, R. (1998, June 4). Bilingual classes in attack: California vote turns on the pressure here. *Seattle Post-Intelligencer,* p. B1.

Zitzow, D., & Estes, G. (1981). The heritage consistency continuum in counseling Native American children. In Spring Conference on Contemporary American Issues (Ed.), *American Indian issues in higher education* (pp. 133–139).

Zuniga, M.E. (1997). Counseling Mexican American seniors: An overview. *Journal of Multicultural Counseling and Development, 25,* 142–155.

◆ Author Index